D0086074

# WINDOW ON HUMANITY

## *A Concise Introduction to Anthropology*

**Conrad Phillip Kottak**

*University of Michigan*

Boston   Burr Ridge, IL   Dubuque, IA   New York   San Francisco   St. Louis
Bangkok   Bogotá   Caracas   Kuala Lumpur   Lisbon   London   Madrid   Mexico City
Milan   Montreal   New Delhi   Santiago   Seoul   Singapore   Sydney   Taipei   Toronto

The McGraw·Hill Companies

Higher Education

This book is printed on acid-free paper.

1 2 3 4 5 6 7 8 9 0 DOC/DOC 0 9 8 7

ISBN: 978-0-07-340527-8
MHID: 0-07-340527-2

Editor in Chief: Michael Ryan
Publisher: Frank Mortimer
Sponsoring Editor: Gina Boedeker
Developmental Editor: Kate Scheinman
Editorial Coordinator: Evan Bock
Marketing Manager: Leslie Oberhuber
Media Project Manager: Jessalyn Clark
Text Permissions Coordinator: Karyn L. Morrison
Production Editor: Leslie LaDow
Manuscript Editor: Chet Gottfried
Designer: Preston Thomas
Photo Research Coordinator: Alexandra Ambrose
Art Editor: Sonia Brown
Production Supervisor: Dennis Fitzgerald
Composition: 10/12 Times by ICC Macmillan
Printing: 45 # New Era Matte Plus by R.R. Donnelley & Sons
PMS: 287

**Cover:** © Amelia Walchi, 2003

**Credits:** The credits section for this book begins on page C-1 and is considered an extension of the copyright page.

**Library of Congress Cataloging-in-Publication Data**

Kottak, Conrad Phillip.
    Window on humanity : a concise introduction to anthropology / Conrad Phillip Kottak. — 3rd ed.
        p. cm.
    Includes bibliographical references and index.
    ISBN-13: 978-0-07-340527-8 (alk. paper)
    ISBN-10: 0-07-340527-2 (alk. paper)
    1. Anthropology.  I. Title.
GN25.K68 2008
301—dc22                                                              2007030052

The Internet addresses listed in the text were accurate at the time of publication. The inclusion of a Web site does not indicate an endorsement by the authors or McGraw-Hill, and McGraw-Hill does not guarantee the accuracy of the information presented at these sites.
**www.mhhe.com**

*To My Wife,*
*Isabel Wagley Kottak*

**Also available from McGraw-Hill by Conrad Phillip Kottak**

*Anthropology: The Exploration of Human Diversity,* 12th ed. (2008)

*Cultural Anthropology,* 12th ed. (2008)

*Mirror for Humanity: A Concise Introduction to Cultural Anthropology,* 6th ed. (2008)

*On Being Different: Diversity and Multiculturalism in the North American Mainstream,* 3rd ed. (2008) (with Kathryn A. Kozaitis)

*Assault on Paradise: The Globalization of a Little Community in Brazil,* 4th ed. (2006)

# BRIEF CONTENTS

# TABLE OF CONTENTS

---

# CHAPTER 3   Evolution, Genetics, and Human Variation  47

# CHAPTER 4   The Primates 69

# CHAPTER 19    CULTURAL EXCHANGE AND SURVIVAL  416

# ANTHROPOLOGY TODAY BOXES

# ABOUT THE AUTHOR

**_Conrad Phillip Kottak_** (A.B. Columbia College, 1963; Ph.D. Columbia University, 1966) is a professor and former chair (1996–2006) of the Department of Anthropology at the University of Michigan, where he has taught since 1968. He is a member of the American Academy of Arts and Sciences. In 1991 he was honored for his teaching by the University and the State of Michigan. In 1992 he received an excellence in teaching award from the College of Literature, Sciences, and the Arts of the University of Michigan. And in 1999 the American Anthropological Association (AAA) awarded Professor Kottak the AAA/Mayfield Award for Excellence in the Undergraduate Teaching of Anthropology.

Professor Kottak has done ethnographic fieldwork in Brazil (since 1962), Madagascar (since 1966), and the United States. His general interests are in the processes by which local cultures are incorporated—and resist incorporation—into larger systems. This interest links his earlier work on ecology and state formation in Africa and Madagascar to his more recent research on global change, national and international culture, and the mass media.

The fourth edition of Kottak's popular case study *Assault on Paradise,* based on his fieldwork in Arembepe, Bahia, Brazil, was published in 2006 by McGraw-Hill. In a research project during the 1980s, Kottak blended ethnography and survey research in studying "Television's Behavioral Effects in Brazil." That research is the basis of Kottak's book *Prime-Time Society: An Anthropological Analysis of Television and Culture* (Wadsworth 1990)—a comparative study of the nature and impact of television in Brazil and the United States.

Kottak's other books include *The Past in the Present: History, Ecology and Cultural Variation in Highland Madagascar* (1980), *Researching American Culture: A Guide for Student Anthropologists* (1982) (both University of Michigan Press), and *Madagascar: Society and History* (1986) (Carolina Academic Press). With Kathryn A. Kozaitis, Kottak is the co-author of *On Being Different: Diversity and Multiculturalism in the North American Mainstream* (3rd ed., McGraw-Hill, 2008). The most recent editions (twelfth) of his longer texts *Anthropology: The Exploration of Human Diversity* and *Cultural Anthropology* were published by McGraw-Hill in 2007. In addition to

*Window on Humanity: A Concise Introduction to Anthropology* (this book), Kottak is also the author of *Mirror for Humanity: A Concise Introduction to Cultural Anthropology,* sixth edition, published in 2008.

Conrad Kottak's articles have appeared in academic journals, including *American Anthropologist, Journal of Anthropological Research, American Ethnologist, Ethnology, Human Organization,* and *Luso-Brazilian Review.* He also has written for more popular journals, including *Transaction/SOCIETY, Natural History, Psychology Today,* and *General Anthropology.*

In recent research projects, Kottak and his colleagues have investigated the emergence of ecological awareness in Brazil, the social context of deforestation and biodiversity conservation in Madagascar, and popular participation in economic development planning in northeastern Brazil. Since 1999 Professor Kottak has been active in the University of Michigan's Center for the Ethnography of Everyday Life, supported by the Alfred P. Sloan Foundation. In that capacity, for a research project titled "Media, Family, and Work in a Middle-Class Midwestern Town," Kottak has investigated how middle-class families draw on various media in planning, managing, and evaluating their choices and solutions with respect to the competing demands of work and family.

Conrad Kottak appreciates comments about his books from professors and students. He can be readily reached by e-mail at the following Internet address: ckottak@bellsouth.net.

# PREFACE

*Window on Humanity* is intended to provide a concise, lower-cost introduction to general (four-field) anthropology. The combination of shorter length and lower cost increases the instructor's options for assigning additional reading—cases studies, readers, and other supplements—in a semester course. *Window* may also work well in a quarter system, since traditional anthropology texts may be too long for a one-quarter course.

Since 1968, I've regularly taught Anthropology 101 (Introduction to Anthropology) to a class of 375 to 550 students. I continue to believe that effective textbooks are rooted in enthusiasm for and enjoyment of one's own teaching experience.

As a college student, I was drawn to anthropology by its breadth and because of what it could tell me about the human condition, present and past. Since then, I've been fortunate in spending my teaching career at a university (the University of Michigan) that values and unites anthropology's four subdisciplines. I have daily contact with members of all the subfields, and as a teacher of the four-field introductory anthropology course, I'm happy to keep up with those subfields. I believe that anthropology has compiled an impressive body of knowledge about human diversity in time and space, and I'm eager to introduce that knowledge in the pages that follow. I believe strongly in anthropology's capacity to enlighten and inform. Anthropology's subject matter is intrinsically fascinating, and its focus on diversity helps students understand and interact with their fellow human beings in an increasingly interconnected world and an increasingly diverse North America.

I decided to write my first textbook back in 1972, when there were far fewer introductory anthropology texts than there are today. The texts back then tended to be overly encyclopedic. I found them too long and too unfocused for my course and my image of contemporary anthropology. The field of anthropology was changing rapidly. Anthropologists were writing about a "new archaeology" and a "new ethnography." Fresh fossil finds and biochemical studies were challenging our understanding of human and primate evolution. Studies of monkeys and apes in their natural settings were contradicting conclusions based on work in zoos. Studies of language as it actually is used in society were revolutionizing overly formal and static linguistic models. In cultural anthropology, symbolic and interpretive approaches were joining ecological and materialist ones.

Today there are new issues and approaches, such as molecular anthropology and new forms of spatial and historical analysis. The fossil and archaeological records expand every day. Profound changes have affected the people and societies ethnographers traditionally have studied. In cultural anthropology it's increasingly difficult to know when to write in the present and when to write in the past tense. Anthropology hasn't lost its excitement. Yet many texts ignore change—except maybe with a chapter tacked on at the end—and write as though anthropology and the people it studies were the same as they were a generation ago. While any competent anthropology text must present anthropology's core, it also should demonstrate anthropology's relevance to today's world. *Window on Humanity* has a specific set of goals.

## ✧ GOALS

This book has three main goals. My first goal was to offer a concise, up-to-date, relatively low-cost four-field introduction to anthropology. Anthropology is a *science*—a "systematic field of study or body of knowledge that aims, through experiment, observation, and deduction, to produce reliable explanations of phenomena, with reference to the material and physical world" (*Webster's New World Encyclopedia* 1993, p. 937). Anthropology is a humanistic science devoted to discovering, describing, and explaining similarities and differences in time and space. In *Mirror for Man,* one of the first books I ever read in anthropology, I was impressed by Clyde Kluckhohn's (1944) description of anthropology as "the science of human similarities and differences" (p. 9). Kluckhohn's statement of the need for such a field still stands: "Anthropology provides a scientific basis for dealing with the crucial dilemma of the world today: how can peoples of different appearance, mutually unintelligible languages, and dissimilar ways of life get along peaceably together?" (p. 9).

Anthropology is a science with clear links to the humanities, as it brings a comparative and cross-cultural perspective to forms of creative expression. One might say that anthropology is among the most humanistic academic fields because of its fundamental respect for human diversity. Anthropologists routinely listen to, record, and attempt to represent voices and perspectives from a multitude of times, places, nations, and cultures. Through its four subfields, anthropology brings together biological, social, cultural, linguistic, and historical approaches. Multiple and diverse perspectives offer a fuller understanding of what it means to be human than is provided by academic fields that lack anthropology's broad vision and cross-cultural approach.

My second goal was to write a book that would be good for students. This book would be user-friendly in layout, writing style, approach, and pedagogy. By discussing current events in relation to anthropology's core, it would show students how anthropology affects their lives. Throughout this book I've attempted to be fair and objective in covering various and sometimes diverging approaches, but I make my own views known and write in the first person when it seems appropriate. I've heard colleagues who have used other textbooks complain that some authors seem so intent on presenting every conceivable theory about an issue that students are bewildered by the array of possibilities. Anthropology should not be made so complicated that it is impossible for beginning students to appreciate and understand it. The textbook author, like the instructor, must be able to guide the student.

My third goal was to write a book that professors, as well as students, would appreciate. The organization of this text is intended to cover core concepts and basics while also discussing prominent current interests.

# ✦ CONTENT AND ORGANIZATION

*Window on Humanity* covers the core and basics of all four subfields while also examining current issues and approaches.

In Chapter 1, anthropology is introduced as an integrated four-field discipline, with academic and applied dimensions, that examines human biological and cultural diversity in time and space. Anthropology is discussed as a comparative and holistic science, featuring biological, social, cultural, linguistic, humanistic, and historical approaches. Chapter 2 considers ethics and methods in physical anthropology, archaeology, and cultural anthropology.

The chapters on physical anthropology and archaeology (3–8) offer up-to-date answers to several key questions: When did we originate, and how did we become what we are? What role do genes, the environment, society, and culture play in human variation and diversity? What can we tell about our origins and nature from the study of our nearest relatives—nonhuman primates? When and how did the primates originate? What key features of their early adaptations are still basic to our abilities, behavior, and perceptions? How did hominids develop from our primate ancestors? When, where, and how did the first hominins emerge and expand? What about the earliest real humans? How do we explain biological diversity in our own species, *Homo sapiens*? What major transitions have taken place since the emergence of *Homo sapiens*? The origin of food production (the domestication of plants and animals) was a major change in human adaptation, with profound implications for society and culture. The spread and intensification of food production are tied to the appearance of the first towns, cities, and states and the emergence of social stratification and major inequalities.

The chapters on cultural anthropology (9–19) are organized to place related content close together. Culture and language are covered in Chapters 9 and 10. The chapter "Ethnicity and Race" has been moved from Chapter 10 to Chapter 17, following the advice of several readers and my own feeling that it would fit better near related material toward the end of the book. "Political Systems" (Chapter 12) logically follows "Making a Living" (Chapter 11). Chapters 13 and 14 ("Families, Kinship, and Marriage" and "Gender," respectively) also form a coherent unit.

The chapter on religion (15) covers not just traditional religious practices but also contemporary world religions and religious movements. It is followed by four chapters (16–19) that form a natural unit exploring sociocultural transformations and expressions in the modern world. This concluding unit represents one of the key differences between this anthropology text and others. Several important questions are addressed in these four chapters: How and why did the modern world system emerge? How has world capitalism affected patterns of stratification and inequality within and among nations? What were colonialism, imperialism, and Communism, and what are their legacies? How are race and ethnicity socially constructed and handled in different societies, and how do they generate prejudice, discrimination, and conflict? How do economic development and globalization affect the peoples, societies, and communities among which anthropologists traditionally have worked? How do people today actively interpret and confront the world system and the products of globalization? What factors threaten continued human diversity? How can anthropologists work to ensure the preservation of that diversity?

Let me also focus here on two chapters present in *Window on Humanity* but not found consistently in other anthropology texts: "Ethnicity and Race" (Chapter 17) and "Gender" (Chapter 14). I believe that systematic consideration of ethnicity, race, and gender is vital in an introductory anthropology text. Anthropology's distinctive four-field approach can shed special light on these subjects. Race and gender studies are fields in which anthropology always has taken the lead. I'm convinced that anthropology's special contributions to understanding the biological, social, cultural, and linguistic dimensions of ethnicity, race, and gender should be highlighted in any introductory text. So significant to anthropology do I consider ideas about race that I have moved to Chapter 1 a discussion of problems with the race concept that was previously in Chapter 3.

## ✦ NEW IN THE THIRD EDITION

There are some changes in chapter order and content. "Ethnicity and Race" has been moved from Chapter 10 to Chapter 17. Material on colonialism formerly in Chapter 18 has been combined with historical material on the world system in a new Chapter 16, "The World System and Colonialism." The discussion of development anthropology has been moved from the chapter titled "Colonialism and Development" in the last edition to a new chapter (18) on applied anthropology. The discussion of applied anthropology formerly in Chapter 1 is now in Chapter 18, "Applying Anthropology." Chapter 18 highlights the importance of this second dimension of anthropology. All chapters have been updated, and some have been revised substantially (1, 3, 5, 6, 16, 17, 18, and 19). Charts, tables, and statistics have been updated with the most recent figures available. Five new end-of-chapter boxes are included, to bring home anthropology's relevance to current issues and events. The focus on global themes, trends, and issues has been strengthened even further in this edition.

## ✦ CHAPTER-BY-CHAPTER CHANGES

### Chapter 1: What Is Anthropology?

A substantially revised Chapter 1 introduces anthropology as a four-field, integrated, biocultural discipline that focuses on human biological and cultural diversity in time and space. Anthropology is discussed as a comparative and holistic science, with links to the natural and social sciences and the humanities. The four subfields are described in greater detail than in the last edition. Now in Chapter 1 is a discussion of problems with the race concept that previously was in Chapter 3. A new box on anthropological fieldwork in northern Kenya concludes the chapter. Applying anthropology has been removed from this chapter to its own (18).

### Chapter 2: Ethics and Methods

Chapter 2 focuses on ethical issues, research methods, and dating techniques. The ethical issues anthropologists increasingly confront are highlighted. Students learn how anthropologists do their work and how that work is relevant in understanding ourselves. This chapter has been updated throughout. The chapter concludes with a new box describing the work of an anthropologist doing public archaeology in New Orleans in the wake of Hurricane Katrina.

## Chapter 3: Evolution, Genetics, and Human Variation

Chapter 3 discusses natural selection and other evolutionary principles, along with genetics. I try to provide a gentle, yet complete, introduction to these difficult topics. This chapter has been revised substantially. The discussion of natural selection has been revised and includes a new section on peppered moths. The chapter contains a new discussion of evolution as theory and fact. There is an expanded discussion of prevailing theories of inheritance when Mendel did his experiments. Recent research on high-altitude adaptation is highlighted in a new box. There is a new discussion of disease and evolution.

## Chapter 4: The Primates

Chapter 4 describes primate traits and trends, the major primate groups, and primate evolution. Also included is information on endangered primates and on hunting by chimpanzees. Again, I've tried to cover the basics—what's interesting and relevant about primates—while avoiding the more confusing classificatory terminology that some other texts provide. In this chapter and throughout the third edition, hominins (the human line and its ancestors after the split from the African apes) are distinguished now from hominids, which include humans, chimps, and gorillas. The discussion of Miocene apes examines several possible common ancestors for humans and the apes, including *Pierolapithecus* from Spain. Also discussed are the Toumai discovery from Chad and *Orrorin tugenensis* from Kenya—possible early hominins.

## Chapter 5: Early Hominins

Chapter 5, which has been rewritten substantially, considers early hominins—their fossils and tool making—from *Ardipithecus* and the australopithecines to the advent of *Homo*. The latest finds and interpretations are covered. A new section titled "What Makes Us Human?" begins the chapter by examining bipedalism, the brain, childhood dependency, tools, and teeth as human features and their importance at various stages of human evolution. All charts and tables have been updated. New photos have been added to illustrate diversity among early hominins.

## Chapter 6: The Genus *Homo*

This chapter has been rewritten substantially. The discussions of *H. habilis, H. rudolfensis,* and early *H. erectus,* formerly in Chapter 5, now, more appropriately, begin Chapter 6. Based on discoveries confirming the expansion of early *H. erectus* (sometimes called *H. ergaster*) out of Africa, Chapter 6 describes recent fossil finds in Europe. There is new material on archaic *H. sapiens*. A new box argues that anatomically modern humans arrived in Europe earlier—but overlapped with Neandertals less—than was previously thought.

# Chapter 7: The First Farmers

An updated Chapter 7 examines the origins and implications of food production (the domestication of plants and animals). The seven world centers of domestication are identified and discussed, with a focus on the first farmers and herders in the Middle East and the first farmers in Mexico and adjacent areas. A new section titled "Geography and the Spread of Food Production" shows how the geography of the Old World facilitated the diffusion of plants, animals, technology, and information.

# Chapter 8: The First Cities and States

Chapter 8 examines the emergence of towns, cities, chiefdoms, and states. Its examples include the Middle East, India/Pakistan, China, Mesoamerica, and Peru. Students learn how archaeologists make inferences about ancient societies from contemporary ethnographic studies. This illustrates the text's overall focus on anthropology as a four-field discipline in which findings from one subfield are integral to the others. Chapter 8 parallels the structure of Chapter 7, which begins with theory and explanation and then discusses cases.

# Chapter 9: Culture

This chapter, which examines the anthropological concept of culture, including its symbolic and adaptive features, has been updated based on recent writing and statistics. A new discussion distinguishes between the moral and methodological meanings of cultural relativism.

# Chapter 10: Language and Communication

Chapter 10 introduces methods and topics in linguistic anthropology, including nonverbal communication, descriptive and historical linguistics, sociolinguistics, and language and culture. A new section examines primate communication and differences between call systems and language. A new box on restoring lost languages, with a focus on Native American languages, concludes the chapter.

# Chapter 11: Making a Living

Chapter 11 surveys economic anthropology, including adaptive strategies (systems of food production) and exchange systems. Included is a discussion of recent legal rulings affecting the San people of Botswana. The idea of industrial alienation is illustrated here by Ong's study of Malaysian factory women. The discussion of potlatching has been revised. The concluding box on scarcity has been updated based on the author's 2006 revisit to Madagascar.

# Chapter 12: Political Systems

Using case material from various societies, Chapter 12 discusses political systems, in terms of scale and types of conflict resolution. The section on "Foraging Bands" has been revised. The discussion of status, formerly in the chapter "Ethnicity and Race," has been moved here, where it fits more appropriately.

## Chapter 13: Families, Kinship, and Marriage

Chapter 13 discusses families, households, descent groups, and marriage cross-cultur-ally, and also with reference to updated U.S. and Canadian census data. Various defini-tions of *family* now are considered. The discussion of marriage examines exogamy, endogamy, the incest taboo, caste, postmarital residence rules, marital exchanges, replacement marriage, and plural marriage cross-culturally. Also covered are divorce and same-sex marriage, updated to reflect recent events and legal decisions in the United States and Canada. There is a new section titled "Although Tabooed, Incest Does Happen."

## Chapter 14: Gender

A thoroughly updated Chapter 14 examines cross-cultural similarities and differences in male and female roles, rights, and responsibilities. Systems of gender stratification and multiple genders are examined. There is information on contemporary gender roles and issues, including the feminization of poverty. The latest relevant census data are included.

## Chapter 15: Religion

Chapter 15 surveys time-honored anthropological approaches to religion while also dis-cussing contemporary world religions and religious movements. This chapter concludes with a box on Islam's expansion. The section on contemporary world religions has been revised and updated, with a new table and figure illustrating numbers of adherents.

## Chapter 16: The World System and Colonialism

This chapter brings together historical material previously included in Chapters 17 and 18 of the last edition. Topics include the emergence and nature of the modern world system, including industrial and postindustrial systems of stratification and their impact on nonindustrial societies. Also discussed are colonial systems and development poli-cies that have impinged on the people and societies anthropologists traditionally have studied. Major sections examine neoliberalism, Communism and its fall, and postso-cialist transitions. The chapter concludes with an updated discussions of global energy consumption.

## Chapter 17: Ethnicity and Race

This repositioned chapter (from 10 to 17) now is placed nearer related material in adjacent chapters. It discusses the social construction of race and ethnicity and offers cross-cultural examples of variation in racial classification and ethnic relations. This chapter has been thoroughly updated, with the most recent sources and census data for the United States and Canada available in key tables. There is new material on Iraq and on an ethnically diverse United States, whose population now exceeds 300 million people.

## Chapter 18: Applying Anthropology

In the last edition, applied anthropology was discussed under "Anthropology and Its Applications," in Chapter 1. Now this second dimension of anthropology has its own chapter, placed near related material in adjacent chapters. Examples of applied anthropology from the four subfields are provided. The section on development anthropology (formerly discussed with colonialism) has been moved here, where it belongs as an important focus of applied anthropology. I've rewritten the sections on urban and medical anthropology, including recent studies. The chapter introduction has been totally rewritten. There is an expanded discussion of ethical dilemmas in applied anthropology.

## Chapter 19: Cultural Exchange and Survival

Chapter 19 continues the examination of how development and globalization affect the peoples, societies, and communities in which anthropologists traditionally have worked. Using recent examples, it shows how local people actively confront the world system and the products of globalization. There is a major new section on indigenous peoples. The chapter concludes with a final consideration of the role of the anthropologist in ensuring the continuance and preservation of cultural diversity.

---

## → PEDAGOGY

This third edition incorporates suggestions made by users of my other texts as well as reviewers of previous editions of *Window on Humanity*. The result, I hope, is a sound, well-organized, interesting, and "user-friendly" introduction to cultural anthropology.

*Window for Humanity* contains "Anthropology Today" boxes at the end of each chapter, intended to give students a chance to consider anthropology's relevance to today's world and to their own lives. Some boxes examine current events or debates. Others are more personal accounts, which add human feeling to the presentation of cultural anthropology's subject matter. Many boxes illustrate a point with examples familiar to students from their enculturation or everyday experience.

A glossary defining key terms presented in each chapter is found at the end of the book, along with a bibliography of references cited.

End-of-chapter summaries are numbered to make major points stand out.

---

## → SUPPLEMENTS

Visit our Online Learning Center Web site at www.mhhe.com/kottakwoh3 for robust student and instructor resources.

# For Students

Student resources include self-quizzes (multiple choice, true or false, essay), Internet exercises, and chapter study aids.

# For Instructors

The password-protected instructor portion of the Web site includes the instructor's manual, a comprehensive computerized test bank, PowerPoint lecture slides, and a variety of additional instructor resources.

## ✦ ACKNOWLEDGMENTS

I'm grateful to many colleagues at McGraw-Hill. When I started working on this edition, Monica Eckman, at that time McGraw-Hill's senior editor for anthropology, offered her support and enthusiasm. Since then, I've enjoyed meeting and working with Gina Boedeker, McGraw-Hill's sponsoring editor for anthropology. As developmental editor, Kate Scheinman once again did an excellent job of synthesizing the new reviews and helped keep things moving on a quick schedule. I look forward to working with Frank Mortimer, McGraw-Hill's publisher of anthropology.

I would like to thank Leslie La Dow for her excellent work as production editor, guiding the manuscript through production. Dennis Fitzgerald, production supervisor, worked with the printer to make sure everything came out right. I want to thank Maria Perez and Britt Halvorson for their excellent work on the supplements for this book. I also thank Chet Gottfried for his copyediting, and Preston Thomas for conceiving and executing the design.

Sonia Brown and Alex Ambrose also deserve thanks as art editor and photo research coordinator. Thanks, too, to Jessalyn Clark, media project manager, for creating the OLC. I also thank Karyn Morrison, who has handled the literary permissions, and David Shapiro for his excellent work proofreading this and other editions of my various books.

I'm very grateful to prepublication reviewers of this book and of various editions of *Window on Humanity: A Concise Introduction to Anthropology,* who include:

Terri Aihoshi, *Grant MacEwan College*
Sue L. Aki, *University of Texas at San Antonio*
Linda Allen, *Kirkwood Community College*
Diane Everett Barbolla, *San Diego Mesa College*
Joshua Barker, *University of Toronto*
Jeffrey P. Blick, *Georgia College & State University*
Beau Bowers, *Central Piedmont Community College*
Jim Brady, *California State University, Los Angeles*
Larisa Lee Broyles, *State University, San Bernardino*
Stephen Childs, *Valdosta State University*
William L. Coleman, *University of North Carolina, Greensboro*
Leslie Dawson, *Grant MacEwan College*
Connie Deroche, *Cape Breton University*

Barbra E. Erickson, *California State University–Fullerton*
Jason M. Fancher, *Washington State University*
Les W. Field, *University of New Mexico*
Elizabeth Fortenbery, *Pierce Community College*
Elizabeth Fuller-Tarbox, *State University of New York–Potsdam*
Dan Gardiner, *Mohawk College*
Christopher Hays, *University of Wisconsin-Washington County*
Marc Healy, *Elgin Community College*
Katherine Hirschfeld, *University of Oklahoma*
Hilary Kahn, *Indiana University–Indianapolis*
Patricia Kelly-Spurles, *Mount Allison University*
Yin Lam, *University of Victoria*
Jami Leibowitz, *East Carolina University*
William Leons, *University of Toledo*
Daniel Maher, *Westark College*
Garry Morgan, *Northwestern College*
Martin Oppenheimer, *Kansas State University*
Mary Patterson, *The University of Melbourne, Australia*
Gerald F. Reid, *Sacred Heart University*
Carolyn Rock, *Valdosta State University*
Rita C. Rodabaugh, *Central Piedmont Community College*
Eugene E. Ruyle, *California State University, Long Beach*
Jon A. Schlenker, *University of Maine at Augusta*
Andris Skreija, *University of Nebraska–Omaha*
Betty A. Smith, *Kennesaw State University*
Shannon Speed, *University of Texas at Austin*
Emily Stovel, *Ripon College*
Ted Swedenburg, *University of Arkansas*
Mark Tromans, *Broward Community College*
Helen Vallianatos, *University of Alberta*
Salena Wakim, *Orange Coast College*
Thomas Williamson, *St. Olaf College*

Students, too, regularly share their insights about my various texts via e-mail. Anyone—student or instructor—with access to e-mail can reach me at the following address: ckottak@bellsouth.net.

My family offered me understanding, support, and inspiration during the preparation of *Window on Humanity*. Dr. Nicholas Kottak, another doctor of anthropology, regularly shares his insights with me, as does Isabel Wagley Kottak, my companion in the field and in life for more than four decades, to whom this book is dedicated.

During a teaching career that began in 1968, I have benefited from the knowledge, help, and advice of so many friends, colleagues, teaching assistants, and students that I cannot fit their names into a short preface. I hope they know who they are and accept my thanks.

Feedback from students, professors, and teaching assistants keeps me up to date on the interests, needs, and views of the people for whom *Window on Humanity* is written. As stated previously, I believe that effective textbooks are based in enthusiastic practice—in the enjoyment of teaching. I hope that this product of my experience will be helpful to others.

**Conrad Phillip Kottak**
*Ann Arbor, Michigan*
*and Johns Island,*
*South Carolina*
*ckottak@bellsouth.net*

# CHAPTER 1

❦

# WHAT IS ANTHROPOLOGY?

❖ **Human Adaptability**

Adaptation, Variation, and Change

❖ **General Anthropology**

❖ **Human Biological Diversity and the Race Concept**

Explanatory Approaches

Cultural Forces Shape Human Biology

❖ **The Subdisciplines of Anthropology**

Cultural Anthropology

Archaeological Anthropology

Biological, or Physical, Anthropology

Linguistic Anthropology

❖ **Anthropology and Other Academic Fields**

❖ **Applied Anthropology**

*Anthropology Today: Remote and Poked, Anthropology's Dream Tribe*

---

That's just human nature." "People are pretty much the same all over the world." Such opinions, which we hear in conversations, in the mass media, and in a dozen scenes in daily life, promote the erroneous idea that people in other countries have the same desires, feelings, values, and aspirations that we do. Such statements proclaim that because people are essentially the same, they are eager to receive the ideas, beliefs, values, institutions, practices, and products of an expansive North American culture. Often this assumption turns out to be wrong.

Anthropology offers a broader view—a distinctive comparative, cross-cultural perspective. Most people think that anthropologists study nonindustrial societies, and they do. My research has taken me to remote villages in Brazil and Madagascar, a large island off the southeast coast of Africa. In Brazil I sailed with fishers in simple sailboats on Atlantic waters. Among Madagascar's Betsileo people I worked in rice fields and took part in ceremonies in which I entered tombs to rewrap the corpses of decaying ancestors.

However, anthropology is much more than the study of nonindustrial peoples. It is a comparative science that examines all societies, ancient and modern, simple and complex. Most of the other social sciences tend to focus on a single society, usually an industrial nation such as the United States or Canada. Anthropology offers a unique cross-cultural perspective, constantly comparing the customs of one society with those of others.

To become a cultural anthropologist, one normally does *ethnography* (the firsthand, personal study of local settings). Ethnographic fieldwork usually entails spending a year or more in another society, living with the local people and learning about their way of life. No matter how much the ethnographer discovers about the society, he or she

1

remains an alien there. That experience of alienation has a profound impact. Having learned to respect other customs and beliefs, anthropologists can never forget that there is a wider world. There are normal ways of thinking and acting other than our own.

## ✦ HUMAN ADAPTABILITY

Anthropologists study human beings wherever and whenever they find them—in a Turkish café, a Mesopotamian tomb, or a North American shopping mall. Anthropology is the exploration of human diversity in time and space. Anthropology studies the whole of the human condition: past, present, and future; biology, society, language, and culture. Of particular interest is the diversity that comes through human adaptability.

Humans are among the world's most adaptable animals. In the Andes of South America, people wake up in villages 16,000 feet above sea level and then trek 1,500 feet higher to work in tin mines. Tribes in the Australian desert worship animals and discuss philosophy. People survive malaria in the tropics. Men have walked on the moon. The model of the starship *Enterprise* in Washington's Smithsonian Institution symbolizes the desire to "seek out new life and civilizations, to boldly go where no one has gone before." Wishes to know the unknown, control the uncontrollable, and create order out of chaos find expression among all peoples. Creativity, adaptability, and flexibility are basic human attributes, and human diversity is the subject matter of anthropology.

Students often are surprised by the breadth of **anthropology,** which is the study of the human species and its immediate ancestors. Anthropology is a uniquely comparative and **holistic** science. Holism refers to the study of the whole of the human condition: past, present, and future; biology, society, language, and culture. (See the box at the end of this chapter for an account of the varied techniques that anthropologists have used to study the Ariaal people of northern Kenya since the 1970s.)

People share *society*—organized life in groups—with other animals, including baboons, wolves, and even ants. Culture, however, is distinctly human. **Cultures** are traditions and customs, transmitted through learning, that form and guide the beliefs and behavior of the people exposed to them. Children learn such a tradition by growing up in a particular society, through a process called enculturation. Cultural traditions include customs and opinions, developed over the generations, about proper and improper behavior. These traditions answer such questions as: How should we do things? How do we make sense of the world? How do we tell right from wrong? What is right, and what is wrong? A culture produces a degree of consistency in behavior and thought among the people who live in a particular society.

The most critical element of cultural traditions is their transmission through learning rather than through biological inheritance. Culture is not itself biological, but it rests on certain features of human biology. For more than a million years, humans have had at least some of the biological capacities on which culture depends. These abilities are to learn, to think symbolically, to use language, and to employ tools and other products in organizing their lives and adapting to their environments.

Anthropology confronts and ponders major questions of human existence as it explores human biological and cultural diversity in time and space. By examining ancient bones and tools, we unravel the mysteries of human origins. When did our ancestors separate from those remote great-aunts and great-uncles whose descendants are the apes? Where and when did *Homo sapiens* originate? How has our species changed? What are we now, and where are we going? How have changes in culture and society influenced biological change? Our genus, *Homo,* has been changing for more than 1 million years. Humans continue to adapt and change both biologically and culturally.

## Adaptation, Variation, and Change

**Adaptation** refers to the processes by which organisms cope with environmental forces and stresses, such as those posed by climate and *topography* or terrains, also called land-forms. How do organisms change to fit their environments, such as dry climates or high mountain altitudes? Like other animals, humans use biological means of adaptation. But humans are unique in also having cultural means of adaptation. Table 1-1 summarizes the cultural and biological means that humans use to adapt to high altitudes.

Mountainous terrains pose particular challenges, those associated with high altitude and oxygen deprivation. Consider four ways (one cultural and three biological) in which humans may cope with low oxygen pressure at high altitudes. Illustrating cultural (technological) adaptation would be a pressurized airplane cabin equipped with oxygen masks. There are three ways of adapting biologically to high altitudes: genetic adaptation, long-term physiological adaptation, and short-term physiological adaptation. First, native populations of high-altitude areas, such as the Andes of Peru and the Himalayas of Tibet and Nepal, seem to have acquired certain genetic advantages for life at very high altitudes. The Andean tendency to develop a voluminous chest and lungs probably has a genetic basis. Second, regardless of their genes, people who grow up at a high

## TABLE 1-1

### Forms of Cultural and Biological Adaptation (to High Altitude)

| Form of Adaptation | Type of Adaptation | Example |
|---|---|---|
| Technology | Cultural | Pressurized airplane cabin with oxygen masks |
| Genetic adaptation (occurs over generations) | Biological | Larger "barrel chests" of native highlanders |
| Long-term physiological adaptation (occurs during growth and development of the individual organism) | Biological | More efficient respiratory system, to extract oxygen from "thin air" |
| Short-term physiological adaptation (occurs spontaneously when the individual organism enters a new environment) | Biological | Increased heart rate, hyperventilation |

altitude become physiologically more efficient there than genetically similar people who have grown up at sea level would be. This illustrates long-term physiological adaptation during the body's growth and development. Third, humans also have the capacity for short-term or immediate physiological adaptation. Thus, when lowlanders arrive in the highlands, they immediately increase their breathing and heart rates. Hyperventilation increases the oxygen in their lungs and arteries. As the pulse also increases, blood reaches their tissues more rapidly. All these varied adaptive responses—cultural and biological—achieve a single goal: maintaining an adequate supply of oxygen to the body.

As human history has unfolded, the social and cultural means of adaptation have become increasingly important. In this process, humans have devised diverse ways of coping with the range of environments they have occupied in time and space. The rate of cultural adaptation and change has accelerated, particularly during the past 10,000 years. For millions of years, hunting and gathering of nature's bounty—*foraging*—was the sole basis of human subsistence. However, it took only a few thousand years for **food production** (the cultivation of plants and domestication of animals), which originated some 12,000–10,000 years ago, to replace foraging in most areas. Between 6000 and 5000 B.P. (before the present), the first civilizations arose. These were large, powerful, and complex societies, such as ancient Egypt, that conquered and governed large geographic areas.

Much more recently, the spread of industrial production has profoundly affected human life. Throughout human history, major innovations have spread at the expense of earlier ones. Each economic revolution has had social and cultural repercussions. Today's global economy and communications link all contemporary people, directly or indirectly, in the modern world system. People must cope with forces generated by progressively larger systems—region, nation, and world. The study of such contemporary adaptations generates new challenges for anthropology: "The cultures of world peoples need to be constantly rediscovered as these people reinvent them in changing historical circumstances" (Marcus and Fischer 1986, p. 24).

## → GENERAL ANTHROPOLOGY

The academic discipline of anthropology, also known as **general anthropology** or "four-field" anthropology, includes four main subdisciplines or subfields. They are sociocultural, archaeological, biological, and linguistic anthropology. (From here on, the shorter term *cultural anthropology* will be used as a synonym for "sociocultural anthropology.") Of the subfields, cultural anthropology has the largest membership. Most departments of anthropology teach courses in all four subfields.

There are historical reasons for the inclusion of four subfields in a single discipline. The origin of anthropology as a scientific field, and of American anthropology in particular, can be traced to the nineteenth century. Early American anthropologists were concerned especially with the history and cultures of the native peoples of North America. Interest in the origins and diversity of Native Americans brought together studies of customs, social life, language, and physical traits. Anthropologists still are pondering such questions as, Where did Native Americans come from? How many waves of migration brought them to the New World? What are the linguistic, cultural, and biological links among Native Americans and between them and Asia? (Note that a unified

Early American anthropology was especially concerned with the history and cultures of Native North Americans. Ely S. Parker, or Ha-sa-no-an-da, was a Seneca Indian who made important contributions to early anthropology. Parker also served as Commissioner of Indian Affairs for the United States.

four-field anthropology did not develop in Europe, where the subfields tend to exist separately.)

There also are logical reasons for the unity of American anthropology. Each subfield considers variation in time and space (that is, in different geographic areas). Cultural and archaeological anthropologists study (among many other topics) changes in social life and customs. Archaeologists use studies of living societies to imagine what life might have been like in the past. Biological anthropologists examine evolutionary changes in physical form, for example, anatomical changes that might have been associated with the origin of tool use or language. Linguistic anthropologists may reconstruct the basics of ancient languages by studying modern ones.

The subfields influence each other as anthropologists talk to each other, read books and journals, and meet in professional organizations. Anthropologists share certain key assumptions. Perhaps the most fundamental is the idea that sound conclusions about "human nature" cannot be derived from studying a single population, nation, society, or cultural tradition. A comparative, cross-cultural approach is essential.

General anthropology explores the basics of human biology, society, and culture and considers their interrelations. The four-field approach has been particularly effective in examining the relation between biology (e.g., "race"—see below) and culture. Almost 70 years ago, the famed anthropologist Ruth Benedict realized, "In World history, those who have helped to build the same culture are not necessarily of one race, and those of the same race have not all participated in one culture" (Benedict 1940, Ch. 2). This statement is even truer in today's globalizing world. How do contemporary anthropologists deal with issues of human biological diversity and race?

## ✦ HUMAN BIOLOGICAL DIVERSITY AND THE RACE CONCEPT

The photos in this book offer only a glimpse of the range of human biological variation. Additional illustration comes from your own experience. Look around you in your classroom or at the mall or multiplex. Inevitably you'll see people whose ancestors lived in many lands. The first (Native) Americans had to cross a land bridge that once linked Siberia to North America. For later immigrants, perhaps including your own parents or grandparents, the voyage may have been across the sea or overland from nations to the south. They came for many reasons. Some came voluntarily, while others were brought here in chains. The scale of migration in today's world is so vast that millions of people routinely cross national borders or live far from the homelands of their grandparents. Now meeting every day are diverse human beings whose biological features reflect adaptation to a wide range of environments other than the ones they now inhabit. Physical contrasts are evident to anyone. Anthropology's job is to explain them.

Historically, scientists have approached the study of human biological diversity in two main ways: (1) racial classification (now largely abandoned) versus (2) the current explanatory approach, which focuses on understanding specific differences. First we'll consider problems with **racial classification** (the attempt to assign humans to discrete categories [purportedly] based on common ancestry). Then we'll offer some explanations for specific aspects of human biological diversity (in this case light versus dark skin color). *Biological differences are real, important, and apparent to us all.* Modern scientists find it most productive to seek *explanations* for this diversity, rather than trying to pigeonhole people into categories called races.

What is race anyway? In theory, a biological race would be a geographically isolated subdivision of a species. (A *species* is a population whose members can interbreed to produce offspring that can live and reproduce.) Such a *subspecies* would be capable of interbreeding with other subspecies of the same species, but it would not actually do so because of its geographic isolation. Some biologists also use "race" to refer to "breeds," as of dogs or roses. Thus, a pit bull and a Chihuahua would be different races of dogs. Such domesticated "races" have been bred by humans for generations. Humanity (*Homo sapiens*) lacks such races because human populations have not been isolated enough from one another to develop into such discrete groups. Nor have humans experienced controlled breeding like that which has created the various kinds of dogs and roses.

A race is supposed to reflect shared *genetic* material (inherited from a common ancestor), but early scholars instead used *phenotypical* traits (usually skin color) for racial classification. **Phenotype** refers to an organism's evident traits, its "manifest biology"—anatomy and physiology. Humans display hundreds of evident (detectable) physical traits. They range from skin color, hair form, eye color, and facial features (which are visible) to blood groups and enzyme production (which become evident through testing).

Racial classifications based on phenotype raise the problem of deciding which traits are most important. Should races be defined by height, weight, body shape, facial features, teeth, skull form, or skin color? Like their fellow citizens, early European and American scientists gave priority to skin color. Many school books and encyclopedias still proclaim the existence of three great races: the white, the black, and the yellow. This overly simplistic classification was compatible with the political use of race during the colonial period of the late 19th and early 20th centuries. Such a tripartite scheme kept white Europeans neatly separate from their African, Asian, and Native American subjects. Colonial empires began to break up, and scientists began to question established racial categories, after World War II.

Politics aside, one obvious problem with such racial labels is that they don't accurately describe skin color. "White" people are more pink, beige, or tan than white. "Black" people are various shades of brown, and "yellow" people are tan or beige. These terms also have been dignified by more scientific-*sounding* synonyms—Caucasoid, Negroid, and Mongoloid—which actually have no more of a scientific basis than do white, black, and yellow.

It's true also that many human populations don't fit neatly into any one of the three "great races." For example, where does one put the Polynesians? *Polynesia* is a triangle

The photos in this chapter illustrate only a small part of the range of human biological diversity. Shown here is a Bai minority woman, from Shapin, in China's Yunnan province.

A young man from the Marquesas Islands in Polynesia.

A Native American: a Chiquitanos Indian woman from Bolivia.

A Native Australian.

of South Pacific islands formed by Hawaii to the north, Easter Island to the east, and New Zealand to the southwest. Does the bronze skin color of Polynesians place them with the Caucasoids or the Mongoloids? Some scientists, recognizing this problem, enlarged the original tripartite scheme to include the Polynesian race. Native Americans present an additional problem. Are they red or yellow? Again, some scientists add a fifth race—the red, or Amerindian—to the major racial groups.

Many people in southern India have dark skins, but scientists have been reluctant to classify them with black Africans because of their Caucasoid facial features and hair form. Some, therefore, have created a separate race for these people. What about the Australian aborigines, hunters and gatherers native to the most isolated continent? By skin color, one might place some Native Australians in the same race as tropical Africans. However, similarities to Europeans in hair color (light or reddish) and facial features have led some scientists to classify them as Caucasoids. But there is no evidence that Australians are closer genetically or historically to either of these groups than they are to Asians. Recognizing this problem, scientists often regard Native Australians as a separate race.

Finally, consider the San ("Bushmen") of the Kalahari Desert in southern Africa. Scientists have perceived their skin color as varying from brown to yellow. Those who regard San skin as yellow have placed them in the same category as Asians. In theory, people of the same race share more recent common ancestry with each other than they do with any others; but there is no evidence for recent common ancestry between San and Asians. More reasonably, the San are classified as members of the Capoid (from the Cape of Good Hope) race, which is seen as being different from other groups inhabiting tropical Africa.

Similar problems arise when any single trait is used as a basis for racial classification. An attempt to use facial features, height, weight, or any other phenotypical trait is fraught with difficulties. For example, consider the Nilotes, natives of the upper Nile region of Uganda and Sudan. Nilotes tend to be tall and to have long, narrow noses. Certain Scandinavians also are tall, with similar noses. Given the distance between their homelands, to classify them as members of the same race makes little sense. There is no reason to assume that Nilotes and Scandinavians are more closely related to each other than either is to shorter (and nearer) populations with different kinds of noses.

Would it be better to base racial classifications on a combination of physical traits? This would avoid some of the problems just discussed, but others would arise. First, skin color, stature, skull form, and facial features (nose form, eye shape, lip thickness) don't go together as a unit. For example, people with dark skin may be tall or short and have hair ranging from straight to very curly. Dark-haired populations may have light or dark skin, along with various skull forms, facial features, and body sizes and shapes. The number of combinations is very large, and the amount that heredity (versus environment) contributes to such phenotypical traits is often unclear.

There is a final objection to racial classification based on phenotype. The phenotypical characteristics on which races are based supposedly reflect genetic material that is shared and that has stayed the same for long periods of time. But phenotypical similarities and differences don't necessarily have a genetic basis. Because of changes in the environment that affect individuals during growth and development, the range of phenotypes characteristic of a population may change without any genetic change. There are several examples. In the early 20th century, the anthropologist Franz Boas

(1940/1966) described changes in skull form among the children of Europeans who had migrated to the United States. The reason for this wasn't a change in genes, since the European immigrants tended to marry among themselves. Some of their children had been born in Europe and merely raised in the United States. Something in the new environment, probably in the diet, was producing this change. We know now that changes in average height and weight produced by dietary differences in a few generations are common and have nothing to do with race or genetics.

## Explanatory Approaches

Traditional racial classification assumed that biological characteristics were determined by heredity and were stable (immutable) over long periods of time. We know now that a biological similarity doesn't necessarily indicate recent common ancestry. Dark skin color, for example, can be shared by tropical Africans and Native Australians for reasons other than common ancestry. It is not possible to *define human races* biologically. Still, scientists have made much progress in *explaining* variation in skin color, along with many other expressions of human biological diversity. We shift now from classification to *explanation,* in which natural selection plays a key role.

First recognized by Charles Darwin and Alfred Russel Wallace, **natural selection** is the process by which the forms most fit to survive and reproduce in a given environment—such as the tropics—do so in greater numbers than others in the same population do. Over the years, the less fit organisms die out and the favored types survive by producing more offspring. The role of natural selection in producing variation in skin color will illustrate the explanatory approach to human biological diversity. Comparable explanations have been provided for many other aspects of human biological variation.

*Melanin,* the primary determinant of human skin color, is a chemical substance manufactured in the epidermis, or outer skin layer. The melanin cells of darker-skinned people produce more and larger granules of melanin than do those of lighter-skinned people. By screening out ultraviolet radiation from the sun, melanin offers protection against a variety of maladies, including sunburn and skin cancer.

Before the 16th century, most of the world's very dark-skinned populations lived in the **tropics,** a belt extending about 23 degrees north and south of the equator, between the Tropic of Cancer and the Tropic of Capricorn. The association between dark skin color and a tropical habitat existed throughout the Old World, where humans and their ancestors have lived for millions of years. The darkest populations of Africa evolved not in shady equatorial forests but in sunny open grassland, or savanna, country.

Outside the tropics, skin color tends to be lighter. Moving north in Africa, for example, there is a gradual transition from dark brown to medium brown. Average skin color continues to lighten as one moves through the Middle East, into southern Europe, through central Europe, and to the north. South of the tropics skin color also is lighter. In the Americas, by contrast, tropical populations don't have very dark skin. This is because the settlement of the New World, by light-skinned Asian ancestors of Native Americans, was relatively recent, probably dating back no more than 18,000 years.

How, aside from migrations, can we explain the geographic distribution of skin color? Natural selection provides an answer. In the tropics, with intense ultraviolet

Before the 16th century, almost all the very dark-skinned populations of the world lived in the tropics, as does this Samburu woman from Kenya.

Very light skin color, illustrated in this photo of a blond, blue-eyed North Sea German fisherman, maximizes absorption of ultraviolet radiation by those few parts of the body exposed to direct sunlight during northern winters. This helps prevent rickets.

radiation from the sun, unprotected humans face the threat of severe sunburn, which can increase susceptibility to disease. This confers a selective *dis*advantage (i.e., less success in surviving and reproducing) on lighter-skinned people in the tropics (unless they stay indoors or use cultural products, like umbrellas or lotions, to screen sunlight). Sunburn also impairs the body's ability to sweat. This is a second reason light skin color, given tropical heat, can diminish the human ability to live and work in equatorial climates. A third disadvantage of having light skin color in the tropics is that exposure to ultraviolet radiation can cause skin cancer (Blum 1961).

A fourth, but very important, factor affecting the geographic distribution of human skin color has to do with vitamin D. W. F. Loomis (1967) focused on the role of ultraviolet radiation in stimulating the manufacture of vitamin D by the human body. The unclothed human body can produce its own vitamin D when exposed to sufficient sunlight. But in a cloudy environment that also is so cold that people have to clothe themselves most of the year (such as northern Europe, where very light skin color evolved), clothing interferes with the body's manufacture of vitamin D. A shortage of vitamin D diminishes the absorption of calcium in the intestines. A nutritional disease known as *rickets,* which softens and deforms the bones, can develop. In women, deformation of the pelvic bones from rickets can interfere with childbirth. During northern winters, light skin color maximizes the absorption of ultraviolet radiation and the manufacture of vitamin D by the few parts of the body that are exposed to direct sunlight. There has been selection against dark skin color in northern areas because melanin screens out ultraviolet radiation.

Considering vitamin D production, light skin is an advantage in the cloudy north but a disadvantage in the sunny tropics. In the tropics, dark skin color protects the body against an *overproduction* of vitamin D by screening out ultraviolet radiation. Too much vitamin D can lead to a potentially fatal condition (*hypervitaminosis D*), in which calcium deposits build up in the body's soft tissues. Kidney failure, gallstones, joint problems, and circulation problems can result from hypervitaminosis D—making it a selective disadvantage and making light skin maladaptive in the tropics.

This discussion of skin color shows that common ancestry, the presumed basis of race, is not the only reason for biological similarities. Natural selection can produce the same results in separate and distant populations, for example, Africans and southern Indians. Guided by the scientific method, biologists and anthropologists now focus on specific biological differences, such as skin color, and try to explain them.

## Cultural Forces Shape Human Biology

Anthropology's comparative, biocultural perspective recognizes that environmental factors, including cultural forces, constantly mold human biology, as we saw in the case of skull form among children of European migrants to the United States. (**Biocultural** refers to the inclusion and combination of both biological and cultural perspectives and approaches to comment on or solve a particular issue or problem.) Culture is a key environmental force in determining how human bodies grow and develop. Cultural traditions promote certain activities and abilities, discourage others, and set standards of physical well-being and attractiveness. Physical activities, including sports, which are influenced by culture, help build the body. For example, North American girls are encouraged to pursue, and therefore do well in competition involving figure skating, gymnastics, track and field, swimming, diving, and many other sports. Brazilian girls, although excelling in the team sports of basketball and volleyball, haven't fared nearly as well in individual sports as have their American and Canadian counterparts. Why are people encouraged to excel as athletes in some nations but not others? Why do people in some countries invest so much time and effort in competitive sports that their bodies change significantly as a result?

Cultural standards of attractiveness and propriety influence participation and achievement in sports. Americans run or swim not just to compete but to keep trim and fit. Brazil's beauty standards accept more fat, especially in female buttocks and hips. Brazilian men have had some international success in swimming and running, but Brazil rarely sends female swimmers or runners to the Olympics. One reason Brazilian women avoid competitive swimming in particular may be that sport's effects on the body. Years of swimming sculpt a distinctive physique: an enlarged upper torso, a massive neck, and powerful shoulders and back. Successful female swimmers tend to be big, strong, and bulky. The countries that produce them most consistently are the United States, Canada, Australia, Germany, the Scandinavian nations, the Netherlands, and the former Soviet Union, where this body type isn't as stigmatized as it is in Latin countries. Swimmers develop hard bodies, but Brazilian culture says that women should be soft, with big

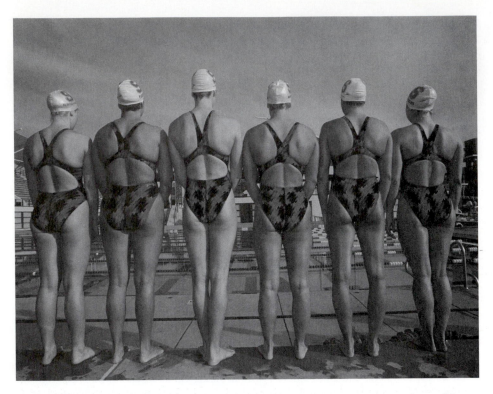

Years of swimming sculpt a distinctive physique: an enlarge upper torso, a massive neck, and powerful shoulders and back. Shown here are members of the Stanford University swim team.

hips and buttocks, not big shoulders. Many young female swimmers in Brazil choose to abandon the sport rather than the "feminine" body ideal.

## ❖ THE SUBDISCIPLINES OF ANTHROPOLOGY

## Cultural Anthropology

**Cultural anthropology** is the study of human society and culture, the subfield that describes, analyzes, interprets, and explains social and cultural similarities and differences. To study and interpret cultural diversity, cultural anthropologists engage in two kinds of activity: ethnography (based on fieldwork) and ethnology (based on cross-cultural comparison). **Ethnography** provides an account of a particular community, society, or culture. During ethnographic fieldwork, the ethnographer gathers data that he or she organizes, describes, analyzes, and interprets to build and present that account, which may be in the form of a book, article, or film. Traditionally, ethnographers have lived in small communities and studied local behavior, beliefs, customs, social life, economic activities, politics, and religion.

The anthropological perspective derived from ethnographic field work often differs radically from that of economics or political science. Those fields focus on national and official organizations and policies and often on elites. However, the groups that anthropologists traditionally have studied usually have been relatively poor and powerless, as are most people in the world today. Ethnographers often observe discriminatory practices directed toward such people, who experience food shortages, dietary deficiencies, and other aspects of poverty. Political scientists tend to study programs that national planners develop, while anthropologists discover how these programs work on the local level.

Cultures are not isolated. As noted by Franz Boas (1940/1966) many years ago, contact between neighboring tribes always has existed and has extended over enormous areas." Human populations construct their cultures in interaction with one another, and not in isolation" (Wolf 1982, p. ix). Villagers increasingly participate in regional, national, and world events. Exposure to external forces comes through the mass media, migration, and modern transportation. City and nation increasingly invade local communities with the arrival of tourists, development agents, government and religious officials, and political candidates. Such linkages are prominent components of regional, national, and international systems of politics, economics, and information. These larger systems increasingly affect the people and places anthropology traditionally has studied. The study of such linkages and systems is part of the subject matter of modern anthropology.

**Ethnology** examines, interprets, analyzes, and compares the results of ethnography—the data gathered in different societies. It uses such data to compare and contrast and to make generalizations about society and culture. Looking beyond the particular to the more general, ethnologists attempt to identify and explain cultural differences and similarities, to test hypotheses, and to build theory to enhance our understanding of how social and cultural systems work. Ethnology gets its data for comparison not just from ethnography but also from the other subfields, particularly from archaeological anthropology, which reconstructs social systems of the past. (Table 1-2 summarizes the main contrasts between ethnography and ethnology.)

## Archaeological Anthropology

**Archaeological anthropology** (more simply, "archaeology") reconstructs, describes, and interprets human behavior and cultural patterns through material remains. At sites where people live or have lived, archaeologists find artifacts, material items that humans have made, used, or modified, such as tools, weapons, camp sites, buildings, and garbage. Plant and animal remains and ancient garbage tell stories about consumption

| TABLE 1-2 | |
|---|---|
| **Ethnography and Ethnology—Two Dimensions of Cultural Anthropology** | |
| **Ethnography** | **Ethnology** |
| Requires fieldwork to collect data | Uses data collected by a series of researchers |
| Often descriptive | Usually synthetic |
| Group/community specific | Comparative/cross-cultural |

and activities. Wild and domesticated grains have different characteristics, which allow archaeologists to distinguish between gathering and cultivation. Examination of animal bones reveals the ages of slaughtered animals and provides other information useful in determining whether species were wild or domesticated.

Analyzing such data, archaeologists answer several questions about ancient economies. Did the group get its meat from hunting, or did it domesticate and breed animals, killing only those of a certain age and sex? Did plant food come from wild plants or from sowing, tending, and harvesting crops? Did the residents make, trade for, or buy particular items? Were raw materials available locally? If not, where did they come from? From such information, archaeologists reconstruct patterns of production, trade, and consumption.

Archaeologists have spent much time studying potsherds, fragments of earthenware. Potsherds are more durable than many other artifacts, such as textiles and wood. The quantity of pottery fragments allows estimates of population size and density. The discovery that potters used materials that were not available locally suggests systems of trade. Similarities in manufacture and decoration at different sites may be proof of cultural connections. Groups with similar pots may be historically related. Perhaps they shared common cultural ancestors, traded with each other, or belonged to the same political system.

Many archaeologists examine paleoecology. *Ecology* is the study of interrelations among living things in an environment. The organisms and environment together constitute an *ecosystem,* a patterned arrangement of energy flows and exchanges. Human

An archaeological team works at Harappa, one site from an ancient Indus River civilization dating back some 4,800 years.

ecology studies ecosystems that include people, focusing on the ways in which human use "of nature influences and is influenced by social organization and cultural values" (Bennett 1969, pp. 10–11). *Paleoecology* looks at the ecosystems of the past.

In addition to reconstructing ecological patterns, archaeologists may infer cultural transformations, for example, by observing changes in the size and type of sites and the distance between them. A city develops in a region where only towns, villages, and hamlets existed a few centuries earlier. The number of settlement levels (city, town, village, hamlet) in a society is a measure of social complexity. Buildings offer clues about political and religious features. Temples and pyramids suggest that an ancient society had an authority structure capable of marshaling the labor needed to build such monuments. The presence or absence of certain structures, like the pyramids of ancient Egypt and Mexico, reveals differences in function between settlements. For example, some towns were places where people came to attend ceremonies. Others were burial sites; still others were farming communities.

Archaeologists also reconstruct behavior patterns and lifestyles of the past by excavating. This involves digging through a succession of levels at a particular site. In a given area, through time, settlements may change in form and purpose, as may the connections between settlements. Excavation can document changes in economic, social, and political activities.

Although archaeologists are best known for studying prehistory, that is, the period before the invention of writing, they also study the cultures of historical and even living peoples. Studying sunken ships off the Florida coast, underwater archaeologists have been able to verify the living conditions on the vessels that brought ancestral African Americans to the New World as enslaved people. In a research project begun in 1973 in Tucson, Arizona, archaeologist William Rathje has learned about contemporary life by studying modern garbage. The value of "garbology," as Rathje calls it, is that it provides "evidence of what people did, not what they think they did, what they think they should have done, or what the interviewer thinks they should have done" (Harrison, Rathje, and Hughes 1994, p. 108). What people report may contrast strongly with their real behavior as revealed by garbology. For example, the garbologists discovered that the three Tucson neighborhoods that reported the lowest beer consumption actually had the highest number of discarded beer cans per household (Podolefsky and Brown 1992, p. 100)! Rathje's garbology also has exposed misconceptions about how much of different kinds of trash are in landfills: While most people thought that fast-food containers and disposable diapers were major waste problems, in fact they were relatively insignificant compared with paper, including environmentally friendly, recyclable paper (Rathje and Murphy 2001).

## Biological, or Physical, Anthropology

The subject matter of **biological,** or **physical, anthropology** is human biological diversity in time and space. The focus on biological variation unites five special interests within biological anthropology:

1. Human evolution as revealed by the fossil record (paleoanthropology)
2. Human genetics

3. Human growth and development
4. Human biological plasticity (the body's ability to change as it copes with stresses, such as heat, cold, and altitude)
5. The biology, evolution, behavior, and social life of monkeys, apes, and other nonhuman primates

These interests link physical anthropology to other fields: biology, zoology, geology, anatomy, physiology, medicine, and public health. Osteology—the study of bones—helps paleoanthropologists, who examine skulls, teeth, and bones, to identify human ancestors and to chart changes in anatomy over time. A paleontologist is a scientist who studies fossils. A paleoanthropologist is one sort of paleontologist, one who studies the fossil record of human evolution. Paleoanthropologists often collaborate with archaeologists, who study artifacts, in reconstructing biological and cultural aspects of human evolution. Fossils and tools often are found together. Different types of tools provide information about the habits, customs, and lifestyles of the ancestral humans who used them.

More than a century ago, Charles Darwin noticed that the variety that exists within any population permits some individuals (those with the favored characteristics) to do better than others at surviving and reproducing. Genetics, which developed later, enlightens us about the causes and transmission of this variety. However, it isn't just genes that cause variety. During any individual's lifetime, the environment works along with heredity to determine biological features. For example, people with a genetic tendency to be tall will be shorter if they are poorly nourished during childhood. Thus, biological anthropology also investigates the influence of environment on the body as it grows and matures. Among the environmental factors that influence the body as it develops are nutrition, altitude, temperature, and disease, as well as cultural factors, such as the standards of attractiveness we considered previously.

Biological anthropology (along with zoology) also includes primatology. The primates include our closest relatives—apes and monkeys. Primatologists study their biology, evolution, behavior, and social life, often in their natural environments. Primatology assists paleoanthropology, because primate behavior may shed light on early human behavior and human nature.

## Linguistic Anthropology

We don't know (and probably never will) when our ancestors acquired the ability to speak, although biological anthropologists have looked to the anatomy of the face and the skull to speculate about the origin of language. And primatologists have described the communication systems of monkeys and apes. We do know that well-developed, grammatically complex languages have existed for thousands of years. Linguistic anthropology offers further illustration of anthropology's interest in comparison, variation, and change. **Linguistic anthropology** studies language in its social and cultural context, across space and over time. Some linguistic anthropologists make inferences about universal features of language, linked perhaps to uniformities in the human brain. Others reconstruct ancient languages by comparing their contemporary descendants and in so doing make discoveries about history. Still others study linguistic differences to discover varied perceptions and patterns of thought in different cultures.

Historical linguistics considers variation in time, such as the changes in sounds, grammar, and vocabulary between Middle English (spoken from approximately A.D. 1050 to 1550) and modern English. **Sociolinguistics** investigates relationships between social and linguistic variation. No language is a homogeneous system in which everyone speaks just like everyone else. How do different speakers use a given language? How do linguistic features correlate with social factors, including class and gender differences (Tannen 1990)? One reason for variation is geography, as in regional dialects and accents. Linguistic variation also is expressed in the bilingualism of ethnic groups. Linguistic and cultural anthropologists collaborate in studying links between language and many other aspects of culture, such as how people reckon kinship and how they perceive and classify colors.

## ❖ ANTHROPOLOGY AND OTHER ACADEMIC FIELDS

As mentioned previously, one of the main differences between anthropology and the other fields that study people is holism, anthropology's unique blend of biological, social, cultural, linguistic, historical, and contemporary perspectives. Paradoxically, while distinguishing anthropology, this breadth is what also links it to many other disciplines. Techniques used to date fossils and artifacts have come to anthropology from physics, chemistry, and geology. Because plant and animal remains often are found with human bones and artifacts, anthropologists collaborate with botanists, zoologists, and paleontologists.

As a discipline that is both scientific and humanistic, anthropology has links with many other academic fields. Anthropology is a **science**—a "systematic field of study or body of knowledge that aims, through experiment, observation, and deduction, to produce reliable explanations of phenomena, with reference to the material and physical world" (*Webster's New World Encyclopedia* 1993, p. 937). The following chapters present anthropology as a humanistic science devoted to discovering, describing, understanding, and explaining similarities and differences in time and space among humans and our ancestors. Clyde Kluckhohn (1944) described anthropology as "the science of human similarities and differences" (p. 9). His statement of the need for such a field still stands: "Anthropology provides a scientific basis for dealing with the crucial dilemma of the world today: how can peoples of different appearance, mutually unintelligible languages, and dissimilar ways of life get along peaceably together?" (p. 9). Anthropology has compiled an impressive body of knowledge that this textbook attempts to encapsulate.

Besides its links to the natural sciences (e.g., geology, zoology), and social sciences (e.g., sociology, psychology), anthropology also has strong links to the humanities. The humanities include English, comparative literature, classics, folklore, philosophy, and the arts. These fields study languages, texts, philosophies, arts, music, performances, and other forms of creative expression. Ethnomusicology, which studies forms of musical expression on a worldwide basis, is especially closely related to anthropology.

Also linked is folklore, the systematic study of tales, myths, and legends from a variety of cultures. One might well argue that anthropology is among the most humanistic of all academic fields because of its fundamental respect for human diversity. Anthropologists listen to, record, and represent voices from a multitude of nations and cultures. Anthropology values local knowledge, diverse worldviews, and alternative philosophies. Cultural anthropology and linguistic anthropology in particular bring a comparative and nonelitist perspective to forms of creative expression, including language, art, narratives, music, and dance, viewed in their social and cultural context.

## ✦ APPLIED ANTHROPOLOGY

Anthropology is not a science of the exotic carried on by quaint scholars in ivory towers. Rather, anthropology has a lot to tell the public. Anthropology's foremost professional organization, the American Anthropological Association (AAA), has formally acknowledged a public service role by recognizing that anthropology has two dimensions: (1) academic anthropology and (2) practicing or **applied anthropology.** The latter refers to the application of anthropological data, perspectives, theory, and methods to identify, assess, and solve contemporary social problems. As Erve Chambers (1987, p. 309) states it, applied anthropology is the "field of inquiry concerned with the relationships between anthropological knowledge and the uses of that knowledge in the world beyond anthropology." More and more anthropologists from the four subfields now work in such "applied" areas as public health, family planning, business, economic development, and cultural resource management.

Applied anthropology encompasses any use of the knowledge and/or techniques of the four subfields to identify, assess, and solve practical problems. Because of anthropology's breadth, it has many applications. For example, applied medical anthropologists consider both the sociocultural and the biological contexts and implications of disease and illness. Perceptions of good and bad health, along with actual health threats and problems, differ among societies. Various ethnic groups recognize different illnesses, symptoms, and causes and have developed different health-care systems and treatment strategies.

Applied archaeology, usually called *public archaeology,* includes such activities as cultural resource management, contract archaeology, public educational programs, and historic preservation. An important role for public archaeology has been created by legislation requiring evaluation of sites threatened by dams, highways, and other construction activities. To decide what needs saving, and to preserve significant information about the past when sites cannot be saved, is the work of **cultural resource management (CRM).** CRM involves not only preserving sites but also allowing their destruction if they are not significant. The "management" part of the term refers to the evaluation and decision-making process. Cultural resource managers work for federal, state, and county agencies and other clients. Applied cultural anthropologists sometimes work with the public archaeologists, assessing the human problems generated by the proposed change and determining how they can be reduced. Table 1-3 relates anthropology's four subfields to its two dimensions.

| TABLE 1-3 | |
|---|---|
| **The Four Subfields and Two Dimensions of Anthropology** | |
| **Anthropology's Subfields (General Anthropology)** | **Examples of Application (Applied Anthropology)** |
| Cultural anthropology | Development anthropology |
| Archaeological anthropology | Cultural resource management (CRM) |
| Biological or physical anthropology | Forensic anthropology |
| Linguistic anthropology | Study of linguistic diversity in classrooms |

## ANTHROPOLOGY TODAY

### Remote and Poked, Anthropology's Dream Tribe

*"Been on any digs lately?"* Anthropologists are accustomed to that question, after announcing their profession. Often people confuse anthropology with archaeology, which is one—but just one—of anthropology's four subfields. Many anthropologists do dig in the ground, but others dig into the intricacies of human biology and living cultural expression. Anthropologists are known for their close observation of human behavior in natural settings and their focus on diversity. It is typical of the anthropological approach to go right to—and live with—the local people, whether in northern Kenya, as described here, or in middle-class America.

Anthropologists study human biology and culture in varied times and places and in a rapidly changing world. This news story focuses on a remote population, the Ariaal of northern Kenya, whom anthropologists have been studying since the 1970s. This account previews the multifaceted research interests that anthropologists have. Among the Ariaal, anthropologists have studied a range of topics, including kinship and marriage customs, conflict, and even biomedical issues such as illness and body type and function. As you read this account, consider, too, what anthropologists get from the people being studied and vice versa.

Anthropologists and other researchers have long searched the globe for people isolated from the modern world. The Ariaal, a nomadic community of about 10,000 people in northern Kenya, have been seized on by researchers since the 1970's, after one anthropologist, Elliot Fratkin—stumbled upon them and began publishing his accounts of their lives. . .

Other researchers have done studies on everything from their cultural practices to their testosterone levels. *National Geographic* focused on the Ariaal in 1999, in an article on vanishing cultures.

But over the years, more and more Ariaal—like the Masai and the Turkana in Kenya and the Tuaregs and Bedouins elsewhere in Africa—are settling down. Many have emigrated closer to Marsabit, the nearest town, which has cellphone reception and even sporadic Internet access.

The scientists continue to arrive in Ariaal country, with their notebooks, tents

*Continued*

## ANTHROPOLOGY TODAY

and bizarre queries, but now they document a semi-isolated people straddling modern life and more traditional ways.

"The era of finding isolated tribal groups is probably over," said Dr. Fratkin, a professor at Smith College who has lived with the Ariaal for long stretches and is regarded by some of them as a member of the tribe.

For Benjamin C. Campbell, a biological anthropologists at Boston University who was introduced to the Ariaal by Dr. Fratkin, their way of life, diet and cultural practices make them worthy of study.

Other academics agree. Local residents say they have been asked over the years how many livestock they own (many), how many times they have had diarrhea in the last month (often) and what they ate the day before yesterday (usually meat, milk or blood).

Ariaal women have been asked about the work they do, which seems to exceed that of the men, and about local marriage customs, which compel their prospective husbands to hand over livestock to their parents before the ceremony can take place. . . .

The researchers may not know this, but the Ariaal have been studying them all these years as well.

The Ariaal note that foreigners slather white liquid on their very white skin to protect them from the sun, and that many favor short pants that show off their legs and the clunky boots on their feet. Foreigners often partake of the local food but drink water out of bottles and munch on strange food in wrappers between meals, the Ariaal observe.

The scientists leave tracks as well as memories behind. For instance, it is not uncommon to see nomads in T-shirts bearing university logos, gifts from departing academics.

In Lewogoso Lukumai, a circle of makeshift huts near the Ndoto Mountains, nomads rushed up to a visitor and asked excitedly in the Samburu language, "Where's Elliot?"

They meant Dr. Fratkin, who describes in his book "Ariaal Pastoralists of Kenya" how in 1974 he stumbled upon the Ariaal, who had been little known until then. With money from the University of London and the Smithsonian Institution, he was traveling north from Nairobi in search of isolated agropastoralist groups in Ethiopia. But a coup toppled Haile Selassie, then the emperor, and the border between the countries was closed. So as he sat in a bar in Marsabit, a boy approached and, mistaking him for a tourist, asked if he wanted to see the elephants in a nearby forest. When the aspiring anthropologist declined, the boy asked if he wanted to see a traditional ceremony at a local village instead. That was Dr. Fratkin's introduction to the Ariaal, who share cultural traits with the Samburu and Rendille tribes of Kenya.

Soon after, he was living with the Ariaal, learning their language and customs while fighting off mosquitoes and fleas in his hut of sticks covered with grass.

The Ariaal wear sandals made from old tires and many still rely on their cows, camels and goats to survive. Drought is a regular feature of their world, coming in regular intervals and testing their durability.

"I was young when Elliot first arrived," recalled an Ariaal elder known as Lenampere in Lewogoso Lukumai, a settlement that moves from time to time to a new patch of sand. "He came here and lived with us. He drank milk and blood with us. After him, so many others came.". . .

Not all African tribes are as welcoming to researchers, even those with the necessary permits from government bureaucrats. But the Ariaal have a reputation for cooperating—in exchange, that is, for pocket money. "They think I'm stupid for asking dumb questions," said Daniel Lemoille, headmaster of the school in Songa, a village outside of Marsabit for Ariaal nomads who have settled down, and a frequent research assistant for visiting professors. "You have to try to explain that these same questions are asked to people all over the world and that their answers will help advance science.". . .

The Ariaal have no major gripes about the studies, although the local chief in Songa, Stephen Lesseren, who wore a Boston University T-shirt the other day, said he wished their work would lead to more tangible benefits for his people.

"We don't mind helping people get their Ph.D.'s," he said. "But once they get their Ph.D.'s, many of them go away. They don't send us their reports. . . . We want feedback. We want development."

Even when conflicts break out in the area, as happened this year as members of rival tribes slaughtered each other, victimizing the Ariaal, the research does not cease. With tensions still high, John G. Galaty, an anthropologist at McGill University in Montreal who studies ethnic conflicts, arrived in northern Kenya to question them.

In a study in *The International Journal of Impotence Research*, Dr. Campbell found that Ariaal men with many wives showed less erectile dysfunction than did men of the same age with fewer spouses.

Dr. Campbell's body image study, published in the *Journal of Cross-Cultural Psychology* this year, also found that Ariaal men are much more consistent than men in other parts of the world in their views of the average man's body [one like their own] and what they think women want [one like their own].

Dr. Campbell came across no billboards or international magazines in Ariaal country and only one television in a local restaurant that played CNN, leading him to contend that Ariaal men's views of their bodies were less affected by media images of burly male models with six-pack stomachs and rippling chests.

To test his theories, a nonresearcher without a Ph.D. showed a group of Ariaal men a copy of *Men's Health* magazine full of pictures of impossibly well-sculpted men and women. The men looked on with rapt attention and admired the chiseled forms.

"That one, I like," said one nomad who was up in his years, pointing at a photo of a curvy woman who was clearly a regular at the gym. Another old-timer gazed at the bulging pectoral muscles of a male bodybuilder in the magazine and posed a question that got everybody talking. Was it a man, he asked, or a very, very strong woman?

*Source*: "Remote and Poked, Anthropology's Dream Tribe," by Marc Lacey from *The New York Times*, December 18, 2005, Reprinted by permission.

## SUMMARY

1. Anthropology is the holistic, biocultural, and comparative study of humanity. It is the systematic exploration of human biological and cultural diversity across time and space. Examining the origins of, and changes in, human biology and culture, anthropology provides explanations for similarities and differences among humans and their societies.
2. The four subfields of general anthropology are (socio)cultural, archaeological, biological, and linguistic. All consider variation in time and space. Each also examines adaptation—the process by which organisms cope with environmental stresses.
3. Anthropology's biocultural perspective is a particularly effective way of approaching the topics of human biological diversity and "race." Because of a range of problems involved in classifying humans into racial categories, contemporary scientists focus on specific differences, such as in skin color, and try to explain them. Biological similarities between groups may reflect—rather than common ancestry (the assumed basis of race)—similar but independent adaptation to similar natural selective forces. Cultural forces mold human biology, including our body types and images.
4. Cultural anthropology explores the cultural diversity of the present and the recent past. Archaeology reconstructs cultural patterns, often of prehistoric populations. Biological anthropology documents diversity involving fossils, genetics, growth and development, bodily responses, and nonhuman primates. Linguistic anthropology considers diversity among languages. It also studies how speech changes in social situations and over time.
5. Concerns with biology, society, culture, and language link anthropology to many other fields—natural sciences, social sciences, and humanities.
6. Anthropology has two dimensions: academic and applied. The latter uses anthropological perspectives, theory, methods, and data to identify, assess, and solve social problems. The fields in which applied anthropologists work include business, government, economic development, education, and social services, action, and outreach. Applied anthropologists come from all four subfields.

## KEY TERMS

adaptation (p. 3)
anthropology (p. 2)
applied anthropology (p. 18)
archaeological anthropology (p. 13)
biocultural (p. 11)
biological (or physical) anthropology
    (p. 15)
cultural anthropology (p. 12)
cultural resource management (CRM)
    (p. 18)
culture (p. 2)
ethnography (p. 12)

ethnology (p. 13)
food production (p. 4)
general anthropology (p. 4)
holistic (p. 2)
linguistic anthropology (p. 16)
natural selection (p. 9)
phenotype (p. 6)
racial classification (p. 6)
science (p. 17)
sociolinguistics (p. 17)
tropics (p. 9)

# CHAPTER 2

## ETHICS AND METHODS

I n Chapter 1, we learned about anthropology and its subfields. Chapter 2 begins with a consideration of the ethical dimensions of anthropology, then turns to a discussion of research methods in physical anthropology, archaeology, and cultural anthropology. (Linguistic methods are discussed in Chapter 10.)

As the main organization representing the breadth of anthropology (all four subfields, academic and applied dimensions), the American Anthropological Association (AAA) believes that generating and appropriately using knowledge of the peoples of the world, past and present, is a worthy goal. The mission of the AAA is to advance anthropological research and encourage the spread of anthropological knowledge through publications, teaching, public education, and application. Part of that mission is to help educate AAA members about ethical obligations and challenges (http://www.aaanet.org).

## ⇨ ETHICS AND ANTHROPOLOGY

Anthropologists are increasingly mindful of the fact that science exists in society, and in the context of law and ethics. Anthropologists can't study things simply because they happen to be interesting or of value to science. As anthropologists conduct research and engage in other professional activities, ethical issues inevitably arise. Anthropologists typically have worked abroad, outside their own society. In the context of international contacts and cultural diversity, different value systems will meet, and often compete. To guide its members in making decisions involving ethics and values, the AAA offers a Code of Ethics.

The most recent code was approved in 1998 and updated in 1999. The code's preamble states that anthropologists have obligations to their scholarly field, to the wider society and culture, and to the human species, other species, and the environment. This code's aim is to offer guidelines and to promote discussion and education rather than to investigate allegations of misconduct. The AAA code addresses several contexts in which anthropologists work. Its main points may be summarized.

> Anthropologists should be open and honest about their research projects with all parties affected by the research. These parties should be informed about the nature, procedures, purpose(s), potential impacts, and source(s) of support for the research. Researchers should not compromise anthropological ethics in order to conduct research. They should pay attention to proper relations between themselves as guests and the host nations and communities where they work. The AAA does not advise anthropologists to avoid taking stands on issues. Indeed, seeking to shape actions and policies may be as ethically justifiable as inaction.

The full Code of Ethics is available at the AAA website (http://www.aaanet.org).

Physical anthropologists and archaeologists, in particular, often work as members of international teams. These teams typically include researchers from several countries, including the *host country*—the place (e.g., Ethiopia) where the research takes place. In **paleoanthropology** (aka *human paleontology*)—the study of human evolution through the fossil record—physical anthropologists and archaeologists often work together. Although the physical anthropologists are more interested in bones and the archaeologists in artifacts, their work may proceed jointly, as they try to infer the relation between the physical and cultural features of the remains they are examining.

Anthropologists must inform officials and colleagues in the host country about the purpose, funding, and likely results, products, and impacts of their research. They need to negotiate the matter of where the materials produced by the research will be analyzed and stored—in the host country or in the anthropologists' country—and for how long. To whom do research materials such as bones, artifacts, and blood samples belong? What kinds of restrictions will apply to their use?

The anthropologist's primary ethical obligation is to the people, species, and materials he or she studies. **Informed consent** (agreement to take part in the research—after having been informed about its nature, procedures, and possible impacts) should be obtained from anyone who provides information or who might be affected by the research. Although nonhuman primates can't give informed consent, primatologists still must take steps to ensure that their research doesn't endanger the animals. Either government agencies or nongovernmental organizations (NGOs) may be entrusted with protecting primates. If this is the case, the anthropologist will need their permission and informed consent to conduct research.

With living humans, informed consent is a necessity, not only in gathering information, but especially in obtaining biological samples, such as blood or urine. The research subjects must be told how the samples will be collected, used, and identified, and about the potential costs and benefits to them. Informed consent is needed from anyone providing data or information, owning materials being studied, or otherwise having an interest that might be affected by the research.

It is appropriate for North American anthropologists working in another country to (1) include host country colleagues in their research planning and requests for funding, (2) establish truly collaborative relationships with those colleagues and their institutions before, during, and after field work, (3) include host country colleagues in dissemination, including publication, of the research results, and (4) ensure that something is "given back" to host country colleagues. For example, research equipment and technology are allowed to remain in the host country. Or funding is provided for host country colleagues to do research, attend international meetings, or visit foreign institutions— especially those where their international collaborators work.

## ✦ RESEARCH METHODS IN PHYSICAL ANTHROPOLOGY AND ARCHAEOLOGY

There are all sorts of specialized research interests, topics, and methods within both physical anthropology and archaeology. (Given space limitations only some of them can be covered here.)

## Multidisciplinary Approaches

Scientists from diverse fields—for example, soil science and **paleontology** (the study of ancient life through the fossil record)—collaborate with anthropologists in the study of sites where fossils or artifacts have been found. *Palynology,* the study of ancient plants through pollen samples, is used to determine a site's environment at the time of occupation. Physical anthropologists and archaeologists turn to physicists and chemists for help with dating techniques. Physical anthropologists representing a subspecialty known as *bioarchaeology* may complement the picture of ancient life at a particular site by examining human skeletons to reconstruct their physical traits, health status, and diet (Larsen 2000). Evidence for social status may endure in hard materials—bones, jewels, buildings—through the ages. During life, bone growth and stature are influenced by diet. Genetic differences aside, taller people often are that way because they eat better than shorter people do. Differences in the chemical composition of groups of bones at a site may help distinguish privileged nobles from less fortunate commoners.

Anthropologists work with geologists, geographers, and other scientists in using satellite images to find ancient footpaths, roads, canals, and irrigation systems as well as patterns of flooding and deforestation, which can then be investigated on the ground. Aerial photos (taken from airplanes) and satellite images are forms of *remote sensing* used in site location. Anthropologists have used satellite imagery to identify, and then investigate on the ground, regions where deforestation is especially severe and where people and biodiversity, including nonhuman primates, may be at risk (Green and Sussman 1990; Kottak 1999; Kottak, Gezon, and Green 1994).

## Primatology

Primate behavior has been observed in zoos (e.g., de Waal 1998) and through experimentation (e.g., Harlow 1971), but the most significant studies have been done in natural settings, among free-ranging apes, monkeys, and lemurs. Since the 1950s, when primatologists began their shift from zoos to natural settings, numerous studies have been done of apes (chimps, gorillas, orangutans, and gibbons), monkeys (e.g., baboons, macaques), and lemurs (e.g., Madagascar's indrii, sifaka, and ring-tailed lemurs). *Arboreal* primates (those that spend most of their time in the trees) are difficult to see and follow, but they typically make a lot of noise. Their howls and calls can be studied and teach us about how primates communicate. Studies of primate social systems and behavior, including their mating patterns, infant care, and patterns of contact and dispersal, suggest hypotheses about behavior that humans do or do not share with our nearest relatives—and also with our hominid ancestors.

## Anthropometry

Physical anthropologists use various techniques to study nutrition, growth, and development. **Anthropometry** is the measurement of human body parts and dimensions, including skeletal parts (*osteometry*). Anthropometry is done on living people as well as on skeletal remains from sites. Body mass and composition provide measures of nutritional status in living people. Body mass is calculated from height and weight. The *body mass index* ($kg/m^2$) is the ratio of weight in kilograms divided by height in meters squared. An adult body mass above 30 is considered at risk of overweight, while one below 18 is at risk of underweight or malnutrition.

## Bone Biology

Central to physical anthropology is **bone biology** (or skeletal biology)—the study of bone as a biological tissue, including its genetics; cell structure; growth, development, and decay; and patterns of movement (*biomechanics*) (Katzenberg and Saunders, eds. 2000). The interpretation of fossil remains relies on understanding the structure and function of the skeleton. **Paleopathology** is the study of disease and injury in skeletons from archaeological sites. Some forms of cancer leave evidence in the bone. Breast cancer, for example, may spread (metastasize) skeletally, leaving holes or lesions in bones and skull. Certain infectious diseases (e.g., syphilis and tuberculosis) also mark bone, as do injuries and nutritional deficiencies (e.g., rickets, a vitamin D deficiency that deforms the bones).

In forensic anthropology, physical anthropologists work in a legal context, assisting coroners, medical examiners, and law enforcement agencies in recovering,

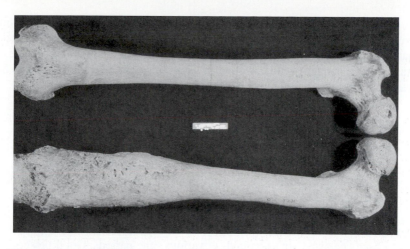

Two adult femora. The top one is normal in size and shape. The bottom one shows swelling and a ragged surface resulting from the chronic bacterial infection called osteomyelitis. These bones are from the Mississippian period Hazel site in Arkansas.

analyzing, and identifying human remains and determining the cause of death (Nafte 2000; Prag and Neave 1997). For example, when unknown skeletal remains are found, the police and the Delaware Medical Examiner's Office call on University of Delaware physical anthropologist Karen Rosenberg to help identify the body. By examining the bones, Rosenberg can determine characteristics, such as the height, age, and sex of the person. She notes that "the police authorities always ask for the race of an unidentified person. But racial categories are, in part, culturally defined and in any case are not closed biological 'types.' Recently I identified a skeleton as possibly being Caucasian, then on subsequent examinations thought he might be African American. In actuality, when the identification was made, he turned out to be Hispanic" (Rosenberg, quoted in Moncure 1998).

## Molecular Anthropology

**Molecular anthropology** uses genetic analysis (of DNA sequences) to assess evolutionary links. Through molecular comparison, evolutionary distance among living species, along with dates of most recent common ancestry, can be estimated. Molecular studies also have been used to assess and date the origins of modern humans and to examine their relation to extinct human groups such as the Neandertals, which lived in Europe between 130,000 and 28,000 years ago.

Molecular anthropologists examine relationships among ancient and contemporary populations and among species. It's well established, for example, that humans and chimpanzees have more than 98 percent of their DNA in common. Molecular anthropologists also reconstruct waves and patterns of migration and settlement. A *haplogroup* is a biological lineage (a large group of related people) defined by a specific cluster of genetic traits that occur together. Native Americans have four major haplogroups, which also are linked to East Asia. For nonhuman primates, molecular anthropologists use

DNA sequences to identify parentage, and to calculate kinship and degree of inbreeding within primate colonies. Molecular anthropologists also use "genetic clocks" to estimate divergence time (date of most recent common ancestry) among species (e.g., humans, chimps, and gorillas—5 million to 8 million years ago) and of various human groups (e.g., Neandertals and modern humans).

# Paleoanthropology

Paleoanthropologists study early hominids through fossil remains. **Fossils** are remains (e.g., bones), traces, or impressions (e.g., footprints) of ancient life. Typically, a team composed of scientists, students, and local workers participates in a paleoanthropological study. Such teams may include physical anthropologists, archaeologists, paleontologists, geologists, palynologists, paleoecologists, physicists, and chemists. Paleontologists help locate fossil beds containing remains of animals that can be dated and that are known to have coexisted with hominids at various time periods. Good preservation of faunal remains may suggest that hominid fossils have survived as well. Sometimes it's impossible to date the hominid fossils and artifacts found at a given site by using the most accurate and direct (radiometric) methods. In this case, comparison of the faunal remains at that site with similar, but more securely dated, fauna at another site may suggest a date for those animal fossils and the hominids and artifacts associated with them (see Gugliotta 2005).

# Survey and Excavation

Once potential sites have been identified, more intensive surveying begins in the search for hominid traces—bones or tools. Only hominids work rock to make tools and move rock fragments over long distances (see Watzman 2006). Some early hominid sites are strewn with thousands of tools. Typically, archaeologists, paleoanthropologists, and paleontologists combine both local (excavation) and regional (systematic survey) perspectives. They recognize that sites may not be discrete and isolated, but parts of larger systems.

## *Systematic Survey*

Archaeologists and paleoanthropologists have two basic field work strategies: systematic survey and excavation. **Systematic survey** provides a regional perspective by gathering information on settlement patterns over a large area. *Settlement pattern* refers to the distribution of sites within a region. Regional surveys reconstruct settlement patterns by addressing several questions: Where were sites located? How big were they? What kinds of buildings did they have? How old are the sites? Ideally, a systematic survey involves walking over the entire survey area and recording the location and size of all sites. From artifacts found on the surface, the surveyor estimates when each site was occupied.

## *Excavation*

During an **excavation,** scientists recover remains by digging through the layers of deposits that make up a site. These layers or strata are used to establish the time order of

An archaeologist drives in another stake for a large grid at an excavation site in Teotihuacan, Mexico. Such a grid enables the researchers to record the exact location of any artifact or feature found at the site.

the materials encountered during the dig. This relative chronology is based on the principle of *superposition:* In an undisturbed sequence of strata, the oldest layer is on the bottom. Each successive layer above is younger than the one below. Thus, artifacts and fossils from lower strata are older than those recovered from higher strata in the same deposit. This relative time ordering of material remains lies at the heart of archaeological, paleoanthropological, and paleontological research.

The archaeological and fossil records are so rich, and excavation is so labor-intensive and expensive, that nobody digs a site without a good reason. Sites are excavated because they are endangered, or because they answer specific research questions. Cultural resource management (CRM) focuses on managing the preservation of archaeological sites that are threatened by modern development. Many countries require archaeological impact studies before construction can take place. If a site is at risk and the development cannot be stopped, CRM archaeologists are called in to salvage what information they can from the site. (See the box at the end of this chapter.) Another reason a site may be chosen for excavation is that it is well suited to answer specific research questions. An archaeologist studying the origins of agriculture wouldn't want to excavate a large, fortified hilltop city with a series of buildings dating to a period well after the first appearance of farming communities. Rather, he or she would look for a small hamlet-size site located near good farmland and a water source. Such a site would have evidence of an early occupation dating to the period when farming communities first appeared in that region.

## ✦ KINDS OF ARCHAEOLOGY

Archaeologists pursue diverse research topics, using a wide variety of methods. Experimental archaeologists try to replicate ancient techniques and processes (e.g., tool making) under controlled conditions. Historical archaeologists use written records as guides and supplements to archaeological research. They work with remains more recent—often much more recent—than the advent of writing. Colonial archaeologists, for instance, use historical records as guides to locate and excavate postcontact sites in North and South America, and to verify or question written accounts. Classical archaeologists usually are affiliated with university departments of classics or the history of art, rather than with anthropology departments. These classical scholars focus on the literate civilizations of the Old World, such as Greece, Rome, and Egypt. Classical archaeologists often are as (or more) interested in art—styles of architecture and sculpture—as in the social, political, and economic variables that typically interest the anthropologist. Underwater archaeology is a growing field that investigates submerged sites, most often shipwrecks. Special techniques, including remotely operated vehicles like the one shown in the movie *Titanic*, are used, but divers also do underwater survey and excavation.

## ✦ DATING THE PAST

The archaeological record hasn't revealed every ancient society that has existed on Earth; nor is the fossil record a representative sample of all the plants and animals that ever have lived. Some species and body parts are better represented than others are, for many reasons. Hard parts, such as bones and teeth, preserve better than do soft parts, such as flesh and skin. The chances of fossilization increase when remains are buried in a newly forming sediment, such as silt, gravel, or sand. Good places for bones to be buried include swamps, floodplains, river deltas, lakes, and caves. The species that inhabit such areas have a better chance to be preserved than do animals that live in other habitats. Fossilization also is favored in areas with volcanic ash. Once remains do get buried, chemical conditions must be right for fossilization to occur. If the sediment is too acidic, even bones and teeth will dissolve. The study of the processes that affect the remains of dead animals is called **taphonomy,** from the Greek *taphos*, which means "tomb." Such processes include scattering by carnivores and scavengers, distortion by various forces, and the possible fossilization of the remains.

The conditions under which fossils are found also influence the fossil record. For example, fossils are more likely to be uncovered through erosion in arid areas than in wet areas. Sparse vegetation allows wind to scour the landscape and uncover fossils. The fossil record has been accumulating longer and is more extensive in Europe than in Africa because civil engineering projects and fossil hunting have been going on longer in Europe than in Africa. A world map showing where fossils have been found does not indicate the true range of ancient animals. Such a map tells us more about ancient geological activity, modern erosion, or recent human activity—such as paleontological research or road building. In considering the primate fossil record in later chapters, we'll see that certain areas provide more abundant fossil evidence for particular time periods. This doesn't necessarily mean that primates were not living elsewhere at the same time.

Nor does failure to find a fossil species in a particular place always mean that species did not live there. In the words of paleoanthropologist Christopher Stringer, "absence of evidence does not necessarily prove evidence of absence" (quoted in Gugliotta 2005).

We've seen that *paleontology* is the study of ancient life through the fossil record and that *paleoanthropology* is the study of ancient humans and their immediate ancestors. These fields have established a time frame, or *chronology*, for the evolution of life. Scientists use several techniques to date fossils. These methods offer different degrees of precision and are applicable to different periods of the past.

## Relative Dating

Chronology is established by assigning dates to geologic layers (strata) and to the material remains, such as fossils and artifacts, within them. Dating may be relative or absolute. **Relative dating** provides a time frame in relation to other strata or materials rather than absolute dates in numbers. Many dating methods are based on the geological study of **stratigraphy,** the science that examines the ways in which earth sediments accumulate in layers known as *strata* (singular, *stratum*). Soil that erodes from a hillside into a valley covers, and is younger than, the soil deposited there previously. Stratigraphy permits relative dating. That is, the fossils in a given stratum are younger than those in the layers below them and older than those in the layers above them. We may not know the exact or absolute dates of the fossils, but we can place them in time relative to remains in other layers. Changing environmental forces, such as lava flows and the alternation of land and sea, cause different materials to be deposited in a given sequence of strata; this allows scientists to distinguish between the strata.

Remains of animals and plants that lived at the same time are found in the same stratum. When fossils are found within a stratigraphic sequence, scientists know their dates relative to fossils in other strata; this is relative dating. When fossils are found in a particular stratum, the associated geological features (such as frost patterning) and remains of particular plants and animals offer clues about the climate at the time of deposition.

## Absolute Dating

Fossils can be dated more precisely, with dates in numbers (**absolute dating**), by using several methods. For example, the $^{14}C$, or carbon-14, technique is used to date organic remains. This is a *radiometric* technique (so called because it measures radioactive decay). $^{14}C$ is an unstable radioactive isotope of normal carbon, $^{12}C$. Cosmic radiation entering the earth's atmosphere produces $^{14}C$, and plants take in $^{14}C$ as they absorb carbon dioxide. $^{14}C$ moves up the food chain as animals eat plants and as predators eat other animals.

With death, the absorption of $^{14}C$ stops. This unstable isotope starts to break down into nitrogen ($^{14}N$). It takes 5,730 years for half the $^{14}C$ to change to nitrogen; this is the half-life of $^{14}C$. After another 5,730 years only one-quarter of the original $^{14}C$ will remain. After yet another 5,730 years only one-eighth will be left. By measuring the proportion of $^{14}C$ in organic material, scientists can determine a fossil's date of death, or the date of an ancient campfire. However, because the half-life of $^{14}C$ is short, this dating technique is less dependable for specimens older than 40,000 years than it is for more recent remains.

Fortunately, other radiometric dating techniques are available for earlier periods. One of the most widely used is the potassium-argon (K/A) technique. $^{40}$K is a radioactive isotope of potassium that breaks down into argon-40, a gas. The half-life of $^{40}$K is far longer than that of $^{14}$C—1.3 *billion* years. With this method, the *older* the specimen, the more reliable the dating. Furthermore, whereas $^{14}$C dating can be done only on organic remains, K/A dating can be used only for inorganic substances: rocks and minerals.

$^{40}$K in rocks gradually breaks down into argon-40. That gas is trapped in the rock until the rock is heated intensely (as with volcanic activity), at which point it may escape. When the rock cools, the breakdown of potassium into argon resumes. Dating is done by reheating the rock and measuring the escaping gas.

In Africa's Great Rift Valley, which runs down eastern Africa and in which early hominid fossils abound, past volcanic activity permits K/A dating. In studies of strata containing fossils, scientists find out how much argon has accumulated in rocks since they were last heated. They then determine, using the standard $^{40}$K deterioration rate (half-life), the date of that heating. Considering volcanic rocks at the top of a stratum with fossil remains, scientists establish that the fossils are *older than*, say, 1.8 million years. By dating the volcanic rocks below the fossil remains, they determine that the fossils are *younger than*, say, 2 million years. Thus, the age of the fossils is set at between 2 million and 1.8 million years. Note that absolute dating is that in name only; it may give ranges of numbers rather than exact dates.

Many fossils were discovered before the advent of modern stratigraphy. Often we can no longer determine their original stratigraphic placement. Furthermore, fossils aren't always discovered in volcanic layers. Like $^{14}$C dating, the K/A technique applies to a limited period of the fossil record. Because the half-life of $^{40}$K is so long, the technique cannot be used with materials less than 500,000 years old.

Other radiometric dating techniques can be used to cross-check K/A dates, again by using minerals surrounding the fossils. One such method, *uranium series dating*, measures fission tracks produced during the decay of radioactive uranium ($^{238}$U) into lead. Two other radiometric techniques are especially useful for fossils that cannot be dated by $^{14}$C (up to 40,000 before the present, or B.P.) or $^{40}$K (more than 500,000 B.P.). These methods are *thermoluminescence* (TL) and *electron spin resonance* (ESR). Both TL and ESR measure the electrons that are constantly being trapped in rocks and minerals (Shreeve 1992). Once a date is obtained for a rock found associated with a fossil, that date also can be applied to that fossil. The time spans for which the various absolute dating techniques are applicable are summarized in Table 2-1.

# ✦ RESEARCH METHODS IN CULTURAL ANTHROPOLOGY

Cultural anthropology and sociology share an interest in social relations, organization, and behavior. However, important differences between these disciplines arose from the kinds of societies each traditionally studied. Initially sociologists focused on the industrial West; anthropologists, on nonindustrial societies. Different methods of data collection and analysis emerged to deal with those different kinds of societies. To study large-scale, complex nations, sociologists came to rely on questionnaires and other

| TABLE 2-1 | | | |
|---|---|---|---|

**Absolute Dating Techniques**

| Technique | Abbreviation | Materials Dated | Effective Time Range |
|---|---|---|---|
| Carbon-14 | $^{14}C$ | Organic materials | Up to 40,000 years |
| Potassium-argon | K/A and $^{40}K$ | Volcanic rock | Older than 500,000 years |
| Uranium series | $^{238}U$ | Minerals | Between 1,000 and 1,000,000 years |
| Thermoluminescence | TL | Rocks and minerals | Between 5,000 and 1,000,000 years |
| Electron spin resonance | ESR | Rocks and minerals | Between 1,000 and 1,000,000 years |

means of gathering masses of quantifiable data. For many years sampling and statistical techniques have been basic to sociology, whereas statistical training has been less common in anthropology (although this is changing somewhat as anthropologists increasingly work in modern nations).

Traditional ethnographers studied small, nonliterate (without writing) populations and relied on ethnographic methods appropriate to that context. "Ethnography is a research process in which the anthropologist closely observes, records, and engages in the daily life of another culture—an experience labeled as the fieldwork method—and then writes accounts of this culture, emphasizing descriptive detail" (Marcus and Fischer 1986, p. 18). One key method described in this quote is **participant observation**—taking part in the events one is observing, describing, and analyzing.

Anthropology started to separate from sociology around 1900. Early students of society, such as the French scholar Émile Durkheim, were among the founders of both sociology and anthropology. Comparing the organization of simple and complex societies, Durkheim studied the religions of Native Australians (Durkheim 1912/2001), as well as mass phenomena (such as suicide rates) in modern nations (Durkheim 1897/1951). Eventually anthropology would specialize in the former, sociology in the latter.

## ❖ ETHNOGRAPHY: ANTHROPOLOGY'S DISTINCTIVE STRATEGY

Anthropology developed into a separate field as early scholars worked on Indian (Native American) reservations and traveled to distant lands to study small groups of foragers (hunters and gatherers) and cultivators. Traditionally, the process of becoming a cultural anthropologist has required a field experience in another society. Early ethnographers lived in small-scale, relatively isolated societies with simple technologies and economies.

Ethnography thus emerged as a research strategy in societies with greater cultural uniformity and less social differentiation than are found in large, modern, industrial nations. Traditionally, ethnographers have tried to understand the whole of a particular culture (or, more realistically, as much as they can, given limitations of time and perception). To pursue this goal, ethnographers adopt a free-ranging strategy for gathering information. In a given society or community, the ethnographer moves from setting to setting, place to place, and subject to subject to discover the totality and interconnectedness of social life. By expanding our knowledge of the range of human diversity, ethnography provides a foundation for generalizations about human behavior and social life. Ethnographers draw on varied techniques to piece together a picture of otherwise alien lifestyles. Anthropologists usually employ several (but rarely all) of the techniques discussed below (see also Bernard 2006).

---

## ✦ ETHNOGRAPHIC TECHNIQUES

The characteristic *field techniques* of the ethnographer include the following:

1.  Direct, firsthand observation of behavior, including *participant observation*.
2.  Conversation with varying degrees of formality, from the daily chitchat that helps maintain rapport and provides knowledge about what is going on, to prolonged *interviews,* which can be unstructured or structured.
3.  The *genealogical method*.
4.  Detailed work with *key consultants,* or *informants,* about particular areas of community life.
5.  In-depth interviewing, often leading to the collection of *life histories* of particular people (narrators).
6.  Discovery of local (native) beliefs and perceptions, which may be compared with the ethnographer's own observations and conclusions.
7.  Problem-oriented research of many sorts.
8.  Longitudinal research—the continuous long-term study of an area or site.
9.  Team research—coordinated research by multiple ethnographers.

## Observation and Participant Observation

Ethnographers must pay attention to hundreds of details of daily life, seasonal events, and unusual happenings. They should record what they see as they see it. Things never will seem quite as strange as they do during the first few weeks in the field. The ethnographer eventually gets used to, and accepts as normal, cultural patterns that initially were alien. Staying a bit more than a year in the field allows the ethnographer to repeat the season of his or her arrival, when certain events and processes may have been missed because of initial unfamiliarity and culture shock.

Many ethnographers record their impressions in a personal *diary,* which is kept separate from more formal *field notes*. Later, this record of early impressions will help point out some of the most basic aspects of cultural diversity. Such aspects include

Bronislaw Malinowski (1884–1942), who was born in Poland but spent most of his professional life in England, did fieldwork in the Trobriand Islands from 1914 to 1918. Malinowski is generally considered to be the father of ethnography. Does this photo suggest anything about his relationship with Trobriand villagers?

distinctive smells, noises people make, how they cover their mouths when they eat, and how they gaze at others. These patterns, which are so basic as to seem almost trivial, are part of what Bronislaw Malinowski called "the imponderabilia of native life and of typical behavior" (Malinowski 1922/1961, p. 20). These features of culture are so fundamental that natives take them for granted. They are too basic even to talk about, but the unaccustomed eye of the fledgling ethnographer picks them up. Thereafter, becoming familiar, they fade to the edge of consciousness. Initial impressions are valuable and should be recorded. First and foremost, ethnographers should try to be accurate observers, recorders, and reporters of what they see in the field.

Ethnographers strive to establish *rapport,* a good, friendly working relationship based on personal contact, with their hosts. One of ethnography's most characteristic procedures is participant observation, which means that we take part in community life as we study it. As human beings living among others, we cannot be totally impartial and detached observers. We take part in many events and processes we are observing and trying to comprehend. By participating, we may learn why people find such events meaningful, as we see how they are organized and conducted.

In Arembepe, Brazil, I learned about fishing by sailing on the Atlantic with local fishers. I gave Jeep rides to malnourished babies, to pregnant mothers, and once to a teenage girl possessed by a spirit. All those people needed to consult specialists outside the village. I danced on Arembepe's festive occasions, drank libations commemorating new births, and became a godfather to a village girl. Most anthropologists have similar field experiences. The common humanity of the student and the studied, the ethnographer and the research community, makes participant observation inevitable.

## Conversation, Interviewing, and Interview Schedules

Participating in local life means that ethnographers constantly talk to people and ask questions. As their knowledge of the local language and culture increases, they understand more. There are several stages in learning a field language. First is the naming phase—asking name after name of the objects around us. Later we are able to pose more complex questions and understand the replies. We begin to understand simple conversations between two villagers. If our language expertise proceeds far enough, we eventually become able to comprehend rapid-fire public discussions and group conversations.

One data-gathering technique I have used in both Arembepe and Madagascar involves an ethnographic survey that includes an interview schedule. In 1964, my fellow field-workers and I attempted to complete an interview schedule in each of Arembepe's 160 households. We entered almost every household (fewer than 5 percent refused to participate) to ask a set of questions on a printed form. Our results provided us with a census and basic information about the village. We wrote down the name, age, and gender of each household member. We gathered data on family type, religion, present and previous jobs, income, expenditures, diet, possessions, and many other items on our eight-page form.

Although we were doing a survey, our approach differed from the survey research design routinely used by sociologists and other social scientists working in large, industrial nations. That survey research, discussed below, involves sampling (choosing a small, manageable study group from a larger population). We did not select a partial sample from the total population. Instead, we tried to interview in all households in the community (that is, to have a total sample). We used an interview schedule rather than a questionnaire. With the **interview schedule,** the ethnographer talks face to face with people, asks the questions, and writes down the answers. *Questionnaire* procedures tend to be more indirect and impersonal; often the respondent fills in the form.

Our goal of getting a total sample allowed us to meet almost everyone in the village and helped us establish rapport. Decades later, Arembepeiros still talk warmly about how we were interested enough in them to visit their homes and ask them questions. We stood in sharp contrast to the other outsiders the villagers had known, who considered them too poor and backward to be taken seriously.

Like other survey research, however, our interview schedule did gather comparable quantifiable information. It gave us a basis for assessing patterns and exceptions in village life. Our schedules included a core set of questions that were posed to everyone. However, some interesting side issues often came up during the interview, which we would pursue then or later.

We followed such leads into many dimensions of village life. One woman, for instance, a midwife, became the key cultural consultant we sought out later when we wanted detailed information about local childbirth. Another woman had done an internship in an Afro-Brazilian cult (*candomblé*) in the city. She still went there regularly to study, dance, and get possessed. She became our candomblé expert.

A young interviewer at work on the campus of the University of Southern California (USC). Does this strike you as a formal or an informal interview?

Thus, our interview schedule provided a structure that *directed but did not confine* us as researchers. It enabled our ethnography to be both quantitative and qualitative. The quantitative part consisted of the basic information we gathered and later analyzed statistically. The qualitative dimension came from our follow-up questions, open-ended discussions, pauses for gossip, and work with key consultants.

## The Genealogical Method

As ordinary people, many of us learn about our own ancestry and relatives by tracing our genealogies. Various computer programs now allow us to trace our "family tree" and degrees of relationship. The **genealogical method** is a well-established ethnographic technique. Early ethnographers developed notation and symbols to deal with kinship, descent, and marriage. Genealogy is a prominent building block in the social organization of nonindustrial societies, where people live and work each day with their close kin. Anthropologists need to collect genealogical data to understand current social relations and to reconstruct history. In many nonindustrial societies, kin links are basic to social life. Anthropologists even call such cultures "kin-based societies." Everyone is related, and spends most of his or her time with relatives. Rules of behavior attached to particular kin relations are basic to everyday life (see Carsten 2004). Marriage also is crucial in organizing non-industrial societies because strategic marriages between villages, tribes, and clans create political alliances.

## Key Cultural Consultants

Every community has people who by accident, experience, talent, or training can provide the most complete or useful information about particular aspects of life. These people are **key cultural consultants,** also called *key informants*. In Ivato, the Betsileo village in Madagascar where I spent most of my time, a man named Rakoto was particularly knowledgeable about village history. However, when I asked him to work with me on a genealogy of the fifty to sixty people buried in the village tomb, he called in his cousin Tuesdaysfather, who knew more about that subject. Tuesdaysfather had survived an epidemic of influenza that ravaged Madagascar, along with much of the world, around 1919. Immune to the disease himself, Tuesdaysfather had the grim job of burying his kin as they died. He kept track of everyone buried in the tomb. Tuesdaysfather helped me with the tomb genealogy. Rakoto joined him in telling me personal details about the deceased villagers.

## Life Histories

In nonindustrial societies as in our own, individual personalities, interests, and abilities vary. Some villagers prove to be more interested in the ethnographer's work and are more helpful, interesting, and pleasant than others are. Anthropologists develop likes and dislikes in the field as we do at home. Often, when we find someone unusually interesting, we collect his or her **life history.** This recollection of a lifetime of experiences provides a more intimate and personal cultural portrait than would be possible otherwise. Life histories, which may be recorded or videotaped for later review and analysis, reveal how specific people perceive, react to, and contribute to changes that affect their lives. Such accounts can illustrate diversity, which exists within any community, since the focus is on how different people interpret and deal with some of the same problems. Many ethnographers include the collection of life histories as an important part of their research strategy.

## Local Beliefs and Perceptions, and the Ethnographer's

One goal of ethnography is to discover local (native) views, beliefs, and perceptions, which may be compared with the ethnographer's own observations and conclusions. In the field, ethnographers typically combine two research strategies, the emic (native-oriented) and the etic (scientist-oriented). These terms, derived from linguistics, have been applied to ethnography by various anthropologists. Marvin Harris (1968/2001) popularized the following meanings of the terms: An **emic** approach investigates how local people think. How do they perceive and categorize the world? What are their rules for behavior? What has meaning for them? How do they imagine and explain things? Operating emically, the ethnographer seeks the "native viewpoint," relying on local people to explain things and to say whether something is significant or not. The term **cultural consultant,** or *informant*, refers to individuals the ethnographer gets to know in the field, the people who teach him or her about their culture, who provide the emic perspective.

The **etic** (scientist-oriented) approach shifts the focus from local observations, categories, explanations, and interpretations to those of the anthropologist. The etic approach realizes that members of a culture often are too involved in what they are doing to interpret their cultures impartially. Operating etically, the ethnographer emphasizes what he or she (the observer) notices and considers important. As a trained scientist, the ethnographer should try to bring an objective and comprehensive viewpoint to the study of other cultures. Of course, the ethnographer, like any other scientist, is also a human being with cultural blinders that prevent complete objectivity. As in other sciences, proper training can reduce, but not totally eliminate, the observer's bias. But anthropologists do have special training to compare behavior between different societies.

What are some examples of emic versus etic perspectives? Consider our holidays. For North Americans, Thanksgiving Day has special significance. In our view (emically) it is a unique cultural celebration that commemorates particular historical themes. But a wider, etic, perspective sees Thanksgiving as just one more example of the postharvest festivals held in many societies. Another example: Local people (including many Americans) may believe that chills and drafts cause colds, which scientists know are caused by germs. In cultures that lack the germ theory of disease, illnesses are emically explained by various causes, ranging from spirits to ancestors to witches. *Illness* refers to a culture's (emic) perception and explanation of bad health, whereas *disease* refers to the scientific (etic) explanation of poor health, involving known pathogens.

Ethnographers typically combine emic and etic strategies in their fieldwork. The statements, perceptions, categories, and opinions of local people help ethnographers understand how cultures work. Local beliefs are also interesting and valuable in themselves. However, people often fail to admit, or even recognize, certain causes and consequences of their behavior. This is as true of North Americans as it is of people in other societies.

## Problem-Oriented Ethnography

Although anthropologists are interested in the whole context of human behavior, it is impossible to study everything. Most ethnographers now enter the field with a specific problem to investigate, and they collect data relevant to that problem (see Chiseri-Strater and Sunstein 2001; Kutsche 1998). Local people's answers to questions are not the only data source. Anthropologists also gather information on factors such as population density, environmental quality, climate, physical geography, diet, and land use. Sometimes this involves direct measurement—of rainfall, temperature, fields, yields, dietary quantities, or time allocation (Bailey 1990; Johnson 1978). Often it means that we consult government records or archives.

The information of interest to ethnographers is not limited to what local people can and do tell us. In an increasingly interconnected and complicated world, local people lack knowledge about many factors that affect their lives. Our local consultants may be as mystified as we are by the exercise of power from regional, national, and international centers.

## Longitudinal Research

Geography limits anthropologists less now than in the past, when it could take months to reach a field site, and return visits were rare. New systems of transportation allow anthropologists to widen the area of their research and to return repeatedly. Ethnographic reports now routinely include data from two or more field stays. **Longitudinal research** is the long-term study of a community, region, society, culture, or other unit, usually based on repeated visits.

One example of such research is the longitudinal study of Gwembe District, Zambia. This study, planned in 1956 as a longitudinal project by Elizabeth Colson and Thayer Scudder, continues with Colson, Scudder, and their associates of various nationalities. Thus, as is often the case with longitudinal research, the Gwembe study also illustrates team research—coordinated research by multiple ethnographers (Colson and Scudder 1975; Scudder and Colson 1980). Four villages, in different areas, have been followed for more than five decades. Periodic village censuses provide basic data on population, economy, kinship, and religious behavior. Censused people who have moved are traced and interviewed to see how their lives compare with those of people who have stayed in the villages.

A series of different research questions have emerged, while basic data on communities and individuals continue to be collected. The first focus of study was the impact of a large hydroelectric dam, which subjected the Gwembe people to forced resettlement. The dam also spurred road building and other activities that brought the people of Gwembe more closely in touch with the rest of Zambia. In subsequent research Scudder and Colson (1980) examined how education provided access to new opportunities as it also widened a social gap between people with different educational levels. A third study then examined a change in brewing and drinking patterns, including a rise in alcoholism, in relation to changing markets, transportation, and exposure to town values (Colson and Scudder 1988).

## Team Research

As mentioned, longitudinal research often is team research. My own field site of Arembepe, Brazil, for example, first entered the world of anthropology as a field-team village in the 1960s. It was one of four sites for the now defunct Columbia-Cornell-Harvard-Illinois Summer Field Studies Program in Anthropology. For at least three years, that program sent a total of about twenty undergraduates annually, the author included, to do brief summer research abroad. We were stationed in rural communities in four countries: Brazil, Ecuador, Mexico, and Peru. Since my wife, Isabel Wagley-Kottak, and I began studying it in 1962, Arembepe has become a longitudinal field site. Three generations of researchers have monitored various aspects of change and development. The community has changed from a village into a town and illustrates the process of globalization at the local level. Its economy, religion, and social life have been transformed (see Kottak 2006).

Brazilian and American researchers worked with us on team research projects during the 1980s (on television's impact) and the 1990s (on ecological awareness and environmental risk perception). Graduate students from the University of Michigan have drawn on our baseline information from the 1960s as they have studied various topics in Arembepe. In 1990 Doug Jones, a Michigan student doing biocultural research, used Arembepe as a field site to investigate standards of physical attractiveness. In 1996–1997, Janet Dunn studied family planning and changing female reproductive strategies. Chris

O'Leary, who first visited Arembepe in summer 1997, investigated a striking aspect of religious change there—the arrival of Protestantism; his dissertation (O'Leary 2002) research then examined changing food habits and nutrition in relation to globalization. Arembepe is thus a site where various field-workers have worked as members of a longitudinal team. The more recent researchers have built on prior contacts and findings to increase knowledge about how local people meet and manage new circumstances.

## ✦ SURVEY RESEARCH

As anthropologists work increasingly in large-scale societies, they have developed innovative ways of blending ethnography and survey research (Fricke 1994). Before examining such combinations of field methods, let's consider survey research and the main differences between survey research and ethnography. Working mainly in large, populous nations, sociologists, political scientists, and economists have developed and refined the **survey research** design, which involves sampling, impersonal data collection, and statistical analysis. Survey research usually draws a **sample** (a manageable study group) from a much larger population. By studying a properly selected and representative sample, social scientists can make accurate inferences about the larger population.

In smaller-scale societies and communities, ethnographers get to know most of the people. Given the greater size and complexity of nations, survey research cannot

Janet Dunn, one of many anthropologists who have worked in Arembepe. Where is Arembepe, and what kinds of research have been done there?

help being more impersonal. Survey researchers call the people they study *respondents*. These are people who respond to questions during a survey. Sometimes survey researchers interview them personally. Sometimes, after an initial meeting, they ask respondents to fill out a questionnaire. In other cases researchers mail or e-mail questionnaires to randomly selected sample members or have paid assistants interview or telephone them. In a **random sample,** all members of the population have an equal statistical chance of being chosen for inclusion. A random sample is selected by randomizing procedures, such as tables of random numbers, which are found in many statistics textbooks.

Probably the most familiar example of sampling is the polling used to predict political races. The media hire agencies to estimate outcomes and do exit polls to find out what kinds of people voted for which candidates. During sampling, researchers gather information about age, gender, religion, occupation, income, and political party preference. These characteristics (**variables**—attributes that vary among members of a sample or population) are known to influence political decisions.

Many more variables affect social identities, experiences, and activities in a modern nation than in the small communities where ethnography grew up. In contemporary North America hundreds of factors influence our behavior and attitudes. These social predictors include our religion; the region of the country we grew up in; whether we come from a town, suburb, or city; and our parents' professions, ethnic origins, and income levels.

Ethnography can be used to supplement and fine-tune survey research. Anthropologists can transfer the personal, firsthand techniques of ethnography to virtually any setting that includes human beings. A combination of survey research and ethnography can provide new perspectives on life in **complex societies** (large and populous societies with social stratification and central governments). Preliminary ethnography also can help develop culturally appropriate questions for inclusion in surveys.

In any complex society, many predictor variables (*social indicators*) influence behavior and opinions. Because we must be able to detect, measure, and compare the influence of social indicators, many contemporary anthropological studies have a statistical foundation. Even in rural fieldwork, more anthropologists now draw samples, gather quantitative data, and use statistics to interpret them (see Bernard 2006; Bernard, ed. 1998). Quantifiable information may permit a more precise assessment of similarities and differences among communities. Statistical analysis can support and round out an ethnographic account of local social life.

However, in the best studies, the hallmark of ethnography remains: Anthropologists enter the community and get to know the people. They participate in local activities, networks, and associations in the city, town, or countryside. They observe and experience social conditions and problems. They watch the effects of national and international policies and programs on local life. The ethnographic method and the emphasis on personal relationships in social research are valuable gifts that cultural anthropology brings to the study of any society.

# ANTHROPOLOGY TODAY

## *Archaeologist in New Orleans Finds a Way to Help the Living*

*One role for anthropologists is to help communities preserve their culture in the face of threat or disaster. The following account describes the work of an anthropologist doing public archaeology in New Orleans in the wake of Hurricane Katrina. Cultural resource management, as discussed here, is one form of applied anthropology: the application of anthropological perspectives, theory, methods, and data to identify, assess, and solve social problems.*

"That's a finger bone."

Shannon Lee Dawdy kneeled in the forlorn Holt graveyard to touch a thimble-size bone poking up out of the cracked dirt. She examined it without revulsion, with the fascination of a scientist and with the sadness of someone who loves New Orleans.

Dr. Dawdy, a 38-year-old assistant professor of anthropology at the University of Chicago, is one of the more unusual relief workers among the thousands who have come to the devastated expanses of Louisiana, Mississippi and Texas in the aftermath of Hurricanes Katrina and Rita. She is officially embedded with the Federal Emergency Management Agency [FEMA] as a liaison to the state's historic preservation office.

Her mission is to try to keep the rebuilding of New Orleans from destroying what is left of its past treasures and current culture.

While much of the restoration of the battered Gulf Coast is the effort of engineers and machines, the work of Dr. Dawdy, trained as an archaeologist, an anthropologist and a historian, shows that the social sciences have a role to play as well. "It's a way that archaeology can contribute back to the living," she said," which it doesn't often get to do."

Holt cemetery, a final resting place for the city's poor, is just one example of what she wants to preserve and protect.

Other New Orleans graveyards have gleaming mausoleums that keep the coffins above the marshy soil. But the coffins of Holt are buried, and the ground covering many of them is bordered with wooden frames marked with makeshift headstones.

Mourners decorate the graves with votive objects: teddy bears for children and an agglomeration of objects, including ice chests, plastic jack-o'-lanterns and chairs, on the graves of adults. There is the occasional liquor bottle. . . .

Many of the objects on the graves were washed away by the storm, or shifted from one part of the graveyard to another. Dr. Dawdy has proposed treating the site as archaeologists would an ancient site in which objects have been exposed on the surface by erosion.

Before the hurricanes, the cemetery was often busy, a hub of activity on All Soul's Day, when people came to freshen the grave decorations.

"The saddest thing to me now was how few people we see," she said, looking at the empty expanse and the scarred live oaks. "I realize we're having enough trouble taking care of the living," she added, but the lack of activity in a city normally so close to the spirits of the past "drove home how far out of whack things are." . . .

Treating Holt as an archaeological site means the government should not treat the votive artifacts as debris, she said, but as the religious artifacts that they are, with some effort to restore the damaged site, to find the objects and at least record where they came from.

*Continued*

# ANTHROPOLOGY TODAY

FEMA simply tries to clean up damaged areas, and its Disaster Mortuary Operational Response Teams—called Dmort—deal with the bodies of the dead and address problems in cemeteries that might lead to disease.

If such places are destroyed, Dr. Dawdy said, "then people don't feel as connected there." She added that they might be more willing to come back to a damaged city if they felt they were returning to a recognizable home.

Though she has deep emotional ties to New Orleans, Dr. Dawdy was born in Northern California. She came here in 1994 to write her master's thesis for the College of William & Mary, and, "I wrote it all day," she said. "If I had written a minimum of five pages, I could come out for a parade at night." Over the eight weeks it took to finish the project, she said: "I fell in love with New Orleans. I really consider it the home of my heart."

She started a pilot program at the University of New Orleans, working with city planners and grants for research projects that involved excavation, oral history and hands-on work with the city to safeguard its buried treasures.

She left that job to earn a double doctorate at the University of Michigan in anthropology and history that focused on French colonial times in New Orleans, then landed a coveted faculty position at the University of Chicago. . . .

Even before Hurricane Katrina, Dr. Dawdy had found ways to return to New Orleans. In 2004, she made an intriguing discovery while researching a possible archaeological site under an old French Quarter parking garage slated for demolition. Property records and advertisements from the 1820s said that the site had been the location of a hotel with an enticing name: the Rising Sun Hotel.

Dr. Dawdy found a January 1821 newspaper advertisement for the hotel in which its owners promised to "maintain the character of giving the best entertainment, which this house has enjoyed for twenty years past."

It went on: "Gentlemen may here rely upon finding attentive Servants. The bar will be supplied with genuine good Liquors; and at the Table, the fare will be of the best the market or the season will afford." . . .

New Orleans, she noted, has always been known for its libertine lifestyle. The French all but abandoned the city as its colony around 1735 as being unworthy of the nation's support as a colony. Novels like "Manon Lescaut" portrayed the city as a den of iniquity and corruption, and across Europe, "they thought the locals were basically a bunch of rogues, immoral and corrupt," Dr. Dawdy said.

She added that she saw parallels to today, as some skepticism emerges about rebuilding the city. Dr. Dawdy characterized that posture as, "Those people in New Orleans aren't worth saving, because they're all criminals anyway." But even if the devastation makes it hard to envision the road back, the city, she said, is worth fighting for.

"The thing about New Orleans that gives me hope is they are so tied to family, place, history," Dr. Dawdy said. "If anyone is going to stick it out, out of a sense of history, out of a sense of tradition, it is New Orleans."

*Source:* "Archaeologist in New Orleans Finds a Way to Help the Living," by John R. Schwartz from *The New York Times*, January 3, 2006. Reprinted by permission.

# SUMMARY

1. Because science exists in society, and in the context of law and ethics, anthropologists can't study things simply because they happen to be interesting or of scientific value. Anthropologists have obligations to their scholarly field, to the wider society and culture (including that of the host country), and to the human species, other species, and the environment.

2. Physical anthropologists and archaeologists pursue diverse research topics, using varied methods and often working together. At an archaeological site, physical anthropologists may complement the picture of ancient life by examining skeletons to reconstruct their physical traits, health status, and diet. Remote sensing may be used to locate ancient footpaths, roads, canals, and irrigation systems, which can then be investigated on the ground.

3. Studies of primates suggest hypotheses about behavior that humans do or do not share with our nearest relatives—and also with our hominid ancestors. Anthropometry, the measurement of human body parts and dimensions, is done on living people and on skeletal remains from sites.

4. Central to physical anthropology is bone biology—the study of bone genetics; cell structure; growth, development, and decay; and patterns of movement. Paleopathology is the study of disease and injury in skeletons from archaeological sites. Molecular anthropology uses genetic analysis (of DNA sequences) to assess evolutionary relationships.

5. Archaeologists combine both local (excavation) and regional (systematic survey) perspectives. Sites are excavated because they are in danger of being destroyed or because they address specific research interests. There are many kinds of archaeology, such as historical, classical, and underwater archaeology.

6. The fossil record is not a representative sample of all the plants and animals that have ever lived. Hard parts, such as bones and teeth, preserve better than soft parts, such as flesh and skin, do. Anthropologists and paleontologists use stratigraphy and radiometric techniques to date fossils. Carbon-14 ($^{14}$C) dating is most effective with fossils less than 40,000 years old. Potassium-argon (K/A) dating can be used for fossils older than 500,000 years.

7. Ethnographic methods include firsthand and participant observation, rapport building, interviews, genealogies, work with key consultants or informants, collection of life histories, discovery of local beliefs and perceptions, problem-oriented and longitudinal research, and team research. Ethnographers work in communities and form personal relationships with local people as they study their lives.

8. An interview schedule is a form an ethnographer completes as he or she visits a series of households. Key consultants, or informants, teach us about particular areas of local life. Life histories dramatize the fact that culture bearers are individuals. Such case studies document personal experiences with culture and culture change. Genealogical information is particularly useful in societies in which principles of kinship and marriage organize social and political life. Emic approaches focus on native perceptions and explanations. Etic approaches give

priority to the ethnographer's own observations and conclusions. Longitudinal research is the systematic study of an area or site over time.

9. Traditionally, anthropologists worked in small-scale societies; sociologists, in modern nations. Different techniques developed to study such different kinds of societies. Anthropologists do their fieldwork in communities and study the totality of social life. Sociologists use surveys and study samples to make inferences about a larger population. Anthropologists may employ ethnographic procedures to study cities, towns, or rural areas.

## KEY TERMS

absolute dating (p. 31)
anthropometry (p. 26)
bone biology (p. 26)
complex societies (p. 42)
cultural consultant (p. 38)
emic (p. 38)
etic (p. 38)
excavation (p. 28)
fossils (p. 28)
genealogical method (p. 37)
informed consent (p. 24)
interview schedule (p. 36)
key cultural consultants (p. 38)
life history (p. 38)

longitudinal research (p. 40)
molecular anthropology (p. 27)
paleoanthropology (p. 24)
paleontology (p. 25)
paleopathology (p. 26)
participant observation (p. 33)
random sample (p. 42)
relative dating (p. 31)
sample (p. 41)
stratigraphy (p. 31)
survey research (p. 41)
systematic survey (p. 28)
taphonomy (p. 30)
variables (p. 42)

# CHAPTER 3

# EVOLUTION, GENETICS, AND HUMAN VARIATION

Compared with other animals, humans have uniquely varied ways—cultural and biological—of evolving, of adapting to environmental stresses. Exemplifying *cultural* adaptation, we manipulate our artifacts and behavior in response to environmental conditions. We turn up thermostats or travel to Florida in the winter. We turn on fire hydrants, swim, or ride in air-conditioned cars to escape the summer's heat. Although such reliance on culture has increased in the course of human evolution, people haven't stopped adapting biologically. As in other species, human populations adapt genetically in response to environmental forces, and individuals react physiologically to stresses. Thus, when we work in the sun, sweating occurs spontaneously, cooling the skin and reducing the temperature of subsurface blood vessels.

We are ready now for a more detailed look at the principles that determine human biological adaptation, variation, and change.

## ✦ THE ORIGIN OF SPECIES

During the 18th century, many scholars became interested in human origins, biological diversity, and our position within the classification of plants and animals. At that time, the commonly accepted explanation for the origin of species came from Genesis, the first book of the Bible: God had created all life during six days of Creation. According to **creationism,** biological similarities and differences originated at the Creation. Characteristics of life forms were seen as immutable; they could not change. Through

According to creationism all life originated during the six days of creation described in the Bible. Catastrophism proposed that fires and floods, including the biblical deluge involving Noah's ark (depicted in this painting by the American artist Edward Hicks), destroyed certain species.

calculations based on genealogies in the Bible, the biblical scholars James Ussher and John Lightfoot even purported to trace the Creation to a very specific time: October 23, 4004 B.C., at 9 A.M.

Carolus Linnaeus (1707–1778) developed the first comprehensive (and still influential) classification, or taxonomy, of plants and animals. He grouped life forms on the basis of similarities and differences in their physical characteristics. He used traits such as the presence of a backbone to distinguish vertebrates from invertebrates and the presence of mammary glands to distinguish mammals from birds. Linnaeus viewed the differences between life forms as part of the Creator's orderly plan. He thought that biological similarities and differences had been established at the time of Creation and had not changed.

Fossil discoveries during the 18th and 19th centuries raised doubts about creationism. Fossils showed that different kinds of life once had existed. If all life had originated at the same time, why weren't ancient species still around? Why weren't contemporary plants and animals found in the fossil record? A modified explanation combining creationism with **catastrophism** arose to replace the original doctrine. In this view, fires, floods, and other catastrophes, including the biblical flood involving Noah's ark, had destroyed ancient species. After each destructive event, God had created again, leading to contemporary species. How did the catastrophists explain certain clear similarities between fossils and modern animals? They argued that some ancient species had managed to survive in isolated areas. For example, after the biblical flood, the progeny of the animals saved on Noah's ark spread throughout the world.

## Theory and Fact

The alternative to creationism and catastrophism was *transformism,* also called **evolution.** Evolutionists believe that species arise from others through a long and gradual process of transformation, or descent with modification. Charles Darwin became the best known of the evolutionists. However, he was influenced by earlier scholars, including his own grandfather. In a book called *Zoonomia* published in 1794, Erasmus Darwin had proclaimed the common ancestry of all animal species.

Charles Darwin also was influenced by Sir Charles Lyell, the father of geology. During Darwin's famous voyage to South America aboard the *Beagle,* he read Lyell's influential book *Principles of Geology* (1837/1969), which exposed him to Lyell's principle of **uniformitarianism.** Uniformitarianism states that the present is the key to the past. Explanations for past events should be sought in the long-term action of ordinary forces that still operate today. Thus, natural forces (rainfall, soil deposition, earthquakes, and volcanic action) gradually have built and modified geological features such as mountain ranges. The earth's structure has been transformed gradually through natural forces operating for millions of years (see Weiner 1994).

Uniformitarianism was a necessary building block for evolutionary theory. It cast serious doubt on the belief that the world was only 6,000 years old. It would take much longer for such ordinary forces as rain and wind to produce major geological changes. The longer time span also allowed enough time for the biological changes that fossil discoveries were revealing. Darwin applied the ideas of uniformitarianism and long-term transformation to living things. He argued that all life forms are ultimately related and that the number of species has increased over time. (For more on science, evolution, and creationism, see Futuyma 1995; Gould 1999; Wilson 2002.)

Charles Darwin provided a theoretical framework for understanding evolution. He offered natural selection as a powerful evolutionary mechanism that could explain the origin of species, biological diversity, and similarities among related life forms. Darwin proposed a *theory of evolution* in the strict sense. A **theory** is a set of ideas formulated (by reasoning from known facts) to explain something. The main value of a theory is to promote new understanding. A theory suggests patterns, connections, and relationships that may be confirmed by new research. The *fact* of evolution (that evolution has occurred) was known earlier, for example by Erasmus Darwin. The *theory* of evolution, through natural selection (*how* evolution occurred), was Darwin's major contribution. Actually, natural selection wasn't Darwin's unique discovery. Working independently, the naturalist Alfred Russel Wallace had reached a similar conclusion (Shermer 2002). In a joint paper read to London's Linnaean Society in 1858, Darwin and Wallace made their discovery public. Darwin's book *On the Origin of Species* (1859/1958) offered much fuller documentation.

**Natural selection** is the process by which the forms most fit to survive and reproduce in a given environment do so in greater numbers than others in the same population.

More than survival of the fittest, natural selection is differential reproductive success. Natural selection is a natural process that leads to a result. Natural selection operates when there is competition for strategic resources (those necessary for life) such as food and space between members of the population. There is also the matter of finding mates. You can win the competition for food and space and have no mate and thus have no impact on the future of the species. For natural selection to work on a particular population, there must be variety within that population, as there always is.

The giraffe's neck can illustrate how natural selection works on variety within a population. In any group of giraffes, there always is variation in neck length. When food is adequate, the animals have no problem feeding themselves. But when there is pressure on strategic resources, so that dietary foliage is not as abundant as usual, giraffes with longer necks have an advantage. They can feed off the higher branches. If this feeding advantage permits longer-necked giraffes to survive and reproduce even slightly more effectively than shorter-necked ones, giraffes with longer necks will transmit more of their genetic material to future generations than will giraffes with shorter necks.

An incorrect alternative to this (Darwinian) explanation would be the inheritance of acquired characteristics. That is the idea that in each generation, individual giraffes strain their necks to reach just a bit higher. This straining somehow modifies their genetic material. Over generations of strain, the average neck gradually gets longer through the accumulation of small increments of neck length acquired during the lifetime of each generation of giraffes. This is *not* how evolution works. If it did work in this way, weight lifters could expect to produce especially muscular babies. Workouts that promise no gain without the pain apply to the physical development of individuals, not species. Instead, evolution works as the process of natural selection takes advantage of the variety that already is present in a population. That's how giraffes got their necks.

Evolution through natural selection continues today. For example, in human populations there is differential resistance to disease, as we'll see in the discussion of sickle-cell anemia below. One classic recent example of natural selection is the peppered moth, which can be light or dark (in either case with black speckles, thus the name "peppered). A change in this species illustrates recent natural selection (in our own industrial age) through what has been called *industrial melanism*. Great Britain's industrialization changed the environment so as to favor darker moths (those with more melanin) rather than the lighter-colored ones that were favored previously. During the 1800s industrial pollution increased; soot coated buildings and trees, turning them a darker color. The previously typical peppered moth, which had a light color, now stood out against the dark backgrounds of sooty buildings and trees. Such light-colored moths were easily visible to their predators. Through mutations (see below), a new strain of peppered moth, with a darker phenotype, was favored. Because these darker moths were fitter—that is, harder to detect—in polluted environments, they survived and reproduced in greater numbers than lighter moths did. We see how natural selection may favor darker moths in polluted environments and lighter-colored moths in nonindustrial or less polluted environments because of their variant abilities to merge in with their environmental colors and thus avoid predators.

Evolutionary theory is used to explain. The goal of science is to increase understanding through explanation: showing how and why the thing (or class of things)

A speckled peppered moth and a black one alight on a soot-blackened tree. Which phenotype is favored in this environment? How could this adaptive advantage change?

to be understood (e.g., the variation within species, the geographic distribution of species, the fossil record) depends on other things. Explanations rely on associations and theories. An association is an observed relationship between two or more variables, such as the length of a giraffe's neck and the number of its offspring, or an increase in the frequency of dark moths as industrial pollution spreads. A theory is more general, suggesting or implying associations and attempting to explain them. A thing or event, for example, the giraffe's long neck, is explained if it illustrates a general principle or association, such as the concept of adaptive advantage. The truth of a scientific statement (e.g., evolution occurs because of differential reproductive success due to variation within the population) is confirmed by repeated observations.

## ✦ GENETICS

Charles Darwin recognized that for natural selection to operate, there must be variety in the population undergoing selection. Documenting and explaining such variety among humans—human biological diversity—is one of anthropology's major concerns. Genetics, a science that emerged after Darwin, helps us understand the causes of biological variation. We now know that DNA (deoxyribonucleic acid) molecules make up genes and chromosomes, which are the basic hereditary units. Biochemical changes (mutations) in DNA provide much of the variety on which natural selection operates. Through sexual reproduction, recombination of the genetic traits of mother and father in each generation leads to new arrangements of the hereditary units received from each parent. Such genetic recombination also adds variety on which natural selection may operate.

**Mendelian genetics** studies the ways in which chromosomes transmit genes across the generations. *Biochemical genetics* examines structure, function, and changes in DNA. **Population genetics** investigates natural selection and other causes of genetic variation, stability, and change in breeding populations.

## Mendel's Experiments

In 1856, in a monastery garden, the Austrian monk Gregor Mendel began a series of experiments that were to reveal the basic principles of genetics. Mendel studied the inheritance of seven contrasting traits in pea plants. For each trait there were only two forms. For example, plants were either tall (6 to 7 feet) or short (9 to 18 inches), with no intermediate forms. The ripe seeds could be either smooth and round or wrinkled. The peas could be either yellow or green, again with no intermediate colors.

When Mendel began his experiments, one of the prevailing beliefs about heredity was what has been called the "paint-pot" theory. According to this theory, the traits of the two parents blended in their children much as two pigments are blended in a can of paint. Children therefore were a unique mixture of their parents, and when these children married and reproduced, their traits would blend inextricably with those of their spouses. However, prevailing notions about heredity also recognized that occasionally the traits of one parent might swamp those of the other. If children looked far more like their mother than their father, people might say that her "blood" was stronger than his. Occasionally, too, there would be a "throwback," a child who was the image of his or her grandparent or who possessed a distinctive chin or nose characteristic of a whole line of descent.

Through his experiments with pea plants, Mendel discovered that heredity is determined by discrete particles or units. Although traits could disappear in one generation, they reemerged in their original form in later generations. For example, Mendel crossbred pure strains of tall and short plants. Their offspring were all tall. This was the first descending, or first filial, generation, designated $F_1$. Mendel then interbred the plants of the $F_1$ generation to produce a generation of grandchildren, the $F_2$ generation. In this generation, short plants reappeared. Among thousands of plants in the $F_2$ generation, there was approximately one short plant for every three tall ones.

From similar results with the other six traits, Mendel concluded that although a **dominant** form could mask the other form in *hybrid,* or mixed, individuals, the dominated trait—the **recessive**—was not destroyed; it wasn't even changed. Recessive traits would appear in unaltered form in later generations because genetic traits were inherited as discrete units.

These basic genetic units that Mendel described were factors (now called genes or alleles) located on **chromosomes.** Chromosomes are arranged in matching (homologous) pairs. Humans have 46 chromosomes, arranged in 23 pairs, one in each pair from the father and the other from the mother.

For simplicity, a chromosome may be pictured as a surface (see Figure 3-1) with several positions, to each of which we assign a lowercase letter. Each position is a **gene.** Each gene determines, wholly or partially, a particular biological trait, such as whether

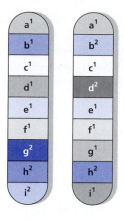

**FIGURE 3-1**

*Simplified Representation of a Normal Chromosome Pair* Letters indicate genes; superscripts indicate alleles.

one's blood is type A, B, or O. **Alleles** (for example, $b^1$ and $b^2$ in Figure 3-1) are biochemically different forms of a given gene. In humans, A, B, AB, and O blood types reflect different combinations of alleles of a particular gene.

In Mendel's experiments, the seven contrasting traits were determined by genes located on seven different pairs of chromosomes. The gene for height occurred in one of the seven pairs. When Mendel crossbred pure tall and pure short plants to produce his $F_1$ generation, each of the offspring received an allele for tallness (T) from one parent and one for shortness (t) from the other. These offspring were mixed, or **heterozygous,** with respect to height; each had two dissimilar alleles of that gene. Their parents, in contrast, had been **homozygous,** possessing two identical alleles of that gene (see Hartl and Jones 2002).

In the next generation ($F_2$), after the mixed plants were interbred, short plants reappeared in the ratio of one short to three talls. Knowing that shorts produced only shorts, Mendel could assume that they were genetically pure. Another fourth of the $F_2$ plants produced only talls. The remaining half, like the $F_1$ generation, were heterozygous; when interbred, they produced three talls for each short (Figure 3-2).

Dominance produces a distinction between **genotype,** or hereditary makeup, and *phenotype,* or expressed physical characteristics. Genotype is what you really are genetically; phenotype is what you appear as. Mendel's peas had three genotypes—TT, Tt, and tt—but only two phenotypes—tall and short. Because of dominance, the heterozygous plants were just as tall as the genetically pure tall ones. How do Mendel's discoveries apply to humans? Although some of our genetic traits follow Mendelian laws, with only two forms—dominant and recessive—other traits are determined differently.

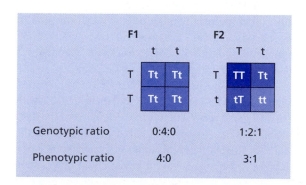

**FIGURE 3-2    *Punnett Squares of a Homozygous Cross and a Heterozygous Cross*** These squares show how phenotypic ratios of the $F_1$ and $F_2$ generation are generated. Colors show genotypes.

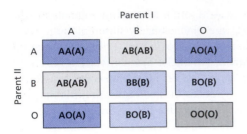

**FIGURE 3-3**    *Determinants of Phenotypes (Blood Groups) in the ABO System*  The four phenotypes—A, B, AB, and O—are indicated in parentheses and by color.

For instance, three alleles determine whether our blood type is A, B, AB, or O. People with two alleles for type O have that blood type. However, if they received a gene for either A or B from one parent and one for O from the other, they will have blood type A or B. In other words, A and B are both dominant over O. A and B are said to be *codominant*. If people inherit a gene for A from one parent and one for B from the other, they will have type AB blood, which is chemically different from the other varieties, A, B, and O.

These three alleles produce four phenotypes—A, B, AB, and O—and six different genotypes—OO, AO, BO, AA, BB, and AB (Figure 3-3). There are fewer phenotypes than genotypes because O is recessive to both A and B.

## Independent Assortment

Through additional experiments, Mendel also formulated his law of **independent assortment.** He discovered that traits are inherited independently of one another. For example, he bred pure round yellow peas with pure wrinkled green ones. All the $F_1$ generation peas were round and yellow, the dominant forms. But when Mendel interbred the $F_1$ generation to produce the $F_2$, four phenotypes turned up. Round greens and wrinkled yellows had been added to the original round yellows and wrinkled greens. The independent assortment and recombination of genetic traits provide one of the main ways by which variety is produced in any population.

An organism develops from a fertilized egg, or *zygote,* created by the union of two sex cells, one from each parent. The zygote grows rapidly through **mitosis,** or ordinary cell division, which continues as the organism grows. The special process by which sex cells are produced is called **meiosis.** Unlike ordinary cell division, in which two cells emerge from one, in meiosis four cells are produced from one. Each has half the genetic material of the original cell. In human meiosis, four cells, each with 23 individual chromosomes, are produced from an original cell with 23 pairs.

With fertilization of egg by sperm, the father's 23 chromosomes combine with the mother's 23 to recreate the pairs in every generation. However, the chromosomes sort independently, so that a child's genotype is a random combination of the DNA of its four grandparents. It is conceivable that one grandparent will contribute very little to its grandchild's heredity. Independent assortment of chromosomes is a major source of variety because the parents' genotypes can be assorted in $2^{23}$, or more than 8 million, different ways.

## ➔ POPULATION GENETICS

Population genetics studies stable and changing populations in which most breeding normally takes place (see Gillespie 2004; Hartl 2000). The term **gene pool** refers to all the alleles, genes, chromosomes and genotypes within a breeding population—the "pool" of genetic material available. When population geneticists use the term *evolution,* they have a more specific definition in mind than the one given earlier ("descent with modification over the generations"). For geneticists, **genetic evolution** is defined as change in gene frequency, that is, in the frequency of alleles in a breeding population from generation to generation. Any factor that contributes to such a change can be considered a *mechanism of genetic evolution.* Those mechanisms include natural selection, mutation, random genetic drift, and gene flow (see Mayr 2001).

## ✦ MECHANISMS OF GENETIC EVOLUTION

### Natural Selection

The first mechanism of genetic evolution is natural selection, which remains the best explanation for evolution. Essential to understanding evolution through natural selection is the distinction between genotype and phenotype. Genotype refers just to hereditary factors—genes and chromosomes. Phenotype—the organism's evident biological characteristics—develops over the years as the organism is influenced by particular environmental forces. (See the photo of the identical twins on this page). Identical twins have exactly the same genotype, but their actual biology, their

Twin Wade on the left is bigger and taller than his brother Wyatt. How can this be if they are identical?

phenotypes, may differ as a result of variation in the environments in which they have been raised. Also, because of dominance, individuals with different genotypes may have identical phenotypes (like Mendel's tall pea plants). Natural selection can operate only on phenotype—on what is exposed, not on what is hidden. For example, a harmful recessive gene can't be eliminated from the gene pool if it is masked by a favored dominant.

Phenotype includes not only outward physical appearance, but also internal organs, tissues, and cells and physiological processes and systems. Many biological reactions to foods, disease, heat, cold, sunlight, and other environmental factors are not automatic, genetically programmed responses but the product of years of exposure to particular environmental stresses. Human biology is not set at birth but has considerable *plasticity*. That is, it is changeable, being affected by the environmental forces, such as diet and altitude, that we experience as we grow up (see Bogin 2001).

The environment works on the genotype to build the phenotype, and certain phenotypes do better in some environments than other phenotypes do. However, remember that favored phenotypes can be produced by different genotypes. Because natural selection works only on genes that are expressed, maladaptive recessives can be removed only when they occur in homozygous form. When a heterozygote carries a maladaptive recessive, its effects are masked by the favored dominant. The process of perfecting the fit between organisms and their environment is gradual.

## *Directional Selection*

After several generations of selection, gene frequencies will change. Adaptation through natural selection will have occurred. Once that happens, those traits that have proved to be the most **adaptive** (favored by natural selection) in that environment will be selected again and again from generation to generation. Given such *directional selection,* or long-term selection of the same trait(s), maladaptive recessive alleles will be removed from the gene pool.

Directional selection will continue as long as environmental forces stay the same. However, if the environment changes, new selective forces start working, favoring different phenotypes. This also happens when part of the population colonizes a new environment. Selection in the changed, or new, environment continues until a new equilibrium is reached. Then there is directional selection until another environmental change or migration takes place. Over millions of years, such a process of successive adaptation to a series of environments has led to biological modification and branching. The process of natural selection has led to the tremendous array of plant and animal forms found in the world today.

Selection also operates through competition for mates in a breeding population. Males may openly compete for females, or females may choose to mate with particular males because they have desirable traits. Obviously, such traits vary from species to species. Familiar examples include color in birds; male birds, such as cardinals, tend to be more brightly colored than females are. Colorful males have a selective advantage because females like them better. As, over the generations, females have opted for colorful mates, the alleles responsible for color have built up in the species. **Sexual selection,** based on differential success in mating, is the term for this process in which certain traits of one sex are selected because of advantages they confer in winning mates.

Selection operates *only* on traits that are present in a population. A favorable mutation *may* occur, but a population doesn't normally come up with a new genotype or phenotype just because one is needed or desirable. Many species have become extinct because they weren't sufficiently varied to adapt to environmental shifts.

## Stabilizing Selection

We've seen that natural selection *reduces* variety in a population through directional selection—by favoring one trait or allele over another. Selective forces also can work to *maintain* variety through *stabilizing selection,* by favoring a **balanced polymorphism,** in which the frequencies of two or more alleles of a gene remain constant from generation to generation. This may be because the phenotypes they produce are neutral, or equally favored, or equally opposed, by selective forces. Sometimes a particular force favors (or opposes) one allele, while a different but equally effective force favors (or opposes) the other allele.

One well-studied example involves two alleles, $Hb^A$ and $Hb^S$, that affect the production of the beta strain (Hb) of human hemoglobin. Hemoglobin, which is located in our red blood cells, carries oxygen from our lungs to the rest of the body via the circulatory system. The allele that produces normal hemoglobin is $Hb^A$. Another allele, $Hb^S$, produces a different hemoglobin. Individuals who are homozygous for $Hb^S$ suffer from *sickle-cell anemia.* Such anemia, in which the red blood cells are shaped like crescents or sickles, is associated with a disease that is usually fatal. This condition interferes with the blood's ability to store oxygen. It increases the heart's burden by clogging the small blood vessels.

Given the fatal disease associated with $Hb^S$, geneticists were surprised to discover that certain populations in Africa, India, and the Mediterranean had very high frequencies of $Hb^S$. In some West African populations, that frequency is around 20 percent. Researchers eventually discovered that both $Hb^A$ and $Hb^S$ are maintained because selective forces in certain environments favor the heterozygote over either homozygote.

Initially, scientists wondered why, if most $Hb^S$ homozygotes died before they reached reproductive age, the harmful allele hadn't been eliminated. Why was its frequency so high? The answer turned out to lie in the heterozygote's greater fitness. Only people who were homozygous for $Hb^S$ died from sickle-cell anemia. Heterozygotes suffered very mild anemia, if any. On the other hand, although people homozygous for $Hb^A$ did not suffer from anemia, they were much more susceptible to *malaria*—a killer disease that continues to plague *Homo sapiens* in the tropics.

The heterozygote, with one sickle-cell allele and one normal one, was the fittest phenotype for a malarial environment. Heterozygotes have enough abnormal hemoglobin, in which malaria parasites cannot thrive, to protect against malaria. They also have enough normal hemoglobin to fend off sickle-cell anemia. The $Hb^S$ allele has been maintained in these populations because the heterozygotes survived and reproduced in greater numbers than did people with any other phenotype.

The example of the sickle-cell allele demonstrates the relativity of evolution through natural selection: Adaptation and fitness are in relation to specific environments. Traits are not adaptive or maladaptive for all times and places. Even harmful alleles can be selected if heterozygotes have an advantage. Moreover, as the environment changes, favored phenotypes and gene frequencies can change. In malaria-free environments, normal-hemoglobin homozygotes reproduce more effectively than heterozygotes do. With no malaria, the frequency of $Hb^S$ declines because $Hb^S$ homozygotes can't compete in survival and reproduction with the other types. This has happened in areas of West Africa where malaria has been reduced through drainage programs and insecticides. Selection against $Hb^S$ also has occurred in the United States among Americans descended from West Africans (Diamond 1997).

## Mutation

The second mechanism of genetic evolution is mutation. Mutations, which occur spontaneously and regularly, provide new biochemical forms—variety—on which natural selection may operate. **Mutations** are changes in the DNA molecules of which genes and chromosomes are built. If a mutation occurs in a sex cell that combines with another as a fertilized egg, the new organism will carry the mutation in every cell. This may or may not, depending on dominance, result in a biochemical difference between the mutant child and the parent.

## Random Genetic Drift

The third mechanism of genetic evolution is **random genetic drift.** This is a change in allele frequency that results not from natural selection but from chance. To understand why, compare the sorting of alleles to a game involving a bag of 12 marbles, 6 red and 6 blue. In step 1, you draw six marbles from the bag. Statistically, your chances of drawing three reds and three blues are less than those of getting four of one color and two of the other. Step 2 is to fill a new bag with 12 marbles on the basis of the ratio of marbles you drew in step 1. Assume that you drew four reds and two blues: The new bag will have eight red marbles and four blue ones. Step 3 is to draw six marbles from the new bag. Your chances of drawing blues in step 3 are lower than they were in step 1, and the probability of drawing all reds increases. If you do draw all reds, the next bag (step 4) will have only red marbles.

Although genetic drift can operate in any population, large or small, *fixation* due to drift is more rapid in small populations. Fixation refers to the total replacement of blue marbles by red marbles—or, to use a human example, of blue eyes by brown eyes. The history of the human line is characterized by a series of small populations, migrations, and fixation due to genetic drift. One cannot understand human origins, human genetic variation, and a host of other important anthropological topics without recognizing the importance of genetic drift.

This game is analogous to random genetic drift operating over the generations. The blue marbles were lost purely by chance. Alleles, too, can be lost by chance rather than because of any disadvantage they confer. Lost alleles can reappear in a gene pool only through mutation.

# Gene Flow

The fourth mechanism of genetic evolution is **gene flow,** the exchange of genetic material between populations of the same species. Gene flow, like mutation, works in conjunction with natural selection by providing variety on which selection can work. Gene flow may consist of direct interbreeding between formerly separated populations of the same species (e.g., Europeans, Africans, and Native Americans in the United States), or it may be indirect.

Consider the following hypothetical case (Figure 3-4). In a certain part of the world live six local populations of a certain species. $P_1$ is the western-most of these populations. $P_2$, which interbreeds with $P_1$, is located 50 miles to the east. $P_2$ also interbreeds with $P_3$, located 50 miles east of $P_2$. Assume that each population interbreeds with, and only with, the adjacent populations. $P_6$ is located 250 miles from $P_1$ and does not directly interbreed with $P_1$, but it is tied to $P_1$ through the chain of interbreeding that ultimately links all six populations.

Assume further that some allele exists in $P_1$ that isn't particularly advantageous in its environment. Because of gene flow, this allele may be passed on to $P_2$, by it to $P_3$, and so on, until it eventually reaches $P_6$. In $P_6$ or along the way, the allele may encounter an environment in which it does have a selective advantage. If this happens, it may serve, like a new mutation, as raw material on which natural selection can operate.

Alleles are spread through gene flow even when selection is not operating on the allele. In the long run, natural selection works on the variety within a population, whatever its source: mutation, drift, or gene flow. Selection and gene flow have worked together to spread the $Hb^S$ allele in Central Africa. Frequencies of $Hb^S$ in Africa reflect not only the intensity of malaria but also the length of time gene flow has been going on (Livingstone 1969).

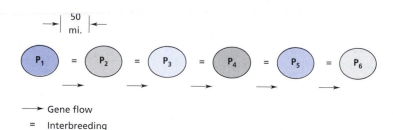

**FIGURE 3-4   *Gene Flow between Local Populations*** $P_1$–$P_6$ are six local populations of the same species. Each interbreeds (=) only with its neighbor(s). Although members of $P_6$ never interbreed with $P_1$, $P_6$ and $P_1$ are linked through gene flow. Genetic material that originates in $P_1$ eventually will reach $P_6$, and vice versa, as it is passed from one neighboring population to the next. Because they share genetic material in this way, $P_1$–$P_6$ remain members of the same species. In many species, local populations distributed throughout a larger territory than the 250 miles depicted here are linked through gene flow.

Gene flow is important in the study of the origin of species. A **species** is a group of related organisms whose members can interbreed to produce offspring that can live and reproduce. A species has to be able to reproduce itself through time. We know that horses and donkeys belong to different species because their offspring cannot meet the test of long-term survival. A horse and a donkey may breed to produce a mule, but mules are sterile. So are the offspring of lions with tigers. Gene flow tends to prevent **speciation**—the formation of new species—unless subgroups of the same species are separated for a sufficient length of time.

When gene flow is interrupted, and isolated subgroups are maintained, new species may arise. Imagine that an environmental barrier arises between $P_3$ and $P_4$, so that they no longer interbreed. If over time, as a result of isolation, $P_1$, $P_2$, and $P_3$ become incapable of interbreeding with the other three populations, speciation will have occurred.

## ✦ HUMAN BIOLOGICAL ADAPTATION

In Chapter 1 we examined a range of problems involved in trying to *classify* humans into racial categories. Given those problems, contemporary scientists focus on specific biological differences and try to *explain* them. Because of extensive gene flow and interbreeding, *Homo sapiens* has not evolved subspecies or distinct races. There are no sharp genetic breaks among human populations of the sort we would associate with discrete races. Instead, there are gradual genetic shifts called *clines*. Biological similarities between groups may reflect—rather than common ancestry—similar but independent adaptations to similar natural selective forces, such as degrees of ultraviolet radiation from the sun in the case of skin color. Let's consider additional examples of human biological diversity that reflect adaptation to environmental stresses, such as disease, diet, and climate. There is abundant evidence for human genetic adaptation and thus for evolution (change in gene frequency) through selection working in specific environments. One example is the adaptive value of the $Hb^S$ heterozygote and its spread in malarial environments, which was discussed previously. Adaptation and evolution go on in specific environments. There is no generally or ideally adaptive allele and no perfect phenotype. Nor can an allele be assumed to be maladaptive for all times and all places. We have seen that even $Hb^S$, which produces a lethal anemia, has a selective advantage in the heterozygous form in malarial environments.

Also, alleles that once were maladaptive may lose their disadvantage if the environment shifts. Color blindness (disadvantageous for hunters and forest dwellers) and a form of genetically determined diabetes are examples. Today's environment contains medical techniques that allow people with such conditions to live fairly normal lives. Formerly maladaptive alleles thus have become neutral with respect to selection. With thousands of human genes now known, new genetic traits are discovered almost every day. Such studies tend to focus on genetic abnormalities, because of their medical and treatment implications.

## Genes and Disease

According to the *World Health Report,* published by the World Health Organization (WHO) in Geneva, Switzerland, tropical diseases affect more than 10 percent of the world's population. Malaria, the most widespread of these diseases, afflicts between 350 million and 500 million people annually (World Malaria Report 2005). Schistosomiasis (snail fever), a waterborne parasitic disease, affects more than 200 million.

The malaria threat has been spreading. Brazil had 560,000 cases in 1988, versus 100,000 in 1977. Worldwide, the number of malaria cases rose from 270 million in 1990 to over 350 million today. Contributing to this rise is the increasing resistance of parasites to drugs used to treat malaria (World Malaria Report 2005). However, hundreds of millions of people are genetically resistant. Sickle-cell hemoglobin is the best known of the genetic antimalarials (Diamond 1997). Microbes have been major selective agents for humans, particularly before the arrival of modern medicine. Some people are genetically more susceptible to certain diseases than others are, and the distribution of human blood types continues to change in response to natural selection.

After food production emerged around 10,000 years ago, infectious diseases posed a mounting risk and eventually became the foremost cause of human mortality. Food production favors infection for several reasons. Cultivation sustains larger, denser populations and a more sedentary lifestyle than does hunting and gathering. People live closer to each other and to their own wastes, making it easier for microbes to survive and to find hosts. Domesticated animals also transmit diseases to people.

Until 1977, when the last case of smallpox was reported, smallpox had been a major threat to humans and a determinant of blood group frequencies (Diamond 1990, 1997). The smallpox virus is a mutation from one of the pox viruses that plague such domesticated animals as cows, sheep, goats, horses, and pigs. Smallpox appeared in human beings after people and animals started living together. Smallpox epidemics have played important roles in world history, often killing one-fourth to one-half of the affected populations.

The ABO blood groups have figured in human resistance to smallpox. Blood is typed according to the protein and sugar compounds on the surface of the red blood cells. Different substances (compounds) distinguish between type A and type B blood. Type A cells trigger the production of *antibodies* in B blood, so that A cells clot in B blood. The different substances work like chemical passwords; they help us distinguish our own cells from invading cells, including microbes, we ought to destroy. The surfaces of some microbes have substances similar to ABO blood group substances. We don't produce antibodies to substances similar to those on our own blood cells. We can think of this as a clever evolutionary trick by the microbes to deceive their hosts, because we don't normally develop antibodies against our own biochemistry.

People with A or AB blood are more susceptible to smallpox than are people with type B or type O. Presumably this is because a substance on the smallpox virus mimics the type A substance, permitting the virus to slip by the defenses of the type A individual. By contrast, type B and type O individuals produce antibodies against smallpox because they recognize it as a foreign substance.

The relation between type A blood and susceptibility to smallpox was first suggested by the low frequencies of the A allele in areas of India and Africa where smallpox had been endemic. A comparative study done in rural India in 1965–1966, during a virulent smallpox epidemic, did much to confirm this relationship. Drs. F. Vogel and M. R. Chakravartti analyzed blood samples from smallpox victims and their uninfected

In New York City in 1947, the appearance of nine cases of smallpox, including two deaths, spurred a very successful mass vaccination program. Shown here, lines of people wait to be vaccinated at the New York Health Department on April 14, 1947.

siblings (Diamond 1990). The researchers found 415 infected children, none ever vaccinated against smallpox. All but eight of the infected children had an uninfected (also unvaccinated) sibling.

The results of the study were clear: Susceptibility to smallpox varied with ABO type. Of the 415 infected children, 261 had the A allele; 154 lacked it. Among their 407 uninfected siblings, the ratio was reversed. Only 80 had the A allele; 327 lacked it. The researchers calculated that a type A or type AB person had a seven times greater chance of getting smallpox than did an O or B person.

In most human populations, the O allele is more common than A and B combined. A is most common in Europe;

The smallpox threat made the cover of Cosmopolitan magazine.

B frequencies are highest in Asia. Since smallpox was once widespread in the Old World, we might wonder why natural selection didn't eliminate the A allele entirely. The answer appears to be this: Other diseases spared the type A people and penalized those with other blood groups.

For example, type O people seem to be especially susceptible to the bubonic plague—the "Black Death" that killed a third of the population of medieval Europe. Type O people are also more likely to get cholera, which has killed as many people in India as smallpox has. On the other hand, blood group O may increase resistance to syphilis. The ravages of that sexually transmitted disease, which may have originated in the New World, may explain the very high frequency of type O blood among the native populations of Central and South America. The distribution of human blood groups appears to represent a compromise among the selective effects of many diseases.

In the case of diseases for which there are no cures, genetic resistance maintains its significance. There is genetic variation in susceptibility to the HIV virus, for example. We know that people exposed to HIV vary in their risk of developing AIDS and in the rate at which the disease progresses. AIDS is widespread in many African nations (and in the United States, France, and Brazil). Particularly in Africa, where treatment strategies now used in the industrial nations are not widely available, the death rate from AIDS could eventually (let us hope it does not) rival that of past epidemics of smallpox and plague. If so, AIDS could cause large shifts in human gene frequencies—again illustrating the ongoing operation of natural selection.

## Lactose Tolerance

Many traits that illustrate human biological adaptation are not under simple genetic control. Genetic determination of such traits may be likely but unconfirmed, or several genes may interact to influence the trait in question. Sometimes there is a genetic component, but the trait also responds to stresses encountered during growth. We speak of **phenotypical adaptation** when adaptive changes occur during the individual's lifetime. Phenotypical adaptation is made possible by biological plasticity—our ability to change in response to the environments we encounter as we grow (see Bogin 2001; Frisancho 1993).

Genes and phenotypical adaptation work together to produce a biochemical difference between human groups in the ability to digest large amounts of milk—an adaptive advantage when other foods are scarce and milk is available. All milk, whatever its source, contains a complex sugar called *lactose*. The digestion of milk depends on an enzyme called *lactase*, which works in the small intestine. Among all mammals except humans and some of their pets, lactase production ceases after weaning, so that these animals can no longer digest milk.

Lactase production and the ability to tolerate milk vary between populations. About 90 percent of northern Europeans and their descendants are lactose tolerant; they can digest several glasses of milk with no difficulty. Similarly, about 80 percent of two African populations, the Tutsi of Rwanda and Burundi in East Africa and the Fulani of Nigeria in West Africa, produce lactase and digest milk easily. Both these groups traditionally have been herders. However, such nonherders as the Yoruba and

Igbo in Nigeria, the Baganda in Uganda, the Japanese and other Asians, Eskimos, South American Indians, and many Israelis cannot digest lactose (Kretchmer 1972/1975).

The variable human ability to digest milk seems to be a difference of degree. Some populations can tolerate very little or no milk, but others are able to metabolize much greater quantities. Studies show that people who move from no-milk or low-milk

## ANTHROPOLOGY TODAY

### *Three Adaptations to Thin Air*

*We've seen that humans have access to varied ways of adapting to environmental stresses, such as disease, heat, cold, humidity, sunlight, and altitude, as described here. Not only do humans evolve and adapt genetically over the generations, they also have the ability to use culture (e.g., tools) to adapt. Remember, too, the discussion of human biological plasticity: our ability to respond adaptively as we grow and develop biologically from childhood to adulthood. Pay attention in this box to the dramatically different ways in which three populations adapt to high altitudes. The biological diversity we observe among contemporary and prehistoric humans has many causes.*

Prehistoric and contemporary human populations living at altitudes of at least 8,000 feet (2,500 meters) above sea level may provide unique insights into human evolution, reports an interdisciplinary group of scientists.

Indigenous highlanders living in the Andean Altiplano in South America, in the Tibetan Plateau in Asia, and at the highest elevations of the Ethiopian Highlands in east Africa have evolved three distinctly different biological adaptations for surviving in the oxygen-thin air found at high altitude.

"To have examples of three geographically dispersed populations adapting in different ways to the same stress is very unusual," said Cynthia Beall, a physical anthropologist at Case Western Reserve University in Cleveland, Ohio. "From an evolutionary standpoint the question becomes, Why do these differences exist?. . ."

"High-altitude populations offer a unique natural lab that allows us to follow [many] lines of evidence—archaeological, biological, climatological—to answer intriguing questions about social, cultural, and biological adaptations," said Mark Aldenderfer, an archaeologist at the University of California, Santa Barbara. . . .

The Andean and Tibetan plateaus rise some 13,000 feet (4 kilometers) above sea level. As prehistoric hunter-gatherers moved into these environments, they . . . likely suffered acute hypoxia, a condition created by a diminished supply of oxygen to body tissues. At high altitudes the air is much thinner than at sea level. As a result, a person inhales fewer oxygen molecules with each breath. Symptoms of hypoxia, sometimes known as mountain sickness, include headaches, vomiting, sleeplessness, impaired thinking, and an inability to sustain long periods of physical activity. At elevations above 25,000 feet (7,600 meters), hypoxia can kill.

The Andeans adapted to the thin air by developing an ability to carry more oxygen in each red blood cell. That is: They breathe at the same rate as people who live at sea diets to high-milk diets increase their lactose tolerance; this suggests some phenotypical adaptation. We can conclude that no simple genetic trait accounts for the ability to digest milk. Lactose tolerance appears to be one of many aspects of human biology governed both by genes and by phenotypical adaptation to environmental conditions.

level, but the Andeans have the ability to deliver oxygen throughout their bodies more effectively than people at sea level do.

"Andeans counter having less oxygen in every breath by having higher hemoglobin concentrations in their blood," Beall said. Hemoglobin is the protein in red blood cells that ferries oxygen through the blood system. Having more hemoglobin to carry oxygen through the blood system than people at sea level counterbalances the effects of hypoxia.

Tibetans compensate for low oxygen content much differently. They increase their oxygen intake by taking more breaths per minute than people who live at sea level.

"Andeans go the hematological route, Tibetans the respiratory route," Beall said.

In addition, Tibetans may have a second biological adaptation, which expands their blood vessels, allowing them to deliver oxygen throughout their bodies more effectively than sea-level people do.

Tibetans' lungs synthesize larger amounts of a gas called nitric oxide from the air they breathe. "One effect of nitric oxide is to increase the diameter of blood vessels, which suggests that Tibetans may offset low oxygen content in their blood with increased blood flow," Beall said.

A pilot study Beall conducted of Ethiopian highlanders living at 11,580 feet (3,530 meters) suggests that—unlike the Tibetans—they don't breathe more rapidly than people at sea level and aren't able to more effectively synthesize nitric oxide. Nor do the Ethiopians have higher hemoglobin counts than sea-level people, as the Andeans do.

Yet despite living at elevations with low oxygen content, "the Ethiopian highlanders were hardly hypoxic at all," Beall said. "I was genuinely surprised."

So what adaptation have the Ethiopian highlanders' bodies evolved to survive at high altitude? "Right now we have no clue how they do it," Beall said. . . .

Knowing how long the populations have been living at the top of the world is crucial to answering the evolutionary question of whether these adaptations are the result of differences in the founding populations, random genetic mutations, or the passage of time.

Archaeologists, paleontologists, and climatologists are pooling their knowledge to pinpoint when some of these early migrations to the high plateaus occurred.

Aldenderfer . . . says cultural adaptations would have to occur first.

"The ability to survive in such harsh environments required control of fire, an expanded tool kit that included bone needles to make complicated clothing that protected the body in a significant way, and the cultural flexibility to change subsistence practices," he said.

*Continued*

## ANTHROPOLOGY TODAY

Climatologists' changing understanding of the nature of the last ice age is contributing to archaeological efforts.

Ice-core and other evidence show that, rather than being a monolithic period lasting 100,000 years with frigid temperatures and glacial landscapes, the Ice Age included long periods of relatively mild weather.

"Through most of the 20th century it was thought that the Tibetan Plateau was covered by a monstrous ice sheet during the last glacial maximum, about 21,000 years ago," Aldenderfer said. "People couldn't live on an ice sheet. So archaeologists wouldn't even bother to look for sites from that time period."

[Now] knowing the Tibetan Plateau more closely resembled Arctic tundra has led to the discovery of new sites. Archaeological evidence suggests hunter-gatherers occupied the Tibetan Plateau some 25,000 to 20,000 years ago. People began moving into the Andean Altiplano around 11,500 to 11,000 years ago.

What motivated prehistoric people to move into the harsh and challenging conditions presented by high altitude?

"The highlands offered an attractive option with a landscape that was open and pristine," Aldenderfer said. "People probably started out moving up and down for short terms, and then gradually settled at the higher elevations."

Changing environmental conditions also created "new opportunities and new constraints," he said.

In South America, for example, the maritime environment began transforming as temperatures warmed, glaciers retreated, and sea levels rose. Large mammals such as mammoths and mastodons gradually went extinct, as did other herbivores. Warmer temperatures allowed plants and animals to move to higher elevations, creating resource-rich patches of habitat in highland areas. . . .

Similar processes likely occurred in Tibet. Prehistoric people occupied the landscape during the interglacial process, when conditions were relatively benign and hunting was plentiful, Aldenderfer said.

"Suddenly [thereafter] it gets really cold. Biomass declined precipitously. It becomes very arid because of wind-flow patterns. The landscape becomes one of very patchy vegetation, rocky. And the huge herds of gazelle, antelope, and sheep wax and wane," Alenderfer said. "What happens? . . . Finding biological differences suggests they toughed it out and adapted."

*Source:* Hillary Mayell, "Three High-Altitude Peoples, Three Adaptations to Thin Air," *National Geographic News,* February 25, 2004. Reprinted by permission of National Geographic.

---

# SUMMARY

1. In the 18th century, Carolus Linnaeus developed biological taxonomy. He viewed differences and similarities among organisms as part of God's orderly plan rather than as evidence for evolution. Charles Darwin and Alfred Russel Wallace proposed that natural selection could explain the origin of species, biological diversity, and similarities among related life forms. Natural selection requires variety in the population undergoing selection.

2. Through breeding experiments with peas in 1856, Gregor Mendel discovered that genetic traits pass on as units. These are now known to be chromosomes, which occur in homologous pairs. Alleles, some dominant, some recessive, are the chemically different forms that occur at a given genetic locus. Mendel also formulated the law of independent assortment. Each of the seven traits he studied in peas was inherited independently of all the others. Independent assortment of chromosomes and their recombination provide some of the variety needed for natural selection. But the major source of such variety is mutation, a chemical change in the DNA molecules of which genes are made.

3. Population genetics studies gene frequencies in stable and changing populations. Natural selection is the most important mechanism of evolutionary change. Others are mutation, random genetic drift, and gene flow. Given environmental change, nature selects traits already present in the population. If variety is insufficient to permit adaptation to the change, extinction is likely. New types don't appear just because they are needed.

4. One well-documented case of natural selection in contemporary human populations is that of the sickle-cell allele. In homozygous form, the sickle-cell allele, $Hb^S$, produces an abnormal hemoglobin. This clogs the small blood vessels, impairing the blood's capacity to store oxygen. The result is sickle-cell anemia, which is usually fatal. Homozygotes for normal hemoglobin are susceptible to malaria and die in great numbers. Heterozygotes get only mild anemia and are resistant to malaria. In a malarial environment, the heterozygote has the advantage.

5. Other mechanisms of genetic evolution complement natural selection. Random genetic drift operates most obviously in small populations, where pure chance can easily change allele frequencies. Gene flow and interbreeding keep subgroups of the same species genetically connected and thus impede speciation.

6. Differential resistance to infectious diseases such as smallpox has influenced the distribution of human blood groups. There are genetic antimalarials, such as the sickle-cell allele. Phenotypical adaptation refers to adaptive changes that occur in an individual's lifetime in response to the environment the organism encounters as it grows. Lactose tolerance is due partly to phenotypical adaptation. Biological similarities between geographically distant populations may be due to similar but independent genetic changes rather than to common ancestry. Or they may reflect similar physiological responses to common stresses during growth.

## KEY TERMS

adaptive (p. 56)

alleles (p. 53)

balanced polymorphism (p. 57)

catastrophism (p. 48)

chromosomes (p. 52)

creationism (p. 47)

dominant (p. 52)

evolution (p. 49)

gene (p. 52)

gene flow (p. 59)

gene pool (p. 54)
genetic evolution (p. 55)
genotype (p. 53)
heterozygous (p. 53)
homozygous (p. 53)
independent assortment (p. 54)
meiosis (p. 54)
Mendelian genetics (p. 52)
mitosis (p. 54)
mutations (p. 58)

natural selection (p. 49)
phenotypical adaptation (p. 63)
population genetics (p. 52)
random genetic drift (p. 58)
recessive (p. 52)
sexual selection (p. 56)
speciation (p. 60)
species (p. 60)
theory (p. 49)
uniformitarianism (p. 49)

# CHAPTER 4

## THE PRIMATES

**P**rimatology is the study of nonhuman primates—fossil and living apes, monkeys, and prosimians—including their behavior and social life. Primatology is fascinating in itself, but it also helps anthropologists make inferences about the early social organization of *hominids* (members of the zoological family that includes fossil and living humans). Of particular relevance to humans are two kinds of primates:

1.  Those whose ecological adaptations are similar to our own: **terrestrial** monkeys and apes—that is, primates that live on the ground rather than in the trees.
2.  Those that are most closely related to us: the great apes, specifically the chimpanzees and gorillas.

## ✦ OUR PLACE AMONG PRIMATES

Similarities between humans and apes are evident in anatomy, brain structure, genetics, and biochemistry. The physical similarities between humans and apes are recognized

**69**

in zoological **taxonomy**—the assignment of organisms to categories (*taxa*; singular, *taxon*) according to their relationship and resemblance. Many similarities between organisms reflect their common *phylogeny*—their genetic relatedness based on common ancestry. In other words, organisms share features they have inherited from the same ancestor. Humans and apes belong to the same taxonomic superfamily Hominoidea (hominoids). Monkeys are placed in two others (Ceboidea and Cercopithecoidea). This means that humans and apes are more closely related to each other than either is to monkeys.

Figure 4-1 summarizes the various levels of classification used in zoological taxonomy. Each lower-level unit belongs to the higher-level unit above it. Thus, looking toward the bottom of Figure 4-1, similar species belong to the same genus (plural, *genera*). Similar genera make up the same family, and so on through the top of Figure 4-1, where similar phyla (plural of *phylum*) are included in the same kingdom. The highest (most inclusive) taxonomic level is the *kingdom*. At that level, animals are distinguished from plants.

At the lowest level of taxonomy, a species may have subspecies. These are its more or less—but not yet totally—isolated subgroups. Subspecies can coexist in time and space. For example, the Neandertals, who thrived between 130,000 and 28,000 years ago, often are assigned not to a separate species but merely to a different subspecies of *Homo sapiens*. Just one subspecies of *Homo sapiens* survives today.

The similarities used to assign organisms to the same taxon are called **homologies,** similarities they have jointly inherited from a common ancestor. Table 4-1 summarizes

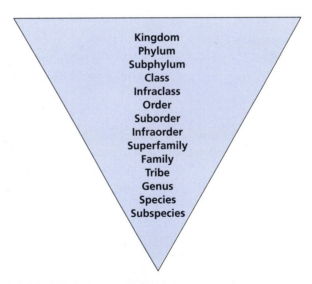

**FIGURE 4-1** *The Principal Classificatory Units of Zoological Taxonomy* Moving down the figure, the classificatory units become more exclusive, so that "Kingdom" at the top is the most inclusive unit and "Subspecies" at the bottom is the most exclusive.

## TABLE 4-1

### The Place of Humans (*Homo sapiens*) in Zoological Taxonomy

Homo sapiens *is an Animal, Chordate, Vertebrate, Mammal, Primate, Anthropoid, Catarrhine, Hominoid, Hominid and Hominin. (Table 4-2 shows the taxonomic placement of the other primates.)*

| Taxon | Scientific (Latin) Name | Common (English) Name |
|---|---|---|
| Kingdom | Animalia | Animals |
| Phylum | Chordata | Chordates |
| Subphylum | Vertebrata | Vertebrates |
| Class | Mammalia | Mammals |
| Infraclass | Eutheria | Eutherians |
| Order | Primates | Primates |
| Suborder | Anthropoidea | Anthropoids |
| Infraorder | Catarrhini | Catarrhines |
| Superfamily | Hominoidea | Hominoids |
| Family | Hominidae | Hominids |
| Tribe | Hominini | Hominins |
| Genus | *Homo* | Humans |
| Species | *Homo sapiens* | Recent humans |
| Subspecies | *Homo sapiens sapiens* | Anatomically modern humans |

the place of humans in zoological taxonomy. We see in Table 4-1 that we are mammals, members of the class Mammalia. This is a major subdivision of the kingdom Animalia. Mammals share certain traits, including mammary glands, that set them apart from other taxa, such as birds, reptiles, amphibians, and insects. Mammalian homologies indicate that all mammals share more recent common ancestry with each other than they do with any bird, reptile, or insect.

Humans are mammals that, at a lower taxonomic level, belong to the *order* Primates. Another mammalian order is Carnivora: the carnivores (dogs, cats, foxes, wolves, badgers, weasels). Rodentia (rats, mice, beavers, squirrels) form yet another mammalian order. The primates share structural and biochemical homologies that distinguish them from other mammals. These resemblances were inherited from their common early primate ancestors after those early primates became reproductively isolated from the ancestors of the other mammals.

## ✦ HOMOLOGIES AND ANALOGIES

Organisms should be assigned to the same taxon on the basis of homologies. The extensive biochemical homologies between apes and humans confirm our common ancestry and support our traditional joint classification as hominoids (see Table 4-2). For example, it is estimated that humans, chimpanzees, and gorillas have more than 98 percent of their DNA in common.

## TABLE 4-2

### Primate Taxonomy

*Major subdivisions of the two primate suborders:* Prosimii *and* Anthropoidea. *Humans are anthropoids who belong to the superfamily* Hominoidea, *along with the apes.*

| Suborder | Infraorder | Superfamily | Family |
|---|---|---|---|
| Prosimii (Prosimians) | Lemuriformes (Lemurs) | Lemuroidea | Daubentoniidae (Aye-ayes) Indridae (Indri) Lemuridae (Lemurs) |
| | Lorisiformes (Lorises) | Lorisoidea | Lorisidae |
| | Tarsiiformes (Tarsiers) | Tarsioidea | Tarsiidae |
| Anthropoidea (Anthropoids) | Platyrrhini (Platyrrhines—New World monkeys) | Ceboidea | Callitrichidae (Tamarins and marmosets) Cebidae |
| | Catarrhini (Catarrhines— Old World monkeys, apes, and humans) | Cercopithecoidea | Cercopithecidae (Old World monkeys) |
| | | Hominoidea (Hominoids) | Hylobatidae (Gibbons and siamangs) Pongidae (Pongids—orangutans) Hominidae (Hominids—gorillas, chimpanzees, and humans) |

SOURCE: "Classification of Primates," ed. by R. Martin, from *The Cambridge Encyclopedia of Human Evolution* S. Jones, R. Martin, and D. Pilbeam, pp. 20–21. Reprinted by permission of Cambridge University Press.

However, common ancestry isn't the only reason for similarities between species. Similar traits also can arise if species experience similar selective forces and adapt to them in similar ways. We call such similarities **analogies.** The process by which analogies are produced is called **convergent evolution.** For example, fish and porpoises share many analogies resulting from convergent evolution to life in the water. Like fish, porpoises, which are mammals, have fins. They are also hairless and streamlined for efficient locomotion. Analogies between birds and bats (wings, small size, light bones) illustrate convergent evolution to flying (see Angier 1998).

In theory, only homologies should be used in taxonomy. With reference to the hominoids, there is no doubt that humans, gorillas, and chimpanzees are more closely related

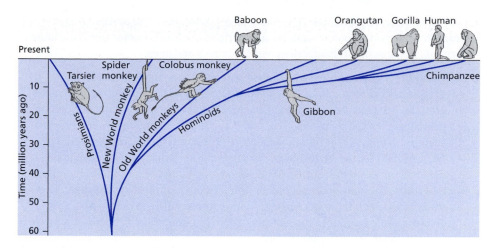

**FIGURE 4-2** *Primate Family Tree* When did the common ancestors of all the primates live?

*SOURCE:* From Roger Lewin, *Human Evolution: An Illustrated Introduction*, 3rd ed., p. 44. Copyright © 1993. Reprinted by permission of Blackwell Scientific Publishing Ltd.

to each other than any of the three is to orangutans, which are Asiatic apes (Ciochon 1983). *Hominidae* is the name of the zoological family that includes hominids—fossil and living humans. Because chimps and gorillas share a more recent common ancestor with humans than they do with the orangutan, many scientists now also place gorillas and chimps in the hominid family. **Hominid** would then refer to the zoological family that includes fossil and living humans, chimpanzees, gorillas, and their common ancestors. This leaves the orangutan (genus *Pongo*) as the only member of the pongid family (*Pongidae*). If chimps and gorillas are classified as hominids, what do we call the group that leads to humans but not to chimps and gorillas? For that, some scientists insert a taxonomic level called *tribe* between family and genus. The tribe *hominini* describes all the human species that ever have existed (including the extinct ones) and excludes chimps and gorillas. When scientists use the word **hominin** today, they mean pretty much the same thing as when they used the word *hominid* 20 years ago (Greiner 2003). Table 4-2 and Figure 4-2 illustrate our degree of relatedness to other primates.

## ↝ WHAT MAKES A PRIMATE?

Primates have adapted to diverse ecological niches. Some primates are active during the day; others, at night. Some eat insects; others, fruits; others, shoots, leaves, and bulk vegetation; and others, seeds or roots. Some primates live on the ground; others live in trees. However, because the earliest primates were tree dwellers, modern primates share homologies reflecting their common **arboreal** heritage.

Many trends in primate evolution are best exemplified by the **anthropoids:** monkeys, apes, and humans, which constitute the suborder *Anthropoidea*. The other primate suborder, *Prosimii*, includes lemurs, lorises, and tarsiers. These **prosimians** are more distant relatives of humans than are monkeys and apes. The primate trends—most developed in the anthropoids—can be summarized briefly. Together they constitute an anthropoid heritage that humans share with monkeys and apes.

1.  *Grasping.* Primates have five-digited feet and hands that are suited for grasping. Certain features of hands and feet that were originally adaptive for arboreal life have been transmitted across the generations to contemporary primates. Flexible hands and feet that could encircle branches were important features in the early primates' arboreal life. Thumb opposability might have been favored by the inclusion of insects in the early primate diet. Manual dexterity makes it easier to catch insects attracted to abundant arboreal flowers and fruits. Humans and many other primates have **opposable thumbs:** The thumb can touch the other fingers. Some primates also have grasping feet. However, in adapting to bipedal (two-footed) locomotion, humans eliminated most of the foot's grasping ability.

2.  *Smell to Sight.* Several anatomic changes reflect the shift from smell to sight as the primates' most important means of obtaining information. Monkeys, apes, and humans have excellent *stereoscopic* (able to see in depth) and color vision. The portion of the brain devoted to vision expanded, while the area concerned with smell shrank.

3.  *Nose to Hand.* Sensations of touch, conveyed by *tactile* organs, also provide information. The tactile skin on a dog's or cat's nose transmits information. Cats' tactile hairs, or whiskers, also serve this function. In primates, however, the main touch organ is the hand, specifically the sensitive pads of the "fingerprint" region.

4.  *Brain Complexity.* The proportion of brain tissue concerned with memory, thought, and association has increased in primates. The primate ratio of brain size to body size exceeds that of most mammals.

5.  *Parental Investment.* Most primates give birth to a single offspring rather than a litter. Because of this, growing primates receive more attention and have more learning opportunities than do other mammals. Learned behavior is an important part of primate adaptation.

6.  *Sociality.* Primates tend to be social animals that live with others of their species. The need for longer and more attentive care of offspring places a selective value on support by a social group.

## ✦ PROSIMIANS

The primate order has two suborders: prosimians and anthropoids. The early history of the primates is limited to prosimianlike animals known through the fossil record. The first anthropoids, ancestral to monkeys, apes, and humans, appeared more than 50 million years ago. Some prosimians managed to survive in Africa and Asia because they were adapted to nocturnal life. As such, they did not compete with anthropoids, which are active during the day. Prosimians (lemurs) in Madagascar had no anthropoid competitors until people colonized that island some 1,500 years ago.

In their behavior and biology, Madagascar's *lemurs*, with 33 species, show adaptations to an array of environments or ecological niches. Their diets and times of activity differ. Lemurs eat fruits, other plant foods, eggs, and insects. Some are nocturnal; others are active during the day. Some are totally arboreal; others spend some time in the trees and some on the ground. Another kind of prosimian is the *tarsier,* today confined to Indonesia, Malaysia, and the Philippines. From the fossil record, we know that 50 million years ago, several genera of tarsierlike prosimians lived in North America and Europe, which were much warmer then than they are now (Boaz 1997). The one genus of tarsier that survived is totally nocturnal. Active at night, tarsiers don't directly compete with anthropoids, which are active during the day. *Lorises* are other nocturnal prosimians found in Africa and Asia.

## ✦ PRIMATE TRENDS: ANTHROPOID TRAITS

All anthropoids share resemblances that can be considered trends in primate evolution in the sense that these traits are fully developed neither in the fossils of primates that lived prior to 50 million years ago nor among contemporary prosimians.

All anthropoids have overlapping fields of vision, permitting them to see things in depth. With reduction of the snout, anthropoid eyes are placed forward in the skull and look directly ahead. The fields of vision of our eyes overlap. Depth perception, impossible without overlapping visual fields, proved adaptive in the trees. Tree-dwelling primates that could judge distance better because of depth perception survived and reproduced in greater numbers than did those that could not.

The abilities to see in depth and in color may have developed together. Both helped early anthropoids interpret their arboreal world. Superior vision made it easier to distinguish edible insects, fruits, berries, and leaves. Furthermore, having color and depth vision makes it easier to groom—to remove burrs, insects, and other small objects from other primates' hair. Grooming is one way of forming and maintaining social bonds.

Visual and tactile changes have been interrelated. Monkeys, apes, and humans have neither tactile muzzle skin nor "cat's whiskers." Instead, fingers are the main touch organs. The ends of the fingers and toes are sensitive tactile pads. Forward placement of the eyes and depth vision allow anthropoids to pick up small objects, hold them in front of their eyes, and appraise them. Our ability to thread a needle reflects an intricate interplay of hands and eyes that took millions of years to achieve. Manual dexterity, including the opposable thumb, confers a tremendous advantage in examining and manipulating objects and is essential to a major human adaptive capacity: tool making. Among monkeys, thumb opposability is indispensable for feeding and grooming.

Another trend is increased size of the *cranium* (skull) to fit a larger brain. The brain-to-body size ratio is greater among anthropoids than among prosimians. Even more important, the brain's outer layer—concerned with memory, association, and integration—is relatively larger. Monkeys, apes, and humans store an array of visual images in their memories, which permits them to learn more. The ability to learn from experience

Primates have five-digited feet and hands, well suited for
grasping. Flexible hands and feet that could encircle branches
were important features in the early primates' arboreal life.
In adapting to bipedal (two-footed) locomotion, hominids
eliminated most of the foot's grasping ability—illustrated here
by the chimpanzee.

and from other group members is a major reason for the success of the anthropoids compared to most other mammals.

## ✦ Monkeys

The anthropoid suborder has two infraorders: *platyrrhines* (New World monkeys) and *catarrhines* (Old World monkeys, apes, and humans). The catarrhines (sharp-nosed) and platyrrhines (flat-nosed) take their names from Latin terms that describe the placement of the nostrils. Old World monkeys, apes, and humans are all catarrhines. Being placed in the same taxon (infraorder in this case) means that Old World monkeys, apes, and humans are more closely related to each other than to New World monkeys. In other words, one kind of monkey (Old World) is more like a human than it is like another kind of monkey (New World). The New World monkeys were reproductively isolated from the catarrhines before the latter diverged into the Old

A woolly spider monkey, aka muriqui, from Monte Clares, Brazil. The long arms and elongated prehensile tail create a spider-like image for this New World monkey.

World monkeys, apes, and humans. This is why New World monkeys are assigned to a different infraorder.

All New World monkeys and many Old World monkeys are arboreal. Whether in the trees or on the ground, however, monkeys move differently from apes and humans. Their arms and legs move parallel to one another, as dogs' legs do. This contrasts with the tendency toward *orthograde posture,* the straight and upright stance of apes and humans. Unlike apes, which have longer arms than legs, and humans, who have longer legs than arms, monkeys have arms and legs of about the same length. Most monkeys also have tails, which help them maintain balance in the trees. Apes and humans lack tails. The apes' tendency toward orthograde posture is most evident when they sit down. When they move about, chimps, gorillas, and orangutans habitually use all four limbs.

## New World Monkeys

New World monkeys live in the forests of Central and South America. Unlike Old World monkeys, many New World monkeys have *prehensile,* or grasping, tails. Sometimes the prehensile tail has tactile skin, which permits it to work like a hand, for instance, in conveying food to the mouth. Old World monkeys, however, have developed their own characteristic anatomic specializations. They have rough patches of skin on the buttocks, adapted to sitting on hard rocky ground and rough branches. If the primate you see in the zoo has such patches, it's from the Old World. If it has a prehensile tail, it's a New World monkey. Among the anthropoids, there's only one nocturnal animal, a New World monkey called the night monkey or owl monkey. All other monkeys and apes, and humans, too, of course, are diurnal—active during the day.

## Old World Monkeys

The Old World monkeys have both terrestrial and arboreal species. Baboons and many macaques are terrestrial monkeys. Certain traits differentiate terrestrial and arboreal primates. Arboreal primates tend to be smaller. Smaller animals can reach a greater variety of foods in trees and shrubs, where the most abundant foods are located at the ends of branches. Arboreal monkeys typically are lithe and agile. They escape from the few predators in their environment—snakes and monkey-eating eagles—through alertness and speed. Large size, by contrast, is advantageous for terrestrial primates in dealing with their predators, which are more numerous on the ground.

This mandrill (Papio sphinx) is a brightly colored terrestrial Old World (African) monkey. Related to the baboon, which shares the same genus name (Papio), mandrills live in family groups consisting of an adult male, several females, and their young. Illustrating sexual dimorphism, female color is drabber and size smaller than in the male.

Another contrast between arboreal and terrestrial primates is in sexual dimorphism—marked differences in male and female anatomy and temperament (see Fedigan 1992). Sexual dimorphism tends to be more marked in terrestrial than in arboreal species. Baboon and macaque males are larger and fiercer than are females of the same species. However, it's hard to tell, without close inspection, the sex of an arboreal monkey.

Of the terrestrial monkeys, the baboons of Africa and the (mainly Asiatic) macaques have been the subjects of many studies. Terrestrial monkeys have specializations in anatomy, psychology, and social behavior that enable them to cope with terrestrial life. Adult male baboons, for example, are fierce-looking animals that can weigh 100 pounds (45 kilograms). They display their long, projecting canines to intimidate predators and when confronting other baboons. Faced with a predator, a male baboon can puff up his ample mane of shoulder hair, so that the would-be aggressor perceives the baboon as larger than he actually is.

Longitudinal field research shows that, near the time of puberty, baboon and macaque males typically leave their home troop for another. Because males move in and out, females form the stable core of the terrestrial monkey troop (Cheney and Seyfarth 1990; Hinde 1983). By contrast, among chimpanzees and gorillas, females are more likely to emigrate and seek mates outside their natal social groups (Bradley et al. 2004; Rodseth et al. 1991; Wilson and Wrangham 2003). Among terrestrial monkeys, then, the core group consists of females; among apes it is made up of males.

## ✧ APES

The Old World monkeys have their own separate superfamily (Cercopithecoidea), while humans and the apes together compose the hominoid superfamily (Hominoidea). Among the hominoids, the so-called great apes are orangutans, gorillas, and chimpanzees. Humans could be included here, too; we are sometimes called "the third African ape." The lesser (smaller) apes are the gibbons and siamangs of Southeast Asia and Indonesia.

Apes live in forests and woodlands. The light and agile gibbons, which are skilled brachiators, are completely arboreal. (*Brachiation* is hand-over-hand movement through the trees.) The heavier gorillas, chimpanzees, and adult male orangutans spend considerable time on the ground. Nevertheless, ape behavior and anatomy reveal past and present adaptation to arboreal life. For example, apes still build nests to sleep in trees. Apes have longer arms than legs, which is adaptive for brachiation (see Figure 4-3). The structure of the shoulder and clavicle (collarbone) of the apes and humans suggests that we had a brachiating ancestor. In fact, young apes still do brachiate. Adult apes tend to be too heavy to brachiate safely. Their weight is more than many branches can withstand. Gorillas and chimps now use the long arms they have inherited from their more arboreal ancestors for life on the ground. The terrestrial locomotion of chimps and gorillas is called *knuckle-walking*. In it, long arms and callused knuckles support the trunk as the apes amble around, leaning forward.

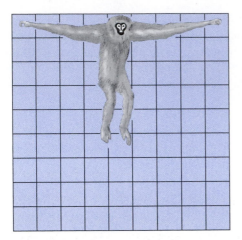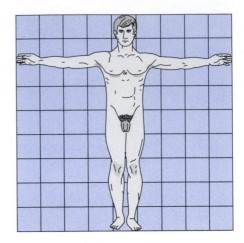

**FIGURE 4-3**    *The Limb Ratio of the Arboreal Gibbon and Terrestrial* **Homo**  How does this anatomical difference fit the modes of locomotion used by gibbons and humans?

# Gibbons

Gibbons are widespread in the forests of Southeast Asia, especially in Malaysia. Smallest of the apes, male and female gibbons have about the same average height (3 feet, or 1 meter) and weight (12 to 25 pounds, or 5 to 10 kilograms). Gibbons spend most of their time just below the forest canopy (treetops). For efficient brachiation, gibbons have long arms and fingers, with short thumbs. Slenderly built, gibbons are the most agile apes. They use their long arms for balance when they occasionally walk erect on the ground or along a branch. Gibbons are the preeminent arboreal specialists among the apes. They subsist on a diet mainly of fruits, with occasional insects and small animals. Gibbons and siamangs, their slightly larger relatives, tend to live in *primary groups,* which are composed of a permanently bonded male and female and their preadolescent offspring.

# Orangutans

There are two existing species of orangutan, Asiatic apes that belong to the genus *Pongo*. Highly endangered, contemporary orangs are confined to two Indonesian islands (Dreifus 2000; Mayell 2004*a*). Sexual dimorphism is marked, with the adult male weighing more than twice as much as the female. The orangutan male, like his human counterpart, is intermediate in size between chimps and gorillas. Some orang males exceed 200 pounds (90 kilograms). With only half the gorilla's bulk, male orangs can be more arboreal, although they typically climb, rather than swing through, the trees. The smaller size of females and young permits them to make fuller use of the trees. Orangutans have a varied diet of fruit, bark, leaves, and insects. Because orangutans live in jungles and feed in trees, they are especially difficult to study. However, field reports about orangutans in their natural setting (MacKinnon 1974; van Schaik 2004) have clarified their behavior and social organization. Orangs tend to be solitary animals. Their tightest social units consist of females and preadolescent young. Males forage alone.

# Gorillas

With just one species, *Gorilla gorilla,* there are three subspecies of gorillas. The western lowland gorilla is the animal you normally see in zoos. This, the smallest subspecies of gorilla, lives mainly in forests in the Central African Republic, Congo, Cameroon, Gabon, Equatorial Guinea, and Nigeria. The eastern lowland gorilla, of which there are only four in captivity, is slightly larger and lives in eastern Congo. There are no mountain gorillas, the third subspecies, in captivity, and it's estimated that no more than 650 of these animals survive in the wild. These are the largest gorillas with the longest hair (to keep them warm in their mountainous habitat). They are also the rarest gorillas, which Dian Fossey (1983) and other scientists have studied in Rwanda, Uganda, and eastern Congo.

Full-grown male gorillas may weigh 400 pounds (180 kilograms) and stand 6 feet tall (183 centimeters). Like most terrestrial primates, gorillas show marked sexual dimorphism. The average adult female weighs half as much as the male. Gorillas spend little time in the trees. It's hard for an adult male to move his bulk about in a tree. When gorillas sleep in trees, they build nests, which are usually no more than 10 feet (3 meters) off the ground. By contrast, the nests of chimps and female orangs may be 100 feet (30 meters) above the ground.

Most of the gorilla's day is spent feeding. Gorillas move through jungle undergrowth eating ground plants, leaves, bark, fruits, and other vegetation. Like most primates, gorillas live in social groups. The troop is a common unit of primate social organization, consisting of multiple males and females and their offspring. Although troops with up to 30 gorillas have been observed, most gorillas live in groups of from 10 to 20. Gorilla troops tend to have fairly stable memberships, with little shifting between troops (Fossey 1983). Each troop has a silverback male, so designated because of the strip of white hair that extends down his back. This is the physical sign of full maturity among the male gorillas. The silverback is usually the only breeding male in the troop, which is why gorilla troops are sometimes called "one-male groups." However, a few younger, subordinate males may also adhere to such a one-male group (Harcourt, Fossey, and Sabater-Pi 1981; Schaller 1963).

# Chimpanzees

Chimpanzees belong to the genus *Pan,* which has two species: *Pan troglodytes* (the common chimpanzee) and *Pan paniscus* (the bonobo or "pygmy" chimpanzee) (de Waal 1997; Susman 1987). Like humans, chimps are closely related to the gorilla, although there are some obvious differences. Like gorillas, chimps live in tropical Africa, but they range over a larger area and more varied environments than gorillas do. The common chimp, *Pan troglodytes,* lives in western central Africa (Gabon, Congo, Cameroon), as well as in western Africa (Sierra Leone, Liberia, Gambia) and eastern Africa (Congo, Uganda, and Tanzania). Bonobos live in remote and densely forested areas of just one country—the Democratic Republic of Congo (DRC). Common chimps live mainly in tropical rain forests but also in woodlands and mixed forest-woodland-grassland areas, such as the Gombe Stream National Park, Tanzania, where Jane Goodall (1996) and other researchers began to study them in 1960.

There are dietary differences between chimps and gorillas. Gorillas eat large quantities of green bulk vegetation, but chimps, like orangutans and gibbons, prefer fruits. Chimps are actually omnivorous, adding animal protein to their diet by capturing small mammals, birds' eggs, and insects.

Chimps are lighter and more arboreal than gorillas are. The adult male's weight—between 100 and 200 pounds (45 to 90 kilograms)—is about a third that of the male gorilla. There is much less sexual dimorphism among chimps than among gorillas. Females approximate 88 percent of the average male height. This is similar to the ratio of sexual dimorphism in *Homo sapiens.*

Several scientists have studied wild chimps, and we know more about the full range of their behavior and social organization than we do about the other apes (see Wrangham et al., eds. 1994; Wilson and Wrangham 2003). The long-term research of Jane Goodall and others at Gombe provides especially useful information. Approximately 150 chimpanzees range over Gombe's 30 square miles (80 square kilometers). Goodall (1986, 1996) has described communities of about 50 chimps, all of which know one another and interact from time to time. Communities regularly split up into smaller groups: a mother and her offspring; a few males; males, females, and young; and occasionally solitary animals. The social networks of males are more closed than are those of females, which are more likely to migrate and mate outside their natal group than males are (Wrangham et al., eds. 1994).

When chimps, which are very vocal, meet, they greet one another with gestures, facial expressions, and calls. They hoot to maintain contact during their daily rounds. Like baboons and macaques, chimps exhibit dominance relationships through attacks and displacement. Some adult females outrank younger males, although females do not display as strong dominance relationships among themselves as males do. Males occasionally cooperate in hunting parties.

## Bonobos

Ancestral chimps, and especially humans, eventually spread out of the forests and into woodlands and more open habitats. Bonobos, which belong to the species *Pan panis-cus,* apparently never left the protection of the trees. Up to 10,000 bonobos survive in the humid forests south of the Zaire River, in the Democratic Republic of Congo. Despite their common name—the *pygmy* chimpanzee—bonobos can't be distinguished from chimpanzees by size. Adult males of the smallest subspecies of chimpanzee average 95 pounds (43 kilograms), and females average 73 pounds (33 kilograms). These figures are about the same for bonobos (de Waal 1995, 1997).

Although much smaller than the males, female bonobos seem to rule. De Waal (1995, 1997) characterizes bonobo communities as female-centered, peace-loving, and egalitarian. The strongest social bonds are among females, although females also bond with males. The male bonobo's status reflects that of his mother, to whom he remains closely bonded for life.

The frequency with which bonobos have sex—and use it to avoid conflict—makes them exceptional among the primates. Despite frequent sex, the bonobo reproductive rate doesn't exceed that of the chimpanzee. A female bonobo gives birth every 5 or

6 years. Then, like chimps, female bonobos nurse and carry around their young for up to 5 years. Bonobos reach adolescence around 7 years of age. Females, which first give birth at age 13 or 14, are full grown by 15 years.

How do we know that bonobos use sexual activity to avoid conflict? According to de Waal:

> First, anything, including food, that arouses the interest of more than one bonobo at a time tends to result in sexual contact. If two bonobos approach a cardboard box thrown into their enclosure, they will briefly mount each other before playing with the box. Such situations lead to squabbles in most other species. But bonobos are quite tolerant, perhaps because they use sex to divert attention and to diffuse tension. Second, bonobo sex often occurs in aggressive contexts totally unrelated to food. A jealous male might chase another away from a female, after which the two males reunite and engage in scrotal rubbing. Or after a female hits a juvenile, the latter's mother may lunge at the aggressor, an action that is immediately followed by genital rubbing between the two adults. (De Waal 1995, p. 87)

## ✦ SIMILARITIES BETWEEN HUMANS AND OTHER PRIMATES

There is a substantial gap between nonhuman primate society and fully developed human culture. However, studies of primates have revealed many similarities. Scholars used to contend that learned (versus instinctive) behavior separates humans from other animals. We know now that monkeys and apes also rely on learning. Many of the differences between humans and other primates are differences in degree rather than in kind. For example, monkeys learn from experiences, but humans learn much more. Another example: Chimpanzees and orangutans make tools for specific tasks (see Mayell 2003), but human reliance on tools is much greater.

## Learning

Common to monkeys, apes, and humans is the fact that behavior and social life are not rigidly programmed by the genes. All these animals learn throughout their lives. In several cases, an entire monkey troop has learned from the experiences of some of its members. In one group of Japanese macaques, a three-year-old female monkey started washing dirt off sweet potatoes before she ate them. First her mother, then her age peers, and finally the entire troop began washing sweet potatoes too. The direction of learning was reversed when members of another macaque troop learned to eat wheat. After the dominant males had tried the new food, within four hours the practice had spread throughout the troop. Changes in learned behavior seem to spread more quickly from the top down than from the bottom up.

For monkeys as for people, the ability to learn, to profit from experience, confers a tremendous adaptive advantage, permitting them to avoid fatal mistakes. Faced with environmental change, primates don't have to wait for a genetic or physiological response. Learned behavior and social patterns can be modified instead.

Learned behavior among wild chimps includes rudimentary tool manufacture. At Tanzania's Gombe Stream National Park, chimps use specially prepared twigs to "fish" for termites.

## Tools

Anthropologists used to distinguish humans from other animals as tool users, and there is no doubt that *Homo* does employ tools much more than any other animal does. However, tool use also turns up among several nonhuman species. For example, in the Galápagos Islands off western South America, there is a "woodpecker finch" that selects twigs to dig out insects and grubs from tree bark. Sea otters use rocks to break open mollusks, which are important in their diet. Beavers are famous for dam construction.

When it became obvious that people weren't the only tool users, anthropologists started contending that only humans make tools with foresight, that is, with a specific purpose in mind. Chimpanzees show that this, too, is false. In 1960, Jane Goodall (1996) began observing wild chimps—including their tool use and hunting behavior—at Gombe Stream National Park in Tanzania, East Africa. From the work of Goodall and many other researchers we know that wild chimps regularly make tools.

Chimps living in the Tai forest of Ivory Coast make and use stone tools to break open hard, golfball-sized nuts (Mercader, Panger, and Boesch 2002). At specific sites, the chimps gather their nuts, place them on tree stumps, which are used as anvils, and pound the nuts with heavy stones. To break open the nuts requires considerable force, which must be managed carefully. When too much force is applied, the nuts shatter into inedible pieces. The chimps also must select hammer stones suited to smashing the nuts and carry them to where the nut trees grow—sophisticated behavior for an animal. Nut cracking is a learned skill, with mothers showing their young how to do it.

The most studied form of tool making by chimps involves "termiting." Chimps make tools to probe termite hills. They choose twigs, which they modify by removing leaves and peeling off bark to expose the sticky surface beneath. They carry the twigs to termite hills, dig holes with their fingers, and insert the twigs. Finally, they pull out the twigs and dine on termites that were attracted to the sticky surface.

Learning to termite takes time, and many Gombe chimps never master it. Twigs with certain characteristics must be chosen. Furthermore, once the twig is in the hill and the chimp judges that termites are crawling on its surface, the chimp must quickly flip the twig as it pulls it out so that the termites are on top. Otherwise they fall off as the twig comes out of the hole. This is an elaborate skill that neither all chimps nor human observers have been able to master.

## Predation and Hunting

Like tool making and language, hunting once was cited as a distinctive human activity unshared with our ape relatives. Again, however, primate research shows that what was previously thought to be a difference of kind is a difference of degree. The diets of other terrestrial primates are not exclusively vegetarian, as was once thought. Baboons kill and eat young antelopes, and researchers have repeatedly observed hunting by chimpanzees.

For several years John Mitani, David Watts, and other researchers have been observing chimpanzees at Ngogo in Uganda's Kibale National Park. This is the largest chimp community ever described in the wild. In 1998 it consisted of 26 adult males, 40 adult females, 16 adolescent males, 5 adolescent females, and 30 infants and juveniles (Mitani and Watts 1999). The large community size permits the formation of large hunting parties, which contributes to hunting success. Hunting parties at Ngogo included an average of 26 individuals (almost always adult and adolescent males). Most hunts (78 percent) resulted in at least one prey animal being caught—a much higher success rate than that among lions (26 percent), hyenas (34 percent), or cheetahs (30 percent). In most hunts (81 percent) the Ngogo chimps managed to catch multiple animals (three on average). The favored prey, at Ngogo as in other chimp communities, was the red colobus monkey.

As described by Mitani and Watts (1999), hunting by chimps is both opportunistic and planned. Opportunistic hunting took place when chimps encountered potential prey as they moved about during the day. Other hunts were organized patrols, in which the chimps became silent and moved together in a single file. They would stop, look up into the trees, scan, and change direction several times. Attentive to any arboreal movement, they would stop and search whenever they detected motion. After they spotted a monkey, the chase would begin. Encountering no prey, the chimps would go on patrolling, sometimes for several hours.

It turns out that chimps eat meat almost as much as some human hunter-gatherers do (Kopytoff 1995; Stanford 1999; Stanford and Bunn, eds. 2001). According to anthropologist Craig Stanford (1999), chimps may consume a quarter pound of meat a day when they hit their hunting stride. This meat intake is comparable to that of some contemporary groups of hunter-gatherers.

## ✦ DIFFERENCES BETWEEN HUMANS AND OTHER PRIMATES

The preceding sections have emphasized similarities between humans and other primates. *Homo* has elaborated substantially on certain tendencies shared with the apes. A unique concentration and combination of characteristics make humans distinct. However, the savanna or open grassland niche in which early humans evolved also selected certain traits that are not so clearly foreshadowed by the apes.

### Sharing and Cooperation

Early humans lived in small social groups called bands, with economies based on hunting and gathering (foraging). Until fairly recently (12,000 to 10,000 years ago), all humans based their subsistence on hunting and gathering and lived in bands. Some such societies even managed to survive into the modern world, and ethnographers have studied them. From those studies we can conclude that in human bands, the strongest and most aggressive members do not dominate, as they do in a troop of terrestrial monkeys. Sharing and curbing of aggression are as basic to technologically simple humans as dominance and threats are to baboons.

We've seen that bonobos use sex to curb aggression and reduce conflict, and that male chimps cooperate in hunting. Humans appear to be the most cooperative of the primates—in the food quest and other social activities. Except for meat sharing by chimps, the ape tendency is to forage individually. Monkeys also fend for themselves in getting food. Among human foragers, men generally hunt and women gather. Men and women bring resources back to the camp and share them. Older people who did not engage in the food quest get food from younger adults. Nourished and protected by younger band members, elders live past the reproductive age and are respected for their knowledge and experience. The amount of information stored in a human band is far greater than that in any other primate society. Sharing, cooperation, and language are intrinsic to information storage. Through millions of years of adaptation to an omnivorous diet, hominins came to rely, more than any other primate, on hunting, food sharing, and cooperative behavior.

### Mating and Kinship

Among baboons, chimpanzees, and bonobos, most mating occurs when females enter **estrus,** during which they ovulate. Receptive females form temporary bonds with, and mate with, males. Human females, by contrast, lack a visible estrus cycle, and their ovulation is concealed. Neither a woman's sexual receptivity nor her readiness to conceive is physically evident, as it is in chimps and bonobos. Not knowing when ovulation is occurring, humans maximize their reproductive success by mating throughout the year. Human pair bonds for mating tend to be more exclusive and more durable than are those of chimps or bonobos. Related to our more constant sexuality, all human societies have some form of marriage. Marriage gives mating a reliable basis and grants to each spouse special, though not always exclusive, sexual rights in the other.

Marriage creates another major contrast between humans and nonhumans: exogamy and kinship systems. Most cultures have rules of exogamy requiring marriage outside one's kin or local group. Coupled with the recognition of kinship, exogamy confers adaptive advantages. It creates ties between the spouses' groups of origin. Their children have relatives, and therefore allies, in two kin groups rather than just one. The key point here is that ties of affection and mutual support between members of different local groups tend to be absent among primates other than *Homo*. There is a tendency among primates to disperse at adolescence. Among chimps and gorillas, females tend to migrate, seeking mates in other groups. Both male and female gibbons leave home when they become sexually mature. Once they find mates and establish their own territories, ties with their natal groups cease. Among terrestrial monkeys, males leave the troop at puberty, eventually finding places elsewhere. Although kin ties are maintained between female monkeys, no close lifelong links are preserved through males.

Humans choose mates from outside the natal group, and usually at least one spouse moves. However, *humans maintain lifelong ties with sons and daughters*. The systems of kinship and marriage that preserve these links provide a major contrast between humans and other primates.

## ✦ PRIMATE EVOLUTION

The fossil record offers evidence for no more than 5 percent of extinct types of primates. Such small numbers provide the merest glimpse of the diverse bioforms—living beings—that have existed on earth.

With reference to the primate fossil record, we'll see that different geographic areas provide more abundant fossil evidence for different time periods. This doesn't necessarily mean that primates were not living elsewhere at the same time. Discussions of primate and human evolution must be tentative because the fossil record is limited and spotty. Much is subject to change as knowledge increases. A key feature of science is to recognize the tentativeness and uncertainty of knowledge. Scientists, including fossil hunters, constantly seek out new evidence and devise new methods, such as DNA comparison, to improve their understanding, in this case of primate and human evolution.

## ✦ CHRONOLOGY

We learned in Chapter 2 that the remains of animals and plants that lived at the same time are found in the same stratum. Based on fossils found in stratigraphic sequences, the history of vertebrate life has been divided into three main eras. The *Paleozoic* was the era of ancient life—fishes, amphibians, and primitive reptiles. The *Mesozoic* was the era of middle life—reptiles, including the dinosaurs. The *Cenozoic* is the era of recent life—birds and mammals. Each era is divided into periods, and the periods are divided into epochs. (See Figure 4-4.)

| Era | Period | |
|---|---|---|
| Cenozoic | Quaternary | 1.8 m.y.a. |
| | Tertiary | 65 m.y.a. |
| Mesozoic | Cretaceous | 146 m.y.a. |
| | Jurassic | 208 m.y.a. |
| | Triassic | 245 m.y.a. |
| Paleozoic | Permian | 286 m.y.a. |
| | Carboniferous | 360 m.y.a. |
| | Devonian | 410 m.y.a. |
| | Silurian | 440 m.y.a. |
| | Ordovician | 505 m.y.a. |
| | Cambrian | 544 m.y.a. |
| Proterozoic | Neoproterozoic | 900 m.y.a. |
| | Mesoproterozoic | 1,600 m.y.a. |
| | Paleoproterozoic | 2,500 m.y.a. |
| Archaean | | 3,800 m.y.a. |
| Hadean | | 4,500 m.y.a. |

FIGURE 4-4  *Geological Time Scales*  The geological time scale, based on stratigraphy. Eras are subdivided into periods, and periods, into epochs. In what era, period, and epoch did *Homo* originate?

| Era | Period | Epoch | Climate and Life Forms |
|---|---|---|---|
| Cenozoic | Quaternary | Holocene<br>11,000 B.P. | Transition to agriculture; emergence of states |
| | | Pleistocene<br>128 m.y.a. | Climatic fluctuations, glaciation; *Homo, A. boisei* |
| | Tertiary | Pliocene<br>5 m.y.a. | *A. robustus, A. africanus, A. afarensis, A. anamensis, Ardipithecus* |
| | | Miocene<br>23 m.y.a. | Cooler and drier grasslands spread in middle latitudes; Africa collides with Eurasia (16 m.y.a.) |
| | | Oligocene<br>38 m.y.a. | Cooler and drier in the north; anthropoids in Africa (Fayum); separation of catarrhines and platyrrhines; separation of hylobatids from pongids and hominids |
| | | Eocene<br>54 m.y.a. | Warm tropical climates become widespread; modern orders of mammals appear; prosimianlike primates abundant; anthropoids appear |
| | | Paleocene<br>65 m.y.a. | First major mammal radiation |

**FIGURE 4-4** *Geological Time Scales—Concluded* Periods and epochs of the Cenozoic era.

Anthropologists are concerned with the Cenozoic *era*, which includes two *periods*: Tertiary and Quaternary. Each of these periods is subdivided into *epochs*. The Tertiary had five epochs: Paleocene, Eocene, Oligocene, Miocene, and Pliocene. The Quaternary includes just two epochs: Pleistocene and Holocene, or Recent. Figure 4-4 gives the approximate dates of these epochs. Sediments from the Paleocene epoch (65 to 54 **m.y.a.**—million years ago) have yielded fossil remains of diverse small mammals, some possibly ancestral to the primates. Prosimianlike fossils abound in strata dating from the Eocene (54 to 36 m.y.a.). The first anthropoid fossils date to the Eocene and the early Oligocene (36 to 23 m.y.a.). Hominoids became widespread during the Miocene (23 to 5 m.y.a.). Hominins first appeared in the late Miocene, just before the Pliocene (5 to 2 m.y.a.) (Figure 4-4).

## ✦ EARLY PRIMATES

When the Mesozoic era ended, and the Cenozoic era began, some 65 million years ago, North America was connected to Europe but not to South America. (The Americas joined around 20 million years ago.) Over millions of years, the continents have "drifted" to their present locations, carried along by the gradually shifting plates of the earth's surface (Figure 4-5).

During the Cenozoic, most land masses had tropical or subtropical climates. The Mesozoic era had ended with a massive worldwide extinction of plants and animals, including the dinosaurs. Thereafter, mammals replaced reptiles as the dominant large land animals. Trees and flowering plants soon proliferated, supplying arboreal foods for the primates that eventually evolved to fill the new niches.

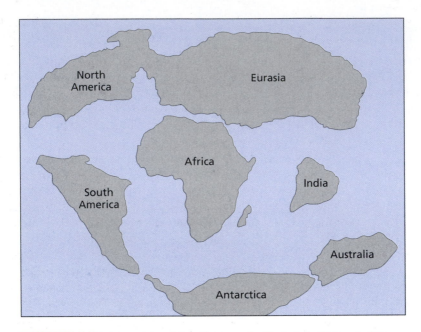

**FIGURE 4-5**    *Placement of Continents at the End of the Mesozoic*    When the Mesozoic era ended, and the Cenozoic began, some 65 million years ago, North America was connected to Europe, but not to South America.

According to the *arboreal theory,* primates became primates by adapting to arboreal life. The primate traits and trends discussed previously developed as adaptations to life high up in the trees. A key feature was the importance of sight over smell. Changes in the visual apparatus were adaptive in the trees, where depth perception facilitated leaping. Grasping hands and feet were used to crawl along slender branches. Grasping feet anchored the body as the primate reached for foods at the ends of branches. Early primates probably had omnivorous diets based on foods available in the trees, such as flowers, fruits, berries, gums, leaves, and insects. The early Cenozoic era witnessed a proliferation of flowering plants, attracting insects that were to figure prominently in many primate diets.

## Early Cenozoic Primates

There is considerable fossil evidence that a diversified group of primates lived, mainly in Europe and North America, during the second epoch of the Cenozoic, the Eocene. On that basis it is likely that the earliest primates lived during the first epoch of the Cenozoic, the Paleocene (65–54 m.y.a.). The status of several fossils as possible Paleocene primates has been debated. Because there is no consensus on this matter, such fossils are not discussed here.

A tiny primate skull found recently in China (Malkin 2004; Ni et al. 2004) confirms that early primates lived in Asia near the start of the Eocene. A team of Chinese paleontologists led by Xijun Ni found the new primate species, *Teilhardina asiatica*, in China's Hunan Province. The tiny 55-million-year-old skull, with most of its teeth intact, is the most complete skull ever found of a euprimate. (The term *euprimate* refers to the first mammals that shared characteristics such as forward-facing eyes and a relatively large braincase with modern primates.) Fragments of euprimates, all dating to around 55 m.y.a., have been found in Europe and North America. The discovery of a euprimate in Asia means that primates were already widespread by then and that their common ancestor must have evolved even earlier.

In primate evolution, the Eocene (54–38 m.y.a.) was the age of the prosimians, with at least 60 genera in two main families. They lived in North America, Europe, Africa, and Asia. Ancestral lemurs reached Madagascar from Africa late in the Eocene. They must have traveled across the Mozambique Channel, which was narrower then than it is now, on thick mats of vegetation. Such naturally formed "rafts" have been observed forming in East African rivers, then floating out to sea.

Sometime during the Eocene, ancestral anthropoids branched off from the prosimians by becoming more diurnal (active during the day) and by strengthening the trend favoring vision over smell. Some Eocene prosimians had larger brains and eyes, and smaller snouts, than others did. These were the ancestors of the anthropoids. Anthropoid eyes are rotated more forward when compared with lemurs and lorises. Also, anthropoids have a fully enclosed bony eye socket, which lemurs and lorises lack. And unlike lemurs and lorises, anthropoids lack a rhinarium, a moist nose continuous with the upper lip. Anthropoids have a dry nose, separate from the upper lip. By the end of the Eocene, many prosimian species had become extinct, reflecting competition from the first anthropoids.

## Oligocene Anthropoids

During the Oligocene epoch (38–23 m.y.a.), anthropoids became the most numerous primates. Most of our knowledge of early anthropoids is based on fossils from Egypt's Fayum deposits. This area is a desert today, but 36–31 million years ago it was a tropical rain forest.

The anthropoids of the Fayum lived in trees and ate fruits and seeds. Compared with prosimians, they had fewer teeth, reduced snouts, larger brains, and increasingly forward-looking eyes. Of the Fayum anthropoid fossils, the *parapithecid* family is the more primitive and is perhaps ancestral to the New World monkeys. The parapithecids were very small (2 to 3 pounds, 0.9 to 1.4 kilograms), with similarities to living marmosets and tamarins, small South American monkeys.

The *propliopithecid* family seems ancestral to the catarrhines—Old World monkeys, apes, and humans. The propliopithecids share with the later catarrhines a distinctive dental formula: 2.1.2.3, meaning two incisors, one canine, two premolars, and three molars. (The formula is based on one-fourth of the mouth, either the right or left side of the upper or lower jaw.) The more primitive primate dental formula is 2.1.3.3. Most other primates, including prosimians and New World monkeys, have the second formula, with three premolars instead of two. Besides the Fayum, Oligocene deposits with primate bones have been found in North and West Africa, southern Arabia, China, Southeast Asia, and North and South America.

The Oligocene was a time of major geological and climatic change: North America and Europe separated and became distinct continents; the Great Rift Valley system of East Africa formed; India drifted into Asia; and a cooling trend began, especially in the Northern Hemisphere, where primates disappeared.

---

## ✦ MIOCENE HOMINOIDS

The earliest hominoid fossils date to the Miocene epoch (23–5 m.y.a.), which is divided into three parts: lower, middle, and upper or late. The early Miocene (23–16 m.y.a.) was a warm and wet period, when forests covered East Africa. Recall that Hominoidea is the superfamily that includes fossil and living apes and humans. For simplicity's sake, the earliest **hominoids** are here called proto-apes, or simply apes. Although some of these may be ancestral to living apes, none is identical, or often even very similar, to modern apes.

### *Proconsul*

The *Proconsul* group represents the most abundant and successful anthropoids of the early Miocene. This group lived in Africa and includes three species. These early Miocene proto-apes had teeth with similarities to those of living apes. But their skeleton below the neck was more monkey-like. Some *Proconsul* species were the size of a small monkey; others, the size of a chimpanzee, usually with marked sexual dimorphism. Their dentition suggests they ate fruits and leaves. *Proconsul* probably contained the last common ancestor shared by the Old World monkeys and the apes. By the middle Miocene, *Proconsul* had been replaced by Old World monkeys and apes.

### Later Miocene Apes

During the early Miocene (23–16 m.y.a.), Africa had been cut off by water from Europe and Asia. But during the middle Miocene, Arabia drifted into Eurasia, providing a land connection between Africa, Europe, and Asia. Migrating both ways—out of and into Africa—after 16 m.y.a. were various animals, including hominoids. Proto-apes were the most common primates of the middle Miocene (16–10 m.y.a.). Over 20 species have been discovered. (See Figure 4-6.)

Perhaps the most remarkable Miocene ape was *Gigantopithecus*—almost certainly the largest primate that ever lived. Confined to Asia, it persisted for millions of years, from the Miocene until 400,000 years ago, when it coexisted with members of our own genus, *Homo erectus*. Some people think *Gigantopithecus* is not extinct yet, and that we know it today as the yeti and bigfoot (Sasquatch).

With a fossil record consisting of nothing more than jaw bones and teeth, it is difficult to say for sure just how big *Gigantopithecus* was. Based on ratios of jaw and tooth size to body size in other apes, various reconstructions have been made. One has *Gigantopithecus* weighing 1,200 pounds (544 kilograms) and standing 10 feet (3 meters) tall (Ciochon, Olsen, and James 1990). Another puts the height at 9 feet (2.7 meters) and cuts the weight in half (Simons and Ettel 1970). All agree, however, that *Gigantopithecus* was the largest ape that ever lived. There have been at least two species of

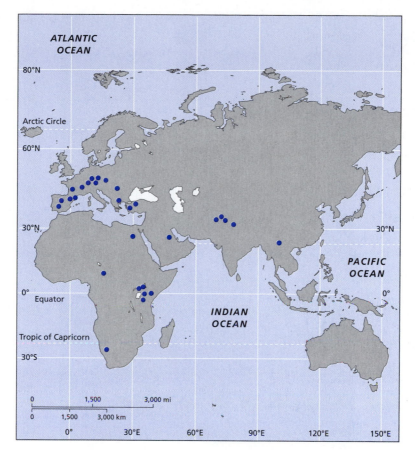

**FIGURE 4-6**    *The Geographic Distribution of Known Miocene Apes*

SOURCE: From *Introduction to Physical Anthropology*, 6th ed. by Robert Jurmain and Harry Nelson, p. 302. Copyright © 1994. Reprinted with permission of Wadsworth, a division of Thomson Learning: www.thomsonrights.com. Fax (800) 730-2215.

*Gigantopithecus:* one coexisted with *H. erectus* in China and Vietnam, and the other, much earlier (5 m.y.a.), lived in northern India.

## *Pierolapithecus catalaunicus*

In November 2004, Spanish anthropologists announced their discovery of what may be the last common ancestor of all the world's living great apes, including hominins (Moyà-Solà et al. 2004). The new ape species, named *Pierolapithecus catalaunicus*, lived around 13 million years ago, during the middle Miocene. This ancient ape could be the last common ancestor of humans, chimpanzees, gorillas, and orangutans. The find comes from a new and rich fossil site, near the village of Hostalets de Pierola in Catalonia, Spain. The name *Pierolapithecus* combines part of the village's name with the Greek word for "ape," while *catalaunicus* commemorates Catalonia, the province where both the village and Barcelona are located.

A reconstruction of *Gigantopithecus* by Russell Ciochon and Bill Munns. Munns is shown here with "Giganto." What would be the likely environmental effects of a population of such large apes?

The *Pierolapithecus* bones include much of the skull, hand and foot bones, three vertebrae, two complete ribs, and large pieces of a dozen others. The find appears to represent a single adult male that weighed about 75 pounds (34 kilograms). Like chimps and gorillas, *Pierolapithecus* was well adapted for tree climbing and knuckle-walking on the ground. Based on the shape of the single surviving tooth, it was probably a fruit eater. Several features distinguished *Pierolapithecus* from the lesser apes (gibbons and siamangs) and monkeys. Its rib cage, lower spine, and wrist suggest it climbed the way modern great apes do. The ape's chest, or thorax, is wider and flatter than that of monkeys and is the earliest modern apelike thorax yet found in the fossil record.

In the current timetable of primate evolution, the lineage of monkeys split off some 25 m.y.a. from the hominoid line, which led to apes and humans. The ancestors of the lesser apes separated from those of the great apes some 16–14 m.y.a. Then, around

11–10 m.y.a., the orangutan line diverged from that leading to the African apes and humans. Yet another split took place when the gorilla line branched off from the line leading to chimpanzees and hominins. Around 7–6 m.y.a., another split in the lineage led to the various early hominins, to be examined in the next chapter. Some intriguing fossils dating from that critical time period have been discovered recently.

## "Toumai"

In July 2001 anthropologists working in Central Africa—in northern Chad's Djurab Desert (Figure 4-7)—unearthed the 6-to-7-million-year-old skull of the oldest possible human ancestor yet found. This discovery consists of a nearly complete skull, two lower

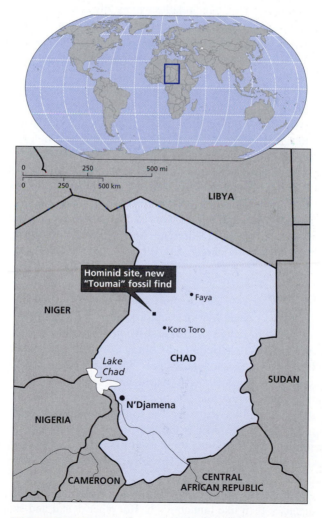

**FIGURE 4-7**  *Location of Toumai Discovery*

jaw fragments, and three teeth. It dates to the time period when humans and chimps would have been diverging from a common ancestor. "It takes us into another world, of creatures that include the common ancestor, the ancestral human and the ancestral chimp," George Washington University paleobiologist Bernard Wood said (quoted in Gugliotta 2002). The discovery was made by a 40-member multinational team led by the French paleoanthropologist Michel Brunet. The actual discoverer was the university undergraduate Ahounta Djimdoumalbaye, who spied the skull embedded in sandstone. The new fossil was dubbed *Sahelanthropus tchadensis,* referring to the northern Sahel region of Chad where it was found. The fossil is also known as "Toumai," a local name meaning "hope of life."

The discovery team identified the skull as that of an adult male with a chimp-sized brain (320–380 cubic centimeters), heavy brow ridges, and a relatively flat, humanlike face. Toumai's habitat included savanna, forests, rivers, and lakes—and abundant animal life such as elephants, antelope, horses, giraffes, hyenas, hippopotamuses, wild boars, crocodiles, fish, and rodents. The animal species enabled the team to date the site where Toumai was found (by comparison with radiometrically dated sites with similar fauna).

Was Toumai the "missing link," a common ancestor, a gorilla ancestor (as Wolpoff et al. [2002] suggest), or the earliest hominin known to science? The discovery of Toumai moves scientists close to the time when humans and the African apes diverged from a common ancestor (see Weiss 2005). As we would expect in a fossil so close to the common ancestor, Toumai blends apelike and human characteristics. Although the brain was chimp-sized, the tooth enamel was thicker than a chimp's enamel, suggesting a diet that included not just fruits, but also tougher vegetation of a sort typically found in the savanna. Also, Toumai's snout did not protrude as far as a chimp's—making it more humanlike, and the canine tooth was shorter than those of other apes. "The fossil is showing the first glimmerings of evolution in our direction," according to University of California at Berkeley anthropologist Tim White (quoted in Gugliotta 2002).

## Orrorin tugenensis

In January 2001 Brigitte Senut, Martin Pickford, and others reported the discovery, near the village of Tugen in Kenya's Baringo district, of possible early hominin fossils they called *Orrorin tugenensis* (Aiello and Collard 2001; Senut et al. 2001). The find consisted of 13 fossils from at least 5 individuals. The fossils include pieces of jaw with teeth, isolated upper and lower teeth, arm bones, and a finger bone. *Orrorin* appears to have been a chimp-sized creature that climbed easily and walked on two legs when on the ground. Its date of 6 million years is close to the time of the common ancestor of humans and chimps. The fossilized left femur (thigh bone) suggests upright bipedalism (walking with two feet), while the thick right humerus (upper arm bone) suggests tree-climbing skills. Animal fossils found in the same rocks indicate *Orrorin* lived in a wooded environment.

*Orrorin's* upper incisor, upper canine, and lower premolar are more like the teeth of a female chimpanzee than like human teeth. But other dental and skeletal features, especially bipedalism, led the discoverers to assign *Orrorin* to the hominin lineage.

*Orrorin* lived after Toumai but before *Ardipithecus kadabba,* discovered in Ethiopia, also in 2001, and dated to 5.8–5.5 m.y.a. The hominin status of *Ardipithecus,* to be considered at the beginning of the next chapter, is more generally accepted than is that of either Toumai or *Orrorin tugenensis.*

## ANTHROPOLOGY TODAY

### *Endangered Primates*

Deforestation poses a special risk for the primates because 90 percent of the 190 living primate species live in tropical forests—in Africa, Asia, South America, and Central America. As the earth's human population swells, the populations of the nonhuman primates are shrinking. According to the Convention on International Trade in Endangered Species (ratified in 1973), all nonhuman primates are now endangered or soon to be endangered. The apes (gibbons, gorillas, orangutans, and chimps) are in the "most endangered" category. Mountain gorillas, which once ranged widely in the forested mountains of East Africa, are now limited to a small area near the war-ravaged borders of Rwanda, the DRC, and Uganda. Other severely threatened species include the golden lion tamarin monkey of southeastern Brazil, the cotton-top tamarin of Colombia, the lion-tailed macaque of southern India, the woolly monkeys of Amazonia, and the orangutan of Southeast Asia.

A combination of forest clearing and forest fires has been deadly to orangutans in Sumatra and Borneo in Indonesia (see Dreifus 2000). Sumatra, which is losing 1,000 orangs a year, has an estimated population of fewer than 6,000 left. A road for loggers and miners that penetrated the orangutan range in Sumatra led to contact with humans that proved fatal to hundreds of the animals. Borneo has been devastated by fires in recent years, leaving some 10,000–15,000 orangs, compared with 60,000 in 1980. Habitat destruction and fragmentation can isolate small groups of animals, leaving them vulnerable to extinction due to loss of genetic diversity. Primate populations are slow to recover from such threats. Ape species, for example, are slow reproducers, rarely having more than three to four offspring over a lifetime (Stern 2000).

Although the destruction of their forest habitats is the main reason the primates are disappearing, it isn't the only reason. Another threat is human hunting of primates for bush meat (Viegas 2000). In Amazonia, West Africa, and Central Africa, primates are a major source of food. People kill thousands of monkeys each year. Human hunters are less of a threat to primates in Asia. In India, Hindus avoid monkey meat because the monkey is sacred, while Moslems avoid it because monkeys are considered unclean and not fit for human consumption.

People also hunt primates for their skins and pelts; poachers sell their body parts as trophies and ornaments. Africans use the skins of black-and-white colobus monkeys for cloaks and head-dresses, and American and European tourists buy coats and rugs made from colobus pelts. In Amazonia, ocelot and jaguar hunters shoot monkeys to bait the traps they set for the cats.

Primates also are killed when they are agricultural pests. In some areas of Africa and Asia, baboons and macaques raid the crops on which people depend for subsistence. Between 1947 and 1962, the government of Sierra Leone held annual drives to rid farm areas of monkeys, and between 15,000 and 20,000 primates perished each year.

*Continued*

## ANTHROPOLOGY TODAY

A final reason for the demise of the primates is the capture of animals for use in labs or as pets. Although this threat is minor compared with deforestation and the hunting of primates for food, it does pose a serious risk to certain endangered species in heavy demand. One of the species most hurt by this trade is the chimpanzee, which has been widely used in biomedical research.

## SUMMARY

1. Humans, apes, monkeys, and prosimians are primates. The primate order is subdivided into suborders, superfamilies, families, tribes, genera, species, and subspecies. Organisms in any subdivision (taxon) of a taxonomy are assumed to share more recent ancestry with each other than they do with organisms in other taxa. But it's sometimes hard to tell the difference between homologies, which reflect common ancestry, and analogies, biological similarities that develop through convergent evolution.

2. Prosimians are the older of the two primate suborders. Some 40 million years ago, anthropoids displaced prosimians from niches their ancestors once occupied. Tarsiers and lorises are prosimians that survived by adapting to nocturnal life. Lemurs survived on the island of Madagascar.

3. Anthropoids include humans, apes, and monkeys. All share fully developed primate trends, such as depth and color vision. Other anthropoid traits include a shift in tactile areas to the fingers. The New World monkeys are all arboreal. Old World monkeys include both terrestrial species (e.g., baboons and macaques) and arboreal ones. The great apes are orangutans, gorillas, chimpanzees, and bonobos. The lesser apes are gibbons and siamangs.

4. Gibbons and siamangs live in Southeast Asian forests. These apes are slight, arboreal animals whose mode of locomotion is brachiation. Sexual dimorphism, slight among gibbons, is marked among orangutans, which are confined to two Indonesian islands. Sexually dimorphic gorillas, the most terrestrial apes, are vegetarians confined to equatorial Africa. Two species of chimpanzees live in the forests and woodlands of tropical Africa. Chimps are less sexually dimorphic, more numerous, and more omnivorous than gorillas are. Terrestrial monkeys (baboons and macaques) live in troops. Baboon males, the troop's main protectors, are twice the size of females.

5. There are significant differences between humans and other primates. But similarities are also extensive, and many differences are of degree rather than of kind. The ability to learn, which is the basis of culture, is an adaptive advantage available to many nonhuman primates. Chimpanzees make tools for several purposes. They also hunt and share meat.

6. Important differences between humans and other primates remain. Aggression and dominance are characteristic of terrestrial monkeys. Sharing and cooperation are equally significant in human bands. Connected with sharing among humans is a traditional division of subsistence labor by age and gender. Only humans have systems of kinship and marriage that permit us to maintain lifelong ties with relatives in different local groups.

7. Primates have lived during the past 65 million years, the Cenozoic era, with seven epochs: Paleocene, Eocene, Oligocene, Miocene, Pliocene, Pleistocene, and Recent. The arboreal theory states that primates evolved by adapting to life high up in the trees.

8. The first (prosimianlike) fossils clearly identified as primates lived during the Eocene (54–38 m.y.a.), mainly in North America and Europe. During the Oligocene (38–23 m.y.a.), anthropoids became the most numerous primates. The parapithecid family may be ancestral to the New World monkeys. The propliopithecid family seems ancestral to the catarrhines—Old World monkeys, apes, and humans.

9. The earliest hominoid fossils are from the Miocene (23–5 m.y.a.). Africa's *Proconsul* group contained the last common ancestor shared by the Old World monkeys and the apes. Since the middle Miocene (16–10 m.y.a.), Africa, Europe, and Asia have been connected. Proto-apes spread beyond Africa and became the most common primates of the middle Miocene. Asia's *Gigantopithecus*, the largest primate ever to live, persisted for millions of years, finally coexisting with *Homo erectus. Pieropithecus catalaunicus*, which lived around 13 million years ago, could be the last common ancestor of humans, chimpanzees, gorillas and orangutans.

10. Anthropologists have yet to identify the fossils of the common ancestors of humans, gorillas, and chimps. However, biochemical evidence strongly suggests that the diversification into ancestral gorillas, chimps, and hominins began in Africa during the late Miocene. A skull found in 2001 in northern Chad, dated at 6 to 7 million years old, officially named *Sahelanthropus tchadensis*, more commonly called "Toumai," may or may not be the earliest hominin yet known, as may the somewhat less ancient *Orrorin tugenensis*, found in Kenya in 2001.

# KEY TERMS

| | |
|---|---|
| analogies (p. 72) | homologies (p. 70) |
| anthropoids (p. 73) | m.y.a. (p. 89) |
| arboreal (p. 73) | opposable thumbs (p. 74) |
| convergent evolution (p. 72) | primatology (p. 69) |
| estrus (p. 86) | prosimians (p. 73) |
| hominin (p. 73) | taxonomy (p. 70) |
| hominid (p. 73) | terrestrial (p. 69) |
| hominoids (p. 92) | |

# CHAPTER 5

# Early Hominins

---

## ✦ What Makes Us Human?

In trying to determine whether a fossil is a human ancestor, should we look for traits that make us human today? Sometimes yes; sometimes no. We do look for similarities in DNA, including mutations shared by certain lineages but not others. But what about such key human attributes as bipedal locomotion, a long period of childhood dependency, big brains, and the use of tools and language? Some of these key markers of humanity are fairly recent—or have origins that are impossible to date. And ironically, some of the physical markers that have led scientists to identify certain fossils as early hominins rather than apes are features that have been lost during subsequent human evolution.

## Bipedalism

Postcranial (below the skull) material from *Ardipithecus* (5.8–4.4 m.y.a.), as described in the box at the end of this chapter, suggests a capacity for upright bipedal locomotion. Indeed, it was the shift toward this form of moving around that led to the distinctive hominin way of life. **Bipedalism**—upright two-legged locomotion—is the key feature differentiating early hominins from the apes. African fossil discoveries suggest that hominin bipedalism is more than five million years old.

Reconstruction of Australopithecus running bipedally with a pebble tool in hand. Along with tool use and manufacture, bipedalism is a key part of being human.

Bipedalism is considered to be an adaptation to an open grassland or savanna habitat. Scientists have suggested several advantages of bipedalism in such an environment: the ability to see over long grass, to carry items back to a home base, and to reduce the body's exposure to solar radiation. The fossil and archaeological records confirm that upright bipedal locomotion preceded stone tool manufacture and the expansion of the hominin brain. However, although the earliest hominins could move bipedally through open country during the day, they also preserved enough of an apelike anatomy to make them good climbers. They could take to the trees to sleep at night and to escape terrestrial predators.

One explanation for bipedalism centers on environmental changes that swept Africa more than 5 million years ago. During the late Miocene, as the global climate became cooler and drier, grasslands in sub-Saharan Africa expanded. The rain forests contracted, shrinking the habitat available to arboreal primates (Wilford 1995). Also, at about the same time, a geological shift deepened the Rift Valley, which runs through Ethiopia, Kenya, and Tanzania. The sinking of the valley thrust up mountains. This left the land west of the valley more humid and arboreal, while the east became more arid and dominated by savanna. The common ancestors of hominins and chimpanzees were divided as a result. Those adapting to the humid west became the chimpanzee family. Those in the east had to forge a new life in an open environment (Coppens 1994).

At least one branch of the eastern primates—those that became hominins—ventured more and more into open country seeking food, but retreating to the trees to escape predators and to sleep at night. To move about more efficiently, and perhaps also to keep a lookout above the grasses for food or predators, these primates started standing up and walking on two legs. Presumably, this adaptation enhanced their chances of surviving and passing on genes that favored this stance and gait, leading eventually to bipedal hominins (Wilford 1995).

Yet another factor may have contributed to bipedalism. Early hominins might have found the intense tropical heat of the savanna very stressful. Most savanna-dwelling animals have built-in ways of protecting their brains from overheating as their body temperatures rise during the day. This isn't true of humans, nor is it likely to have been true of early hominins. The only way we can protect our brains is by keeping our bodies cool. Could it be that early hominins stood up to cool off? Studies with scale models of primates suggest that quadrupedalism exposes the body to 60 percent more solar radiation than does bipedalism. The upright body also could catch the cooler breezes above the ground (Wilford 1995).

## Brains, Skulls, and Childhood Dependency

Compared with contemporary humans, early hominins had very small brains. *Australopithecus afarensis,* a bipedal hominin that lived more than 3 million years ago, had a cranial capacity (430 cm$^3$—cubic centimeters) that barely surpassed the chimp average (390 cm$^3$). The form of the *afarensis* skull also is like that of the chimpanzee, although the brain-to-body size ratio may have been larger. Brain size has increased during hominin evolution, especially with the advent of the genus *Homo.* But this increase had to overcome some obstacles. Larger skulls demand larger birth canals, but the requirements of upright bipedalism impose limits on the expansion of the human pelvic opening. If the opening is too large, the pelvis doesn't provide sufficient support for the trunk. Locomotion suffers, and posture problems develop. If, by contrast, the birth canal is too narrow, mother and child (without the modern option of Caesarean section) may die. Natural selection has struck a balance between the structural demands of upright posture and the tendency toward increased brain size—the birth of immature and dependent children whose brains and skulls grow dramatically for several years after birth.

## Tools

Given what is known (see Chapter 4) about tool use and manufacture by the great apes, it is likely that early hominins shared this ability as a homology with the apes. We'll see later that the first evidence for hominin stone tool manufacture is dated to 2.5 m.y.a. Upright bipedalism would have permitted the use of tools and weapons against predators and competitors in an open grassland habitat. Bipedal locomotion also allowed early hominins to carry things, perhaps including scavenged parts of carnivore kills. We know that primates have generalized abilities to adapt through learning. It would be amazing if early hominins, who are much more closely related to us than the apes are, didn't have even greater cultural abilities than contemporary apes have.

## Teeth

One example of an early hominin trait that has been lost during subsequent human evolution is big back teeth. (Indeed a pattern of overall dental reduction has characterized human evolution.) As they adapted to the savanna, with its gritty, tough, and fibrous vegetation, it was adaptively advantageous for early hominins to have large back teeth and thick tooth enamel. This permitted thorough chewing of tough, fibrous vegetation and mixture with salivary enzymes to permit digestion of foods that otherwise would not have been digestible. The churning, rotary motion associated with such chewing also favored reduction of the canines and first premolars (bicuspids). These front teeth are much sharper and longer in the apes than in early hominins. The apes use their sharp self-honing teeth to pierce fruits. Males also flash their big sharp canines to intimidate and impress others, including potential mates. Although bipedalism seems to have characterized the human lineage since it split from the line leading to the African apes, many other "human" features came later. Yet other early hominin features, such as large back teeth and thick enamel—which we don't have now—offer clues about who was a human ancestor back then.

## ✦ CHRONOLOGY OF HOMININ EVOLUTION

Recall that the term **hominin** is used to designate the human line after its split from ancestral chimps. **Hominid** refers to the taxonomic family that includes humans and the African apes and their immediate ancestors. In this book *hominid* is used when there is doubt about the hominin status of the fossil (e.g., with Toumai, as described in Chapter 4). Although recent fossil discoveries have pushed the hominin lineage back to almost 6 million years, humans actually haven't been around too long when the age of the earth is considered. If we compare earth's history to a 24-hour day (with 1 second equaling 50, 000 years),

> Earth originates at midnight;
> the earliest fossils were deposited at 5:45 A.M.;
> the first vertebrates appeared at 9:02 P.M.;
> the earliest mammals, at 10:45 P.M.;
> the earliest primates, at 11:43 P.M.;
> the earliest hominins, at 11:57 P.M.;
> and *Homo sapiens* arrives 36 seconds before midnight. (Wolpoff, 1999, p. 10)

Although the first hominins appeared late in the Miocene epoch, for the study of hominin evolution, the Pliocene (5 to 2 m.y.a.), Pleistocene (2 m.y.a. to 10,000 B.P.), and Recent (10,000 B.P. to the present) epochs are most important. Until the end of the Pliocene, the main hominin genus was *Australopithecus,* which lived in sub-Saharan Africa. By the start of the Pleistocene, *Australopithecus* had evolved into *Homo*.

## ✦ THE EARLIEST HOMININS

Recent discoveries of fossils and tools have increased our knowledge of hominid and hominin evolution. The most significant recent discoveries have been made in Africa—Kenya, Tanzania, Ethiopia, and Chad. These finds come from different sites and may be the remains of individuals who lived hundreds of thousands of years apart. Furthermore, geological processes operating over thousands or millions of years inevitably distort fossil remains. Table 5-1 summarizes the major events in hominid and hominin evolution. You should consult it throughout this chapter and the next one.

---

**TABLE 5-1**

**Dates and Geographic Distribution of Major Hominoid, Hominid, and Hominin Fossil Groups**

| Fossil Group | Dates, m.y.a. | Known Distribution |
|---|---|---|
| Hominoid | | |
| *Pierolapithecus catalaunicus* | 13 | Spain |
| Hominid | | |
| Common ancestor of hominids | 8? | East Africa |
| "Toumai" | 7–6 | Chad |
| *Orrorin tugenensis* | 6 | Kenya |
| Hominins | | |
| *Ardipithecus kadabba* | 5.8–5.5 | Ethiopia |
| *Ardipithecus ramidus* | 4.4 | Ethiopia |
| Australopithecines | | |
| A. anamensis | 4.2 | Kenya |
| A. afarensis | 3.8–3.0 | East Africa (Laetoli, Hadar) |
| A. garhi | 2.5 | Ethiopia |
| Robusts | 2.6–1.2 | East and South Africa |
| A. robustus | 2.0?–1.0? | South Africa |
| (aka *Paranthropus*) | | |
| A. boisei | 2.6?–1.0 | East Africa |
| Graciles | | |
| A. africanus | 3.0–2.0? | South Africa |
| *Homo* | | |
| H. habilis/H. rudolfensis | 2.4?–1.7? | East Africa |
| H. ergaster/H. erectus | 1.7?–0.3? | Africa, Asia, Europe |
| *Homo sapiens* | 0.3–present | |
| Archaic *H. sapiens* | 0.3–0.28 (300,000–28,000) | Africa, Asia, Europe |
| Neandertals | 0.13–0.28 (130,000–28,000) | Europe, Middle East, North Africa |
| Anatomically modern humans (AMHs) | 0.15?–present (150,000–present) | Worldwide (after 20,000 B.P.) |

## *Ardipithecus*

As we see in the box at the end of this chapter, early hominins assigned to *Ardipithecus kadabba* lived during the late Miocene, between 5.8 and 5.5 million years ago. Some Miocene hominins eventually evolved into a varied group of Pliocene–Pleistocene hominins known as the *australopithecines*—for which we have an abundant fossil record. This term reflects their one-time classification as members of a distinct taxonomic subfamily, the "Australopithecinae." We now know that the various species of *Australopithecus* discussed in this chapter do not form a distinct subfamily within the order Primates, but the name "australopithecine" has stuck to describe them. Today the distinction between the **australopithecines** and later hominins is made on the genus level. The australopithecines are assigned to the genus *Australopithecus (A.);* later humans, to *Homo (H.).*

Ardipithecus (*ramidus*) fossils were first discovered at Aramis in Ethiopia by Berhane Asfaw, Gen Suwa, and Tim White. Dating to 4.4 m.y.a., these *Ardipithecus ramidus* fossils consisted of the remains of some 17 individuals, with cranial, facial, dental, and upper limb bones. The box at the end of the chapter discusses much older *Ardipithecus* (*kadabba*) fossils, dating back to 5.8 m.y.a., very near the time of the common ancestor of humans and the African apes. The *kadabba* find consists of 11 specimens, including a jaw bone with teeth, hand and foot bones, fragments of arm bones, and a piece of collarbone. At least five individuals are represented. These creatures were apelike in size, anatomy, and habitat. They lived in a wooded area rather than the open grassland or savanna habitat where later hominins proliferated. As of this writing, because of its probable bipedalism, *Ardipithecus kadabba* is recognized as the earliest known hominin, with the Toumai find from Chad, dated to 7–6 m.y.a., and *Orrorin tugenensis* from Kenya, dated to 6 m.y.a. (see Chapter 4), possibly even older hominins.

## ✦ THE VARIED AUSTRALOPITHECINES

In the scheme followed here, *Australopithecus* had at least six species:

1. *A. anamensis* (4.2 to 3.9 m.y.a.)
2. *A. afarensis* (3.8? to 3.0 m.y.a.)
3. *A. africanus* (3.0? to 2.0? m.y.a.)
4. *A. garhi* (2.5 m.y.a.)
5. *A. robustus* (2.0? to 1.0? m.y.a.)
6. *A. boisei* (2.6? to 1.0 m.y.a.)

The dates given for each species are approximate because an organism isn't a member of one species one day and a member of another species the next day. Nor could the same dating techniques be used for all the finds. The South African australopithecine fossils (*A. africanus* and *A. robustus*), for example, come from a nonvolcanic area where radiometric dating could not be done. Dating of those fossils has been based mainly on stratigraphy. The hominin fossils from the volcanic regions of East Africa usually have radiometric dates.

### *Australopithecus anamensis*

Ardipithecus ramidus may (or may not) have evolved into *A. anamensis,* a bipedal hominin from northern Kenya, whose fossil remains were reported first by Maeve Leakey and Alan Walker in 1995 (Leakey et al. 1995; Rice 2002). *A.anamensis* consists of 78 fragments from two sites: Kanapoi and Allia Bay. The fossils include upper and lower jaws, cranial fragments, and the upper and lower parts of a leg bone (tibia). The Kanapoi fossils date to 4.2 m.y.a., and those at Allia Bay to 3.9 m.y.a. The molars have thick enamel, and the apelike canines are large. Based on the tibia, *anamensis* weighed about 110 pounds (50 kilograms). This would have made it larger than either the earlier *Ardipithecus* or the later *A. afarensis*. Its anatomy implies that *anamensis* was bipedal. Because of its date and

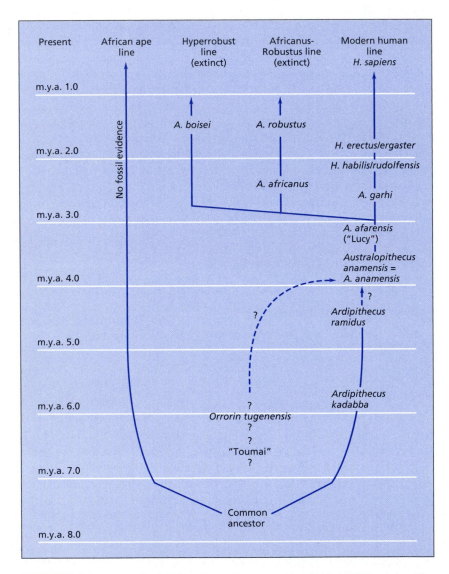

**FIGURE 5-1**    *Phylogenetic Tree for African Apes, Hominids, and Hominins*    The presumed divergence date for ancestral chimps and hominins was between 6 and 8 m.y.a. Branching in later hominin evolution is also shown. For more exact dates, see the text and Table 5-1.

its location in the East African Rift valley, *A. anamensis* may be ancestral to *A. afarensis* (3.8–3.0 m.y.a.) which usually is considered ancestral to all the later australopithecines (*garhi, africanus, robustus*, and *boisei*) as well as to *Homo* (Figure 5-1).

## *Australopithecus afarensis*

The hominin species known as **A. afarensis** includes fossils found at two sites, Laetoli in northern Tanzania and Hadar in the Afar region of Ethiopia. Laetoli is earlier (3.8 to 3.6 m.y.a.). The Hadar fossils probably date to between 3.3 and 3.0 m.y.a. Thus, based on the current evidence, *A. afarensis* lived between about 3.8 and 3.0 m.y.a. Research directed by Mary Leakey was responsible for the Laetoli finds. The Hadar discoveries resulted from an international expedition directed by D. C. Johanson and M. Taieb. The two sites have yielded significant samples of early hominin fossils. There are two dozen specimens from Laetoli, and the Hadar finds include the remains of between 35 and 65 individuals. The Laetoli remains are mainly teeth and jaw fragments, along with some very informative fossilized footprints. The Hadar sample includes skull fragments and postcranial material, most notably 40 percent of the complete skeleton of a tiny hominin female, dubbed "Lucy," who lived around 3 m.y.a.

An ancient trail of hominin footprints fossilized in volcanic ash. Mary Leakey found this 230-foot (70-meter) trail at Laetoli, Tanzania, in 1979. It dates from 3.6 m.y.a and confirms that A. afarensis was a striding biped.

Although the hominin remains at Laetoli and Hadar were deposited half a million years apart, their many resemblances explain their placement in the same species, *A. afarensis*. These fossils forced a reinterpretation of the early hominin fossil record. *A. afarensis*, although clearly a hominin, was so similar in many ways to chimps and gorillas that our common ancestry with the African apes must be very recent, certainly no more than 8 m.y.a. *Ardipithecus* and *A. anamensis* are even more apelike. These discoveries show that hominins are much closer to the apes than the previously known fossil record had suggested. Studies of the learning abilities and biochemistry of chimps and gorillas have taught a valuable lesson about homologies that the fossil record is now confirming.

The *A. afarensis* finds, which have been much more completely described than *Ardipithecus* and *A. anamensis*, make this clear. The many apelike features are surprising in definite hominins that lived as recently as 3 m.y.a. Discussion of hominin fossils requires a brief review of dentition. Moving from front to back, on either side of the upper or lower jaw, humans (and apes) have two incisors, one canine, two premolars, and three molars. Our dental formula is 2.1.2.3, for a total of 8 teeth on each side, upper and lower—32 teeth in all—if we have all our "wisdom teeth" (our third molars). Now back to the australopithecines. Like apes, and unlike modern humans, *A. afarensis* had sharp canine teeth that projected beyond the other teeth. Also like apes, their lower premolar was pointed and projecting to sharpen the upper canine. It had one long cusp and one tiny bump that hints at the bicuspid premolar that eventually developed in hominin evolution.

There is, however, evidence that powerful chewing associated with savanna vegetation was entering the *A. afarensis* feeding pattern. When the coarse, gritty, fibrous vegetation of grasslands and semidesert enters the diet, the back teeth change to accommodate heavy chewing stresses. Massive back teeth, jaws, and facial and cranial structures suggest a diet demanding extensive grinding and powerful crushing. *A. afarensis* molars are large (see Figure 5-2). The lower jaw (mandible) is thick and is buttressed with a bony ridge behind the front teeth. The cheekbones are large and flare out to the side for the attachment of powerful chewing muscles.

The skull of *A. afarensis* contrasts with those of later hominins. The cranial capacity barely surpasses the chimp average. Below the neck, however—particularly in regard to locomotion—*A. afarensis* was unquestionably human. Early evidence of striding bipedalism comes from Laetoli, where volcanic ash, which can be dated directly by the K/A technique, covered a trail of footprints of two or three hominins walking to a water hole. These prints leave no doubt that a small striding biped lived in Tanzania by 3.6 m.y.a. The structure of the pelvic, hip, leg, and foot bones also confirms that upright bipedalism was *A. afarensis's* mode of locomotion.

Although bidepal, *A. afarensis* still contrasts in many ways with later hominins. Sexual dimorphism is especially marked. The male–female contrast in jaw size in *A. afarensis* was more marked than in the orangutan. There was a similar contrast in body size. *A. afarensis* females, such as Lucy, stood between 3 and 4 feet (.9 and 1.2 meters) tall; males might have reached 5 feet (1.5 meters). *A. afarensis* males weighed perhaps twice as much as the females did (Wolpoff 1999). Table 5-2 summarizes data on the various australopithecines, including mid-sex body weight and brain size. Mid-sex means midway between the male average and the female average.

Lucy and her kind were far from dainty. Lucy's muscle-engraved bones are much more robust than ours are. With only rudimentary tools and weapons, early hominins needed powerful and resistant bones and muscles. Lucy's arms are longer relative to her legs than are those of later hominins. Here again her proportions are more apelike than ours are. Although Lucy neither brachiated nor knuckle-walked, she was probably a much better climber than modern people are, and she spent some of her day in the trees.

The *A. afarensis* fossils show that as recently as 3.0 m.y.a., our ancestors had a mixture of apelike and hominin features. Canines, premolars, and skulls were much more apelike than most scholars had imagined would exist in such a recent ancestor.

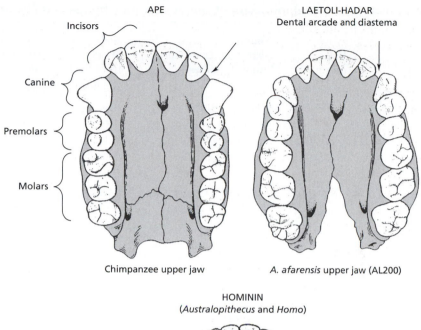

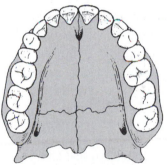

**FIGURE 5-2**    *Comparison of Dentition in Ape, Human, and* **A.** **afarensis** *Palates*

On the other hand, the molars, chewing apparatus, and cheekbones foreshadowed later hominin trends, and the pelvic and limb bones were indisputably hominin. The hominin pattern was being built from the ground up.

The pelvis, the lower spine, the hip joint, and the thigh bone change in accordance with the stresses of bipedal locomotion. With bipedalism, the pelvis forms a sort of basket that balances the weight of the trunk and supports this weight with less stress. Fossilized spinal bones (vertebrae) show that the australopithecine spine had the lower spine (lumbar) curve characteristic of *Homo*. This curvature helps transmit the weight of the upper body to the pelvis and the legs. The pelvises of the australopithecines were similar but not identical to those of *Homo*. The most significant contrast is a narrower

**TABLE 5-2**

**Facts about the Australopithecines Compared with Chimps and *Homo***

| Species | Dates (m.y.a.) | Known Distribution | Important Sites | Body Weight (Mid-Sex) | Brain Size (Mid-Sex) (cm³) |
|---|---|---|---|---|---|
| Anatomically modern humans (AMHs) | 150,000 to present | | | 132 lb/60 kg | 1,350 |
| *Pan troglodytes* (chimpanzee) | Modern | | | 93 lb/42 kg | 390 |
| A. boisei | 2.6? to 1.2 | E. Africa | Olduvai, East Turkana | 86 lb/39 kg | 490 |
| A. robustus | 2.0? to 1.0? | S. Africa | Kromdraai, Swartkrans | 81 lb/37 kg | 540 |
| A. africanus | 3.0 to 2.0? | S. Africa | Taung, Sterkfontein, Makapansqat | 79 lb/36 kg | 490 |
| A. afarensis | 3.8 to 3.0 | E. Africa | Hadar, Laetoli | 77 lb/35 kg | 430 |
| A. anamensis | 4.2 to 3.9 | Kenya | Kanapoi Allia Bay | Insufficient data | No published skulls |
| Ardipithecus | 5.8 to 4.4 | Ethiopia | Aramis | Insufficient data | No published skulls |

australopithecine birth canal (Tague and Lovejoy 1986). Expansion of the birth canal is a trend in hominin evolution. The width of the birth canal is related to the size of the skull and brain. *A. afarensis* had a small cranial capacity. Even in later australopithecines, brain size did not exceed 600 cubic centimeters. Undoubtedly, the australopithecine skull grew after birth to accommodate a growing brain, as it does (much more) in *Homo*. However, the brains of the australopithecines expanded less than ours do. In the australopithecines, the cranial sutures (the lines where the bones of the skull eventually come together) fused relatively earlier in life. Young australopithecines must have depended on their parents and kin for nurturance and protection. Those years of childhood dependency would have provided time for observation, teaching, and learning. This may provide indirect evidence for a rudimentary cultural life.

## Gracile and Robust Australopithecines

The fossils of *A. africanus* and *A. robustus* come from South Africa. In 1924, the anatomist Raymond Dart coined the term *Australopithecus africanus* to describe the first

(Left) Profile view of an *A. africanus* (gracile) skull (Sterkfontein 5). The cranium, discovered by Dr. Robert Broom and J.T. Robinson in April 1947, dates back to 2.9–2.4 m.y.a. (Right) Profile view of an *A. boisei* skull—Olduvai Hominid (OH) 5, originally called *Zinjanthropus boisei*. This skull of a young male, discovered by Mary Leakey in 1959 at Olduvai Gorge, Tanzania, dates back 1.8 million years.

fossil representative of this species, the skull of a juvenile that was found accidentally in a quarry at Taung, South Africa. Radiometric dates are lacking for this nonvolcanic region, but the fossil hominins found at the five main South African sites appear (from stratigraphy) to have lived between 3 and 1 m.y.a.

There were two groups of South African australopithecines: **gracile** (*A. africanus*) and **robust** (*A. robustus*). "Gracile" indicates that members of *A. africanus* were smaller and slighter, less robust, than were members of *A. robustus*. There were also very robust—*hyperrobust*—australopithecines in East Africa. In the classification scheme used here, these have been assigned to *A. boisei*. However, some scholars consider *A. robustus* and *A. boisei* to be regional variants of just one species, usually called *robustus* (sometimes given its own genus, *Paranthropus*).

Graciles and robusts probably descend from *A. afarensis,* which itself was gracile in form, or from a South African version of *A. afarensis.* Some scholars have argued that the graciles lived before (3.0 to 2.0? m.y.a.) and were ancestral to the robusts (2.0? to 1.0? m.y.a.). Others contend that the graciles and the robusts were separate species that may have overlapped in time. (Classifying them as members of different species implies they were reproductively isolated from each other in time or space.) Other paleoanthropologists view the gracile and robust australopithecines as different ends of a continuum of variation in a single *polytypic species*—one with considerable phenotypic variation.

The trend toward enlarged back teeth, chewing muscles, and facial buttressing, which already is noticeable in *A. afarensis,* continues in the South African australopithecines. However, the canines are reduced, and the premolars are fully bicuspid. Dental form and function changed as dietary needs shifted from cutting and slashing to chewing and grinding. The mainstay of the australopithecine diet was the vegetation of the savanna.

In the South African australopithecines, both deciduous ("baby") and permanent molars and premolars are massive, with multiple cusps. The later australopithecines had bigger back teeth than did the earlier ones. However, this evolutionary trend ended with

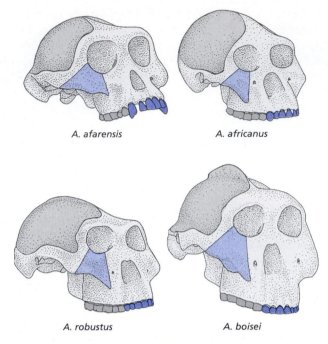

*A. afarensis*                    *A. africanus*

*A. robustus*                    *A. boisei*

Shown above are *A. afarensis, A. africanus, A. robustus,* and *A. boisei.*
What are the main differences you notice among these four types of
early hominins?

early *Homo,* which had much smaller back teeth, reflecting a dietary change that will
be described later.

Contrasts with *Homo* in the front teeth are less marked. But they are still of interest because of what they tell us about sexual dimorphism. *A. africanus*'s canines were
more pointed, with larger roots, than *Homo*'s are. Still, the *A. africanus* canines were
only 75 percent the size of the canines of *A. afarensis.* Despite this canine reduction,
there was just as much canine sexual dimorphism in *A. africanus* as there had been in
*A. afarensis* (Wolpoff 1999). Sexual dimorphism in general was much more pronounced
among the early hominins than it is among *Homo sapiens. A. africanus* females were
about 4 feet (1.2 meters), and males 5 feet (1.5 meters), tall. The average female probably had no more than 60 percent the weight of the average male (Wolpoff 1980*a*). (That
figure contrasts with today's average female-to-male weight ratio of about 88 percent.)

Teeth, jaw, face, and skull changed to fit a diet based on tough, gritty, fibrous
grasslands vegetation. A massive face housed large upper teeth and provided a base for
the attachment of powerful chewing muscles. Australopithecine cheekbones were elongated and massive structures that anchored large chewing muscles running up the jaw.
Another set of robust chewing muscles extended from the back of the jaw to the sides
of the skull. In the more robust australopithecines (*A. robustus* in South Africa and
*A. boisei* in East Africa), these muscles were strong enough to produce a *sagittal crest,*

a bony ridge on the top of the skull. Such a crest forms as the bone grows. It develops from the pull of the chewing muscles as they meet at the midline of the skull.

Overall robustness, especially in the chewing apparatus, increased through time among the australopithecines. This trend was most striking in *A. boisei,* which survived through 1.0 m.y.a in East Africa. Compared with their predecessors, the later australopithecines tended to have larger overall size, skulls, and back teeth. They also had thicker faces, more prominent crests, and more rugged muscle markings on the skeleton. By contrast, the front teeth stayed the same size.

Brain size (measured as cranial capacity, in cubic centimeters—cm$^3$) increased only slightly between *A. afarensis* (430 cm$^3$), *A. africanus* (490 cm$^3$), and *A. robustus* (540 cm$^3$) (Wolpoff 1999). These figures can be compared with an average cranial capacity of 1,350 cm$^3$ in *Homo sapiens.* The modern range goes from less than 1,000 cm$^3$ to more than 2,000 cm$^3$ in normal adults. The cranial capacity of chimps (*Pan troglodytes*) averages 390 cm$^3$ (see Table 5-2). The brains of gorillas (*Gorilla gorilla*) average around 500 cm$^3$, which is within the australopithecine range, but gorilla body weight is much greater.

## ✦ The Australopithecines and Early *Homo*

Between 3 and 2 m.y.a., the ancestors of *Homo* split off and became reproductively isolated from the later australopithecines, such as *A. boisei,* which coexisted with *Homo* until around 1.0 m.y.a. The first evidence for speciation is dental. The fossil sample of hominin teeth from East Africa dated to 2 m.y.a. has two clearly different sizes of teeth. One set is huge, the largest molars and premolars in hominin evolution; these teeth belong to *A. boisei.* The other group of (smaller) teeth belonged to our probable ancestor, *H. habilis,* the first exemplar of the genus *Homo.*

By 1.7 m.y.a., the difference was even more evident. Two hominin groups occupied different environmental niches in Africa. One of them, *Homo*—by then *Homo erectus*—had a larger brain and a reproportioned skull; it had increased the areas of the brain that regulate higher mental functions. These were our ancestors, hominins with greater capacities for culture than the australopithecines had. *H. erectus* hunted and gathered, made sophisticated tools, and eventually displaced its sole surviving cousin species, *A. boisei.*

*A. boisei* of East Africa, the hyperrobust australopithecines, had mammoth back teeth. *A. boisei* females had bigger back teeth than did earlier australopithecine males. *A. boisei* became ever more specialized with respect to one part of the traditional australopithecine diet, concentrating on coarse vegetation with a high grit content.

The separation that led to speciation between *A. boisei* and early *Homo* took time. And why, if two new *species* were forming, is one of them assigned to a new genus, *Homo*? This classification is done in retrospect, since we know that one species survived and evolved into a contemporary descendant whereas the other one became extinct. Hindsight shows us their very different lifeways, which suggest their placement in different genera.

We still don't know why, how, and exactly when the split between *Australopithecus* and *Homo* took place. Scholars have defended many different models, or theoretical schemes, to interpret the early hominin fossil record. Because new finds have so often forced reappraisals, most scientists are willing to modify their interpretation when given new evidence.

The model of Johanson and White (1979), who coined the term *A. afarensis*, proposes that *A. afarensis* split into two groups. One group, the ancestors of *Homo,* became reproductively isolated from other hominins between 3 and 2 m.y.a. This group appeared as ***Homo habilis,*** a term coined by L. S. B. and Mary Leakey for the first members of the genus *Homo. H. habilis* lived between 2 m.y.a. and about 1.7 m.y.a., by which time it had evolved into *H. erectus.* Other members of *A. afarensis* evolved into the various kinds of australopithecines (*A. africanus, A. robustus,* and hyperrobust *A. boisei,* the last member to become extinct).

---

## ✦ Oldowan Tools

It may have been *Homo*'s increasing hunting proficiency that forced *A. boisei* into becoming an ever-more-specialized vegetarian. Tool making also might have had something to do with the split. The simplest obviously manufactured tools were discovered in 1931 by L. S. B. and Mary Leakey at Olduvai Gorge, Tanzania. This site gave the tools their name—Oldowan pebble tools. The oldest tools from Olduvai are about 1.8 million years old. Still older (2.5 to 2.0 m.y.a.) stone implements have been found in Ethiopia, Congo, and Malawi (Asfaw, White, and Lovejoy 1999; Lemonick and Dorfman 1999).

Stone tools consist of cores and flakes. The *core* is the piece of rock from which flakes are removed; the core can be worked to become a tool itself. A *chopper* is a tool made by flaking the edge of such a core on one side. **Oldowan pebble tools** represent the world's oldest formally recognized stone tools. With the use of cores about the size of a tennis ball, flakes were struck off one or both sides to form a chopping or cutting edge.

Core tools or choppers are the most common stone tools found at early African tool sites. Some may have been used for food processing—by pounding, breaking, or bashing. Other "choppers" may have been only cores from which flakes, used for cutting or scraping, were removed. Flakes probably were used mainly as cutters, for example, to dismember game carcasses. Crushed fossil animal bones indicate that stones were used to break open marrow cavities. Also, Oldowan deposits include pieces of bone or horn with scratch marks suggesting they were used to dig up tubers or insects.

Oldowan core and flake tools of the sort widely used between 2.0 and 1.5 m.y.a. are shown in the photos on the next page. The flake tool in the lower photo is made of chert, whereas most Oldowan tools at Olduvai Gorge were made from basalt, which is locally more common and coarser.

For decades anthropologists have debated the identity of the earliest stone tool makers. The first *Homo habilis* find got its name (*habilis* is Latin for "able") for its presumed ability (and presumably first among hominins) to make tools. Recently the story has grown more complicated, with a discovery making it very likely that one kind of australopithecine also made and habitually used stone tools.

Oldowan core tools or choppers are the most common stone tools found at early African tool sites. Some may have been used for food processing, by pounding, breaking, or bashing. Other "choppers" may have been only cores from which flakes, used for cutting or scraping, were removed. Above, a chopper core tool; below, a flake tool.

## *A. garhi* and Early Stone Tools

In 1999 an international team reported the discovery, in Ethiopia, of a new species of hominin, along with the earliest traces of animal butchery (Asfaw, White, and Lovejoy 1999). These new fossils, dating to 2.5 m.y.a., may be the remains of a direct human ancestor and an evolutionary link between *Australopithecus* and the genus *Homo*. At the same site was evidence that antelopes and horses had been butchered with the world's earliest stone tools. When scientists excavated these hominin fossils, they were shocked to find a combination of unforeseen skeletal and dental features. They named the specimen *Australopithecus garhi*. The word *garhi* means "surprise" in the Afar language. Evidence that large mammals were being butchered shows that early stone technologies were aimed at getting meat and marrow from big game. This signals a dietary revolution that eventually may have allowed an invasion of new habitats and continents (*Berkleyan* 1999).

In 1997 the Ethiopian archaeologist Sileshi Semaw announced he had found the world's earliest stone tools, dating to 2.5 m.y.a., at the nearby Ethiopian site of Gona. But which human ancestor had made these tools, he wondered, and what were they used for? The 1999 discoveries by Asfaw, White, and their colleagues provided answers, identifying *A. garhi* as the best candidate for toolmaker (*Berkleyan* 1999).

The association, in the same area at the same time, of *A. garhi,* animal butchery, and the earliest stone tools suggests that the australopithecines were toolmakers, with some capacity for culture. Nevertheless, cultural abilities developed exponentially with *Homo*'s appearance and expansion. With increasing reliance on hunting, tool making,

## ANTHROPOLOGY TODAY

### *Another Branch of Early Human Ancestors*

*Based on molecular genetic calculations, scientists have surmised for decades that a lot was happening in hominid evolution between 7 and 5 million years ago. Now the fossil record is bearing them out. Recent discoveries of possible hominin ancestors, such as Toumai (*Sahelanthropus tchadensis*) and Orrorin tugenensis, were discussed in Chapter 4. Described here are fossils accepted more generally as hominins, assigned to the genus* Ardipithecus, *found in 2001 in Ethiopia. Written in 2004, this account reports a change in the designation of the* Ardipithecus *fossils. Originally they were considered to be an earlier subspecies of a previously known* Ardipithecus *species (*Ardipithecus ramidus*), which lived around 4.4 million years ago. Now they have been assigned to their own species,* Ardipithecus kadabba, *which is considered to be ancestral to the later* Ardipithecus. *Furthermore, the authors of the article on which this story is based make the controversial suggestion that these fossils, along with Toumai and Orrorin, may all belong to the same genus. These recent discoveries push the hominin lineage back to around 6 million years ago, near the time when the chimp–human split is assumed to have occurred based on molecular calculations.*

Another species has been added to the family tree of early human ancestors—and to controversies over how straight or tangled were the branches of that tree.

Long before *Homo erectus, Australopithecus afarensis* (Lucy, more than three million years ago) and several other distant kin, scientists are reporting today, there lived a primitive hominid [hominin] species in what is now Ethiopia about 5.5 million to 5.8 million years ago.

That would make the newly recognized species one of the earliest known human ancestors, perhaps one of the first to emerge after the chimpanzee and human lineages diverged from a common ancestor some six million to eight million years ago. . . .

When the first fossil bones and teeth of this hominid [hominin] were described three years ago, paleoanthropologists tentatively identified it as a more apelike subspecies that they named *Ardipithecus ramidus kadabba.* The original ramidus species was found in 1994 in 4.4-million-year-old sediments, also in Ethiopia.

But with more discoveries and a closer study, especially of the teeth, the scientists decided that the kadabba fossils from five individuals were distinctive enough to qualify as a separate species, *Ardipithecus kadabba.* In that case, the scientists added, kadabba was not a subspecies, but the likely and other cultural abilities, *Homo* eventually became the most efficient exploiter of the savanna niche. The last surviving members of *A. boisei* may have been forced into ever-more-marginal areas. They eventually became extinct. By 1 m.y.a., a single species of hominin, *H. erectus,* not only had rendered other hominin forms extinct but also had expanded the hominin range to Asia and Europe. An essentially human strategy of adaptation, incorporating hunting as a fundamental ingredient of a generalized foraging economy, had emerged. Despite regional variation, it was to be the basic economy for our genus until 11,000 years ago.

direct ancestor of ramidus. But there were too few skeletal bones yet to learn much about other aspects of kadabba.

The description and interpretation of the new hominid [hominin] species appear today in the journal *Science*. The authors of the report are Dr. Yohannes Haile-Selassie of the Cleveland Museum of Natural History, Dr. Gen Suwa of the University of Tokyo and Dr. Tim D. White of the University of California, Berkeley.

The kadabba fossils were found in the Middle Awash valley about 180 miles northeast of Addis Ababa, the Ethiopian capital. These are arid badlands now, but in the time of the early hominids [hominins] the land was wooded and more hospitable.

Dr. Haile-Selassie said the shapes and wear patterns of six teeth in particular were "significant in understanding how the dentition evolved from an apelike common ancestor into the earliest hominids [hominins]." They were also critical, he said, in differentiating the earlier and later species of the genus *Ardipithecus*.

Other scientists familiar with the research, but not involved in it, said they agreed or were at least inclined to agree with the authors' designation of a separate species for the fossils. But they were not so sure about the authors' proposal that the fossils were so similar to those of two other recently discovered early species that all

three species might have actually belonged to a single genus of closely related hominids [hominins].

The other two hominid species are *Sahelanthropus tchadensis,* found in Chad and thought to be 6 million to 7 million years old, and *Orrorin tugenensis,* a 6 million-year-old specimen from Kenya. The two are primitive apelike creatures not much bigger than a modern chimp. Although the analysis of these remains is not complete, and still subject to debate, each has been classified as a separate genus and species. In their report on kadabba, Dr. Haile-Selassie and his colleagues concluded, "Given the limited data currently available, it is possible that all of these remains represent specific or subspecific variation within a single genus."

Dr. White, one of the most experienced paleoanthropologists, emphasized this point in a telephone interview. "These earliest hominids are all very, very similar," he said. "When you look at these three snapshots we have, we are struck by the great biological similarity, not by pronounced differences, not by great lineage diversity."

But in an accompanying commentary in the journal, Dr. David R. Begun, a paleontologist at the University of Toronto, questioned this interpretation. He said it was unlikely that all three of the early

*Continued*

## ANTHROPOLOGY TODAY

hominids belonged to a single genus, noting instead that the three exhibited evidence of striking diversity.

Dr. Begun conceded that "the level of uncertainty in the available direct evidence at this time renders irreconcilable differences of opinion inevitable."

The differences, broadly speaking, take the form of two images of what the hominid family tree looks like—a ladder or a bush. A growing number of scientists, finding multiple species of hominids that overlapped in time, contend that in response to new or changed circumstances hominids evolved along many diverse lines—a bush with many branches.

Dr. Begun, in a telephone interview, emphasized that he was not disagreeing with the designation of the new species, but was "merely presenting an alternative" to the single-genus interpretation. "The material is so fragmentary," he said, "that we really can't know, and so our differences often are a reflection of different philosophies and experience in research." . . .

*Source:* John Noble Wilford, "Another Branch of Early Human Ancestors Is Reported by Scientists," *New York Times*, March 5, 2004, late ed.—final, sec. A, p. 14, col. 1. Reprinted by permission.

## SUMMARY

1. Hominins lived during the late Miocene, Pliocene (5.0 to 2 m.y.a.), and Pleistocene (2 m.y.a. to 10,000 B.P.) epochs. The australopithecines had appeared by 4.2 m.y.a. The six species of *Australopithecus* were *A. anamensis* (4.2 m.y.a.), *A. afarensis* (3.8 to 3.0 m.y.a.), *A. africanus* (3.0 to 2.0? m.y.a.), *A. garhi* (2.5 m.y.a.), *A. robustus* (2.0? to 1.0? m.y.a.), and *A. boisei* (2.6? to 1.0 m.y.a.). The earliest identifiable hominin remains date to between 7.0 m.y.a. and 5.8 m.y.a. The "Toumai" find from northern Chad is a possible early hominin, as is *Orrorin tugenensis* from Kenya. More generally accepted hominin remains from Ethiopia are classified as *Ardipithecus kadabba* (5.8–5.5 m.y.a.) and *ramidus* (4.4 m.y.a.). Next comes *A. anamensis,* then a group of fossils from Hadar, Ethiopia, and Laetoli, Tanzania, classified as *A. afarensis.*

2. These earliest hominins shared many primitive features, including slashing canines, elongated premolars, a small apelike skull, and marked sexual dimorphism. Still, *A. afarensis* and its recently discovered predecessors were definite hominins. In *A. afarensis* this is confirmed by large molars and, more important, by skeletal evidence (e.g., in Lucy) for upright bipedalism.

3. Remains of two later groups, *A. africanus* (graciles) and *A. robustus* (robusts), were found in South Africa. Both groups show the australopithecine trend toward a powerful chewing apparatus. They had large molars and premolars and large and robust faces, skulls, and muscle markings. All these features are more pronounced in the robusts than they are in the graciles. The basis of the australopithecine diet was savanna vegetation. These early hominins may also have hunted small animals and scavenged the kills of predators.

4. Early *Homo, H. habilis* (2.0? to 1.7 m.y.a.), evolved into *H. erectus* (1.7 m.y.a. to 300,000 B.P.). By 2.0 m.y.a. there is ample evidence for two distinct hominin groups: early *Homo* and *A. boisei,* the hyperrobust australopithecines. The latter eventually became extinct around 1.0 m.y.a. *A. boisei* became increasingly specialized, dependent on tough, coarse, gritty, fibrous savanna vegetation. The australopithecine trend toward dental, facial, and cranial robustness continued with *A. boisei,* but these structures were reduced as *H. habilis* evolved into *H. erectus.*

5. Pebble tools dating to between 2.5 and 2.0 m.y.a. have been found in Ethiopia, Congo, and Malawi. Scientists have disagreed about their maker, some arguing that only early *Homo* could have made them. Evidence has been presented that *A. garhi* made pebble tools around 2.5 m.y.a. Cultural abilities developed exponentially with *Homo*'s appearance and evolution.

# KEY TERMS

*A. afarensis* (p. 107)
australopithecines (p. 105)
bipedalism (p. 100)
gracile (p. 111)
hominid (p. 103)

hominin (p. 103)
*Homo habilis* (p. 114)
Oldowan pebble tools (p. 114)
robust (p. 111)

# CHAPTER 6

❧

# THE GENUS *HOMO*

## ✦ EARLY *HOMO*

As we saw in Chapter 5, at 2 million years ago, there is East African evidence for two distinct hominin groups: early *Homo* and *A. boisei,* the hyperrobust australopithecines, which became extinct around 1.0 m.y.a. *A. boisei* became increasingly specialized, dependent on tough, coarse, gritty, fibrous savanna vegetation. The australopithecine trend toward dental, facial, and cranial robustness continued with *A. boisei.* However, these structures were reduced as early forms of *Homo* evolved into *H. ergaster* (or early *H. erectus*) by 1.8–1.7 m.y.a. By that date *Homo* had generalized the subsistence quest to the hunting of large animals to supplement the gathering of vegetation and scavenging.

## *H. rudolfensis* **and** *H. habilis*

In 1972, in an expedition led by Richard Leakey, Bernard Ngeneo unearthed a skull designated KNM-ER 1470. The name comes from its catalog number in the Kenya National Museum (KNM) and its discovery location (East Rudolph—ER)—east of Lake Rudolph, at a site called Koobi Fora. The 1470 skull attracted immediate attention because of its unusual combination of a large brain (775 cm³) and very large molars. Its brain size was more human than that of the australopithecine, but its molars recalled those of the hyperrobust australopithecine. Some paleoanthropologists attributed the large skull and teeth to a very large body, assuming that this had been one *big hominin.*

Meet two kinds of early *Homo*. On the left KNM-ER 1813. On the right KNM-ER 1470. The latter (1470) has been classified as *H. rudolfensis*. What's the classification of 1813?

But no postcranial remains were found with 1470, nor have they been found with any later discovery of a 1470-like specimen.

How to interpret KNM-ER 1470? On the basis of its brain size, it seemed to belong in *Homo*. On the basis of its back teeth, it seemed more like *Australopithecus*. There also are problems with dating. The best dating guess in 1.8 m.y.a., but another estimate suggests that 1470 may be as old as 2.4 m.y.a. Originally, some paleoanthropologists assigned 1470 to *H. habilis,* while others saw it as an unusual australopithecine. In 1986, it received its own species name, *Homo rudolfensis,* from the lake near which it was found. This label has stuck—although it isn't accepted by all paleoanthropologists. Those who find *H. rudolfensis* to be a valid species emphasize its contrasts with *H. habilis*. Note the contrasts in the two skulls in the photo above. KNM-ER 1813, on the left, is considered *H. habilis;* KNM-ER 1470, on the right, is *H. rudolfensis*. The *habilis* skull has a more marked brow ridge and a depression behind it, whereas 1470 has a less pronounced brow ridge and a longer, flatter face. Some think that *rudolfensis* lived earlier than and is ancestral to *habilis*. Some think that *rudolfensis* and *habilis* are simply male and female members of the same species—*H. habilis*. Some think they are separate species that coexisted in time and space (from about 2.4 m.y.a. to about 1.7 m.y.a.). Some think that one or the other gave rise to *H. erectus* (also known in Africa as *H. ergaster*). The debate continues. The only sure conclusion is that several different kinds of hominin lived in Africa before and after the advent of *Homo*.

## *H. habilis* and *H. ergaster/erectus*

L. S. B. and Mary Leakey gave the name ***Homo habilis*** to the earliest members of our genus, first found at Olduvai Gorge in Tanzania. Olduvai's oldest layer, Bed I, dates to 1.8 m.y.a. This layer has yielded both small-brained *A. boisei* (average 490 cm³) fossils and *H. habilis* skulls, with cranial capacities between 600 and 700 cm³.

Another important *habilis* find was made in 1986 by Tim White of the University of California, Berkeley. OH62 (Olduvai Hominid 62) is the partial skeleton of a female *H. habilis* from Olduvai Bed I. This was the first find of a *H. habilis* skull with a significant amount of skeletal material. OH62, dating to 1.8 m.y.a., consists of parts of the skull, the right arm, and both legs. This fossil was surprising because of its small size and its apelike limb bones. Scientists had assumed that *H. habilis* would be taller than Lucy (*A. afarensis*), moving gradually in the direction of *H. erectus*. According to expectations, even a female *H. habilis* should have stood somewhere between Lucy's 3 feet (0.9 meter) and the 5 to 6 feet (1.5 to 1.8 meters) of *H. erectus*. However, not only was OH62 just as tiny as Lucy, its arms were longer and more apelike than expected. The limb proportions suggested greater tree-climbing ability than later hominins had. *H. habilis* may still have sought occasional refuge in the trees.

The small size and primitive proportions of *H. habilis* were unexpected given what was already known about early *H. erectus* in East Africa. (Some paleoanthropologists use the term *Homo ergaster* to refer to the earliest *H. erectus* fossils in Africa. Here I follow the more traditional scheme of calling them *Homo erectus*.) In deposits near Lake Turkana, Kenya, Richard Leakey had uncovered two *H. erectus* skulls dating to 1.6 m.y.a. By that date, **Homo erectus** had already attained a cranial capacity of 900 cm$^3$, along with a modern body shape and height. An amazingly complete young male *H. erectus* fossil (WT15,000) found at West Turkana in 1984 by Kimoya Kimeu, a collaborator of the Leakeys, has confirmed this. WT15,000, also known as the Nariokotome boy, was a 12-year-old male who had already reached 5 feet 5 inches (1.67 meters). He might have grown to 6 feet had he lived.

The sharp contrast between the OH62 *H. habilis* (1.8 m.y.a.) and early *H. erectus* (1.7–1.6 m.y.a.) suggests an acceleration in hominin evolution during that 100,000–200,000-year period. This fossil evidence may support a **punctuated equilibrium** model of the early hominin fossil record. In this view, long periods of equilibrium, during which species change little, are interrupted (punctuated) by sudden changes—evolutionary jumps. Apparently hominins changed very little below the neck between Lucy (*A. afarensis*) and *H. habilis*. Then, between 1.8 and 1.6 m.y.a., a profound change—an evolutionary leap—took place. *H. erectus* looks much more human than *H. habilis* does.

The hominin fossil record exemplifies both gradual and rapid change. Evolution can be slow or fast depending on the rate of environmental change, the speed with which geographic barriers rise or fall, and the effectiveness of the group's adaptive response. There is no doubt that the pace of hominin evolution sped up around 1.8 m.y.a. This spurt resulted in the emergence (in less than 200,000 years) of *H. erectus*. This was followed by a long period of relative stability. One possible key to the rapid emergence of *H. erectus* was a dramatic change in adaptive strategy: greater reliance on hunting through larger body size, along with improved tools and other cultural means of adaptation.

Significant changes in technology occurred during the 200,000-year evolutionary spurt between Bed I (1.8 m.y.a.) and Lower Bed II (1.6 m.y.a) at Olduvai. Tool making got more sophisticated soon after the advent of *H. erectus* in Africa. Out of the crude tools in Bed I evolved better-made and more varied tools. Edges were straighter, for example, and differences in form suggest functional differentiation—that is, the tools were being made and used for different jobs, such as smashing bones or digging for tubers.

The more sophisticated tools aided in hunting and gathering. With the new tools, *Homo* could obtain meat on a more regular basis and dig and process tubers, roots, nuts, and seeds more efficiently. New tools that could batter, crush, and pulp coarse vegetation also reduced chewing demands.

With changes in the types of foods consumed, the burden on the chewing apparatus eased. Chewing muscles developed less, and supporting structures, such as jaws and cranial crests, also were reduced. With less chewing, jaws developed less, and so there was no place to put large teeth. The size of teeth, which form before they erupt, is under stricter genetic control than jaw size and bone size are. Natural selection began to operate against the genes that caused large teeth. In smaller jaws, large teeth now caused dental crowding, impaction, pain, sickness, fever, and sometimes death (there were no dentists).

Some of the main contrasts between *Australopithecus* and early *Homo* are in dentition. *H. erectus* back teeth are smaller; and the front teeth, relatively larger than australopithecine teeth. *H. erectus* used its front teeth to pull, twist, and grip objects. A massive ridge over the eyebrows (a *superorbital torus*) provided buttressing against the forces exerted in these activities.

As hunting became more important to *H. erectus*, encounters with large animals increased. Individuals with stronger skulls had better-protected brains and better survival rates. Given the dangers associated with larger prey, and without sophisticated spear or arrow technology, which developed later, natural selection favored the thickening of certain areas for better protection against blows and falls (Boaz and Ciochon 2004). The base of the skull expanded dramatically, with a ridge of spongy bone (an *occipital bun*) across the back, for the attachment of massive neck muscles. The frontal and parietal (side) areas of the skull also increased, indicating expansion in those areas of the brain. Finally, average cranial capacity expanded from about 500 cm$^3$ in the australopithecines to 1,000 cm$^3$ in *H. erectus*, which is within the modern range of variation.

## ✣ OUT OF AFRICA I: *H. ERECTUS*

Biological and cultural changes enabled *H. erectus* to exploit a new adaptive strategy—gathering and hunting. *H. erectus* pushed the hominin range beyond Africa—to Asia and Europe. Small groups broke off from larger ones and moved a few miles away. They foraged new tracts of edible vegetation and carved out new hunting territories. Through population growth and dispersal, *H. erectus* gradually spread and changed. Hominins were following an essentially human lifestyle based on hunting and gathering. This basic pattern survived until recently in marginal areas of the world, although it is now fading rapidly.

This chapter begins around 2 million years ago, with the transition to *Homo*. It ends in the less distant past, with the advent of anatomically modern humans. We focus

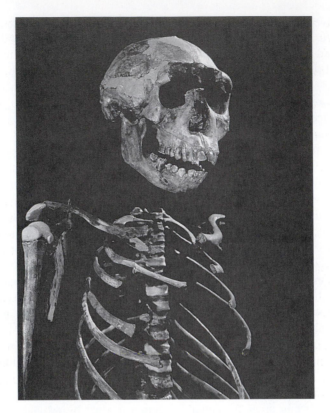

This photo shows the early (1.6 m.y.a) *Homo erectus* WT15,000, or Nariokotome boy, found in 1984 near Lake Turkana, Kenya. This is the most complete *Homo erectus* ever found.

in this chapter on the biological and cultural changes that led from early *Homo,* through intermediate forms, to those anatomically modern humans (AMHs).

## Paleolithic Tools

The stone-tool-making techniques that evolved out of the Oldowan, or pebble tool, tradition and that lasted until about 15,000 years ago are described by the term **Paleolithic** (from Greek roots meaning "old" and "stone"). The Paleolithic, or Old Stone Age, has three divisions: Lower (early), Middle, and Upper (late). Each part is roughly associated with a particular stage in human evolution. The Lower Paleolithic is roughly associated with *H. erectus;* the Middle Paleolithic with archaic *H. sapiens,* including the Neandertals of Western Europe and the Middle East; and the Upper Paleolithic with anatomically modern humans.

The best stone tools are made from rocks such as flint that fracture sharply and in predictable ways when hammered. Quartz, quartzite, chert, and obsidian also are suitable. Each of the three main divisions of the Paleolithic had its typical *tool-making traditions*—coherent patterns of tool manufacture. The main Lower Paleolithic tool-making tradition used by *H. erectus* was the **Acheulian,** named after the French village of St. Acheul, where it was first identified.

Like Oldowan tools, the characteristic Acheulian tool, the hand ax, consisted of a modified core of rock. Flakes removed from the core when it was struck with a hammerstone also were used as tools. Flakes, smaller tools with finer cutting edges, became progressively more important in human evolution, particularly in Middle and Upper Paleolithic tool making.

Acheulian tools were an advance over pebble tools in several ways. Early hominins had made simple tools by picking up pebbles the size of tennis balls and chipping off a few flakes from one end to form a rough and irregular edge. They used these pebble tools (and some of the flakes as well) for a variety of purposes, such as smashing animal bones to extract marrow. The Acheulian technique involved chipping the core all over rather than at one end only. The core was converted from a round piece of rock into a flattish oval hand ax about 6 inches (15 centimeters) long. Its cutting edge was far superior to that of the pebble tool (see Figure 6-1).

Hand axes, along with digging sticks made of bone, horn, and wood, were used to dig edible roots and other foods from the ground. Hunters made tools with a sharper cutting edge to skin and cut up their prey. Cleavers—core tools with a straight edge at one end—were used for heavy chopping and hacking at the sinews of larger animals. Flakes were used to make incisions and for finer work. The Acheulian tradition illustrates trends in the evolution of technology: greater efficiency, manufacture of tools for specific tasks, and an increasingly complex technology. These trends became even more obvious with the advent of *H. sapiens.*

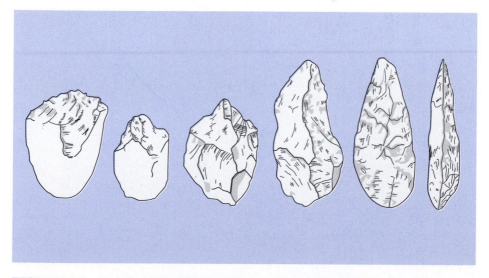

**FIGURE 6-1**   *Evolution in Tool Making*   Finds at Olduvai Gorge and elsewhere show how pebble tools (the first tool at the left) evolved into the Acheulian hand ax of *H. erectus.* This drawing begins with an Oldowan pebble tool and moves through crude hand axes to fully developed Acheulian tools associated with *H. erectus.*

# Adaptive Strategies of *H. erectus*

Interrelated changes in biology and culture have increased human adaptability—the capacity to live in and modify an ever-wider range of environments. Improved tools helped *H. erectus* increase its range (see Figure 6-2). Biological changes also increased hunting efficiency. *H. erectus* had a rugged but essentially modern skeleton that permitted long-distance stalking and endurance during the hunt. The *H. erectus* body was much larger and longer-legged than those of previous hominins, permitting longer-distance hunting of large prey. There is archaeological evidence of *H. erectus*'s success in hunting elephants, horses, rhinos, and giant baboons.

An increase in cranial capacity has been a trend in human evolution. The average *H. erectus* brain (about 1,000 cm³) doubled the australopithecine average. The capacities of *H. erectus* skulls range from 800 to 1,250 cm³, well above the modern minimum.

*H. erectus* had an essentially modern, though very robust, skeleton with a brain and body closer in size to *H. sapiens* than to *Australopithecus*. Still, several anatomical contrasts, particularly in the cranium, distinguish *H. erectus* from modern humans. Compared with moderns, *H. erectus* had a lower and more sloping forehead accentuated by a large brow ridge above the eyes. Skull bones were thicker, and, as noted, average cranial capacity was smaller. The brain case was lower and flatter than in *H. sapiens,* with spongy bone development at the lower rear of the skull. Seen from behind, the *H. erectus* skull has a broad-based angular shape that has been compared to a half-inflated football and a hamburger bun (Figure 6-3). The *H. erectus* face, teeth, and jaws were larger than

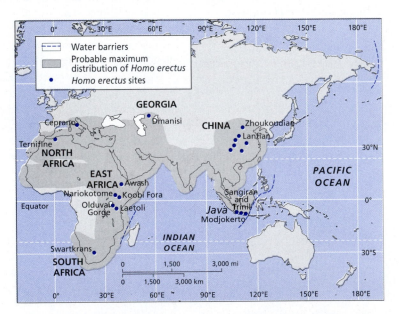

**FIGURE 6-2**    *The Sites of Discovery of Homo erectus and Its Probable Maximum Distribution*

SOURCE: From C. J. Jolly and R. White, *Physical Anthropology and Archaeology*, 5th ed. (New York: McGraw-Hill, 1995), p. 271. Reprinted by permission of The McGraw-Hill Companies.

those in contemporary humans but smaller than those in *Australopithecus*. The front teeth were especially large, but molar size was well below the australopithecine average. Presumably, this reduction reflected changes in diet or food processing.

Hearths at various sites confirm that fire was part of the human adaptive kit by this time. Early evidence for human control over fire has been found in Israel, dating back to almost 800,000 years ago (Gugliotta 2004), and possibly at Swartkrans, South Africa, dated to 1.6–1.0 m.y.a. Fire provided protection against cave bears and saber-toothed tigers. It permitted *H. erectus* to occupy cave sites, including Zhoukoudian, near Beijing in China, which has yielded the remains of more than 40 specimens of *H. erectus*. Fire widened the range of climates open to human colonization. It may have played a role in the expansion out of Africa. Its warmth enabled people to survive winter cold in temperate regions. Human control over fire offered other advantages, such as cooking, which breaks down vegetable fibers and tenderizes meat. Cooking kills parasites and makes meat more digestible, thus reducing strain on the chewing apparatus.

## The Evolution and Expansion of *H. erectus*

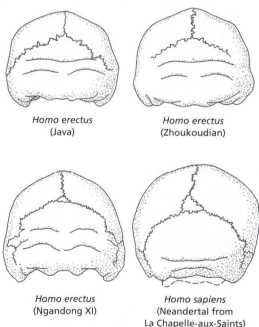

Homo erectus
(Java)

Homo erectus
(Zhoukoudian)

Homo erectus
(Ngandong XI)

Homo sapiens
(Neandertal from
La Chapelle-aux-Saints)

**FIGURE 6-3**   *Rear Views of Three Skulls of* **H. erectus** *and One of "Archaic"* **Homo sapiens** *(a Neandertal)*  Note the more angular shape of the *H. erectus* skulls, with the maximum breadth low down, near the base.

*SOURCE:* From C. J. Jolly and R. White, *Physical Anthropology and Archaeology,* 5th ed. (New York: McGraw-Hill, 1995), p. 268. Reprinted by permission of The McGraw-Hill Companies.

The archaeological record of *H. erectus* activities can be combined with the fossil evidence to provide a more complete picture of our Lower Paleolithic ancestors. We now consider some of the fossil data, whose geographic distribution is shown in Figure 6-2. Early *H. erectus* remains, found by Richard Leakey's team at East and West Turkana, Kenya, and dated to around 1.6 m.y.a., including the Nariokotome boy, were discussed previously.

One fairly complete skull, one large mandible, and two partial skulls—one of a young adult male (780 cm³) and one of an adolescent female (650 cm³)—were found recently at the Dmanisi site in the former Soviet Republic of Georgia. They have been assigned a date of 1.7–1.75 m.y.a. There are notable similarities between the two partial skulls and that of the Nariokotome boy (1.6 m.y.a.). Chopping tools of comparable age associated with the Kenyan and Georgian fossils also are similar. The most recent (2001) Georgian skull find is the most primitive, with a stronger resemblance to *H. habilis* than is the case with the other Dmanisi fossils. Primitive characteristics of this skull include its large canine teeth and small cranial capacity (Vekua, Lordkipanidze, and Rightmire 2002). This specimen may be that of a teenage girl whose skull had not yet reached full size, but whose canines had. The simplest explanation for the anatomical diversity observed at Dmanisi is that *H. erectus* was at least as variable a species as is *H. sapiens.*

Many paleoanthropologists now assign the Nariokotome and Dmanisi finds to a new species, *Homo ergaster,* intermediate between *H. habilis* and *H. erectus.* Others simply consider all these Dmanisi fossils early *H. erectus.* Whatever their designation, the Dmanisi finds suggest a rapid spread, by 1.7 m.y.a., of early *Homo* out of Africa and into Eurasia (Figure 6-2).

The Dmanisi fossils are the most ancient undisputed human fossils outside Africa. How did those hominins get to Georgia? The most probable answer is meat. As hominins became more carnivorous, they expanded their home ranges in accordance with those of the animals they hunted. The bigger bodies and brains of early *Homo* (compared with the australopithecines) required more energy to run. Meat-rich diets provided higher-quality protein as fuel. The australopithecines had smaller bodies and brains, and so they could live mainly on plants. They probably used a limited range at the edge of forests, not too deep in or too exposed far out on the savanna. Once hominins developed stronger bodies and high-protein meat diets, they could—indeed had to—spread out. They ranged farther to find meat, and this expansion eventually led them out of Africa, into Eurasia (Georgia) and eventually Asia (see Wilford 2000).

In 1891, the Indonesian island of Java yielded the first *H. erectus* fossil find, popularly known as "Java man." Eugene Dubois, a Dutch army surgeon, had gone to Java to discover a transitional form between apes and humans. Of course, we now know that the transition to hominin had taken place much earlier than the *H. erectus* period and occurred in Africa. However, Dubois's good luck did lead him to the most ancient human fossils discovered at that time. Excavating near the village of Trinil, Dubois found parts of a *H. erectus* skull and a thigh bone. During the 1930s and 1940s, excavations in Java uncovered additional remains. The various Indonesian *H. erectus* fossils date back at least 700,000, and perhaps as much as 1.6 million, years. Fragments of a skull and a lower jaw found in northern China at Lantian may be as old as the oldest Indonesian fossils. Other *H. erectus* remains, of uncertain date, have been found in Algeria and Morocco in North Africa.

*H. erectus* remains also have been found in Upper Bed II at Olduvai, Tanzania, in association with Acheulian tools. African *H. erectus* fossils also come from Ethiopia, Eritrea, and South Africa (in addition to Kenya and Tanzania). The time span of *H. erectus* in East Africa was long. *H. erectus* fossils have been found in Bed IV at Olduvai, dating to 500,000 B.P., about the same age as the Beijing fossils described below.

The largest group of *H. erectus* fossils was found in the Zhoukoudian cave in China. The Zhoukoudian ("Peking"—now Beijing—"man") site, excavated from the late 1920s to the late 1930s, was a major find for the human fossil record. Zhoukoudian yielded remains of tools, hearths, animal bones, and more than 40 hominins, including five skulls. The analysis of these remains led to the conclusion that the Java and

Zhoukoudian fossils were examples of the same broad stage of human evolution. Today they are commonly classified together as *H. erectus*. The Zhoukoudian individuals lived more recently than did the Javanese *H. erectus,* between 670,000 and 410,000 years ago, when the climate in China was colder and moister than it is today. The inference about the climate has been made on the basis of the animal remains found with the human fossils. The people at Zhoukoudian ate venison, and seed and plant remains suggest they were both gatherers and hunters.

What about Europe? A cranial fragment found at Ceprano, Italy, in 1994 has been assigned a date of 800,000 B.P. Other probable *H. erectus* remains have been found in Europe, but their dates are uncertain. All are later than the Ceprano skull, and they usually are classified as late *H. erectus,* or transitional between *H. erectus* and early *H. sapiens.*

## ✦ ARCHAIC *H. SAPIENS*

Africa, which was center stage during the australopithecine period, is joined by Asia and Europe during the *H. erectus* and *H. sapiens* periods of hominin evolution. European fossils and tools have contributed disproportionately to our knowledge and interpretation of early (archaic) *H. sapiens*. This doesn't mean that *H. sapiens* evolved in Europe or that most early *H. sapiens* lived in Europe. Indeed, the fossil evidence suggests that *H. sapiens*, like *H. erectus* before it, originated in Africa. *H. sapiens* lived in Africa for tens of thousands of years before starting the settlement of Europe around 50,000 B.P. (see the box at the end of this chapter). There were probably many more humans in the tropics than in Europe during the ice ages. We merely *know more* about recent human evolution in Europe because archaeology and fossil hunting—not human evolution—have been going on longer there than in Africa and Asia.

Recent discoveries, along with reinterpretation of the dating and the anatomical relevance of some earlier finds, are filling in the gap between *H. erectus* and archaic *H. sapiens*. **Archaic *H. sapiens*** (300,000? to 28,000 B.P.) encompasses the earliest

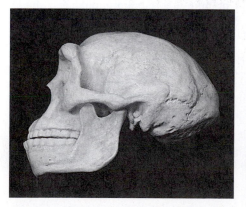

Meet *Homo erectus*. On the left is a reconstruction of one of the *H. erectus* skulls from Zhoukoudian, China. On the right, an attempt to render *H. erectus* in the flesh.

### TABLE 6-1

**Summary of Data on *Homo* Fossil Groups**

*Fossil representatives of the genus* Homo, *compared with anatomically modern humans (AMHs) and* chimps (Pan troglodytes)

| Species | Dates | Known Distribution | Important Sites | Brain Size (in cm³) |
|---|---|---|---|---|
| Anatomically modern humans (AMHs) | 130,000 B.P. to present | Worldwide | Beijing, New York, Paris, Nairobi | 1,350 |
| Neandertals | 130,000 to 28,000 B.P. | Europe, southwestern Asia | La Chapelle-aux-Saints | 1,430 |
| Archaic *Homo sapiens* | 300,000 to 28,000 B.P. | Africa, Europe, Asia | Kabwe, Arago, Dali, Mount Carmel caves | 1,135 |
| *Homo erectus* | 1.7 m.y.a. to 300,000 B.P. | Africa, Asia, Europe | East + West Turkana, Olduvai, Zhoukoudian, Java, Ceprano | 900 |
| *Pan troglodytes* | Modern | Central Africa | Gombe, Mahale | 390 |

members of our species, along with the **Neandertals** (*H. sapiens neanderthalensis*—130,000 to 28,000 B.P.) of Europe and the Middle East and their Neandertal-like contemporaries in Africa and Asia. Brain size in archaic *H. sapiens* was within the modern human range. (The modern average, remember, is about 1,350 cm³.) (See Table 6-1.) A rounding out of the brain case was associated with the increased brain size. As Jolly and White (1995) put it, evolution was pumping more brain into the *H. sapiens* cranium—like filling a football with air.

## Ice Ages of the Pleistocene

Traditionally and correctly, the geological epoch known as the **Pleistocene** has been considered the epoch of human life. Its subdivisions are the Lower Pleistocene (2 to 1 m.y.a.), the Middle Pleistocene (1 m.y.a. to 130,000 B.P.), and the Upper Pleistocene (130,000 to 10,000 B.P.). These subdivisions refer to the placement of geological strata containing, respectively, older, intermediate, and younger fossils. The Lower Pleistocene extends from the start of the Pleistocene to the advent of the ice ages in the Northern Hemisphere around 1 million years ago.

Each subdivision of the Pleistocene is associated with a particular group of hominins. Late *Australopithecus* and early *Homo* lived during the Lower Pleistocene. *Home erectus* spanned most of the Middle Pleistocene. *Homo sapiens* appeared late in the Middle Pleistocene and was the sole hominin of the Upper Pleistocene.

During the second million years of the Pleistocene, there were several ice ages, or **glacials,** major advances of continental ice sheets in Europe and North America. These periods were separated by **interglacials,** long warm periods between the major glacials. (Scientists used to think there were four main glacial advances, but the picture has grown more complex.) With each advance, the world climate cooled and continental ice sheets—massive glaciers—covered the northern parts of Europe and North America. Climates that are temperate today were arctic during the glacials.

During the interglacials, the climate warmed up and the *tundra*—the cold, treeless plain—retreated north with the ice sheets. Forests returned to areas, such as southwestern France, that had had tundra vegetation. The ice sheets advanced and receded several times during the last glacial, the *Würm* (75,000 to 12,000 B.P.). Brief periods of relative warmth during the Würm (and other glacials) are called *interstadials,* in contrast to the longer interglacials. Hominin fossils found in association with animals known to occur in cold or warm climates, respectively, permit us to date them to glacial or interglacial (or interstadial) periods.

## *H. antecessor* and *H. heidelbergensis*

In northern Spain's Atapuerca mountains, the site of Gran Dolina has yielded the remains of 780,000-year-old hominins that Spanish researchers call *H. antecessor* and see as a possible common ancestor of the Neandertals and anatomically modern humans. At the nearby cave of Sima dos Huesos a team led by Juan Luis Arsuaga has found thousands of fossils representing at least 33 hominins of all ages. Almost 300,000 years old, they may represent an early stage of Neandertal evolution (Lemonick and Dorfman 1999).

A massive hominin jaw was discovered in 1907 in a gravel pit at Mauer near Heidelberg, Germany. Originally called "Heidelberg man" or *Homo heidelbergensis,* the jaw appears to be around 500,000 years old. The deposits that yielded this jaw also contained fossil remains of several animals, including bear, bison, deer, elephant, horse, and rhinoceros. Recently, some anthropologists have revived the species name *H. heidelbergensis* to refer to a group of fossil hominins that in this text are described as either late *H. erectus* or archaic *H. sapiens*. This group would include hominins (very roughly) dated between 700,000 and 200,000 years ago and found in different parts of the world including Europe, Africa, and Asia. Such fossils, here assigned to either *H. erectus* or archaic *H. sapiens,* would be transitional between *H. erectus* and later hominin forms such as the Neandertals and anatomically modern humans.

Archaic *H. sapiens* lived during the last part of the *Middle Pleistocene*—during the *Mindel* (second) glacial, the interglacial that followed it, and the following *Riss* (third) glacial. The distribution of the fossils and tools of archaic *H. sapiens,* which have been found in Europe, Africa, and Asia, shows that *Homo*'s tolerance of environmental diversity had increased. For example, the Neandertals and their immediate ancestors managed to survive extreme cold in Europe. Archaic *H. sapiens* occupied the Arago cave in southeastern France at a time when Europe was bitterly cold. The only Riss glacial site with facial material, Arago, was excavated in 1971. It produced a partially intact skull, two jaw bones, and teeth from a dozen individuals. With an apparent date of about 200,000 B.P., the Arago fossils have mixed features that seem transitional between *H. erectus* and the Neandertals.

## ✦ THE NEANDERTALS

Neandertals were first discovered in Western Europe. The first one was found in 1856 in a German valley called Neander Valley—*tal* is the German word for valley. Scientists had trouble interpreting the discovery. It was clearly human and similar to modern Europeans in many ways, yet different enough to be considered strange and abnormal. This was 35 years before Dubois discovered the first *H. erectus* fossils in Java and almost 70 years before the first australopithecine was found in South Africa. Darwin's *On the Origin of Species,* published in 1859, had not yet appeared to offer a theory of evolution through natural selection. There was no framework for understanding human evolution. Over time, the fossil record filled in, along with evolutionary theory. There have been numerous subsequent discoveries of Neandertals in Europe and the Middle East and of archaic human fossils with similar features in Africa and Asia. The similarities and differences between Neandertals and other relatively recent hominins have become clearer.

Fossils that are not Neandertals but that have similar features (such as large faces and brow ridges) have been found in Africa and Asia. The Kabwe skull from Zambia (130,000 B.P.) is an archaic *H. sapiens* with a Neandertal-like brow ridge. Archaic Chinese fossils with Neandertal-like features have been found at Maba and Dali. Neandertals have been found in Central Europe and the Middle East. For example, Neandertal fossils found at the Shanidar cave in northern Iraq date to around 60,000 B.P., as does a Neandertal skeleton found at Israel's Kebara cave (Shreeve 1992). At the Israeli site of Tabun on Mount Carmel, a Neandertal female skeleton was excavated in 1932. She was a contemporary of the Shanidar Neandertals, and her brow ridges, face, and teeth show typical Neandertal robustness.

## Cold-Adapted Neandertals

By 75,000 B.P., after an interglacial interlude, Western Europe's hominins (Neandertals, by then) again faced extreme cold as the Würm glacial began. To deal with this environment, they wore clothes, made more elaborate tools, and hunted reindeer, mammoths, and woolly rhinos. Neandertal technology, a Middle Paleolithic tradition called **Mousterian,** improved considerably during the Würm glacial.

The Neandertals were stocky, with large trunks relative to limb length—a phenotype that minimizes surface area and thus conserves heat. Another adaptation to extreme cold was the Neandertal face, which has been likened to a *H. erectus* face that has been pulled forward by the nose. This extension increased the distance between outside air and the arteries that carry blood to the brain and was adaptive in a cold climate. The brain is sensitive to temperature changes and must be kept warm. The massive nasal cavities of Neandertal fossils suggest long, broad noses. This would expand the area for warming and moistening air.

Neandertal characteristics also include huge front teeth, broad faces, and large brow ridges, and ruggedness of the skeleton and musculature. What activities were associated with these anatomical traits? Neandertal teeth probably did many jobs later done by tools (Brace 1995; Rak 1986). The front teeth show heavy wear, suggesting that they were used for varied purposes, including chewing animal hides to make soft winter clothing out of them. The massive Neandertal face showed the stresses of constantly using the front teeth for holding and pulling.

## The Neandertals and Modern People

Generations of scientists have debated whether the Neandertals were ancestral to modern Europeans. The current prevailing view, denying this ancestry, proposes that *H. erectus* split into separate groups, one ancestral to the Neandertals, the other ancestral to **anatomically modern humans (AMHs),** who first reached Europe around 50,000 B.P. (Early AMHs in Western Europe often are referred to as *Cro-Magnon,* after the earliest fossil find of an anatomically modern human, in France's Dorgon Valley in Les Eyzies region, in 1868.) The current predominant view is that modern humans evolved in Africa and eventually colonized Europe, displacing the Neandertals there.

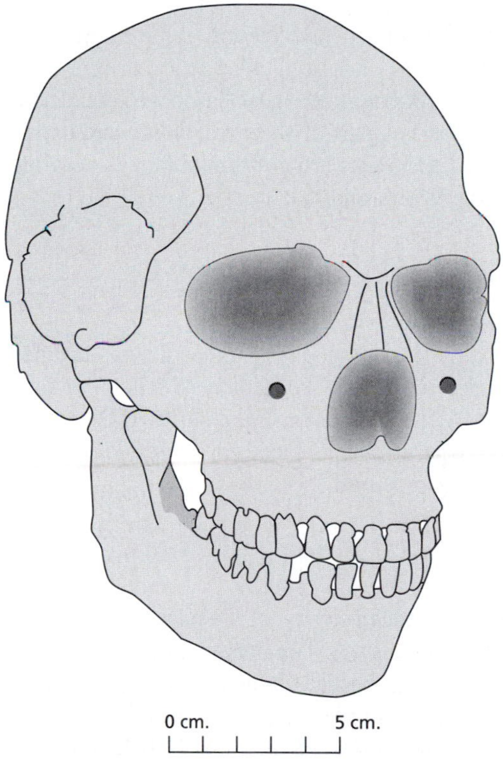

Consider the contrasts between the Neandertals and AMHs. Like *H. erectus* before them, the Neandertals had heavy brow ridges and slanting foreheads. However, average Neandertal cranial capacity (more than 1,400 cm$^3$) exceeded the modern average. Neandertal jaws were large, providing support for huge front teeth, and their faces were massive. The bones and skull were generally more rugged and had greater sexual dimorphism—particularly in the face and skull—than do those of AMHs. In some Western European fossils, these contrasts between Neandertals and AMHs are accentuated—giving a stereotyped, or *classic Neandertal,* appearance.

Those scientists who still believe that Neandertals could have contributed to the ancestry of modern Europeans cite certain fossils to support their view. For example, the Central European site of Mladeč (31,000 to 33,000 B.P.) has yielded remains of several hominins that combine Neandertal robustness with modern features. Wolpoff (1999) also

0 cm.          5 cm.

**FIGURE 6-4**  *Skhūl V*  This anatomically modern human with some archaic features was recently redated to 100,000 B.P. This is one of several fossils found at Skhūl, Israel. Formerly dated to 32,000 B.P., this fossil group once seemed transitional between Neandertals and *H. sapiens sapiens.*

notes modern features in the late Neandertals found at l'Hortus in France and Vindija in Croatia. The fossil remains of a four-year-old boy discovered at Largo Velho in Portugal in 1999 and dated to 24,000 B.P. also shows mixed Neandertal and modern features.

Fossils from Israel's Mount Carmel site of Skhūl also combine archaic and modern features. But most analyses stress the "modernness" of the Skhūl fossils, which date to 100,000 B.P. Another group of modern-looking and similarly dated (92,000 B.P.) skulls comes from the Israeli site of Qafzeh. The Skhūl and Qafzeh fossils cast serious doubt on the Neandertal ancestry of AMHs in Europe and the Middle East. The skulls from Skhūl (Figure 6-4) and Qafzeh have a modern, rather than a Neandertal, shape and are classified as AMHs. Their brain cases are higher, shorter, and rounder than Neandertal skulls. There is a more filled-out forehead region, which rises more vertically above the brows. A marked chin is another modern feature. Still, Skhūl and Qafzeh, although early AMHs, do retain distinct brow ridges, though reduced from their archaic *H. sapiens* ancestor.

Given these early dates from Israel, AMHs may have inhabited the Middle East before the Neandertals did. Ofer Bar-Yosef (1987) has suggested that during the last (Würm) glacial period, which began around 75,000 B.P., Western European Neandertals spread east and south (and into the Middle East) as part of a general southward expansion of cold-adapted fauna. AMHs, in turn, followed warmer-climate fauna south into Africa, returning to the Middle East once the Würm ended.

## ✦ ANATOMICALLY MODERN HUMANS

Most current interpretations of the fossil evidence and dating favor the replacement hypothesis, which denies the Neandertal ancestry of AMHs. Rather, AMHs seem likely to have evolved from an archaic *H. sapiens* African ancestor. Eventually, AMHs spread to other areas, including Western Europe, where they replaced, or interbred with, the Neandertals, whose robust traits eventually disappeared.

## Out of Africa II

In 1987 a group of molecular geneticists at the University of California at Berkeley offered support for the idea that modern humans (AMHs) arose fairly recently in Africa, then spread out and colonized the world. Rebecca Cann, Mark Stoneking, and Allan C. Wilson (1987) analyzed genetic markers in placentas donated by 147 women whose ancestors came from Africa, Europe, the Middle East, Asia, New Guinea, and Australia.

The researchers focused on mitochondrial DNA (mtDNA). This genetic material is located in the cytoplasm (the outer part of a cell—not the nucleus) of cells. Ordinary DNA, which makes up the genes that determine most physical traits, is found in the nucleus and comes from both parents. But only the mother contributes mitochondrial DNA to the fertilized egg. The father plays no part in mtDNA transmission, just as the

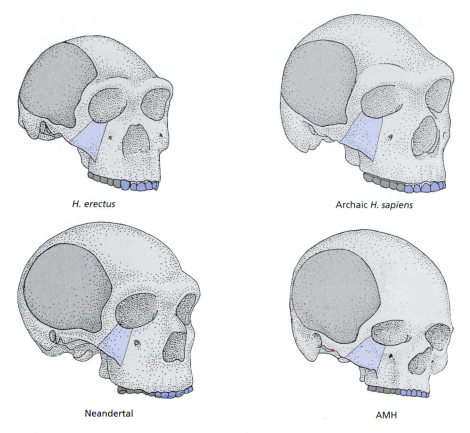

*H. erectus*          Archaic *H. sapiens*

Neandertal          AMH

Compare these drawings of *H. erectus*, archaic *H. sapiens*, Neandertal, and an anatomically modern human (AMH). What are the main differences you notice? Is the Neandertal more like *H. erectus* or the AMH?

mother has nothing to do with the transmission of the Y chromosome, which comes from the father and determines the sex of the child.

To establish a "genetic clock," the Berkeley researchers measured the variation in mtDNA in their 147 tissue samples. They cut each sample into segments to compare with the others. By estimating the number of mutations that had taken place in each sample since its common origin with the 146 others, the researchers drew an evolutionary tree with the help of a computer.

That tree started in Africa and then branched in two. One group remained in Africa, while the other one split off, carrying its mtDNA to the rest of the world. The variation in mtDNA was greatest among Africans. This suggests they have been evolving the longest. The Berkeley researchers concluded that everyone alive today has mtDNA that descends from a woman (dubbed "Eve") who lived in sub-Saharan Africa around 200,000 years ago. Eve was not the only woman alive then; she was just the only one whose descendants have included a daughter in each generation up to the present. Because mtDNA passes exclusively through females, mtDNA lines disappear whenever a woman has no children or has only sons. The details of the Eve theory suggest that her descendants left Africa no more than 135,000 years ago. They eventually displaced the Neandertals in Europe and went on to colonize the rest of the world.

## Recent Fossil and Archaeological Evidence

Besides the DNA dating, fossil and archaeological evidence has been accumulating to support the African origin, perhaps by 150,000 years ago, of AMHs. A major find was announced in 2003: the 1997 discovery in an Ethiopian valley of three anatomically modern skulls—two adults and a child. When found, the fossils had been fragmented so badly that their reconstruction took several years. Tim White and Berhane Asfaw were coleaders of the international team that made the find near the village of Herto, 140 miles northeast of Addis Ababa. All three skulls were missing the lower jaw. The skulls showed evidence of cutting and handling, suggesting they had been detached from their bodies and used—perhaps ritually—after death. A few teeth, but no other bones, were found with the skulls, again suggesting their deliberate removal from the body. Layers of volcanic ash allowed geologists to date them to 154,000–160,000 B.P. The people represented by the skulls had lived on the shore of an ancient lake, where they hunted and fished. The skulls were found along with hippopotamus and antelope bones and some 600 tools, including blades and hand axes.

Except for a few archaic characteristics, the Herto skulls are anatomically modern—long with broad midfaces, featuring tall, narrow nasal bones. The cranial vaults are high, falling within modern dimensions. These finds provide additional support for the view that modern humans originated in Africa and then spread into Europe and Asia (Wilford 2003).

From South Africa comes further evidence. At Border Cave, a remote rock shelter, fossil remains dating back perhaps 150,000 years are believed to be those of early modern humans. The remains of at least five AMHs have been discovered, including the nearly complete skeleton of a four- to six-month-old infant buried in a shallow grave. Excavations at Border Cave also have produced some 70,000 stone tools, along with the remains of several mammal species, including elephants, believed to have been hunted by the ancient people who lived there.

A complex of South African caves near the Klasies River Mouth was occupied by a group of hunter-gatherers some 120,000 years ago. Fragmentary bones suggest how those people looked. A forehead fragment has a modern brow ridge. There is a thin-boned cranial fragment and a piece of jaw with a modern chin. The archaeological evidence suggests that these cave dwellers did coastal gathering and used Middle Paleolithic stone tools.

If those people were anatomically modern, were they behaviorally modern as well? Several archaeologists believe they've found early evidence for behavioral modernity in Africa. For example, South Africa's Blombos Cave has yielded evidence that apparent AMHs were making bone awls and weapon points more than 70,000 years ago. Earlier excavations in Congo's Katanda region had uncovered barbed bone harpoon points dating back 80,000 to 90,000 years (Yellen, Brooks, and Cornelissen 1995).

## ✧ ADVANCES IN TECHNOLOGY

In Europe, Upper Paleolithic tool making traditionally is associated with AMHs. In Africa earlier AMHs made varied tools. The people who lived at the Klasies River Mouth cave sites made Middle Paleolithic tools, as did Neandertals in Europe and the Middle East. However, some of the early African tool finds at Blombos Cave and in Katanda are more reminiscent of the European Upper Paleolithic. AMHs in Europe made tools in a variety of traditions, collectively known as **Upper Paleolithic** because of the tools' location in the upper, or more recent, layers of sedimentary deposits. Some cave deposits have Middle Paleolithic Mousterian tools (made by Neandertals) at lower levels and increasing numbers of Upper Paleolithic tools at higher levels.

The Upper Paleolithic traditions of early AMHs all emphasized **blade tools.** Blades were hammered off a prepared core, as in Mousterian technology, but a blade is longer than a flake—its length is more than twice its width. Blades were chipped off cores 4 to 6 inches (10 to 15 centimeters) high by hitting a punch made of bone or antler with a hammerstone (Figure 6-5). Blades were then modified to produce a variety of special-purpose implements. Some were composite tools that were made by joining reworked blades to other materials.

The blade-core method was faster than the Mousterian and produced 15 times as much cutting edge from the same amount of material. More efficient tool production might have been especially valued by people whose economy depended on cooperative hunting of mammoths, woolly rhinoceroses, bison, wild horses, bears, wild cattle, wild boars, and—principally—reindeer. It has been estimated that approximately 90 percent of the meat eaten by Western Europeans between 25,000 and 15,000 B.P. came from reindeer.

Upper Paleolithic bone tools have survived: knives, pins, needles with eyes, and fishhooks. The needles suggest that clothes sewn with thread—made from the sinews of animals—were being worn. Fishhooks and harpoons confirm an increased emphasis on fishing.

With increasing technological differentiation, specialization, and efficiency, humans have become increasingly adaptable. Through heavy reliance on cultural means of adaptation, *Homo* has become (in numbers and range) the most successful primate by far. The hominid range

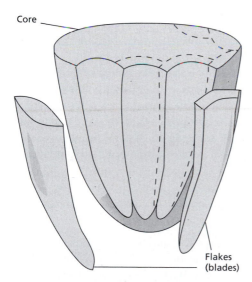

Core

Flakes (blades)

**FIGURE 6-5** *Upper Paleolithic Blade-Tool Making* Blades are flakes that are detached from a specially prepared core. A punch (usually a piece of bone or antler) and a hammerstone (not shown here) were used to knock the blade off the core.

expanded significantly in Upper Paleolithic times with the colonization of two new continents—North America and South America (see below). (Australia was colonized by at least 60,000 B.P.)

## → GLACIAL RETREAT

Consider now one regional example, Western Europe, of the consequences of glacial retreat. The Würm glacial ended in Europe between 17,000 and 12,000 years ago, with the melting of the ice sheet in northern Europe (Scotland, Scandinavia, northern Germany, and Russia). As the ice retreated, the tundra and steppe vegetation grazed by reindeer and other large herbivores gradually moved north. Some people moved north, too, following their prey.

Shrubs, forests, and more solitary animals appeared in southwestern Europe. With most of the big-game animals gone, Western Europeans were forced to use a greater variety of foods. To replace specialized economies based on big game, more generalized adaptations developed during the 5,000 years of glacial retreat.

As seas rose, conditions more encouraging to marine life developed in the shallower, warmer offshore waters, where the quantity and variety of edible species increased tremendously. Furthermore, because rivers now flowed more gently into the oceans, fish such as salmon could ascend rivers to spawn. Flocks of birds that nested in seaside marshes migrated across Europe during the winter. Even inland Europeans could take advantage of new resources, such as migratory birds and springtime fish runs.

Although hunting remained important, southwestern European economies became less specialized. A wider range, or broader spectrum, of plant and animal life was being hunted, gathered, collected, caught, and fished. This was the beginning of what anthropologist Kent Flannery (1969) has called the *broad-spectrum revolution*. It was revolutionary because, in the Middle East, it led to food production—human control over the reproduction of plants and animals. In a mere 10,000 years—after more than a million years during which hominids had subsisted by foraging for natural resources—food production based on plant cultivation and animal domestication replaced hunting and gathering in most areas.

## → SETTLING THE AMERICAS

Another effect of continental glaciation was to expose—during several periods of glacial advance—*Beringia*, the Bering land bridge that once connected North America and Siberia. Submerged today under the Bering Sea, Beringia was once a vast area of dry land, several hundred miles wide. The original settlers of the Americas came from Northeast Asia. Living in Beringia thousands of years ago, these ancestors of Native Americans didn't realize they were embarking on the colonization of a new continent. They were merely big-game hunters who, over the generations, moved gradually eastward as they spread their camps and followed their prey—woolly mammoths and other

**FIGURE 6-6** *A Clovis Spear Point* Such points were attached to spears used by Paleoindians of the North American plains between 12,000 and 11,000 B.P. Are there sites with comparable ages in South America?

tundra-adapted herbivores. Other ancient hunters entered North America along the shore by boat, fishing and hunting sea animals.

This was truly a "new world" to its earliest colonists, as it would be to the European voyagers who rediscovered it thousands of years later. Its natural resources, particularly its big game, never before had been exploited by humans. Early bands followed the game south. Although ice sheets covered most of what is now Canada, colonization gradually penetrated the heartland of what is now the United States. Successive generations of hunters followed game through unglaciated corridors, breaks in the continental ice sheets. Other colonists spread by boat down the Pacific coast.

In North America's rolling grasslands, early American Indians, *Paleoindians,* hunted horses, camels, bison, elephants, mammoths, and giant sloths. The **Clovis tradition**—a sophisticated stone technology based on a point that was fastened to the end of a hunting spear (Figure 6-6)—flourished between 12,000 and 11,000 B.P. in the Central Plains, on their western margins, and over a large area of what is now the eastern United States. Indeed, spear points made in the Clovis tradition have been found in all 48 of the continental United States (Green 2006).

The Clovis people were not the first settlers of the Americas. Thousands of miles to the south of the Clovis area, the Monte Verde archaeological site in south central Chile dates to 13,500 B.P. (Green 2006). This evidence for the early occupation of southern South America (along with other lines of evidence) suggests that the first migration of humans into the Americas may date back 18,000 years. Analysis of DNA—bolstered, some anthropologists believe, by anatomical evidence—suggests that the Americas were settled by more than one *haplogroup,* a lineage marked by one or more specific genetic mutations. The various early colonists (as many as four or five haplogroups, some anthropologists believe) came at different times, perhaps by different routes, and had different physiques and genetic markers, which continue to be discovered and debated (see Bonnichsen and Schneider 2000).

As hunters benefiting from the abundance of big game, bands of foragers gradually spread through the Americas. As they moved, these early Americans learned to cope with a great diversity of environments. Thousands of years later, their descendants independently invented food production, paving the way for the emergence of states based on agriculture and trade in Mexico and Peru. New World food production emerged 3,000 to 4,000 years later than in the Middle East, as did the first states, a story to be told in the next two chapters.

# ANTHROPOLOGY TODAY

## *Improved Science Puts Modern Humans in Europe Earlier*

*For more than a century anthropologists have known of the overlap between archaic (Neandertal) and anatomically modern humans (AMHs) in Europe. This story reports on the implications of recent revisions and recalibrations in the radiocarbon dating technique that has been applied to Neandertals and AMHs in Europe. Radiocarbon ($C^{14}$) dating is most useful for remains that are 50,000 years old or less. The revised dating described here suggests that modern humans have been in Europe longer than previously thought—perhaps for 50,000 years—and that their time of overlap with the Neandertals was less than previously thought, perhaps no more than 2,000 years in western Europe.*

New advances in radiocarbon dating are threatening to upend old theories about when modern humans migrated to Europe from Africa and how rapidly they advanced. The research casts new light on significant patterns of human migration into Central and Western Europe in the crucial period from 50,000 to 35,000 years ago, scientists say. It suggests that the dispersal of anatomically modern *Homo sapiens* into Europe was more rapid than previously thought.

That, in turn, would mean that their coexistence with Neanderthals was briefer and that their introduction of cave art, symbolic artifacts and personal ornamentation occurred much earlier.

"Evidently the native Neanderthal populations of Europe succumbed much more rapidly to competition from the expanding biologically modern populations than previous estimates have generally assumed," Paul Mellars, an archaeologist at the University of Cambridge in England, wrote in an article appearing today in the journal *Nature*.

Although other scientists have for several years been pondering the implications of the revised radiocarbon dating for archaeological research throughout the world, Dr. Mellars's description of the new techniques and their significance is the first comprehensive review of the subject in a major journal. The most pronounced discrepancies between radiocarbon and actual ages coincide with the fateful epoch when modern people first made themselves at home in Europe.

For years, it had been thought that modern humans from Africa began arriving in Western Europe at least 40,000 years ago, and so could have competed and mingled with the local population for at least 12,000 years. The revised dating of fossils and artifacts leaves much less time for two species to have been in close contact.

Dr. Mellars concludes from the revised chronology that the overlap between Neanderthals and new arrivals must be shortened to about 6,000 years in Central and Northern Europe, perhaps only 1,000 to 2,000 years in regions like western France.

Katerina Harvati, a paleontologist at the Max-Planck Institute for Evolutionary Anthropology in Leipzig, Germany, said these advances "can potentially lead to a breakthrough in our understanding of this critical time period in European prehistory."

Dr. Harvati agreed that the new chronology suggested "an earlier appearance of early modern human complex behaviors and an earlier Neanderthal extinction and also suggests a shorter coexistence interval of the two species."

Radiocarbon dating, introduced shortly after World War II, has been widely used in measuring time in prehistory, back to the method's effective limit of 50,000 years ago. It assumes that the proportion of radioactively unstable carbon 14 to stable carbon 12 has remained virtually constant in Earth's atmosphere through this time period. It works by measuring the rate of decay of carbon 14 in once living materials, like plant and animal remains.

Although scientists once estimated the dating uncertainty to be no more than several hundred years, they came to suspect two potential sources of greater error. One was contamination of test samples by intrusions of more recent carbon. The other was fluctuations in proportions of carbon 14 to carbon 12, which scientists came to recognize as a consequence to variations in cosmic radiation reaching the upper atmosphere.

Recent research at the University of Oxford, Dr. Mellars said, has led to a more effective filtration process to reduce contamination in test samples. Other investigations of deep-sea sediments off Venezuela and ice-core records from Greenland yielded evidence of carbon variation problems, which turned out to be especially pronounced between 30,000 and 40,000 years ago. Accordingly, radio carbon dates were recalibrated.

The revised dates, for example, show that a standard radiocarbon reading of 40,000 years translated into a calendar age of 43,000. Even more consequential, a date of 35,000 years is revised to an actual age of 40,500, Dr. Mellars reported.

If correct, the new chronology means that fossil and archaeological evidence, especially in the crucial 30,000-to-40,000-year period, is much older than once estimated. Modern people may have arrived in Europe slightly earlier, but the extinction of the Neanderthals, previously thought to have occurred around 30,000 years ago, is now subject to greater revision because the standard dating yielded the most serious underestimates of true ages.

The degree of age discrepancies is also illustrated by the revised date for the splendid wall art in Chauvet cave in southern France. The charcoal used to produce the Chauvet drawings was originally dated around 31,000 to 32,000 years ago. A team of scientists reported in 2004 in the journal *Science* a revised date closer to 36,000.

In previous estimates, the modern human dispersal through Europe occurred 43,000 to 36,000 years ago. The 7,000-year period implies an overall dispersal rate of about 0.3 kilometer a year, less than two-tenths of a mile. Starting somewhat earlier, the faster dispersal over 5,000 years is now clocked at 0.4 kilometer a year.

Dr. Mellars cautioned that the revised dating based on new research must be viewed as provisional, concluding that the implications of the new studies "will need to be kept under active and vigilant review."

*Source:* John Noble Wilford, "Improved Science Puts Modern Humans in Europe Earlier," *New York Times*, February 23, 2006, p. A10. Reprinted by permission.

## SUMMARY

1. Dental, facial, and cranial robustness was reduced as *H. habilis* evolved into *H. erectus,* who extended the hominid food quest to the hunting of large animals. *H. erectus,* with a much larger body, had smaller back teeth but larger front teeth and supporting structures, including a massive eyebrow ridge. The Lower Paleolithic Acheulian tradition provided *H. erectus* with better tools. *H. erectus*'s average cranial capacity doubled the australopithecine average. Tool complexity and archaeological evidence for cooperative hunting suggest a long period of enculturation and learning. *H. erectus* extended the hominid range beyond Africa to Asia and Europe.

2. The oldest *H. erectus* skulls yet found come from Kenya and Georgia (in Eurasia) and date back some 1.75–1.6 million years. At Olduvai Gorge, Tanzania, geological strata spanning more than a million years demonstrate a transition from Oldowan tools to the Acheulian implements of *H. erectus. H. erectus* persisted for more than a million years, evolving into archaic *H. sapiens* by the Middle Pleistocene epoch, some 300,000 years ago. Fire allowed *H. erectus* to expand into cooler areas, to cook, and to live in caves.

3. The classic Neandertals, who inhabited Western Europe during the early part of the Würm glacial, were among the first hominid fossils found. With no examples of *Australopithecus* or *H. erectus* yet discovered, the differences between them and modern humans were accentuated. Even today, anthropologists tend to exclude the classic Neandertals from the ancestry of Western Europeans. The ancestors of AMHs (anatomically modern humans) were other archaic *H. sapiens* groups, most probably those in Africa. AMH fossil finds such as Herto (160,000–154,000 B.P.), Skhūl (100,000 B.P.), Qafzeh (92,000 B.P.), and South African sites are cited to support the contention that the Neandertals (130,000 to 28,000 B.P.) and AMHs were contemporaries, rather than ancestor and descendant.

4. The classic Neandertals adapted physically and culturally to bitter cold. Their tool kits were much more complex than those of preceding humans. Their front teeth were among the largest to appear in human evolution. The Neandertals manufactured Mousterian flake tools. AMHs made Upper Paleolithic blade tools. The changeover from Neandertal to modern appears to have occurred in Western Europe by 28,000 B.P.

5. As glacial ice melted, foraging patterns were generalized, adding fish, fowl, and plant foods to the diminishing big-game supply. The broad-spectrum revolution, based on a wide variety of dietary resources, began in the Middle East somewhat earlier than in Europe. As we will see in Chapter 7, it culminated in the first food-producing economies in the Middle East around 10,000 B.P.

6. Humans entered the Americas perhaps as long as 18,000 years ago. Pursuing big game or moving by boat along the northern Pacific Coast, they gradually moved into North America. Adapting to different environments, Native Americans developed a variety of cultures. Some continued to rely on big game. Others became broad-spectrum foragers.

## Key Terms

Acheulian (p. 125)
anatomically modern humans
 (AMHs) (p. 133)
archaic *Homo sapiens* (p. 129)
blade tools (p. 137)
Clovis tradition (p. 139)
glacials (p. 131)
*Homo erectus* (p. 122)

*Homo habilis* (p. 121)
interglacials (p. 131)
Mousterian (p. 132)
Neandertals (p. 130)
Paleolithic (p. 124)
Pleistocene (p. 130)
punctuated equilibrium (p. 122)
Upper Paleolithic (p. 137)

# CHAPTER 7

❧

# THE FIRST FARMERS

❖ **The First Farmers and Herders in the Middle East**

Genetic Changes and Domestication

Food Production and the State

❖ **Other Old World Farmers**

❖ **The First American Farmers**

Early Farming in the Mexican Highlands

From Early Farming to the State

❖ **Explaining the Neolithic**

Geography and the Spread of Food Production

*Anthropology Today: On the Iceman's Trail*

In Chapter 6, we considered the economic implications of the end of the Ice Age in Europe. With glacial retreat, foragers pursued a more generalized economy, focusing less on large animals. This was the beginning of what Kent Flannery (1969) has called the **broad-spectrum revolution.** This refers to the period beginning around 15,000 B.P. in the Middle East and 12,000 B.P. in Europe, during which a wider range, or broader spectrum, of plant and animal life was hunted, gathered, collected, caught, and fished. It was revolutionary because, in the Middle East, it led to **food production**—human control over the reproduction of plants and animals.

After 15,000 B.P., throughout the inhabited world, as the big-game supply diminished, foragers had to pursue new resources. Human attention shifted from large-bodied, slow reproducers (such as mammoths) to species such as fish, mollusks, and rabbits that reproduce quickly and prolifically (Hayden 1981). For example, the Japanese site of Nittano (Akazawa 1980), on an inlet near Tokyo, offers evidence of broad-spectrum foraging. Nittano was occupied several times between 6000 and 5000 B.P. by members of the *Jomon* culture, for which 30,000 sites are known in Japan. The Jomon people hunted deer, pigs, bears, and antelope. They also ate fish, shellfish, and plants. Jomon sites have yielded the remains of 300 species of shellfish and 180 species of edible plants (including berries, nuts, and tubers) (Akazawa and Aikens 1986).

Early experiments in food production were the most significant form of broad-spectrum resource use in the post-Ice Age world. By 10,000 B.P., a major economic shift was under way in the Middle East (Turkey, Iraq, Iran, Syria, Jordan, and Israel). People started intervening in the reproductive cycles of plants and animals. No longer simply harvesting nature's bounty, they grew their own food and modified the characteristics of the plants and animals in their diet. By 10,000 B.P., domesticated plants and animals were part of the broad spectrum of resources used by Middle Easterners. By 7500 B.P.,

| TABLE 7-1 |
| --- |

### The Transition to Food Production in the Middle East

| Era | Dates (B.P.) |
| --- | --- |
| Origin of state (Sumer) | 5500 |
| Increasing specialization in food production | 7500–5500 |
| Early dry farming and caprine domestication | 10,000–7500 |
| Seminomadic hunting and gathering (e.g., Natufians) | 12,000–10,000 |

most Middle Easterners were moving away from a broad-spectrum foraging pattern toward more specialized economies based on fewer species, which were domesticates. They were becoming farmers and herders (see Bellwood 2004).

Kent Flannery (1969) has proposed a series of eras during which the Middle Eastern transition to farming and herding took place (Table 7-1). The era of seminomadic hunting and gathering (12,000 to 10,000 B.P.) encompasses the last stages of broad-spectrum foraging. This was the period just before the first domesticated plants (wheat and barley) and animals (goats and sheep) were added to the diet. Next came the era of early dry farming (of wheat and barley) and caprine domestication (10,000 to 7500 B.P.). *Dry farming* refers to farming without irrigation; such farming depended on rainfall. *Caprine* (from *capra,* Latin for "goat") refers to goats and sheep, which were domesticated during this era.

During the era of increasing specialization in food production (7500 to 5500 B.P.), new crops were added to the diet, along with more productive varieties of wheat and barley. Cattle and pigs were domesticated. By 5500 B.P., agriculture extended to the alluvial plain of the Tigris and Euphrates rivers (Figure 7-1), where early Mesopotamians lived in walled towns, some of which grew into cities. Metallurgy and the wheel were invented. After 2 million years of stone-tool making, *H. sapiens* was living in the Bronze Age.

The archaeologist V. Gordon Childe (1951) used the term *Neolithic Revolution* to describe the origin and impact of food production—plant cultivation and animal domestication. **Neolithic,** which means "New Stone Age," was coined to refer to techniques of grinding and polishing stone tools. However, the main significance of the Neolithic was the new total economy rather than just the tool-making techniques. *Neolithic* now refers to the cultural period in a given region in which the first signs of domestication are present. The Neolithic economy based on food production produced substantial changes in human lifestyles. The pace of social and cultural change increased enormously.

## ✦ THE FIRST FARMERS AND HERDERS IN THE MIDDLE EAST

Middle Eastern food production arose in the context of four environmental zones. From highest to lowest, they are high plateau (5,000 feet, or 1,500 meters), Hilly Flanks, piedmont steppe (treeless plain), and alluvial desert—the area watered by the Tigris and Euphrates rivers (100 to 500 feet, or 30 to 150 meters). The **Hilly Flanks** is a subtropical woodland zone that flanks those rivers to the north (Figure 7-1).

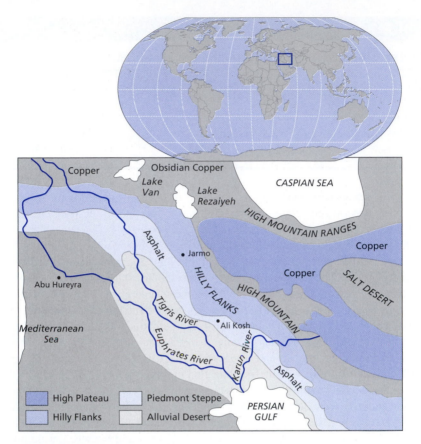

**FIGURE 7-1**    *The Vertical Economy of the Ancient Middle East*
Geographically close but contrasting environments were linked by seasonal
movements and trade patterns of broad-spectrum foragers. Traded resources
included copper, obsidian, and asphalt, located in particular zones. As people
traveled and traded, they removed plants from the zones where they grew
wild in the Hilly Flanks into adjacent zones where humans became agents of
selection.

It was once thought that food production began in oases in the alluvial desert.
(*Alluvial* describes rich, fertile soil deposited by rivers and streams.) This arid region
was where Mesopotamian civilization arose later. Today, we know that although the
world's first civilization (Mesopotamian) did indeed develop in this zone, irrigation,
a late invention (7000 B.P.), was necessary to farm the alluvial desert. Plant cultivation and animal domestication started not in the dry river zone but in areas with reliable rainfall.

The archaeologist Robert J. Braidwood (1975) proposed instead that food production started in the Hilly Flanks, or subtropical woodland, zone, where wild wheat
and barley would have been most abundant (see Figure 7-1). In 1948, a team headed

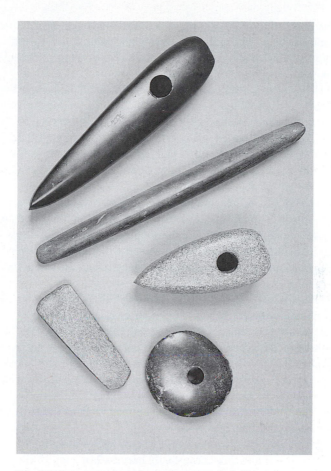

"Neolithic" was coined to refer to techniques of grinding and polishing stone tools, like these axes and hammers from Austria, Hungary, and the Czech Republic. Was the new tool-making style the most significant thing about the Neolithic?

by Braidwood started excavations at Jarmo, an early food-producing village inhabited between 9000 and 8500 B.P., located in the Hilly Flanks. We now know, however, that there were farming villages earlier than Jarmo (Figure 7-1) in zones adjacent to the Hilly Flanks. One example is Ali Kosh, a village in the foothills (piedmont steppe) of the Zagros Mountains. By 9000 B.P., the people of Ali Kosh were herding goats, intensively collecting various wild plants, and harvesting wheat during the late winter and early spring (Hole, Flannery, and Neely 1969).

Climate change played a role in the origin of food production (Smith 1995). The end of the Ice Age brought greater regional and local variation in climatic conditions. Lewis Binford (1968) proposed that in certain areas of the Middle East (such as the Hilly Flanks), local environments were so rich in resources that foragers could adopt **sedentism**—sedentary (settled) life in villages. Binford's prime example is the widespread Natufian culture (12,500 to 10,500 B.P.), based on broad-spectrum foraging. The **Natufians,** who collected wild cereals and hunted gazelles, had year-round villages. They were able to stay in the same place (early villages) because they could harvest nearby wild cereals for six months.

Donald Henry (1989, 1995) documented a climate change toward warmer, more humid, conditions just before the Natufian period. This expanded the altitude range of wild wheat and barley, thus enlarging the available foraging area and allowing a longer harvest season. Wheat and barley ripened in the spring at low altitudes, in the summer at middle altitudes, and in the fall at high altitudes. As locations for their villages, the Natufians chose central places where they could harvest wild cereals in all three zones.

Around 11,000 B.P., this favorable foraging pattern was threatened by a second climate change—to drier conditions. As many wild cereal habitats dried up, the optimal zone for foraging shrank. Natufian villages were now restricted to areas with permanent water. As population continued to grow, some Natufians attempted to maintain productivity by transferring wild cereals to well-watered areas, where they started cultivating.

In the view of many scholars, the people most likely to adopt a new subsistence strategy, such as food production, would be those having the most trouble in following their traditional subsistence strategy (Binford 1968; Flannery 1973; Wenke 1996). Thus, those ancient Middle Easterners living outside the area where wild foods were most abundant would be the most likely to experiment and to adopt new subsistence strategies. This would have been especially true as the climate dried up. Recent archaeological finds support this hypothesis that food production began in *marginal areas,* such as the piedmont steppe, rather than in the optimal zones, such as the Hilly Flanks, where traditional foods were most abundant.

Even today, wild wheat grows so densely in the Hilly Flanks that one person working just an hour with Neolithic tools can easily harvest 2 pounds (1 kilogram) of wheat (Harlan and Zohary 1966). People would have had no reason to invent cultivation when wild grain was ample to feed them. Wild wheat ripens rapidly and can be harvested over a three-week period. According to Flannery, over that time period a family of experienced plant collectors could harvest enough grain—2,200 pounds (1,000 kilograms)—to feed themselves for a year. But after harvesting all that wheat, they'd need a place to put it. They could no longer maintain a nomadic lifestyle, since they'd need to stay close to their grain.

In the Middle East, sedentary village life developed before farming and herding did. The Natufians had no choice but to build villages near the densest stands of wild grains. They needed a place to keep their grain. Furthermore, sheep and goats came to graze on the stubble that remained after humans had harvested the grain. The fact that basic plants and animals were available in the same area also favored village life. Hilly Flanks foragers built houses, dug storage pits for grain, and made ovens to roast it.

Natufian settlements, occupied year-round, show permanent architectural features and evidence for the processing and storage of wild grains. One such site is Abu Hureyra, Syria (see Figure 7-1), which initially was occupied by Natufian foragers around 11,000 to 10,500 B.P. Then it was abandoned—to be reoccupied later by food producers, between 9500 and 8000 B.P. From the Natufian period, Abu Hureyra has yielded the remains of grinding stones, wild plants, and gazelle bones (Jolly and White 1995).

Prior to domestication, the favored Hilly Flanks zone had the densest human population. Eventually, its excess population started to spill over into adjacent areas. Colonists from the Flanks tried to maintain their traditional broad-spectrum foraging in these marginal zones. But with sparser wild foods available, they had to experiment with new subsistence strategies. Eventually, population pressure forced people in the marginal zones to become the first food producers (Binford 1968; Flannery 1969). *Early cultivation began as an attempt to copy, in a less favorable environment, the dense stands of wheat and barley that grew wild in the Hilly Flanks.*

The Middle East is a region that for thousands of years has had a *vertical economy*. (Other examples include Peru and **Mesoamerica**—Middle America, including Mexico, Guatemala, and Belize.) A vertical economy exploits environmental zones that, although close together in space, contrast with one another in altitude, rainfall, overall climate, and vegetation (Figure 7-1). Such a close juxtaposition of varied environments allowed broad-spectrum foragers to use different resources in different seasons.

Early seminomadic foragers in the Middle East had followed game from zone to zone. In winter they hunted in the piedmont steppe region, which had winter rains rather than snow and provided winter pasture for game animals 12,000 years ago. (Indeed it is still used for winter grazing by herders today.) When winter ended, the steppe dried up. Game moved up to the Hilly Flanks and high plateau country as the snow melted. Pasture land became available at higher elevations. Foragers gathered as they climbed, harvesting wild grains that ripened later at higher altitudes. Sheep and goats followed the stubble in the wheat and barley fields after people had harvested the grain.

The four Middle Eastern environmental zones shown in Figure 7-1 also were tied together through trade. Certain resources were confined to specific zones. Asphalt, used as an adhesive in the manufacture of sickles, came from the steppe. Copper and turquoise sources were located in the high plateau. Contrasting environments were therefore linked in two ways: by foragers' seasonal migration and by trade. (See the box at the end of the chapter.)

The movement of people, animals, and products between zones—plus population increase supported by highly productive broad-spectrum foraging—was a precondition for the emergence of food production. As they traveled between zones, people carried seeds into new habitats. Mutations, genetic recombinations, and human selection led to new kinds of wheat and barley. Some of the new varieties were better adapted to the steppe and, eventually, the alluvial desert than the wild forms had been.

# Genetic Changes and Domestication

What are the main differences between wild and domesticated plants? The seeds of domesticated cereals, and often the entire plant, are larger. Compared with wild plants, crops produce a higher yield per unit of area. Domesticated plants also lose their natural

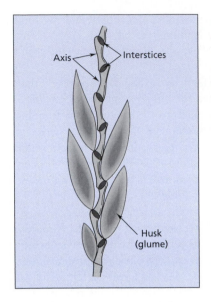

**FIGURE 7-2**    *A Head of Wheat or Barley*   In the wild, the axis comes apart as its parts fall off one by one. The connecting parts (interstices) are tough and don't come apart in domesticated grains. In wild grains, the husks are hard. In domestic plants, they are brittle, which permits easy access to the grain. How did people deal with hard husks before domestication?

seed dispersal mechanisms. Cultivated beans, for example, have pods that hold together, rather than shattering as they do in the wild. Domesticated cereals have tougher connective tissue holding the seedpods to the stem.

Grains of wheat, barley, and other cereals occur in bunches at the end of a stalk (Figure 7-2). The grains are attached to the stalk by an *axis,* plural *axes.* In wild cereals, this axis is brittle. Sections of the axis break off one by one, and a seed attached to each section falls to the ground. This is how wild cereals spread their seeds and propagate their species. But a brittle axis is a problem for people. Imagine the annoyance experienced by broad-spectrum foragers as they tried to harvest wild wheat, only to have the grain fall off or be blown away.

In very dry weather, wild wheat and barley ripen—their axes totally disintegrating—in just three days (Flannery 1973). The brittle axis must have been even more irritating to people who planted the seeds and waited for the harvest. But fortunately, certain stalks of wild wheat and barley happened to have tough axes. These were the ones whose seeds people saved to plant the following year.

Another problem with wild cereals is that the edible portion is enclosed in a tough husk. This husk was too tough to remove with a pounding stone. Foragers had to roast the grain to make the husk brittle enough to come off. However, some wild plants happened to have genes for brittle husks. Humans chose the seeds of these plants (which would have germinated prematurely in nature) because they could be more effectively prepared for eating.

People also selected certain features in animals (Smith 1995). Sometime after sheep were domesticated, advantageous new phenotypes arose. Wild sheep aren't woolly; wool coats were products of domestication. Although it's hard to imagine, a wool coat offers protection against extreme heat. Skin temperatures of sheep living in very hot areas are much lower than temperatures on the surface of their wool. Woolly sheep, but not their wild ancestors, could survive in hot, dry alluvial lowlands. Wool had an additional advantage: its use for clothing.

What are some of the differences between wild and domesticated animals? Plants got larger with domestication, while animals got smaller, probably because smaller animals are easier to control. Middle Eastern sites document changes in the horns of domesticated goats. Such change may have been genetically linked to some other desirable trait that has left no skeletal evidence behind.

## Food Production and the State

The shift from foraging to food production was gradual. The knowledge of how to grow crops and breed livestock didn't immediately convert Middle Easterners into full-time farmers and herders. Domesticated plants and animals began as minor parts of a broad-spectrum economy. Foraging for fruits, nuts, grasses, grains, snails, and insects continued.

Over time, Middle Eastern economies grew more specialized, geared more exclusively toward crops and herds. The former marginal zones became centers of the new economy and of population increase and emigration. Some of the increasing population spilled back into the Hilly Flanks, where people eventually had to intensify production by cultivating. Domesticated crops could now provide a bigger harvest than could the grains that grew wild there. Thus, in the Hilly Flanks, too, farming eventually replaced foraging as the economic mainstay.

Farming colonies spread down into drier areas. By 7000 B.P., simple irrigation systems had developed, tapping springs in the foothills. By 6000 B.P., more complex irrigation techniques made agriculture possible in the arid lowlands of southern Mesopotamia. In the alluvial desert plain of the Tigris and Euphrates rivers, a new economy based on irrigation and trade fueled the growth of an entirely new form of society. This was the *state,* a social and political unit featuring a central government, extreme contrasts of wealth, and social classes. The process of state formation is examined in the next chapter.

Simple irrigation systems were being used in the Middle East by 7000 B.P. By 6000 B.P., complex irrigation techniques made agriculture possible in the arid lowlands of southern Mesopotamia. Here in Sudan, we see a fairly simple, ox-powered irrigation system.

We now understand why the first farmers lived neither in the alluvial lowlands, where the Mesopotamian state arose around 5500 B.P., nor in the Hilly Flanks, where wild plants and animals abounded. Food production began in marginal zones, such as the piedmont steppe, where people experimented at reproducing, artificially, the dense grain stands that grew wild in the Hilly Flanks. As seeds were taken to new environments, new phenotypes were favored by a combination of natural and human selection. The spread of cereal grains outside their natural habitats was part of a system of migration and trade between zones, which had developed in the Middle East during the broad-spectrum period. Food production also owed its origin to the need to intensify production to feed an increasing human population—the legacy of thousands of years of productive foraging.

## ✤ OTHER OLD WORLD FARMERS

The path from foraging to farming was one that people followed independently in at least seven world areas. As we'll see later in this chapter, three were in the Americas. Four were in the Old World, including the very first farmers and herders in the Middle East. In each of these seven centers, people independently invented domestication— albeit of different sets of crops and animals.

Food production also spread out from the Middle East and other centers of domestication. This happened through trade; through diffusion of plants, animals, products, and information; and through the actual migration of farmers, who in some cases displaced native foragers. The crops and livestock that were first domesticated in the Middle East spread westward to northern Africa, including Egypt's Nile Valley, and into Europe (Price 2000). Trade also extended eastward from the Middle East to India and Pakistan. In Egypt, an agricultural economy based on plants and animals originally domesticated in the Middle East led to a pharaonic civilization. Another early civilization eventually arose in western Pakistan.

Excavations in southern Egypt have uncovered very early pottery and cattle. Located in the eastern Sahara and southern Egypt, Nabta Playa is a basin that, during prehistoric summers, filled with water. Over several millennia this temporary lake attracted people who used it for social and ceremonial activities (Wendorf and Schild 2000). The earliest settlements (11,000–9300 B.P.) at Nabta were small summer camps of herders of domesticated cattle. (Note the very early, and perhaps independent, domestication of cattle here.) According to Wendorf and Schild (2000), Nabta Playa provides early evidence for what anthropologists have called the "African cattle complex," in which cattle are used economically for their milk and blood, rather than killed for their meat (except on ceremonial occasions). At first, Nabta was occupied only seasonally, as people came over from the Nile, or from better-watered areas to the south. They returned to those areas in the fall.

By 9,000 B.P. people were living at Nabta Playa year-round. To survive in the desert, they dug large, deep wells and lived in well-organized villages, with small huts arranged in straight lines. Plant remains show they collected sorghum, millets, legumes (peas and beans), tubers, and fruits. These were wild plants, so the economy was not fully Neolithic. By 8800 B.P. they were making their own pottery, possibly the earliest pottery in Egypt. By 8100 B.P., sheep and goats had diffused in from the Middle East (see also Edwards 2004).

Around 8000 B.P., communities on Europe's Mediterranean shores, in Greece, Italy, and France, started shifting from foraging to farming, using imported species. By 7000 B.P., there were fully sedentary farming villages in Greece and Italy. By 6000 B.P., there were thousands of farming villages as far east as Russia and as far west as northern France (see Bogaard 2004). By chance, we can even meet a man from one of those European Neolithic villages. The "Iceman" discovered in the Italian Alps in 1991 (see the box at the end of this chapter) came from a village of farmers who raised wheat, barley, sheep, and goats.

Compared with the Middle East, less is known about early farmers in such Old World areas as sub-Saharan Africa, South and Southeast Asia, and China. Partly this reflects the poorer preservation of archaeological remains in hot, moist habitats. Mostly it reflects the need for more archaeological research in such areas. In Pakistan's Indus River Valley, ancient cities (Harappa and Mohenjo-daro) emerged slightly later than did the first Mesopotamian city-states. Domestication and state formation in the Indus Valley probably were influenced by developments in, and trade with, the Middle East. Still, archaeological research confirms the early (8000 B.P.) presence of domesticated goats, sheep, cattle, wheat, and barley in Pakistan (Meadow 1991).

China also was one of the first world areas to develop farming, based on millet and rice. Millet is a tall, coarse cereal grass still grown in northern China. This grain, which today feeds a third of the world's population, is used in contemporary North America mainly as birdseed. By 7500 B.P., two kinds of millet supported early farming communities in northern China, along the Yellow River. Millet cultivation paved the way for widespread village life and eventually for Shang dynasty civilization, based on irrigated agriculture, between 3600 and 3100 B.P. (See Chapter 8.) The northern Chinese also had domesticated dogs, pigs, and possibly cattle, goats, and sheep by 7000 B.P. (Chang 1977).

Recent discoveries by Chinese archaeologists suggest that rice was domesticated in the Yangtze River corridor of southern China as early as 8400 B.P. (Smith 1995). Other early rice comes from the 7,000-year-old site Hemudu, on Lake Dongting in southern China. The people of Hemudu used both wild and domesticated rice, along with domesticated water buffalo, dogs, and pigs. They also hunted wild game (Jolly and White 1995).

It appears that food production arose independently at least seven times in different world areas. Figure 7-3 is a map highlighting those seven areas: the Middle East, north China, south China, sub-Saharan Africa, central Mexico, the south central Andes, and the eastern United States. A different set of major foods was domesticated, at different times, in each area, as we see in Table 7-2. Some grains, such as millet and rice, were domesticated more than once. Millet grows wild in China and Africa, where it became an important food crop, as well as in Mexico, where it did not. Indigenous African rice, grown only in West Africa, belongs to the same genus as Asian rice. Pigs and probably cattle were independently domesticated in the Middle East, China, and sub-Saharan Africa. Independent domestication of the dog was virtually a worldwide phenomenon, including the Western Hemisphere. We turn now to archaeological sequences in the Americas.

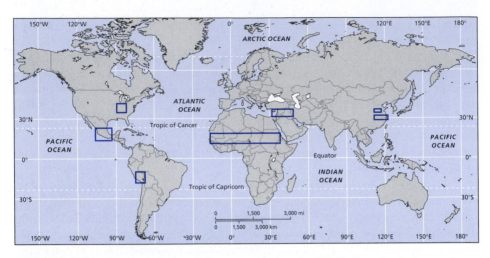

**FIGURE 7-3**    *Seven World Areas Where Food Production Was Independently Invented*
Do any of these areas surprise you?

*SOURCE:* B. D. Smith, *The Emergence of Agriculture* (New York: Scientific American Library, W. H. Freeman, 1999), p. 12.

## TABLE 7-2

### Seven World Areas Where Food Production Was Independently Invented

| World Area | Major Domesticated Plants/Animals | Earliest Date (B.P.) |
|---|---|---|
| Middle East | Wheat, barley<br>Sheep, goats, cattle, pigs | 10,000 |
| South China<br>(Yangtze River corridor) | Rice<br>Water buffalo, dogs, pigs | 8500–6500 |
| North China<br>(Yellow River) | Millet<br>Dogs, pigs, chickens | 7500 |
| Sub-Saharan Africa | Sorghum, pearl millet,<br>African rice | 4000 |
| Central Mexico | Maize, beans, squash<br>Dogs, turkeys | 4700 |
| South Central Andes | Potato, quinoa, beans<br>Camelids (llama, alpaca),<br>guinea pigs | 4500 |
| Eastern United States | Goosefoot, marsh elder,<br>sunflower, squash | 4500 |

*SOURCE:* Data compiled from B. D. Smith, *The Emergence of Agriculture* (New York: Scientific American Library, W. H. Freeman, 1999).

# ✦ The First American Farmers

*Homo* did not, of course, originate in the Western Hemisphere. Never have fossils of Neandertals or earlier hominins been found in North or South America. The settlement of the Americas was one of the major achievements of anatomically modern humans. This colonization continued the trends toward population increase and expansion of geographic range that have marked human evolution generally.

Spreading gradually through the Americas, early Native Americans occupied a variety of environments. Their descendants would independently invent food production, paving the way for the emergence of states based on agriculture and trade in Mexico and Peru. New World food production emerged 3,000 to 4,000 years later than in the Middle East, as did the first states. The most significant contrast between Old and New World food production involved animal domestication, which was much more important in the Old World than in the New World. The animals that had been hunted during the early American big-game tradition either became extinct before people could domesticate them or were not domesticable. The largest animal ever domesticated in the New World (in Peru, around 4500 B.P.) was the llama. Early Peruvians and Bolivians ate llama meat and used that animal as a beast of burden (Flannery, Marcus, and Reynolds 1989). They bred the llama's relative, the alpaca, for its wool. Peruvians also added animal protein to their diet by raising and eating guinea pigs and ducks. The turkey was domesticated in Mesoamerica and in the southwestern United States. Lowland South Americans domesticated a type of duck. The dog is the only animal that was domesticated throughout the New World.

There were no cattle, sheep, or goats in the areas of the Americas where food production arose. As a result, neither herding nor the kinds of relationships that developed between herders and farmers in many parts of the Middle East, Europe, Asia, and Africa emerged in the precolonial Americas. The New World crops were different, although staples as nutritious as those of the Old World were domesticated from native wild plants.

Three *caloric staples,* major sources of carbohydrates, were domesticated by Native American farmers. **Maize,** or corn, first domesticated in highland Mexico, became the caloric staple in Mesoamerica and Central America; it eventually spread to coastal Peru. The other two staples were root crops: white ("Irish") potatoes, first domesticated in the Andes, and **manioc,** or cassava, a tuber first cultivated in the South American lowlands. Other crops added variety to New World diets and made them nutritious. Beans and squash, for example, provided essential proteins, vitamins, and minerals. Maize, beans, and squash were the basis of the Mesoamerican diet.

Food production was invented independently in three areas of the Americas: Mesoamerica, the eastern United States, and the south central Andes. Mesoamerica is discussed in detail in the next section. Food plants known as goosefoot and marsh elder, along with the sunflower and a species of squash, were domesticated by Native Americans in the eastern United States by 4500 B.P. These crops supplemented a diet based mainly on hunting and gathering. They never became caloric staples like maize, wheat, rice, millet, manioc, and potatoes. Eventually maize diffused from Mesoamerica into what is now the United States, reaching both the Southwest and the eastern area just mentioned. Maize provided a more reliable caloric staple for Native North American farming. In what is now Peru and Bolivia, six species appear to have been domesticated more or less together in the highland valleys and basins of the south central Andes between 5000 and 4000 B.P. These domesticates were the potato, quinoa (a cereal grain), beans, llamas, alpacas, and guinea pigs (Smith 1995).

## Early Farming in the Mexican Highlands

Long before Mexican highlanders developed a taste for maize, beans, and squash, they hunted as part of a pattern of broad-spectrum foraging. Mammoth remains dated to 11,000 B.P. have been found along with spear points in the basin that surrounds Mexico City. However, small animals were more important than big game, as were the grains, pods, fruits, and leaves of wild plants.

In the *Valley of Oaxaca,* in Mexico's southern highlands, between 10,000 and 4000 B.P., foragers concentrated on certain wild animals—deer and rabbits—and plants—cactus leaves and fruits, and tree pods, especially mesquite (Flannery, ed. 1986). Those early Oaxacans dispersed to hunt and gather in fall and winter. But they came together in late spring and summer, forming larger groups to harvest seasonally available plants. Cactus fruits appeared in the spring. Since summer rains would reduce the fruits to mush and since birds, bats, and rodents competed for them, cactus collection required hard work by large groups of people. The edible pods of the mesquite, available in June, also required intensive gathering.

In fall, these early Oaxacan foragers gathered a wild grass known as **teocentli,** or *teosinte,* the wild ancestor of maize. Sometime between 7000 and 4000 B.P., teocentli-maize underwent a series of genetic changes like those described earlier for Middle Eastern wheat and barley. These changes included increases in the number of kernels per cob, cob size, and the number of cobs per stalk (Flannery 1973). Such steps toward domestication made it increasingly profitable to collect wild maize and eventually to plant maize.

As people harvested teocentli, they took back to camp a greater proportion of plants with tough axes and stalks. These were the plants most likely to hold together during harvesting and least likely to disintegrate on the way back home. Now teocentli depended on humans for its survival, since it lacked the natural means of dispersal—a brittle axis or stalk. If humans chose plants with tough axes inadvertently, their selection of plants with soft husks must have been intentional. Their selection of corn ears with larger cobs, more kernels per cob, and more cobs per plant was also intentional.

Eventually, people started planting maize in the alluvial soils of valley floors. This was the zone where foragers had traditionally congregated for the annual summer harvest of mesquite pods. By 4000 B.P., a type of maize had been developed that provided more food than the mesquite pods did. Once that happened, people started cutting down mesquite trees and replacing them with corn fields.

## From Early Farming to the State

Eventually, food production led to the *early village farming community*. Permanent villages sustained by farming were occupied year-round. The earliest such settlements in Mesoamerica developed around 3500 B.P., in two kinds of environment. One was

As maize cultivation spread, genetic changes led to higher yields and more productive farming. Pressures to intensify cultivation helped improve water-control systems, such as the canal irrigation shown in this mural by Diego Rivera.

humid lowlands, along the Gulf Coast of Mexico and the Pacific Coast of Mexico and Guatemala. Here, maize farming in rich soils was combined with gathering and hunting of several species of wild plants and animals.

Early village farming communities also emerged in one part of the Mexican highlands. In the Valley of Oaxaca in southern Mexico, winter frosts are absent, and simple irrigation permitted the establishment of early permanent villages based on maize farming. Water close to the surface allowed early farmers to dig wells right in their corn fields. Using pots, they dipped water out of these wells and poured it on their growing plants, a technique known as *pot irrigation*. The earliest year-round Mesoamerican farming depended on reliable rainfall, pot irrigation, or access to humid river bottomlands.

The subsequent spread of maize farming resulted in further genetic changes, higher yields, higher human populations, and more intensive farming. Pressures to intensify cultivation led to improvements in early water-control systems. New varieties of fast-growing maize eventually appeared, expanding the range of areas that could be cultivated. Increasing population and irrigation also helped spread maize farming.

The gradual transformation of broad-spectrum foraging into intensive cultivation laid the foundation for the emergence of the state in Mesoamerica—some 3,000 years later than in the Middle East. A state is a form of social and political organization that has a formal, central government and a division of society into classes. The process of state formation in Mesoamerica is examined further in the next chapter.

## ✦ EXPLAINING THE NEOLITHIC

Several factors had to converge to make domestication happen and to promote its spread (see also Diamond 1997). Most plants, and especially animals, aren't easy—or particularly valuable—to domesticate. Thus, of some 148 large animal species that seem potentially domesticable, only 14 actually have been domesticated. A mere dozen among 200,000 known plant species account for 80 percent of the world's farm production. Those 12 caloric staples are wheat, corn (maize), rice, barley, sorghum, soybeans, potatoes, cassava (manioc), sweet potatoes, sugar cane, sugar beets, and bananas.

The first domestication occurred, as we have seen, at a particular place and time—in the Middle East about 10,000 years ago.

Domestication rested on a combination of conditions and resources that had not come together previously. The development of a full-fledged Neolithic economy required settling down. Sedentism, such as that adopted by ancient Natufian hunter-gatherers, was especially attractive when several species of plants and animals were available locally for foraging and eventual domestication. The Middle East had such species, along with a Mediterranean climate favorable to the origin and spread of the Neolithic economy. Among those species were several self-pollinating plants, the easiest wild plants to domesticate, including wheat, which required few genetic changes for domestication. We've seen that the Natufians adopted sedentism prior to farming. They lived off abundant wild grain and the animals attracted to the stubble left after the harvest. Eventually, with climate change, population growth, and the need for people to sustain themselves in the marginal zones, hunter-gatherers started cultivating. In Mesoamerica, the shift from teocentli to maize required more genetic changes, so the domestication process took longer. The lack of domesticable animals in Mesoamerica, except for dogs and turkeys, also retarded the emergence of food production, sedentism, and a full-fledged Neolithic economy.

Compared with other world areas, the Middle East had the largest Mediterranean climate with the highest species diversity. As we saw previously, this was an area of vertical economy and closely packed microenvironments. Such diverse terrains and habitats concentrated in a limited area offered a multiplicity of plant species, as well as goats, sheep, pigs, and cattle. The first farmers eventually domesticated several crops: two kinds of wheat, barley, lentils, peas, and chickpeas (garbanzo beans). As in Mesoamerica, where corn (supplying carbohydrate) was supplemented by squash and beans (supplying protein), the Neolithic diet of the Middle East combined caloric staples such as wheat and barley with protein-rich pulses such as lentils, peas, and chickpeas.

Anthropologists once thought, erroneously, that domestication would happen almost automatically—once people gained sufficient knowledge of plants and animals and their reproductive habits to figure out how to make domestication work. Anthropologists now realize that foragers have an excellent knowledge of plants, animals, and their reproductive characteristics, and that some other trigger is needed to start and sustain the process of domestication. A full-fledged Neolithic economy requires a minimal set of nutritious domesticates. Some world areas, for example, North America (north of Mesoamerica), managed independently to invent domestication, but the inventory of available plants and animals was too meager to maintain a Neolithic economy. The early domesticates—squash, sunflower, sumpweed, and goosefoot—had to be supplemented by hunting and gathering. A full Neolithic economy and sedentism did not develop in the east, southeast, and southwest of what is now the United States until maize diffused in from Mesoamerica—more than 3,000 years after the first domestication in the eastern United States.

## Geography and the Spread of Food Production

As Jared Diamond (1997, Ch. 10) observes convincingly, the geography of the Old World facilitated the diffusion of plants, animals, technology (e.g., wheels and vehicles), and information (e.g., writing). Most crops in Eurasia were domesticated just once and spread rapidly in an east–west direction. The first domesticates spread from the Middle East to Egypt, North Africa, Europe, India, and eventually China (which, however, also had its own domesticates, as we have seen). By contrast, there was much less diffusion of American domesticates. Some important crops (e.g., beans and chili peppers) were domesticated twice, in Mesoamerica and again in South America.

Figure 7-4 shows that Eurasia has a much broader east–west expanse than do Africa or the Americas, which are arranged north–south. This is important because climates are more likely to be similar moving across thousands of miles east–west than north–south. In Eurasia, plants and animals could spread more easily east–west than north–south because of common day lengths and similar seasonal variations. More radical climatic contrasts have hindered north–south diffusion. In the Americas, for example, although the distance between the cool Mexican highlands and the South American highlands is just 1,200 miles, those two similar zones are separated by a low, hot, tropical region, which supports very different plant species than the highlands. Such environmental barriers to diffusion kept the Neolithic societies (of Mesoamerica and South America) more separate and independent in the Americas than they were in Eurasia. In fact, maize was the only crop that spread in the Americas before Columbus. And it took some 3,000 years for maize to reach what is now the United States, where productive Neolithic economies eventually did develop.

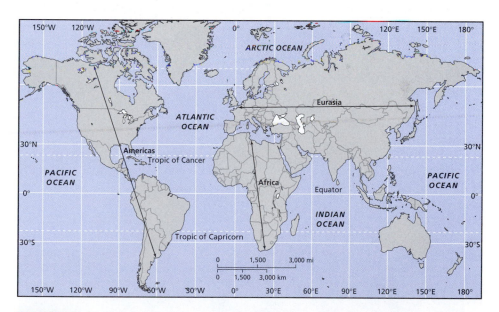

**FIGURE 7-4**  *Major Axes of the Continents*  Note the breadth of the east-west axis in Eurasia, compared with the much narrower east-west spreads in Africa, North America, and South America. Those three continents have north-south as their major axes.

*SOURCE:* J. M. Diamond, *Guns, Germs, and Steel: The Fates of Human Societies* (New York: W. W. Norton 1997), p. 177. Used by permission.

# ANTHROPOLOGY TODAY

## On the Iceman's Trail

*This news brief describes a late Neolithic Alpine European: the glacially preserved "Iceman" found in the Italian Alps in 1991. This find is significant because of its state of preservation and its combination of a human cadaver with clothing and possessions, including stone and metal (copper) tools. The Iceman probably came from an Alpine farming village, perhaps the archaeological site mentioned here. He was on an autumn hunting trip when he was killed and eventually frozen. DNA analysis of the contents of his stomach has shown that he ate wheat (cultivated) and red deer (hunted) for his last meal (Fountain 2002). The Neolithic, which began some 10,000 years ago in the Middle East, had spread to Western*
*Europe by 6500 B.P. Note that the Iceman died around 5200 B.P.—relatively late in the Neolithic. Although he was a Neolithic man, he lived as close to the present day as he did to the origins of Neolithic farming, which occurred in the Middle East at least 5,200 years before the Iceman's death.*

Like a never-ending *CSI* episode, scientists have been scrutinizing the oldest mummy ever found with nearly all that forensic science has to offer. They have learned what the man ate, his age, his health and they think they know more about how he died. Now they've answered another question— where he lived.

The latest series of tests on the mysterious, 5,200-year-old Iceman reveal the 46-year-old stuck close to home.

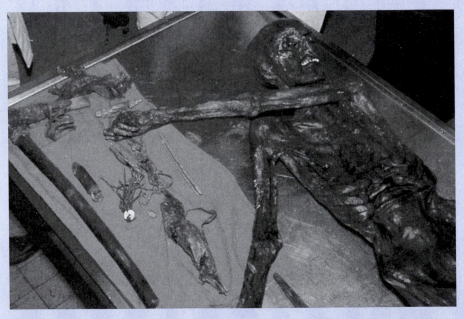

Meet the Iceman. Since his frozen body emerged from a glacier in the Italian Alps in 1991, scientists have come to realize he is the closest we may ever come to meeting a real person from the Stone Age. How would you evaluate his state of preservation?

Hikers first found the mummified man frozen in a glacier in the Alps between Italy and Austria in 1991. Researchers have since nicknamed the specimen "Ötzi," after the Ötztal area where he was found.

To trace the ancient man's where-abouts, researchers led by Wolfgang Müller of the Australian National University in Canberra studied the different forms of elements in the Iceman's teeth, bones and intestines and compared them with types found in soil and water in the area.

They found the 5-foot-2-inch-tall man likely spent his entire life within 37 miles mostly south of the location where he was discovered. That would mean the Iceman lived most of his life in what is now Italy. His mummified remains are still in Italy—at a refrigerated museum designed just for him in the northern city of Bolzano. . . .

The Iceman has revealed much about the Neolithic Copper Age of Europe. The frozen corpse was still clothed in goatskin leggings and a grass cloak, while a cop-per-headed ax and a quiver full of arrows were lying nearby. Now researchers say they can confidently link him with an ancient community that once settled in the region.

"I think it is important to know whether the Iceman was a chance wanderer in the Alps or whether he had migrated from farther away—or whether he was liv-ing in the local area during most of his life," said Müller. "We can now say that the latter was the case."

To reach that conclusion, Müller turned to chemistry.

Elements such as strontium, oxygen and argon occur in different forms, known as isotopes. Isotopes differ in the number of neutrons they carry in each atom. By com-paring the ratio of one isotope found in the water or soil of a region to that found in the body tissue, researchers can locate the source of the Iceman's food or water and link him to that region.

Isotopes in Ötzi's teeth reveal where he spent his youth, since dental enamel is fixed at the time that the tooth is formed. Isotopes in his bones reflect where he spent most of his adult life, since bones are remineralized every 10 to 20 years. And isotopes taken from the mummy's intestine shed light on where he spent his final hours.

Müller and his colleagues also ana-lyzed the chemical makeup of minerals that had been leached into Ötzi's water supplies to try and further narrow down his stomp-ing grounds. . . .

Since the Alpine mountains around where the Iceman was found host miner-als with a range of distinctive elements and isotopes, it was possible to link Ötzi with very specific locations. . . .

Oxygen isotopes from Ötzi's tooth enamel matched those found in valleys just south of where he was found. And in fact, Fricke and Müller suggest that an archaeo-logical site of a small Neolithic village in the nearby Eisack Valley may very well be where Ötzi spent his youth.

Isotopes and minerals from the Icc-man's thighbones reflect those found in soil and water between the more northern loca-tion where he was found and his childhood one, suggesting he roamed at a slightly higher altitude as an adult.

To determine where the Iceman spent his final days, Müller's team analyzed argon found in white mica from Ötzi's intestines that could have come from a grinding stone used to mash the wheat that he had eaten just hours before his death.

The mica matched pieces found in the Etsch Valley, a region west of the Iceman's assumed childhood home. All locations fall within a 37-mile area. So if Ötzi spent his life close to home, what was he doing in the mountain peaks on that fateful day? . . .

*Continued*

## ANTHROPOLOGY TODAY

Theories about how the Iceman died have varied wildly since his discovery, but some evidence suggests foul play.

Scientists first believed Ötzi may have been a shepherd who was returning with his flock when he encountered some kind of trouble, hurt his ribs and then fled to the mountains to escape. Then, overtaken by exhaustion, Ötzi propped his copper-headed ax against a rock and lay down or collapsed. Analysis of Ötzi's bones show he suffered from arthritis and so may have needed a rest after scrambling to the alpine ridge where he was discovered.

In 2001, scientists X-rayed the mummy's body and made a shocking discovery: The radiologist noticed what looked like a dense object in the body's shoulder. Further scrutiny showed it was an arrowhead lodged deep inside his shoulder.

One of the first to see the frozen mummy in the alpine glacier later revealed that it appeared Ötzi was clutching a knife in his right hand when he was found. Further analysis showed Ötzi had a deep wound in the same hand and had traces of blood from four different people on his clothes and weapons.

All of these revelations cleared away previous theories that the Iceman might have fallen asleep and died of hypothermia. A new picture emerged suggesting he was attacked and fought back with a hand knife. He eventually fled but was struck by an arrow as he ran away. He reached the top of the mountains, but was exhausted and bleeding and collapsed on the ground, and there he lay for more than 5,000 years.

That's the story for now anyway.

As scientists are learning, the Iceman holds seemingly endless clues, and theories about his life and death could evolve as forensic tools designed to catch new clues improve.

*Source:* "On the Iceman's Trail Scientists Trace Whereabouts of Man Who Died 5,200 Years Ago," by Dean Schabner and Amanda Diamond from *ABC News*, October 31, 2003.

## SUMMARY

1. After 15,000 B.P., as the big-game supply diminished, foragers sought out new foods. By 10,000 B.P., domesticated plants and animals were part of a broad spectrum of resources used by Middle Easterners. By 7500 B.P., most Middle Easterners were moving away from broad-spectrum foraging toward more specialized food-producing economies. *Neolithic* refers to the period when the first signs of domestication appeared.

2. Braidwood proposed that food production started in the Hilly Flanks zone. Others questioned this: The wild grain supply in that zone already provided an excellent diet for the Natufians and other ancient Middle Easterners. There would have been no incentive to domesticate.

3. Ancient Middle Eastern foragers migrated seasonally in pursuit of game. They also collected wild plant foods as they ripened at different altitudes. As they moved about, these foragers took grains from the Hilly Flanks zone where they grew wild, to adjacent areas. Humans became agents of selection, preferring plants with certain attributes. Population spilled over from the Hilly Flanks into

adjacent areas like the piedmont steppe. In such marginal zones people started cultivating plants. They were trying to duplicate the dense wild grains of the Hilly Flanks.

4. After the harvest, sheep and goats fed off the stubble of these wild plants. Animal domestication occurred as people started selecting certain features and behavior and guiding the reproduction of goats, sheep, cattle, and pigs. Gradually, food production spread into the Hilly Flanks. Later, with irrigation it spread down into Mesopotamia's alluvial desert, where the first cities, states, and civilizations developed by 5500 B.P. Food production then spread west from the Middle East into North Africa and Europe and east to India and Pakistan.

5. There were seven independent inventions of food production: in the Middle East, sub-Saharan Africa, northern and southern China, Mesoamerica, the south central Andes, and the eastern United States.

6. The transition to food production took place thousands of years later in the New World, where the most important domesticates were maize, potatoes, and manioc. The llama of the central Andes was the largest animal domesticated in the New World, where herding traditions analogous to those of the Old World did not develop. Economic similarities between the hemispheres must be sought in foraging and farming.

7. The earliest New World farming was in Mesoamerica. At Oaxaca, in Mexico's southern highlands, maize was gradually added to a broad-spectrum diet between 7000 and 4000 B.P. The first permanent villages, supported by maize cultivation, arose in the lowlands and in a few frost-free areas of the highlands. In the Valley of Mexico, quick-growing maize made year-round village life possible and paved the way for the emergence of civilization and city life.

8. Several factors, including a diversity of useful plant and animal species and early sedentism, combined to promote the first domestication in the ancient Middle East. The first domesticates spread rapidly across Eurasia, facilitated by climatic similarities across a broad territorial expanse. In the Americas, food production emerged later and spread less rapidly—and never as successfully—because of north–south contrasts. Another factor that slowed the Neolithic transition in the Americas was the lack of large animals suitable for domestication.

## KEY TERMS

broad-spectrum revolution (p. 144)
food production (p. 144)
Hilly Flanks (p. 145)
maize (p. 155)
manioc (p. 155)

Mesoamerica (p. 149)
Natufians (p. 148)
Neolithic (p. 145)
sedentism (p. 147)
teocentli (p. 156)

# CHAPTER 8

# THE FIRST CITIES AND STATES

## ✦ THE ORIGIN OF THE STATE

As food-producing economies spread and became more productive, chiefdoms, and eventually states, developed in many parts of the world. A **state** is a form of social and political organization that has a formal, central government and a division of society into classes. The first states developed in Mesopotamia by 5500 B.P. and in Mesoamerica some 3,000 years later. Chiefdoms were precursors to states, with privileged and effective leaders—chiefs—but lacking the sharp class divisions that characterize states. By 7000 B.P. in the Middle East and 3200 B.P. in Mesoamerica, there is evidence for what archaeologists call the elite level, indicating a chiefdom or a state.

How and why did chiefdoms and states originate? Compared with foraging, food production could support larger and denser populations. Also, the complexity of the division of social and economic labor tended to grow as food production spread and intensified. Systems of political authority and control typically develop to handle regulatory problems encountered as the population grows or the economy increases in scale and diversity. Anthropologists have identified the causes of state formation and reconstructed the rise of several states. A systemic perspective recognizes that multiple factors always contribute to state formation, with the effects of one magnifying those of the others. Although some contributing factors have appeared again and again, no single one is always present. In other words, state formation has generalized rather than universal causes.

## Hydraulic Systems

One suggested cause of state formation is the need to regulate *hydraulic* (water-based) agricultural economies (Wittfogel 1957). In certain arid areas, such as ancient Egypt and Mesopotamia, states have emerged to manage systems of irrigation, drainage, and flood control. However, hydraulic agriculture is neither a sufficient nor a necessary condition for the rise of the state. That is, many societies with irrigation never experienced state formation, and states have developed without hydraulic systems.

But hydraulic agriculture does have certain implications. Water control increases production in arid lands. Because of its labor demands and its ability to feed more people, irrigated agriculture fuels population growth. This in turn leads to enlargement of the system. The expanding hydraulic system supports larger and denser concentrations of people. Conflicts over access to water and irrigated land become more frequent. Political authorities may arise to regulate production, as well as interpersonal and intergroup relations. Large hydraulic works can sustain towns and cities and become essential to their subsistence. Regulators protect the economy by mobilizing crews to maintain and repair the hydraulic system. These life-and-death functions enhance the authority of state officials. Thus, growth in hydraulic systems is often (as in Mesopotamia, Egypt, and the Valley of Mexico), but not always, associated with state formation.

## Long-Distance Trade Routes

Another theory is that states arise at strategic locations in regional trade networks. These sites include points of supply or exchange, such as crossroads of caravan routes, and places (e.g., mountain passes and river narrows) situated to threaten or halt trade between centers. Here again, however, the cause is generalized but neither necessary nor sufficient. Long-distance trade has been important in the evolution of many states, including those of Mesopotamia and Mesoamerica. Such exchange does develop eventually in all states, but it can follow rather than precede state formation. Furthermore, long-distance trade also occurs in societies where no states developed, such as those of Papua New Guinea.

## Population, War, and Circumscription

Robert Carneiro (1970) put forth an influential theory that incorporates three factors working together instead of a single cause of state formation. (We call a theory involving multiple factors or variables a **multivariate** theory.) Wherever and whenever *environmental circumscription* (or *resource concentration*), *increasing population,* and *warfare* exist, suggested Carneiro, state formation will begin. Environmental circumscription may be physical or social. Physically circumscribed environments include small islands and, in arid areas, river plains, oases, and valleys with streams. Social circumscription exists when neighboring societies block expansion, emigration, or access to resources. When strategic resources are concentrated in limited areas—even when no obstacles to migration exist—the effects are similar to those of circumscription.

Coastal Peru, one of the world's most arid areas, illustrates the interaction of environmental circumscription, warfare, and population increase. The earliest cultivation there was limited to valleys with springs. Each valley was circumscribed by the Andes Mountains to the east, the Pacific Ocean to the west, and desert regions to the north and south. The advent of food production triggered population increase (Figure 8-1). In each valley, villages got bigger. Colonists split off from the old villages and founded new ones. With more villages and people, a scarcity of land developed. Rivalries and raiding developed among villages in the same valley.

Population pressure and land shortages were developing in all the valleys. Because the valleys were circumscribed, when one village conquered another, the losers had to submit to the winners—they had nowhere else to go. Conquered villagers could keep their land only if they agreed to pay tribute to their conquerors. To do this, they had to intensify production, using new techniques to produce more food. By working harder, they managed to pay tribute while meeting their own subsistence needs. Villagers brought new areas under cultivation by means of irrigation and terracing.

Those early inhabitants of the Andes didn't work harder because they chose to do so. They were *forced* to pay tribute, accept political domination, and intensify production by factors beyond their control. Once established, all these trends accelerated. Population grew, warfare intensified, and villages eventually were united in chiefdoms. The first states developed when one chiefdom in a valley conquered the others (Carneiro 1990). Eventually, different valleys began to fight. The winners brought the losers into growing states and empires, which eventually expanded from the coast to the highlands. By the 16th century, from their capital, Cuzco, in the high Andes, the Inca ruled one of the major empires of the tropics.

Carneiro's theory is very useful, but again, the association between population density and state organization is generalized rather than universal. States do tend to have large and dense populations (Stevenson 1968). However, population increase and warfare within a circumscribed environment did not trigger state formation in highland Papua New Guinea. Certain valleys there are socially or physically circumscribed and have population densities similar to those of many states. Warfare also was present, but no states emerged. Again, we are dealing with an important theory that explains many but not all cases of state formation.

Early states arose in different places, and for many reasons. In each case, interacting causes (often comparable ones) magnified each other's effects. To explain any instance of state formation, we must search for the specific changes in access to resources and in regulatory problems that fostered stratification and state machinery. We must remember also that chiefdoms and states don't inevitably arise from food production. Anthropologists know of, and have studied, many societies that maintained Neolithic economies without ever developing chiefdoms or states. Similarly there are chiefdoms that never developed into states, just as there are foragers who never adopted food production, even when they knew about it. Recall from the last chapter those early food producers in what is now the eastern United States who had to keep on hunting and gathering for the bulk of their subsistence because the foods they had domesticated (e.g., sunflower, marsh elder) could not provide a complete diet.

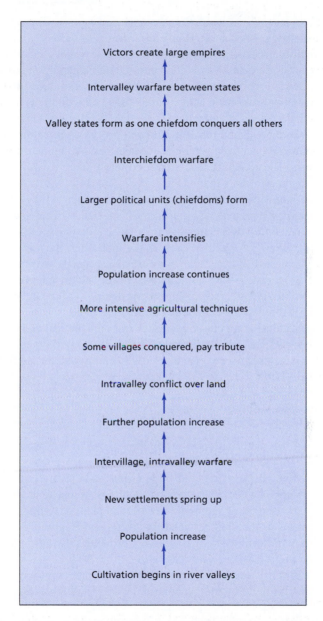

**FIGURE 8-1**    *Carneiro's Multivariate Approach to the Origin of the State as Applied to Coastal Peru*  In this very arid area, food production developed in narrow river valleys where water for cultivation was available (resource concentration). With cultivation, the population increased. Population pressure on land led to warfare, and some villages conquered others. Physical circumscription meant that the losers had no way to escape. The process accelerated as the population grew and as warfare and cultivation intensified. Chiefdoms, states, and empires eventually developed.

# ❖ ATTRIBUTES OF STATES

Certain attributes distinguished states from earlier forms of society:

1. A state controls a specific territory, such as the Nile Valley or the Valley of Mexico. The large expanse of a state contrasts with the much smaller territories controlled by kin groups and villages in prestate societies. Early states were expansionist; they arose from competition among chiefdoms, as the most powerful chiefdom conquered others, extended its rule over a larger territory, and managed to hold on to, and rule, the land and people acquired through conquest.

2. Early states had productive farming economies, supporting dense populations, often in cities. The agricultural economies of early states usually involved some form of water control or irrigation.

3. Early states used tribute and taxation to accumulate, at a central place, resources needed to support hundreds, or thousands, of specialists. These states had rulers, a military, and control over human labor.

4. States are stratified into social classes. In the first states, the non-food-producing population consisted of a tiny elite, plus artisans, officials, priests, and other specialists. Most people were commoners. Slaves and prisoners constituted the lowest rung of the social ladder. Rulers stayed in power by combining personal ability, religious authority, economic control, and force.

5. Early states had imposing public buildings and monumental architecture, including temples, palaces, and storehouses.

6. Early states developed some form of record-keeping system, usually a written script. (Fagan 1996)

# ❖ STATE FORMATION IN THE MIDDLE EAST

In the last chapter we saw that food production arose in the ancient Middle East around 10,000 B.P. In the ensuing process of change, the center of population growth shifted from the zone where wheat and barley grew wild (Hilly Flanks) to adjacent areas (piedmont steppe) where those grains were first domesticated. By 6000 B.P., population was increasing most rapidly in the alluvial plain of southern Mesopotamia. (**Mesopotamia** refers to the area between the Tigris and Euphrates rivers in what is now southern Iraq and southwestern Iran.) This growing population supported itself through irrigation and intensive river valley agriculture. By 5500 B.P. towns had grown into cities (Gates 2003). The earliest city-states were Sumer (southern Iraq) and Elam (southwestern Iran), with their capitals at Uruk (Warka) and Susa, respectively.

## Urban Life

The first towns arose around 10,000 years ago in the Middle East. Over the generations houses of mud brick were built and rebuilt in the same place. Substantial *tells* or mounds arose from the debris of a succession of such houses. The Middle East and Asia have thousands of such mounds, only a few of which have been excavated. These sites have yielded remains of ancient community life, including streets, buildings, terraces, court-yards, wells, and other artifacts.

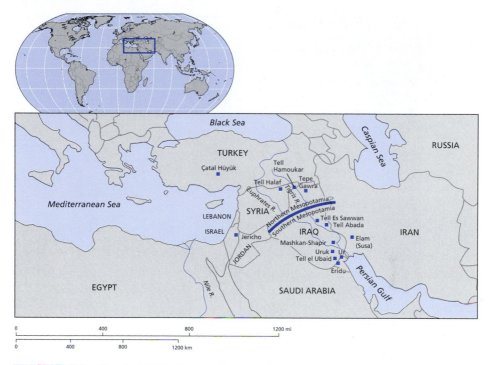

**FIGURE 8-2**   *Sites in Middle Eastern State Formation*

The earliest known town was Jericho, located in what now is Israel, below sea level at a well-watered oasis (Figure 8-2). From the lowest (oldest) level, we know that around 11,000 years ago, Jericho was first settled by Natufian foragers. Occupation continued thereafter, through and beyond biblical times, when "Joshua fit the battle of Jericho, and the walls came tumbling down" (Laughlin 2006).

During the phase just after the Natufians, the earliest known town appeared. It was an unplanned, densely populated settlement with round houses and some 2,000 people. At this time, well before the invention of pottery, Jericho was surrounded by a sturdy wall, with a massive tower. The wall may have been built initially as a flood barrier rather than for defense. Around 9000 B.P. Jericho was destroyed, to be rebuilt later. The new occupants lived in square houses with finished plaster floors. They buried their dead beneath their homes, a pattern seen at other sites, such as Çatal Hüyük in Turkey (see below). Pottery reached Jericho around 8000 B.P. (Gowlett 1993).

Long-distance trade, especially of obsidian, a volcanic glass used to make tools and ornaments, became important in the Middle East between 9500 and 7000 B.P. One town that prospered from this trade was Çatal Hüyük in Anatolia, Turkey (DeMarco 1997). A grassy mound 65 feet (20 meters) high holds the remains of this 9,000-year-old town, probably the largest settlement of the Neolithic age. Çatal Hüyük was located on a river, which deposited rich soil for crops, created a lush environment for animals, and was harnessed for irrigation by 7000 B.P. Over the mound's 32 acres (12.9 hectares), up

The world's earliest known town was Jericho, located in what is now Israel.
Jericho was first settled by Natufian foragers around 11,000 B.P. This round tower
dates back 8,000 years.

to 10,000 people once lived in crowded mud-brick houses packed so tight that residents
entered from their roofs.

Shielded by a defensive wall, Çatal Hüyük flourished between 8000 and 7000 B.P.
Its individual mud-brick dwellings, rarely larger than a suburban American bedroom,
had separate areas reserved for ritual and secular uses. In a given house, the ritual images
(wall paintings) were placed along the walls that faced north, east, or west, but never
south. That area was reserved for cooking and other domestic tasks. The dwellings at
Çatal Hüyük were entered through the roof, and people had to crawl through holes from
room to room, somewhat like moving between chambers of a cave.

Two or three generations of a family were buried beneath their homes. In one
dwelling, archaeologists found remains of 17 individuals, mostly children. After two or
three generations of family burials, the dwelling was burned. The site was then covered
with fine dirt, and a floor laid for a new dwelling.

Çatal Hüyük's residents, though living in a town, acted independently in family
groups without any apparent control by a priestly or political elite. The town never
became a full-fledged city with centralized organization. Just as it lacked priests,

Çatal Hüyük never had leaders who controlled or managed trade and production (Fagan 1996). Food was stored and processed not collectively, but on a smaller, domestic scale (DeMarco 1997).

## The Elite Level

The first pottery (ceramics) dates back a bit more than 8,000 years, when it first reached Jericho. Before that date, the Neolithic is called the prepottery Neolithic. By 7000 B.P., pottery had become widespread in the Middle East. Archaeologists consider pottery shape, finishing, decoration, and type of clay as features used for dating. The geographic distribution of a given pottery style may indicate trade or alliance spanning a large area at a particular time.

An early and widespread pottery style, the **Halafian,** was first found at Tell Halaf in the mountains of northern Syria. Halafian (7500–6500 B.P.) refers to a delicate ceramic style. It also describes the period during which the elite level and the first chiefdoms emerged. The low number of Halafian ceramics suggests they were luxury goods associated with a social hierarchy.

By 7000 B.P. chiefdoms had emerged in the Middle East. The Ubaid period (7000–6000 B.P.) is named for a southern Mesopotamian pottery type first discovered at a small site, Tell el-Ubaid, located near the major city of Ur in southern Iraq. Similar pottery has been discovered in the deep levels of the Mesopotamian cities of Ur, Uruk, and Eridu. Ubaid pottery is associated with advanced chiefdoms and perhaps the earliest states. It diffused rapidly over a large area, becoming more widespread than earlier ceramic styles such as the Halafian.

## Social Ranking and Chiefdoms

It is easy for archaeologists to identify early states. Evidence for state organization includes monumental architecture, central storehouses, irrigation systems, and written records. In Mesoamerica, chiefdoms are easy to detect archaeologically. Ancient Mexican chiefdoms left behind stone works, such as temple complexes and the huge carved Olmec heads. Mesoamericans also had a penchant for marking their elites with durable ornaments and prestige goods, including those buried with chiefs and their families. Early Middle Eastern chiefs were less ostentatious in their use of material markers of prestige, making their chiefdoms somewhat harder to detect archaeologically (Flannery 1999).

On the basis of the kinds of status distinctions within society, the anthropologist Morton Fried (1960) divided societies into three types: egalitarian, ranked, and stratified. An **egalitarian society,** most typically found among foragers, lacks status distinctions except for those based on age, gender, and individual qualities, talents, and achievements. Thus, depending on the society, adult men, elder women, talented musicians, or ritual specialists might receive special respect for their activities or knowledge. In egalitarian societies, status distinctions usually are not inherited. The child of a respected person will not receive special recognition because of his or her parent, but must earn such respect.

**Ranked societies,** in contrast, do have hereditary inequality. But they lack **stratification** (sharp social divisions—*strata*—based on unequal access to wealth and power) into noble and commoner classes. In ranked societies, individuals tend to be ranked in terms of their genealogical distance from the chief. Closer relatives of the chief have higher rank or social status than more distant ones do. But there is a continuum of status, with many individuals and kin groups ranked about equally, which can lead to competition for positions of leadership.

Not all ranked societies are chiefdoms. Robert Carneiro (1991) has distinguished between two kinds of ranked societies, only the second of which is a chiefdom. In the first type, exemplified by some Indians of North America's Pacific Northwest, there were hereditary differences in rank among individuals, but villages were independent of one another and not ranked in relation to each other. Exemplifying the second type were the Cauca of Colombia and the Natchez of the southeastern United States. These ranked societies had become **chiefdoms,** societies in which relations among villages as well as among individuals were unequal. The smaller villages had lost their autonomy and were under the authority of leaders who lived at larger villages. According to Kent Flannery (1999), *only those ranked societies with such loss of village autonomy should be called chiefdoms.* In chiefdoms, there always is inequality—differences in rank—among both individuals and communities.

In Mesopotamia, Mesoamerica, and Peru, chiefdoms were precursors to **primary states** (states that arose on their own, and not through contact with other state societies—see Wright 1994). Primary states emerged from competition among chiefdoms, as one chiefdom managed to conquer its neighbors and to make them part of a larger political unit (Flannery 1995).

Archaeological evidence for chiefdoms in Mesoamerica dates back more than 3,000 years. Mesoamerican chiefdoms are easy to detect archaeologically because they were flamboyant in the way they marked their aristocracy. High-status families deformed the heads of their infants and buried them with special symbols and grave goods. In burials, prestige goods show a continuum from graves with many, to less, to none, of precious materials, such as jade and turquoise (Flannery 1999).

The first Middle Eastern states developed between 6000 and 5500 B.P. The first societies based on rank, including the first chiefdoms, emerged during the preceding 1,500 years. In the Middle East, the archaeological record of the period after 7300 B.P. reveals behavior typical of chiefdoms, including exotic goods used as markers of status, along with raiding and political instability. Early Middle Eastern chiefdoms included both the Halafian culture of northern Iraq and the Ubaid culture of southern Iraq, which eventually spread north.

As in Mesoamerica, ancient Middle Eastern chiefdoms had cemeteries where chiefly relatives were buried with distinctive items: vessels, statuettes, necklaces, and high-quality ceramics. Such goods were buried with children too young to have earned prestige on their own, but who happened to be born into elite families. In the ancient village of Tell es-Sawwan, infant graves show a continuum of richness from six statuettes, to three statuettes, to one statuette, to none. Such signs of slight gradations in social status are exactly what one expects in ranked societies (Flannery 1999).

Such burials convince Flannery (1999) that hereditary status differences were present in the Middle East by 7000 B.P. But had the leaders of large villages extended their authority to the smaller villages nearby? Is there evidence for the loss of village autonomy, converting simple ranked societies into chiefdoms? One clue that villages were linked in political units is the use of a common canal to irrigate several villages. This suggests a way of resolving disputes among farmers over access to water, for example, by appeal to a strong leader. By later Halafian times in northern Mesopotamia, there is evidence for such multivillage alliances (Flannery 1999). Another clue to the loss of village autonomy is the emergence of a two-tier settlement hierarchy, with small villages clustering around a large village, especially one with public buildings. There is evidence for this pattern in northern Mesopotamia during the Halafian period (Watson 1983).

## Advanced Chiefdoms

In northeastern Syria, near the border with Iraq, archaeologists have been excavating an ancient settlement that once lay on a major trade route. This large site, Tell Hamoukar, dates back more than 5,500 years (Wilford 2000). Its remains suggest that advanced chiefdoms arose in northern areas of the Middle East independently of the better-known city-states of southern Mesopotamia, in southern Iraq (Wilford 2000).

The oldest layer yet uncovered at Tell Hamoukar contains traces of villages dating back 6,000 years. By 5700 B.P. the settlement was a prosperous town of 32 acres (13 hectares) enclosed by a defensive wall 10 feet high and 13 feet wide (3 meters high and 4 meters wide). The site had fine pottery and large ovens—evidence of food preparation on an institutional scale. The site has yielded pieces of large cooking pots, animal bones, and traces of wheat, barley, and oats for baking and brewing. The archaeologist McGuire Gibson, one of the excavators, believes that food preparation on this scale is evidence of a ranked society in which elites were organizing people and resources (Wilford 2000). Most likely they were hosting and entertaining in a chiefly manner.

Also providing evidence for social ranking are the seals used to mark containers of food and other goods. Some of the seals are small, with only simple incisions or cross-hatching. Others are larger and more elaborate, presumably for higher officials to stamp more valuable goods. Gibson suspects the larger seals with figurative scenes were held by the few people who had greater authority. The smaller, simply incised seals were used by many more people with less authority (Wilford 2000).

## The Rise of the State

In southern Mesopotamia at this time (5700 B.P.), an expanding population and increased food production from irrigation were changing the social landscape even more drastically than in the north. Irrigation had allowed Ubaid communities to spread along the Euphrates River. Travel and trade were expanding, with water serving as the highway system. Such raw materials as hardwood and stone, which southern Mesopotamia lacked, were imported via river routes. Population density increased as new settlements appeared. Social and economic networks now linked communities on the rivers in the south and in the foothills to the north. Settlements spread north into what is now Syria. Social differentials also increased. Priests and political leaders joined expert potters and other specialists. These non-food-producers were supported by the larger population of farmers and herders (Gilmore-Lehne 2000).

Economies were being managed by central leadership. Agricultural villages had grown into cities, some of which were ruled by local kings. The Uruk period (6000–5200 B.P.), which succeeded the Ubaid period, takes its name from a prominent southern city-state located more than 400 miles (644 kilometers) south of Tell Hamoukar (Table 8-1). The Uruk period established Mesopotamia as "the cradle of civilization" (see Pollock 1999).

There is no evidence of Uruk influence at Tell Hamoukar until 5200 B.P., when some Uruk pottery showed up. When southern Mesopotamians expanded north, they found advanced chiefdoms, which were not yet states. The fact that writing originated in Sumer, in southern Mesopotamia, indicates a more advanced, state-organized society there. The first writing presumably developed to handle record keeping for a centralized economy.

Writing initially was used to keep accounts, reflecting the needs of trade. Rulers, nobles, priests, and merchants were the first to benefit from it. Writing spread from Mesopotamia to Egypt by 5000 B.P. The earliest writing was pictographic, for example, with pictorial symbols of horses used to represent them. Early Mesopotamian scribes used a stylus (writing implement) to scrawl symbols on raw clay. This writing left a wedge-shaped impression on the clay, called **cuneiform** writing, from the Latin word for "wedge." Both the Sumerian (southern Mesopotamia) and Akkadian (northern Mesopotamia) languages were written in cuneiform (Gowlett 1993).

Writing and temples played key roles in the Mesopotamian economy. For the historic period after 5600 B.P., when writing was invented, there are temple records of

## TABLE 8-1

### Archaeological Periods in Middle Eastern State Formation

| Dates | Period | Age |
|---|---|---|
| 3000–2539 B.P. | Neo-Babylonian | Iron Age |
| 3600–3000 B.P. | Kassite | |
| 4000–3600 B.P. | Old Babylonian | Bronze Age |
| 4150–4000 B.P. | Third Dynasty of Ur | |
| 4350–4150 B.P. | Akkadian | |
| 4600–4350 B.P. | Early Dynastic III | |
| 4750–4600 B.P. | Early Dynastic II | |
| 5000–4750 B.P. | Early Dynastic I | |
| 5200–5000 B.P. | Jemdet Nasr | |
| 6000–5200 B.P. | Uruk | Chalcolithic |
| 7500–6000 B.P. | Ubaid (southern Mesopotamia)–<br>Halaf (northern Mesopotamia) | |
| 10,000–7000 B.P. | | Neolithic |

Early Mesopotamian scribes used a stylus to scrawl symbols on raw clay. This writing, called *cuneiform,* left a wedge-shaped impression on the clay. What languages were written in cuneiform?

economic activities. States can exist without writing, but literacy facilitates the flow and storage of information. As the economy expanded, trade, manufacture, herding, and grain storage were centrally managed. Temples collected and distributed meat, dairy products, crops, fish, clothing, tools, and trade items. Potters, metalworkers, weavers, sculptors, and other artisans perfected their crafts.

Prior to the invention of **metallurgy** (knowledge of the properties of metals, including their extraction and processing and the manufacture of metal tools), raw copper was shaped by hammering. If copper is hammered too long, it hardens and becomes brittle, with a risk of cracking. But once heated (annealed) in a fire, copper becomes malleable again. Such annealing of copper was an early form of metallurgy. A vital step for metallurgy was the discovery of **smelting,** the high-temperature process by which pure metal is produced from an ore. Ores, including copper ore, have a much wider distribution than does native copper, which initially was traded as a luxury good because of its rarity (Gowlett 1993).

When and how smelting was discovered is unknown. But after 5000 B.P., metal-lurgy evolved rapidly. The Bronze Age began when alloys of arsenic and copper, or tin and copper (in both cases known as **bronze**), became common and greatly extended the use of metals. Bronze flows more easily than copper does when heated to a similar temperature, so bronze was more convenient for metal casting. Early molds were carved in stone, as shaped depressions to be filled with molten metal. A copper ax cast from such a mold has been found in northern Mesopotamia and predates 5000 B.P. Thereafter, other metals came into common use. By 4500 B.P. golden objects were found in royal burials at Ur.

Iron ore is distributed more widely than is copper ore. Iron, when smelted, can be used on its own; there is no need for tin or arsenic to make a metal alloy (bronze). The Iron Age began once high-temperature iron smelting was mastered. In the Old World after 3200 B.P. iron spread rapidly. Formerly valued as highly as gold, iron crashed in value when it became plentiful (Gowlett 1993).

The Mesopotamian economy, based on craft production, trade, and intensive agriculture, spurred population growth and an increase in urbanism. Sumerian cities were protected by a fortress wall and surrounded by a farming area. By 4800 B.P., Uruk, the largest early Mesopotamian city, had a population of 50,000. As irrigation and the population expanded, communities fought over water. People sought protection in the fortified cities (Adams 1981), which defended themselves when neighbors or invad-ers threatened.

By 4600 B.P., secular authority had replaced temple rule. The office of military coordinator developed into kingship. This change shows up architecturally in palaces and royal tombs. The palace raised armies and supplied them with armor, chariots, and metal armaments. At Ur's royal cemetery, by 4600 B.P. monarchs were being buried with soldiers, charioteers, and ladies in waiting. These subordinates were killed at the time of royal burial to accompany the monarch to the afterworld.

Agricultural intensification made it possible for the number of people supported by a given area to increase. Population pressure on irrigated fields helped create a strati-fied society. Land became scarce private property that was bought and sold. Some peo-ple amassed large estates, and their wealth set them off from ordinary farmers. These landlords joined the urban elite, while sharecroppers and serfs toiled in the fields. By 4600 B.P., Mesopotamia had a well-defined class structure, with complex stratification into nobles, commoners, and slaves.

## ❖ OTHER EARLY STATES

In northwestern India and Pakistan, the Indus River Valley (or *Harappan*) state, with major cities at Harappa and Mohenjo-daro, takes its name from the river valley along which it extended. (Figure 8-3 maps the four great early river-valley states of the Old World: Mesopotamia, Egypt, India/Pakistan, and northern China.) Trade and the spread of writing from Mesopotamia may have played a role in the emergence of the Harap-pan state around 4600 B.P. Located in Pakistan's Punjab Province, the ruins of Harappa were the first to be identified as part of the Indus River Valley civilization. At its peak,

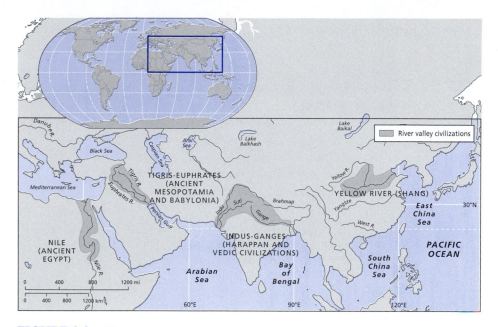

**FIGURE 8-3**   *The Four Great Early River-Valley States of the Old World*   By approximately 4000 B.P. urban life had been established along the Tigris and Euphrates rivers in Mesopotamia, the Nile River in Egypt, the Indus and Ganges rivers in India/Pakistan, and the Yellow River in China.

*SOURCE:* Based on Map 1-1, Chapter 1, "Birth of Civilization," in A. M. Craig, W. A. Graham, et al, *The Heritage of World Civilizations, Volume I, to 1650,* 4th ed. (Upper Saddle River, NJ: Pearson Education, 1997). Adapted by permission.

the Indus River Valley state incorporated 1,000 cities, towns, and villages, spanning 280,000 square miles (725,000 square kilometers). This state flourished between 4600 and 3900 B.P. It displayed such features of state organization as urban planning, social stratification, and an early writing system, which remains undeciphered. The Harappans maintained a uniform system of weights, and their cities had carefully planned residential areas with wastewater systems. An array of products from sophisticated craft industries included ceramic vessels made on potter's wheels (Meadow and Kenoyer 2000).

The Indus River Valley state collapsed, apparently through warfare, around 3900 B.P. Its cities became largely depopulated. Skeletons of massacre victims have been found in the streets of Mohenjo-daro. Harappa continued to be occupied, but on a much smaller scale than previously (Meadow and Kenoyer 2000).

The first Chinese state, dating to 3750 B.P., was that of the Shang dynasty. It arose in the Huang He (Yellow) River area of northern China, where wheat was the dietary staple. This state was characterized by urbanism, palatial (as well as domestic) architecture, human sacrifice, and a sharp division between social classes. Burials of the aristocracy were marked by ornaments of stone, including jade. The Shang had bronze metallurgy and an elaborate writing system. In warfare they used chariots and took prisoners (Gowlett 1993; Trigger 2003).

This bronze vessel was commissioned during China's Shang
dynasty. The small elephant on top forms the handle of the lid. Wine
was poured through the spout formed by the big elephant's trunk.
Three notable features of the Shang dynasty were bronze, writing,
and social stratification.

Like Mesopotamia and China, many early civilizations came to rely on metallurgy. At Nok Nok Tha in northern Thailand, metalworking goes back 6,000 years. In
Peru's Andes metalworking appeared around 4000 B.P. The ancient inhabitants of the
Andes were skilled workers of bronze, copper, and gold. They also are well known
for their techniques of pottery manufacture. Their arts, crafts, and agricultural knowledge compared well with those of Mesoamerica at its height, to which we now turn.
Note that both Mesoamerican and Andean state formation were truncated by Spanish
conquest. The Aztecs of Mexico were conquered in A.D. 1519; and the Inca of Peru,
in 1532.

## ✦ STATE FORMATION IN MESOAMERICA

In the last chapter we examined the independent inventions of farming in the Middle
East and Mesoamerica. The processes of state formation that took place in these areas
also were comparable, beginning with ranked societies and chiefdoms, and ending with
fully formed states and empires. The first monumental buildings (temple complexes) in
the Western Hemisphere were constructed by Mesoamerican chiefdoms in many areas,
from the Valley of Mexico to Guatemala. These chiefdoms influenced one another as
they traded materials, such as obsidian, shells, jade, and pottery. (Figure 8-4 maps major
sites in the emergence of Mesoamerican food production, chiefdoms, and states.)

**FIGURE 8-4**    *Major Sites in the Emergence of Food Production and the State in Mesoamerica*

SOURCE: From C. J. Jolly and R. White, *Physical Anthropology and Archaeology,* 5th ed., (New York: McGraw-Hill, 1995), p. 115. Reprinted by permission of the McGraw-Hill companies.

## Early Chiefdoms and Elites

The Olmec built a series of ritual centers on Mexico's southern Gulf Coast between 3,200 and 2,500 years ago. Three of these centers, each from a different century, are known. Earthen mounds were grouped into plaza complexes, presumably for religious use. Such centers show that Olmec chiefs could marshal human labor to construct such mounds. The Olmec were also master sculptors; they carved massive stone heads, perhaps as images of their chiefs or their ancestors.

There is evidence, too, that trade routes linked the Olmec with other parts of Mesoamerica, such as the Valley of Oaxaca in the southern highlands and the Valley of Mexico (see Figure 8-4). By 3000 B.P. a ruling elite had emerged in Oaxaca. The items traded at that time between Oaxaca and the Olmec were for elite consumption. High-status Oaxacans wore ornaments made of mussel shells from the coast. In return, the Olmec elite imported mirrors and jade made by Oaxacan artisans. Chiefdoms in Oaxaca developed canal and well irrigation, exported magnetite mirrors, and used adobes (mud bricks), stucco, and stone masonry. Chiefdoms in the Olmec area farmed river levees, built mounds of earth, and carved colossal stone heads.

The Olmec are famous for their huge carved stone heads, but other early Mexican chiefdoms also had accomplished artists and builders, who used adobes and lime plaster and constructed stone buildings, precisely oriented 8 degrees north of east. The period between 3200 and 3000 B.P. was one of rapid social change in Mexico. Mesoamerica's chiefdoms were linked by trade and exchange. Many competing chiefly centers were intensifying agriculture, exchanging trade goods, and borrowing ideas, including art motifs and styles, from each other. Archaeologists now believe it was the *intensity of competitive interaction*—rather than the supremacy of any one chiefdom—that made social change so rapid. The social and political landscape of Mexico around 3000 B.P. was one in which 25 or so chiefly centers were (1) sufficiently separate and autonomous to adapt to local zones and conditions; and (2) sufficiently interacting and competitive to borrow and incorporate new ideas and innovations as they arose in other regions (Flannery and Marcus 2000).

It used to be thought that a single chiefdom could become a state on its own. Archaeologists know now that state formation involves one chiefdom incorporating several others into the emerging state it controls, and making changes in its own infrastructure as it acquires and holds on to new territories, followers, and goods. Warfare and attracting followers are two key elements in state formation.

Many chiefdoms have dense populations, intensive agriculture, and settlement hierarchies that include hamlets, villages, and perhaps towns. These factors pave the way for greater social and political complexity. Political leaders emerge, and military success (in raiding) often solidifies their position. Such figures attract lots of followers, who are loyal to their leader. Warfare enables leaders to incorporate new lands and people. Success in warfare leads to states becoming even more densely occupied and in control of new lands. States, unlike chiefdoms, can acquire labor and land and hold on to them. States have armies, warfare, developed political hierarchies, law codes, and military force, which can be used in fact or as a threat.

The Olmec and Oaxaca were just two of many flamboyant early Mexican chiefdoms that once thrived in the area from the Valley of Mexico to Guatemala. Oaxaca went on to develop a state as early as the Teotihuacan state in the Valley of Mexico. Oaxaca and other highland areas came to overshadow the Olmec area and the Mesoamerican lowlands in general. By 2500 B.P. the Zapotec state at Oaxaca had developed a distinctive art style, perfected at its capital city of Monte Alban. The Zapotec state lasted almost 2,000 years, until it—along with the rest of Mexico—was conquered by Spain (see Blanton 1999; Marcus and Flannery 1996).

As the Olmec chiefdoms were declining, the elite level was spreading throughout Mesoamerica. By A.D. 1 (2000 B.P.), the Valley of Mexico, located in the highlands where Mexico City now stands, came to prominence in Mesoamerican state formation. In this large valley **Teotihuacan** flourished between 1900 and 1300 B.P. (A.D. 100 and 700).

## States in the Valley of Mexico

The Valley of Mexico is a large basin surrounded by mountains. The valley has rich volcanic soils, but rainfall isn't always reliable. The northern part of the valley, where the huge city and state of Teotihuacan eventually arose, is colder and drier than the south. Frosts there limited farming until quick-growing varieties of maize were developed. Until 2500 B.P., most people lived in the warmer and wetter southern part of the valley, where rainfall made farming possible. After 2500 B.P., new maize varieties and small-scale irrigation appeared. Population increased and began to spread north.

By A.D. 1 Teotihuacan was a town of 10,000 people. It governed a territory of a few thousand square kilometers and perhaps 50,000 people (Parsons 1974). Teotihuacan's growth reflected its agricultural potential. Perpetual springs permitted irrigation of a large alluvial plain. Rural farmers supplied food for the growing urban population.

By this time, a clear **settlement hierarchy** had emerged. This is a ranked series of communities that differ in size, function, and building types. The settlements at the top of the hierarchy were political and religious centers. Those at the bottom were rural villages. Such a three-level settlement hierarchy (capital city, smaller urban centers, and rural villages) provides archaeological evidence of state organization (Wright and Johnson 1975).

The Pyramid of the Sun, Teotihuacan's largest structure, is shown in the upper part of the photo. At its height around A.D. 500, Teotihuacan was larger than imperial Rome. The mobilization of manual labor to build such structures is one of the costs of state organization.

Along with state organization went large-scale irrigation, status differentiation, and complex architecture. Teotihuacan thrived between A.D. 100 and 700. It grew as a planned city built on a grid pattern, with the Pyramid of the Sun at its center. By A.D. 500, the population of Teotihuacan had reached 130,000, making it larger than imperial Rome. Farmers were one of its diverse specialized groups, along with artisans, merchants, and political, religious, and military personnel.

After A.D. 700 Teotihuacan declined in size and power. By A.D. 900 its population had shrunk to 30,000. Between A.D. 900 and 1200, the Toltec period, the population scattered, and small cities and towns sprang up throughout the valley. People also left the Valley of Mexico to live in larger cities—like Tula, the Toltec capital—on its edge (see Figure 8-4).

Population increase (including immigration by the ancestors of the Aztecs) and urban growth returned to the Valley of Mexico between A.D. 1200 and 1520. During the **Aztec** period (A.D. 1325 to 1520) there were several cities, the largest of which— Tenochtitlan, the capital—may have surpassed Teotihuacan at its height. A dozen Aztec towns had more than 10,000 people. Fueling this population growth was intensification of agriculture, particularly in the southern part of the valley, where the drainage of lake bottoms and swamps added new cultivable land (Parsons 1976).

Another factor in the renaissance of the Valley of Mexico was trade. Local manufacture created products for a series of markets. The major towns and markets were located on the lake shores, with easy access to canoe traffic. The Aztec capital stood on an island in the lake. In Tenochtitlan, the production of luxury goods was more prestigious and more highly organized than that of pottery, basket making, and weaving. Luxury producers, such as stone workers, feather workers, and gold- and silversmiths, occupied a special position in Aztec society. The manufacture of luxury goods for export was an important part of the economy of the Aztec capital (Hassig 1985; Santley 1985).

## ✦ Why States Collapse

States can be fragile and decomposable, falling apart along the same cleavage lines (e.g., regional political units) that were forged together to form the state originally. Various factors could threaten their economies and political institutions. Invasion, disease, famine, or prolonged drought could upset the balance. A state's citizens might harm the environment, usually with economic costs. For example, farmers and smelters might cut down trees. Such deforestation promotes erosion and leads to a decline in the water supply. Overuse of land may deplete the soil of the nutrients needed to grow crops.

### The Mayan Decline

Generations of scholars have debated the decline of classic Mayan civilization around A.D. 900 (1700–1100 B.P.). Classic Mayan culture, featuring several competing states, flourished between A.D. 300 and 900 in parts of what are now Mexico, Honduras, El Salvador, Guatemala, and Belize. The ancient Maya are known for their monuments (temples and pyramids), calendars, mathematics, and hieroglyphic writing.

The major archaeological site of Tikal in verdant Guatemala.

Archaeological clues to Mayan decline have been found at Copán, in western Honduras. This classic Mayan royal center, the largest site in the southeastern part of the Mayan area, covered 29 acres. It was built on an artificial terrace overlooking the Copán River. Its rulers inscribed their monuments with accounts of their coronation, their lineage history, and reports of important battles. The Maya dated their monuments with the names of kings and when they reigned. One monument at Copán was intended to be the ruler's throne platform, but only one side had been finished. The monument bears a date, A.D. 822, in a section of unfinished text. Copán has no monuments with later dates. The site probably was abandoned by A.D. 830.

Environmental factors implicated in Copán's demise may have included erosion and soil exhaustion due to overpopulation and overfarming. Overfarming contributes to deforestation and erosion. Hillside farmhouses in particular had debris from erosion—erosion probably caused by overfarming of the hillsides that began as early as A.D. 750—that caused many farm sites to be abandoned, with some eventually buried by erosion debris. Food stress and malnutrition were clearly present at Copán, where 80 percent of the buried skeletons display signs of anemia, due to iron deficiency. One skull shows anemia severe enough to have been the cause of death. Even the nobility were malnourished. One noble skull, known to be such from its carved teeth and cosmetic deformation, also has telltale signs of anemia: spongy areas at its rear (Annenberg/CPB Exhibits 2000).

Just as the origins of states, and their causes, are diverse, so are the reasons for state decline. The Mayan state was not as powerful as once was assumed; it was fragile and vulnerable. Increased warfare and political competition destabilized many of its dynasties and governments. Archaeologists now stress the role of warfare in Mayan state decline. Hieroglyphic texts document increased warfare among many Mayan cities. From the period just before the collapse, there is archaeological evidence for increased concern with fortifications (moats, ditches, walls, and palisades) and moving to defensible locations. Archaeologists have evidence of the burning of structures, the projectile points from spears, and some of the bodies of those killed. Some sites were abandoned, with the people fleeing into the forests to occupy perishable huts. (Copán, as we have seen, was depopulated soon after A.D. 822.) Archaeologists now believe that social, political, and military upheaval and competition had as much as or more to do with

## ANTHROPOLOGY TODAY

### Pseudo-Archaeology

The study of prehistory has spawned popular-culture creations, including movies, TV programs, and books. In these fictional works, the anthropologists (and the natives as well) usually don't bear much resemblance to their real-life counterparts. Unlike Indiana Jones, normal and reputable archaeologists don't have nonstop adventures—fighting Nazis, lashing whips, or rescuing antiquities. The archaeologist's profession isn't a matter of raiding lost arks or of going on crusades but of reconstructing lifeways through the analysis of material remains, in order to understand culture and human behavior.

Much of the popular nonfiction dealing with prehistory also is suspect. Through books and the mass media, we have been exposed to the ideas of popular writers such as Thor Heyerdahl and Erich von Daniken. Heyerdahl, a well-known diffusionist, believed that developments in one world area were usually based on ideas borrowed from another. Von Daniken carried diffusionism one step further, proposing that major human achievements had been borrowed from beings from space who have visited us at various periods of our past. Heyerdahl and von Daniken seemed to share (with some science-fiction writers) a certain contempt for human inventiveness

and originality. They took the position that major changes in ancient human life styles were the results of outside instruction or interference rather than the achievements of the natives of the places where the changes took place.

In *The Ra Expeditions* (Heyerdahl 1971), for example, world traveler and adventurer Heyerdahl argued that his voyage in a papyrus boat from the Mediterranean to the Caribbean demonstrated that ancient Egyptians could have navigated to the New World. (The boat was modeled on an ancient Egyptian vessel, but Heyerdahl and his crew took along such modern conveniences as a radio and canned goods.) Heyerdahl maintained that given the possibility of ancient transatlantic voyages, Old World people could have influenced the emergence of civilization in the Americas.

What is the scientific evaluation of Heyerdahl's contention? Even if Old World ancients had reached the New World, they couldn't have done much to propel Native Americans toward state organization because the New World wasn't yet ready for food production and the state. When Egypt became a major power capable of sending scouts across the seas, around 5,000 years ago, Mexicans were broad-spectrum foragers. The gradual nature of the Mesoamerican transition from foraging to food production is demonstrated clearly the Mayan decline and abandonment of cities than did natural environmental factors (Marcus, personal communication).

Formerly archaeologists tended to explain state origin and decline mainly in terms of natural environmental factors, such as climate change, habitat destruction, and demographic pressure (see Weiss 2005). Archaeologists now see state origins and declines more fully—in social and political terms—because we can read the texts. And the Mayan texts document competition and warfare between dynasties jockeying for position and power. Warfare was indeed a creator and a destroyer of ancient chiefdoms and states. What's its role in our own?

by archaeological sequences in such sites as Oaxaca and the Valley of Mexico. Had foreign inputs been important, they would have shown up in the material remains that constitute the archaeological record.

Beginning some 2,000 years ago, states fully comparable to those of Mesopotamia and Egypt began to rise and fall in the Mexican highlands. This occurred more than 1,000 years after the height of ancient Egyptian influence, between 3600 and 3400 B.P. Had Egypt or any other ancient Old World state contributed to the rise or the fall of Mesoamerican civilization, we would expect this influence to have been exerted during Egypt's heyday as an ancient power—not 1,500 years later.

There is abundant archaeological evidence for the gradual, evolutionary emergence of food production and the state in the Middle East, in Mesoamerica, and in Peru. This evidence effectively counters the diffusionist theories about how and why human achievements, including farming and the state, began. Popular theories to the contrary, changes, advances, and setbacks in ancient American social life were the products of the ideas and activities of the Native Americans themselves.

There is no valid evidence for Old World interference before the European Age of Discovery which began late in the 15th century. Francisco Pizzaro conquered Peru's Inca state in 1532, 11 years after its Mesoamerican counterpart, Tenochtitlan, the Aztec capital, fell to Spanish conquistadores in 1521. (We do have abundant archaeological, as well as written, evidence for this recent, historically known contact between Europeans and Native Americans.)

The archaeological record also casts doubt on contentions that the advances of earthlings came with extraterrestrial help, as Erich von Daniken argued in his book *Chariots of the Gods* (1971), and as Discovery-type TV sometimes suggests. Abundant, well-analyzed archaeological data from the Middle East, Mesoamerica, and Peru tell a clear story. Plant and animal domestication, the state, and city life were not brilliant discoveries, inventions, or secrets that humans needed to borrow from extraterrestrials. They were long-term, gradual processes, developments with down-to-earth causes and effects. They required thousands of years of orderly change, not some chance meeting in the high Andes between an ancient Inca chief and a beneficent Johnny Appleseed from Aldebaran.

This is not to deny, by the way, that intelligent life and civilizations at a variety of technological levels—some more, some less advanced than Earth—may exist throughout the galaxy or even that

*Continued*

## ANTHROPOLOGY TODAY

extraterrestrials may have occasionally ventured into this relatively isolated outer spiral arm of the Milky Way galaxy and even visited Earth itself. However, even if extraterrestrials have been on Earth, archaeological evidence suggests that their starship commanders observed a prime directive of noninterference in the affairs of less-advanced planets. There is no scientifically valid evidence for the rapid kind of change that sustained extraterrestrial intervention would have produced.

## SUMMARY

1. States develop to handle regulatory problems as the population grows and the economy gets more complex. Multiple factors contribute to state formation. Some appear repeatedly, but no single factor is always present.

2. A state is a society with a formal, central government and a division of society into classes. The first cities and states, supported by irrigated farming, developed in southern Mesopotamia between 6000 and 5500 B.P. Evidence for early state organization includes monumental architecture, central storehouses, irrigation systems, and written records.

3. Towns predate pottery in the Middle East. The first towns grew up 10,000 to 9,000 years ago. The first pottery dates back just over 8,000 years. Halafian (7500–6500 B.P.) refers to a pottery style and to the period when the first chiefdoms emerged. Ubaid pottery (7000–6000 B.P.) is associated with advanced chiefdoms and perhaps the earliest states. Most state formation occurred during the Uruk period (6100–5100 B.P.).

4. Based on the status distinctions they include, societies may be divided into egalitarian, ranked, and stratified. In egalitarian societies, status distinctions are not usually inherited. Ranked societies have hereditary inequality, but they lack stratification. Stratified societies have sharp social divisions—social classes or strata—based on unequal access to wealth and power. Ranked societies with loss of village autonomy are chiefdoms.

5. Mesopotamia's economy was based on craft production, trade, and intensive agriculture. Writing, invented by 5600 B.P., was first used to keep accounts for trade. With the invention of smelting, the Bronze Age began just after 5000 B.P.

6. In northwestern India and Pakistan, the Indus River Valley state flourished from 4600 to 3900 B.P. The first Chinese state, dating to 3750 B.P., was that of the Shang dynasty in northern China. The major early states of the Western Hemisphere were in Mesoamerica and Peru.

7. States arose between 2500 and 1600 B.P. (500 B.C. and A.D. 400) in Mesoamerica. Between 3,200 and 3,000 B.P., intense competitive interaction among the many chiefdoms in Mesoamerica at that time fueled rapid social change. Some chiefdoms would develop into states (e.g., Oaxaca, Valley of Mexico). Others (e.g., Olmec) would not. By A.D. 1 (2000 B.P.), the Valley of Mexico had come to

prominence. In this large valley in the highlands, Teotihuacan thrived between A.D. 100 and 700. Tenochtitlan, the capital of the Aztec state (A.D. 1325 to 1520), may have surpassed Teotihuacan at its height.

8. States may collapse when they fail to keep social and economic order or to protect themselves against outsiders. The Mayan state fell in the face of increased warfare among competing dynasties.

## KEY TERMS

Aztec (p. 182)

bronze (p. 176)

chiefdoms (p. 172)

cuneiform (p. 174)

egalitarian society (p. 171)

Halafian (p. 171)

Mesopotamia (p. 168)

metallurgy (p. 175)

multivariate (p. 165)

primary states (p. 172)

ranked societies (p. 172)

settlement hierarchy (p. 181)

smelting (p. 175)

state (p. 164)

stratification (p. 172)

Teotihuacan (p. 181)

# CHAPTER 9

# CULTURE

In Chapter 1 we saw that humans share *society,* organized life in groups, with other animals—social animals, such as monkeys, wolves, and ants. Other animals, especially the great apes, have rudimentary cultural abilities, but only humans have fully elaborated cultures—distinctive traditions and customs transmitted over the generations through learning and through language.

The concept of culture has long been basic to anthropology. Well over a century ago, in his book *Primitive Culture,* the British anthropologist Edward Tylor proposed that cultures, systems of human behavior and thought, obey natural laws and therefore can be studied scientifically. Tylor's definition of culture still offers an overview of the subject matter of anthropology and is widely quoted.

"Culture . . . is that complex whole which includes knowledge, belief, arts, morals, law, custom, and any other capabilities and habits acquired by man as a member of society" (Tylor 1871/1958, p. 1). The crucial phrase here is "acquired . . . as a member of society." Tylor's definition focuses on attributes that people acquire not through biological inheritance but by growing up in a particular society in which they are exposed to a specific cultural tradition. **Enculturation** is the process by which a child *learns* his or her culture.

## ✦ WHAT IS CULTURE?

### Culture Is Learned

The ease with which children absorb any cultural tradition rests on the uniquely elaborated human capacity to learn. Other animals may learn from experience, so that, for

Cultures have strikingly different standards of personal space, such as how far apart people should stand in normal encounters and interactions. Contrast the distance between the American businessmen with the closeness, including touching, of the two rabbis in Jerusalem. Have you noticed such differences in your own interactions with others?

example, they avoid fire after discovering that it hurts. Social animals also learn from other members of their group. Wolves, for instance, learn hunting strategies from other pack members. Such social learning is particularly important among monkeys and apes, our closest biological relatives. But our own *cultural learning* depends on the uniquely developed human capacity to use **symbols,** signs that have no necessary or natural connection to the things they stand for or signify.

On the basis of cultural learning, people create, remember, and deal with ideas. They grasp and apply specific systems of symbolic meaning. Anthropologist Clifford Geertz defined culture as ideas based on cultural learning and symbols. Cultures have been characterized as sets of "control mechanisms—plans, recipes, rules, instructions, what computer engineers call programs for the governing of behavior" (Geertz 1973, p. 44). These programs are absorbed by people through enculturation in particular traditions. People gradually internalize a previously established system of meanings and symbols, which helps guide their behavior and perceptions throughout their lives.

Every person begins immediately, through a process of conscious and unconscious learning and interaction with others, to internalize, or incorporate, a cultural tradition through the process of enculturation. Sometimes culture is taught directly, as when parents tell their children to say "thank you" when someone gives them something or does them a favor.

Culture also is transmitted through observation. Children pay attention to the things that go on around them. They modify their behavior not just because other people tell them to do so but as a result of their own observations and growing awareness of what their culture considers right and wrong. Culture also is absorbed unconsciously. North Americans acquire their culture's notions about how far apart people should stand when they talk (see the box at the end of this chapter), not by being told directly to maintain a certain distance but through a gradual process of observation, experience, and conscious and unconscious behavior modification. No one tells Latins to stand closer together than North Americans do; they learn to do so as part of their cultural tradition.

## Culture Is Shared

Culture is an attribute not of individuals per se but of individuals as members of *groups*. Culture is transmitted in society. Don't we learn our culture by observing, listening, talking, and interacting with many other people? Shared beliefs, values, memories, and expectations link people who grow up in the same culture. Enculturation unifies people by providing us with common experiences.

People in the United States sometimes have trouble understanding the power of culture because of the value that American culture places on the idea of the individual. Americans are fond of saying that everyone is unique and special in some way. However, in American culture individualism itself is a distinctive shared value. Individualism is transmitted through hundreds of statements and settings in our daily lives. From the late Mr. Rogers on TV to parents, grandparents, and teachers, our enculturative agents insist that we are all "someone special."

Today's parents were yesterday's children. If they grew up in North America, they absorbed certain values and beliefs transmitted over the generations. People become agents in the enculturation of their children, just as their parents were for them. Although a culture constantly changes, certain fundamental beliefs, values, worldviews, and child-rearing practices endure. Consider a simple American example of enduring shared enculturation. As children, when we didn't finish a meal, our parents may have reminded us of starving children in some foreign country, just as our grandparents might have done a generation earlier. The specific country changes (China, India, Bangladesh, Ethiopia, Somalia, Rwanda—what was it in your home?). Still, American culture goes on transmitting the idea that by eating all our brussels sprouts or broccoli, we can justify our own good fortune, compared to a hungry child in an impoverished or war-ravaged country.

## Culture Is Symbolic

Symbolic thought is unique and crucial to humans and to cultural learning. A symbol is something verbal or nonverbal, within a particular language or culture, that comes to stand for something else. Anthropologist Leslie White defined culture as

> dependent upon symbolling. . . . Culture consists of tools, implements, utensils,
> clothing, ornaments, customs, institutions, beliefs, rituals, games, works of art,
> language, etc. (White 1959, p. 3)

For White, culture originated when our ancestors acquired the ability to use symbols, that is, to originate and bestow meaning on a thing or event, and, correspondingly, to grasp and appreciate such meanings (White 1959, p. 3).

There need be no obvious, natural, or necessary connection between the symbol and what it symbolizes. The familiar pet that barks is no more naturally a *dog* than it is a *chien, Hund,* or *mbwa,* the words for "dog" in French, German, and Swahili, respectively. Language is one of the distinctive possessions of *Homo sapiens*. No other animal has developed anything approaching the complexity of language, with its multitude of symbols.

Symbols often are linguistic. There also are myriad nonverbal symbols, such as flags, which stand for various countries, and the arches that symbolize a particular hamburger chain. Holy water is a potent symbol in Roman Catholicism. As is true of all symbols, the association between a symbol (water) and what is symbolized (holiness) is arbitrary and conventional. Water probably is not intrinsically holier than milk, blood, or other natural liquids. Nor is holy water chemically different from ordinary water. Holy water is a symbol within Roman Catholicism, which is part of an international cultural system. A natural thing has been associated arbitrarily with a particular meaning for Catholics, who share common beliefs and experiences that are based on learning and that are transmitted across the generations.

For hundreds of thousands of years, humans have shared the abilities on which culture rests—the abilities to learn, to think symbolically, to manipulate language, and to use tools and other cultural products in organizing their lives and coping with their environments. Every contemporary human population has the ability to use symbols and thus to create and maintain culture. Our nearest relatives—chimpanzees and gorillas—have rudimentary cultural abilities. However, no other animal has elaborated cultural abilities to the extent that *Homo* has.

## Culture and Nature

Culture takes the natural biological urges we share with other animals and teaches us how to express them in particular ways. People have to eat, but culture teaches us what, when, and how. In many cultures people have their main meal at noon, but most North Americans prefer a large dinner. English people eat fish for breakfast, but North Americans prefer hot cakes and cold cereals. Brazilians put hot milk into strong coffee, whereas many North Americans pour cold milk into a weaker brew. Midwesterners dine at five or six, Spaniards at ten.

Cultural habits, perceptions, and inventions mold "human nature" into many forms. People have to eliminate wastes from their bodies. But some cultures teach people to defecate standing, while others tell them to do it sitting down. Peasant women in the Andean highlands squat in the streets and urinate, getting all the privacy they need from their massive skirts. All these habits are parts of cultural traditions that have converted natural acts into cultural customs.

Our culture—and cultural changes—affect how we perceive nature, human nature, and "the natural." Through science, invention, and discovery, cultural advances have overcome many "natural" limitations. We prevent and cure diseases such as polio and smallpox, which felled our ancestors. We use Viagra to enhance or restore sexual potency. Through cloning, scientists have challenged the way we think about biological identity and the meaning of life itself. Culture, of course, does not always protect us from natural threats. Hurricanes, floods, earthquakes, and other natural forces regularly overthrow our wishes to modify the environment through building, development, and expansion. Can you think of other ways in which nature strikes back at culture?

## Culture Is All-Encompassing

For anthropologists, culture includes much more than refinement, good taste, sophistication, education, and appreciation of the fine arts. Not only college graduates but all people are "cultured." The most interesting and significant cultural forces are those that affect people every day of their lives, particularly those that influence children during enculturation.

*Culture,* as defined anthropologically, encompasses features that are sometimes regarded as trivial or unworthy of serious study, such as those of "popular" culture. To understand contemporary North American culture, we must consider television, fast-food restaurants, sports, and games. As a cultural manifestation, a rock star may be as interesting as a symphony conductor (or vice versa); a comic book may be as significant as a book-award winner.

## Culture Is Integrated

Cultures are not haphazard collections of customs and beliefs. Cultures are integrated, patterned systems. If one part of the system (the overall economy, for instance) changes, other parts change as well. For example, during the 1950s most American women planned domestic careers as homemakers and mothers. Most of today's college women, by contrast, expect to get paying jobs when they graduate.

What are some of the social repercussions of this particular economic change? Attitudes and behavior regarding marriage, family, and children have changed. Late marriage, "living together," and divorce have become more common. The average age at first marriage for American women rose from 20 in 1955 to 25 in 2003. The comparable figures for men were 23 and 27 (U.S. Census Bureau 2004). The number of currently divorced Americans quadrupled from 4 million in 1970 to about 22 million in 2004 (Statistical Abstract of the United States 2006). Work competes with marriage and family responsibilities and reduces the time available to invest in child care.

Cultures are integrated not simply by their dominant economic activities and related social patterns but also by sets of values, ideas, symbols, and judgments. Cultures train their individual members to share certain personality traits. A set of characteristic **core values** (key, basic, central values) integrates each culture and helps distinguish it from others. For instance, the work ethic and individualism are core values that have integrated American culture for generations. Different sets of dominant values influence the patterns of other cultures.

## Culture Can Be Adaptive and Maladaptive

Humans have both biological and cultural ways of coping with environmental stresses. Besides our biological means of adaptation, we also use "cultural adaptive kits," which contain customary activities and tools that aid us. Although humans continue to adapt biologically, reliance on social and cultural means of adaptation has increased during human evolution and plays a crucial role.

Sometimes, adaptive behavior that offers short-term benefits to particular subgroups or individuals may harm the environment and threaten the group's long-term

Cultures are integrated systems. When one behavior pattern changes, others also change. During the 1950s, most American women expected to have careers as wives, mothers, and domestic managers. As more and more women have entered the workforce, attitudes toward work and family have changed. On the top, mom and kids do the dishes in 1952. On the bottom (taken in January 2005), nuclear expert and Deputy Director of ISIS (Institute for Science & International Security) Corey Hinderstein uses her office in Washington, D.C., to monitor nuclear activities all over the globe.

survival. Economic growth may benefit some people while it depletes resources needed for society at large or for future generations. Thus, cultural traits, patterns, and inventions can also be *maladaptive,* threatening the group's continued existence (survival and reproduction). Air conditioners help us deal with heat, as fires and furnaces protect us against the cold. Automobiles permit us to make a living by getting us from home to workplace. But the by-products of such "beneficial" technology often create new problems. Chemical emissions increase air pollution, deplete the ozone layer, and contribute to global warming. Many cultural patterns such as overconsumption and pollution appear to be maladaptive in the long run. Can you think of others?

## Culture and the Individual: Agency and Practice

Generations of anthropologists have theorized about the relationship between the "system," on one hand, and the "person" or "individual" on the other. The system can refer to various concepts, including culture, society, social relations, or social structure. Individual human beings always make up, or constitute, the system. But, living within that system, humans also are constrained (to some extent, at least) by its rules and by the actions of other individuals. Cultural rules provide guidance about what to do and how to do it, but people don't always do what the rules say should be done. People use their culture actively and creatively, rather than blindly following its dictates. Humans aren't passive beings who are doomed to follow their cultural traditions like programmed robots. Cultures are dynamic and constantly changing. People learn, interpret, and manipulate the same rule in different ways—or they emphasize different rules that better suit their interests. Culture is *contested:* Different groups in society struggle with one another over whose ideas, values, goals, and beliefs will prevail. Even common symbols may have radically different *meanings* to different individuals and groups in the same culture. Golden arches may cause one person to salivate while another plots a vegetarian protest. The same flag may be waved to support or oppose a given war.

Even when they agree about what should be done, people don't always do as their culture directs or as other people expect. Many rules are violated, some very often (for example, automobile speed limits). Some anthropologists find it useful to distinguish between ideal and real culture. The *ideal culture* consists of what people say they should do and what they say they do. *Real culture* refers to their actual behavior as observed by the anthropologist.

Culture is both public and individual, both in the world and in people's minds. Anthropologists are interested not only in public and collective behavior but also in how *individuals* think, feel, and act. The individual and culture are linked because human social life is a process in which individuals internalize the meanings of *public* (i.e., cultural) messages. Then, alone and in groups, people influence culture by converting their private (and often divergent) understandings into public expressions (D'Andrade 1984).

Conventionally culture has been seen as social glue transmitted across the generations, binding people through their common past, rather than as something being continually created and reworked in the present. The tendency to view culture as an entity rather than as a process is changing. Contemporary anthropologists now emphasize how day-to-day action, practice, or resistance can make and remake culture (Gupta and Ferguson, eds. 1997*b*). *Agency* refers to the actions that individuals take, both alone and in groups, in forming and transforming cultural identities.

The approach to culture known as *practice theory* (Ortner 1984) recognizes that individuals within a society or culture have diverse motives and intentions and different degrees of power and influence. Such contrasts may be associated with gender, age, ethnicity, class, and other social variables. Practice theory focuses on how such varied individuals—through their ordinary and extraordinary actions and practices—manage to influence, create, and transform the world they live in. Practice theory appropriately recognizes a reciprocal relation between culture (the system—see above) and the individual. The system shapes how individuals experience and respond to external events, but individuals also play an active role in how society functions and changes. Practice theory recognizes both constraints on individuals and the flexibility and changeability of cultures and social systems.

## Levels of Culture

We distinguish between different levels of culture: national, international, and subcultural. In today's world these distinctions are increasingly important. **National culture** embodies those beliefs, learned behavior patterns, values, and institutions that are shared by citizens of the same nation. **International culture** extends beyond and across national boundaries. Because culture is transmitted through learning rather than genetically, cultural traits can spread through borrowing or *diffusion* from one group to another.

Because of diffusion, migration, colonialism, and globalization, many cultural traits and patterns have acquired international scope. The contemporary United States, Canada, Great Britain, and Australia share cultural traits they have inherited from their common linguistic and cultural ancestors in Great Britain. Roman Catholics in many different countries share beliefs, symbols, experiences, and values transmitted by their church. The World Cup has become an international cultural event, as people in many countries know the rules of, play, and follow soccer.

Cultures also can be smaller than nations (see Jenks 2004). Although people who live in the same country share a national cultural tradition, all cultures also contain diversity. Individuals, families, communities, regions, classes, and other groups within a culture have different learning experiences as well as shared ones. **Subcultures** are different symbol-based patterns and traditions associated with particular groups in the same complex society. In large or diverse nations such as the United States or Canada, a variety of subcultures originate in region, ethnicity, language, class, and religion. The religious backgrounds of Jews, Baptists, and Roman Catholics create subcultural differences between them. While sharing a common national culture, U.S. northerners and southerners also differ in their beliefs, values, and customary behavior as a result of national and regional history. French-speaking Canadians sometimes pointedly contrast with English-speaking people in the same country. Italian Americans have ethnic traditions different from those of Irish, Polish, and African Americans.

Illustrating the international level of culture, Roman Catholics in different nations share knowledge, symbols, beliefs, and values transmitted by their church. Here we see a prayer vigil in Seoul, Korea. In addition to religious conversion, what other forces work to spread international culture?

Nowadays, many anthropologists are reluctant to use the term *subculture*. They feel that the prefix *sub-* is offensive because it means "below." *Subcultures* thus may be perceived as "less than" or somehow inferior to a dominant, elite, or national culture. In this discussion of levels of culture, I intend no such implication. My point is simply that nations may contain many different culturally defined groups. As mentioned earlier, culture is contested. Various groups may strive to promote the correctness and value of their own practices, values, and beliefs in comparison with those of other groups or the nation as a whole.

## Ethnocentrism, Cultural Relativism, and Human Rights

**Ethnocentrism** is the tendency to view one's own culture as superior and to apply one's own cultural values in judging the behavior and beliefs of people raised in other cultures. We hear ethnocentric statements all the time. Ethnocentrism contributes to social solidarity, a sense of value and community, among people who share a cultural tradition. People everywhere think that the familiar explanations, opinions, and customs are true, right, proper, and moral. They regard different behavior as strange, immoral, or savage. Often other societies are not considered fully human. Their members may be castigated as cannibals, thieves, or people who do not bury their dead.

Among several tribes in the Trans-Fly region of Papua New Guinea homosexuality was valued over heterosexuality (see the chapter in this book on gender). Men who grew up in the Etoro tribe (Kelly 1976) favored oral sex between men, while their neighbors the Marind-anim encouraged men to engage in anal sex. (In both groups heterosexual coitus was stigmatized and allowed only for reproduction.) Etoro men considered Marind-anim anal sex to be disgusting, while seeing nothing abnormal about their own oral homosexual practices.

Opposing ethnocentrism is **cultural relativism,** the viewpoint that behavior in one culture should not be judged by the standards of another culture. This position also can present problems. At its most extreme, cultural relativism argues that there is no superior, international, or universal morality, that the moral and ethical rules of all cultures deserve equal respect. In the extreme relativist view, Nazi Germany would be evaluated as nonjudgmentally as Athenian Greece.

In today's world, human rights advocates challenge many of the tenets of cultural relativism. For example, several societies in Africa and the Middle East have traditions of female genital modification (FGM). *Clitoridectomy* is the removal of a girl's clitoris. *Infibulation* involves sewing the lips (labia) of the vagina, to constrict the vaginal opening. Both procedures reduce female sexual pleasure, and, it is believed in some cultures, the likelihood of adultery. Such practices have been opposed by human rights advocates, especially women's rights groups. The idea is that the tradition infringes on a basic human right—disposition over one's body and one's sexuality. Some African countries have banned or otherwise discouraged the procedures, as have Western nations that receive immigration from such cultures. Similar issues arise with circumcision and other male genital operations. Is it right for a baby boy to be circumcised without his permission, as has been done routinely in the United States? Is it proper to require adolescent boys to undergo collective circumcision to fulfill cultural tradition, as has been done in parts of Africa and Australia?

Some would argue that the problems with relativism can be solved by distinguishing between methodological and moral relativism. In anthropology, cultural relativism is not a moral position, but a methodological one. It states: To understand another culture fully, you must try to see how the people in that culture see things. What motivates them—what are they thinking—when they do those things? Such an approach does not preclude making moral judgments or taking action. When faced with Nazi atrocities, a methodological relativist would have a moral obligation to stop doing anthropology and take action to intervene. In the FGM example, one only can understand the *motivations* for the practice by looking at the situation from the point of view of those who engage in it. Having done this, one then faces the moral question of whether to intervene to stop it. We should recognize as well that different people and groups living in the same society—for example, women and men, old and young, the more and less powerful—can have widely different views about what is proper, necessary, and moral.

The idea of **human rights** invokes a realm of justice and morality beyond and superior to the laws and customs of particular countries, cultures, and religions (see R. Wilson, ed. 1996). Human rights include the right to speak freely, to hold religious beliefs without persecution, and not to be murdered, injured, or enslaved or imprisoned without charge. Such rights are seen as *inalienable* (nations cannot abridge or terminate them) and international (larger than and superior to individual nations and cultures).

Four United Nations documents describe nearly all the human rights that have been internationally recognized. Those documents are the U.N. Charter; the Universal Declaration of Human Rights; the Covenant on Economic, Social and Cultural Rights; and the Covenant on Civil and Political Rights.

Alongside the human rights movement has arisen an awareness of the need to preserve cultural rights. Unlike human rights, **cultural rights** are vested not in individuals but in *groups,* such as religious and ethnic minorities and indigenous societies. Cultural rights include a group's ability to preserve its culture, to raise its children in the ways of its forebears, to continue its language, and not to be deprived of its economic base by the nation in which it is located (Greaves 1995). The related notion of indigenous **intellectual property rights (IPR)** has arisen in an attempt to conserve each society's cultural base—its core beliefs, knowledge, and practices (see Merry 2006). Much traditional cultural knowledge has commercial value. Examples include ethnomedicine (traditional medical knowledge and techniques), cosmetics, cultivated plants, foods, folklore, arts, crafts, songs, dances, costumes, and rituals (see Nazarea 2006). According to the IPR concept, a particular group may determine how indigenous knowledge and its products may be used and distributed and the level of compensation required.

The notion of cultural rights is related to the idea of cultural relativism, and the problem discussed previously arises again. What does one do about cultural rights that interfere with human rights? I believe that anthropology's main job is to present accurate accounts and explanations of cultural phenomena. The anthropologist doesn't have to approve infanticide, cannibalism, or torture to record their existence and determine their causes and the motivations behind them. However, each anthropologist has a choice about where he or she will do fieldwork. Some anthropologists choose not to study a particular culture because they discover in advance or early in fieldwork that behavior they consider morally repugnant is practiced there. Anthropologists respect human diversity. Most ethnographers try to be objective, accurate, and sensitive in their accounts of other cultures. However, objectivity, sensitivity, and a cross-cultural perspective don't mean that anthropologists have to ignore international standards of justice and morality. What do you think?

## ✦ Universality, Generality, and Particularity

Anthropologists agree that cultural learning is uniquely elaborated among humans and that all humans have culture. Anthropologists also accept a doctrine termed in the 19th century "the psychic unity of man." This means that although *individuals* differ in their emotional and intellectual tendencies and capacities, all human *populations* have equivalent capacities for culture. Regardless of their genes or their physical appearance, people can learn *any* cultural tradition.

To understand this point, consider that contemporary Americans and Canadians are the genetically mixed descendants of people from all over the world. Our ancestors were biologically varied, lived in different countries and continents, and participated in hundreds of cultural traditions. However, early colonists, later immigrants, and their descendants all have become active participants in American and Canadian life. All now share a common national culture.

To recognize biopsychological equality is not to deny differences among populations. In studying human diversity in time and space, anthropologists distinguish among the universal, the generalized, and the particular. Certain biological, psychological, social, and cultural features are **universal,** found in every culture. Others are merely **generalities,** common to several but not all human groups. Still other traits are **particularities,** unique to certain cultural traditions.

## Universals and Generalities

Biologically based universals include a long period of infant dependency, year-round (rather than seasonal) sexuality, and a complex brain that enables us to use symbols, languages, and tools. Among the social universals is life in groups and in some kind of family (see Brown 1991). Generalities occur in certain times and places but not in all cultures. They may be widespread, but they are not universal. One cultural generality that is present in many but not all societies is the *nuclear family,* a kinship group consisting of parents and children. Although many middle-class Americans ethnocentrically view the nuclear family as a proper and "natural" group, it is not universal. It is absent, for example, among the Nayars, who live on the Malabar Coast of India. The Nayars live in female-headed households, and husbands and wives do not live together. In many other societies, the nuclear family is submerged in larger kin groups, such as extended families, lineages, and clans.

One reason for generalities is diffusion. Societies can share the same beliefs and customs because of borrowing or through (cultural) inheritance from a common cultural ancestor. Speaking English is a generality shared by North Americans and Australians because both countries had English settlers. Another reason for generalities is domination, as in colonial rule, when customs and procedures are imposed on one culture by another one that is more powerful. In many countries, use of the English language reflects colonial history. More recently, English has spread through diffusion to many other countries, as it has become the world's foremost language for business and travel and in the context of globalization.

## Particularity: Patterns of Culture

A cultural particularity is a trait or feature of culture that is not generalized or widespread; rather it is confined to a single place, culture, or society. Yet because of cultural diffusion, which has accelerated through modern transportation and communication systems, traits that once were limited in their distribution have become more widespread. Traits that are useful, that have the capacity to please large audiences, and that don't clash with the cultural values of potential adopters are more likely to diffuse than others are. Still, certain cultural particularities persist. One example would be a particular food dish (e.g., pork barbeque with a mustard-based sauce available only in South Carolina, or the pastie—beef stew baked in pie dough characteristic of Michigan's upper peninsula). Besides diffusion which, for example, has spread McDonald's food outlets, once confined to San Bernadino, California, across the globe, there are other reasons why cultural particularities are increasingly rare. Many cultural traits are shared as cultural universals and as a result of independent invention. Facing similar problems, people in different places have come up with similar solutions. Again and again, similar cultural causes have produced similar cultural results.

At the level of the individual cultural trait or element (e.g, bow and arrow, hot dog, MTV), particularities may be getting rarer. But at a higher level, particularity is more obvious. Different cultures emphasize different things. *Cultures are integrated and patterned differently and display tremendous variation and diversity.* When cultural traits are borrowed, they are modified to fit the culture that adopts them. They are reintegrated—patterned anew—to fit their new setting. MTV in Germany or Brazil isn't at all the same thing as MTV in the United States. As was stated in the earlier section "Culture Is Integrated," patterned beliefs, customs, and practices lend distinctiveness to particular cultural traditions.

Consider universal life-cycle events, such as birth, puberty, marriage, parenthood, and death, that many cultures observe and celebrate. The occasions (e.g., marriage, death) may be the same and universal, but the patterns of ceremonial observance may be dramatically different. Cultures vary in just which events merit special celebration. Americans, for example, regard expensive weddings as more socially appropriate than lavish funerals. However, the Betsileo of Madagascar take the opposite view. The marriage ceremony is a minor event that brings together just the couple and a few close relatives. However, a funeral is a measure of the deceased person's social position and lifetime achievement, and it may attract a thousand people. Why use money on a house, the Betsileo say, when one can use it on the tomb where one will spend eternity in the company of dead relatives? How unlike contemporary Americans' dreams of home ownership and preference for quick and inexpensive funerals. Cremation, an increasingly common option in the United States, would horrify the Betsileo, for whom ancestral bones and relics are important ritual objects.

Cultures vary tremendously in their beliefs, practices, integration, and patterning. By focusing on and trying to explain alternative customs, anthropology forces us to reappraise our familiar ways of thinking. In a world full of cultural diversity, contemporary American culture is just one cultural variant, more powerful perhaps, but no more natural, than the others.

## ✧ Mechanisms of Cultural Change

Why and how do cultures change? One way is **diffusion** or borrowing of traits between cultures. Such exchange of information and products has gone on throughout human history because cultures never have been truly isolated. Contact between neighboring groups has always existed and has extended over vast areas (Boas 1940/1966). Diffusion is *direct* when two cultures trade with, intermarry among, or wage war on one another. Diffusion is *forced* when one culture subjugates another and imposes its customs on the dominated group. Diffusion is *indirect* when items or traits move from group A to group C via group B without any firsthand contact between A and C. In this case, group B might consist of traders or merchants who take products from a variety of places to new markets. Or group B might be geographically situated between A and C, so that what it gets from A eventually winds up in C, and vice versa. In today's world, much international diffusion is indirect—culture spread by the mass media and advanced information technology.

**Acculturation,** a second mechanism of cultural change, is the exchange of cultural features that results when groups have continuous firsthand contact. The cultures of either or both groups may be changed by this contact (Redfield, Linton, and Herskovits 1936). With acculturation, parts of the cultures change, but each group remains distinct. One example of acculturation is a *pidgin,* a mixed language that develops to ease communication between members of different cultures in contact. This usually happens in situations of trade or colonialism. Pidgin English, for example, is a simplified form of English. It blends English grammar with the grammar of a native language. Pidgin English was first used for commerce in Chinese ports. Similar pidgins developed later in Papua New Guinea and West Africa. In situations of continuous contact, cultures have also exchanged and blended foods, recipes, music, dances, clothing, tools, and technologies.

**Independent invention**—the process by which humans innovate, creatively finding solutions to problems—is a third mechanism of cultural change. Faced with comparable problems and challenges, people in different societies have innovated and changed in similar ways, which is one reason cultural generalities exist. One example is the independent invention of agriculture in the Middle East and Mexico. Over the course of human history, major innovations have spread at the expense of earlier ones. Often a major invention, such as agriculture, triggers a series of subsequent interrelated changes. These economic revolutions have social and cultural repercussions. Thus in both Mexico and the Middle East, agriculture led to many social, political, and legal changes, including notions of property and distinctions in wealth, class, and power (see Naylor 1996).

## ✦ GLOBALIZATION

The term **globalization** encompasses a series of processes, including diffusion, migration, and acculturation, working to promote change in a world in which nations and people are increasingly interlinked and mutually dependent. Promoting such linkages are economic and political forces, as well as modern systems of transportation and communication. The forces of globalization include international commerce and finance, travel and tourism, transnational migration, the media, and various high-tech information flows (see Appadurai, ed. 2001; Ong and Collier, eds. 2005; Scholte 2000). During the Cold War, which ended with the fall of the Soviet Union, the basis of international alliance was political, ideological, and military. More recent international pacts have shifted toward trade and economic issues. New economic unions (which have met considerable resistance in their member nations) have been created through the North American Free Trade Agreement (NAFTA), the World Trade Organization (WTO), and the European Union (EU).

Long-distance communication is easier, faster, and cheaper than ever, and extends to remote areas. I can now e-mail or call families in Arembepe, Brazil, which lacked phones or even postal service when I first began to study the community. The mass media help propel a globally spreading culture of consumption. Within nations and across their borders, the media spread information about products, services, rights, institutions, lifestyles, and the perceived costs and benefits of globalization. Emigrants transmit information and resources transnationally, as they maintain their ties with home (phoning, faxing, e-mailing, making visits, sending money). In a sense such people live multilocally—in different places and cultures at once. They learn to play various social roles and to change behavior and identity depending on the situation (see Cresswell 2006).

Local people must cope increasingly with forces generated by progressively larger systems—region, nation, and world. An army of outsiders now intrudes on

## ANTHROPOLOGY TODAY

### *Touching, Affection, Love, and Sex*

Comparing the United States to Brazil—or virtually any Latin nation—we can see a striking cultural contrast between a culture that discourages physical contact and demonstrations of affection and one in which the contrary is true.

"Don't touch me." "Take your hands off me." Such statements are not uncommon in North America, but they are virtually never heard in Brazil, the Western Hemisphere's second most populous country. Brazilians like to be touched (and kissed) more than North Americans do. The world's cultures have strikingly different notions about displays of affection and about matters of personal space. When North Americans talk, walk, and dance, they maintain a certain distance from others—their personal space. Brazilians, who maintain less physical distance, interpret this as a sign of coldness. When conversing with a North American, the Brazilian characteristically moves in as the North American "instinctively" retreats. In these body movements, neither Brazilian nor North American is trying consciously to be especially friendly or unfriendly. Each

is merely executing a program written on the self by years of exposure to a particular cultural tradition. Because of different ideas about proper social space, cocktail parties in international meeting places such as the United Nations can resemble an elaborate insect mating ritual as diplomats from different cultures advance, withdraw, and sidestep.

One easily evident cultural difference between Brazil and the United States involves kissing, hugging, and touching. Middle-class Brazilians teach their kids—both boys and girls—to kiss (on the cheek, two or three times, coming and going) every adult relative they ever see. Given the size of Brazilian extended families, this can mean hundreds of people. Females continue kissing throughout their lives. They kiss male and female kin, friends, relatives of friends, friends of relatives, friends of friends and, when it seems appropriate, more casual acquaintances. Males go on kissing their female relatives and friends. Until they are adolescents, boys also kiss adult male relatives. Brazilian men, brothers, cousins, nephews and uncles, and friends, typically greet each other with hearty handshakes and a traditional male hug (*abraço*). The people everywhere. Tourism has become the world's number one industry (see Holden 2005). Economic development agents and the media promote the idea that work should be for cash rather than mainly for subsistence. Indigenous peoples and traditional societies have devised various strategies to deal with threats to their autonomy, identity, and livelihood (Maybury-Lewis 2002). New forms of political mobilization and cultural expression, including the rights movements discussed previously, are emerging from the interplay of local, regional, national, and international cultural forces.

closer the relationship, the tighter and longer-lasting the embrace. Many Brazilian men keep on kissing their fathers and uncles throughout their lives. Could it be that homophobia (fear of homosexuality) prevents American men from engaging in such displays of affection with other men? Are American women more likely to show affection toward each other than American men are?

Like other North Americans who spend time in a Latin culture, I miss the numerous kisses and handshakes when I get back to the United States. After several months in Brazil, I find North Americans rather cold and impersonal. Many Brazilians share this opinion. I have heard similar feelings expressed by Italian Americans as they compare themselves with North Americans of different ethnic backgrounds.

According to clinical psychologist David E. Klimek, who has written about intimacy and marriage in the United States, "in American society, if we go much beyond simple touching, our behavior takes on a minor sexual twist" (Slade 1984). North Americans define demonstrations of affection between males and females with reference to marriage. Love and affection are supposed to unite the married pair, and they blend into sex. When a wife asks her husband for "a little affection," she may mean, or he may think she means, sex.

A certain lack of clarity in North American definitions of love, affection, and sex is evident on Valentine's Day, which used to be just for lovers. Valentines used to be sent to wives, husbands, girlfriends, and boyfriends. Now, after years of promotion by the greeting card industry, they also go to mothers, fathers, sons, daughters, aunts, and uncles. There is a blurring of sexual and nonsexual affection. In Brazil, Lovers' Day retains its autonomy. Mother, father, and children each have their own separate days of recognition.

It's true, of course, that in a good marriage love and affection exist alongside sex. Nevertheless, affection does not necessarily imply sex. The Brazilian culture shows that there can be rampant kissing, hugging, and touching without sex—or fears of improper sexuality. In Brazilian culture, physical demonstrations help cement many kinds of close personal relationships that have no sexual component.

## SUMMARY

1. Culture refers to customary behavior and beliefs that are passed on through enculturation. Culture rests on the human capacity for cultural learning. Culture encompasses shared rules for conduct that are internalized in human beings. Such rules lead people to think and act in characteristic ways.

2. Other animals learn, but only humans have cultural learning, dependent on symbols. Humans think symbolically—arbitrarily bestowing meaning on things and events. By convention, a symbol stands for something with which it has no necessary or natural relation. Symbols have special meaning for people who share memories, values, and beliefs because of common enculturation. People absorb cultural lessons consciously and unconsciously.

3. Cultural traditions mold biologically based desires and needs in particular directions. Everyone is cultured, not just people with elite educations. Cultures may be integrated and patterned through economic and social forces, key symbols, and core values. Cultural rules don't rigidly dictate our behavior. There is room for creativity, flexibility, diversity, and disagreement within societies. Cultural means of adaptation have been crucial in human evolution. Aspects of culture can also be maladaptive.

4. There are levels of culture, which can be larger or smaller than a nation. Diffusion, migration, colonialism, and globalization have carried cultural traits and patterns to different areas. Such traits are shared across national boundaries. Nations also include cultural differences associated with ethnicity, region, and social class.

5. Using a comparative perspective, anthropology examines biological, psychological, social, and cultural universals and generalities. There are also unique and distinctive aspects of the human condition. North American cultural traditions are no more natural than any others. Mechanisms of cultural change include diffusion, acculturation, and independent invention. Globalization describes a series of processes that promote change in our world in which nations and people are increasingly interlinked and mutually dependent.

## KEY TERMS

acculturation (p. 201)
core values (p. 192)
cultural relativism (p. 197)
cultural rights (p. 198)
diffusion (p. 200)
enculturation (p. 188)
ethnocentrism (p. 196)
generalities (p. 199)
globalization (p. 201)

human rights (p. 197)
independent invention (p. 201)
intellectual property rights (IPR) (p. 198)
international culture (p. 195)
national culture (p. 195)
particularities (p. 199)
subcultures (p. 195)
symbols (p. 189)
universal (p. 199)

# CHAPTER 10

❦

# LANGUAGE AND COMMUNICATION

Depending on where we live, North Americans have certain stereotypes about how people in other regions talk. Some stereotypes, spread by the mass media, are more generalized than others are. Most Americans think they can imitate a "Southern accent." We also have nationwide stereotypes about speech in New York City (the pronunciation of *coffee,* for example) and Boston ("I pahked the kah in Hahvahd Yahd").

Regional patterns influence the way all Americans speak. In whichever state, college students from out of state easily recognize that their in-state classmates speak differently. In-state students, however, have difficulty hearing their own speech peculiarities because they are accustomed to them and view them as normal.

It is sometimes thought that midwesterners don't have accents. This belief stems from the fact that midwestern dialects don't have many stigmatized linguistic variants— speech patterns that people in other regions recognize and look down on, such as *r*lessness and *dem, dese*, and *dere* (instead of *them, these,* and *there*).

Far from having no accents, midwesterners, even in the same high school, exhibit linguistic diversity (see Eckert 1989, 2000). Dialect differences are immediately obvious to people, like me, who come from other parts of the country. One of the best examples of variable midwestern speech, involving vowels, is pronunciation of the *e* sound (called the /e/ phoneme), in such words as *ten, rent, French, section, lecture, effect, best,* and *test.* In southeastern Michigan, where I live and teach, there are four different ways of pronouncing this *e* sound. Speakers of Black English and immigrants from Appalachia often pronounce *ten* as *tin,* just as Southerners habitually do. Some Michiganders say *ten,* the correct pronunciation in Standard English. However, two other pronunciations also are common. Instead of *ten,* many Michiganders say *tan,* or *tun* (as though they were using the word *ton,* a unit of weight).

My students often astound me with their pronunciation. One day I met one of my Michigan-raised teaching assistants in the hall. She was deliriously happy. When I asked why, she replied, "I've just had the best suction."

"What?" I said.

She finally spoke more precisely. "I've just had the best saction." She considered this a clearer pronunciation of the word *section.*

Another TA complimented me, "You luctured to great effuct today." After an exam a student lamented that she had not done her "bust on the tust."

The truth is, regional patterns affect the way we all speak.

## ✦ LANGUAGE

Linguistic anthropology illustrates anthropology's characteristic interests in diversity, comparison, and change—but here the focus is on language. Language, spoken (*speech*) and written (*writing*—which has existed for about 6,000 years), is our primary means of communication. Like culture in general, of which language is a part, language is transmitted through learning. Language is based on arbitrary, learned associations between words and the things they stand for. Unlike the communication systems of other animals, language allows us to discuss the past and future, share our experiences with others, and benefit from their experiences.

Anthropologists study language in its social and cultural context (see Bonvillain 2003; Salzmann 2003). Some linguistic anthropologists reconstruct ancient languages by comparing their contemporary descendants and in so doing make discoveries about history. Others study linguistic differences to discover the varied worldviews and patterns of thought in a multitude of cultures. Sociolinguists examine dialects and styles in a single language to show how speech reflects social differences, as in the above discussion of regional speech contrasts. Linguistic anthropologists also explore the role of language in colonization and globalization (Geis 1987; Thomas 1999).

## ✦ NONHUMAN PRIMATE COMMUNICATION

### Call Systems

Only humans speak. No other animal has anything approaching the complexity of language. The natural communication systems of other primates (monkeys and apes) are **call systems.** These vocal systems consist of a limited number of sounds—*calls*—that are produced only when particular environmental stimuli are encountered. Such calls may be varied in intensity and duration, but they are much less flexible than language because they are automatic and can't be combined. When primates encounter food and danger simultaneously, they can make only one call. They can't combine the calls for food and danger into a single utterance, indicating that both are present. At some point in human evolution, however, our ancestors began to combine calls and to understand the combinations. The number of calls also expanded, eventually becoming too great to be transmitted even partly through the genes. Communication came to rely almost totally on learning.

Although wild primates use call systems, the vocal tract of apes is not suitable for speech. Until the 1960s, attempts to teach spoken language to apes suggested that they lack linguistic abilities. In the 1950s, a couple raised a chimpanzee, Viki, as a member of their family and systematically tried to teach her to speak. However, Viki learned only four words ("mama," "papa," "up," and "cup").

# Sign Language

More recent experiments have shown that apes can learn to use, if not speak, true language (Fouts 1997; Miles 1983). Several apes have learned to converse with people through means other than speech. One such communication system is American Sign Language, or ASL, which is widely used by deaf and mute Americans. ASL employs a limited number of basic gesture units that are analogous to sounds in spoken language. These units combine to form words and larger units of meaning.

The first chimpanzee to learn ASL was Washoe, a female. Captured in West Africa, Washoe was acquired by R. Allen Gardner and Beatrice Gardner, scientists at the University of Nevada in Reno, in 1966, when she was a year old. Four years later, she moved to Norman, Oklahoma, to a converted farm that had become the Institute for Primate Studies. Washoe revolutionized the discussion of the language-learning abilities of apes. At first she lived in a trailer and heard no spoken language. The researchers always used ASL to communicate with each other in her presence. The chimp gradually acquired a vocabulary of more than 100 signs representing English words (Gardner, Gardner, and Van Cantfort, eds. 1989). At the age of two, Washoe began to combine as many as five signs into rudimentary sentences such as "you, me, go out, hurry."

The second chimp to learn ASL was Lucy, Washoe's junior by one year. Lucy died, or was murdered by poachers, in 1986, after having been introduced to "the wild" in Africa in 1979 (Carter 1988). From her second day of life until her move to Africa, Lucy lived with a family in Norman, Oklahoma. Roger Fouts, a researcher from the nearby Institute for Primate Studies, came two days a week to test and improve Lucy's knowledge of ASL. During the rest of the week, Lucy used ASL to converse with her foster parents. After acquiring language, Washoe and Lucy exhibited several human traits: swearing, joking, telling lies, and trying to teach language to others (Fouts 1997).

When irritated, Washoe called her monkey neighbors at the institute "dirty monkeys." Lucy insulted her "dirty cat." On arrival at Lucy's place, Fouts once found a pile of excrement on the floor. When he asked the chimp what it was, she replied, "dirty, dirty," her expression for feces. Asked whose "dirty, dirty" it was, Lucy named Fouts's coworker, Sue. When Fouts refused to believe her about Sue, the chimp blamed the excrement on Fouts himself.

**Cultural transmission** of a communication system through learning is a fundamental attribute of language. Washoe, Lucy, and other chimps have tried to teach ASL to other animals, including their own offspring. Washoe has taught gestures to other

Apes, such as these Congo chimpanzees, use call systems to communicate in the wild. Their vocal systems consist of a limited number of sounds—calls—that are produced only when particular environmental stimuli are encountered.

institute chimps, including her son Sequoia, who died in infancy (Fouts, Fouts, and Van Cantfort 1989).

Because of their size and strength as adults, gorillas are less likely subjects than chimps for such experiments. Lean adult male gorillas in the wild weigh 400 pounds (180 kilograms), and full-grown females can easily reach 250 pounds (110 kilograms). Because of this, psychologist Penny Patterson's work with gorillas at Stanford University seems more daring than the chimp experiments. Patterson raised her now full-grown female gorilla, Koko, in a trailer next to a Stanford museum. Koko's vocabulary surpasses that of any chimp. She regularly employs 400 ASL signs and has used about 700 at least once.

Koko and the chimps also show that apes share still another linguistic ability with humans: **productivity.** Speakers routinely use the rules of their language to produce entirely new expressions that are comprehensible to other native speakers. I can, for example, create "baboonlet" to refer to a baboon infant. I do this by analogy with

English words in which the suffix -*let* designates the young of a species. Anyone who speaks English immediately understands the meaning of my new word. Koko, Washoe, Lucy, and others have shown that apes also are able to use language productively. Lucy used gestures she already knew to create "drinkfruit" for watermelon. Washoe, seeing a swan for the first time, coined "waterbird." Koko, who knew the gestures for "finger" and "bracelet," formed "finger bracelet" when she was given a ring.

Chimps and gorillas have a rudimentary capacity for language. They may never have invented a meaningful gesture system in the wild. However, given such a system, they show many humanlike abilities in learning and using it. Of course, language use by apes is a product of human intervention and teaching. The experiments mentioned here do not suggest that apes can invent language (nor are human children ever faced with that task). However, young apes have managed to learn the basics of gestural language. They can employ it productively and creatively, although not with the sophistication of human ASL users.

Apes also have demonstrated linguistic **displacement.** Absent in call systems, this is a key ingredient in language. Normally, each call is tied to an environmental stimulus such as food. Calls are uttered only when that stimulus is present. Displacement means that humans can talk about things that are not present. We don't have to see the objects before we say the words. Human conversations are not limited by place. We can discuss the past and future, share our experiences with others, and benefit from theirs.

Patterson has described several examples of Koko's capacity for displacement (Patterson 1978). The gorilla once expressed sorrow about having bitten Penny three days earlier. Koko has used the sign "later" to postpone doing things she doesn't want to do. Table 10-1 summarizes the contrasts between language, whether sign or spoken, and call systems.

Certain scholars doubt the linguistic abilities of chimps and gorillas (Sebeok and Umiker-Sebeok, eds. 1980; Terrace 1979). These people contend that Koko and the

## TABLE 10-1

### Language Contrasted with Call Systems

| Human Language | Primate Call Systems |
|---|---|
| Has the capacity to speak of things and events that are not present (displacement). | Are stimuli-dependent; the food call will be made only in the presence of food; it cannot be faked. |
| Has the capacity to generate new expressions by combining other expressions (productivity). | Consist of a limited number of calls that cannot be combined to produce new calls. |
| Is group specific in that all humans have the capacity for language, but each linguistic community has its own language, which is culturally transmitted. | Tend to be species specific, with little variation among communities of the same species for each call. |

chimps are comparable to trained circus animals and don't really have linguistic ability. However, in defense of Patterson and the other researchers (Hill 1978; Van Cantfort and Rimpau 1982), only one of their critics has worked with an ape. This was Herbert Terrace, whose experience teaching a chimp sign language lacked the continuity and personal involvement that have contributed so much to Patterson's success with Koko.

No one denies the huge difference between human language and gorilla signs. There is a major gap between the ability to write a book or say a prayer and the few hundred gestures employed by a well-trained chimp. Apes aren't people, but they aren't just animals either. Let Koko express it: When asked by a reporter whether she was a person or an animal, Koko chose neither. Instead, she signed "fine animal gorilla" (Patterson 1978).

## ✈ Nonverbal Communication

Language is our principal means of communicating, but it isn't the only one we use. We *communicate* when we transmit information about ourselves to others and receive such information from them. Our facial expressions, bodily stances, gestures, and movements, even if unconscious, convey information and are part of our communication styles. Deborah Tannen (1990) discusses differences in the communication styles of American men and women, and her comments go beyond language. She notes that American girls and women tend to look directly at each other when they talk, whereas American boys and men do not. Males are more likely to look straight ahead rather than turn and make eye contact with someone, especially another man, seated beside them. Also, in conversational groups, American men tend to relax and sprawl out. American women may adopt a similar relaxed posture in all-female groups, but when they are with men, they tend to draw in their limbs and adopt a tighter stance.

**Kinesics** is the study of communication through body movements, stances, gestures, and facial expressions. Related to kinesics is the examination of cultural differences in personal space discussed in the chapter "Culture." Linguists pay attention not only to what is said but to how it is said, and to features besides language itself that convey meaning. A speaker's enthusiasm is conveyed not only through words, but also through facial expressions, gestures, and other signs of animation. We use gestures, such as a jab of the hand, for emphasis. We vary our intonation and the pitch or loudness of our voices. We communicate through strategic pauses, and even by being silent. An effective communication strategy may be to alter pitch, voice level, and grammatical forms, such as declaratives ("I am . . ."), imperatives ("Go forth . . ."), and questions ("Are you . . . ?"). Culture teaches us that certain manners and styles should accompany certain kinds of speech. Our demeanor, verbal and nonverbal, when our favorite team is winning would be out of place at a funeral, or when a somber subject is being discussed.

Culture always plays a role in shaping the "natural." Cross-culturally, nodding does not always mean affirmative, nor does head shaking from side to side always mean negative. Brazilians wag a finger to mean no. Americans say "uh huh" to affirm, whereas in Madagascar a similar sound is made to deny. Americans point with their fingers; the people of Madagascar point with their lips. Patterns of "lounging around" vary too. Outside, when resting, some people may sit or lie on the ground; others squat; others lean against a tree.

Body movements communicate social differences. In Japan, bowing is a regular part of social interaction, but different bows are used depending on the social status of the people who are interacting. In Madagascar and Polynesia, people of lower status should not hold their heads above those of people of higher status. When one approaches someone older or of higher status, one bends one's knees and lowers one's head as a sign of respect. In Madagascar, one always does this, for politeness, when passing between two people. Although our gestures, facial expressions, and body stances have roots in our primate heritage, and can be seen in the monkeys and the apes, they have not escaped cultural shaping. Language, which is so highly dependent on the use of symbols, is the domain of communication in which culture plays the strongest role.

## ✦ THE STRUCTURE OF LANGUAGE

The scientific study of a spoken language (**descriptive linguistics**) involves several interrelated areas of analysis: phonology, morphology, lexicon, and syntax. **Phonology,** the study of speech sounds, considers which sounds are present and significant in a given language. **Morphology** studies the forms in which sounds combine to form *morphemes*—words and their meaningful parts. Thus, the word *cats* would be analyzed as containing two morphemes—*cat,* the name for a kind of animal, and *-s,* a morpheme indicating plurality. A language's **lexicon** is a dictionary containing all its morphemes and their meanings. **Syntax** refers to the arrangement and order of words in phrases and sentences. For example, do nouns usually come before or after verbs? Do adjectives normally precede or follow the nouns they modify?

## Speech Sounds

From the movies and TV, and from meeting foreigners, we know something about foreign accents and mispronunciations. We know that someone with a marked French accent doesn't pronounce *r* like an American does. But at least someone from France can distinguish between "craw" and "claw," which someone from Japan may not be able to do. The difference between *r* and *l* makes a difference in English and in French, but it doesn't in Japanese. In linguistics we say that the difference between *r* and *l* is *phonemic* in English and French but not in Japanese. In English and French *r* and *l* are phonemes but not in Japanese. A **phoneme** is a sound contrast that makes a difference, that differentiates meaning.

We find the phonemes in a given language by comparing *minimal pairs,* words that resemble each other in all but one sound. The words have different meanings, but they differ in just one sound. The contrasting sounds are therefore phonemes in that language. An example in English is the minimal pair *pit/bit*. These two words are distinguished by a single sound contrast between /p/ and /b/ (we enclose phonemes in slashes). Thus /p/ and /b/ are phonemes in English. Another example is the different vowel sound of *bit* and *beat* (Figure 10-1). This contrast serves to distinguish these two words and the two vowel phonemes written /I/ and /i/ in English.

Standard (American) English (SE), the "region-free" dialect of TV network newscasters, has about 35 phonemes—at least 11 vowels and 24 consonants. The number

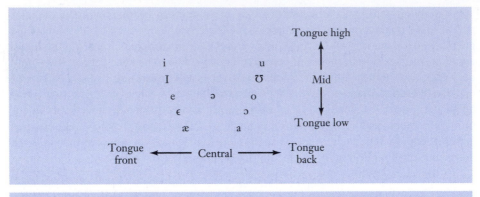

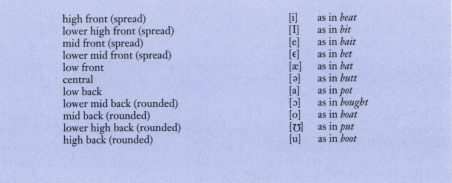

| | | |
|---|---|---|
| high front (spread) | [i] | as in *beat* |
| lower high front (spread) | [I] | as in *bit* |
| mid front (spread) | [e] | as in *bait* |
| lower mid front (spread) | [ɛ] | as in *bet* |
| low front | [æ] | as in *bat* |
| central | [ə] | as in *butt* |
| low back | [a] | as in *pot* |
| lower mid back (rounded) | [ɔ] | as in *bought* |
| mid back (rounded) | [o] | as in *boat* |
| lower high back (rounded) | [ʊ] | as in *put* |
| high back (rounded) | [u] | as in *boot* |

**FIGURE 10-1**     *Vowel phonemes in Standard American English*  They are shown according to height of tongue and tongue position at front, center, or back of mouth. Phonetic symbols are identified by English words that include them; note that most are minimal pairs.

*SOURCE:* Adaptation of excerpt and Figure 2-1 from *Aspects of Language,* 3rd ed. by Dwight Bolinger and Donald Sears, copyright © 1981 by Harcourt Brace Jovanovich, Incl, reprinted by permission of the publisher.

of phonemes varies from language to language—from 15 to 60, averaging between 30 and 40. The number of phonemes also varies between dialects of a given language. In North American English, for example, vowel phonemes vary noticeably from dialect to dialect. Readers should pronounce the words in Figure 10-1, paying attention to (or asking someone else) whether they distinguish each of the vowel sounds. Most North Americans don't pronounce them all.

**Phonetics** is the study of speech sounds in general, what people actually say in various languages, like the differences in vowel pronunciation described in the discussion of midwestern speech at the beginning of the chapter. **Phonemics** studies only the *significant* sound contrasts (phonemes) of a given language. In English, like /r/ and /l/ (remember *craw* and *claw*), /b/ and /v/ also are phonemes, occurring in minimal pairs like *bat* and *vat*. In Spanish, however, the contrast between [b] and [v] doesn't distinguish meaning, and they therefore are not phonemes (we enclose sounds that are not phonemic in brackets). Spanish speakers normally use the [b] sound to pronounce words spelled with either *b* or *v*.

In any language a given phoneme extends over a phonetic range. In English the phoneme /p/ ignores the phonetic contrast between the [pʰ] in *pin* and the [p] in *spin*. Most English speakers don't even notice that there is a phonetic difference. The [pʰ] is aspirated, so that a puff of air follows the [p]. The [p] in *spin* is not. (To see the difference, light a match, hold it in front of your mouth, and watch the flame as you pronounce the two words.) The contrast between [pʰ] and [p] *is* phonemic in some languages, such as Hindi (spoken in India). That is, there are words whose meaning is distinguished only by the contrast between an aspirated and an unaspirated [p].

Native speakers vary in their pronunciation of certain phonemes, such as the /e/ phoneme in the midwestern United States. This variation is important in the evolution of language. With no shifts in pronunciation, there can be no linguistic change. The section on sociolinguistics below considers phonetic variation and its relationship to social divisions and the evolution of language.

## ✦ LANGUAGE, THOUGHT, AND CULTURE

The well-known linguist Noam Chomsky (1957) has argued that the human brain contains a limited set of rules for organizing language, so that all languages have a common structural basis. (Chomsky calls this set of rules *universal grammar*.) That people can learn foreign languages and that words and ideas translate from one language to another supports Chomsky's position that all humans have similar linguistic abilities and thought processes. Another line of support comes from creole languages. Such languages develop from pidgins, languages that form in situations of acculturation, when different societies come into contact and must devise a system of communication. Pidgins based on English and native languages developed through trade and colonialism in China, Papua New Guinea, and West Africa. Eventually, after generations of being spoken, pidgins may develop into *creole languages*. These are more mature languages, with developed grammatical rules and native speakers (people who learn the language as their primary one during enculturation).

Creoles are spoken in several Caribbean societies. Gullah, which is spoken by African Americans on coastal islands in South Carolina and Georgia, is a creole language. Supporting the idea that creoles are based on universal grammar is the fact that such languages all share certain features. Syntactically, all use particles (e.g., will, was) to form future and past tenses and multiple negation to deny or negate (e.g., he don't got none). Also, all form questions by changing inflection rather than by changing word order. For example, "You're going home for the holidays?" (with a rising tone at the end) rather than "Are you going home for the holidays?"

## The Sapir-Whorf Hypothesis

Other linguists and anthropologists take a different approach to the relation between language and thought. Rather than seeking universal linguistic structures and processes, they believe that different languages produce different ways of thinking. This position sometimes is known as the **Sapir-Whorf hypothesis** after Edward Sapir (1931) and his student Benjamin Lee Whorf (1956), its prominent early advocates. Sapir and Whorf argued that the grammatical categories of particular languages lead their speakers to think about things in different ways. For example, English divides time into past, present, and future. Hopi, a language of the Pueblo region of the Native American Southwest, does not. Rather, Hopi distinguishes between events that exist or have existed (what we use present and past to discuss) and those that don't or don't yet (our future events, along with imaginary and hypothetical events). Whorf argued that this difference leads Hopi speakers to think about time and reality in different ways than English speakers do.

A similar example comes from Portuguese, which employs a future subjunctive verb form, introducing a degree of uncertainty into discussions of the future. In English we routinely use the future tense to talk about something we think will happen. We don't feel the need to qualify "The sun'll come out tomorrow," by adding "if it doesn't go supernova." We don't hesitate to proclaim "I'll see you next year," even when we can't be absolutely sure we will. The Portuguese future subjunctive qualifies the future event, recognizing that the future can't be certain. Our way of expressing the future as certain is so ingrained that we don't even think about it, just as the Hopi don't see the need to distinguish between present and past, both of which are real, while the future remains hypothetical. It seems, however, that language does not tightly restrict thought, because cultural changes can produce changes in thought and in language, as we'll see in the next section (see also Gumperz and Levinson, eds. 1996).

Shown here (in 1995) is Leigh Jenkins, who was or is director of Cultural Preservation for the Hopi tribal council. The Hopi language would not distinguish between *was* and *is* in the previous sentence. For the Hopi, present and past are real and are expressed grammatically in the same way while the future remains hypothetical and has a different grammatical expression.

# Focal Vocabulary

A lexicon (or vocabulary) is a language's dictionary, its set of names for things, events, and ideas. Lexicon influences perception. Thus, Eskimos (or Inuit) have several distinct words for different types of snow that in English are all called *snow*. Most English speakers never notice the differences between these types of snow and might have trouble seeing them even if someone pointed them out. Eskimos recognize and think about differences in snow that English speakers don't see because our language gives us just one word.

Similarly, the Nuer of Sudan have an elaborate vocabulary to describe cattle. Eskimos have several words for snow and Nuer have dozens for cattle because of their particular histories, economies, and environments (Brown 1958; Eastman 1975). When the need arises, English speakers can also elaborate their snow and cattle vocabularies. For example, skiers name varieties of snow with words that are missing from the lexicons of Florida retirees. Similarly, the cattle vocabulary of a Texas rancher is much more ample than that of a salesperson in a New York City department store. Such specialized sets of terms and distinctions that are particularly important to certain groups (those with particular *foci* of experience or activity) are known as **focal vocabulary.**

Vocabulary is the area of language that changes most readily. New words and distinctions, when needed, appear and spread. For example, who would have "faxed" anything a generation ago? Names for items get simpler as they become common and important. A television has become a *TV,* an automobile a *car,* and a digital video disc a *DVD*.

Language, culture, and thought are interrelated. Opposing the Sapir-Whorf hypothesis, however, it might be more accurate to say that changes in culture produce changes in language and thought than to say the reverse. Consider differences between female and male Americans regarding the color terms they use (Lakoff 2004). Distinctions implied by such terms as *salmon, rust, peach, beige, teal, mauve, cranberry,* and *dusky orange* aren't in the vocabularies of most American men. However, many of them weren't even in American women's lexicons 50 years ago. These changes reflect changes in American economy, society, and culture. Color terms and distinctions have increased with the growth of the fashion and cosmetic industries. A similar contrast (and growth) in Americans' lexicons shows up in football, basketball, and hockey vocabularies. Sports fans, more often males than females, use more terms concerning, and make more elaborate distinctions between, the games they watch, such as hockey (see Table 10-2). Thus, cultural contrasts and changes affect lexical distinctions (for instance, *peach* versus *salmon*) within semantic domains (for instance, color terminology). **Semantics** refers to a language's meaning system.

The ways in which people divide up the world—the lexical contrasts they perceive as meaningful or significant—reflect their experiences (see Bicker, Sillitoe, and Pottier, eds. 2004). Anthropologists have discovered that certain sets of vocabulary items evolve in a determined order. For example, after studying more than 100 languages, Berlin and Kay (1969/1992) discovered 10 basic color terms: *white, black, red, yellow, blue, green, brown, pink, orange,* and *purple* (they evolved in more or less that order). The number of terms varied with cultural complexity. Representing one extreme were Papua New

A scene from the May 2005, Ice Hockey World Championship finals in Vienna, Austria. The Czech Republic beat Canada 3–0. How would a hockey insider use focal vocabulary to describe this situation?

## TABLE 10-2

### Focal Vocabulary for Hockey

*Insiders have special terms for the major elements of the game*

| Elements of Hockey | Insiders' Term |
| --- | --- |
| puck | biscuit |
| goal/net | pipes |
| penalty box | sin bin |
| hockey stick | twig |
| helmet | bucket |
| space between a goalie's leg pads | five hole |

Guinea cultivators and Australian hunters and gatherers, who used only two basic terms, which translate as *black* and *white* or *dark* and *light*. At the other end of the continuum were European and Asian languages with all the color terms. Color terminology was most developed in areas with a history of using dyes and artificial coloring.

## → SOCIOLINGUISTICS

No language is a uniform system in which everyone talks just like everyone else. The field of **sociolinguistics** investigates relationships between social and linguistic variation (Romaine 2000; Trudgill 2000). How do different speakers use a given language? How do linguistic features correlate with social diversity and stratification, including class, ethnic, and gender differences (Tannen 1990; Tannen, ed. 1993)? How is language used to express, reinforce, or resist power (Geis 1987; Lakoff 2000)?

Sociolinguists focus on features that vary systematically with social position and situation. To study variation, sociolinguists must observe, define, and measure variable use of language in real-world situations. To show that linguistic features correlate with social, economic, and political differences, the social attributes of speakers also must be measured and related to speech (Fasold 1990; Labov 1972*a*).

Variation within a language at a given time is historical change in progress. The same forces that, working gradually, have produced large-scale linguistic change over the centuries are still at work today. Linguistic change doesn't occur in a vacuum but in society. When new ways of speaking are associated with social factors, they are imitated, and they spread. In this way, a language changes.

## Linguistic Diversity within Nations

As an illustration of the linguistic variation encountered in all nations, consider the contemporary United States. Ethnic diversity is revealed by the fact that millions of Americans learn first languages other than English. Spanish is the most common. Most of those people eventually become bilinguals, adding English as a second language. In many multilingual (including colonized) nations, people use two languages on different occasions—one in the home, for example, and the other on the job or in public.

Whether bilingual or not, we all vary our speech in different contexts; we engage in **style shifts.** In certain parts of Europe, people regularly switch dialects. This phenomenon, known as **diglossia.** applies to "high" and "low" variants of the same language, for example, in German and Flemish (spoken in Belgium). People employ the high variant at universities and in writing, professions, and the mass media. They use the low variant for ordinary conversation with family members and friends.

Just as social situations influence our speech, so do geographical, cultural, and socioeconomic differences. Many dialects coexist in the United States with Standard (American) English (SE). SE itself is a dialect that differs, say, from "BBC English," which is the preferred dialect in Great Britain. Different dialects are equally effective as systems of communication, which is language's main job. Our tendency to think of particular dialects as cruder or more sophisticated than others is a social rather than a linguistic judgment. We rank certain speech patterns as better or worse because we

Ethnic and linguistic diversity characterize many nations, especially in big cities, as is illustrated by this California sign written in seven languages: Chinese, Korean, Spanish, Vietnamese, Japanese, Tagalog, and English.

recognize that they are used by groups that we also rank. People who say *dese, dem*, and *dere* instead of *these, them*, and *there* communicate perfectly well with anyone who recognizes that the *d* sound systematically replaces the *th* sound in their speech. However, this form of speech has become an indicator of low social rank. We call it, like the use of *ain't*, "uneducated speech." The use of *dem, dese*, and *dere* is one of many phonological differences that Americans recognize and look down on.

## Gender Speech Contrasts

Comparing men and women, there are differences in phonology, grammar, and vocabulary, and in the body stances and movements that accompany speech (Eckert and McConnell-Ginet 2003; Lakoff 2004; Tannen 1990). In phonology, American women tend to pronounce their vowels more peripherally ("rant," "rint" when saying the word "rent"), whereas men tend to pronounce theirs more centrally ("runt"). In public contexts, Japanese women tend to adopt an artificially high voice, for the sake of politeness, according to their traditional culture. Women tend to be more careful about uneducated speech. This trend shows up in both the United States and England. Men may adopt working-class speech because they associate it with masculinity. Perhaps women pay more attention to the media, in which standard dialects are employed.

According to Robin Lakoff (2004), the use of certain types of words and expressions has been associated with women's traditional lesser power in American society (see also Coates 1986; Romaine 1999; Tannen 1990; Tannen, ed. 1993). For example, *Oh dear, Oh fudge,* and *Goodness!* are less forceful than *Hell* and *Damn.* Watch the lips of a disgruntled athlete in a televised competition, such as a football game. What's the likelihood he's saying "Phooey on you"? Women, by contrast, are more likely to use such adjectives as *adorable, charming, sweet, cute, lovely,* and *divine* than men are.

Let's return to sports and color terminology for additional illustration of differences in lexical (vocabulary) distinctions that men and women make. Men typically know more terms related to sports, make more distinctions among them (e.g., runs versus points), and try to use the terms more precisely than women do. Correspondingly, influenced more by the fashion and cosmetics industries than men are, women use more color terms and attempt to use them more specifically than men do. Thus, when I lecture on sociolinguistics, and to make this point, I bring an off-purple shirt to class. Holding it up, I first ask women to say aloud what color the shirt is. The women rarely answer with a uniform voice, as they try to distinguish the actual shade (mauve, lavender, lilac, violet, or some other purplish hue). Then I ask the men, who consistently answer as one, "PURPLE." Rare is the man who on the spur of the moment can imagine the difference between *fuchsia* and *magenta*.

Differences in the linguistic strategies and behavior of men and women are examined in several books by the well-known sociolinguist Deborah Tannen (1990; ed. 1993). Tannen uses the terms "rapport" and "report" to contrast women's and men's overall linguistic styles. Women, says Tannen, typically use language and the body movements that accompany it to build rapport, social connections with others. Men, on the other hand, tend to make reports, reciting information that serves to establish a place for themselves in a hierarchy, as they also attempt to determine the relative ranks of their conversation mates.

## Stratification and Symbolic Domination

We use and evaluate speech in the context of *extralinguistic* forces—social, political, and economic. Mainstream Americans evaluate the speech of low-status groups negatively, calling it "uneducated." This is not because these ways of speaking are bad in themselves but because they have come to symbolize low status. Consider variation in the pronunciation of *r*. In some parts of the United States *r* is regularly pronounced, and in other (*r*less) areas it is not. Originally, American *r*less speech was modeled on the fashionable speech of England. Because of its prestige, *r*lessness was adopted in many areas and continues as the norm around Boston and in the South.

New Yorkers sought prestige by dropping their *r*'s in the 19th century, after having pronounced them in the 18th. However, contemporary New Yorkers are going back to the 18th-century pattern of pronouncing *r*'s. What matters, and what governs linguistic change, is not the reverberation of a strong midwestern *r* but *social* evaluation, whether *r*'s happen to be "in" or "out."

Studies of *r* pronunciation in New York City have clarified the mechanisms of phonological change. William Labov (1972*b*) focused on whether *r* was pronounced after vowels in such words as *car, floor, card*, and *fourth*. To get data on how this linguistic variation correlated with social class, he used a series of rapid encounters with employees in three New York City department stores, each of whose prices and locations attracted a different socioeconomic group. Saks Fifth Avenue (68 encounters) catered to the upper middle class, Macy's (125) attracted middle-class shoppers, and S. Klein's (71) had predominantly lower-middle-class and working-class customers. The class origins of store personnel reflected those of their customers.

Having already determined that a certain department was on the fourth floor, Labov approached ground-floor salespeople and asked where that department was. After the salesperson had answered, "Fourth floor," Labov repeated his "Where?" in order to get a second response. The second reply was more formal and emphatic, the salesperson presumably thinking that Labov hadn't heard or understood the first answer. For each salesperson, therefore, Labov had two samples of /r/ pronunciation in two words.

Labov calculated the percentages of workers who pronounced /r/ at least once during the interview. These were 62 percent at Saks, 51 percent at Macy's, but only 20 percent at S. Klein's. He also found that personnel on upper floors, where he asked "What floor is this?" (and where more expensive items were sold), pronounced *r* more often than ground-floor salespeople did.

In Labov's study, *r* pronunciation was clearly associated with prestige. Certainly the job interviewers who had hired the salespeople never counted *r*'s before offering employment. However, they did use speech evaluations to make judgments about how effective certain people would be in selling particular kinds of merchandise. In other words, they practiced sociolinguistic discrimination, using linguistic features in deciding who got certain jobs.

Our speech habits help determine our access to employment and other material resources. Because of this, "proper language" itself becomes a strategic resource—and a path to wealth, prestige, and power (Gal 1989; Thomas and Wareing, eds. 2004). Illustrating this, many ethnographers have described the importance of verbal skill and oratory in politics (Beeman 1986; Bloch, ed. 1975; Brenneis 1988; Geis 1987; Lakoff 2000). Ronald Reagan, known as a "great communicator," dominated American society in the 1980s as a two-term president. Another twice-elected president, Bill Clinton, despite his southern accent, was known for his verbal skills in certain contexts (e.g., televised debates and town-hall meetings). Communications flaws may have helped doom the presidencies of Gerald Ford, Jimmy Carter, and George Bush the elder. Does his or her use of language affect your perception of the current president of the United States?

The French anthropologist Pierre Bourdieu views linguistic practices as *symbolic capital* which properly trained people may convert into economic and social capital. The value of a dialect—its standing in a "linguistic market"—depends on the extent to which it provides access to desired positions in the labor market. In turn, this reflects its legitimation by formal institutions—educational institutions, state, church, and prestige media. Even people who don't use the prestige dialect accept its authority and correctness,

*My dream Was to became a shool teacher.*
*Mrs Stone is rich.*
*I have talents but not opportunity.*
*I ~~have~~ am used to standing behind*
*Mrs Stone.*
*I have been a servant for 40 years.*
*Vickie Figueroa.*

Proper language is a strategic resource, correlated with wealth, prestige, and power.
How is linguistic (and social) stratification illustrated in this photo, including the
handwritten comments below it?

its "symbolic domination" (Bourdieu 1982, 1984). Thus, linguistic forms, which lack
power in themselves, take on the power of the groups they symbolize. The education
system, however (defending its own worth), denies linguistic relativity. It misrepresents
prestige speech as being inherently better. The linguistic insecurity often felt by lower-
class and minority speakers is a result of this symbolic domination.

## Black English Vernacular (BEV)

The sociolinguist William Labov and several associates, both white and black, have conducted detailed studies of what they call **Black English Vernacular (BEV).** (*Vernacular*
means ordinary, casual speech.) BEV is the "relatively uniform dialect spoken by the
majority of black youth in most parts of the United States today, especially in the inner
city areas of New York, Boston, Detroit, Philadelphia, Washington, Cleveland, . . . and
other urban centers. It is also spoken in most rural areas and used in the casual, intimate

speech of many adults" (Labov 1972*a*, p. xiii). This does not imply that all, or even most, African Americans speak BEV.

BEV is a complex linguistic system with its own rules, which linguists have described. The phonology and syntax of BEV are similar to those of southern dialects. This reflects generations of contact between southern whites and blacks, with mutual influence on each other's speech patterns. Many features that distinguish BEV from SE (Standard English) also show up in southern white speech, but less frequently than in BEV.

Linguists disagree about exactly how BEV originated (Rickford 1997). Smitherman (1986) calls it an Africanized form of English reflecting both an African heritage and the conditions of servitude, oppression, and life in America. She notes certain structural similarities between West African languages and BEV. African linguistic backgrounds no doubt influenced how early African Americans learned English. Did they restructure English to fit African linguistic patterns? Or did they quickly learn English from whites, with little continuing influence from the African linguistic heritage? Or, possibly, in acquiring English, did African slaves fuse English with African languages to make a pidgin or creole, which influenced the subsequent development of BEV? Creole speech may have been brought to the American colonies by the many slaves who were imported from the Caribbean during the 17th and 18th centuries. Some slaves may even have learned, while still in Africa, the pidgins or creoles spoken in West African trading forts (Rickford 1997).

Origins aside, there are phonological and grammatical differences between BEV and SE. One phonological difference is that BEV speakers are less likely to pronounce *r* than SE speakers are. Actually, many SE speakers don't pronounce *r*'s that come right before a consonant (ca*r*d) or at the end of a word (car). But SE speakers usually do pronounce an *r* that comes right before a vowel, either at the end of a word (fou*r* o'clock) or within a word (Ca*r*ol). BEV speakers, by contrast, are much more likely to omit such intervocalic (between vowels) *r*'s. The result is that speakers of the two dialects have different *homonyms* (words that sound the same but have different meanings). BEV speakers who don't pronounce intervocalic *r*'s have the following homonyms: Carol/Cal; Paris/pass.

Observing different phonological rules, BEV speakers pronounce certain words differently than SE speakers do. Particularly in the elementary school context, the homonyms of BEV-speaking students typically differ from those of their SE-speaking teachers. To evaluate reading accuracy, teachers should determine whether students are recognizing the different meanings of such BEV homonyms as *passed, past,* and *pass.* Teachers need to make sure students understand what they are reading, which is probably more important than whether they are pronouncing words correctly according to the SE norm.

Phonological rules may lead BEV speakers to omit *-ed* as a past-tense marker and *-s* as a marker of plurality. However, other speech contexts demonstrate that BEV speakers do understand the difference between past and present verbs, and between singular and plural nouns. Confirming this are irregular verbs (e.g., *tell, told*) and irregular plurals (e.g., *child, children*), in which BEV works the same as SE.

SE is not superior to BEV as a linguistic system, but it does happen to be the prestige dialect—the one used in the mass media, in writing, and in most public and professional contexts. SE is the dialect that has the most "symbolic capital." In areas of Germany where there is diglossia, speakers of Plattdeusch (Low German) learn the High German dialect to communicate appropriately in the national context. Similarly, upwardly mobile BEV-speaking students learn SE.

## ✦ HISTORICAL LINGUISTICS

Sociolinguists study contemporary variation in speech, which is language change in progress. **Historical linguistics** deals with longer-term change. Historical linguists can reconstruct many features of past languages by studying contemporary **daughter languages.** These are languages that descend from the same parent language and that have been changing separately for hundreds or even thousands of years. We call the original language from which they diverge the **protolanguage.** Romance languages such as French and Spanish, for example, are daughter languages of Latin, their common protolanguage. German, English, Dutch, and the Scandinavian languages are daughter languages of proto-Germanic. The Romance languages and the Germanic languages all belong to the Indo-European language family. Their common protolanguage is called Proto-Indo-European, PIE. Historical linguists classify languages according to their degree of relationship (see Figure 10-2—PIE family tree).

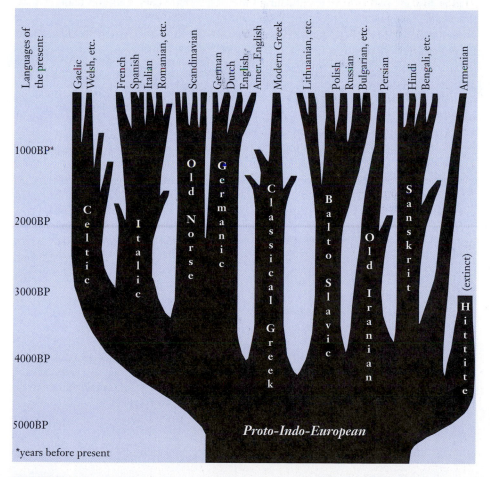

**FIGURE 10-2**    *PIE Family Tree*   Main languages and subgroups of the Indo-European language stock, showing approximate time to their divergence.

Language changes over time. It evolves—varies, spreads, divides into **subgroups** (languages within a taxonomy of related languages that are most closely related). Dialects of a single parent language become distinct daughter languages, especially if they are isolated from one another. Some of them split, and new "granddaughter" languages develop. If people remain in the ancestral homeland, their speech patterns also change. The evolving speech in the ancestral homeland should be considered a daughter language like the others.

A close relationship between languages doesn't necessarily mean that their speakers are closely related biologically or culturally, because people can adopt new languages. In the equatorial forests of Africa, "pygmy" hunters have discarded their ancestral languages and now speak those of the cultivators who have migrated to the area. Immigrants to the United States spoke many different languages on arrival, but their descendants now speak fluent English.

Knowledge of linguistic relationships often is valuable to anthropologists interested in history, particularly events during the past 5,000 years. Cultural features may

## ANTHROPOLOGY TODAY

### Restoring Lost Languages

*Language is a key ingredient in being human. Language and culture go together. Cultural transmission depends on language, and language is a vital part of culture. Contemporary Native Americans display a revived pride in cultural heritage, accompanied by an interest in the languages spoken by their ancestors. Any language helps organize and express modes of thought, systems of meaning, worldviews, and cultural understandings. When languages die, so do meaning systems; cultural diversity is reduced. This account describes one form of cultural heritage management—the science of reconstructing lost languages, known as language revitalization.*

In the new movie about Jamestown, the first permanent English settlement in North America, founded in 1607, the paramount Indian chief Powhatan asks Capt. John Smith where his people came from. The sky?

Responding to the question, translated by an Indian whose smattering of English probably came indirectly from the earlier failed Roanoke colony in North Carolina, Smith replies: "The sky? No. We come from England, an island on the other side of the sea."

The dialogue continues as the interpreter puts Smith's reply in Powhatan's own words, Virginia Algonquian, a language not spoken for more than two centuries. Like most of the 800 or more indigenous languages of North America when Europeans first arrived, Powhatan's became extinct as Indians declined in number, dispersed and lost their cultural identity.

But a small yet growing number of linguists and anthropologists has been busy in recent years recreating such dead or dying Indian speech.

Their field is language revitalization, the science of reconstructing lost languages. One byproduct of the scholarship is the dialogue in Virginia Algonquian for the movie "The New World."

More than moviemaking is behind the research. A revival of ethnic pride and cultural studies among Indians has stimulated Indians' interest in their languages, some (or may not) correlate with the distribution of language families. Groups that speak related languages may (or may not) be more culturally similar to each other than they are to groups whose speech derives from different linguistic ancestors. Of course, cultural similarities aren't limited to speakers of related languages. Even groups whose members speak unrelated languages have contact through trade, intermarriage, and warfare. Ideas and inventions diffuse widely among human groups. Many items of vocabulary in contemporary English, particularly food items such as "beef" and "pork," come from French. Even without written documentation of France's influence after the Norman Conquest of England in 1066, linguistic evidence in contemporary English would reveal a long period of important firsthand contact with France. Similarly, linguistic evidence may confirm cultural contact and borrowing when written history is lacking. By considering which words have been borrowed, we also can make inferences about the nature of the contact.

long dead. Of the more than 15 original Algonquian languages in eastern North America, the two still spoken are Passamaquoddy-Malecite in Maine and Mikmaq in New Brunswick. . . .

The passing of a language diminishes cultural diversity, anthropologists say, and the restoration of at least some part of a language is an act of reclaiming a people's heritage.

Blair A. Rudes, a linguist at the University of North Carolina, Charlotte, who specializes in reconstructing Indian languages, said several Algonquian communities in the East had efforts under way to recover their lost languages and return them to daily use. . . .

When the director of "The New World," Terrence Malick, decided that for authenticity Powhatan should speak in his own language, he called in Dr. Rudes, who has worked . . . in reconstructing the defunct Algonquian language of the Pequot of Connecticut. He is also engaged in language restoration for the Catawba of North Carolina and is collaborating with Helen Rountree, emeritus professor of anthropology at

Old Dominion University, on a dictionary of Virginia Algonquian.

Dr. Rudes was asked what Powhatan and his daughter Pocahontas would say and how they would say it. It was a daunting assignment.

The related Algonquian languages were among the first in America to die out, and no one is known to have spoken Virginia Algonquian since 1785. . . . Just two contemporary accounts—one by Captain Smith and the other by the Jamestown colony secretary, William Strachey—preserved some Virginia Algonquian words, including ones that have passed into modern English as raccoon, terrapin, moccasins and tomahawk. . . .

The first challenge for Dr. Rudes was the limited vocabulary. Smith, the colony leader, set down just 50 Indian words, and Strachey compiled 600. The lists were written phonetically by Englishmen who were not expert in linguistics and whose spelling and pronunciation differed considerably from modern usage, making it difficult to determine the words' actual Indian form.

*Continued*

## ANTHROPOLOGY TODAY

Dr. Rudes had to apply techniques of historical linguistics to rebuilding a language from these sketchy, unreliable word lists. He compared Strachey's recorded words with vocabularies of related Algonquian languages, especially those spoken from the Carolinas north into Canada that had survived longer and are thus better known.

This family of Indian tongues, in one respect, reminded linguists of the Romance languages. Each was distinctive but as closely related as Spanish is to Italian or Italian to Romanian. Comparisons with related languages revealed the common elements of grammar and sentence structure and many similarities in vocabulary. A translation of the Bible into the language once spoken by Massachusetts Indians offered more insights into the grammar. The Munsee Delaware version spoken by coastal Indians from Delaware to New York. . . . may be dead, but its grammar and vocabulary are fairly well known to scholars.

"We have a big fat dictionary of Munsee Delaware," said Dr. Rudes, who adapted some of those words when needed for Virginia Algonquian. Recordings of the last Munsee Delaware speakers, a century ago, were a valuable guide to pronunciations. . . .

Pocahontas would not have said to Smith, if she ever actually did, "I love you." She would have used the verb for love, with a prefix meaning you and a suffix for I. "It is one of the few languages that give greater importance to the listener than the speaker," Dr. Rudes said.

Then there was the problem of creating dialogue reflecting what the Indians would have understood in the early 17th century. This also required changing the script for the initial Powhatan-Smith conversation.

In a paper summarizing his methods, Dr. Rudes said the original script had Smith saying: "The sky? No. From England, a land to the east." At the time, though, a land to the east was for the Indians more myth than reality, he noted, but they probably had already heard about "white-skinned people who lived on islands in the Caribbean."

So Smith's reply was changed to "We came from England, an island on the other side of the sea," and the translator then used documented words of Virginia Algonquian for sky, no, island and sea. The spelling was slightly modified to account for Strachey's misspellings and conform to similar words in other Algonquian speech. Because the word signifying a question is not known in Virginia Algonquian, Dr. Rudes borrowed the word. . . . from a related language. Of course, Powhatan's interpreter could not be expected to have a word for England. He presumably did his best to reproduce what it sounded like in Algonquian, Inkurent, to which he added the general locational ending -unk, meaning at or in. He also followed the practice of naming the place first and adding the word for "we come from there."

*Source:* John Noble Wilford, "Linguists Find the Words, and Pocahontas Speaks Again," *New York Times*, March 7, 2006. Copyright © 2006 The New York Times. Reprinted by permission.

## Summary

1. Wild primates use call systems to communicate. Environmental stimuli trigger calls, which cannot be combined when multiple stimuli are present. Contrasts between language and call systems include displacement, productivity, and cultural transmission. Over time, our ancestral call systems grew too complex

for genetic transmission, and hominid communication began to rely on learning. Humans still use nonverbal communication, such as facial expressions, gestures, and body stances and movements. But language is the main system humans use to communicate. Chimps and gorillas can understand and manipulate nonverbal symbols based on language.

2. No language uses all the sounds the human vocal tract can make. Phonology—the study of speech sounds—focuses on sound contrasts (phonemes) that distinguish meaning. The grammars and lexicons of particular languages can lead their speakers to perceive and think in certain ways.

3. Linguistic anthropologists share anthropology's general interest in diversity in time and space. Sociolinguistics investigates relationships between social and linguistic variation by focusing on the actual use of language. Only when features of speech acquire social meaning are they imitated. If they are valued, they will spread. People vary their speech, shifting styles, dialects, and languages.

4. As linguistic systems, all languages and dialects are equally complex, rule-governed, and effective for communication. However, speech is used, is evaluated, and changes in the context of political, economic, and social forces. Often the linguistic traits of a low-status group are negatively evaluated. This devaluation is not because of linguistic features per se. Rather, it reflects the association of such features with low social status. One dialect, supported by the dominant institutions of the state, exercises symbolic domination over the others.

5. Historical linguistics is useful for anthropologists interested in historical relationships among populations. Cultural similarities and differences often correlate with linguistic ones. Linguistic clues can suggest past contacts between cultures. Related languages—members of the same language family—descend from an original protolanguage. Relationships between languages don't necessarily mean there are biological ties between their speakers because people can learn new languages.

## KEY TERMS

Black English Vernacular (BEV) (p. 221)
call systems (p. 206)
cultural transmission (p. 207)
daughter languages (p. 223)
descriptive linguistics (p. 211)
diglossia (p. 217)
displacement (p. 209)
focal vocabulary (p. 215)
historical linguistics (p. 223)
kinesics (p. 210)
lexicon (p. 211)
morphology (p. 211)

phoneme (p. 211)
phonemics (p. 212)
phonetics (p. 212)
phonology (p. 211)
productivity (p. 208)
protolanguage (p. 223)
Sapir-Whorf hypothesis (p. 214)
semantics (p. 215)
sociolinguistics (p. 217)
style shifts (p. 217)
subgroups (p. 224)
syntax (p. 211)

# CHAPTER 11

# MAKING A LIVING

In today's globalizing world, communities and societies are being incorporated, at an accelerating rate, into larger systems. The origin (around 10,000 years ago) and spread of food production (plant cultivation and animal domestication) led to the formation of larger and more powerful social and political systems. Food production led to major changes in human life. The pace of cultural transformation increased enormously. This chapter provides a framework for understanding a variety of human adaptive strategies and economic systems.

## ✦ ADAPTIVE STRATEGIES

The anthropologist Yehudi Cohen (1974) used the term *adaptive strategy* to describe a society's system of economic production. Cohen argued that the most important reason for similarities between two (or more) unrelated societies is their possession of a similar adaptive strategy. In other words, similar economic causes have similar sociocultural effects. For example, there are clear similarities among societies that have a foraging (hunting and gathering) strategy. Cohen developed a typology of societies based on correlations between their economies and their social features. His typology includes these five adaptive strategies: foraging, horticulture, agriculture, pastoralism, and industrialism. Industrialism is discussed in the chapter, "The World System and Colonialism." The present chapter focuses on the first four adaptive strategies.

# Foraging

Until 10,000 years ago all humans were foragers. However, environmental differences did create substantial contrasts among the world's foragers. Some, like the people who lived in Europe during the ice ages, were big-game hunters. Today, hunters in the Arctic still focus on large animals and herd animals; they have much less vegetation and variety in their diets than do tropical foragers. Moving from colder to hotter areas, the number of species increases. The tropics contain tremendous biodiversity, and tropical foragers typically hunt and gather a wide range of plant and animal species. The same may be true in temperate areas. For example, on the North Pacific Coast of North America, foragers could draw on varied sea, river, and land species, such as salmon and other fish, sea mammals, berries, and mountain goats. Despite differences caused by such environmental variation, all foraging economies have shared one essential feature: People rely on nature to make their living.

Animal domestication (initially of sheep and goats) and plant cultivation (of wheat and barley) began 10,000 to 12,000 years ago in the Middle East. Cultivation based on different crops, such as corn (maize), manioc (cassava), and potatoes, arose independently some 3,000 to 4,000 years later in the Americas. In both hemispheres most foragers eventually turned to food production. Today most foragers have at least some dependence on food production or on food producers (Kent 1992).

The foraging way of life survived into modern times in certain forests, deserts, islands, and very cold areas—places where food production was not practicable with simple technology (see Lee and Daly 1999). In many areas, foragers were exposed to the "idea" of food production but never adopted it because their own economies provided a perfectly adequate and nutritious diet—with a lot less work. In some places, people reverted to foraging after trying food production and abandoning it. In most areas where hunter-gatherers did survive, foraging should be described as "recent" rather than "contemporary." *All modern foragers live in nation-states and depend to some extent on government assistance.* They are in contact with food-producing neighbors as well as with missionaries and other outsiders. We should not view contemporary foragers as isolated or pristine survivors of the Stone Age. Modern foragers are influenced by national and international policies and political and economic events in the world system.

Although foraging is disappearing rapidly as a way of life, we can trace the outlines of Africa's two broad belts of recent foraging. One is the Kalahari Desert of southern Africa. This is the home of the San ("Bushmen"), who include the Ju/'hoansi (see Kent 1996; Lee 2003). The other main African foraging area is the equatorial forest of central and eastern Africa, home of the Mbuti, Efe, and other "pygmies" (Bailey et al. 1989; Turnbull 1965).

People still do subsistence foraging in certain remote forests in Madagascar, Southeast Asia, Malaysia, the Philippines, and on certain islands off the Indian coast. Some of the best-known recent foragers are the aborigines of Australia. Those Native Australians lived on their island continent for more than 60,000 years without developing food production.

The Western Hemisphere also had recent foragers. The Eskimos, or Inuit, of Alaska and Canada are well-known hunters. These (and other) northern foragers now use modern technology, including rifles and snowmobiles, in their subsistence activities (Pelto 1973). The native populations of California, Oregon, Washington, and British Columbia all were foragers, as were those of inland subarctic Canada and the Great Lakes. For many Native Americans, fishing, hunting, and gathering remain important subsistence (and sometimes commercial) activities.

Coastal foragers also lived near the southern tip of South America, in Patagonia. On the grassy plains of Argentina, southern Brazil, Uruguay, and Paraguay, there were other hunter-gatherers. The contemporary Aché of Paraguay usually are called "hunter-gatherers" although they now get just a third of their livelihood from foraging. The Aché also grow crops, have domesticated animals, and live in or near mission posts, where they receive food from missionaries (Hawkes, O'Connell, and Hill 1982; Hill et al. 1987).

Throughout the world, foraging survived mainly in environments that posed major obstacles to food production. (Some foragers took refuge in such areas after the rise of food production, the state, colonialism, or the modern world system.) The difficulties of cultivating at the North Pole are obvious. In southern Africa the Dobe Ju/'hoansi San area studied by Richard Lee and others is surrounded by a waterless belt 43 to 124 miles (70 to 200 kilometers) in breadth (Solway and Lee 1990).

Environmental obstacles to food production aren't the only reason foragers survived. See Figure 11-1 for the distribution of recent hunter-gatherers. Their niches have one thing in common—their marginality. Their environments were not of immediate interest to farmers, herders, or colonialists. The foraging way of life did persist in a few areas that could be

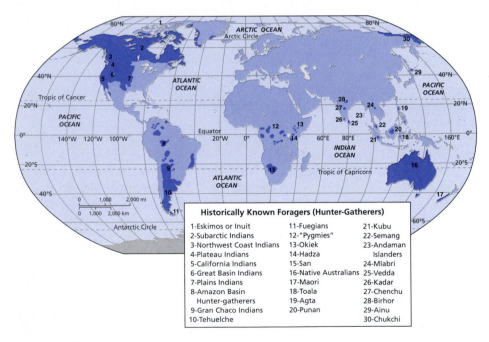

**FIGURE 11-1**    *Worldwide Distribution of Recent Hunter-Gatherers*

*SOURCE:* Adapted from a map by Ray Sim, in Göran Burenhult, ed., *Encyclopedia of Humankind: People of the Stone Age* (McMahons Point, NSW, Australia: Weldon Owen Pty Ltd., 1993), p. 193.

cultivated, even after contact with farmers. Those tenacious foragers, like the indigenous peoples of what is now California and the Pacific Northwest, did not adopt food production, because they were supporting themselves adequately by hunting and gathering. As the modern world system spreads, the number of foragers continues to decline.

Most of the estimated 100,000 San who survive today live in poverty on society's fringes. Each year more and more foragers come under the control of nation-states and are influenced by forces of globalization. As described by Motseta (2006), between 1997 and 2002, the government of Botswana in southern Africa relocated about 3,000 Basarwa San Bushmen outside their ancestral territory, which was converted into a reserve for wildlife protection. The Basarwa received some compensation for their land, along with access to schools, medical facilities, and job training in resettlement centers. However, critics claim this resettlement turned a society of free hunter-gatherers into communities dependent on food aid and government handouts (Motseta 2006).

In 2006 Botswana's High Court ruled that the Basarwa had been wrongly evicted from the "Central Kalahari Game Reserve." In the context of global political action for cultural rights, this verdict was hailed as a victory for indigenous peoples around the world (Motseta 2006). In December 2006 Botswana's attorney general recognized the court order to allow the Basarwa to return to their ancestral lands, while imposing conditions likely to prevent most of them from doing so. Only the 189 people who actually filed the lawsuit would have automatic right of return with their children, compared with some 2,000 Basarwa wishing to return. The others would have to apply for special permits. Returning Basarwa would be allowed to build only temporary structures and to use enough water for subsistence needs. Water would be a major obstacle since the government shut the main well in 2002, and water is scarce in the Kalahari. Furthermore, anyone wishing to hunt would have to apply for a permit. So goes the foraging way of life in the world today.

## Correlates of Foraging

Typologies, such as Cohen's adaptive strategies, are useful because they suggest **correlations**—that is, association or covariation between two or more variables. (Correlated variables are factors that are linked and interrelated, such as food intake and body weight, such that when one increases or decreases, the other changes too.) Ethnographic studies in hundreds of societies have revealed many correlations between the economy and social life. Associated (correlated) with each adaptive strategy is a bundle of particular sociocultural features. Correlations, however, rarely are perfect. Some foragers lack cultural features usually associated with foraging, and some of those features are found in groups with other adaptive strategies.

What, then, are some correlates of foraging? People who subsisted by hunting and gathering often, but not always (see the section on potlatching), lived in band-organized societies. Their basic social unit, the **band,** was a small group of fewer than a hundred people, all related by kinship or marriage. Among some foragers, band size stayed about the same year-round. In others, the band split up for part of the year. Families left to gather resources that were better exploited by just a few people. Later, they regrouped for cooperative work and ceremonies.

One typical characteristic of the foraging life was mobility. In many San groups, as among the Mbuti of Congo, people shifted band membership several times in a lifetime. One might be born, for example, in a band in which one's mother had kin. Later, one's family might move to a band in which the father had relatives. Because bands were exogamous (people married outside their own band) one's parents came from two different bands, and one's grandparents might have come from four. People could join any band to which they had kin or marital links. A couple could live in, or shift between, the husband's and the wife's band.

All human societies have some kind of division of labor based on gender. (See the chapter on gender for more on this.) Among foragers, men typically hunt and fish while women gather and collect, but the specific nature of the work varies among cultures. Sometimes women's work contributes most to the diet. Sometimes male hunting and fishing predominate. Among foragers in tropical and semitropical areas, gathering tends to contribute more to the diet than hunting and fishing do.

All foragers make social distinctions based on age. Often old people receive great respect as guardians of myths, legends, stories, and traditions. Younger people value the elders' special knowledge of ritual and practical matters. Most foraging societies are *egalitarian*. This means that contrasts in prestige are minor and are based on age and gender.

When considering issues of "human nature," we should remember that the egalitarian band was a basic form of human social life for most of our history. Food production has existed less than 1 percent of the time *Homo* has spent on earth. However, it has produced huge social differences. We now consider the main economic features of food-producing strategies.

## ✦ CULTIVATION

In Cohen's typology, the three adaptive strategies based on food production in nonindustrial societies are horticulture, agriculture, and pastoralism. Just as they do in the United States and Canada, people in nonindustrial societies carry out a variety of economic activities. Each adaptive strategy refers to the main economic activity. Pastoralists (herders), for example, consume milk, butter, blood, and meat from their animals as mainstays of their diet. However, they also add grain to their diet by doing some cultivating or by trading with neighbors.

## Horticulture

Horticulture and agriculture are two types of cultivation found in nonindustrial societies. Both differ from the farming systems of industrial nations such as the United States and Canada, which use large land areas, machinery, and petrochemicals. According to Cohen, **horticulture** is cultivation that makes intensive use of *none* of the factors of production: land, labor, capital, and machinery. Horticulturalists use simple tools such as hoes and digging sticks to grow their crops. Their fields lie fallow for varying lengths of time. Horticulture often involves *slash-and-burn* techniques. Here, horticulturalists clear land by cutting down (slashing) and burning forest or bush or by setting fire to the grass covering the plot. The vegetation is broken down, pests are killed, and the ashes remain to fertilize the soil. Crops then are sown, tended, and harvested. Use of the plot is not continuous. Often it is cultivated only for a year or two.

When horticulturalists abandon a plot because of soil exhaustion or a thick weed cover, they clear another piece of land, and the original plot reverts to forest. After several years of fallowing, the cultivator returns to farm the original plot again. Because the relationship between people and land is not permanent, horticulture also is called *shifting cultivation*. Shifting cultivation does not mean that whole villages must move when plots are abandoned. Among the Kuikuru of the South American tropical forest, one village of 150 people remained in the same place for 90 years (Carneiro 1956). Kuikuru houses were large and well made. Because the work involved in building

In slash-and-burn horticulture, the land is cleared by cutting down (slashing) and burning trees and bush, using simple technology. After such clearing, this woman uses a digging stick to plant mountain rice in Madagascar. What might be the environmental effects of slash-and-burn cultivation?

them was substantial, the Kuikuru preferred to walk farther to their fields than to construct a new village. They shifted their plots rather than their settlements. On the other hand, horticulturalists in the montaña (Andean foothills) of Peru lived in small villages of about 30 people (Carneiro 1961/1968). Their houses were small and simple. After a few years in one place, these people built new villages near virgin land. Because their houses were so simple, they preferred rebuilding to walking even a half mile to their fields.

# Agriculture

**Agriculture** requires more labor than horticulture does because it uses land intensively and continuously. The greater labor demands associated with agriculture reflect its use of domesticated animals, irrigation, or terracing.

## *Domesticated Animals*

Many agriculturists use animals as means of production—for transport, as cultivating machines, and for their manure. Asian farmers typically incorporate cattle and/or water buffalo into their agricultural economies. Those rice farmers may use cattle to trample pre-tilled flooded fields, thus mixing soil and water, before transplanting. Many agriculturists attach animals to plows and harrows for field preparation before planting or transplanting. Also, agriculturists typically collect manure from their animals, using it to fertilize their plots, thus increasing yields. Animals are attached to carts for transport and also to implements of cultivation.

## *Irrigation*

While horticulturalists must await the rainy season, agriculturists can schedule their planting in advance because they control water. Like other irrigation experts in the Philippines, the Ifugao water their fields with canals from rivers, streams, springs, and ponds. Irrigation makes it possible to cultivate a plot year after year. Irrigation enriches the soil because the irrigated field is a unique ecosystem with several species of plants and animals, many of them minute organisms, whose wastes fertilize the land.

An irrigated field is a capital investment that usually increases in value. It takes time for a field to start yielding; it reaches full productivity only after several years of cultivation. The Ifugao, like other irrigators, have farmed the same fields for generations. In some agricultural areas, including the Middle East, however, salts carried in the irrigation water can make fields unusable after 50 or 60 years.

## *Terracing*

Terracing is another agricultural technique the Ifugao have mastered. Their homeland has small valleys separated by steep hillsides. Because the population is dense, people need to farm the hills. However, if they simply planted on the steep hillsides, fertile soil and crops would be washed away during the rainy season. To prevent this, the Ifugao

Agriculture requires more labor than horticulture does and uses land intensively and continuously. Labor demands associated with agriculture reflect its use of domesticated animals, irrigation, and terracing. The rice farmers of Luzon in the Philippines, such as the Ifugao, are famous for their irrigated and terraced fields.

cut into the hillside and build stage after stage of terraced fields rising above the valley floor. Springs located above the terraces supply their irrigation water. The labor necessary to build and maintain a system of terraces is great. Terrace walls crumble each year and must be partially rebuilt. The canals that bring water down through the terraces also demand attention.

## Costs and Benefits of Agriculture

Agriculture requires human labor to build and maintain irrigation systems, terraces, and other works. People must feed, water, and care for their animals. But agricultural land can yield one or two crops annually for years, or even generations. An agricultural field does not necessarily produce a higher single-year yield than does a horticultural plot. The first crop grown by horticulturalists on long-idle land may be larger than that from an agricultural plot of the same size. Furthermore, because agriculturists work harder than horticulturalists do, agriculture's yield relative to the labor invested also is lower. Agriculture's main advantage is that the long-term yield per area is far greater and more dependable. Because a single field sustains its owners year after year, there is no need to maintain a reserve of uncultivated land as horticulturalists do. This is why agricultural societies tend to be more densely populated than horticultural ones are.

## Agricultural Intensification: People and the Environment

The range of environments available for food production has widened as people have increased their control over nature. For example, in arid areas of California, where Native Americans once foraged, modern irrigation technology now sustains rich agricultural estates. Agriculturists live in many areas that are too arid for nonirrigators or too hilly for nonterracers. Increasing labor intensity and permanent land use have major demographic, social, political, and environmental consequences.

Thus, because of their permanent fields, agriculturists are sedentary. People live in larger and more permanent communities located closer to other settlements. Growth in population size and density increases contact between individuals and groups. There is more need to regulate interpersonal relations, including conflicts of interest. Economies that support more people usually require more coordination in the use of land, labor, and other resources.

Intensive agriculture has significant environmental effects. Irrigation ditches and paddies (fields with irrigated rice) become repositories for organic wastes, chemicals (such as salts), and disease microorganisms. Intensive agriculture typically spreads at the expense of trees and forests, which are cut down to be replaced by fields. Accompanying such deforestation is loss of environmental diversity (see Srivastava, Smith, and Forno 1999). Agricultural economies grow increasingly specialized. They focus on one or a few caloric staples, such as rice, and on the animals that aid the agricultural economy. Because tropical horticulturalists typically cultivate dozens of plant species simultaneously, a horticultural plot mirrors the botanical diversity that is found in a tropical forest. Agricultural plots, by contrast, reduce ecological diversity by cutting down trees and concentrating on just a few staple foods. Such crop specialization is true of agriculturists both in the tropics (e.g., Indonesian paddy farmers) and outside the tropics (e.g., Middle Eastern irrigation farmers).

Agriculturists attempt to reduce risk in production by favoring stability in the form of a reliable annual harvest and long-term production. Tropical foragers and horticulturalists, by contrast, attempt to reduce risk by relying on multiple species and benefiting from ecological diversity. The agricultural strategy is to put all one's eggs in one big and very dependable basket. The strategy of tropical foragers and horticulturalists is to have several smaller baskets, a few of which may fail without endangering subsistence. The agricultural strategy makes sense when there are lots of children to raise and adults to be fed. Foraging and horticulture, of course, are associated with smaller, sparser, and more mobile populations.

Agricultural economies also pose a series of regulatory problems. How is water to be managed? How are disputes about access to and distribution of water to be resolved? With more people living closer together on more valuable land, agriculturists are more likely to come into conflict than foragers and horticulturalists are. The social and political implications of food production and intensification are examined more fully in the chapter "Political Systems."

## ✈ PASTORALISM

**Pastoralists** live in North Africa, the Middle East, Europe, Asia, and sub-Saharan Africa. These herders are people whose activities focus on such domesticated animals as cattle, sheep, goats, camels, yak, and reindeer. East African pastoralists, like many others, live in symbiosis with their herds. (*Symbiosis* is an obligatory interaction between groups— here humans and animals—that is beneficial to each.) Herders attempt to protect their animals and to ensure their reproduction in return for food and other products, such as leather. Herds provide dairy products and meat.

People use livestock in various ways. Natives of North America's Great Plains, for example, didn't eat, but only rode, their horses. (Europeans reintroduced horses to the Western Hemisphere; the native American horse had become extinct thousands of years earlier.) For Plains Indians, horses served as "tools of the trade," means of production used to *hunt* buffalo, a main target of their economies. So the Plains Indians were not true pastoralists but hunters who used horses—as many agriculturists use animals—as means of production.

Pastoralists, by contrast, typically use their herds for food. They consume their meat, blood, and milk, from which they make yogurt, butter, and cheese. Although some pastoralists rely on their herds more completely than others do, it is impossible to base subsistence solely on animals. Most pastoralists therefore supplement their diet by hunting, gathering, fishing, cultivating, or trading.

The Samis (also known as Lapps or Laplanders) of Norway, Sweden, and Finland domesticated the reindeer, which their ancestors used to hunt, in the 16th century. Like other herders, they follow their animals as they make an annual trek, in this case from coast to interior. Today's Samis use modern technology, such as snowmobiles and four-wheel-drive vehicles, to accompany their herds on their annual nomadic trek. Although their environment is harsher, the Samis, like other herders, live in nation-states and must deal with outsiders, including government officials, as they follow their herds and make their living through animal husbandry, trade, and sales (Hoge 2001).

Unlike foraging and cultivation, which existed throughout the world before the Industrial Revolution, pastoralism was confined almost totally to the Old World. Before European conquest, the only pastoralists in the Americas lived in the Andean region of South America. They used their llamas and alpacas for food and wool and in agriculture and transport. Much more recently, Navajo of the southwestern United States developed a pastoral economy based on sheep, which were brought to North America by Europeans. The populous Navajo became the major pastoral population in the Western Hemisphere.

Two patterns of movement occur with pastoralism: *nomadism* and *transhumance.* Both are based on the fact that herds must move to use pasture available in particular places in different seasons. In pastoral **nomadism,** the entire group—women, men, and children—moves with the animals throughout the year. The Middle East and North Africa provide numerous examples of pastoral nomads. In Iran, for example, the Basseri and the Qashqai ethnic groups traditionally followed a nomadic route more than 300 miles (480 kilometers) long (see Salzman 2004).

With **transhumance,** part of the group moves with the herds, but most people stay in the home village. There are examples from Europe and Africa. In Europe's Alps it is just the shepherds and goatherds—not the whole village—who accompany the flocks to highland meadows in summer. Among the Turkana of Uganda, men and boys accompany the herds to distant pastures, while much of the village stays put and does some horticultural farming. During their annual trek, pastoral nomads trade for crops and other products with more sedentary people. Transhumants don't have to trade for crops. Because only part of the population accompanies the herds, transhumants can maintain year-round villages and grow their own crops.

## ✦ ECONOMIC SYSTEMS

An **economy** is a system of production, distribution, and consumption of resources; *economics* is the study of such systems. Economists focus on modern nations and capitalist systems. Anthropologists have broadened understanding of economic principles by gathering data on nonindustrial economies. Economic anthropology studies economics in a comparative perspective (see Gudeman, ed. 1999; Plattner, ed. 1989; Sahlins 2004; Wilk 1996).

A **mode of production** is a way of organizing production—"a set of social relations through which labor is deployed to wrest energy from nature by means of tools, skills, organization, and knowledge" (Wolf 1982, p. 75). In the capitalist mode of production, money buys labor power, and there is a social gap between the people (bosses and workers) involved in the production process. By contrast, in nonindustrial societies, labor usually is not bought but is given as a social obligation. In such a *kin-based* mode of production, mutual aid in production is one among many expressions of a larger web of social relations.

Societies representing each of the adaptive strategies just discussed (e.g., foraging) tend to have similar modes of production. Differences in the mode of production within a given strategy may reflect differences in environments, target resources, or cultural traditions (Kelly 1995). Thus a foraging mode of production may be based on individual hunters or teams, depending on whether the game is a solitary or a herd animal. Gathering usually is more individualistic than hunting, although collecting teams may assemble when abundant resources ripen and must be harvested quickly. Fishing may be done alone (as in ice or spear fishing) or in crews (as with open-sea fishing and hunting of sea mammals).

## Production in Nonindustrial Societies

Although some kind of division of economic labor related to age and gender is a cultural universal, the specific tasks assigned to each sex and to people of different ages vary (see the chapter "Gender"). Many horticultural societies assign a major productive role to women, but some make men's work primary. Similarly, among pastoralists men generally tend large animals, but in some societies women do the milking. Jobs accomplished through teamwork in some cultivating societies are done in other societies by smaller groups or by individuals working over a longer period.

The Betsileo of Madagascar have two stages of teamwork in rice cultivation: transplanting and harvesting. Both feature a traditional division of labor by age and gender which is well known and repeated across the generations. The first job in transplanting is the trampling of a flooded, previously tilled, field by young men driving cattle, in order to mix earth and water. They bring cattle to the fields just before transplanting. The young men yell at and beat the cattle, striving to drive them into a frenzy so that they will trample the fields properly. Trampling breaks up clumps of earth and mixes irrigation water with soil to form a smooth mud into which women transplant seedlings. Once the tramplers leave the field, older men arrive. With their spades they break up the clumps that the cattle missed. Meanwhile, the owner and other adults uproot rice seedlings and bring them to the field. Women plant the seedlings.

At harvest time, four or five months later, young men cut the rice off the stalks. Young women carry it to the clearing above the field. Older women arrange and stack it. The oldest men and women then stand on the stack, stomping and compacting it. Three days later, young men thresh the rice, beating the stalks against a rock to remove the grain. Older men then attack the stalks with sticks to make sure all the grains have fallen off.

# Means of Production

In nonindustrial societies there is a more intimate relationship between the worker and the means of production than there is in industrial nations. **Means, or factors, of production** include land (territory), labor, and technology.

## *Land*

Among foragers, ties between people and land are less permanent than they are among food producers. Although many bands have territories, the boundaries usually are not marked, and there is no way they can be enforced. The hunter's stake in an animal is more important than where the animal finally dies. A person acquires the rights to use a band's territory by being born in the band or by joining it through a tie of kinship, marriage, or fictive kinship. In Botswana in southern Africa, Ju/'hoansi San women habitually used specific tracts of berry-bearing trees. When a woman changed bands, she immediately acquired a new gathering area.

Among food producers, rights to the means of production also come through kinship and marriage. Descent groups (groups whose members claim common ancestry) are common among nonindustrial food producers. Those who descend from the founder share the group's territory and resources. If the adaptive strategy is horticulture, the estate includes gardens and fallow land for shifting cultivation. As members of a descent group, pastoralists have access to animals to start their own herds, to grazing land, to garden land, and to other means of production.

## *Labor, Tools, and Specialization*

Like land, labor is a means of production. In nonindustrial societies, access to both land and labor comes through social links such as kinship, marriage, and descent. Mutual aid in production is merely one aspect of ongoing social relations that are expressed on many other occasions.

Nonindustrial societies contrast with industrial nations regarding another means of production—technology. In bands and tribes manufacturing often is linked to age and gender. Women may weave and men may make pottery, or vice versa. Most people of a particular age and gender share the technical knowledge associated with that age and gender. If married women customarily make baskets, most married women know how to make baskets. Neither technology nor technical knowledge is very specialized.

Some tribal societies, however, do promote specialization. Among the Yanomami of Venezuela and Brazil, for instance, certain villages manufacture clay pots and others make hammocks. They don't specialize, as one might suppose, because certain raw materials happen to be available near particular villages. Clay suitable for pots is widely available. Everyone knows how to make pots, but not everybody does so. Craft specialization reflects the social and political environment rather than the natural environment. Such specialization promotes trade, which is the first step in creating an alliance with enemy villages (Chagnon 1997).

## Alienation in Industrial Economies

There are significant contrasts between industrial and nonindustrial economies. When factory workers produce for their employer's profit, they may be *alienated* from the items they make: They don't feel strong pride in or personal identification with their products. They see their product as belonging to someone other than the man or woman whose labor actually produced it. In nonindustrial societies, by contrast, people usually see their work through from start to finish and feel a sense of accomplishment.

In nonindustrial societies the economic relation between coworkers is just one aspect of a more general social relation. They aren't just coworkers but kin, in-laws, or celebrants in the same ritual. In industrial nations, people usually don't work with relatives and neighbors. If coworkers are friends, the personal relationship usually develops out of their common employment rather than being based on a previous association.

Thus, industrial workers have impersonal relations with their products, coworkers, and employers. People sell their labor for cash, and the economic domain stands apart from ordinary social life. In nonindustrial societies, however, the relations of production, distribution, and consumption are *social relations with economic aspects*. Economy is not a separate entity but is *embedded* in the society.

### *A Case of Industrial Alienation*

For decades, the government of Malaysia has promoted export-oriented industry, allowing transnational companies to install labor-intensive manufacturing operations in rural Malaysia. The industrialization of Malaysia is part of a global strategy. In search of cheaper labor, corporations headquartered in Japan, Western Europe, and the United States have moved labor-intensive factories to developing countries. Malaysia has hundreds of Japanese and American subsidiaries, which produce garments, foodstuffs, and electronics components. In electronics plants in rural Malaysia, thousands of young women from peasant families now assemble microchips and microcomponents for transistors and capacitors. Aihwa Ong (1987) did a study of electronics assembly workers in an area where 85 percent of the workers were young unmarried females from nearby villages.

Ong found that, unlike village women, female factory workers had to cope with a rigid work routine and constant supervision by men. The discipline that factories value was being taught in local schools, where uniforms helped prepare girls for the factory dress code. Village women wear loose, flowing tunics, sarongs, and sandals, but factory workers had to don tight overalls and heavy rubber gloves, in which they felt constrained. Assembling electronics components requires precise, concentrated labor. Labor in these factories illustrates the separation of intellectual and manual activity—the alienation that Karl Marx considered the defining feature of industrial work. One woman said about her bosses, "They exhaust us very much, as if they do not think that we too are human beings" (Ong 1987, p. 202). Nor does factory work bring women a substantial financial reward, given low wages, job uncertainty, and family claims on wages. Young women typically work just a few years. Production quotas, three daily shifts, overtime, and surveillance take their toll in mental and physical exhaustion.

One response to factory relations of production has been spirit possession (factory women are possessed by spirits). Ong interprets this phenomenon as the women's unconscious protest against labor discipline and male control of the industrial setting. Sometimes possession takes the form of mass hysteria. Spirits have simultaneously invaded as many as 120 factory workers. Weretigers (the Malay equivalent of the werewolf) arrive to avenge the construction of a factory on aboriginal burial grounds. Disturbed earth and grave spirits swarm on the shop floor. First the women see the spirits;

Employees working in a Celestica factory outside Penang, Malaysia. Celestica, which is based in Toronto, Canada, makes electronics for other companies. In Malaysia, thousands of young women from peasant families now assemble electronic components. Unlike village women, female factory workers often face a rigid work routine and constant supervision by men.

then their bodies are invaded. The women become violent and scream abuses. The wer-etigers send the women into sobbing, laughing, and shrieking fits. To deal with posses-sion, factories employ local medicine men, who sacrifice chickens and goats to fend off the spirits. This solution works only some of the time; possession still goes on. Factory women continue to act as vehicles to express their own frustrations and the anger of avenging ghosts.

Ong argues that spirit possession expresses anguish at, and resistance to, capitalist relations of production. By engaging in this form of rebellion, however, factory women avoid a direct confrontation with the source of their distress. Ong concludes that spirit pos-session, while expressing repressed resentment, doesn't do much to modify factory condi-tions. (Other tactics, such as unionization, would do more.) Spirit possession may even help maintain the current system by operating as a safety valve for accumulated tensions.

## ✦ ECONOMIZING AND MAXIMIZATION

Economic anthropologists have been concerned with two main questions:

1.  How are production, distribution, and consumption organized in different societies? This question focuses on *systems* of human behavior and their organization.
2.  What motivates people in different societies to produce, distribute or exchange, and consume? Here the focus is not on systems of behavior but on the *individuals* who participate in those systems.

Anthropologists view both economic systems and motivations in a cross-cultural perspective. Motivation is a concern of psychologists, but it also has been a concern of economists and anthropologists. American economists assume that producers and dis-tributors make decisions rationally, using the *profit motive,* as do consumers when they shop around for the best value. Although anthropologists know that the profit motive is not universal, the assumption that individuals try to maximize profits is basic to capital-ism and to Western economic theory. In fact, the subject matter of economics is often defined as economizing, or the rational allocation of scarce means (or resources) to alternative ends (or uses).

What does that mean? Classical economic theory assumes that our wants are infi-nite while our means are limited. People must make choices about how to use their scarce resources—their time, labor, money, and capital. (The box at the end of this chapter dis-putes the idea that people always make economic choices based on scarcity.) Western economists assume that when confronted with choices and decisions, people tend to make the one that maximizes profit. This is assumed to be the most rational choice.

The idea that individuals choose to maximize profits was a basic assumption of the classical economists of the 19th century and one held by many contemporary econo-mists. However, certain economists now recognize that individuals may be motivated by many other goals. Depending on the society and the situation, people may try to max-imize profit, wealth, prestige, pleasure, comfort, or social harmony. Individuals may want to realize their personal or family ambitions or those of another group to which they belong (see Sahlins 2004).

# Alternative Ends

To what uses do people put their scarce resources? Throughout the world, people devote some of their time and energy to building up a *subsistence fund* (Wolf 1966). In other words, they have to work to eat, to replace the calories they use in daily activity. People also must invest in a *replacement fund*. They must maintain their technology and other items essential to production. If a hoe or plow breaks, they must repair or replace it. They also must obtain and replace items that are essential not to production but to everyday life, such as clothing and shelter.

People everywhere also have to invest in a *social fund*. They must help their friends, relatives, in-laws, and neighbors. It is useful to distinguish between a social fund and a *ceremonial fund*. The latter term refers to expenditures on ceremonies or rituals. To prepare a festival honoring one's ancestors, for example, requires time and the outlay of wealth.

Citizens of nonindustrial states also must allocate scarce resources to a *rent fund*. We think of rent as payment for the use of property. Rent fund, however, has a wider meaning. It refers to resources that people must render to an individual or agency that is superior politically or economically. Tenant farmers and sharecroppers, for example, either pay rent or give some of their produce to their landlords, as peasants did under feudalism.

**Peasants** are small-scale agriculturists who live in nonindustrial states and have rent fund obligations (see Kearney 1996). They produce to feed themselves, to sell their produce, and to pay rent. All peasants have two things in common:

1. They live in state-organized societies.
2. They produce food without the elaborate technology—chemical fertilizers, tractors, airplanes to spray crops, and so on—of modern farming or agribusiness.

Besides paying rent to landlords, peasants must satisfy government obligations, paying taxes in the form of money, produce, or labor. The rent fund is not simply an *additional* obligation for peasants. Often it becomes their foremost and unavoidable duty. Sometimes their own diets suffer as a result. The demands of social superiors may divert resources from subsistence, replacement, social, and ceremonial funds.

Motivations vary from society to society, and people often lack freedom of choice in allocating their resources. Because of obligations to pay rent, peasants may allocate their scarce means toward ends that are not their own but those of government officials. Thus, even in societies in which there is a profit motive, people often are prevented from rationally maximizing self-interest by factors beyond their control.

## ✦ DISTRIBUTION, EXCHANGE

The economist Karl Polanyi (1968) stimulated the comparative study of exchange, and several anthropologists followed his lead. Polanyi defined three principles that guide exchanges: the market principle, redistribution, and reciprocity. These principles all can be present in the same society, but in that case they govern different kinds of transactions. In any society, one of them usually dominates. The principle of exchange that dominates in a given society is the one that allocates the means of production.

# The Market Principle

In today's world capitalist economy, the **market principle** dominates. It governs the distribution of the means of production—land, labor, natural resources, technology, and capital. With market exchange, items are bought and sold, using money, with an eye to maximizing profit, and value is determined by the *law of supply and demand* (things cost more the scarcer they are and the more people want them). Bargaining is characteristic of market-principle exchanges. The buyer and seller strive to maximize—to get their "money's worth." Bargaining doesn't require that the buyer and seller meet. Consumers bargain whenever they shop around or use advertisements or the Internet in their decision making (see Madra 2004).

# Redistribution

**Redistribution** operates when goods, services, or their equivalent move from the local level to a center. The center may be a capital, a regional collection point, or a storehouse near a chief's residence. Products often move through a hierarchy of officials for storage at the center. Along the way officials and their dependents may consume some of them, but the exchange principle here is *re*distribution. The flow of goods eventually reverses direction—out from the center, down through the hierarchy, and back to the common people.

One example of a redistributive system comes from the Cherokee, the original owners of the Tennessee Valley. Productive farmers who subsisted on maize, beans, and squash, supplemented by hunting and fishing, the Cherokee had chiefs. Each of their main villages had a central plaza, where meetings of the chief's council took place and where redistributive feasts were held. According to Cherokee custom, each family farm had an area where the family could set aside part of their annual harvest for the chief. This supply of corn was used to feed the needy, as well as travelers and warriors journeying through friendly territory. This store of food was available to all who needed it, with the understanding that it "belonged" to the chief and was available through his generosity. The chief also hosted the redistributive feasts held in the main settlements (Harris 1978).

# Reciprocity

**Reciprocity** is exchange between social equals, who normally are related by kinship, marriage, or another close personal tie. Because it occurs between social equals, it is dominant in the more egalitarian societies—among foragers, cultivators, and pastoralists. There are three degrees of reciprocity: *generalized, balanced,* and *negative* (Sahlins 1968, 2004; Service 1966). These may be imagined as areas of a continuum defined by these questions:

1. How closely related are the parties to the exchange?
2. How quickly and unselfishly are gifts reciprocated?

Generalized reciprocity, the purest form of reciprocity, is characteristic of exchanges between closely related people. In balanced reciprocity, social distance increases, as does the need to reciprocate. In negative reciprocity, social distance is greatest and reciprocation is most calculated.

With **generalized reciprocity,** someone gives to another person and expects nothing concrete or immediate in return. Such exchanges are not primarily economic transactions but expressions of personal relationships. Most parents don't keep accounts of every penny they spend on their children. They merely hope that the children will respect their culture's customs involving love, honor, loyalty, and other obligations to parents.

Among foragers, generalized reciprocity tends to govern exchanges. People routinely share with other band members (Bird-David 1992; Kent 1992). So strong is the ethic of sharing that most foragers lack an expression for "thank you." To offer thanks would be impolite because it would imply that a particular act of sharing, which is the keystone of egalitarian society, was unusual. Among the Semai, foragers of central Malaysia (Dentan 1979), to express gratitude would suggest surprise at the hunter's success (Harris 1974).

**Balanced reciprocity** applies to exchanges between people who are more distantly related than are members of the same band or household. In a horticultural society, for example, a man presents a gift to someone in another village. The recipient may be a cousin, a trading partner, or a brother's fictive kinsman. The giver expects something in return. This may not come immediately, but the social relationship will be strained if there is no reciprocation.

Exchanges in nonindustrial societies also may illustrate **negative reciprocity,** mainly in dealing with people on the fringes of or outside their social systems. To people who live in a world of close personal relations, exchanges with outsiders are full of ambiguity and distrust. Exchange is one way of establishing friendly relations, but when trade begins, the relationship is still tentative. Often the initial exchange is close to being purely economic; people want to get something back immediately. Just as in market economies, but without using money, they try to get the best possible immediate return for their investment.

Generalized reciprocity and balanced reciprocity are based on trust and a social tie. Negative reciprocity involves the attempt to get something for as little as possible, even if it means being cagey or deceitful or cheating. Among the most extreme and "negative" examples of negative reciprocity was 19th-century horse thievery by North American Plains Indians. Men would sneak into camps and villages of neighboring tribes to steal horses. A similar pattern of livestock (cattle) raiding continues today in East Africa, among tribes such as the Kuria (Fleisher 2000). In these cases, the party that starts the raiding can expect reciprocity—a raid on their own village—or worse. The Kuria hunt down cattle thieves and kill them. It's still reciprocity, governed by "Do unto others as they have done unto you."

One way of reducing the tension in situations of potential negative reciprocity is to engage in "silent trade." One example was the silent trade of the Mbuti pygmy foragers of the African equatorial forest and their neighboring horticultural villagers. There was no personal contact during their exchanges. A Mbuti hunter left game, honey, or another forest product at a customary site. Villagers collected it and left crops in exchange. Often the parties bargained silently. If one felt the return was insufficient, he or she simply left it at the trading site. If the other party wanted to continue trade, it was increased.

## Coexistence of Exchange Principles

In today's North America, the market principle governs most exchanges, from the sale of the means of production to the sale of consumer goods. We also have redistribution. Some of our tax money goes to support the government, but some of it also comes back to us in the form of social services, education, health care, and road building. We also have reciprocal exchanges. Generalized reciprocity characterizes the relationship between parents and children. However, even here the dominant market mentality surfaces in comments about the high cost of raising children and in the stereotypical statement of the disappointed parent: "We gave you everything money could buy."

Exchanges of gifts, cards, and invitations exemplify reciprocity, usually balanced. Everyone has heard remarks like "They invited us to their daughter's wedding, so when ours gets married, we'll have to invite them" and "They've been here for dinner three times and haven't invited us yet. I don't think we should ask them back until they do." Such precise balancing of reciprocity would be out of place in a foraging band, where resources are communal (common to all) and daily sharing based on generalized reciprocity is an essential ingredient of social life and survival.

## Potlatching

One of the most famous cultural practices studied by ethnographers is the **potlatch.** This is a festive event within a regional exchange system among tribes of the North Pacific Coast of North America, including the Salish and Kwakiutl of Washington and British Columbia. Some tribes still practice the potlatch, sometimes as a memorial to the dead (Kan 1986, 1989). At each such event, assisted by members of their communities, potlatch sponsors traditionally gave away food, blankets, pieces of copper, or other items. In return for this, they got prestige. To give a potlatch enhanced one's reputation. Prestige increased with the lavishness of the potlatch, the value of the goods given away in it.

The potlatching tribes were foragers, but atypical ones for relatively recent times. They were sedentary and had chiefs. And unlike the environments of most other recent foragers, theirs wasn't marginal. They had access to a wide variety of land and sea resources. Among their most important foods were salmon, herring, candlefish, berries, mountain goats, seals, and porpoises (Piddocke 1969).

According to classical economic theory, the profit motive is universal, with the goal of maximizing material benefits. How then does one explain the potlatch, in which substantial wealth is given away (and even destroyed—see below)? Christian missionaries considered potlatching to be wasteful and antithetical to the Protestant work ethic. By 1885, under pressure from Indian agents, missionaries, and Indian converts to Christianity, both Canada and the United States had outlawed potlatching. Between 1885 and 1951 the custom went underground. By 1951 both countries had discreetly dropped the antipotlatching laws from the books (Miller n.d.).

Some scholars seized on this view of the potlatch as a classic case of economically wasteful behavior. The economist and social commentator Thorstein Veblen cited potlatching as an example of conspicuous consumption in his influential book *Theory of the Leisure Class* (1899/1992), claiming that potlatching was based on an economically irrational drive for prestige. This interpretation stressed the lavishness and supposed

This historic photo shows Tlingit clan members attending a potlatch at Sitka, Alaska, in 1904. Such ancestral headdresses have been repatriated recently from museums back to Tlingit clans. Have you ever partaken in anything like a potlatch?

wastefulness, especially of the Kwakiutl displays, to support the contention that in some societies people strive to maximize prestige at the expense of their material well-being. This interpretation has been challenged.

Ecological anthropology, also known as *cultural ecology,* is a theoretical school that attempts to interpret cultural practices, such as the potlatch, in terms of their long-term role in helping humans adapt to their environments. Wayne Suttles (1960) and Andrew Vayda (1961/1968) saw potlatching not in terms of its immediate wastefulness, but in terms of its long-term role as a cultural adaptive mechanism. This view also helps us understand similar patterns of lavish feasting throughout the world. Here is the ecological interpretation: *Customs such as the potlatch are cultural adaptations to alternating periods of local abundance and shortage.*

How does this work? Although the natural environment of the North Pacific Coast is favorable, resources do fluctuate from year to year and place to place. Salmon and herring aren't equally abundant every year in a given locality. One village can have a good year while another is experiencing a bad one. Later their fortunes reverse. In this context, the potlatch cycle had adaptive value, and the potlatch was not a competitive display that brought no material benefit.

A village enjoying an especially good year had a surplus of subsistence items, which it could trade for more durable wealth items, such as blankets, canoes, or pieces of copper. Wealth, in turn, by being distributed, could be converted into prestige. Members of several villages were invited to any potlatch and got to take home the resources that were given away. In this way, potlatching linked villages together in a regional economy—an exchange system that distributed food and wealth from wealthy to needy communities. In return, the potlatch sponsors and their villages got prestige. The decision to potlatch was determined by the health of the local economy. If there had been subsistence surpluses, and thus a buildup of wealth over several good years, a village could afford a potlatch to convert its surplus food and wealth into prestige.

The long-term adaptive value of intercommunity feasting becomes clear when a formerly prosperous village had a run of bad luck. Its people started accepting invitations to potlatches in villages that were doing better. The tables were turned as the temporarily rich became temporarily poor and vice versa. The newly needy accepted food and wealth items. They were willing to receive rather than bestow gifts and thus

## ANTHROPOLOGY TODAY

### *Scarcity and the Betsileo*

In the late 1960s my wife and I lived among the Betsileo people of Madagascar, studying their economy and social life (Kottak 1980). Soon after our arrival we met two well-educated schoolteachers (first cousins) who were interested in our research. The woman's father was a congressional representative who became a cabinet minister during our stay. Their family came from a historically important and typical Betsileo village called Ivato, which they invited us to visit with them.

We had traveled to many other Betsileo villages, where often we were displeased with our reception. As we drove up, children would run away screaming. Women would hurry inside. Men would retreat to doorways, where they lurked bashfully. This behavior expressed the Betsileo's great fear of the *mpakafo*. Believed to cut out and devour his victim's heart and liver, the mpakafo is the Malagasy vampire. These cannibals are said to have fair skin and to be very tall. Because I have light skin and stand over six feet tall, I was a natural suspect. The fact that such creatures were not known to travel with their wives helped

convince the Betsileo that I wasn't really a mpakafo.

When we visited Ivato, its people were different—friendly and hospitable. Our very first day there we did a brief census and found out who lived in which households. We learned people's names and their relationships to our schoolteacher friends and to each other. We met an excellent informant who knew all about the local history. In a few afternoons I learned much more than I had in the other villages in several sessions.

Ivatans were so willing to talk because we had powerful sponsors, village natives who had made it in the outside world, people the Ivatans knew would protect them. The schoolteachers vouched for us, but even more significant was the cabinet minister, who was like a grandfather and benefactor to everyone in town. The Ivatans had no reason to fear us because their more influential native son had asked them to answer our questions.

Once we moved to Ivato, the elders established a pattern of visiting us every evening. They came to talk, attracted by the inquisitive foreigners but also by the wine, tobacco, and food we offered. I asked to relinquish some of their stored-up prestige. They hoped their luck would eventually improve so that resources could be recouped and prestige regained.

The potlatch linked local groups along the North Pacific Coast into a regional alliance and exchange network. Potlatching and intervillage exchange had adaptive functions, regardless of the motivations of the individual participants. The anthropologists who stressed rivalry for prestige were not wrong. They were merely emphasizing *motivations* at the expense of an analysis of economic and ecological *systems*.

The use of feasts to enhance individual and community reputations and to redistribute wealth is not peculiar to populations of the North Pacific Coast. Competitive feasting is widely characteristic of nonindustrial food producers. But among most surviving foragers, who live in marginal areas, resources are too meager to support feasting on such a level. In such societies, sharing rather than competition prevails.

questions about their customs and beliefs. I eventually developed interview schedules about various subjects, including rice production. I used these forms in Ivato and in two other villages I was studying less intensively. Never have I interviewed as easily as I did in Ivato.

As our stay neared its end, our Ivatan friends lamented, saying, "We'll miss you. When you leave, there won't be any more cigarettes, any more wine, or any more questions." They wondered what it would be like for us back in the United States. They knew we had an automobile and that we regularly purchased things, including the wine, cigarettes, and food we shared with them. We could afford to buy products they never would have. They commented, "When you go back to your country, you'll need a lot of money for things like cars, clothes, and food. We don't need to buy those things. We make almost everything we use. We don't need as much money as you, because we produce for ourselves."

The Betsileo weren't unusual for nonindustrial people. Strange as it may seem to an American consumer, those rice farmers actually believed *they had all they needed.* The lesson from the Betsileo of the 1960s is that scarcity, which economists view as universal, is variable. Although shortages do arise in nonindustrial societies, the concept of scarcity (insufficient means) is much less developed in stable subsistence-oriented societies than in the societies characterized by industrialism, particularly as the reliance on consumer goods increases.

But, with globalization over the past few decades, significant changes have affected the Betsileo—and most nonindustrial peoples. On my last visit to Ivato, in 2006, the effects of cash and of rapid population increase were evident there—and throughout Madagascar—where the national growth rate has been about 3 percent per year. Madagascar's population doubled between 1966 and 1991— from 6 to 12 million people. Today it stands near 18 million (Kottak 2004). One result of population pressure has been agricultural intensification. In Ivato, farmers who formerly had grown only rice in their rice fields now were using the same land for commercial crops, such as carrots, after the annual rice harvest. Another change affecting Ivato in recent years has been the breakdown of social and political order, fueled by increasing demand for cash.

*Continued*

## ANTHROPOLOGY TODAY

Women hull rice in a Betsileo village. In the village of Ivato, farmers who traditionally grew only rice in their fields now use the same land for commercial crops, such as carrots, after the annual rice harvest.

Cattle rustling has become a growing threat. Cattle thieves (sometimes from neighboring villages) have terrorized peasants who previously felt secure in their villages. Some of the rustled cattle are driven to the coasts for commercial export to nearby islands. Prominent among the rustlers are relatively well-educated young men who have studied long enough to be comfortable negotiating with outsiders, but who have been unable to find formal work, and who are unwilling to work the rice fields like their peasant ancestors. The formal education system has familiarized them with external institutions and norms, including the need for cash. The concepts of scarcity, commerce, and negative reciprocity now thrive among the Betsileo.

I have witnessed other striking evidence of the new addiction to cash during my most recent visits to Betsileo country. Near Ivato's county seat, people now sell precious stones—tourmalines, which were found by chance in local rice fields. We saw an amazing sight: dozens of villagers destroying an ancestral resource, digging up a large rice field, seeking tourmalines—clear evidence of the encroachment of cash on the local subsistence economy.

Throughout the Betsileo homeland, population growth and density are propelling emigration. Locally, land, jobs, and money are all scarce. One woman with ancestors from Ivato, herself now a resident of the national capital (Antananarivo), remarked that half the children of Ivato now lived in that city. Although she was exaggerating, a census of all the descendants of Ivato reveals a substantial emigrant and urban population.

Ivato's recent history is one of increasing participation in a cash economy. That history, combined with the pressure of a growing population on local resources, has made scarcity not just a concept but a reality for Ivatans and their neighbors.

# SUMMARY

1. Cohen's adaptive strategies include foraging (hunting and gathering), horticulture, agriculture, pastoralism, and industrialism. Foraging was the only human adaptive strategy until the advent of food production (farming and herding) 10,000 years ago. Food production eventually replaced foraging in most places. Almost all modern foragers have some dependence on food production or food producers.

2. Horticulture doesn't use land or labor intensively. Horticulturalists cultivate a plot for one or two years (sometimes longer) and then abandon it. There is always a fallow period. Agriculturists farm the same plot of land continuously and use labor intensively. They use one or more of the following: irrigation, terracing, domesticated animals as means of production, and manuring.

3. The pastoral strategy is mixed. Nomadic pastoralists trade with cultivators. Part of a transhumant pastoral population cultivates while another part takes the herds to pasture. Except for some Peruvians and the Navajo, who are recent herders, the New World lacks native pastoralists.

4. Economic anthropology is the cross-cultural study of systems of production, distribution, and consumption. In nonindustrial societies, a kin-based mode of production prevails. One acquires rights to resources and labor through membership in social groups, not impersonally through purchase and sale. Work is just one aspect of social relations expressed in varied contexts.

5. Economics has been defined as the science of allocating scarce means to alternative ends. Western economists assume the notion of scarcity is universal—which it isn't—and that in making choices, people strive to maximize personal profit. In nonindustrial societies, indeed as in our own, people often maximize values other than individual profit.

6. In nonindustrial societies, people invest in subsistence, replacement, social, and ceremonial funds. States add a rent fund: People must share their output with their social superiors. In states, the obligation to pay rent often becomes primary.

7. Besides studying production, economic anthropologists study and compare exchange systems. The three principles of exchange are the market principle, redistribution, and reciprocity, which may coexist in a given society. The primary exchange mode is the one that allocates the means of production.

8. Patterns of feasting and exchanges of wealth among villages are common among nonindustrial food producers, as among the potlatching societies of North America's North Pacific Coast. Such systems help even out the availability of resources over time.

## KEY TERMS

agriculture (p. 234)

balanced reciprocity (p. 245)

band (p. 231)

correlation (p. 231)

economy (p. 238)

generalized reciprocity (p. 245)

horticulture (p. 232)

market principle (p. 244)

means (or factors) of production (p. 239)

mode of production (p. 238)

negative reciprocity (p. 245)

nomadism, pastoral (p. 237)

pastoralists (p. 237)

peasants (p. 243)

potlatch (p. 246)

reciprocity (p. 244)

redistribution (p. 244)

transhumance (p. 237)

# CHAPTER 12

## POLITICAL SYSTEMS

Anthropologists and political scientists share an interest in political systems and organization, but the anthropological approach is global and comparative and includes nonstates as well as the states and nation-states usually studied by political scientists. Anthropological studies have revealed substantial variation in power, authority, and legal systems in different societies. (*Power* is the ability to exercise one's will over others; *authority* is the socially approved use of power.) (See Gledhill 2000; Kurtz 2001; Lewellen 2003; Nugent and Vincent, eds. 2004; Wolf with Silverman 2001.)

## ✦ WHAT IS "THE POLITICAL"?

Recognizing that political organization sometimes is just an aspect of social organization, Morton Fried offered this definition:

> Political organization comprises those portions of social organization that specifically relate to the individuals or groups that manage the affairs of public policy or seek to control the appointment or activities of those individuals or groups. (Fried 1967, pp. 20–21)

This definition certainly fits contemporary North America. Under "individuals or groups that manage the affairs of public policy" come federal, state (provincial), and local (municipal) governments. Those who seek to influence public policy include such

Citizens routinely use collective action to influence public policy. Shown here, members of Citizens for Responsible Growth in Clemson, South Carolina, have mobilized against the construction of a Wal-Mart Super Center on this 35-acre (14-hectare) site. Have your actions ever influenced public policy?

interest groups as political parties, unions, corporations, consumers, activists, action committees, religious groups, and nongovernmental organizations (NGOs).

Fried's definition is much less applicable to nonstates, where it often was difficult to detect any "public policy." For this reason, I prefer to speak of *socio*political organization in discussing the regulation or management of relations among groups and their representatives. Political regulation includes such processes as decision making, social control, and conflict resolution. The study of political regulation draws our attention to those who make decisions and resolve conflicts (are there formal leaders?).

Ethnographic and archaeological studies in hundreds of places have revealed many correlations between economy and social and political organization.

## ✦ TYPES AND TRENDS

Decades ago, the anthropologist Elman Service (1962) listed four types, or levels, of political organization: band, tribe, chiefdom, and state. Today, none of these political entities (*polities*) can be studied as a self-contained form of political organization, since all exist within the context of nation-states and are subject to state control (see Ferguson 2002). There is archaeological evidence for early bands, tribes, and chiefdoms that existed before the first states appeared. However, since anthropology came into being long after the origin of the state, anthropologists never have been able to observe "in the flesh" a band, tribe, or chiefdom outside the influence of some state. There still may be local political leaders (e.g., village heads) and regional figures (e.g., chiefs) of the sort discussed in this chapter, but all now exist and function within the context of state organization.

A **band** refers to a small *kin-based* group (all its members are related by kinship or marriage) found among foragers. **Tribes** had economies based on nonintensive food production (horticulture and pastoralism). Living in villages and organized into kin groups based on common descent (clans and lineages—see the next chapter), tribes lacked a formal government and had no reliable means of enforcing political decisions. **Chiefdom** refers to a form of sociopolitical organization intermediate between the tribe and the state. In chiefdoms, social relations were based mainly on kinship, marriage, descent, age, generation, and gender—just as they were in bands and tribes. Although chiefdoms were kin-based, they featured differential access to resources (some people had more wealth, prestige, and power than others did) and a permanent political structure. The **state** is a form of sociopolitical organization based on a formal government structure and socioeconomic stratification.

The four labels in Service's typology are much too simple to account for the full range of political diversity and complexity known to archaeology and ethnography. We'll see, for instance, that tribes have varied widely in their political systems and institutions. Nevertheless, Service's typology does highlight some significant contrasts in political organization, especially those between states and nonstates. For example, in bands and tribes—unlike states, which have clearly visible governments—political organization did not stand out as separate and distinct from the total social order. In bands and tribes, it was difficult to characterize an act or event as political rather than merely social.

Service's labels "band," "tribe," "chiefdom," and "state" are categories or types within a **sociopolitical typology.** These types are correlated with the adaptive strategies (economic typology) discussed in the chapter "Making a Living." Thus, foragers (an economic type) tended to have band organization (a sociopolitical type). Similarly, many horticulturalists and pastoralists lived in tribes. Although most chiefdoms had farming economies, herding was important in some Middle Eastern chiefdoms. Nonindustrial states usually had an agricultural base.

With food production came larger, denser populations and more complex economies than was the case among foragers. These features posed new regulatory problems, which gave rise to more complex relations and linkages. Many sociopolitical trends reflect the increased regulatory demands associated with food production. Archaeologists have studied these trends through time, and cultural anthropologists have observed them among more contemporary groups.

---

## ✦ BANDS AND TRIBES

This chapter examines a series of societies with different political systems. A common set of questions will be addressed for each one. What kinds of social groups does the society have? How do the groups link up with larger ones? How do the groups represent themselves to each other? How are their internal and external relations regulated? To answer these questions, we begin with bands and tribes and then move on to chiefdoms and states.

# Foraging Bands

Modern hunter-gatherers should not be seen as representative of Stone Age peoples, all of whom also were foragers. Just how much can contemporary foragers tell us about the economic and social relations that characterized humanity before food production? Modern foragers, after all, live in nation-states and an interlinked world. For genera-tions, the pygmies of the Congo have shared a social world and economic exchanges with their neighbors who are cultivators. All foragers now trade with food producers. Most contemporary hunter-gatherers rely on governments and on missionaries for at least part of what they consume.

## *The San*

In the chapter "Making a Living," we saw how the Basarwa San are affected by policies of the government of Botswana, which relocated them after converting their ancestral lands into a wildlife reserve (Motseta 2006). San speakers ("Bushmen") of southern Africa have been influenced by Bantu speakers (farmers and herders) for 2,000 years and by Europeans for centuries. Edwin Wilmsen (1989) sees the San as a rural under-class in a larger political and economic system dominated by Europeans and Bantu food producers. Many San now tend cattle for wealthier Bantu rather than foraging independ-ently. The Basarwa have domesticated animals. Wilmsen also argues that many San descend from herders who were pushed into the desert by poverty or oppression.

Susan Kent (1992, 1996) notes a tendency to stereotype foragers, to treat them all as alike. They used to be stereotyped as isolated, primitive survivors of the Stone Age. A new stereotype sees them as culturally deprived people forced by states, colonialism, or world events into marginal environments. Although this view often is exaggerated, it probably is more accurate than the former one. Modern foragers differ substantially from Stone Age hunter-gatherers.

Kent (1996) stresses variation among foragers, focusing on diversity in time and space among the San. The nature of San life has changed considerably since the 1950s and 1960s, when a series of anthropologists from Harvard University, including Richard Lee, embarked on a systematic study of life in the Kalahari. Lee and others have docu-mented many of the changes in various publications (Lee 1979, 1984, 2003; Silberbauer 1981, Tanaka 1980). Such longitudinal research monitors variation in time, while field-work in many San areas has revealed variation in space. One of the most important contrasts was found to be that between settled (sedentary) and nomadic groups (Kent and Vierich 1989). Although sedentism has increased substantially in recent years, some San groups (along rivers) have been sedentary for generations. Others, including the Dobe Ju/'hoansi San studied by Lee (1984, 2003) and the Kutse San that Kent studied, have retained more of the hunter-gatherer life style.

Modern foragers are not Stone Age relics, living fossils, lost tribes, or noble sav-ages. Still, to the extent that foraging is the basis of their subsistence, modern hunter-gatherers can illustrate links between a foraging economy and other aspects of society and culture. For example, San groups that still are mobile, or that were so until recently, emphasize social, political, and gender equality. A social system based on kinship, reciprocity, and sharing is appropriate for an economy with few people and limited resources. The nomadic pursuit of wild plants and animals tends to discourage permanent settlement, wealth accumulation, and status distinctions. In this context families and bands are adaptive social units.

Foraging bands, small, nomadic or seminomadic social units, formed seasonally when component nuclear families got together. The particular families in a band varied from year to year. Marriage and kinship created ties between members of different bands. Trade and visiting also linked them. Band leaders were leaders in name only. In such an egalitarian society, they were first among equals. Sometimes they gave advice or made decisions, but they had no way to enforce their decisions.

## *The Inuit*

The aboriginal Inuit (Hoebel 1954, 1954/1968), another group of foragers, provide a good example of methods of settling disputes—**conflict resolution**—in stateless societies. All societies have ways of settling disputes (of variable effectiveness) along with cultural rules or norms about proper and improper behavior. *Norms* are cultural standards or guidelines that enable individuals to distinguish between appropriate and inappropriate behavior in a given society (N. Kottak 2002). While rules and norms are cultural universals, only state societies, those with formal governments, have laws that are formulated, proclaimed, and enforced.

Foragers lacked formal **law** in the sense of a legal code with trial and enforcement, but they did have methods of social control and dispute settlement. The absence of law did not mean total anarchy. As described by E. A. Hoebel (1954) in a classic ethnographic study of conflict resolution, a sparse population of some 20,000 Inuit spanned 6,000 miles (9,500 kilometers) of the Arctic region. The most significant social groups were the nuclear family and the band. Personal relationships linked the families and bands. Some bands had headmen. There were also shamans (part-time religious specialists). However, these positions conferred little power on those who occupied them.

Hunting and fishing by men were the primary Inuit subsistence activities. The diverse and abundant plant foods available in warmer areas, where female labor in gathering is important, were absent in the Arctic. Traveling on land and sea in a bitter environment, Inuit men faced more dangers than women did. The traditional male role took its toll in lives, so that adult women outnumbered men. This permitted some men to have two or three wives. The ability to support more than one wife conferred a certain amount of prestige, but it also encouraged envy. (*Prestige* is esteem, respect, or approval for culturally valued acts or qualities.) If a man seemed to be taking additional wives just to enhance his reputation, a rival was likely to steal one of them. Most disputes were between men and originated over women, caused by wife stealing or adultery. If a man discovered that his wife had been having sexual relations without his permission, he considered himself wronged.

The husband had several options. He could try to kill the wife stealer. However, if he succeeded, one of his rival's kinsmen surely would try to kill him in retaliation. One dispute could escalate into several deaths as relatives avenged a succession of murders. No government existed to intervene and stop such a *blood feud* (a murderous feud between families). However, one also could challenge a rival to a song battle. In a public setting, contestants made up insulting songs about each other. At the end of the match, the audience judged one of them the winner. However, if a man whose wife had been stolen won, there was no guarantee she would return. Often she would decide to stay with her abductor.

Thefts are common in societies with marked property differentials, like our own, but thefts are uncommon among foragers. Each Inuit had access to the resources needed to sustain life. Every man could hunt, fish, and make the tools necessary for subsistence. Every woman could obtain the materials needed to make clothing, prepare food, and do domestic work. Inuit men could even hunt and fish in the territories of other local groups. There was no notion of private ownership of territory or animals.

# Tribal Cultivators

As is true of foraging bands, there are no totally autonomous tribes in today's world. Still, there are societies, for example, in Papua New Guinea and in South America's tropical forests, in which tribal principles continue to operate. Tribes typically have a horticultural or pastoral economy and are organized by village life or membership in *descent groups* (kin groups whose members trace descent from a common ancestor). Tribes lack socioeconomic stratification (i.e., a class structure) and a formal government of their own. A few tribes still conduct small-scale warfare, in the form of intervillage raiding. Tribes have more effective regulatory mechanisms than foragers do, but tribal societies have no sure means of enforcing political decisions. The main regulatory officials are village heads, "big men," descent-group leaders, village councils, and leaders of pantribal associations. All these figures and groups have limited authority.

Like foragers, horticulturalists tend to be egalitarian, although some have marked *gender stratification:* an unequal distribution of resources, power, prestige, and personal freedom between men and women (see the chapter "Gender"). Horticultural villages usually are small, with low population density and open access to strategic resources. Age, gender, and personal traits determine how much respect people receive and how much support they get from others. Egalitarianism diminishes, however, as village size and population density increase. Horticultural villages usually have headmen—rarely, if ever, headwomen.

# The Village Head

The Yanomami (Chagnon 1997) are Native Americans who live in southern Venezuela and the adjacent part of Brazil. Their tribal society has about 20,000 people living in 200 to 250 widely scattered villages, each with a population between 40 and 250. The Yanomami are horticulturalists who also hunt and gather. Their staple crops are bananas and plantains (a banana-like crop). There are more significant social groups among the Yanomami than exist in a foraging society. The Yanomami have families, villages, and descent groups. Their descent groups, which span more than one village, are patrilineal (ancestry is traced back through males only) and exogamous (people must marry outside their own descent group). However, local branches of two different descent groups may live in the same village and intermarry.

As has been true in many village-based tribal societies, the only leadership position among the Yanomami is that of **village head** (always a man). His authority, like that of a foraging band's leader, is severely limited. If a headman wants something done, he must lead by example and persuasion. The headman lacks the right to issue orders. He can only persuade, harangue, and try to influence public opinion. For example, if he wants people to clean up the central plaza in preparation for a feast, he must start sweeping it himself, hoping his covillagers will take the hint and relieve him.

When conflict erupts within the village, the headman may be called on as a mediator who listens to both sides. He will give an opinion and advice. If a disputant is unsatisfied, the headman has no power to back his decisions and no way to impose punishments. Like the band leader, he is first among equals.

A Yanomami village headman also must lead in generosity. Because he must be more generous than any other villager, he cultivates more land. His garden provides much of the food consumed when his village holds a feast for another village. The headman represents the village in its dealings with outsiders. Sometimes he visits other villages to invite people to a feast.

The way a person acts as headman depends on his personal traits and the number of supporters he can muster. One village headman, Kaobawa, intervened in a dispute between a husband and a wife and kept him from killing her (Chagnon 1983/1992). He also guaranteed safety to a delegation from a village with which a covillager of his wanted to start a war. Kaobawa was a particularly effective headman. He had demonstrated his fierceness in battle, but he also knew how to use diplomacy to avoid offending other villagers. No one in the village had a better personality for the headmanship. Nor (because Kaobawa had many brothers) did anyone have more supporters. Among the Yanomami, when a group is dissatisfied with a village headman, its members can leave and found a new village; this is done from time to time.

Yanomami society, with its many villages and descent groups, is more complex than a band-organized society. The Yanomami also face more regulatory problems. A headman sometimes can prevent a specific violent act, but there is no government to resolve conflicts and maintain order. In fact, intervillage raiding has been a feature of some areas of Yanomami territory, particularly those studied by Chagnon (1997).

We also must stress that the Yanomami are not isolated from outside events, including missionization. They live in two nation-states, Venezuela and Brazil, and external warfare waged by Brazilian ranchers and miners increasingly has threatened them (Chagnon 1997; Cultural Survival Quarterly 1989; Ferguson 1995). During a Brazilian gold rush between 1987 and 1991, one Yanomami died each day, on average, from external attacks. By 1991, there were some 40,000 Brazilian miners in the Brazilian Yanomami homeland. Some Indians were killed outright. The miners introduced new diseases, and the swollen population ensured that old diseases became epidemic. In 1991, a commission of the American Anthropological Association reported on the plight of the Yanomami (*Anthropology Newsletter,* September 1991). Brazilian Yanomami were dying at a rate of 10 percent annually, and their fertility rate had dropped to zero. Since then, both the Brazilian and the Venezuelan governments have intervened to protect the Yanomami. One Brazilian president declared a huge Yanomami territory off-limits to outsiders. Unfortunately, local politicians, miners, and ranchers have increasingly evaded the ban. The future of the Yanomami remains uncertain.

# The "Big Man"

Many societies of the South Pacific, particularly in the Melanesian Islands and Papua New Guinea, had a kind of political leader that we call the big man. The **big man** (almost always a male) was an elaborate version of the village head, but with one significant difference. The village head's leadership is within one village; the big man had supporters in several villages. The big man therefore was a regulator of *regional* political organization. Here we see the trend toward expansion in the scale of sociopolitical regulation—from village to region.

The Kapauku Papuans live in Irian Jaya, Indonesia (which is on the island of New Guinea). Anthropologist Leopold Pospisil (1963) studied the Kapauku (then 45,000 people), who grow crops (with the sweet potato as their staple) and raise pigs. Their economy is too complex to be described as simple horticulture. The only political figure among the Kapauku was the big man, known as a *tonowi*. A tonowi achieved his status through hard work, amassing wealth in the form of pigs and other native riches.

The term *status* often is used as a synonym for prestige. In that context, "She's got a lot of status" means she's got a lot of prestige; people look up to her. Among social scientists, that's not the primary meaning of "status." Social scientists use *status* more neutrally—for any social position, no matter what the prestige. In this sense, **status** encompasses the various positions that people occupy in society, such as spouse, parent, trading partner, teacher, student, salesperson, big man, and many others. People always occupy multiple statuses (e.g., son, brother, father, big man). Among the statuses we occupy, particular ones dominate in particular settings, such as son or daughter at home and student in the classroom.

Some statuses are **ascribed:** People have little or no choice about occupying them. Age is an ascribed status; we can't choose not to age. One's status as a member of the nobility, or as a male or a female, usually is ascribed; people are born members of a certain social category and remain so all their lives. **Achieved statuses,** by contrast, aren't automatic; they come through choices, actions, efforts, talents, or accomplishments, and may be positive or negative. Examples of achieved statuses include big man, healer, senator, convicted felon, terrorist, salesperson, union member, father, and college student.

The achieved status of big man rested on certain characteristics that distinguished the big man from his fellows: wealth, generosity, eloquence, physical fitness, bravery, and supernatural powers. Men became big men because they had certain personalities. They amassed resources during their own lifetime; they did not inherit their wealth or position. A man who was determined enough could become a big man, creating wealth through hard work and good judgment. Wealth resulted from successful pig breeding and trading. As a man's pig herd and prestige grew, he attracted supporters. He sponsored ceremonial pig feasts in which pigs were slaughtered and their meat distributed to guests.

Unlike the Yanomami village head, a big man's wealth exceeded that of his fellows. His supporters, recognizing his past favors and anticipating future rewards, recognized him as a leader and accepted his decisions as binding. The big man was an important regulator of regional events in Kapauku life. He helped determine the dates for feasts and markets. He persuaded people to sponsor feasts, which distributed pork and wealth. He

The big man persuades people to organize feasts, which distribute pork and wealth. Shown here is such a regional event, drawing on several villages, in Papua New Guinea. Big men owe their status to their individual personalities rather than to inherited wealth or position. Does our society have equivalents of big men?

initiated economic projects requiring the cooperation of a regional community.

The Kapauku big man again exemplifies a generalization about leadership in tribal societies: If someone achieves wealth and widespread respect and support, he or she must be generous. The big man worked hard not to hoard wealth but to be able to give away the fruits of his labor, to convert wealth into prestige and gratitude. A stingy big man would lose his support, his reputation plummeting. Selfish and greedy big men sometimes were murdered by their fellows (Zimmer-Tamakoshi 1997).

Are contemporary North American politicians like Melanesian big men? Politically valuable attributes of a Melanesian big man included wealth, generosity, eloquence, physical fitness, bravery, and supernatural powers. Americans routinely use their own wealth to finance campaigns. Big men get their loyalists to produce and deliver wealth in the form of pigs, just as modern politicians persuade their supporters to make campaign contributions. And, like big men, successful American politicians try to be generous with their supporters. Payback may take the form of a night in the Lincoln bedroom, a strategic dinner invitation, an ambassadorship, or largesse to a place that was particularly supportive.

Big men amass wealth and then give away pigs. Successful American politicians give away "pork." As with the big man, eloquence and communication skills contribute to political success (e.g., Bill Clinton and Ronald Reagan), although lack of such skills isn't necessarily fatal. What about physical fitness? Hair, height, and health are still political advantages. Bravery, for instance, demonstrated through distinguished military service, also helps political careers (e.g., Wesley Clark and John McCain), but it certainly isn't required. Supernatural powers? Candidates who proclaim themselves atheists are as rare as self-identified witches. Almost all political candidates claim to belong to a mainstream religion. Some even present their candidacies as promoting divine wishes. On the other hand, contemporary politics isn't just about personality, as it is in big man systems. We live in a state-organized, stratified society with inherited wealth, power, and privilege, all of which have political implications. As is typical of states, inheritance and kin connections play a role in political success. Just think of Kennedys, Bushes, Gores, Clintons, and Gandhis.

celebrated militarism. As noted previously, the leaders of these associations organized bison hunting and raiding. They also arbitrated disputes during the summer, when many people came together.

Many tribes that adopted this Plains strategy of adaptation had once been foragers for whom hunting and gathering had been individual or small-group affairs. They never had come together previously as a single social unit. Age and gender were available as social principles that could quickly and efficiently forge unrelated people into pantribal groups.

Raiding of one tribe by another, this time for cattle rather than horses, also was common in eastern and southeastern Africa, where pantribal sodalities, including age sets, also developed. Among the pastoral Masai of Kenya, men born during the same four-year period were circumcised together and belonged to the same named group, an age set, throughout their lives. The sets moved through age grades, the most important of which was the warrior grade. Members of the set who wished to enter the warrior grade were at first discouraged by its current occupants, who eventually vacated the warrior grade and married. Members of a set felt a strong allegiance to one another. Masai women lacked comparable set organization, but they also passed through culturally recognized age grades: the initiate, the married woman, and the postmenopausal woman.

To understand the difference between an age set and an age grade, think of a college class, the Class of 2012, for example, and its progress through the university. The age set would be the group of people constituting the Class of 2012, while the first ("freshman"), sophomore, junior, and senior years would represent the age grades.

Not all societies with age grades also have age sets. When there are no sets, men can enter or leave a particular grade individually or collectively, often by going through a predetermined ritual. The grades most commonly recognized in Africa are these:

1. Recently initiated youths
2. Warriors
3. One or more grades of mature men who play important roles in pantribal government
4. Elders, who may have special ritual responsibilities

In certain parts of West Africa and Central Africa, the pantribal sodalities are *secret societies,* made up exclusively of men or women. Like our college fraternities and sororities, these associations have secret initiation ceremonies. Among the Mende of Sierra Leone, men's and women's secret societies were very influential. The men's group, the Poro, trained boys in social conduct, ethics, and religion and supervised political and economic activities. Leadership roles in the Poro often overshadowed village headship and played an important part in social control, dispute management, and tribal political regulation. Age, gender, and ritual can link members of different local groups into a single social collectivity in a tribe and thus create a sense of ethnic identity, of belonging to the same cultural tradition.

## Nomadic Politics

Although many pastoralists, such as the Masai, live in tribes, a range of demographic and sociopolitical diversity occurs with pastoralism. A comparison of pastoralists shows that as regulatory problems increase, political hierarchies become more complex. Political organization becomes less personal, more formal, and less kinship-oriented. The pastoral strategy of adaptation does not dictate any particular political organization. Unlike the Masai and other tribal herders, some pastoralists have chiefs and live in nation-states.

The scope of political authority among pastoralists expands considerably as regulatory problems increase in densely populated regions. Consider two Iranian pastoral nomadic tribes—the Basseri and the Qashqai (Salzman 1974). Starting each year from a plateau near the coast, these groups took their animals to grazing land 17,000 feet (5,400 meters) above sea level. The Basseri and the Qashqai shared this route with one another and with several other ethnic groups.

Use of the same pasture land at different times was carefully scheduled. Ethnic-group movements were tightly coordinated. Expressing this schedule is *il-rah,* a concept common to all Iranian nomads. A group's il-rah is its customary path in time and space. It is the schedule, different for each group, of when specific areas can be used in the annual trek.

Each tribe had its own leader, known as the *khan* or *il-khan.* The Basseri khan, because he dealt with a smaller population, faced fewer problems in coordinating its movements than did the leaders of the Qashqai. Correspondingly, his rights, privileges, duties, and authority were weaker. Nevertheless, his authority exceeded that of any political figure discussed so far. The khan's authority still came from his personal traits rather than from his office. That is, the Basseri followed a particular khan not because of a political position he happened to fill but because of their personal allegiance and loyalty to him as a man. The khan relied on the support of the heads of the descent groups into which Basseri society was divided.

In Qashqai society, however, allegiance shifted from the person to the office. The Qashqai had multiple levels of authority and more powerful chiefs or khans. Managing 400,000 people required a complex hierarchy. Heading it was the il-khan, helped by a deputy, under whom were the heads of constituent tribes, under each of whom were descent-group heads.

A case illustrates just how developed the Qashqai authority structure was. A hailstorm prevented some nomads from joining the annual migration at the appointed time. Although everyone recognized that they were not responsible for their delay, the il-khan assigned them less favorable grazing land, for that year only, in place of their usual pasture. The tardy herders and other Qashqai considered the judgment fair and didn't question it. Thus, Qashqai authorities regulated the annual migration. They also adjudicated disputes between people, tribes, and descent groups.

These Iranian cases illustrate the fact that pastoralism often is just one among many specialized economic activities within complex nation-states and regional systems. As part of a larger whole, pastoral tribes are constantly pitted against other ethnic groups. In these nations, the state becomes a final authority, a higher-level regulator that attempts to limit conflict between ethnic groups. State organization arose not just to manage agricultural economies but also to regulate the activities of ethnic groups within expanding social and economic systems (see Das and Poole, eds. 2004).

## ✦ CHIEFDOMS

Having looked at bands and tribes, we turn to more complex forms of sociopolitical organization—chiefdoms and states. The first states emerged in the Old World about 5,500 years ago. The first chiefdoms developed perhaps a thousand years earlier, but few survive today. In many parts of the world, the chiefdom was a transitional form of organization that emerged during the evolution of tribes into states. State formation began in Mesopotamia (currently Iran and Iraq). It next occurred in Egypt, the Indus Valley of Pakistan and India, and northern China. A few thousand years later states arose in two parts of the Western Hemisphere—Mesoamerica (Mexico, Guatemala, Belize) and the central Andes (Peru and Bolivia). Early states are known as *archaic states*, or nonindustrial states, in contrast to modern industrial nation-states. Robert Carneiro defines the state as "an autonomous political unit encompassing many communities within its territory, having a centralized government with the power to collect taxes, draft men for work or war, and decree and enforce laws" (Carneiro 1970, p. 733).

The chiefdom and the state, like many categories used by social scientists, are *ideal types*. That is, they are labels that make social contrasts seem sharper than they really are. In reality there is a continuum from tribe to chiefdom to state. Some societies had many attributes of chiefdoms but retained tribal features. Some advanced chiefdoms had many attributes of archaic states and thus are difficult to assign to either category. Recognizing this "continuous change" (Johnson and Earle 2000), some anthropologists speak of "complex chiefdoms" (Earle 1987, 1997), which are almost states.

## Political and Economic Systems in Chiefdoms

Chiefdoms developed in several parts of the world, including the circum-Caribbean (e.g., Caribbean islands, Panama, Colombia), lowland Amazonia, what is now the southeastern United States, and Polynesia. Between the emergence and spread of food production and the expansion of the Roman empire, much of Europe was organized at the chiefdom level. Europe reverted to this level for centuries after the fall of Rome in the fifth century A.D. Chiefdoms created the megalithic cultures of Europe, such as the one that built Stonehenge. Bear in mind that chiefdoms and states can fall (disintegrate) as well as rise.

Much of our ethnographic knowledge about chiefdoms comes from Polynesia, where they were common at the time of European exploration. In chiefdoms, social relations are based mainly on kinship, marriage, descent, age, generation, and gender—just as they are in bands and tribes. This is a fundamental difference between chiefdoms and states. States bring nonrelatives together and oblige them all to pledge allegiance to a government.

Unlike bands and tribes, however, chiefdoms are characterized by *permanent political regulation* of the territory they administer. They have a clear-cut and enduring regional political system. Chiefdoms may include thousands of people living in many villages or hamlets. Regulation is carried out by the chief and his or her assistants, who occupy political offices. An **office** is a permanent position, which must be refilled when it is vacated by death or retirement. Because offices are refilled systematically, the structure of a chiefdom endures across the generations, ensuring permanent political regulation.

Stonehenge, England, and an educational display designed for tourists and
visitors. Chiefdoms created the megalithic cultures of Europe, such as the one
that built Stonehenge over 5,000 years ago. Between the emergence and spread
of food production and the expansion of the Roman empire, much of Europe was
organized at the chiefdom level, to which it reverted after the fall of Rome.

In the Polynesian chiefdoms, the chiefs were full-time political specialists in
charge of regulating the economy—production, distribution, and consumption. Polynesian chiefs relied on religion to buttress their authority. They regulated production by
commanding or prohibiting (using religious taboos) the cultivation of certain lands and
crops. Chiefs also regulated distribution and consumption. At certain seasons—often
on a ritual occasion such as a first-fruit ceremony—people would offer part of their
harvest to the chief through his or her representatives. Products moved up the hierarchy,

eventually reaching the chief. Conversely, illustrating obligatory sharing with kin, chiefs sponsored feasts at which they gave back much of what they had received.

Such a flow of resources to and then from a central office is known as *chiefly redistribution*. Redistribution offers economic advantages. If the different areas specialized in particular crops, goods, or services, chiefly redistribution made those products available to the entire society. Chiefly redistribution also played a role in risk management. It stimulated production beyond the immediate subsistence level and provided a central storehouse for goods that might become scarce at times of famine (Earle 1987, 1997).

## Social Status in Chiefdoms

Social status in chiefdoms was based on seniority of descent. Because rank, power, prestige, and resources came through kinship and descent, Polynesian chiefs kept extremely long genealogies. Some chiefs (without writing) managed to trace their ancestry back 50 generations. All the people in the chiefdom were thought to be related to each other. Presumably, all were descended from a group of founding ancestors.

The status of chief was ascribed, based on seniority of descent. The chief would be the oldest child (usually son) of the oldest child of the oldest child, and so on. Degrees of seniority were calculated so intricately on some islands that there were as many ranks as people. For example, the third son would rank below the second, who in turn would rank below the first. The children of an eldest brother, however, would all rank above the children of the next brother, whose children would in turn outrank those of younger brothers. However, even the lowest-ranking person in a chiefdom was still the chief's relative. In such a kin-based context, everyone, even a chief, had to share with his or her relatives.

Because everyone had a slightly different status, it was difficult to draw a line between elites and common people. Other chiefdoms calculated seniority differently and had shorter genealogies than did those in Polynesia. Still, the concern for seniority and the lack of sharp gaps between elites and commoners are features of all chiefdoms.

## Status Systems in Chiefdoms and States

The status systems of chiefdoms and states are similar in that both are based on **differential access** to resources. This means that some men and women had privileged access to power, prestige, and wealth. They controlled strategic resources such as land and water. Earle characterizes chiefs as "an incipient aristocracy with advantages in wealth and lifestyle" (1987, p. 290). Nevertheless, differential access in chiefdoms was tied very much to kinship. The people with privileged access were generally chiefs and their nearest relatives and assistants.

Compared with chiefdoms, archaic states drew a much firmer line between elites and masses, distinguishing at least between nobles and commoners. Kinship ties did not extend from the nobles to the commoners because of *stratum endogamy*—marriage within one's own group. Commoners married commoners; elites married elites.

Such a division of society into socioeconomic strata contrasts strongly with bands and tribes, whose status systems are based on prestige, rather than on differential access to resources. The prestige differentials that do exist in bands reflect special qualities and abilities. Good hunters get respect from their fellows if they are generous. So does a skilled curer, dancer, storyteller—or anyone else with a talent or skill that others appreciate.

In tribes, some prestige goes to descent-group leaders, to village heads, and especially to the big man. All these figures must be generous, however. If they accumulate more resources—such as property or food—than others in the village, they must share them with the others. Since strategic resources are available to everyone, social classes based on the possession of unequal amounts of resources can never exist.

In many tribes, particularly those with patrilineal descent (descent traced through males only), men have much greater prestige and power than women do. The gender contrast in rights may diminish in chiefdoms, where prestige and access to resources are based on seniority of descent, so that some women are senior to some men. Unlike big men, chiefs are exempt from ordinary work and have rights and privileges that are unavailable to the masses. Like big men, however, they still return much of the wealth they take in.

## The Emergence of Stratification

The status system in chiefdoms, although based on differential access, differed from the status system in states because the privileged few were always relatives and assistants of the chief. However, this type of status system didn't last very long. Chiefs would start acting like kings and try to erode the kinship basis of the chiefdom. In Madagascar they

Shown here in Cleveland, Ohio, in January 2004, Rebecca Jemison meets the media after being announced as the winner of Ohio's first ($162 million) "Mega Millions" lottery. Wealth and prestige are not always correlated. Do you think Jemison's prestige will rise as a result of winning the lottery?

### TABLE 12-1

**Max Weber's Three Dimensions of Stratification**

| | | |
|---|---|---|
| wealth | $\longrightarrow$ | economic status |
| power | $\longrightarrow$ | political status |
| prestige | $\longrightarrow$ | social status |

would do this by demoting their more distant relatives to commoner status and banning marriage between nobles and commoners (Kottak 1980). Such moves, if accepted by the society, created separate social strata—*unrelated* groups that differ in their access to wealth, prestige, and power. (A *stratum* is one of two or more groups that contrast in social status and access to strategic resources. Each stratum includes people of both sexes and all ages.) The creation of separate social strata is called **stratification,** and its emergence signified the transition from chiefdom to state. *The presence of stratification is one of the key distinguishing features of a state.*

The influential sociologist Max Weber (1922/1968) defined three related dimensions of social stratification: (1) Economic status, or **wealth,** encompasses all a person's material assets, including income, land, and other types of property. (2) **Power,** the ability to exercise one's will over others—to do what one wants—is the basis of political status. (3) **Prestige**—the basis of social status—refers to esteem, respect, or approval for acts, deeds, or qualities considered exemplary. Prestige, or "cultural capital" (Bourdieu 1984), gives people a sense of worth and respect, which they may often convert into economic advantage (Table 12-1).

In archaic states—for the first time in human evolution—there were contrasts in wealth, power, and prestige between entire groups (social strata) of men and women. Each stratum included people of both sexes and all ages. The **superordinate** (the higher or elite) stratum had privileged access to wealth, power, and other valued resources. Access to resources by members of the **subordinate** (lower or underprivileged) stratum was limited by the privileged group.

## Open- and Closed-Class Systems

Inequalities, which are built into the structure of state-organized societies, tend to persist across the generations. The extent to which they do or don't is a measure of the openness of the stratification system, the ease of social mobility it permits. **Vertical mobility** is an upward or downward change in a person's social status. A truly **open-class system** would facilitate mobility. Individual achievement and personal merit would determine social rank. Hierarchical social statuses would be achieved on the basis of people's efforts. Ascribed statuses (family background, ethnicity, gender, religion) would be less important.

Stratification has taken many forms, including caste, slavery, and class systems. **Caste systems** are closed, hereditary systems of stratification that often are dictated by religion. Hierarchical social status is ascribed at birth, so that people are locked into their parents' social position. Caste lines are clearly defined, and legal and religious sanctions are applied against those who seek to cross them.

In **slavery,** the most inhumane, coercive, and degrading form of legal stratification, people who are conquered or stolen from their homelands become someone's property. In the Atlantic slave trade millions of human beings were treated as commodities. The plantation systems of the Caribbean, the southeastern United States, and Brazil were based on forced slave labor. Lacking control over the means of production as well as their own destinies, slaves were forced to live and work at their master's whim. Defined as lesser—or less than—human beings, slaves lacked legal rights. They could be sold and resold; their families were split apart. Unlike the poorest nonslaves, enslaved people had nothing to sell—not even their own labor (Mintz 1985).

Modern class structures, featuring forms of stratification more open than slavery, caste systems, or the status systems of ancient states, have developed in recent times. Still, socioeconomic stratification continues as a defining feature of all states, archaic or industrial. The elites control a significant part of the means of production, for example, land, herds, water, capital, farms, or factories. Those born at the bottom of the hierarchy have reduced chances of social mobility. Because of elite ownership rights, ordinary people lack free access to resources. Only in states do the elites get to keep their differential wealth. Unlike big men and chiefs, they don't have to give it back to the people whose labor has built and increased it.

## ✦ STATES

Table 12-2 summarizes the information presented so far on bands, tribes, chiefdoms, and states. States, remember, are autonomous political units with social classes and a formal government, based on law. States tend to be large and populous, as compared to bands,

## TABLE 12-2

### Economic Basis of and Political Regulation in Bands, Tribes, Chiefdoms, and States

| Sociopolitical Type | Economic Type | Examples | Type of Regulation |
|---|---|---|---|
| Band | Foraging | Inuit, San | Local |
| Tribe | Horticulture, pastoralism | Yanomami, Masai, Kapauku | Local, temporary, regional |
| Chiefdom | Intensive horticulture, pastoral nomadism, agriculture | Qashqai, Polynesia, Cherokee | Permanent, regional |
| State | Agriculture, industrialism | Ancient Mesopotamia, contemporary U.S., and Canada | Permanent, regional |

tribes, and chiefdoms. Certain statuses, systems, and subsystems with specialized functions are found in all states (see Sharma and Gupta 2006). They include the following:

1. *Population control:* fixing of boundaries, establishment of citizenship categories, and the taking of a census.
2. *Judiciary:* laws, legal procedure, and judges.
3. *Enforcement:* permanent military and police forces.
4. *Fiscal:* taxation.

In archaic states, these subsystems were integrated by a ruling system or government composed of civil, military, and religious officials (Fried 1960).

# Population Control

To know whom they govern, states typically conduct censuses. States demarcate boundaries that separate them from other societies. Customs agents, immigration officers, navies, and coast guards patrol frontiers. Even nonindustrial states have boundary-maintenance forces. In Buganda, an archaic state on the shores of Lake Victoria in Uganda, the king rewarded military officers with estates in outlying provinces. They became his guardians against foreign intrusion.

States also control population through administrative subdivision: provinces, districts, "states," counties, subcounties, and parishes. Lower-level officials manage the populations and territories of the subdivisions.

In nonstates, people work and relax with their relatives, in-laws, and agemates—people with whom they have a personal relationship. Such a personal social life existed throughout most of human history, but food production spelled its eventual decline. After millions of years of human evolution, it took a mere 4,000 years for the population increase and regulatory problems spawned by food production to lead from tribe to chiefdom to state. With state organization, kinship's pervasive role diminished. Descent groups may continue as kin groups within archaic states, but their importance in political organization declines.

States foster geographic mobility and resettlement, severing longstanding ties among people, land, and kin (Smith 2003). Population displacements have increased in the modern world and with globalization. War, famine, and job seeking across national boundaries churn up migratory currents. People in states come to identify themselves by new statuses, both ascribed and achieved—including ethnicity, residence, occupation, party, religion, and team or club affiliation—rather than only as members of a descent group or extended family.

States also manage their populations by granting different rights and obligations to citizens and noncitizens. Status distinctions among citizens are also common. Many archaic states granted different rights to nobles, commoners, and slaves. Unequal rights within state-organized societies persist in today's world. In recent American history, before the Emancipation Proclamation, there were different laws for enslaved and free people. In European colonies, separate courts judged cases involving only natives and cases involving Europeans. In contemporary America, a military code of justice and court system continue to coexist alongside the civil judiciary.

# Judiciary

States have *laws* based on precedent and legislative proclamations. Without writing, laws may be preserved in oral tradition, with justices, elders, and other specialists responsible for remembering them. Oral traditions as repositories of legal wisdom have continued in some nations with writing, such as Great Britain. Laws regulate relations between individuals and groups.

*Crimes* are violations of the legal code, with specified types of punishment. However, a given act, such as killing someone, may be legally defined in different ways (e.g., as manslaughter, justifiable homicide, or first-degree murder). Furthermore, even in contemporary North America, where justice is supposed to be "blind" to social distinctions, the poor are prosecuted more often and more severely than are the rich.

To handle disputes and crimes, all states have courts and judges. Precolonial African states had subcounty, county, and district courts, plus a high court formed by the king or queen and his or her advisers. Most states allow appeals to higher courts, although people are encouraged to solve problems locally.

A striking contrast between states and nonstates is intervention in family affairs. In states, aspects of parenting and marriage enter the domain of public law. Governments step in to halt blood feuds and regulate previously private disputes. States attempt to curb *internal* conflict, but they aren't always successful. About 85 percent of the world's armed conflicts since 1945 have begun within states—in efforts to overthrow a ruling regime or as disputes over tribal, religious, and ethnic minority issues (see Chatterjee 2004). Only 15 percent have been fights across national borders (Barnaby, ed. 1984). Rebellion, resistance, repression, terrorism, and warfare continue (see Nordstrom 2004; Tishkov 2004). Indeed, recent states have perpetrated some of history's bloodiest deeds.

# Enforcement

All states have agents to enforce judicial decisions. Confinement requires jailers. If there is a death penalty, it requires executioners. Agents of the state have the power to collect fines and confiscate property.

As a relatively new form of sociopolitical organization, states have competed successfully with nonstates throughout the world. A government suppresses internal disorder (with police) and guards the nation against external threats (with the military). Military organization helps states subdue neighboring nonstates, but this is not the only reason for the spread of state organization. Although states impose hardships, they also offer advantages. They provide protection from outsiders and preserve internal order. By promoting internal peace, states enhance production. Their economies support massive, dense populations, which supply armies and colonists to promote expansion. A major concern of government is to defend hierarchy, property, and the power of the law.

# Fiscal Systems

A financial or **fiscal** system is needed in states to support rulers, nobles, officials, judges, military personnel, and thousands of other specialists. As in the chiefdom, the state intervenes in production, distribution, and consumption. The state may decree that a certain area will produce certain things or forbid certain activities in particular places. Although, like chiefdoms, states also have redistribution (through taxation), generosity and sharing are played down. Less of what comes in flows back to the people.

In nonstates, people customarily share with relatives, but residents of states face added obligations to bureaucrats and officials. Citizens must turn over a substantial portion of what they produce to the state. Of the resources that the state collects, it reallocates part for the general good and uses another part (often larger) for the elite.

The state does not bring more freedom or leisure to the common people, who usually work harder than do people in nonstates. They may be called on to build monumental public works. Some of these projects, such as dams and irrigation systems, may be economically necessary. People also build temples, palaces, and tombs for the elites.

Markets and trade usually are under at least some state control, with officials overseeing distribution and exchange, standardizing weights and measures, and collecting

## ANTHROPOLOGY TODAY

### *Diwaniyas in Kuwait*

*When we think of politics, we think of government, of federal and state institutions, of Washington, Ottawa, or perhaps our state or provincial capital, city hall, or courthouse. We hear discussions of public service, political offices, and elections—and maybe the economic and political power that goes along with holding office, or with influencing those who hold office. Binding decisions get made at the top levels of government. There are also informal political institutions, which aren't part of the governmental apparatus, but which substantially influence it. Described here are the diwaniyas of Kuwait—informal, local-level meeting places where informal discussions can have formal consequences. Much of Kuwait's decision making, networking, and influence peddling takes place in diwaniyas.*

In the historical fabric of Kuwait, diwaniyas have been men-only political salons—a local equivalent of neighborhood pub and town-hall meeting combined. They serve not only as parlors for chit-chats, but governance, too. Diwaniyas are so integral to Kuwaiti culture that during election season, candidates don't go door to door, but diwaniya to diwaniya. This is where business deals are made and marriages arranged. . . .

Traditionally, most men have an open invitation to attend a diwaniya on any given night, and wealthy families have a large, long room adjacent to their homes expressly for their diwaniya.

Some neighborhoods have a common diwaniya, much like a community center.

At a typical men-only diwaniya . . . the attendees lounge among the partitions of a never-ending couch that follow the contours of the room in one giant U. They usually gather once a week, starting at 8 in the evening and sometimes going past midnight.

As they discuss issues . . . they twirl smoothly polished beads around their fingers and worry aloud whether change has taxes on goods passing into or through the state. Taxes support government and the ruling class, which is clearly separated from the common people in regard to activities, privileges, rights, and obligations. Taxes also support the many specialists—administrators, tax collectors, judges, lawmakers, generals, scholars, and priests. As the state matures, the segment of the population freed from direct concern with subsistence grows.

The elites of archaic states reveled in the consumption of *sumptuary goods*—jewelry, exotic food and drink, and stylish clothing reserved for, or affordable only by, the rich. Peasants' diets suffered as they struggled to meet government demands. Commoners perished in territorial wars that had little relevance to their own needs. Are any of these observations true of contemporary states?

come to Kuwait too fast. The presence of malls and movies, they fret, is breaking down social norms like the taboo against premarital dating.

At the Al-Fanar Center, with its bevy of Body Shops and Benettons, teenage boys say they also have no interest in chattering the night away when they could be flirting. "We like to follow around girls without hijab [veil]," says teenager Abdul Rahman al-Tarket, roaming the mall with his two friends. Mixed [male and female] diwaniyas are still an anomaly. "For me, the diwaniya is a very comfortable place to have people come and see me," says artist Thoraya al-Baqsami, who co-hosts one mixed gathering. "I know many people don't like it, but we are in the 21st century now," she says as she gives a tour of her adjacent gallery. . . .

Many women here say they're happy to leave the diwaniya to the domain of men. But more problematic is that it is the diwaniya at which much of the country's decision making and networking takes place. It is also a forum where a constituent can meet his parliamentary representative and consult him about major problems or minor potholes. The importance of diwaniyas to Kuwaiti society cannot be understated. Kuwait's parliament emerged from a 1921 proposal by diwaniyas. And Sheik Jaber al-Sabah, who dissolved the assembly in 1986, restored it in 1992 following pressure from diwaniyas. . . .

Some here say they wouldn't mind seeing the decline of the diwaniya. Says Kuwait University political scientist Shamlan El-Issa: "The positive aspects are that it helps democracy—men meet every day and talk and complain for two or three hours. The negative is that it replaces the family—men go to work and diwaniya, and never see their wives."

*Source:* Ilene R. Prusher, "Chat Rooms, Bedouin Style," *Christian Science Monitor*, April 26, 2000. © 2000 The Christian Science Monitor (www.csmonitor.com). All rights reserved.

## Summary

1. Although no anthropologist has been able to observe a polity uninfluenced by some state, many anthropologists use a sociopolitical typology that classifies societies as bands, tribes, chiefdoms, or states. Foragers tended to live in egalitarian, band-organized, societies. Personal networks linked individuals, families, and bands. Band leaders were first among equals, with no sure way to enforce decisions. Disputes rarely arose over strategic resources, which were open to all.

2. Political authority and power increased with the growth in population size and density and in the scale of regulatory problems. More people mean more relations among individuals and groups to regulate. Increasingly complex economies pose further regulatory problems.

3. Heads of horticultural villages are local leaders with limited authority. They lead by example and persuasion. Big men have support and authority beyond a single village. They are regional regulators, but temporary ones. In organizing a feast, they mobilize labor from several villages. Sponsoring such events leaves them with little wealth but with prestige and a reputation for generosity.

4. Age and gender also can be used for regional political integration. Among North America's Plains Indians, men's associations (pantribal sodalities) organized raiding and buffalo hunting. Such men's associations tend to emphasize the warrior grade. They serve for offense and defense when there is intertribal raiding for animals. Among pastoralists, the degree of authority and political organization reflects population size and density, interethnic relations, and pressure on resources.

5. The state is an autonomous political unit that encompasses many communities. Its government collects taxes, drafts people for work and war, and decrees and enforces laws. The state is a form of sociopolitical organization based on central government and social stratification—a division of society into classes. Early states are known as archaic, or nonindustrial, states, in contrast to modern industrial nation-states.

6. Unlike tribes, but like states, chiefdoms had permanent regional regulation and differential access to resources. But chiefdoms lacked stratification. Unlike states, but like bands and tribes, chiefdoms were organized by kinship, descent, and marriage. Chiefdoms emerged in several areas, including the circum-Caribbean, lowland Amazonia, the southeastern United States, and Polynesia.

7. Weber's three dimensions of stratification are wealth, power, and prestige. In early states—for the first time in human history—contrasts in wealth, power, and prestige between entire groups of men and women came into being. A socioeconomic stratum includes people of both sexes and all ages. The superordinate—higher or elite—stratum enjoys privileged access to resources.

8. Certain systems are found in all states: population control, judiciary, enforcement, and fiscal. These are integrated by a ruling system or government composed of civil, military, and religious officials. States conduct censuses and demarcate boundaries. Laws are based on precedent and legislative proclamations. Courts and judges handle disputes and crimes. A police force maintains internal order, as a military defends against external threats. A financial or fiscal system supports rulers, officials, judges, and other specialists.

# KEY TERMS

achieved status (p. 260)
age set (p. 263)
ascribed status (p. 260)
band (p. 255)
big man (p. 260)
caste systems (p. 270)
chiefdom (p. 255)
conflict resolution (p. 257)
differential access (p. 268)
fiscal (p. 273)
law (p. 257)
office (p. 266)
open-class system (p. 270)
power (p. 270)

prestige (p. 270)
slavery (p. 271)
sociopolitical typology (p. 255)
pantribal sodality (p. 262)
state (p. 255)
status (p. 260)
stratification (p. 270)
subordinate (p. 270)
superordinate (p. 270)
tribe (p. 255)
vertical mobility (p. 270)
village head (p. 259)
wealth (p. 270)

# CHAPTER 13

❦

# FAMILIES, KINSHIP, AND MARRIAGE

The societies anthropologists traditionally have studied have stimulated a strong interest in families, along with larger systems of kinship and marriage. The wide web of kinship—as vitally important in daily life in nonindustrial societies as work outside the home is in our own—has become an essential part of anthropology because of its importance to the people we study. We are ready to take a closer look at the systems of kinship and marriage that have organized human life for much of our history.

Ethnographers quickly recognize social divisions, or groups, within any society they study. They learn about significant groups by observing their activities and membership. Often people live in the same village or neighborhood or work, socialize, or celebrate together because they are related in some way. A significant kin group might consist of descendants of the same grandfather. These people live in neighboring houses, farm adjoining fields, and help each other in daily tasks. Groups based on other kin links get together less often in that society.

The nuclear family (parents and children) is one kind of kin group that is widespread in human societies. Other kin groups include extended families (families consisting of three or more generations) and descent groups—lineages and clans.

Much of kinship is *culturally constructed,* that is, based on learning and variable from culture to culture (Schneider 1967; McKinnon 2005). Different societies have different kinds of families, households, kin groups, marriage customs, and living arrangements. Consider the term *family,* which is basic, familiar (so much so it even shares its root with *familiar*), and difficult to define in a way that applies to all cultures. A **family** is a group of people (e.g., parents, children, siblings, grandparents, grandchildren, uncles, aunts, nephews, nieces, cousins, spouses, siblings-in-law, parents-in-law, children-in-law) who are considered to be related in some way, for example, by "blood" (common ancestry or descent) or marriage. Some families, such as the nuclear family, are residentially based; its members live together. Others are not; they live apart but come together for family reunions of various sorts from time to time.

Consider a striking contrast between the United States and Brazil, the two most populous countries of the Western Hemisphere, in the meaning and role of family. American adults usually define their family as consisting of their spouse and children. However, when middle-class Brazilians talk about their family ( *família*), they mean their parents, siblings, aunts, uncles, grandparents, and cousins. Later they add their children, but rarely the husband or wife, who has his or her own family. The children are shared by the two families. Because middle-class Americans typically lack an extended family support system, marriage assumes more importance. The husband–wife relationship is supposed to take precedence over either spouse's relationship with his or her own parents. This places a significant strain on North American marriages.

Living in a less mobile society, Brazilians stay in closer face-to-face contact with their relatives, including members of the extended family, than North Americans do. Residents of Rio de Janeiro and São Paulo, two of South America's largest cities, are reluctant to leave those urban centers to live away from family and friends. Brazilians find it hard to imagine, and unpleasant to live in, social worlds without relatives. Contrast this with a characteristic American theme: learning to live with strangers.

---

## ✦ FAMILIES

### Nuclear and Extended Families

A nuclear family is *impermanent;* it lasts only as long as the parents and children remain together. Most people belong to at least two nuclear families at different times in their lives. They are born into a family consisting of their parents and siblings. When they reach adulthood, they may marry and establish a nuclear family that includes the spouse and eventually children. Since most societies permit divorce, some people establish more than one family through marriage.

Anthropologists distinguish between the **family of orientation** (the family in which one is born and grows up) and the **family of procreation** (formed when one marries and has children). From the individual's point of view, the critical relationships are with parents and siblings in the family of orientation and with spouse and children in the family of procreation. In Brazil, as we just saw, the family of orientation predominates, whereas in the United States it is the family of procreation.

In most societies, relations with nuclear family members (parents, siblings, and children) take precedence over relations with other kin. Nuclear family organization is very widespread but not universal, and its significance in society differs greatly from one place to another. In a few societies, such as the classic Nayar case described below, nuclear families are rare or nonexistent. In others, the nuclear family plays no special role in social life. The nuclear family is not always the basis of residence or authority organization. Other social units—most notably descent groups and extended families—can assume many of the functions otherwise associated with the nuclear family.

Consider an example from the former Yugoslavia. Traditionally, among the Muslims of western Bosnia (Lockwood 1975), nuclear families lacked autonomy. Several such families lived in an extended family household called a *zadruga*. The zadruga was headed by a male household head and his wife, the senior woman. It included married sons and their wives and children, and unmarried sons and daughters. Each nuclear family had a sleeping room, decorated and partly furnished from the bride's trousseau. However, possessions—even clothing and trousseau items—were shared by zadruga members. Such a residential unit is known as a *patrilocal* extended family because each couple resides in the husband's father's household after marriage.

The zadruga took precedence over its component units. Social interaction was more usual among the women, the men, or the children of the zadruga than between spouses or between parents and children. There were three successive meal settings—for men, women, and children, respectively. Traditionally, all children over the age of 12 slept together in boys' or girls' rooms. When a woman wished to visit another village, she sought the permission of the male zadruga head. Although men usually felt closer to their own children than to those of their brothers, they were obliged to treat them equally. Children were disciplined by any adult in the household. When a nuclear family broke up, children under age 7 went with the mother. Older children could choose between their parents. Children were considered part of the household where they were born even if their mother left. One widow who remarried had to leave her five children, all over the age of 7, in their father's zadruga, now headed by his brother.

Another example of an alternative to the nuclear family is provided by the Nayars (or Nair), a large and powerful caste on the Malabar Coast of southern India (Gough 1959; Shivaram 1996). Their traditional kinship system was matrilineal (descent traced only through females). Nayar lived in matrilineal extended family compounds called *tarawads*. The tarawad was a residential complex with several buildings, its own temple, granary, water well, orchards, gardens, and land holdings. Headed by a senior woman, assisted by her brother, the tarawad housed her siblings, sisters' children, and other matrikin—matrilineal relatives.

Traditional Nayar marriage seems to have been hardly more than a formality: a kind of coming-of-age ritual. A young woman would go through a marriage ceremony with a man, after which they might spend a few days together at her tarawad. Then the man would return to his own tarawad, where he lived with his sisters, aunts, and other matrikin. Nayar men belonged to a warrior class, who left home regularly for military expeditions, returning permanently to their tarawad on retirement. Nayar women could have multiple sexual partners. Children became members of the mother's tarawad; they were not considered to be relatives of their biological father. Indeed, many Nayar children didn't even know who their biological father (genitor) was. Child care was the responsibility of the tarawad. Nayar society therefore reproduced itself biologically without the nuclear family.

This just-married Khasi couple poses (in 1997) in India's northeastern city of Shillong. The Khasis are matrilineal, tracing descent through women and taking their maternal ancestors' surnames. Women choose their husbands, family incomes are pooled, and extended family households are managed by older women.

## Industrialism and Family Organization

For many Americans and Canadians, the nuclear family is the only well-defined kin group. Family isolation arises from geographic mobility, which is associated with industrialism, so that a nuclear family focus is characteristic of many modern nations. Born into a family of orientation, North Americans leave home for college or work, and the break with parents is under way. Selling our labor on the market, we often move to places where jobs are available. Eventually most North Americans marry and start a family of procreation.

Many married couples live hundreds of miles from their parents. Their jobs have determined where they live. Such a postmarital residence pattern is **neolocality:** Married couples are expected to establish a new place of residence—a "home of their own." Among middle-class North Americans, neolocal residence is both a cultural preference and a statistical norm. Most middle-class Americans eventually establish households and nuclear families of their own.

There are significant differences between middle-class and poorer North Americans. For example, in the lower class the incidence of *expanded family households* (those that include nonnuclear relatives) is greater than it is in the middle class. When an expanded family household includes three or more generations, it is an **extended family household,** such as the zadruga. Another type of expanded family is the *collateral household,* which includes siblings and their spouses and children.

The higher proportion of expanded family households among poorer Americans has been explained as an adaptation to poverty (Stack 1975). Unable to survive economically as nuclear family units, relatives band together in an expanded household and pool their resources. Adaptation to poverty causes kinship values and attitudes to diverge from middle-class norms. Thus, when North Americans raised in poverty achieve financial success, they often feel obligated to provide financial help to a wide circle of less fortunate relatives (see Willie 2003).

## Changes in North American Kinship

Although the nuclear family remains a cultural ideal for many Americans, Table 13-1 and Figure 13-1 show that nuclear families accounted for just 23 percent of American households in 2003–2004. Other domestic arrangements now outnumber the "traditional" American household more than three to one. There are several reasons for this changing household composition. Women increasingly are joining men in the cash workforce. This often removes them from their family of orientation while making

## TABLE 13-1

### Changes in Family and Household Organization in the United States: 1970 versus 2004

|  | 1970 | 2004 |
|---|---|---|
| Numbers: |  |  |
| Total number of households | 63 million | 112 million |
| Number of people per household | 3.1 | 2.6 |
| Percentages: |  |  |
| Married couples with children | 40% | 23% |
| Family households | 81 | 68 |
| Households with five or more people | 21 | 10 |
| People living alone | 17 | 26 |
| Percentage of single-mother families | 5 | 12 |
| Percentage of single-father families | 0 | 2 |
| Households with own children under 18 | 45 | 32 |

*SOURCE*: From U.S. Census data in J. M. Fields, "America's Families and Living Arrangements: 2003," *Current Population Reports*, P20-553, November 2004. http://www.census.gov/prod/2004pubs/p20-553.pdf, p. 4; J. M. Fields and L. M. Casper, "America's Families and Living Arrangement: Population Characteristics, 2000," *Current Population Reports*, P20-537, June 2001. http://www.census.gov/prod/2001pubs/p20-537.pdf; U.S. Census Bureau, *Statistical Abstract of the United States 2006*, Tables 55, 56, and 65. http://www.census.gov/prod/www/statistical_abstract.html.

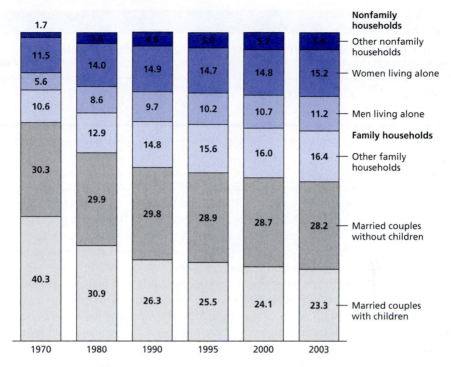

**FIGURE 13-1**   *Households by Type: Selected Years, 1970 to 2003 (percent distribution)*

SOURCE: U.S Census Bureau, *Current Population Survey*, March and Annual Social and Economic Supplements: 1970 to 2003; Fields 2004.

it economically feasible to delay marriage. Furthermore, job demands compete with romantic attachments. The median age at first marriage for American women jumped from 20.8 years in 1970 to 25.3 in 2003. The comparable ages for men were 23.2 and 27.1 (Fields 2004).

Also, the U.S. divorce rate has risen, making divorced Americans much more common today than they were in 1970. Between 1970 and 2003 the number of divorced Americans quintupled—some 22 million in 2003 versus 4.3 million in 1970. (Note, however, that each divorce creates two divorced people). Table 13-2 shows the ratio of divorces to marriages in the United States for selected years between 1950 and 2003. The major jump in the American divorce rate took place between 1960 and 1980. During that period the ratio of divorces to marriage doubled. Since 1980 the ratio has stayed the same, around 50 percent. That is, each year there are about half as many new divorces as there are new marriages.

The rate of growth in single-parent families also has outstripped population growth, quadrupling from fewer than 4 million in 1970 to more than 16 million in 2003. (The overall American population in 2003 was 1.4 times its size in 1970.) The percentage of children living in fatherless (mother-headed, no resident dad) households in 2003 was more than twice the 1970 rate while the percentage in motherless (father-headed,

**TABLE 13-2**

### Ratio of Divorces to Marriages per 1,000 U.S. Population, Selected Years, 1950–2003

| 1950 | 1960 | 1970 | 1980 | 1990 | 2000 | 2003 |
|------|------|------|------|------|------|------|
| 23%  | 26%  | 33%  | 50%  | 48%  | 49%  | 51%  |

SOURCE: U.S. Census Bureau, *Statistical Abstract of the United States 2006*, Table 71, p. 64. http://www.census.gov/prod/www/statistical_abstract.html.

no resident mom) homes increased fivefold. About 57 percent of American women and 60 percent of American men were currently married in 2004, versus 60 and 65 percent, respectively, in 1970 (Fields 2004; Fields and Casper 2001). To be sure, contemporary Americans maintain social lives through work, friendship, sports, clubs, religion, and organized social activities. However, the growing isolation from kin that these figures suggest may well be unprecedented in human history.

Table 13-3 documents comparable changes in family and household size in the United States and Canada between 1975 and 2004. Those figures confirm a general trend toward smaller families and living units in North America (see also Hansen and Garey, eds. 1998). This trend is also detectable in western Europe and other industrial nations.

Immigrants often are shocked by what they perceive as weak kinship bonds and lack of proper respect for family in contemporary North America. In fact, most of the people whom middle-class North Americans see every day are either nonrelatives or members of the nuclear family. On the other hand, Stack's (1975) study of welfare-dependent families in a ghetto area of a midwestern city shows that regular sharing with nonnuclear relatives is an important strategy that the urban poor use to adapt to poverty.

**TABLE 13-3**

### Household and Family Size in the United States and Canada, 1980 versus 2004

|                          | 1980 | 2004 |
|--------------------------|------|------|
| *Average family size:*   |      |      |
| United States            | 3.3  | 3.1  |
| Canada                   | 3.4  | 3.0  |
| *Average household size:*|      |      |
| United States            | 2.9  | 2.6  |
| Canada                   | 2.9  | 2.6  |

SOURCE: J. M. Fields, "America's Families and Living Arrangements: 2003," *Current Population Reports*, P20-553, November 2004. http://www.census.gov/prod/2004pubs/p20-553.pdf, pp. 3–4. U.S. Census Bureau, *Statistical Abstract of the United States, 2004–5; Statistics Canada*, 2001 Census. http://www.statcan.ca/english/Pgdb/famil53a.htm, http://www.statcan.ca/english/Pgdb/famil40a.htm.

In contemporary North America, single-parent families have increased at a rapid rate. In 1960, 88 percent of American children lived with both parents, compared with 68 percent today. This divorced mom, Valerie Jones, enjoys a candlelight dinner with her kids. What do you see as the main differences between nuclear families and single-parent families?

## The Family among Foragers

Foraging societies are far removed from industrial nations in terms of social complexity, but they do feature geographic mobility, which is associated with nomadic or semi-nomadic hunting and gathering. Here again, the nuclear family often is the most significant kin group, although in no foraging society is it the only group based on kinship. The two basic social units of traditional foraging societies are the nuclear family and the band.

Unlike middle-class couples in industrial nations, foragers don't usually reside neolocally. Instead, they join a band in which either the husband or the wife has relatives. However, couples and families may move from one band to another several times. Although nuclear families are ultimately as impermanent among foragers as they are in any other society, they are usually more stable than bands are.

Many foraging societies lacked year-round band organization. The Native American Shoshone of Utah and Nevada provide an example. The resources available to the Shoshone were so meager that for most of the year families traveled alone through the countryside hunting and gathering. In certain seasons families assembled to hunt cooperatively as a band, but after just a few months together they dispersed.

In neither industrial nor foraging economies are people permanently tied to the land. The mobility and the emphasis on small, economically self-sufficient family units promote the nuclear family as a basic kin group in both types of societies.

## ✦ DESCENT

We've seen that the nuclear family is important in industrial nations and among foragers. The analogous group among nonindustrial food producers is the descent group. A **descent group** is a *permanent* social unit whose members claim common ancestry. Descent group members believe they all descend from those common ancestors. The group endures even though its membership changes, as members are born and die, move in and move out. Often, descent-group membership is determined at birth and is lifelong. In this case, it is an ascribed status.

## Descent Groups

Descent groups frequently are exogamous (members seek their mates from other descent groups). Two common rules serve to admit certain people as descent-group members while excluding others. With a rule of **patrilineal descent,** people automatically have lifetime membership in their father's group. The children of the group's men join the group, but the children of the group's women are excluded. With **matrilineal descent,** people join the mother's group automatically at birth and stay members throughout life. Matrilineal descent groups therefore include only the children of the group's women. (In Figures 13-2 and 13-3, which show patrilineal and matrilineal descent groups, respectively, the triangles stand for males and the circles for females.) Matrilineal and patrilineal descent are types of **unilineal descent.** This means the descent rule uses one line only, either the male or the female line. Patrilineal descent is much more common

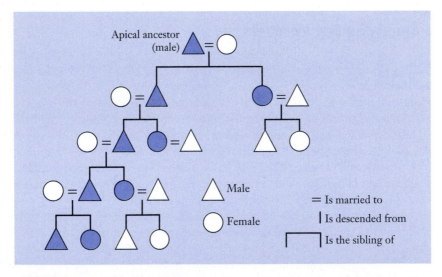

**FIGURE 13-2** *A Patrilineage Five Generations Deep* Lineages are based on demonstrated descent from an apical ancestor. With patrilineal descent, children of the group's men (shaded) are included as descent-group members. Children of the group's women are excluded; they belong to *their* father's patrilineage.

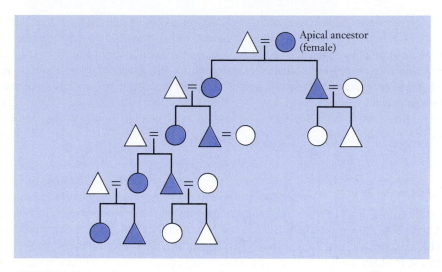

**FIGURE 13-3**    *A Matrilineage Five Generations Deep*  Matrilineages are based on demonstrated descent from a female ancestor. Only the children of the group's women (shaded) belong to the matrilineage. The children of the group's men are excluded; they belong to *their* mother's matrilineage.

than matrilineal descent is. In a sample of 564 societies (Murdock 1957), about three times as many were found to be patrilineal (247 to 84).

Descent groups may be **lineages** or **clans.** Common to both is the belief that members descend from the same *apical ancestor,* the person who stands at the apex, or top, of the common genealogy. For example, Adam and Eve are the apical ancestors of the biblical Jews, and, according to the Bible, of all humanity. Since Eve is said to have come from Adam's rib, Adam stands as the original apical ancestor for the patrilineal genealogy laid out in the Bible.

How do lineages and clans differ? A lineage uses *demonstrated descent.* Members recite the names of their forebears from the apical ancestor through the present. (This doesn't mean their recitations are accurate, only that lineage members think they are.) In the Bible the litany of men who "begat" other men is a demonstration of genealogical descent for a large patrilineage that ultimately includes Jews and Arabs (who share Abraham as their last common apical ancestor).

Unlike lineages, clans use *stipulated descent.* Clan members merely say they descend from the apical ancestor, without trying to trace the actual genealogical links. The Betsileo of Madagascar have both clans and lineages. Descent may be demonstrated for the most recent 8–10 generations, then stipulated for the more remote past—sometimes with mermaids and vaguely defined foreign royalty mentioned among the founders (Kottak 1980). Like the Betsileo, many societies have both lineages and clans. In such a case, clans have more members and cover a larger geographical area than lineages do. Sometimes a clan's apical ancestor is not a human at all but an animal or plant (called a *totem*).

The economic types that usually have descent group organization are horticulture, pastoralism, and agriculture. Such societies tend to have several descent groups. Any one of them may be confined to a single village, but usually they span more than one village. Two or more local branches of different descent groups may live in the same village. Descent groups in the same village or different villages may establish alliances through frequent intermarriage.

## Lineages, Clans, and Residence Rules

As we've seen, descent groups, unlike families, are permanent and enduring units, with new members added in every generation. Members have access to the lineage estate, where some of them must live, in order to benefit from and manage that estate across the generations. An easy way to keep members at home is to have a rule about who belongs to the descent group and where they should live after they get married. Patrilineal and matrilineal descent, and the postmarital residence rules that usually accompany them, ensure that about half the people born in each generation will spend their lives on the ancestral estate.

**Patrilocality** is the rule that when a couple marries, it moves to the husband's community, so that their children will grow up in their father's village. Patrilocality is associated with patrilineal descent. This makes sense. If the group's male members are expected to exercise their rights in the ancestral estate, it's a good idea to raise them on that estate and to keep them there after they marry. This can be done by having wives move to the husband's village, rather than vice versa.

A less common postmarital residence rule, often associated with matrilineal descent, is **matrilocality:** Married couples live in the wife's community, and their children grow up in their mother's village. This rule keeps related women together. Together, patrilocality and matrilocality are known as *unilocal* rules of postmarital residence.

## ✣ MARRIAGE

"Love and marriage," "marriage and the family": These familiar phrases show how we link the romantic love of two individuals to marriage, and how we link marriage to reproduction and family creation. But marriage is an institution with significant roles and functions in addition to reproduction. What is marriage, anyway?

No definition of marriage is broad enough to apply easily to all societies and situations. A commonly quoted definition comes from *Notes and Queries on Anthropology:*

> Marriage is a union between a man and a woman such that the children born
> to the woman are recognized as legitimate offspring of both partners. (Royal
> Anthropological Institute 1951, p. 111)

This definition isn't valid universally for several reasons. In many societies, marriages unite more than two spouses. Here we speak of *plural marriages,* as when a man weds two (or more) women, or a woman weds a group of brothers—an arrangement called *fraternal polyandry* that is characteristic of certain Himalayan cultures. In the Brazilian community of Arembepe, people can choose among various forms of marital union. Most people live in long-term "common-law" domestic partnerships that are not legally sanctioned. Some have civil marriages, which are licensed and legalized by a justice of the peace. Still others go through religious ceremonies, so they are united in "holy matrimony," although not legally. And some have both civil and religious ties. The different forms of union permit someone to have multiple spouses (e.g., one common-law, one civil, one religious) without ever getting divorced.

Some societies recognize various kinds of same-sex marriages. In Sudan, a Nuer woman could marry a woman if her father had only daughters but no male heirs, who are necessary if his patrilineage is to survive. He might ask his daughter to stand as a son in order to take a bride. This daughter would become the socially recognized husband of another woman (the wife). This was a symbolic and social relationship rather than a sexual one. The "wife" had sex with a man or men (whom her female "husband" had to approve) until she got pregnant. The children born to the wife were accepted as the offspring of both the female husband and the wife. Although the female husband was not the actual *genitor,* the biological father, of the children, she was their *pater,* or socially recognized father. What's important in this Nuer case is *social* rather than *biological paternity.* We see again how kinship is socially constructed. The bride's children were considered the legitimate offspring of her female husband, who was biologically a woman but socially a man, and the descent line continued.

## Incest and Exogamy

In nonindustrial societies, a person's social world includes two main categories—friends and strangers. Strangers are potential or actual enemies. Marriage is one of the primary ways of converting strangers into friends, of creating and maintaining personal and political alliances, relationships of affinity. **Exogamy,** the practice of seeking a mate outside one's own group, has adaptive value because it links people into a wider social network that nurtures, helps, and protects them in times of need.

**Incest** refers to sexual relations with a relative. All cultures have taboos against it. However, although the taboo is a cultural universal, cultures define their kin, and thus incest, differently. When unilineal descent is very strongly developed, the parent who belongs to a different descent group than your own isn't considered a relative. Thus, with strict patrilineality, the mother is not a relative but a kind of in-law who has married a member of your own group—your father. With strict matrilineality, the father isn't a relative because he belongs to a different descent group.

The Lakher of Southeast Asia are strictly patrilineal (Leach 1961). Using the male ego (the reference point, the person in question) in Figure 13-4, let's suppose that ego's father and mother get divorced. Each remarries and has a daughter by a second marriage. A Lakher always belongs to his or her father's group, all the members of which (one's *agnates,* or patrikin) considered too closely related to marry because they are members of the same patrilineal descent group. Therefore, ego can't marry his father's daughter by the second marriage, just as in contemporary North America it's illegal for half-siblings to marry.

However, in contrast to our society, where all half-siblings are tabooed in marriage, the Lakher would permit ego to marry his mother's daughter by a different father.

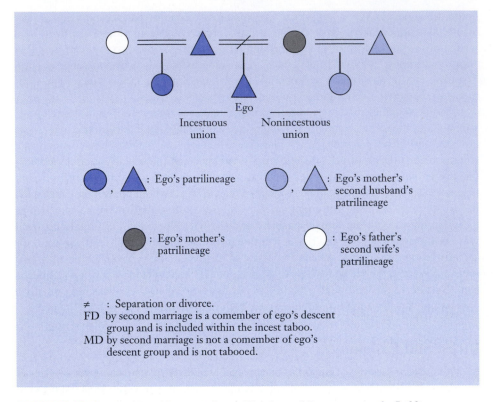

**FIGURE 13-4**    *Patrilineal Descent-Group Identity and Incest among the Lakher*

She is not ego's relative because she belongs to her own father's descent group rather than ego's. The Lakher illustrate very well that definitions of relatives, and therefore of incest, vary from culture to culture.

## Although Tabooed, Incest Does Happen

There is no simple or universally accepted explanation for the fact that all cultures ban incest. Do primate studies offer any clues? Research with primates does show that adolescent males (among monkeys) or females (among apes) often move away from the group in which they were born (Rodseth et al. 1991). This emigration reduces the frequency of incestuous unions, but it doesn't eliminate them. DNA testing of wild chimps has confirmed incestuous unions between adult sons and their mothers, who reside in the same group. Human behavior with respect to mating with close relatives may express a generalized primate tendency, in which we see both urges and avoidance.

A cross-cultural study of 87 societies (Meigs and Barlow 2002) revealed that incest did occur in several of them. For example, among the Yanomami, Chagnon reported that "incest, far from being feared, is widely practiced" (1967, p.66). Meyer Fortes observed about the Ashanti: "In the old days it [incest] was punished by death. Nowadays the culprits are heavily fined" (Fortes 1950, p.257). Among 24 Ojibwa individuals from whom he obtained information about incest, A. Irving Hallowell found eight cases of parent–child incest and ten cases of brother–sister incest (Hallowell 1955, pp. 294–95).

In ancient Egypt, sibling marriage apparently was allowed not just for royalty but for commoners as well, in at least some districts. Based on official census records from Roman Egypt (first to third centuries A.D.) preserved on papyrus, 24 percent of all documented marriages in the Arsinoites district were between brothers and sisters. In the second century A.D., the rates were 37 percent for the city of Arsinoe and 19 percent for the surrounding villages. These figures are much higher than any other documented levels of inbreeding among humans (Scheidel 1997).

According to Anna Meigs and Kathleen Barlow (2002), for Western societies with nuclear family organization, father–daughter incest is most common with stepfathers, but it also happens with biological fathers, especially those who were absent or did little caretaking of their daughters in childhood (Williams and Finkelhor 1995). In a carefully designed study, Linda M. Williams and David Finkelhor (1995) found father–daughter incest to be least likely when there was substantial paternal parenting of daughters who were four to five years old. This experience enhanced the father's parenting skills and his feelings of nurturance, protectiveness, and identification with his daughter, thus reducing the risk of incest.

It has been argued (Hobhouse 1915; Lowie 1920/1961) that the incest taboo is universal because incest horror is instinctive: Humans have a genetically programmed disgust toward incest. Because of this feeling, early humans banned it. However, cultural universality doesn't necessarily entail an instinctual basis. Fire making, for example, is a cultural universal, but it certainly isn't an ability transmitted by the genes. Furthermore, if people really did have an instinctive horror of mating with blood relatives, a formal incest taboo would be unnecessary. No one would do it. However, as we have just seen, and as social workers, judges, psychiatrists, and psychologists know, incest is more common than we might suppose.

# Endogamy

The practice of exogamy pushes social organization outward, establishing and preserving alliances among groups. In contrast, rules of **endogamy** dictate mating or marriage within a group to which one belongs. Endogamic rules are less common but are still familiar to anthropologists. Indeed, most cultures *are* endogamous units, although they usually do not need a formal rule requiring people to marry someone from their own society. In our own society, classes and ethnic groups are quasi-endogamous groups. Members of an ethnic or religious group often want their children to marry within that group, although many of them do not do so. The outmarriage rate varies among such groups, with some more committed to endogamy than others.

## Caste

An extreme example of endogamy is India's caste system, which was formally abolished in 1949, although its structure and effects linger. Castes are stratified groups in which membership is ascribed at birth and is lifelong. Indian castes are grouped into five major categories, or *varna*. Each is ranked relative to the other four, and these categories extend throughout India. Each varna includes a large number of castes (*jati*), each of which includes people within a region who may intermarry. All the jati in a single varna in a given region are ranked, just as the varna themselves are ranked.

Occupational specialization often sets off one caste from another. A community may include castes of agricultural workers, merchants, artisans, priests, and sweepers. The untouchable varna, found throughout India, includes castes whose ancestry, ritual status, and occupations are considered so impure that higher-caste people consider even casual contact with untouchables to be defiling.

The belief that intercaste sexual unions lead to ritual impurity for the higher-caste partner has been important in maintaining endogamy. A man who has sex with a lower-caste woman can restore his purity with a bath and a prayer. However, a woman who has intercourse with a man of a lower caste has no such recourse. Her defilement cannot be undone. Because the women have the babies, these differences protect the purity of the caste line, ensuring the pure ancestry of high-caste children. Although Indian castes are endogamous groups, many of them are internally subdivided into exogamous lineages. Traditionally this meant that Indians had to marry a member of another descent group from the same caste. This shows that rules of exogamy and endogamy can coexist in the same society.

## ✦ MARITAL RIGHTS AND SAME-SEX MARRIAGE

The British anthropologist Edmund Leach (1955) observed that, depending on the society, several kinds of rights are allocated by marriage. According to Leach, marriage can, but doesn't always, accomplish the following:

1.  Establish the legal father of a woman's children and the legal mother of a man's.
2.  Give either or both spouses a monopoly in the sexuality of the other.
3.  Give either or both spouses rights to the labor of the other.
4.  Give either or both spouses rights over the other's property.
5.  Establish a joint fund of property—a partnership—for the benefit of the children.
6.  Establish a socially significant "relationship of affinity" between spouses and their relatives.

The discussion of same-sex marriage that follows will serve to illustrate the six rights just listed by seeing what happens in their absence. What if same-sex marriages, which by and large remain illegal in the United States, were legal? Could a same-sex marriage establish legal parentage of children born to one or both partners after the partnership is formed? In the case of a different-sex marriage, children born to the wife after the marriage takes place usually are defined legally as her husband's regardless of whether he is the genitor.

Nowadays, of course, DNA testing makes it possible to establish paternity, just as modern reproductive technology makes it possible for a lesbian couple to have one or both partners artificially inseminated. When same-sex marriage is legal, the social construction of kinship easily can make both partners parents. If a Nuer woman married to a woman can be the pater of a child she did not father, why can't two lesbians be the *maters* (socially recognized mothers) of a child one of them did not father?

On December 21, 2005, Sir Elton John (right) married his long-time domestic partner, David Furnish. The ceremony took place in the town chapel in Windsor, England, where, eight months earlier, Prince Charles had married Camilla Parker-Bowles. The John-Furnish union took place on the first day on which same-sex couples were allowed a legal status comparable to marriage—including the same social security, pension, tax, and inheritance rights—in England and Wales. (The law took effect earlier that week in Northern Ireland and Scotland.)

And if a married different-sex couple can adopt a child and have it be theirs through the social and legal construction of kinship, the same logic could be applied to a gay male or lesbian couple.

Continuing with Leach's list of the rights transmitted by marriage, same-sex marriage certainly could give each spouse rights to the sexuality of the other. Same-sex marriages, as forms of monogamous commitment, have been endorsed by representatives of many religions, including Unitarians, Quakers (the Society of Friends), and reform Jewish synagogues (Eskridge 1996). In June 2003 a court ruling established same-sex marriages as legal in the province of Ontario, Canada. On June 28, 2005, Canada's House of Commons voted to guarantee full marriage rights to same-sex couples throughout that nation. On May 17, 2004, Massachusetts became the first state in the United States to allow same-sex couples to marry. In Vermont (as of 2000), Connecticut (2005), and New Jersey (2006), gay civil unions have been granted marital rights. In reaction to same-sex marriage, voters in more than 25 U.S. states have approved measures in their state constitutions defining marriage as an exclusively heterosexual union.

Legal same-sex marriages can easily give each spouse rights to the other spouse's labor and its products. Some societies do allow marriage between members of the same biological sex. Several Native American groups had figures known as *berdaches*. These were biological men who assumed many of the mannerisms, behavior patterns, and tasks of women. Sometimes berdaches married men, who shared the products of their labor from hunting and traditional male roles, as the berdache fulfilled the traditional wifely role. Also, in some Native American cultures, a marriage of a "manly-hearted woman" to another woman brought the traditional male–female division of labor to their household. The manly woman hunted and did other male tasks, while the wife played the traditional female role.

There's no logical reason why same-sex marriage cannot give spouses rights over the other's property. But in the United States, the same inheritance rights that apply to male–female couples usually do not apply to same-sex couples. For instance, even in the absence of a will, property can pass to a widow or a widower without going through probate. The wife or husband pays no inheritance tax. This benefit is not available to gay men and lesbians. When a same-sex partner is in a nursing home, prison, or hospital, the other partner may not have the same visiting rights as would a husband, wife, or biological relative (Weston 1991).

What about Leach's fifth right—to establish a joint fund of property—to benefit the children? Here again, gay and lesbian couples are at a disadvantage. If there are children, property is separately, rather than jointly, transmitted. Some organizations do make staff benefits, such as health and dental insurance, available to same-sex domestic partners.

Finally, there is the matter of establishing a socially significant "relationship of affinity" between spouses and their relatives. In many societies, one of the main roles of marriage is to establish an alliance between groups, in addition to the individual bond. Affinals are relatives through marriage, such as a brother-in-law or mother-in-law. For same-sex couples in contemporary North America, affinal relations are problematic. In an unofficial union, terms like "daughter-in-law" and "mother-in-law" may sound strange. Many parents are suspicious of their children's sexuality and lifestyle choices and may not recognize a relationship of affinity with a child's partner of the same sex.

This discussion of same-sex marriage has been intended to illustrate the different kinds of rights that typically accompany marriage, by seeing what may happen when there is a permanent pair bond without legal sanction. In the United States, with the exception of Connecticut, Massachusetts, New Jersey, and Vermont, such unions are illegal. As we have seen, same-sex unions have been recognized in different historical and cultural settings. In certain African cultures, including the Igbo of Nigeria and the Lovedu of South Africa, women could marry other women. In situations in which women, such as prominent market women in West Africa, are able to amass property and other forms of wealth, they may take a wife. Such marriage allows the prominent woman to strengthen her social status and the economic importance of her household (Amadiume 1987).

## ✦ Marriage across Cultures

Outside industrial societies, marriage often is more a relationship between groups than one between individuals. We think of marriage as an individual matter. Although the bride and groom usually seek their parents' approval, the final choice (to live together, to marry, to divorce) lies with the couple. The idea of romantic love symbolizes this individual relationship.

In nonindustrial societies, although there can be romantic love, (Goleman 1992), marriage is a group concern. People don't just take a spouse; they assume obligations to a group of in-laws. When residence is patrilocal, for example, a woman must leave the community where she was born. She faces the prospect of spending the rest of her life in her husband's village, with his relatives. She may even have to transfer her major allegiance from her own group to her husband's.

## Bridewealth and Dowry

In societies with descent groups, people enter marriage not alone but with the help of the descent group. Descent-group members often have to contribute to the **bridewealth,** a customary gift before, at, or after the marriage from the husband and his kin to the wife and her kin. Another word for bridewealth is *brideprice,* but this term is inaccurate because people with the custom don't usually think of marriage as a commercial relationship between a man and an object that can be bought and sold.

Bridewealth compensates the bride's group for the loss of her companionship and labor. More important, it makes the children born to the woman full members of her husband's descent group. For this reason, the institution also is called **progeny price.** Rather than the woman herself, it is her children who are permanently transferred to the husband's group. Whatever we call it, such a transfer of wealth at marriage is common in patrilineal groups. In matrilineal societies, children are members of the mother's group, and there is no reason to pay a progeny price.

**Dowry** is a marital exchange in which the wife's group provides substantial gifts to the husband's family. Dowry, best known from India but also practiced in Europe, correlates with low female status. Women are perceived as burdens. When husbands and their families take a wife, they expect to be compensated for the added responsibility.

Bridewealth exists in many more cultures than dowry does, but the nature and quantity of transferred items differ. In many African societies, cattle constitute bridewealth, but the number of cattle given varies from society to society. As the value of bridewealth increases, marriages become more stable. Bridewealth is insurance against divorce.

Imagine a patrilineal society in which a marriage requires the transfer of about 25 cattle from the groom's descent group to the bride's. Michael, a member of descent group A, marries Sarah from group B. His relatives help him assemble the bridewealth. He gets the most help from his close agnates—his older brother, father, father's brother, and closest patrilineal cousins.

The distribution of the cattle once they reach Sarah's group mirrors the manner in which they were assembled. Sarah's father, or her oldest brother if the father is dead, receives her bridewealth. He keeps most of the cattle to use as bridewealth for his sons' marriages. However, a share also goes to everyone who will be expected to help when Sarah's brothers marry.

When Sarah's brother David gets married, many of the cattle go to a third group—C, which is David's wife's group. Thereafter, they may serve as bridewealth to still other groups. Men constantly use their sisters' bridewealth cattle to acquire their own wives. In a decade, the cattle given when Michael married Sarah will have been exchanged widely.

In such societies marriage entails an agreement between descent groups. If Sarah and Michael try to make their marriage succeed but fail to do so, both groups may conclude that the marriage can't last. Here it becomes especially obvious that marriages are relationships between groups as well as between individuals. If Sarah has a younger sister or niece (her older brother's daughter, for example), the concerned parties may agree to Sarah's replacement by a kinswoman.

However, incompatibility isn't the main problem that threatens marriage in societies with bridewealth. Infertility is a more important concern. If Sarah has no children, she and her group have not fulfilled their part of the marriage agreement. If the relationship is to endure, Sarah's group must furnish another woman, perhaps her younger sister, who can have children. If this happens, Sarah may choose to stay in her husband's village. Perhaps she will someday have a child. If she does stay on, her husband will have established a plural marriage.

Most nonindustrial food-producing societies, unlike most industrial nations, allow **plural marriages,** or *polygamy*. There are two varieties; one is common and the other is very rare. The more common variant is **polygyny,** in which a man has more than one wife. The rare variant is **polyandry,** in which a woman has more than one husband. If the infertile wife remains married to her husband after he has taken a substitute wife provided by her descent group, this is polygyny.

## Durable Alliances

It is possible to exemplify the group-alliance nature of marriage by examining still another common practice—continuation of marital alliances when one spouse dies.

### Sororate

What happens if Sarah dies young? Michael's group will ask Sarah's group for a substitute, often her sister. This custom is known as the **sororate** (Figure 13-5). If Sarah has no sister, or if all her sisters already are married, another woman from her group may be available. Michael marries her, there is no need to return the bridewealth, and the alliance continues.

The sororate exists in both matrilineal and patrilineal societies. In a matrilineal society with matrilocal postmarital residence, a widower may remain with his wife's group by marrying her sister or another female member of her matrilineage (Figure 13-5).

### Levirate

What happens if the husband dies? In many societies, the widow may marry his brother. This custom is known as the **levirate** (Figure 13-5). Like the sororate, it is a continuation marriage that maintains the alliance between descent groups, in this case by replacing the husband with another member of his group. The implications of the levirate vary with age. One study found that in African societies the levirate, although widely permitted, rarely involves cohabitation of the widow and her new husband. Furthermore, widows don't automatically marry the husband's brother just because they are allowed to. Often they prefer to make other arrangements (Potash 1986).

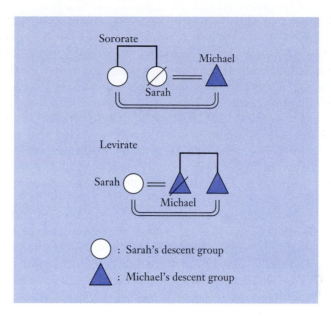

**FIGURE 13-5**   *Sororate and Levirate*

# ✣ DIVORCE

In some societies marriages may seem to go on forever, but in our own they are fairly brittle. Ease of divorce varies across cultures. What factors work for and against divorce? As we've seen, marriages that are political alliances between groups are more difficult to dissolve than are marriages that are more individual affairs, of concern mainly to the married couple and their children. Substantial bridewealth may decrease the divorce rate for individuals; replacement marriages (levirate and sororate) also work to preserve group alliances. Divorce tends to be more common in matrilineal than in patrilineal societies. When residence is matrilocal (in the wife's home village), the wife may simply send off a man with whom she's incompatible.

Among the Hopi of the American Southwest, houses were owned by matrilineal clans, with matrilocal postmarital residence. The household head was the senior woman of that household, which also included her daughters and their husbands and children. A son-in-law had no important role there; he returned to his own mother's home for his clan's social and religious activities. In this matrilineal society, women were socially and economically secure and the divorce rate was high. Consider the Hopi of Oraibi (Orayvi) pueblo, northeastern Arizona (Levy 1992; Titiev 1992). In a study of the marital histories of 423 Oraibi women, Mischa Titiev found 35 percent to have been divorced at least once. Jerome Levy found that 31 percent of 147 adult women had been divorced and remarried at least once. For comparison, of all ever-married women in the United States, only 4 percent had been divorced in 1960, 10.7 percent in 1980, and 11.5 percent in 2004. Titiev characterizes Hopi marriages as unstable. Part of this brittleness was due to conflicting loyalties to matrikin versus spouse. Most Hopi divorces appear to have been matters of personal choice. Levy generalizes that, cross-culturally, high divorce rates are correlated with a secure female economic position. In Hopi society women were secure in their home and land ownership and in the custody of their children. In addition, there were no formal barriers to divorce.

Divorce is harder in a patrilineal society, especially when substantial bridewealth would have to be reassembled and repaid if the marriage failed. A woman residing patrilocally (in her husband's household and community) might be reluctant to leave him. Unlike the Hopi, where the kids stay with the mother, in patrilineal, patrilocal societies the children of divorce would be expected to remain with their father, as members of his patrilineage. From the women's perspective this is a strong impediment to divorce.

Among foragers, different factors favor or oppose divorce. What factors work against durable marriages? Since foragers tend to lack descent groups, the political alliance functions of marriage are less important to them than they are to food producers. Foragers also tend to have minimal material possessions. The process of dissolving a joint fund of property is less complicated when spouses do not hold substantial resources in common. What factors work in opposition to divorce among foragers? In societies in which the family is an important year-round unit with a gender-based division of labor, ties between spouses tend to be durable. Also, sparse populations mean few alternative spouses if a marriage doesn't work out.

In contemporary Western societies, we have the idea that romantic love is necessary for a good marriage (see Ingraham 1999). When romance fails, so may the marriage. Or it may not fail, if the other rights associated with marriage, as discussed previously in this chapter, are compelling. Economic ties and obligations to children, along with other factors, such as concern about public opinion, or simple inertia, may keep marriages intact after sex, romance, or companionship fade.

## ✦ PLURAL MARRIAGES

In contemporary North America, where divorce is fairly easy and common, polygamy (marriage to more than one spouse at the same time) is against the law. Marriage in industrial nations joins individuals, and relationships between individuals can be severed more easily than can those between groups. North Americans practice *serial monogamy:* Individuals have more than one spouse but never, legally, more than one at the same time. As stated earlier, the two forms of polygamy are polygyny and polyandry. Polyandry is practiced in only a few societies, notably among certain groups in Tibet, Nepal, and India. Polygyny is much more common.

### Polygyny

We must distinguish between the social approval of plural marriage and its actual frequency in a particular society. Many cultures approve of a man's having more than one wife. However, even when polygyny is encouraged, most people are monogamous, and polygyny characterizes only a fraction of the marriages. Why?

One reason is equal sex ratios. In the United States, about 105 males are born for every 100 females. In adulthood the ratio of men to women equalizes, and eventually it reverses. The average North American woman outlives the average man. In many nonindustrial societies as well, the male-biased sex ratio among children reverses in adulthood.

The custom of men marrying later than women also promotes polygyny. Among Nigeria's Kanuri people (Cohen 1967), men got married between the ages of 18 and 30; women, between 12 and 14. The age difference between spouses meant there were more widows than widowers. Most of the widows remarried, some in polygynous unions. Among the Kanuri and in other polygynous societies, such as the Tiwi of northern Australia, widows made up a large number of the women involved in plural marriages (Hart, Pilling, and Goodale 1988).

In certain societies, the first wife requests a second wife to help with household chores. The second wife's status is lower than that of the first; they are senior and junior wives. The senior wife sometimes chooses the junior one from among her close kinswomen. Among the Betsileo of Madagascar, the different wives always lived in different villages. A man's first and senior wife, called "Big Wife," lived in the village where he cultivated his best rice field and spent most of his time. High-status men with several rice fields and multiple wives had households near each field. They spent most of their time with the senior wife but visited the others throughout the year.

Members of the Uighur ethnic group, this polygynous family includes two wives, six children, and one husband. They sit in front of their house at the Buzak Commune, near Khotan, Xinjiang Province, People's Republic of China. Would you expect most marriages to be polygynous in a society that allows polygyny?

Plural wives can play important political roles in nonindustrial states. The king of the Merina, a populous society in the highlands of Madagascar, had palaces for each of his 12 wives in different provinces. He stayed with them when he traveled through the kingdom. They were his local agents, overseeing and reporting on provincial matters. The king of Buganda, the major precolonial state of Uganda, took hundreds of wives, representing all the clans in his nation. Everyone in the kingdom became the king's in-law, and all the clans had a chance to provide the next ruler. This was a way of giving the common people a stake in the government.

These examples show there is no single explanation for polygyny. Its context and function vary from society to society and even within the same society. Some men are polygynous because they have inherited a widow from a brother. Others have plural wives because they seek prestige or want to increase household productivity. Men and women with political and economic ambitions cultivate marital alliances that serve their aims. In many societies, including the Betsileo of Madagascar and the Igbo of Nigeria, women arrange the marriages.

## ANTHROPOLOGY TODAY

### *Social Security, Kinship Style*

My book *Assault on Paradise,* fourth edition (Kottak 2006), describes social relations in Arembepe, the Brazilian fishing community I've studied since the 1960s. When I first studied Arembepe I was struck by how similar its social relations were to those in the egalitarian, kin-based societies anthropologists have studied traditionally. The twin assertions "We're all equal here" and "We're all relatives here" were offered repeatedly as Arembepeiros' own summaries of the nature and basis of local life. Like members of a clan (who claim to share common ancestry, but who can't say exactly how they are related), most villagers couldn't trace precise genealogical links to their distant kin. "What difference does it make, as long as we know we're relatives?"

As in most nonindustrial societies, close personal relations were either based or modeled on kinship. A degree of community solidarity was promoted, for example, by the myth that everyone was kin. However, social solidarity was actually much *less* developed in Arembepe than in societies with clans and lineages—which use genealogy to include some people, and *exclude* others, from membership in a given descent group. Intense social solidarity demands that some people be excluded. By asserting they all were related—that is, by excluding no one—Arembepeiros were actually weakening kinship's potential strength in creating and maintaining group solidarity.

Rights and obligations always are associated with kinship and marriage. In Arembepe, the closer the kin connection and the more formal the marital tie, the greater the rights and obligations. Couples could be married formally or informally. The most common union was a stable common-law marriage. Less common, but with more prestige, was legal (civil) marriage, performed by a justice of the peace and conferring inheritance rights. The union with the most prestige combined legal validity with a church ceremony.

The rights and obligations associated with kinship and marriage comprised the local social security system, but people had

# Polyandry

Polyandry is rare and is practiced under very specific conditions. Most of the world's polyandrous peoples live in South Asia—Tibet, Nepal, India, and Sri Lanka. In some of these areas, polyandry seems to be a cultural adaptation to mobility associated with customary male travel for trade, commerce, and military operations. Polyandry ensures there will be at least one man at home to accomplish male activities within a gender-based division of labor. Fraternal polyandry is also an effective strategy when resources are scarce. Brothers with limited resources (in land) pool their resources in expanded (polyandrous) households. They take just one wife. Polyandry restricts the number of wives and heirs. Less competition among heirs means that land can be transmitted with minimal fragmentation.

to weigh the benefits of the system against its costs. The most obvious cost was this: Villagers had to share in proportion to their success. As ambitious men climbed the local ladder of success, they got more dependents. To maintain their standing in public opinion, and to guarantee they could depend on others in old age, they had to share. However, sharing was a powerful leveling mechanism. It drained surplus wealth and restricted upward mobility.

How, specifically, did this leveling work? As is often true in stratified nations, Brazilian national cultural norms are set by the upper classes. Middle- and upper-class Brazilians usually marry legally and in the church. Even Arembepeiros knew this was the only "proper" way to marry. The most successful and ambitious local men copied the behavior of elite Brazilians. By doing so, they hoped to acquire some of their prestige.

However, legal marriage drained individual wealth, for example, by creating a responsibility to help one's in-laws financially. Such obligations could be regular and costly. Obligations to kids also increased

with income because successful people tended to have more living children. Children were valued as companions and as an eventual economic benefit to their parents. Boys especially were prized because their economic prospects were so much brighter than those of girls.

Children's chances of survival surged dramatically in wealthier households with better diets. The normal household diet included fish—usually in a stew with tomatoes, onions, palm oil, vinegar, and lemon. Dried beef replaced fish once a week. Roasted manioc flour was the main source of calories and was eaten at all meals. Other daily staples included coffee, sugar, and salt. Fruits and vegetables were eaten in season. Diet was one of the main contrasts between households. The poorest people didn't eat fish regularly; often they subsisted on manioc flour, coffee, and sugar. Better-off households supplemented the staples with milk, butter, eggs, rice, beans, and more ample portions of fresh fish, fruits, and vegetables.

Adequate incomes bought improved diets and provided the means and confidence

*Continued*

## ANTHROPOLOGY TODAY

to seek out better medical attention than was locally available. Most of the kids born in the wealthier households survived. But this meant more mouths to feed, and (since the heads of such households usually wanted a better education for their children) it meant increased expenditures on schooling. The correlation between economic success and large families was a siphoner of wealth that restricted individual economic advance. Tomé, a fishing entrepreneur, envisioned a life of constant hard work if he was to feed, clothe, and educate his growing family. Tomé and his wife had never lost a child. But he recognized that his growing family would, in the short run, be a drain on his resources. "But in the end, I'll have successful sons to help their mother and me, if we need it, in our old age."

Arembepeiros knew who could afford to share with others; success can't be concealed in a small community. Villagers based their expectations of others on this knowledge. Successful people had to share with more kin and in-laws, and with more distant kin, than did poorer people. Success-

ful captains and boat owners were expected to buy beer for ordinary fishers; store owners had to sell on credit. As in bands and tribes, any well-off person was expected to exhibit a corresponding generosity. With increasing wealth, people were also more frequently asked to enter ritual kin relationships. Through baptism—which took place twice a year when a priest visited, or which could be done outside—a child acquired two godparents. These became the coparents (*compadres*) of the baby's parents. The fact that ritual kinship obligations increased with wealth was another factor limiting individual economic advance.

We see that kinship, marriage, and ritual kinship in Arembepe had costs and benefits. The costs were limits on the economic advance of individuals. The primary benefit was social security—guaranteed help from kin, in-laws, and ritual kin in times of need. Benefits, however, came only after costs had been paid: that is, only to those who had lived "proper" lives, not deviating too noticeably from local norms, especially those about sharing.

## SUMMARY

1. Kinship and marriage organize social and political life in nonindustrial societies. One widespread kin group is the nuclear family, consisting of a married couple and their children. Other groups, such as extended families and descent groups, may assume functions usually associated with the nuclear family. Nuclear families tend to be especially important in foraging and industrial societies.

2. In contemporary North America, the nuclear family is the characteristic kin group for the middle class. Expanded households and sharing with extended family kin occur more frequently among the poor, who may pool their resources in dealing with poverty. Today, however, even in the American middle class, nuclear family households are declining as single-person households and other domestic arrangements increase.

3. The descent group is a basic kin group among nonindustrial food producers (farmers and herders). Unlike families, descent groups have perpetuity, lasting for generations. Descent-group members share and manage an estate. Lineages are

based on demonstrated descent; clans, on stipulated descent. Unilineal (patrilineal and matrilineal) descent is associated with unilocal (patrilocal and matrilocal, respectively) postmarital residence.

4. All societies have an incest taboo. Because kinship is socially constructed, the taboo applies to different relatives in different societies. Human behavior with respect to mating with close relatives may express a generalized primate tendency, illustrating both urges and avoidance. But types, risks, and avoidance of incest also reflect specific kinship structures. Exogamy extends social and political ties outward; endogamy does the reverse. Endogamic rules are common in stratified societies. One extreme example is India, where castes are the endogamous units.

5. The discussion of same-sex marriage, which, by and large, is illegal in the United States, illustrates the various rights that go along with marriage. Marriage establishes the legal parents of children. It gives spouses rights to the sexuality, labor, and property of the other. And it establishes a socially significant "relationship of affinity" between spouses and each other's relatives.

6. In societies with descent groups, marriages are relationships between groups as well as between spouses. With bridewealth, the groom and his relatives transfer wealth to the bride and her relatives. As the bridewealth's value increases, the divorce rate declines. Bridewealth customs show that marriages among nonindustrial food producers create and maintain group alliances. So do the sororate, by which a man marries the sister of his deceased wife, and the levirate, by which a woman marries the brother of her deceased husband.

7. The ease and frequency of divorce vary across cultures. When marriage is a matter of intergroup alliance, as is typically true in societies with descent groups, divorce is less common. A large fund of joint property also complicates divorce.

8. Many societies permit plural marriages. The two kinds of polygamy are polygyny and polyandry. The former involves multiple wives; the latter, multiple husbands. Polygyny is much more common than polyandry.

## KEY TERMS

bridewealth (p. 295)
clan (p. 287)
descent group (p. 286)
dowry (p. 295)
endogamy (p. 291)
exogamy (p. 289)
extended family household (p. 282)
family (p. 279)
family of orientation (p. 279)
family of procreation (p. 279)
incest (p. 289)
levirate (p. 296)

lineage (p. 287)
matrilineal descent (p. 286)
matrilocality (p. 288)
neolocality (p. 281)
patrilineal descent (p. 286)
patrilocality (p. 288)
plural marriages (p. 296)
polyandry (p. 296)
polygyny (p. 296)
progeny price (p. 295)
sororate (p. 296)
unilineal descent (p. 286)

# CHAPTER 14

## GENDER

Because anthropologists study biology, society, and culture, they are in a unique position to comment on nature (biological predispositions) and nurture (environment) as determinants of human behavior. Human attitudes, values, and behavior are limited not only by our genetic predispositions—which often are difficult to identify—but also by our experiences during enculturation. Our attributes as adults are determined both by our genes and by our environment during growth and development.

Questions about nature and nurture emerge in the discussion of human sex–gender roles and sexuality. Men and women differ genetically. Women have two X chromosomes, and men have an X and a Y. The father determines a baby's sex because only he has the Y chromosome to transmit. The mother always provides an X chromosome.

The chromosomal difference is expressed in hormonal and physiological contrasts. Humans are sexually dimorphic, more so than some primates, such as gibbons (small tree-living Asiatic apes) and less so than others, such as gorillas and orangutans. **Sexual dimorphism** refers to differences in male and female biology besides the contrasts in breasts and genitals. Women and men differ not just in primary (genitalia and reproductive organs) and secondary (breasts, voice, hair distribution) sexual characteristics, but in average weight, height, strength, and longevity. Women tend to live longer than men and have excellent endurance capabilities. In a given population, men tend to be taller and to weigh more than women do. Of course, there is a considerable overlap between the sexes in terms of height, weight, and physical strength, and there has been a pronounced reduction in sexual dimorphism during human biological evolution.

Just how far, however, do such genetically and physiologically determined differences go? What effects do they have on the way men and women act and are treated in different societies? Anthropologists have discovered both similarities and differences in the roles of men and women in different cultures. The predominant anthropological position on sex–gender roles and biology may be stated as follows:

> The biological nature of men and women [should be seen] not as a narrow enclosure limiting the human organism, but rather as a broad base upon which a variety of structures can be built. (Friedl 1975, p. 6)

Although in most societies men tend to be somewhat more aggressive than women, many of the behavioral and attitudinal differences between the sexes emerge from culture rather than biology. *Sex* differences are biological, but *gender* encompasses all the traits that a culture assigns to and inculcates in males and females. "Gender," in other words, refers to the cultural construction of male and female characteristics (Rosaldo 1980*b*).

Given the "rich and various constructions of gender" within the realm of cultural diversity, Susan Bourque and Kay Warren (1987) note that the same images of masculinity and femininity do not always apply. Anthropologists have gathered systematic ethnographic data about similarities and differences involving gender in many cultural settings (Bonvillain 2001; Brettell and Sargent 2005; Gilmore 2001; Mascia-Lees and Black 2000; Nanda 2000; Ward and Edelstein 2006). Anthropologists can detect recurrent themes and patterns involving gender differences. They also can observe that gender roles vary with environment, economy, adaptive strategy, and type of political system. Before we examine the cross-cultural data, some definitions are in order.

The realm of cultural diversity contains richly different social constructions and expressions of gender roles, as is illustrated by these Wodaabe male celebrants in Niger. (Look closely for suggestions of diffusion.) For what reasons do men decorate their bodies in our society?

**Gender roles** are the tasks and activities a culture assigns to the sexes. Related to gender roles are **gender stereotypes,** which are oversimplified but strongly held ideas about the characteristics of males and females. **Gender stratification** describes an unequal distribution of rewards (socially valued resources, power, prestige, human rights, and personal freedom) between men and women, reflecting their different positions in a social hierarchy. According to Ann Stoler (1977), the economic determinants of gender status include freedom or autonomy (in disposing of one's labor and its fruits) and social power (control over the lives, labor, and produce of others).

In stateless societies, gender stratification often is more obvious in regard to prestige than it is in regard to wealth. In her study of the Ilongots of northern Luzon in the Philippines, Michelle Rosaldo (1980a) described gender differences related to the positive cultural value placed on adventure, travel, and knowledge of the external world. More often than women, Ilongot men, as headhunters, visited distant places. They acquired knowledge of the external world, amassed experiences there, and returned to express their knowledge, adventures, and feelings in public oratory. They received acclaim as a result. Ilongot women had inferior prestige because they lacked external experiences on which to base knowledge and dramatic expression. On the basis of Rosaldo's study and findings in other stateless societies, Ong (1989) argues that we must distinguish between prestige systems and actual power in a given society. High male prestige may not entail economic or political power held by men over their families.

## ✦ RECURRENT GENDER PATTERNS

Ethnologists compare ethnographic data from several cultures (i.e., cross-cultural data) to discover and explain differences and similarities. Data relevant to the cross-cultural study of gender can be drawn from the domains of economics, politics, domestic activity, kinship, and marriage. Table 14-1 shows cross-cultural data from 185 randomly selected societies on the division of labor by gender.

Remembering the discussion in the chapter "Culture" of universals, generalities, and particularities, the findings in Table 14-1 about the division of labor by gender illustrate generalities rather than universals. That is, among the societies known to ethnography, there is a very strong tendency for men to build boats, but there are exceptions. One was the Hidatsa, a Native American group in which the women made the boats used to cross the Missouri River. (Traditionally, the Hidatsa were village farmers and bison hunters on the North American Plains; they now live in North Dakota.) Another exception: Pawnee women worked wood; this is the only Native American group that assigned this activity to women. (The Pawnee, also traditionally Plains farmers and bison hunters, originally lived in what is now central Nebraska and central Kansas; they now live on a reservation in north central Oklahoma.)

Exceptions to cross-cultural generalizations may involve societies or individuals. That is, a society like the Hidatsa can contradict the cross-cultural generalization that men build boats by assigning that task to women. Or, in a society where the cultural expectation is that only men build boats, a particular woman or women can contradict that expectation by doing the male activity. Table 14-1 shows that in a sample of 185 societies, certain activities ("swing activities") are assigned to either or both men and

## TABLE 14-1

### Generalities in the Division of Labor by Gender, Based on Data from 185 Societies

| Generally Male Activities | Swing (Male or Female) Activities | Generally Female Activities |
|---|---|---|
| Hunting of large aquatic animals (e.g., whales, walrus) | Making fire | Gathering fuel (e.g., firewood) |
| Smelting of ores | Body mutilation | Making drinks |
| Metalworking | Preparing skins | Gathering wild vegetal foods |
| Lumbering | Gathering small land animals | Dairy production (e.g., churning) |
| Hunting large land animals | Planting crops | Spinning |
| Working wood | Making leather products | Doing the laundry |
| Hunting fowl | Harvesting | Fetching water |
| Making musical instruments | Tending crops | Cooking |
| Trapping | Milking | Preparing vegetal food (e.g., processing cereal grains) |
| Building boats | Making baskets | |
| Working stone | Carrying burdens | |
| Working bone, horn, and shell | Making mats | |
| Mining and quarrying | Caring for small animals | |
| Setting bones | Preserving meat and fish | |
| Butchering* | Loom weaving | |
| Collecting wild honey | Gathering small aquatic animals | |
| Clearing land | Clothing manufacture | |
| Fishing | Making pottery | |
| Tending large herd animals | | |
| Building houses | | |
| Preparing the soil | | |
| Making nets | | |
| Making rope | | |

*All the activities above "butchering" are almost always done by men; those from "butchering" through "making rope" usually are done by men.
*SOURCE:* Murdock and Provost 1973.

women. Among the most important of such activities are planting, tending, and harvesting crops. We'll see below that some societies customarily assign more farming chores to women, whereas others call on men to be the main farm laborers. Among the tasks almost always assigned to men (Table 14-1), some (e.g., hunting large animals on land

and sea) seem clearly related to the greater average size and strength of males. Others, such as working wood and making musical instruments, seem more culturally arbitrary. And women, of course, are not exempt from arduous and time-consuming physical labor, such as gathering firewood and fetching water. In Arembepe, Bahia, Brazil, women routinely transported water in five-gallon tins, balanced on their heads, from wells and lagoons located long distances from their homes.

Both women and men have to fit their activities into 24-hour days. Based on cross-cultural data, Table 14-2 shows that the time and effort spent in subsistence activities by men and women tend to be about equal. If anything, men do slightly less subsistence work than women do. Think about how female domestic activities could have been specified in greater detail in Table 14-1. The original coding of the data in Table 14-1 probably illustrates a male bias in that extradomestic activities received much more prominence than domestic activities did. For example, is collecting wild honey (listed in Table 14-1) more necessary or time-consuming than cleaning a baby's bottom (absent from Table 14-1)? Also, notice that Table 14-1 does not mention trade and market activity, in which either or both men and women are active.

Cross-culturally the subsistence contributions of men and women are roughly equal (Table 14-2). But in domestic activities and child care, female labor predominates, as we see in Tables 14-3 and 14-4. Table 14-3 shows that in about half the societies studied, men did virtually no domestic work. Even in societies where men did some domestic chores, the bulk of such work was done by women. Adding together their subsistence activities and their domestic work, women tend to work more hours than men do. Has this changed in the contemporary world?

## TABLE 14-2

### Time and Effort Expended on Subsistence Activities by Men and Women*

| | |
|---|---|
| More by men | 16 |
| Roughly equal | 61 |
| More by women | 23 |

*Percentage of 88 randomly selected societies for which information was available on this variable.
*SOURCE:* Whyte 1978.

## TABLE 14-3

### Who Does the Domestic Work?*

| | |
|---|---|
| Males do virtually none | 51 |
| Males do some, but mostly done by females | 49 |

*Percentage of 92 randomly selected societies for which information was available on this variable.
*SOURCE:* Whyte 1978.

## TABLE 14-4

### Who Has Final Authority over the Care, Handling, and Discipline of Infant Children (under Four Years Old)?*

| | |
|---|---|
| Males have more say | 18 |
| Roughly equal | 16 |
| Females have more say | 66 |

*Percentage of 67 randomly selected societies for which information was available on this variable.
*SOURCE:* Whyte 1978.

What about child care? Women tend to be the main caregivers in most societies, but men often play a role. Table 14-4 uses cross-cultural data to answer the question, "Who—men or women—has final authority over the care, handling, and discipline of children younger than four years?" Women have primary authority over infants in two-thirds of the societies. Given the critical role of breast-feeding in ensuring infant survival, it makes sense, for infants especially, for the mother to be the primary caregiver.

There are differences in male and female reproductive strategies. Women work to ensure their progeny will survive by establishing a close bond with each baby. It's also advantageous for a woman to have a reliable mate to ease the child-rearing process and ensure the survival of her children. (Again, there are exceptions, for example, the matrilineal Nayars discussed in the previous chapter). Women can have only so many babies during their reproductive years, which begin after menarche (the advent of first menstruation) and end with menopause (cessation of menstruation.) Men, in contrast, have a longer reproductive period, which can last into the elder years. If they choose to do so, men can enhance their reproductive success by impregnating several women over a longer time period. Although men do not always have multiple mates, they do have a greater tendency to do so than women do (see Tables 14-5, 14-6, and 14-7). Among the societies known to ethnography, polygyny is much more common than polyandry (see Table 14-5).

Men mate, within and outside marriage, more than women do. Table 14-6 shows cross-cultural data on premarital sex, and Table 14-7 summarizes the data on extramarital sex. In both cases men are less restricted than women are, although the restrictions are equal in about half the societies studied.

## TABLE 14-5

### Does the Society Allow Multiple Spouses?*

| | |
|---|---|
| Only for males | 77 |
| For both, but more commonly for males | 4 |
| For neither | 16 |
| For both, but more commonly for females | 2 |

*Percentage of 92 randomly selected societies.
*SOURCE:* Whyte 1978.

## TABLE 14-6

### Is There a Double Standard with Respect to PREMARITAL Sex*

| | |
|---|---|
| Yes—females are more restricted | 44 |
| No—equal restrictions on males and females | 56 |

*Percentage of 73 randomly selected societies for which information was available on this variable.
*SOURCE:* Whyte 1978.

## TABLE 14-7

### Is There a Double Standard with Respect to EXTRAMARITAL Sex*

| | |
|---|---|
| Yes—females are more restricted | 43 |
| Equal restrictions on males and females | 55 |
| Males punished more severely for transgression | 3 |

*Percentage of 75 randomly selected societies for which information was available on this variable.
*SOURCE:* Whyte 1978.

Double standards that restrict women more than men illustrate gender stratification. Several studies have shown that economic roles affect gender stratification. In one cross-cultural study, Sanday (1974) found that gender stratification decreased when men and women made roughly equal contributions to subsistence. She found that gender stratification was greatest when the women contributed either much more or much less than the men did.

## ✦ GENDER AMONG FORAGERS

In foraging societies gender stratification was most marked when men contributed much *more* to the diet than women did. This was true among the Inuit and other northern hunters and fishers. Among tropical and semitropical foragers, by contrast, gathering usually supplies more food than hunting and fishing do. Gathering generally is women's work. Men usually hunt and fish, but women also do some fishing and may hunt small animals. When gathering is prominent, gender status tends to be more equal than it is when hunting and fishing are the main subsistence activities.

Gender status also is more equal when the domestic and public spheres aren't sharply separated. (*Domestic* means within or pertaining to the home.) Strong differentiation between the home and the outside world is called the **domestic–public dichotomy** or the *private–public contrast*. The outside world can include politics, trade, warfare, or work. Often when domestic and public spheres are clearly separated, public activities have greater prestige than domestic ones do. This can promote gender stratification, because men are more likely to be active in the public domain than women are. Cross-culturally, women's activities tend to be closer to home than men's are. Thus, another reason hunter-gatherers have less gender stratification than food producers do is that the domestic–public dichotomy is less developed among foragers.

Certain roles tend to be more sex-linked than others. Men are the usual hunters and warriors. Given such weapons as spears, knives, and bows, men make better fighters because they are bigger and stronger on average than are women in the same population (Divale and Harris 1976). The male hunter–fighter role also reflects a tendency toward greater male mobility. In foraging societies, women are either pregnant or lactating during much of their childbearing period. Late in pregnancy and after childbirth, carrying a baby limits a woman's movements. However, among the Agta of the Philippines (Griffin and Estioko-Griffin, eds. 1985), women not only gather, but they also hunt with dogs while carrying their babies with them. Still, considering cross-cultural data, women rarely are the primary hunters (Friedl 1975). Warfare, which also requires mobility, is not found in most foraging societies, nor is interregional trade well developed. Warfare and trade are two public arenas that contribute to status inequality of males and females among food producers.

The Ju/'hoansi San illustrate the extent to which the activities and spheres of influence of men and women may overlap among foragers (Draper 1975). Traditional Ju/'hoansi gender roles were interdependent. During gathering, women discovered information about game animals, which they passed on to the men. Men and women spent about the same amount of time away from the camp, but neither worked more than three days a week. The Ju/'hoansi saw nothing wrong in doing the work of the other gender. Men often gathered food and collected water. A general sharing ethos dictated that men distribute meat and that women share the fruits of gathering.

It is among foragers that the public and private spheres are least separate, hierarchy is least marked, aggression and competition are most discouraged, and the rights, activities, and spheres of influence of men and women overlap the most. Our ancestors lived entirely by foraging until 10,000 years ago. Despite the popular stereotype of the club-wielding caveman dragging his mate by the hair, relative gender equality is a much more likely ancestral pattern.

## ✦ GENDER AMONG HORTICULTURALISTS

Gender roles and stratification among cultivators vary widely, depending on specific features of the economy and social structure. Demonstrating this, Martin and Voorhies (1975) studied a sample of 515 horticultural societies, representing all parts of the world. They looked at several factors, including descent and postmarital residence, the percentage of the diet derived from cultivation, and the relative productivity of men and women.

Women turned out to be the main producers in horticultural societies. In 50 percent of those societies, women did most of the cultivating. In 33 percent, contributions to cultivation by men and women were equal (see Table 14-8). In only 17 percent did men do most of the work. Women tended to do a bit more cultivating in matrilineal compared with patrilineal societies. They dominated horticulture in 64 percent of the matrilineal societies versus 50 percent of the patrilineal ones.

## TABLE 14-8

**Male and Female Contributions to Production in Cultivating Societies**

|                                   | Horticulture (percentage of 104 societies) | Agriculture (percentage of 93 societies) |
|-----------------------------------|:------------------------------------------:|:----------------------------------------:|
| Women are primary cultivators     | 50%                                        | 15%                                      |
| Men are primary cultivators       | 17                                         | 81                                       |
| Equal contributions to cultivation| 33                                         | 3                                        |

SOURCE: Martin and Voorhies 1975, p. 283.

# Reduced Gender Stratification—Matrilineal–Matrilocal Societies

Cross-cultural variation in gender status is related to rules of descent and postmarital residence (Friedl 1975; Martin and Voorhies 1975). Among horticulturalists with matrilineal descent and *matrilocality* (residence after marriage with the wife's relatives), female status tends to be high. Matriliny and matrilocality disperse related males, rather than consolidating them. By contrast, patriliny and *patrilocality* (residence after marriage with the husband's kin) keep male relatives together—an advantage given warfare. Matrilineal–matrilocal systems tend to occur in societies where population pressure on strategic resources is minimal and warfare is infrequent.

Women tend to have high status in matrilineal, matrilocal societies for several reasons (see the box at the end of the chapter). Descent-group membership, succession to political positions, allocation of land, and overall social identity all come through female links. Among the matrilineal Malays of Negeri Sembilan, Malaysia (Peletz 1988), matriliny gave women sole inheritance of ancestral rice fields. Matrilocality created solidary clusters of female kin. These Malay women had considerable influence beyond the household (Swift 1963). In such matrilineal contexts, women are the basis of the entire social structure. Although public authority nominally may be assigned to the men, much of the power and decision making actually may belong to the senior women.

# Increased Gender Stratification—Patrilineal–Patrilocal Societies

Martin and Voorhies (1975) link the decline of matriliny and the spread of the **patrilineal–patrilocal complex** (consisting of patrilineality, patrilocality, warfare, and male supremacy) to pressure on resources. Faced with scarce resources, patrilineal–patrilocal cultivators such as the Yanomami often wage warfare against other villages. This favors patrilocality and patriliny, customs that keep related men together in the same village, where they make strong allies in battle. Such societies tend to have a sharp domestic-public dichotomy, and men tend to dominate the prestige hierarchy. Men may use their public roles in warfare and trade and their greater prestige to symbolize and reinforce the devaluation or oppression of women.

In some parts of Papua New Guinea, the patrilineal–patrilocal complex has extreme social repercussions. Regarding females as dangerous and polluting, men may segregate themselves in men's houses (such as this one, located near the Sepik River), where they hide their precious ritual objects from women. Are there places like this in your society?

The patrilineal–patrilocal complex characterizes many societies in highland Papua New Guinea. Women work hard growing and processing subsistence crops, raising and tending pigs (the main domesticated animal and a favorite food), and doing domestic cooking, but they are isolated from the public domain, which men control. Men grow and distribute prestige crops, prepare food for feasts, and arrange marriages. The men even get to trade the pigs and control their use in ritual.

In densely populated areas of the Papua New Guinea highlands, male–female avoidance is associated with strong pressure on resources (Lindenbaum 1972). Men fear all female contacts, including sex. They think that sexual contact with women will weaken them. Indeed, men see everything female as dangerous and polluting. They segregate themselves in men's houses and hide their precious ritual objects from women. They delay marriage, and some never marry.

By contrast, the sparsely populated areas of Papua New Guinea, such as recently settled areas, lack taboos on male–female contacts. The image of woman as polluter fades, heterosexual intercourse is valued, men and women live together, and reproductive rates are high.

## ✦ GENDER AMONG AGRICULTURISTS

When the economy is based on agriculture, women typically lose their role as primary cultivators. Certain agricultural techniques, particularly plowing, have been assigned to men because of their greater average size and strength (Martin and Voorhies 1975). Except when irrigation is used, plowing eliminates the need for constant weeding, an activity usually done by women.

Cross-cultural data illustrate these contrasts in productive roles between agricultural and horticultural economies. Women were the main workers in 50 percent of the horticultural societies surveyed but in only 15 percent of the agricultural groups. Male subsistence labor dominated 81 percent of the agricultural societies but only 17 percent of the horticultural ones (Martin and Voorhies 1975) (see Table 14-8).

With the advent of agriculture, women were cut off from production for the first time in human history. Belief systems started contrasting men's valuable extradomestic labor with women's domestic role, now viewed as inferior. (**Extradomestic** means outside the home; within or pertaining to the public domain.) Changes in kinship and postmarital residence patterns also hurt women. Descent groups and polygyny declined with agriculture, and the nuclear family became more common. Living with her husband and children, a woman was isolated from her kinswomen and cowives. Female sexuality is carefully supervised in agricultural economies; men have easier access to divorce and extramarital sex, reflecting a "double standard."

Still, female status in agricultural societies is not inevitably bleak. Gender stratification is associated with plow agriculture rather than with intensive cultivation per se. Studies of peasant gender roles and stratification in France and Spain (Harding 1975; Reiter 1975), which have plow agriculture, show that people think of the house as the female sphere and the fields as the male domain. However, such a dichotomy is not inevitable, as my own research among Betsileo agriculturists in Madagascar shows.

Betsileo women play a prominent role in agriculture, contributing a third of the hours invested in rice production. They have their customary tasks in the division of labor, but their work is more seasonal than men's is. No one has much to do during the ceremonial season, between mid-June and mid-September. Men work in the rice fields almost daily the rest of the year. Women's cooperative work occurs during transplanting (mid-September through November) and harvesting (mid-March through early May). Along with other members of the household, women do daily weeding in December and January. After the harvest, all family members work together winnowing the rice and then transporting it to the granary.

If we consider the strenuous daily task of husking rice by pounding (a part of food preparation rather than production per se), women actually contribute slightly more than 50 percent of the labor devoted to producing and preparing rice before cooking.

Not just women's prominent economic role but traditional social organization enhances female status among the Betsileo. Although postmarital residence is mainly patrilocal, descent rules permit married women to keep membership in and a strong allegiance to their own descent groups. Kinship is broadly and bilaterally (on both sides— as in contemporary North America) calculated. The Betsileo exemplify Aihwa Ong's (1989) generalization that bilateral (and matrilineal) kinship systems, combined with subsistence economies in which the sexes have complementary roles in food production and distribution, are characterized by reduced gender stratification. Such societies are common among South Asian peasants (Ong 1989).

Traditionally, Betsileo men participate more in politics, but the women also hold political office. Women sell their produce and products in markets, invest in cattle, sponsor ceremonies, and are mentioned during offerings to ancestors. Arranging marriages, an important extradomestic activity, is more women's concern than men's. Sometimes Betsileo women seek their own kinswomen as wives for their sons, reinforcing their own prominence in village life and continuing kin-based female solidarity in the village.

The Betsileo illustrate the idea that intensive cultivation does not necessarily entail sharp gender stratification. We can see that gender roles and stratification reflect not just the type of adaptive strategy but also specific cultural attributes. Betsileo women continue to play a significant role in their society's major economic activity, rice production.

## ✦ PATRIARCHY AND VIOLENCE

**Patriarchy** describes a political system ruled by men in which women have inferior social and political status, including basic human rights. Barbara Miller (1997), in a study of systematic neglect of females, describes women in rural northern India as "the endangered sex." Societies that feature a full-fledged patrilineal–patrilocal complex, replete with warfare and intervillage raiding, also typify patriarchy. Such practices as dowry murders, female infanticide, and clitoridectomy exemplify patriarchy, which extends from tribal societies such as the Yanomami to state societies such as India and Pakistan.

Although more prevalent in certain social settings than in others, family violence and domestic abuse of women are worldwide problems. Domestic violence certainly occurs in neolocal–nuclear family settings, such as Canada and the United States. Cities, with their impersonality and isolation from extended kin networks, are breeding groups for domestic violence.

We've seen that gender stratification typically is reduced in matrilineal, matrifocal, and bilateral societies in which women have prominent roles in the economy and social life. When a woman lives in her own village, she has kin nearby to look after and protect her interests. Even in patrilocal polygynous settings, women often count on the support of their cowives and sons in disputes with potentially abusive husbands.

Such settings, which tend to provide a safe haven for women, are retracting rather than expanding in today's world, however. Isolated families and patrilineal social forms have spread at the expense of matrilineality. Many nations have declared polygyny illegal. More and more women, and men, find themselves cut off from extended kin and families of orientation.

With the spread of the women's rights movement and the human rights movement, attention to domestic violence and abuse of women has increased. Laws have been passed and mediating institutions established. Brazil's female-run police stations for battered women provide an example, as do shelters for victims of domestic abuse in the United States and Canada. But patriarchal institutions do persist in what should be a more enlightened world.

## ✦ GENDER AND INDUSTRIALISM

The domestic–public dichotomy, which is developed most fully among patrilineal–patrilocal food producers and plow agriculturists, also has affected gender stratification in industrial societies, including the United States and Canada. Gender roles have been changing rapidly in North America. The "traditional" idea that "a woman's place is in the home" actually emerged in the United States as industrialism spread after 1900. Earlier, pioneer women in the Midwest and West had been recognized as fully productive workers in farming and home industry. Under industrialism, attitudes about gendered work came to vary with class and region. In early industrial Europe, men, women, and children had flocked to factories as wage laborers. Enslaved Americans of both sexes had done grueling work in cotton fields. With abolition, southern African American women continued working as field hands and domestics. Poor white women labored in the South's early cotton mills. In the 1890s more than 1 million American women held menial and repetitive unskilled factory positions (Margolis 1984; Martin and Voorhies 1975).

After 1900, European immigration produced a male labor force willing to work for wages lower than those of American-born men. Those immigrant men moved into factory jobs that previously had gone to women. As machine tools and mass production further reduced the need for female labor, the notion that women were biologically unfit for factory work began to gain ground (Martin and Voorhies 1975).

Maxine Margolis (1984, 2000) has shown how gendered work, attitudes, and beliefs have varied in response to American economic needs. For example, wartime shortages of men have promoted the idea that work outside the home is women's patriotic duty. During the world wars the notion that women are unfit for hard physical labor faded. Inflation and the culture of consumption also have spurred female employment. When prices or demand rise, multiple paychecks help maintain family living standards.

The steady increase in female paid employment since World War II also reflects the baby boom and industrial expansion. American culture traditionally has defined clerical work, teaching, and nursing as female occupations. With rapid population growth and business expansion after World War II, the demand for women to fill such jobs grew steadily. Employers also found they could increase their profits by paying women lower wages than they would have to pay returning male war veterans.

During the world wars the notion that women were biologically unfit for hard physical labor faded. Shown here is World War II's famous Rosie the Riveter. Is there a comparable poster woman today? What does her image say about modern gender roles?

Margolis (1984, 2000) contends that changes in the economy lead to changes in attitudes toward and about women. Economic changes paved the way for the contemporary women's movement, which also was spurred by the publication of Betty Friedan's book *The Feminine Mystique* in 1963 and the founding of NOW, the National Organization of Women, in 1966. The movement in turn promoted expanded work opportunities for women, including the goal of equal pay for equal work. Between 1970 and 2005, the female percentage of the American workforce rose from 38 to 46 percent. In other words, almost half of all Americans who work outside the home are women. Over 69 million women now have paid jobs, compared with 80 million men. Women now fill more than half (56 percent)

## TABLE 14-9

### Cash Employment of American Mothers, Wives, and Husbands, 1960–2005*

| Year | Percentage of Married Women, Husband Present with Children under 6 | Percentage of All Married Women[†] | Percentage of All Married Men[‡] |
|------|:---:|:---:|:---:|
| 1960 | 19 | 32 | 89 |
| 1970 | 30 | 40 | 86 |
| 1980 | 45 | 50 | 81 |
| 1990 | 59 | 58 | 79 |
| 2005 | 59 | 61 | 77 |

*Civilian population 16 years of age and older.
[†]Husband present.
[‡]Wife present.
SOURCE: *Statistical Abstract of the United States 2007,* Table 582, p. 379; Table 583, p. 379. http://www.census.gov/prod/www/statistical_abstract.html.

of all professional jobs (*Statistical Abstract of the United States 2007*, p. 388). And it's not mainly single women working, as once was the case. Table 14-9 presents figures on the ever-increasing cash employment of American wives and mothers.

Note in Table 14-9 that the cash employment of American married men has been falling while that of American married women has been rising. There has been a dramatic change in behavior and attitudes since 1960, when 89 percent of all married men worked, compared with just 32 percent of married women. The comparable figures in 2005 were 77 percent and 61 percent. Ideas about the gender roles of males and females have changed. Compare your grandparents and your parents. Chances are you have a working mother, but your grandmother was more likely a stay-at-home mom. Your grandfather is more likely than your father to have worked in manufacturing and to have belonged to a union. Your father is more likely than your grandfather to have shared child care and domestic responsibilities. Age at marriage has been delayed for both men and women. College educations and professional degrees have increased. What other changes do you associate with the increase in female employment outside the home?

## The Feminization of Poverty

Alongside the economic gains of many American women stands an opposite extreme: the feminization of poverty, or the increasing representation of women (and their children) among America's poorest people. Women head over half of U.S. households with incomes below the poverty line. In 1959 female-headed households accounted for just one-fourth of the American poor. Since then that figure has more than doubled.

Married couples are much more secure economically than single mothers are. The average income for married-couple families is more than twice that of families maintained by a single woman. The average one-earner family maintained by a single woman had an annual income of $29,307 in 2003. This was less than one-half the mean income ($62,405) of a married-couple household. (*Statistical Abstract of the United States, 2007*, p. 429).

The feminization of poverty isn't just a North American trend. The percentage of female-headed households has been increasing worldwide. In Western Europe, for example, female-headed households rose from 24 percent in 1980 to 31 percent in 1990. The figure ranges from below 20 percent in certain South Asian and Southeast Asian countries to almost 50 percent in certain African countries and the Caribbean (Buvinic 1995).

Why must so many women be solo household heads? Where are the men going, and why are they leaving? Among the causes are male migration, civil strife (men off fighting), divorce, abandonment, widowhood, unwed adolescent parenthood, and, more generally, the idea that children are women's responsibility. Globally, households headed by women tend to be poorer than those headed by men. In one study, the percentage of single-parent families considered poor was 18 percent in Britain, 20 percent in Italy, 25 percent in Switzerland, 40 percent in Ireland, 52 percent in Canada, and 63 percent in the United States.

It is widely believed that one way to improve the situation of poor women is to encourage them to organize. New women's groups can in some cases revive or replace traditional forms of social organization that have been disrupted. Membership in a group can help women to mobilize resources, to rationalize production, and to reduce the risks and costs associated with credit. Organization also allows women to develop self-confidence and to decrease dependence on others. Through such organization, poor women throughout the world are working to determine their own needs and priorities and to change things so as to improve their social and economic situation (Buvinic 1995).

## ✦ WHAT DETERMINES GENDER VARIATION?

We see that gender roles and stratification have varied widely across cultures and through history. Among many foragers and matrilineal cultivators, there is little gender stratification. Competition for resources leads to warfare and the intensification of production. These conditions favor patriliny and patrilocality. To the extent that women lose their productive roles in agricultural societies, the domestic–public dichotomy is accentuated and gender stratification is sharpened. With industrialism, attitudes about gender vary in the context of female extradomestic employment. Gender is flexible and varies with cultural, social, political, and economic factors. The variability of gender in time and space suggests that it will continue to change. The biology of the sexes is not a narrow enclosure limiting humans but a broad base upon which a variety of structures can be built (Friedl 1975).

## ✦ SEXUAL ORIENTATION

**Sexual orientation** refers to a person's habitual sexual attraction to, and sexual activities with, persons of the opposite sex (*heterosexuality*), the same sex (*homosexuality*), or both sexes (*bisexuality*). *Asexuality*, indifference toward, or lack of attraction to either sex, also is a sexual orientation. All four of these forms are found in contemporary North America, and throughout the world. But each type of desire and experience holds different meanings for individuals and groups. For example, an asexual disposition may be acceptable in some places but may be perceived as a character flaw in others. Male–male sexual activity may be a private affair in Mexico, rather than public, socially sanctioned, and encouraged as among the Etoro (see below) of Papua New Guinea (see also Blackwood and Wieringa, eds. 1999; Herdt 1981; Kimmel and Plante 2004; Lancaster and di Leonardo, eds. 1997; Nanda 2000).

Recently in the United States there has been a tendency to see sexual orientation as fixed and biologically based. There is not enough information at this time to determine the extent to which sexual orientation is based on biology. What we can say is that, to some extent at least, all human activities and preferences, including erotic expression, are learned, malleable, and culturally constructed.

In any society, individuals will differ in the nature, range, and intensity of their sexual interests and urges. No one knows for sure why such individual sexual differences exist. Part of the answer probably is biological, reflecting genes or hormones (Wade 2005). Another part may have to do with experiences during growth and development. But whatever the reasons for individual variation, culture always plays a role in molding individual sexual urges toward a collective norm. And such sexual norms vary from culture to culture.

What do we know about variation in sexual norms from society to society, and over time? A classic cross-cultural study (Ford and Beach 1951) found wide variation in attitudes about masturbation, bestiality (sex with animals), and homosexuality. In a single society, such as the United States, attitudes about sex differ over time and with socioeconomic status, region, and rural versus urban residence. However, even in the 1950s, prior to the "age of sexual permissiveness" (the pre-HIV period from the mid-1960s through the 1970s), research showed that almost all American men (92 percent) and more than half of American women (54 percent) admitted to masturbation. In the famous Kinsey report (Kinsey, Pomeroy, and Martin 1948), 37 percent of the men surveyed admitted having had at least one sexual experience leading to orgasm with another male. In a later study of 1,200 unmarried women, 26 percent reported same-sex sexual activities. (Because Kinsey's research relied on nonrandom samples, it should be considered merely illustrative, rather than a statistically accurate representation of, sexual behavior at the time.)

Sex acts with people of the same sex were absent, rare, or secret in only 37 percent of 76 societies for which data were available in the Ford and Beach study (1951). In the others, various forms of same-sex sexual activity were acceptable. Sometimes sexual relations between people of the same sex involved transvestism on the part of one of the partners (see Kulick 1998). Transvestism did not characterize male–male sex among the Sudanese Azande, who valued the warrior role (Evans-Pritchard 1970). Prospective warriors—young men aged 12 to 20—left their families and shared quarters with adult fighting men, who paid bridewealth for, and had sex with, them. During this apprenticeship, the young men did the domestic duties of women. Upon reaching warrior status, these young men took their own younger male brides. Later, retiring from the warrior role, Azande men married women. Flexible in their sexual expression, Azande males had no difficulty shifting from sex with older men (as male brides), to sex with younger men (as warriors), to sex with women (as husbands) (see Murray and Roscoe, eds. 1998).

Consider also the Etoro (Kelly 1976), a group of 400 people who subsist by hunting and horticulture in the Trans-Fly region of Papua New Guinea. The Etoro illustrate the power of culture in molding human sexuality. The following account, based on ethnographic field work by Raymond C. Kelly in the late 1960s, applies only to Etoro males and their beliefs. Etoro cultural norms prevented the male anthropologist who studied them from gathering comparable information about female attitudes. Note, also, that the activities described have been discouraged by missionaries. Since there has been no restudy of the Etoro specifically focusing on these activities, the extent to which these practices continue today is unknown. For this reason, I'll use the past tense in describing them.

Etoro opinions about sexuality were linked to their beliefs about the cycle of birth, physical growth, maturity, old age, and death. Etoro men believed that semen was necessary to give life force to a fetus, which was, they believed, implanted in a woman by an ancestral spirit. Sexual intercourse during pregnancy nourished the growing fetus. The Etoro believed that men had a limited lifetime supply of semen. Any sex act leading to ejaculation was seen as draining that supply, and as sapping a man's virility and vitality. The birth of children, nurtured by semen, symbolized a necessary sacrifice that would lead to the husband's eventual death. Heterosexual intercourse, required only for reproduction, was discouraged. Women who wanted too much sex were viewed as witches, hazardous to their husbands' health. Etoro culture allowed heterosexual intercourse only about 100 days a year. The rest of the time it was tabooed. Seasonal birth clustering shows the taboo was respected.

So objectionable was male–female sex that it was removed from community life. It could occur neither in sleeping quarters nor in the fields. Coitus could happen only in the woods, where it was risky because poisonous snakes, the Etoro claimed, were attracted by the sounds and smells of male–female sex.

Although coitus was discouraged, sex acts between men were viewed as essential. Etoro believed that boys could not produce semen on their own. To grow into men and eventually give life force to their children, boys had to acquire semen orally from older men. From the age of 10 until adulthood, boys were inseminated by older men. No taboos were attached to this. Such oral insemination could proceed in the sleeping area or garden. Every three years, a group of boys around the age of 20 was formally initiated into manhood. They went to a secluded mountain lodge, where they were visited and inseminated by several older men.

Male–male sex among the Etoro was governed by a code of propriety. Although sexual relations between older and younger males were considered culturally essential, those between boys of the same age were discouraged. A boy who took semen from other youths was believed to be sapping their life force and stunting their growth. A boy's rapid physical development might suggest he was getting semen from other boys. Like a sex-hungry wife, he might be shunned as a witch.

These sexual practices among the Etoro rested not on hormones or genes but on cultural beliefs and traditions. The Etoro shared a cultural pattern, which Gilbert Herdt (1984) calls "ritualized homosexuality," with some 50 other tribes in Papua New Guinea, especially in that country's Trans-Fly region. These societies illustrate one extreme of a male–female avoidance pattern that is widespread in Papua New Guinea and indeed in many patrilineal–patrilocal societies.

Flexibility in sexual expression seems to be an aspect of our primate heritage. Both masturbation and same-sex sexual activity exist among chimpanzees and other primates. Male bonobos (pygmy chimps) regularly engage in a form of mutual masturbation known as "penis fencing." Females get sexual pleasure from rubbing their genitals against those of other females (de Waal 1997). Our primate sexual potential is molded by culture, the environment, and reproductive necessity. Heterosexual coitus

## ANTHROPOLOGY TODAY

### Indonesia's Matriarchal Minangkabau Offer an Alternative Social System

*If a patriarchy is a political system ruled by men, what would a matriarchy be? Would a matriarchy be a political system ruled by women, or a political system in which women play a much more prominent role than men do in social and political organization? As you read this account, pay attention to the centrality of Minangkabau women in social, economic, and ceremonial life and as key symbols. Matriliny or matrilineality (reckoning of kinship through females only) is uncommon as an organizing principle in nation-states, such as Indonesia, where the Minangkabau live. But political systems operate at different levels. We see here that matriliny and matriarchy are expressed locally, at the village level, and regionally, where seniority of matrilineal descent serves as a way to rank villages. This account again illustrates the idea that contemporary non-Western societies should not be seen as isolated and pristine social and political systems, but as blends in which different religious, philosophical, and political principles may coexist.*

For the last century, . . . scholars have searched both human history and the continents to find a matriarchy—a society where the power was in the hands of women, not men. Most have concluded that a genuine matriarchy does not exist, perhaps may never have existed.

Anthropologist Peggy Reeves Sanday, Consulting Curator, University of Pennsylvania Museum of Archaeology and Anthropology, disagrees. After years of research among the Minangkabau people of West Sumatra, Indonesia, she has accepted that group's own self-labeling as a "matriarchate," or matriarchy. The problem, she asserts, lies in Western cultural notions of what a matriarchy "should" look like—patriarchy's female-twin.

"Too many anthropologists have been looking for a society where women rule the affairs of everyday life, including government," she said. "That template—and a singular, Western perspective on power—doesn't fit very well when you're looking at non-Western cultures like the Minangkabau of West Sumatra, Indonesia, where males and females are partners for the common good rather than competitors ruled by self-interest. Social prestige accrues to those who promote good relations by following the dictates of custom and religion."

The four million Minangkabau, one of Indonesia's largest ethnic groups, live in the highlands of the province of West Sumatra. Their society is founded on the coexistence of matrilineal custom and a nature-based philosophy called adat. More recently, Islam has been incorporated into the foundation. . . .

The key to Minangkabau matriarchy, according to Sanday, is found in the is practiced in all human societies—which, after all, must reproduce themselves—but alternatives also are widespread (Rathus, Nevid, and Fichner-Rathus 2005). Like gender roles and attitudes more generally, the sexual component of human personality and identity—just how we express our "natural" sexual urges—is a matter that culture and environment determine and limit.

A Minangkabau bride and groom in West Sumatra, Indonesia, where anthropologist Peggy Reeves Sanday has conducted several years of ethnographic fieldwork.

everpresent adat idea [that] "One must nurture growth in humans, animals, and plants so that society will be strong." . . .

The emphasis on nurturing growth yields a unique emphasis on the maternal in daily life. The Minangkabau glorify their mythical Queen Mother and cooperation. In village social relations senior women are associated with the central pillar of the traditional house, which is the oldest pillar because it is the first erected. The oldest village in a group of villages is referred to as the "mother village." When they stage ceremonies in their full ceremonial regalia, women are addressed by the same term reserved for the mythical Queen. Such practices suggest that matriarchy in this society is about making the maternal the center, origin, and foundation, not just of life but of the social order as well.

The power of Minangkabau women extends to the economic and social realms. Women control land inheritance, and husbands move into the households of their wives. . . . During the wedding ceremony the wife collects her husband from his household and, with her female relatives, brings him back to her household to live. In the event of a divorce the husband collects his clothes and leaves. Yet, despite the special position women are accorded in the society, the Minangkabau matriarchy is not the equivalent of female rule.

*Continued*

## ANTHROPOLOGY TODAY

"Neither male nor female rule is possible because of the Minangkabau belief that decision-making should be by consensus," Dr. Sanday said. "In answer to my persistent questions about 'who rules,' I was often told that I was asking the wrong question. Neither sex rules, it was explained to me, because males and females complement one another."

Today, according to Dr. Sanday, while the Minangkabau matriarchy is based largely on adat, Islam also plays a role. Islam arrived in West Sumatra sometime in the 16th century, long after adat customs and philosophy had been established. At first there was an uneasy relationship between adat and Islam and, in the 19th century, a war between adherents of adat customs and fundamentalist beliefs imported from Mecca.

The conflict was resolved by both sides making accommodations. Today, matrilineal adat and Islam are accepted as equally sacred and inviolate.

Resurgent Islamic fundamentalism, nationalism, and expanding capitalism may erode the Minangkabau's nature-based matriarchal culture and the adat that infuses meaning into their lives. [Sanday] remains optimistic that their culture has the innate flexibility to adapt to a changing world. "Had the Minangkabau chosen to fight rather than to accommodate the numerous influences that impinged on their world over the centuries, had they chosen to assert cultural purity, no doubt their 'adat' would have long ago succumbed. The moral of the Minangkabau story is that accommodating differences can preserve a world."

*Source:* Pam Kosty, "Indonesia's Matriarchal Minangkabau Offer an Alternative Social System," May 9, 2000, http://eurekalert.org. Reprinted by permission.

## SUMMARY

1. Gender roles are the tasks and activities that a culture assigns to each sex. Gender stereotypes are oversimplified ideas about attributes of males and females. Gender stratification describes an unequal distribution of rewards by gender, reflecting different positions in a social hierarchy. Cross-cultural comparison reveals some recurrent patterns involving the division of labor by gender and gender-based differences in reproductive strategies. Gender roles and gender stratification also vary with environment, economy, adaptive strategy, level of social complexity, and degree of participation in the world economy.

2. When gathering is prominent, gender status is more equal than when hunting or fishing dominates a foraging economy. Gender status also is more equal when the domestic and public spheres aren't sharply separated. Foragers lack two public arenas that contribute to higher male status among food producers: warfare and organized interregional trade.

3. Gender stratification also is linked to descent and residence. Women's status in matrilineal societies tends to be high because overall social identity comes through female links. Women in many societies, especially matrilineal ones, wield power and make decisions. Scarcity of resources promotes intervillage warfare, patriliny, and patrilocality. The localization of related males is adaptive for

military solidarity. Men may use their warrior role to symbolize and reinforce the social devaluation and oppression of women.

4. With the advent of plow agriculture, women were removed from production. The distinction between women's domestic work and men's "productive" labor reinforced the contrast between men as public and valuable and women as homebound and inferior. Patriarchy describes a political system ruled by men in which women have inferior social and political status, including basic human rights.

5. Americans' attitudes toward gender roles vary with class and region. When the need for female labor declines, the idea that women are unfit for many jobs increases, and vice versa. Factors such as war, falling wages, and inflation help explain female cash employment and Americans' attitudes toward it. Countering the economic gains of many American women is the feminization of poverty. This has become a global phenomenon, as impoverished female-headed households have increased worldwide.

6. There has been a recent tendency to see sexual orientation as fixed and biologically based. But, to some extent at least, all human activities and preferences, including erotic expression, are influenced by culture. Sexual orientation stands for a person's habitual sexual attraction to, and activities with, persons of the opposite sex (heterosexuality), the same sex (homosexuality), or both sexes (bisexuality). Sexual norms vary widely from culture to culture.

## Key Terms

domestic–public dichotomy (p. 310)
extradomestic (p. 314)
gender roles (p. 306)
gender stereotypes (p. 306)
gender stratification (p. 306)

patriarchy (p. 315)
patrilineal–patrilocal complex (p. 312)
sexual dimorphism (p. 304)
sexual orientation (p. 319)

# CHAPTER 15

# RELIGION

❖ **Expressions of Religion**

   Spiritual Beings

   Powers and Forces

   Magic and Religion

   Uncertainty, Anxiety, Solace

   Rituals

   Rites of Passage

   Totemism

❖ **Social Control**

❖ **Kinds of Religion**

❖ **World Religions**

❖ **Religion and Change**

   Revitalization Movements

   Cargo Cults

❖ **Secular Rituals**

   *Anthropology Today: Islam Expanding Globally, Adapting Locally*

The anthropologist Anthony F. C. Wallace defined **religion** as "belief and ritual concerned with supernatural beings, powers, and forces" (1966, p. 5). The supernatural is the extraordinary realm outside (but believed to impinge on) the observable world. It is nonempirical and inexplicable in ordinary terms. It must be accepted "on faith." Supernatural beings—gods and goddesses, ghosts, and souls—are not of the material world. Nor are supernatural forces, some of which may be wielded by beings. Other sacred forces are impersonal; they simply exist. In many societies, however, people believe they can benefit from, become imbued with, or manipulate supernatural forces (see Bowie 2006; Crapo 2003).

Another definition of religion (Reese 1999) focuses on bodies of people who gather together regularly for worship. These congregants or adherents subscribe to and internalize a common system of meaning. They accept (adhere to or believe in) a set of doctrines involving the relationship between the individual and divinity, the supernatural, or whatever is taken to be the ultimate nature of reality. Anthropologists have stressed the collective, shared, and enacted nature of religion, the emotions it generates, and the meanings it embodies. Emile Durkheim (1912/2001), an early scholar of religion, stressed religious *effervescence,* the bubbling up of collective emotional intensity generated by worship. Victor Turner (1969/1995) updated Durkheim's notion, using the term *communitas,* an intense community spirit, a feeling of great social solidarity, equality, and togetherness. The word *religion* derives from the Latin *religare*—"to tie, to bind," but it is not necessary for all members of a given religion to meet together as a common body. Subgroups meet regularly at local congregation sites. They may attend occasional meetings with adherents representing a wider region. And they may form an imagined community with people of similar faith throughout the world.

Like ethnicity and language, religion also is associated with social divisions within and between societies and nations, such as those countries into which Islam has diffused (see the box at the end of this chapter). Religion both unites and divides. Participation in common rites may affirm, and thus maintain, the social solidarity of one religion's adherents. However, as we know from daily headlines, religious difference also may be associated with bitter enmity.

In studying religion cross-culturally, anthropologists pay attention to the social nature and roles of religion as well as to the nature, content, and meaning to people of religious doctrines, acts, events, settings, practitioners, and organizations. We also consider such verbal manifestations of religious beliefs as prayers, chants, myths, texts, and statements about ethics and morality (see Cunningham 1999; Klass 2003; Lehmann, Meyers, and Moro 2005; Stein and Stein 2005). Religion, by either definition offered here, exists in all human societies. It is a cultural universal. However, we'll see that it isn't always easy to distinguish the supernatural from the natural and that different societies conceptualize divinity, supernatural entities, and ultimate realities very differently.

## ✦ EXPRESSIONS OF RELIGION

When did religion begin? No one knows for sure. There are suggestions of religion in Neandertal burials and on European cave walls, where painted stick figures may represent shamans, early religious specialists. Nevertheless, any statement about when, where, why, and how religion arose, or any description of its original nature, can be only speculative. Although such speculations are inconclusive, however, many have revealed important functions and effects of religious behavior. Several theories will be examined now.

## Spiritual Beings

The founder of the anthropology of religion was the Englishman Sir Edward Burnett Tylor (1871/1958). Religion was born, Tylor thought, as people tried to understand conditions and events they could not explain by reference to daily experience. Tylor believed that our ancestors—and contemporary nonindustrial peoples—were particularly intrigued with death, dreaming, and trance. In dreams and trances, people see images they may remember when they wake up or come out of the trance state.

Tylor concluded that attempts to explain dreams and trances led early humans to believe that two entities inhabit the body, one active during the day and the other—a double or soul—active during sleep and trance states. Although they never meet, they are vital to each other. When the double permanently leaves the body, the person dies. Death is departure of the soul. From the Latin for soul, *anima,* Tylor named this belief animism. The soul was one sort of spiritual entity; people remembered various images from their dreams and trances—other spirits. For Tylor, **animism,** the earliest form of religion, was a belief in spiritual beings.

Tylor proposed that religion evolved through stages, beginning with animism. *Polytheism* (the belief in multiple gods) and then *monotheism* (the belief in a single, all-powerful deity) developed later. Because religion originated to explain things people didn't understand, Tylor thought it would decline as science offered better explanations. To an extent, he was right. We now have scientific explanations for many things that religion once elucidated. Nevertheless, because religion persists, it must do something more than explain the mysterious. It must, and does, have other functions and meanings.

## Powers and Forces

Besides animism—and sometimes coexisting with it in the same society—is a view of the supernatural as a domain of impersonal power, or *force,* which people can control under certain conditions. (You'd be right to think of *Star Wars.*) Such a conception of the supernatural is particularly prominent in Melanesia, the area of the South Pacific that includes Papua New Guinea and adjacent islands. Melanesians believed in **mana,** a sacred impersonal force existing in the universe. Mana can reside in people, animals, plants, and objects.

Melanesian mana was similar to our notion of efficacy or luck. Melanesians attributed success to mana, which people could acquire or manipulate in different ways, such as through magic. Objects with mana could change someone's luck. For example, a charm or amulet belonging to a successful hunter might transmit the hunter's mana to the next person who held or wore it. A woman might put a rock in her garden, see her yields improve dramatically, and attribute the change to the force contained in the rock.

Beliefs in manalike forces are widespread, although the specifics of the religious doctrines vary. Consider the contrast between mana in Melanesia and Polynesia (the islands included in a triangular area marked by Hawaii to the north, Easter Island to the east, and New Zealand to the southwest). In Melanesia, one could acquire mana by chance, or by working hard to get it. In Polynesia, however, mana wasn't potentially available to everyone but was attached to political offices. Chiefs and nobles had more mana than ordinary people did.

So charged with mana were the highest chiefs that contact with them was dangerous to the commoners. The mana of chiefs flowed out of their bodies wherever they went. It could infect the ground, making it dangerous for others to walk in the chief's footsteps. It could permeate the containers and utensils chiefs used in eating. Contact between chief and commoners was dangerous because mana could have an effect like an electric shock. Because high chiefs had so much mana, their bodies and possessions were **taboo** (set apart as sacred and off-limits to ordinary people). Contact between a high chief and commoners was forbidden. Because ordinary people couldn't bear as much sacred current as royalty could, when commoners were accidentally exposed, purification rites were necessary.

One function of religion is to explain. A belief in souls explains what happens in sleep, trance, and death. Melanesian mana explains differential success that people can't understand in ordinary, natural terms. People fail at hunting, war, or gardening not because they are lazy, stupid, or inept but because success comes—or doesn't come—from the supernatural world.

The beliefs in spiritual beings (e.g., animism) and supernatural forces (e.g., mana) fit within the definition of religion given at the beginning of this chapter. Most religions include both spirits and impersonal forces. Likewise the supernatural beliefs of contemporary North Americans include beings (gods, saints, souls, demons) and forces (charms, talismans, crystals, and sacred objects).

## Magic and Religion

**Magic** refers to supernatural techniques intended to accomplish specific aims. These techniques include spells, formulas, and incantations used with deities or with impersonal forces. Magicians use *imitative magic* to produce a desired effect by imitating it. If magicians wish to injure or kill someone, they may imitate that effect on an image of the victim. Sticking pins in "voodoo dolls" is an example. With *contagious magic,* whatever is done to an object is believed to affect a person who once had contact with it. Sometimes practitioners of contagious magic use body products from prospective victims—their nails or hair, for example. The spell performed on the body product is believed to reach the person eventually and work the desired result.

We find magic in societies with diverse religious beliefs. It can be associated with animism, mana, polytheism, or monotheism. Magic is neither simpler nor more primitive than animism or the belief in mana.

## Uncertainty, Anxiety, Solace

Religion and magic don't just explain things. They serve emotional needs as well as cognitive (e.g., explanatory) ones. For example, supernatural beliefs and practices can help reduce anxiety. Religion helps people face death and endure life crises. Magical techniques can dispel doubts that arise when outcomes are beyond human control.

Although all societies have techniques to deal with everyday matters, there are certain aspects of people's lives over which they lack control. When people face uncertainty and danger, according to Malinowski, they turn to magic. Malinowski found that the Trobriand Islanders used magic when sailing, a hazardous activity. He proposed that because people can't control matters such as wind, weather, and the fish supply, they turn to magic (Malinowski 1931/1978).

Malinowski noted that it was only when confronted by situations they could not control that Trobrianders, out of psychological stress, turned from technology to magic. Despite our improving technical skills, we can't still control every outcome, and magic persists in contemporary societies. Magic is particularly evident in baseball, where George Gmelch (1978, 2001) describes a series of rituals, taboos, and sacred objects. Like Trobriand sailing magic, these behaviors serve to reduce psychological stress, creating an illusion of magical control when real control is lacking. Even the best pitchers have off days and bad luck. Examples of pitchers' magic include tugging one's

Illustrating baseball magic, Los Angeles Dodgers first baseman Nomar Garciaparra goes through his glove adjustment ritual between pitches during the first inning of a spring training game against the New York Mets Sunday, March 5, 2006, in Vero Beach, Florida. Such rituals are most common in batting and pitching.

cap between pitches, touching the resin bag after each bad pitch, and talking to the ball. Gmelch's conclusions confirm Malinowski's that magic is most prevalent in situations of chance and uncertainty. All sorts of magical behavior surrounded pitching and batting, where uncertainty is rampant, but few rituals involved fielding, where players have much more control. (Batting averages of .350 or higher are very rare after a full season, but a fielding percentage below .900 is a disgrace.)

# Rituals

Several features distinguish **rituals** from other kinds of behavior (Rappaport 1974, 1999). Rituals are formal—stylized, repetitive, and stereotyped. People perform them in special (sacred) places and at set times. Rituals include *liturgical orders*—sequences of words and actions invented prior to the current performance of the ritual in which they occur.

These features link rituals to plays, but there are important differences. Plays have audiences rather than participants. Actors merely *portray* something, but ritual performers—who make up congregations—are *in earnest*. Rituals convey information about the participants and their traditions. Repeated year after year, generation after generation, rituals translate enduring messages, values, and sentiments into action.

Rituals are *social* acts. Inevitably, some participants are more committed than others to the beliefs that lie behind the rites. However, just by taking part in a joint public act, the performers signal that they accept a common social and moral order, one that transcends their status as individuals.

## Rites of Passage

Magic and religion, as Malinowski noted, can reduce anxiety and allay fears. Ironically, beliefs and rituals can also *create* anxiety and a sense of insecurity and danger (Radcliffe-Brown 1962/1965). Anxiety may arise *because* a rite exists. Indeed, participation in a collective ritual may build up stress, whose common reduction, through the completion of the ritual, enhances the solidarity of the participants.

Rites of passage, such as the collective circumcision of teenagers, can be very stressful. The traditional vision quests of Native Americans, particularly the Plains Indians, illustrate **rites of passage** (customs associated with the transition from one place or stage of life to another), which are found throughout the world. Among the Plains Indians, to move from boyhood to manhood, a youth temporarily separated from his community. After a period of isolation in the wilderness, often featuring fasting and drug consumption, the young man would see a vision, which would become his guardian spirit. He would return then to his community as an adult.

The rites of passage of contemporary societies include confirmations, baptisms, bar and bat mitzvahs, and fraternity hazing. Passage rites involve changes in social status, such as from boyhood to manhood and from nonmember to sorority sister. More generally, a rite of passage may mark any change in place, condition, social position, or age.

All rites of passage have three phases: separation, liminality, and incorporation. In the first phase, people withdraw from the group and begin moving from one place or status to another. In the third phase, they reenter society, having completed the rite. The *liminal* phase is the most interesting. It is the period between states, the limbo during which people have left one place or state but haven't yet entered or joined the next (Turner 1967/1974).

**Liminality** always has certain characteristics. Liminal people occupy ambiguous social positions. They exist apart from ordinary distinctions and expectations, living in a time out of time. They are cut off from normal social contacts. A variety of contrasts may demarcate liminality from regular social life. For example, among the Ndembu of Zambia, a chief underwent a rite of passage before taking office. During the liminal period, his past and future positions in society were ignored, even reversed. He was subjected to a variety of insults, orders, and humiliations.

Passage rites often are collective. Several individuals—boys being circumcised, fraternity or sorority initiates, men at military boot camps, football players in summer training camps, women becoming nuns—pass through the rites together as a group.

Passage rites are often collective. A group—such as these initiates in Togo or these Navy trainees in San Diego—passes through the rites as a unit. Such liminal people experience the same treatment and conditions and must act alike. They share communitas, an intense community spirit, a feeling of great social solidarity or togetherness.

## TABLE 15-1

### Oppositions between Liminality and Normal Social Life

| Liminality | Normal Social Structure |
| --- | --- |
| transition | state |
| homogeneity | heterogeneity |
| communitas | structure |
| equality | inequality |
| anonymity | names |
| absence of property | property |
| absence of status | status |
| nakedness or uniform dress | dress distinctions |
| sexual continence or excess | sexuality |
| minimization of sex distinctions | maximization of sex distinctions |
| absence of rank | rank |
| humility | pride |
| disregard of personal appearance | care for personal appearance |
| unselfishness | selfishness |
| total obedience | obedience only to superior rank |
| sacredness | secularity |
| sacred instruction | technical knowledge |
| silence | speech |
| simplicity | complexity |
| acceptance of pain and suffering | avoidance of pain and suffering |

SOURCE: Adapted from *The Ritual Process* by Turner 1969/1974. Copyright © 1969 by Aldine Publishers. Reprinted by permission.

Table 15-1 summarizes the contrasts or oppositions between liminality and normal social life. Most notable is a social aspect of *collective liminality* called **communitas** (Turner 1967/1974), an intense community spirit, a feeling of great social solidarity, equality, and togetherness. People experiencing liminality together form a community of equals. The social distinctions that have existed before or will exist afterward are forgotten temporarily. Liminal people experience the same treatment and conditions and must act alike. Liminality may be marked ritually and symbolically by *reversals* of ordinary behavior. For example, sexual taboos may be intensified, or conversely, sexual excess may be encouraged.

Liminality is basic to every passage rite. Furthermore, in certain societies, including our own, liminal symbols may be used to set off one (religious) group from another, and from society as a whole. Such "permanent liminal groups" (e.g., sects, brotherhoods, and cults) are found most characteristically in nation-states. Such liminal features as humility, poverty, equality, obedience, sexual abstinence, and silence may be required for all sect or cult members. Those who join such a group agree to its rules. As if they were undergoing a passage rite—but in this case a never-ending one—they may rid themselves of their previous possessions and cut themselves off from former social links, including those with family members.

Identity as a member of the group is expected to transcend individuality. Cult members often wear uniform clothing. They may try to reduce distinctions based on age and gender by using a common hair style (shaved head, short hair, or long hair). The Heaven's Gate cult, whose mass suicide garnered headlines in 1997, even used castration to increase *androgyny* (similarity between males and females). With such cults (as in the military), the individual, so important in American culture, is submerged in the collective. This is one reason Americans are so fearful and suspicious of "cults." In a variety of contexts, liminal features signal the distinctiveness or sacredness of groups, persons, settings, and events. Liminal symbols mark entities and circumstances as extraordinary—outside and beyond ordinary social space and routine social events.

Not all collective rites are rites of passage. Most societies observe occasions on which people come together to worship and, in doing so, affirm and reinforce their solidarity. Rituals such as the totemic ceremonies described below are *rites of intensification:* They demand collective adherence to the rules of ritual behavior and create emotions (the collective spiritual effervescence described by Durkheim 1912/2001) that enhance and intensify social solidarity.

## Totemism

Rituals serve the social function of creating temporary or permanent solidarity among people—forming a social community. We see this also in practices known as totemism. Totemism was important in the religions of the Native Australians. *Totems* could be animals, plants, or geographical features. In each tribe, groups of people had particular totems. Members of each totemic group believed themselves to be descendants of their totem. They customarily neither killed nor ate it, but this taboo was lifted once a year, when people assembled for ceremonies dedicated to the totem. These annual rites were believed to be necessary for the totem's survival and reproduction.

Totemism uses nature as a model for society. The totems are usually animals and plants, which are part of nature. People relate to nature through their totemic association with natural species. Because each group has a different totem, social differences mirror natural contrasts. Diversity in the natural order becomes a model for diversity in the social order. However, although totemic plants and animals occupy different niches in nature, on another level they are united because they all are part of nature. The unity of the human social order is enhanced by symbolic association with and imitation of the natural order (Durkheim 1912/2001; Lévi-Strauss 1963; Radcliffe-Brown 1962/1965).

In contemporary nations, too, totems continue to mark groups, such as states and universities (e.g., Badgers, Buckeyes, and Wolverines), professional teams (Lions, and Tigers, and Bears), and political parties (donkeys and elephants). Although the modern context is more secular, one can still witness, in intense college football rivalries, some of the effervescence Durkheim noted in Australian totemic religion and other rites of intensification.

Totems are sacred emblems symbolizing common identity. This is true not just among Native Australians, but also among Native American groups of the North Pacific

Coast of North America, whose totem poles are well known. Their totemic carvings, which commemorated, and told visual stories about, ancestors, animals and spirits, were also associated with ceremonies. In totemic rites, people gather together to honor their totem. In so doing, they use ritual to maintain the social oneness that the totem symbolizes.

## ✦ SOCIAL CONTROL

Religion has meaning for people. It helps them cope with adversity and tragedy. It offers hope that things will get better. Lives can be transformed through spiritual healing. Sinners can repent and be saved—or they can go on sinning and be damned. If the faithful truly internalize a system of religious rewards and punishments, their religion becomes a powerful influence on their beliefs, behavior, and what they teach their children.

Many people engage in religious activity because it seems to work. Prayers get answered. Faith healers heal. Sometimes it doesn't take much to convince the faithful that religious actions are efficacious. Many American Indian people in southwestern Oklahoma use faith healers at high monetary costs, not just because it makes them feel better about the uncertain, but because it works (Lassiter 1998). Each year legions of Brazilians visit a church, Nosso Senhor do Bomfim, in the city of Salvador, Bahia. They vow to repay "Our Lord" (Nosso Senhor) if healing happens. Showing that the vows work, and are repaid, are the thousands of *ex votos,* plastic impressions of every conceivable body part, that adorn the church, along with photos of people who have been cured.

Religion can work by getting inside people and mobilizing their emotions—their joy, their wrath, their righteousness. Émile Durkheim (1912/2001) described the collective "effervescence" that can develop in religious contexts. Intense emotion bubbles up. People feel a deep sense of shared joy, meaning, experience, communion, belonging, and commitment to their religion.

The power of religion affects action. When religions meet, they can coexist peacefully, or their differences can be a basis for enmity and disharmony, even battle. Religious fervor has inspired Christians on crusades against the infidel and has led Muslims to wage jihads, holy wars against non-Islamic peoples. Throughout history, political leaders have used religion to promote and justify their views and policies.

By late September 1996, the Taliban Movement had firmly imposed an extreme form of social control through religious repression on Afghanistan and its people. Led by Muslim clerics, the Taliban aimed to create their version of an Islamic society modeled on the teachings of the Koran (Burns 1997). Various repressive measures were instituted. The Taliban barred women from work and girls from school. Females past puberty were prohibited from talking to unrelated men. Women needed an approved reason, such as shopping for food, to leave their homes. Men, who were required to grow bushy beards, also faced an array of bans—against playing cards, listening to music, keeping pigeons, and flying kites.

To enforce their decrees, the Taliban sent armed enforcers throughout the country. These agents took charge of "beard checks" and other forms of scrutiny on behalf of a religious police force known as the General Department for the Preservation of Virtue and the Elimination of Vice (Burns 1997). By late fall 2001 the Taliban had been over-thrown, with a new interim government established in Kabul, the Afghan capital, on December 22. The collapse of the Taliban followed American bombing of Afghanistan in response to the September 11, 2001, attacks on New York's World Trade Center and Washington's Pentagon. As the Taliban yielded Kabul to victorious northern alliance forces, local men flocked to barbershops to have their beards trimmed or shaved. They were using a key Taliban symbol to celebrate the end of religious repression.

Note that in the case of the Taliban, forms of social control were used to support a strict religious orthodoxy. This wasn't repression in religion's name, but repressive religion. In other countries, secular leaders use religion to justify social control. Seeking power, they use religious rhetoric to get it. The Saudi Arabian government, for example, can be seen as using religion to divert attention from a repressive social policy.

How may leaders mobilize communities and, in so doing, gain support for their own policies? One way is by persuasion; another is by instilling hatred or fear. Consider witchcraft accusations. Witch hunts can be powerful means of social control by creat-ing a climate of danger and insecurity that affects everyone, not just the people who are likely targets. No one wants to seem deviant, to be accused of being a witch. Witch hunts often take aim at people who can be accused and punished with least chance of retaliation. During the great European witch craze, during the 15th, 16th, and 17th cen-turies (Harris 1974), most accusations and convictions were against poor women with little social support.

Witchcraft accusations often are directed at socially marginal or anomalous indi-viduals. Among the Betsileo of Madagascar, for example, who prefer patrilocal postmar-ital residence, men living in their wife's or their mother's village violate a cultural norm. Linked to their anomalous social position, just a bit of unusual behavior (e.g., staying up late at night) on their part is sufficient for them to be called witches and avoided as a result. In tribes and peasant communities, people who stand out economically, especially if they seem to be benefiting at the expense of others, often face witchcraft accusations, leading to social ostracism or punishment. In this case witchcraft accusa-tion becomes a **leveling mechanism,** a custom or social action that operates to reduce status differences and thus to bring standouts in line with community norms—another form of social control.

To ensure proper behavior, religions offer rewards (e.g., the fellowship of the religious community) and punishments (e.g., the threat of being cast out or excommuni-cated). Religions, especially the formal organized ones typically found in state societies, often prescribe a code of ethics and morality to guide behavior. The Judaic Ten Com-mandments laid down a set of prohibitions against killing, stealing, adultery, and other misdeeds. Crimes are breaches of secular laws, as sins are breaches of religious stric-tures. Some rules (e.g., the Ten Commandments) proscribe or prohibit behavior; others prescribe behavior. The Golden Rule, for instance, is a religious guide to do unto others as you would have them do unto you. Moral codes are ways of maintaining order and stability. Codes of morality and ethics are constantly repeated in religious sermons, cat-echisms, and the like. They become internalized psychologically. They guide behavior and produce regret, guilt, shame, and the need for forgiveness, expiation, and absolution when they are not followed.

## ✦ Kinds of Religion

Religion is a cultural universal. But religions exist in particular societies, and cultural differences show up systematically in religious beliefs and practices. For example, the religions of stratified, state societies differ from those of societies with less marked social contrasts and power differentials.

Considering several societies, Wallace (1966) identified four types of religion: shamanic, communal, Olympian, and monotheistic (Table 15-2). The simplest type is shamanic religion. Unlike priests, **shamans** aren't full-time religious officials but part-time religious figures who mediate between people and supernatural beings and forces. All societies have medico-magico-religious specialists. *Shaman* is the general term encompassing curers ("witch doctors"), mediums, spiritualists, astrologers, palm readers, and other diviners. Wallace found shamanic religions to be most characteristic of foraging societies.

Shamans sometimes set themselves off symbolically from ordinary people by assuming a different or ambiguous sex or gender role. (In nation-states, priests, nuns, and vestal virgins do something similar by taking vows of celibacy and chastity.) Among the Chukchee of Siberia (Bogoras 1904) male shamans copied the dress, speech, hair arrangements, and life styles of women. These shamans took other men as husbands and sex partners and received respect for their supernatural and curative expertise. Female shamans could join a fourth gender, copying men and taking wives.

## TABLE 15-2

### Wallace's Typology of Religions

| Type of Religion | Type of Practitioner | Conception of Supernatural | Type of Society |
|---|---|---|---|
| Monotheistic | Priests, ministers, etc. | Supreme being | States |
| Olympian | Priesthood | Hierarchical pantheon with powerful deities | Chiefdoms and archaic states |
| Communal | Part-time specialists; occasional community-sponsored events, including collective rites | Several deities with some control over nature | Food-producing tribes |
| Shamanic | Shaman (part-time practitioner) | Zoomorphic (plants and animals) | Foraging bands |

**Communal religions** have, in addition to shamans, community rituals such as harvest ceremonies and collective rites of passage. Although communal religions lack *full-time* religious specialists, they believe in several deities (**polytheism**) who control aspects of nature. Although some hunter-gatherers, including Australian totemites, have communal religions, these religions are more typical of farming societies.

**Olympian religions,** which arose with state organization and marked social stratification, add full-time religious specialists—professional *priesthoods*. Like the state itself, the priesthood is hierarchically and bureaucratically organized. The term *Olympian* comes from Mount Olympus, home of the classical Greek gods. Olympian religions are polytheistic. They include powerful anthropomorphic gods with specialized functions, for example, gods of love, war, the sea, and death. Olympian *pantheons* (collections of supernatural beings) were prominent in the religions of many nonindustrial nation-states, including the Aztecs of Mexico, several African and Asian kingdoms, and classical Greece and Rome. Wallace's fourth type—**monotheism**—also has priesthoods and notions of divine power, but it views the supernatural differently. In monotheism, all supernatural phenomena are manifestations of, or are under the control of, a single eternal, omniscient, omnipotent, and omnipresent supreme being.

## TABLE 15-3

### Religions of the World, by Estimated Number of Adherents, 2005

| | |
|---|---|
| Christianity | 2.1 billion |
| Islam | 1.3 billion |
| Secular/Nonreligious/Agnostic/Atheist | 1.1 billion |
| Hinduism | 900 million |
| Chinese traditional religion | 394 million |
| Buddhism | 376 million |
| Primal-indigenous | 300 million |
| African traditional and diasporic | 100 million |
| Sikhism | 23 million |
| Juche | 19 million |
| Spiritism | 15 million |
| Judaism | 14 million |
| Baha'i | 7 million |
| Jainism | 4.2 million |
| Shinto | 4 million |
| Cao Dai | 4 million |
| Zoroastrianism | 2.6 million |
| Tenrikyo | 2 million |
| Neo-Paganism | 1 million |
| Unitarian-Universalism | 800,000 |
| Rastafarianism | 600,000 |
| Scientology | 500,000 |

*SOURCE:* Reprinted by permission of Ontario Consultants on Religious Tolerance, www.religioustolerance.org.

Robert Bellah (1978) coined the term "world-rejecting religion" to describe most forms of Christianity. The first world-rejecting religions arose in ancient civilizations, along with literacy and a specialized priesthood. These religions are so-named because of their tendency to reject the natural (mundane, ordinary, material, secular) world and to focus instead on a higher (sacred, transcendent) realm of reality. The divine is a domain of exalted morality to which humans can only aspire. Salvation through fusion with the supernatural is the main goal of such religions.

## ❖ WORLD RELIGIONS

Information on the world's major religions today is provided in Table 15-3 (number of adherents) and Figure 15-1 (percentage of world population). Based on people's claimed religions, Christianity is the world's largest, with some 2.1 billion adherents. Islam, with some 1.3 billion practitioners, is next, followed by Hinduism, then Chinese traditional religion (also known as Chinese folk religion or Confucianism), and Buddhism. More than a billion people claim no official religion, but only about a fifth of them are self-proclaimed atheists. Worldwide, Islam is growing at a rate of about 2.9 percent annually, versus 2.3 percent for Christianity, whose overall growth rate is the same as the rate of world population increase (Ontario Consultants 2001; Adherents. com 2002).

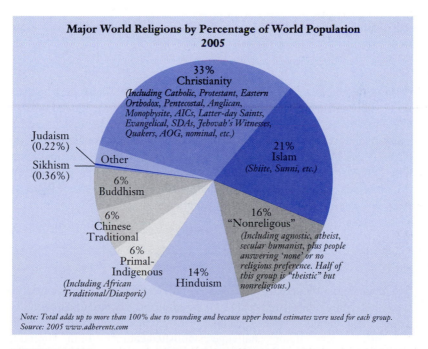

**FIGURE 15-1**    *Major World Religions by Percentage of World Population, 2005*

Colonialism and missionization have abetted the spread of Christianity, the world's largest religion. Shown here, devout Catholics, including a Portuguese nun and several Mozambican women, celebrate the Pope's visit to Mozambique, a former Portuguese colony, in September 1988.

Within Christianity, there is variation in the growth rate. There were an estimated 680 million "born-again" Christians (e.g., Pentecostals and Evangelicals) in the world in 2001, with an annual worldwide growth rate of 7 percent, versus just 2.3 percent for Christianity overall. (This would translate into over 1 billion Pentecostals/Evangelicals by 2007.) The global growth rate of Roman Catholics has been estimated at only 1.3 percent, compared with a Protestant growth rate of 3.3 percent per year (Winter 2001). Much of this explosive growth, especially in Africa, is of a type of Protestantism that would be scarcely recognizable to most Americans, given its incorporation of many animistic elements.

## ✦ RELIGION AND CHANGE

Religious fundamentalists seek order based on strict adherence to purportedly traditional standards, beliefs, rules, and customs. Christian and Islamic fundamentalists recognize, decry, and attempt to redress change, yet they also contribute to change. In a worldwide process, new religions challenge established churches. In the United States, for example, conservative Christian TV hosts have become influential broadcasters and

opinion shapers. In Latin America evangelical Protestantism is winning millions of converts from Roman Catholicism.

Like political organization, religion helps maintain social order. And like political
mobilization, religious energy can be harnessed not just for change but also for revolution. Reacting to conquest or to actual or perceived foreign domination, for instance,
religious leaders may seek to alter or revitalize their society. In an "Islamic Revolution,"
for example, Iranian ayatollahs marshaled religious fervor to create national solidarity
and radical change. We call such movements nativistic movements (Linton 1943) or
revitalization movements (Wallace 1956).

## Revitalization Movements

**Revitalization movements** are social movements that occur in times of change, in
which religious leaders emerge and undertake to alter or revitalize a society. Christianity originated as a revitalization movement. Jesus was one of several prophets who
preached new religious doctrines while the Middle East was under Roman rule. It was
a time of social unrest, when a foreign power ruled the land. Jesus inspired a new, enduring, and major religion. His contemporaries were not so successful.

The Handsome Lake religion arose around 1800 among the Iroquois of New York
State (Wallace 1969). Handsome Lake, the founder of this revitalization movement, was
a leader of one of the Iroquois tribes. The Iroquois had suffered because of their support of the British against the American colonials. After the colonial victory and a wave
of immigration to their homeland, the Iroquois were dispersed on small reservations.
Unable to pursue traditional horticulture and hunting in their homeland, the Iroquois
became heavy drinkers and quarreled among themselves.

Handsome Lake was a heavy drinker who started having visions from heavenly
messengers. The spirits warned him that unless the Iroquois changed their ways, they
would be destroyed. His visions offered a plan for coping with the new order. Witchcraft,
quarreling, and drinking would end. The Iroquois would copy European farming techniques, which, unlike traditional Iroquois horticulture, stressed male rather than female
labor. Handsome Lake preached that the Iroquois should also abandon their communal
long houses and matrilineal descent groups for more permanent marriages and individual family households. The teachings of Handsome Lake produced a new church and
religion, one that still has members in New York and Ontario. This revitalization movement helped the Iroquois adapt to and survive in a modified environment. They eventually gained a reputation among their non-Indian neighbors as sober family farmers.

## Cargo Cults

Like the Handsome Lake religion just discussed, cargo cults are revitalization movements. Such movements may emerge when natives have regular contact with industrial
societies but lack their wealth, technology, and living standards. Some such movements
attempt to *explain* European domination and wealth and to achieve similar success magically by mimicking European behavior and manipulating symbols of the desired life
style. The **cargo cults** of Melanesia and Papua New Guinea weave Christian doctrine

with aboriginal beliefs. They take their name from their focus on cargo—European goods of the sort natives have seen unloaded from the cargo holds of ships and airplanes.

In one early cult, members believed that the spirits of the dead would arrive in a ship. These ghosts would bring manufactured goods for the natives and would kill all the whites. More recent cults replaced ships with airplanes (Worsley 1959/1985). Many cults have used elements of European culture as sacred objects. The rationale is that Europeans use these objects, have wealth, and therefore must know the "secret of cargo." By mimicking how Europeans use or treat objects, natives hope also to come upon the secret knowledge needed to gain cargo.

For example, having seen Europeans' reverent treatment of flags and flagpoles, the members of one cult began to worship flagpoles. They believed the flagpoles were sacred towers that could transmit messages between the living and the dead. Other natives built airstrips to entice planes bearing canned goods, portable radios, clothing, wristwatches, and motorcycles. Near the airstrips they made effigies of towers, airplanes, and radios. They talked into the cans in a magical attempt to establish radio contact with the gods. Can you think of anything in your own society (including the media) that features similar behavior?

Some cargo cult prophets proclaimed that success would come through a reversal of European domination and native subjugation. The day was near, they preached, when natives, aided by God, Jesus, or native ancestors, would turn the tables. Native skins would turn white, and those of Europeans would turn brown; Europeans would die or be killed.

Cargo cults blend aboriginal and Christian beliefs. Melanesian myths told of ancestors shedding their skins and changing into powerful beings and of dead people returning to life. Christian missionaries, who had been in Melanesia since the late 19th century, also spoke of resurrection. The cults' preoccupation with cargo is related to traditional Melanesian big-man systems. In the chapter "Political Systems," we saw that a Melanesian big man had to be generous. People worked for the big man, helping him amass wealth, but eventually he had to give a feast and give away all that wealth.

Because of their experience with big-man systems, Melanesians believed that all wealthy people eventually had to give their wealth away. For decades they had attended Christian missions and worked on plantations. All the while they expected Europeans to return the fruits of their labor as their own big men did. When the Europeans refused to distribute the wealth or even to let natives know the secret of its production and distribution, cargo cults developed.

Like arrogant big men, Europeans would be leveled, by death if necessary. However, natives lacked the physical means of doing what their traditions said they should do. Thwarted by well-armed colonial forces, natives resorted to magical leveling. They called on supernatural beings to intercede, to kill or otherwise deflate the European big men and redistribute their wealth.

Cargo cults are religious responses to the expansion of the world capitalist economy. However, this religious mobilization had political and economic results. Cult participation gave Melanesians a basis for common interests and activities and thus helped pave the way for political parties and economic interest organizations. Previously separated by geography, language, and customs, Melanesians started forming larger groups

A cargo cult in Vanuatu, a country in Melanesia. Boys and men march with spears, imitating Bristish colonial soldiers. Does anything in your own society remind you of a cargo cult?

as members of the same cults and followers of the same prophets. The cargo cults paved the way for political action through which the indigenous peoples eventually regained their autonomy.

## ✦ SECULAR RITUALS

In concluding this discussion of religion, we may recognize some problems with the definition of religion given at the beginning of this chapter. The first problem: If we define religion with reference to supernatural beings, powers, and forces, how do we classify ritual-like behaviors that occur in secular contexts? Some anthropologists believe there are both sacred and secular rituals. Secular rituals include formal, invariant, stereotyped, earnest, repetitive behavior and rites of passage that take place in nonreligious settings.

A second problem: If the distinction between the supernatural and the natural is not consistently made in a society, how can we tell what is religion and what isn't? The Betsileo of Madagascar, for example, view witches and dead ancestors as real people who play roles in ordinary life. However, their occult powers are not empirically demonstrable.

A third problem: The behavior considered appropriate for religious occasions varies tremendously from culture to culture. One society may consider drunken frenzy the surest sign of faith, whereas another may inculcate quiet reverence. Who is to say which is "more religious"?

# ANTHROPOLOGY TODAY

## Islam Expanding Globally, Adapting Locally

*One well-known anthropological definition of religion stresses beliefs and behavior concerned with supernatural beings, powers, and forces. Another definition focuses on congregants—a body of people who gather together regularly for worship, and who accept a set of doctrines involving the relationship between the individual and divinity. Some religions, and the beliefs, affirmations, and forms of worship they promote, have spread widely. Here we see how Islam, a rapidly spreading religion, has adapted locally to various nations and cultures. In this process, although certain fundamentals endure, there is also room for considerable diversity. Local people always assign their own meanings to the messages and social forms, including religion, they receive from outside. Such meanings reflect their cultural backgrounds and experiences. This news brief describes how Islam has adapted successfully to many cultural differences, including linguistic practices, building styles, and the presence of other religions, such as Hinduism, already established in the area.*

One in every five people worldwide is a Muslim, some 1.3 billion believers. Islam is the world's fastest growing religion and it has spread across the globe.

Muslims everywhere agree on the Shahadah, the profession of faith: "There is no God but Allah; Mohammed is the prophet of Allah." But Islam is far from homogeneous—the faith reflects the increasingly diverse areas in which it is practiced.

"Islam is a world religion," said Ali Asani, a Harvard professor of Indo-Muslim Languages and Culture. "If you think about doctrine and theology, when these sets of religious ideas and concepts are transferred to different parts of the world—and Muslims live in many cultures and speak many different languages—the expressions of those doctrines and theology will necessarily be influenced by local culture."

Sometimes such regional distinctions are obvious to even casual observers. Mosques, for example, all share common features—they face Mecca and have a mihrab, or niche, that indicates that direction. Yet they also boast unique architectural elements and décor that suggest whether their location is Iran, Africa, or China. The houses of worship provide what Asani calls "a visual reminder of cultural diversity." Other easily grasped regional distinctions have their origins at the level of language. While Arabic is Islam's liturgical language, used for prayer, most Muslims' understanding of their faith occurs in their local language.

"Languages are really windows into culture," Asani explains. "So very often what you find is that theological Islamic concepts get translated into local idioms." . . .

Some Islamic fundamentalists might frown upon the diversity caused by local characteristics, but such are the predominant forms of Islam. "Rather than discussing Islam, we might more accurately talk about 'Islams' in different cultural contexts," Asani said. "We have Muslim literature from China, for example, where Islamic concepts are understood within a Confucian framework."

In the region of Bengal, now part of the nation of Bangladesh and the Indian state of West Bengal, a popular literary tradition created a context for the arrival of Islam. The concept of the avatar is important to the Hindu tradition, in which these deities become incarnate and descend to Earth to guide the righteous and fight evil.

"What you find in 16th century Bengal is the development of what you might call 'folk literature' where the Islamic idea of the prophet becomes understood within the framework of the avatar," Asani said. "So you have bridges being built between religious traditions as concepts resonate against each other."

This example is quite different from conditions in pre-Islam Arabia, at the time of Mohammed, where the poet held a special place in society. "If you consider the Koran, the word means 'recitation' in Arabic, and it's primarily an oral scripture, intended to be recited aloud and heard; to be performed," Asani said. "Viewed from a literary perspective, its form and structure relate very well to the poetic traditions of pre-Islamic Arabia. It's an example where the format of revelation was determined by the culture. In pre-Islamic Arabia the poet was often considered to be inspired in his poetic compositions by jinn from another world. So when the Prophet Muhammed began receiving revelations which were eventually compiled into the Koran, he was accused of being a poet, to which he responded 'I'm not a poet but a prophet.'" . . .

Islam came to Indonesia with merchants who were not theologians but simply practicing Muslims who people looked to as an example. There were also Sufi teachers who were quite willing to create devotional exercises that fit the way people in Sumatra or Java already practiced their faith. The two largest Muslim groups in Indonesia today, and perhaps in the world, are Muhammadyya and Nahdlatul Ulama. Each of them has over 30 million members, and each began as a local reform movement rooted in the promotion of a more modern education within the framework of Islam. . . .

A large number of Muslims, of course, don't live in Islamic nations at all but as minorities in other countries. The emergence of some minority Muslim communities has been an interesting and important development of the last 25 to 30 years.

Some relatively small communities can have a large impact. The European Muslim populations, for example, have a high component of refugee intellectuals. They've had an effect on their adopted countries, and also on the rest of the Islamic world. . . .

In South Africa the Muslim community is less than three percent of the population—but it's highly visible and highly educated. In the days of apartheid they had the advantage of being an intermediary, a community that was neither black nor white. By the 1980s the younger Muslim leadership became very opposed to apartheid on Islamic grounds and on basic human rights grounds. Muslims became quite active in the African National Congress (ANC). Though they were only a small minority when apartheid was destroyed, a number of Muslims became quite visible in the new South African regime—and throughout the larger Muslim world. Encompassing both Islamic states and minority communities, Islam is the world's fastest growing religion and an increasingly common topic of global conversation. Yet much of the discourse paints the faith with a single brush. As more people become familiar with Islam around the world it may be well for them to first ask, as Professor Asani suggests: "Whose Islam? Which Islam?"

*Source:* Brian Handwerk, "Islam Expanding Globally, Adapting Locally", *National Geographic News,* October 24, 2003, http://news. nationalgeographic.com. Reprinted by permission.

## SUMMARY

1. Religion, a cultural universal, consists of belief and behavior concerned with supernatural beings, powers, and forces. Religion also encompasses the feelings, meanings, and congregations associated with such beliefs and behavior. Anthropological studies have revealed many expressions and functions of religion.

2. Tylor considered animism—the belief in spirits or souls—to be religion's earliest and most basic form. He focused on religion's explanatory role, arguing that religion would eventually disappear as science provided better explanations. Besides animism, yet another view of the supernatural also occurs in nonindustrial societies, seeing the supernatural as a domain of raw, impersonal power or force (called mana in Polynesia and Melanesia). People can manipulate and control mana under certain conditions.

3. When ordinary technical and rational means of doing things fail, people may turn to magic. Often they use magic when they lack control over outcomes. Religion offers comfort and psychological security at times of crisis. On the other hand, rites can also create anxiety. Rituals are formal, invariant, stylized, earnest acts in which people subordinate their particular beliefs to a social collectivity. Rites of passage have three stages: separation, liminality, and incorporation. Such rites can mark any change in social status, age, place, or social condition. Collective rites are often cemented by communitas, a feeling of intense solidarity.

4. Religion establishes and maintains social control through a series of moral and ethical beliefs and real and imagined rewards and punishments, internalized in individuals. Religion also achieves social control by mobilizing its members for collective action.

5. Wallace defines four types of religion: shamanic, communal, Olympian, and monotheistic. Each has its characteristic ceremonies and practitioners. The world's major religions vary in their growth rates, with Islam expanding more rapidly than Christianity. Religion helps maintain social order, but it also can promote change. Revitalization movements blend old and new beliefs and have helped people adapt to changing conditions. There are secular as well as religious rituals.

## KEY TERMS

animism (p. 327)
cargo cults (p. 341)
communal religions (p. 338)
communitas (p. 333)
leveling mechanism (p. 336)
liminality (p. 331)
magic (p. 329)
mana (p. 328)
monotheism (p. 338)

Olympian religions (p. 338)
polytheism (p. 338)
religion (p. 326)
revitalization movements (p. 341)
rites of passage (p. 331)
rituals (p. 330)
shaman (p. 337)
taboo (p. 328)

# CHAPTER 16

❦

# THE WORLD SYSTEM
# AND COLONIALISM

Although fieldwork in small communities is anthropology's hallmark, isolated groups are impossible to find today. Truly isolated societies probably never have existed. For thousands of years, human groups have been in contact with one another. Local societies always have participated in a larger system, which today has global dimensions—we call it the *modern world system,* by which we mean a world in which nations are economically and politically interdependent.

---

## ✦ THE WORLD SYSTEM

The world system and the relations among the countries within it are shaped by the capitalist world economy. A huge increase in international trade during and after the 15th century led to the **capitalist world economy** (Wallerstein 1982, 2004*b*), a single world system committed to production for sale or exchange, with the object of maximizing profits, rather than supplying domestic needs. **Capital** refers to wealth or resources invested in business, with the intent of using the means of production to make a profit.

World-system theory can be traced to the French social historian Fernand Braudel. In his three-volume work *Civilization and Capitalism, 15th–18th Century* (1981, 1982, 1992), Braudel argued that society consists of interrelated parts assembled into a system.

Societies are subsystems of larger systems, with the world system the largest. The key claim of **world-system theory** is that an identifiable social system, based on wealth and power differentials, extends beyond individual countries. That system is formed by a set of economic and political relations that has characterized much of the globe since the 16th century, when the Old World established regular contact with the New World (see Bodley 2003).

According to Wallerstein (1982, 2004*b*), countries within the world system occupy three different positions of economic and political power: core, periphery, and semiperiphery. The geographic center, or **core,** the dominant position in the world system, includes the strongest and most powerful nations. In core nations, "the complexity of economic activities and the level of capital accumulation is the greatest" (Thompson 1983, p. 12). With its sophisticated technologies and mechanized production, the core churns out products that flow mainly to other core countries. Some also go to the periphery and semiperiphery. According to Arrighi (1994), the core monopolizes the most profitable activities, especially the control of world finance.

Semiperiphery and periphery countries have less power, wealth, and influence than the core does. The **semiperiphery** is intermediate between the core and the periphery. Contemporary nations of the semiperiphery are industrialized. Like core nations, they export both industrial goods and commodities, but they lack the power and economic dominance of core nations. Thus Brazil, a semiperiphery nation, exports automobiles to

World capitalism in 21st-century Moscow. On January 31, 2006, in a Moscow electronics store, a potential customer considers a display of TV sets, broadcasting live the annual press conference of Russian President Vladimir Putin.

Nigeria (a periphery nation) and auto engines, orange juice extract, coffee, and shrimp to the United States (a core nation). The **periphery** includes the world's least privileged and powerful countries. Economic activities there are less mechanized than are those in the semiperiphery, although some degree of industrialization has reached even peripheral nations. The periphery produces raw materials, agricultural commodities, and, increasingly, human labor for export to the core and the semiperiphery (Shannon 1996).

In the United States and Western Europe today, immigration—legal and illegal—from the periphery and semiperiphery supplies cheap labor for agriculture in core countries. U.S. states as distant as California, Michigan, and South Carolina make significant use of farm labor from Mexico. The availability of relatively cheap workers from non-core nations such as Mexico (in the United States) and Turkey (in Germany) benefits farmers and business owners in core countries, while also supplying remittances to families in the semiperiphery and periphery. As a result of 21st-century telecommunications technology, cheap labor doesn't even need to migrate to the United States. Thousands of families in India are being supported as American companies "outsource" jobs—from telephone assistance to software engineering—to nations outside the core.

Consider recent moves by IBM, the world's largest information technology company. On June 24, 2005, *The New York Times* reported that IBM was planning to hire more than 14,000 additional workers in India, while laying off some 13,000 workers in Europe and the United States (Lohr 2005). These figures illustrate the ongoing globalization of work and the migration of even skilled jobs to low-wage countries. Its critics accuse IBM of shopping the globe for the cheapest labor, to enhance corporate profits at the expense of wages, benefits, and job security in the United States and other developed countries. In explaining the hiring in India, an IBM senior vice president (quoted in Lohr 2005) cited a surging demand for technology services in India's thriving economy and the opportunity to tap the many skilled Indian software engineers to work on projects around the world. Skilled Western workers must compete now against well-educated workers in such low-wage countries as India, where an experienced software programmer earns one-fifth the average salary of a comparable American worker— $15,000 versus $75,000 (Lohr 2005).

## The Emergence of the World System

As Europeans took to ships, developing a transoceanic trade-oriented economy, people throughout the world entered Europe's sphere of influence. In the 15th century Europe established regular contact with Asia, Africa, and eventually the New World (the Caribbean and the Americas). Christopher Columbus's first voyage from Spain to the Bahamas and the Caribbean in 1492 was soon followed by additional voyages. These journeys opened the way for a major exchange of people, resources, products, ideas, and diseases, as the Old and New Worlds were forever linked (Crosby 2003; Diamond 1997; Fagan 1998; Viola and Margolis 1991). Led by Spain and Portugal, Europeans extracted silver and gold, conquered the natives (taking some as slaves), and colonized their lands (see the box at the end of this chapter).

Previously in Europe as throughout the world, rural people had produced mainly for their own needs, growing their own food and making clothing, furniture, and tools from local products. Production beyond immediate needs was undertaken to pay taxes and to purchase trade items such as salt and iron. As late as 1650 the English diet, like diets in most of the world today, was based on locally grown starches (Mintz 1985). In the 200 years that followed, however, the English became extraordinary consumers of imported goods. One of the earliest and most popular of those goods was sugar (Mintz 1985).

Sugarcane originally was domesticated in Papua New Guinea, and sugar was first processed in India. Reaching Europe via the Middle East and the eastern Mediterranean, it was carried to the New World by Columbus (Mintz 1985). The climate of Brazil and the Caribbean proved ideal for growing sugarcane, and Europeans built plantations there to supply the growing demand for sugar. This led to the development in the 17th century of a plantation economy based on a single cash crop—a system known as *monocrop* production.

The demand for sugar in a growing international market spurred the development of the transatlantic slave trade and New World plantation economies based on slave labor. By the 18th century, an increased English demand for raw cotton led to rapid settlement of what is now the southeastern United States and the emergence there of another slave-based monocrop production system. Like sugar, cotton was a key trade item that fueled the growth of the world system.

## ✦ INDUSTRIALIZATION

By the 18th century the stage had been set for the **Industrial Revolution**—the historical transformation (in Europe, after 1750) of "traditional" into "modern" societies through industrialization of the economy. Industrialization required capital for investment. The established system of transoceanic trade and commerce supplied this capital from the enormous profits it generated. Wealthy people sought investment opportunities and eventually found them in machines and engines to drive machines. Industrialization increased production in both farming and manufacturing. Capital and scientific innovation fueled invention.

European industrialization developed from (and eventually replaced) the *domestic system* of manufacture (or home-handicraft system). In this system, an organizer-entrepreneur supplied the raw materials to workers in their homes and collected the finished products from them. The entrepreneur, whose sphere of operations might span several villages, owned the materials, paid for the work, and arranged the marketing.

## Causes of the Industrial Revolution

The Industrial Revolution began with cotton products, iron, and pottery. These were widely used goods whose manufacture could be broken down into simple routine motions that machines could perform. When manufacturing moved from homes to factories, where machinery replaced handwork, agrarian societies evolved into industrial ones. As factories produced cheap staple goods, the Industrial Revolution led to a dramatic increase in production. Industrialization fueled urban growth and created a new kind of city, with factories crowded together in places where coal and labor were cheap.

The Industrial Revolution began in England rather than in France. Why? Unlike the English, the French didn't have to transform their domestic manufacturing system by industrializing. Faced with an increased need for products, with a late 18th-century population at least twice that of Great Britain, France could simply augment its domestic system of production by drawing in new homes. Thus, the French were able to increase production *without innovating*—they could enlarge the existing system rather than adopt a new one. To meet mounting demand for staples—at home and in the colonies—England had to industrialize.

As its industrialization proceeded, Britain's population began to increase dramatically. It doubled during the 18th century (especially after 1750) and did so again between 1800 and 1850. This demographic explosion fueled consumption, but British entrepreneurs couldn't meet the increased demand with the traditional production methods. This spurred experimentation, innovation, and rapid technological change.

English industrialization drew on national advantages in natural resources. Britain was rich in coal and iron ore, and had navigable waterways and easily negotiated coasts.

*The Art of Stocking-Frame-Work-Knitting.*

*Engrav'd for the Universal Magazine 1750, for J. Hinton at the Kings Arms in S.t Pauls ChurchYard* LONDON.

In the home-handicraft, or domestic, system of production, an organizer supplied raw materials to workers in their homes and collected their products. Family life and work were intertwined, as in this English scene. Is there a modern equivalent to the domestic system of production?

It was a seafaring island-nation located at the crossroads of international trade. These features gave Britain a favored position for importing raw materials and exporting manufactured goods. Another factor in England's industrial growth was the fact that much of its 18th-century colonial empire was occupied by English settler families who looked to the mother country as they tried to replicate European civilization in the New World. These colonies bought large quantities of English staples.

It also has been argued that particular cultural values and religion contributed to industrialization. Many members of the emerging English middle class were Protestant nonconformists. Their beliefs and values encouraged industry, thrift, the dissemination of new knowledge, inventiveness, and willingness to accept change (Weber 1904/1958).

## ✦ SOCIOECONOMIC EFFECTS OF INDUSTRIALIZATION

The socioeconomic effects of industrialization were mixed. English national income tripled between 1700 and 1815 and increased 30 times more by 1939. Standards of comfort rose, but prosperity was uneven. At first, factory workers got wages higher than those available in the domestic system. Later, owners started recruiting labor in places where living standards were low and labor (including that of women and children) was cheap.

Social ills worsened with the growth of factory towns and industrial cities, amid conditions like those Charles Dickens described in *Hard Times*. Filth and smoke polluted the 19th-century cities. Housing was crowded and unsanitary, with insufficient water and sewage disposal facilities. People experienced rampant disease and rising death rates. This was the world of Ebenezer Scrooge, Bob Cratchit, Tiny Tim—and Karl Marx.

## Industrial Stratification

The social theorists Karl Marx and Max Weber focused on the stratification systems associated with industrialization. From his observations in England and his analysis of 19th-century industrial capitalism, Marx (Marx and Engels 1848/1976) saw socioeconomic stratification as a sharp and simple division between two opposed classes: the bourgeoisie (capitalists) and the proletariat (propertyless workers). The bourgeoisie traced its origins to overseas ventures and the world capitalist economy, which had transformed the social structure of northwestern Europe, creating a wealthy commercial class.

Industrialization shifted production from farms and cottages to mills and factories, where mechanical power was available and where workers could be assembled to operate heavy machinery. The **bourgeoisie** were the owners of the factories, mines, large farms, and other means of production. The **working class,** or **proletariat,** was made up of people who had to sell their labor to survive. With the decline of subsistence production and with the rise of urban migration and the possibility of unemployment, the bourgeoisie came to stand between workers and the means of production.

Industrialization hastened the process of *proletarianization*—the separation of workers from the means of production. The bourgeoisie also came to dominate the means of communication, the schools, and other key institutions. *Class consciousness* (recognition of collective interests and personal identification with one's economic group) was a vital part of Marx's view of class. He saw bourgeoisie and proletariat as socioeconomic divisions with radically opposed interests. Marx viewed classes as powerful collective forces that could mobilize human energies to influence the course of history. On the basis of their common experience, workers would develop class consciousness, which could lead to revolutionary change. Although no proletarian revolution was to occur in England, workers did develop organizations to protect their interests and increase their share of industrial profits. During the 19th century, trade unions and socialist parties emerged to express a rising anticapitalist spirit. The concerns of the English labor movement were to remove young children from factories and limit the hours during which women and children could work. The profile of stratification in industrial core nations gradually took shape. Capitalists controlled production, but labor was organizing for better wages and working conditions. By 1900 many governments had factory legislation and social-welfare programs. Mass living standards in core nations rose as population grew.

In today's capitalist world system the class division between owners and workers is now worldwide. However, publicly traded companies complicate the division between capitalists and workers in industrial nations. Through pension plans and personal investments, many American workers now have some proprietary interest in the means of production. They are part-owners rather than propertyless workers. The key difference is that the wealthy have *control* over these means. The key capitalist now is not the factory owner, who may have been replaced by thousands of stockholders, but the CEO or the chair of the board of directors, neither of whom may actually own the corporation.

Modern stratification systems aren't simple and dichotomous. They include (particularly in core and semiperiphery nations) a middle class of skilled and professional workers. Gerhard Lenski (1966) argues that social equality tends to increase in advanced industrial societies. The masses improve their access to economic benefits and political power. In Lenski's scheme, the shift of political power to the masses reflects the growth of the middle class, which reduces the polarization between owning and working classes. The proliferation of middle-class occupations creates opportunities for social mobility. The stratification system grows more complex (Giddens 1973).

Weber faulted Marx for an overly simple and exclusively economic view of stratification. As we saw in the chapter "Political Systems," Weber (1992/1968) defined three dimensions of social stratification: wealth, power, and prestige. Although, as Weber showed, wealth, power, and prestige are separate components of social ranking, they tend to be correlated. Weber also believed that social identities based on ethnicity, religion, race, nationality, and other attributes could take priority over class (social identity based on economic status). In addition to class contrasts, the modern world system *is* cross-cut by collective identities based on ethnicity, religion, and nationality (Shannon 1996). Class conflicts tend to occur within nations, and nationalism has prevented global class solidarity, particularly of proletarians.

Although the capitalist class dominates politically in most countries, growing wealth has made it easier for core nations to grant higher wages (Hopkins and Wallerstein 1982). However, the improvement in core workers' living standards wouldn't have occurred without the world system. The added surplus that comes from the periphery allows core capitalists to maintain their profits while satisfying the demands of core workers. In the periphery, wages and living standards are much lower. The current *world stratification system* features a substantial contrast between both capitalists and workers in the core nations and workers on the periphery.

## ✦ COLONIALISM

World-system theory stresses the existence of a global culture. It emphasizes historical contacts, linkages, and power differentials between local people and international forces. The major forces influencing cultural interaction during the past 500 years have been commercial expansion, industrial capitalism, and the dominance of colonial and core nations (Wallerstein 1982, 2004*b*; Wolf 1982). As state formation had done previously, industrialization accelerated local participation in larger networks. According to Bodley (1985), perpetual expansion is a distinguishing feature of industrial economic systems. Bands and tribes were small, self-sufficient, subsistence-based systems. Industrial economies, by contrast, are large, highly specialized systems in which market exchanges occur with profit as the primary motive (Bodley 1985).

During the 19th century European business interests initiated a concerted search for markets. This process led to European imperialism in Africa, Asia, and Oceania. **Imperialism** refers to a policy of extending the rule of a country or empire over foreign nations and of taking and holding foreign colonies. Imperialism goes back to early states, including Egypt in the Old World and the Incas in the New. A Greek empire was forged by Alexander the Great, and Julius Caesar and his successors spread the Roman empire. More recent examples include the British, French, and Soviet empires (Scheinman 1980).

During the second half of the 19th century, European imperial expansion was aided by improved transportation, which facilitated the colonization of vast areas of sparsely settled lands in the interior of North and South America and Australia. The new colonies purchased masses of goods from the industrial centers and shipped back wheat, cotton, wool, mutton, beef, and leather. The first phase of European colonialism had been the exploration and exploitation of the Americas and the Caribbean after Columbus. A new second phase began as European nations competed for colonies between 1875 and 1914, setting the stage for World War I.

**Colonialism** is the political, social, economic, and cultural domination of a territory and its people by a foreign power for an extended time (see Bremen and Shimizu, eds. 1999; Cooper and Stoler, eds. 1997). If imperialism is almost as old as the state, colonialism can be traced back to the Phoenicians, who established colonies along the eastern Mediterranean 3,000 years ago. The ancient Greeks and Romans were avid colonizers, as well as empire builders.

The first phase of modern colonialism began with the European "Age of Discovery"— of the Americas and of a sea route to the Far East. After 1492, the Spanish, the original conquerors of the Aztecs and the Incas, explored and colonized widely in the New World—the Caribbean, Mexico, the southern portions of what was to become the United States and Central and South America. In South America, Portugal ruled over Brazil. Rebellions and wars aimed at independence ended the first phase of European colonialism by the early 19th century. Brazil declared independence from Portugal in 1822. By 1825 most of Spain's colonies were politically independent. Spain held onto Cuba and the Philippines until 1898, but otherwise withdrew from the colonial field. During the first phase of colonialism, Spain and Portugal, along with Britain and France, were major colonizing nations. The latter two (Britain and France) dominated the second phase.

## British Colonialism

At its peak about 1914, the British empire covered a fifth of the world's land surface and ruled a fourth of its population (see Figure 16-1). Like several other European nations. Britain had two stages of colonialism. The first began with the Elizabethan voyages of the 16th century. During the 17th century, Britain acquired most of the eastern coast of North America, Canada's St. Lawrence basin, islands in the Caribbean, slave stations in Africa, and interests in India.

The British shared the exploration of the New World with the Spanish, Portuguese, French, and Dutch. The British by and large left Mexico, along with Central and South America, to the Spanish and the Portuguese. The end of the Seven Years' War in 1763 forced a French retreat from most of Canada and India, where France previously had competed with Britain (Cody 1998; Farr 1980).

The American revolution ended the first stage of British colonialism. A second colonial empire, on which the "sun never set," rose from the ashes of the first. Beginning in 1788, but intensifying after 1815, the British settled Australia. Britain had acquired Dutch South Africa by 1815. The establishment of Singapore in 1819 provided a base for a British trade network that extended to much of South Asia and along the coast of China. By this time, the empires of Britain's traditional rivals, particularly Spain, had been severely diminished in scope. Britain's position as imperial power and the world's leading industrial nation was unchallenged (Cody 1998; Farr 1980).

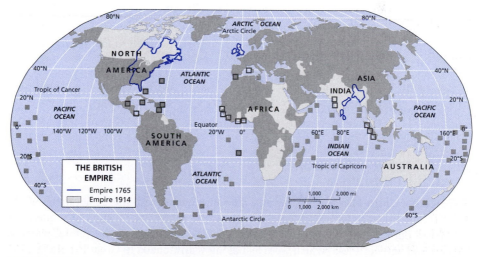

**FIGURE 16-1**    *Map of British Empire in 1765 and 1914*

On January 1, 1900, a British officer in India receives a pedicure from a servant. What does this photo say to you about colonialism? Who gives pedicures in your society?

During the Victorian Era (1837–1901), as Britain's acquisition of territory and of further trading concessions continued, Prime Minister Benjamin Disraeli implemented a foreign policy justified by a view of imperialism as shouldering "the white man's burden"—a phrase coined by the poet Rudyard Kipling. People in the empire were seen as unable to govern themselves, so that British guidance was needed to civilize and Christianize them. This paternalistic and racist doctrine served to legitimize Britain's acquisition and control of parts of central Africa and Asia (Cody 1998).

After World War II, the British empire began to fall apart, with nationalist movements for independence. India became independent in 1947, as did Ireland in 1949. Decolonization in Africa and Asia accelerated during the late 1950s. Today, the ties that remain between Britain and its former colonies are mainly linguistic or cultural rather than political (Cody 1998).

## French Colonialism

French colonialism also had two phases. The first began with the explorations of the early 1600s. Prior to the French revolution in 1789, missionaries, explorers, and traders carved out niches for France in Canada, the Louisiana territory, several Caribbean islands, and parts of India, which were lost along with Canada to Great Britain in 1763 (Harvey 1980).

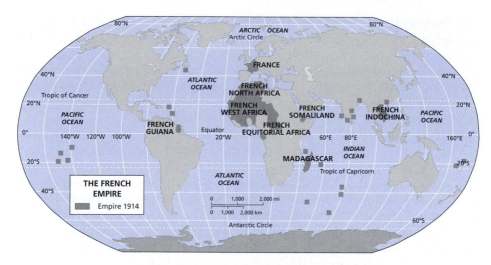

**FIGURE 16-2**    *Map of the French Empire at Its Height around 1914*

The foundations of the second French empire were established between 1830 and 1870. In Great Britain the sheer drive for profit led expansion, but French colonialism was spurred more by the state, church, and armed forces than by pure business interests. France acquired Algeria and part of what eventually became Indochina (Cambodia, Laos, and Vietnam). By 1914 the French empire covered 4 million square miles and included some 60 million people (see Figure 16-2). By 1893 French rule had been fully established in Indochina. Tunisia and Morocco became French protectorates in 1883 and 1912, respectively (Harvey 1980).

To be sure, the French, like the British, had substantial business interests in their colonies, but they also sought, again like the British, international glory and prestige. The French promulgated a *mission civilisatrice,* their equivalent of Britain's "white man's burden." The goal was to implant French culture, language, and religion, Roman Catholicism, throughout the colonies (Harvey 1980).

The French used two forms of colonial rule: *indirect rule,* governing through native leaders and established political structures, in areas with long histories of state organization, such as Morocco and Tunisia; and *direct rule* by French officials in many areas of Africa, where the French imposed new government structures to control diverse societies, many of them previously stateless. Like the British empire, the French empire began to disintegrate after World War II. France fought long—and ultimately futile— wars to keep its empire intact in Indochina and Algeria (Harvey 1980).

## Colonialism and Identity

Many geopolitical labels in the news today had no equivalent meaning before colonialism. Whole countries, along with social groups and divisions within them, were colonial inventions. In West Africa, for example, by geographic logic, several adjacent countries could be one (Togo, Ghana, Ivory Coast, Guinea, Guinea-Bissau, Sierra Leone, Liberia). Instead, they are separated by linguistic, political, and economic contrasts promoted under colonialism.

Hundreds of ethnic groups and "tribes" are colonial constructions (see Ranger 1996). The Sukuma of Tanzania, for instance, were first registered as a single tribe by the colonial administration. Then missionaries standardized a series of dialects into a single Sukuma language into which they translated the Bible and other religious texts. Thereafter, those texts were taught in missionary schools and to European foreigners and other non-Sukuma speakers. Over time this standardized the Sukuma language and ethnicity (Finnstrom 1997).

As in most of East Africa, in Rwanda and Burundi farmers and herders live in the same areas and speak the same language. Historically they have shared the same social world, although their social organization is "extremely hierarchical," almost "castelike" (Malkki 1995, p. 24). There has been a tendency to see the pastoral Tutsis as superior to the agricultural Hutus. Tutsis have been presented as nobles, Hutus as commoners. Yet when distributing identity cards in Rwanda, the Belgian colonizers simply identified all people with more than 10 head of cattle as Tutsi. Owners of fewer cattle were registered as Hutus (Bjuremalm 1997). Years later, these arbitrary colonial registers were used systematically for "ethnic" identification during the mass killings (genocide) that took place in Rwanda in 1994 (as portrayed vividly in the film *Hotel Rwanda*).

## Postcolonial Studies

In anthropology, history, and literature, the field of postcolonial studies has gained prominence since the 1970s (see Ashcroft, Griffiths, and Tiffin 1989; Cooper and Stoler, eds. 1997). **Postcolonial** refers to the study of the interactions between European nations and the societies they colonized (mainly after 1800). In 1914, European empires, which broke up after World War II, ruled more than 85 percent of the world (Petraglia-Bahri 1996). The term "postcolonial" also has been used to describe the second half of the 20th century in general, the period succeeding colonialism. Even more generically, "postcolonial" may be used to signify a position against imperialism and Eurocentrism (Petraglia-Bahri 1996).

The former colonies (*postcolonies*) can be divided into settler, nonsettler, and mixed (Petraglia-Bahri 1996). The settler countries, with large numbers of European colonists and sparser native populations, include Australia and Canada. Examples of nonsettler countries include India, Pakistan, Bangladash, Sri Lanka, Malaysia, Indonesia, Nigeria, Senegal, Madagascar, and Jamaica. All these had substantial native populations and relatively few European settlers. Mixed countries include South Africa, Zimbabwe, Kenya, and Algeria. Such countries had significant European settlement despite having sizable native populations.

Given the varied experiences of such countries, "postcolonial" has to be a loose term. The United States, for instance, was colonized by Europeans and fought a war for independence from Britain. Is the United States a postcolony? It usually isn't perceived as such, given its current world power position, its treatment of native Americans (sometimes called internal colonization), and its annexation of other parts of the world (Petraglia-Bahri 1996). Research in postcolonial studies is growing, permitting a wide-ranging investigation of power relations in varied contexts. Broad topics in the field include the formation of an empire, the impact of colonization, and the state of the postcolony today (Petraglia-Bahri 1996).

## ✦ DEVELOPMENT

During the Industrial Revolution, a strong current of thought viewed industrialization as a beneficial process of organic development and progress. Many economists still assume that industrialization increases production and income. They seek to create in Third World ("developing") countries a process like the one that first occurred spontaneously in 18th-century Great Britain.

We have seen that Britain used the notion of a white man's burden to justify its imperialist expansion and that France claimed to be engaged in a *mission civilisatrice,* a civilizing mission, in its colonies. Both these ideas illustrate an **intervention philosophy,** an ideological justification for outsiders to guide native peoples in specific directions. Economic development plans also have intervention philosophies. John Bodley (1988) argues that the basic belief behind interventions—whether by colonialists, missionaries, governments, or development planners—has been the same for more than 100 years. This belief is that industrialization, modernization, Westernization, and individualism are desirable evolutionary advances and that development schemes that promote them will bring long-term benefits to local people. In a more extreme form, intervention philosophy may pit the assumed wisdom of enlightened colonial or other First World planners against the purported conservatism, ignorance, or "obsolescence" of "inferior" local people.

## Neoliberalism

One currently influential intervention philosophy is neoliberalism. This term encompasses a set of assumptions that have become widespread during the last 25–30 years. Neoliberal policies are being implemented in developing nations, including postsocialist societies (e.g., those of the former Soviet Union). **Neoliberalism** is the current form of the classic economic liberalism laid out in Adam Smith's famous capitalist manifesto, *The Wealth of Nations,* published in 1776, soon after the Industrial Revolution. Smith advocated laissez-faire (hands-off) economics as the basis of capitalism: The government should stay out of its nation's economic affairs. Free trade, Smith thought, was the best way for a nation's economy to develop. There should be no restrictions on manufacturing, no barriers to commerce, and no tariffs. This philosophy is called "liberalism" because it aimed at liberating or freeing the economy from government controls. Economic liberalism encouraged "free" enterprise and competition, with the goal of generating profits. (Note the difference between this meaning of *liberal* and the one that has been popularized on American talk radio, in which "liberal" is used—usually as a derogatory term—as the opposite of "conservative." Ironically, Adam Smith's liberalism is today's capitalist "conservatism.")

Economic liberalism prevailed in the United States until President Franklin Roosevelt's New Deal during the 1930s. The Great Depression produced a turn to Keynesian economics, which challenged liberalism. John Maynard Keynes (1927, 1936) insisted that full employment was necessary for capitalism to grow, that governments and central banks should intervene to increase employment, and that government should promote the common good.

Especially since the fall of Communism (1989–1991), there has been a revival of economic liberalism, now known as neoliberalism, which has been spreading globally. Around the world, neoliberal policies have been imposed by powerful financial institutions such as the International Monetary Fund (IMF), the World Bank, and the Inter-American Development Bank (see Edelman and Haugerud 2004). Neoliberalism entails open (tariff- and barrier-free) international trade and investment. Profits are sought through lowering of costs, whether through improving productivity, laying off workers, or seeking workers who accept lower wages. In exchange for loans, the governments of postsocialist and developing nations have been required to accept the neoliberal premise that deregulation leads to economic growth, which will eventually benefit everyone through a process sometimes called "trickle down." Accompanying the belief in free markets and the idea of cutting costs is a tendency to impose austerity measures that cut government expenses. This can entail reduced public spending on education, health care, and other social services (Martinez and Garcia 2000).

## ✦ THE SECOND WORLD

The labels "First World," "Second World," and "Third World" represent a common, although ethnocentric, way of categorizing nations. The *First World* refers to the "democratic West"—traditionally conceived in opposition to a "Second World" ruled by "Communism." The *Second World* refers to the former Soviet Union and the socialist and once-socialist countries of Eastern Europe and Asia. Proceeding with this classification, the "less-developed countries" or "developing nations" make up the *Third World*.

## Communism

The two meanings of communism involve how it is written, whether with a lowercase (small) or an uppercase (large) *c*. Small-*c* **communism** describes a social system in which property is owned by the community and in which people work for the common good. Large-*C* **Communism** was a political movement and doctrine seeking to overthrow capitalism and to establish a form of communism such as that which prevailed in the Soviet Union (USSR) from 1917 to 1991. The heyday of Communism was a 40-year period from 1949 to 1989, when more Communist regimes existed than at any time before or after. Today only five Communist states remain—China, Cuba, Laos, North Korea, and Vietnam, compared with 23 in 1985.

Communism, which originated with Russia's Bolshevik Revolution in 1917, and took its inspiration from Karl Marx and Friedrich Engels, was not uniform over time or among countries. All Communist systems were *authoritarian* (promoting obedience to authority rather than individual freedom). Many were *totalitarian* (banning rival parties and demanding total submission of the individual to the state). Several features distinguished Communist societies from other authoritarian regimes (e.g., Spain under Franco) and from socialism of a social democratic type. First, the Communist Party monopolized power in every Communist state. Second, relations within the party were highly centralized and strictly disciplined. Third, Communist nations had state owner-ship, rather than private ownership, of the means of production. Finally, all Communist regimes, with the goal of advancing communism, cultivated a sense of belonging to an international movement (Brown 2001).

Social scientists have tended to refer to such societies as socialist rather than Com-munist. Today research by anthropologists is thriving in *postsocialist* societies—those that once emphasized bureaucratic redistribution of wealth according to a central plan (Verdery 2001). In the postsocialist period, states that once had planned economies have been following the neoliberal agenda, by divesting themselves of state-owned resources in favor of privatization. These societies in transition are undergoing democratization and marketization. Some of them have moved toward formal liberal democracy, with political parties, elections, and a balance of powers (Grekova 2001).

## Postsocialist Transitions

Neoliberal economists assumed that dismantling the Soviet Union's planned econ-omy would raise gross domestic product (GDP) and living standards. The goal was to enhance production by substituting a decentralized market system and providing incentives through privatization. In October 1991, Boris Yeltsin, who had been elected president of Russia that June, announced a program of radical market-oriented reform, pursuing a changeover to capitalism. Yeltsin's program of "shock therapy" cut subsi-dies to farms and industries and ended price controls. Since then, postsocialist Russia has faced many problems. The anticipated gains in productivity did not materialize. After the fall of the Soviet Union, Russia's GDP fell by half. Poverty increased, with a quarter of the population now living below the poverty line. Life expectancy and the birth rate declined. Another problem to emerge in the postsocialist transition is corrup-tion. Since 1996, the World Bank and other international organizations have launched anticorruption programs worldwide. *Corruption* is defined as the abuse of public office for private gain.

The World Bank's approach to corruption assumes a clear and sharp distinction between the state (the public or official domain) and the private sphere, and that the two should be kept separate. The idea that the public sphere can be separated neatly from the private sphere is ethnocentric. According to Janine Wedel (2002), postsocialist states provide rich contexts in which to explore variability in relations between public and private domains. Alexei Yurchak (2002, 2005) describes two spheres that operate in Russia today; these spheres do not mesh neatly with the assumption of a public–private split. He calls them the official–public sphere and the personal–public sphere, refer-ring to domains that coexist and sometimes overlap. State officials may respect the law (official–public), while also working with informal or even criminal groups (personal–public). Officials switch from official–public to personal–public behavior all the time, in order to accomplish specific tasks.

In an illustrative case from Poland, a man selling an apartment he had inherited was to pay a huge sum in taxes. He visited the state tax office, where a bureaucrat informed him of how much he was being assessed (official–public). She also told him how to avoid paying it (personal–public). He followed her advice and saved a lot of money. The man didn't know the bureaucrat personally. She didn't expect anything in return, and he didn't offer anything. She said she routinely offers such help.

In postsocialist societies, what is legal (official–public) and what is considered morally correct don't necessarily correspond. The bureaucrat just described seemed still to be operating under the old communist notion that state property (tax dollars in this case) belongs both to everyone and to no one. For further illustration of this view of state property, imagine two people working in the same state-owned construction enterprise. To take home for private use materials belonging to the enterprise (that is, to everyone and no one) is morally acceptable. No one will fault you for it because "everyone does it." However, if a fellow worker comes along and takes materials someone else had planned to take home, that would be stealing and morally wrong (Wedel 2002). In evaluating charges of corruption, anthropologists point out that property notions and spheres of official action in postsocialist societies are in transition.

## ✦ THE WORLD SYSTEM TODAY

The process of industrialization continues today, although nations have shifted their positions within the world system (Table 16-1). By 1900, the United States had become a core nation within the world system and had overtaken Great Britain in iron, coal, and cotton production. In a few decades (1868–1900), Japan had changed from a medieval handicraft economy to an industrial one, joining the semiperiphery by 1900 and moving to the core between 1945 and 1970. Figure 16-3 is a map showing the modern world system.

Twentieth-century industrialization added hundreds of new industries and millions of new jobs. Production increased, often beyond immediate demand, spurring strategies, such as advertising, to sell everything industry could churn out. Mass production gave rise to a culture of consumption, which valued acquisitiveness and conspicuous consumption (Veblen 1934). Industrialization entailed a shift from reliance on renewable

## TABLE 16-1

### Ascent and Decline of Nations within the World System

| Periphery to Semiperiphery | Semiperiphery to Core | Core to Semiperiphery |
|---|---|---|
| United States (1800–1860) | United States (1860–1900) | Spain (1620–1700) |
| Japan (1868–1900) | Japan (1945–1970) | |
| Taiwan (1949–1980) | Germany (1870–1900) | |
| S. Korea (1953–1980) | | |

*SOURCE:* Reprinted by permission of Westview Press from *An Introduction to the World-System Perspective* by Thomas Richard Shannon. Copyright Westview Press 1989, Boulder, Colorado.

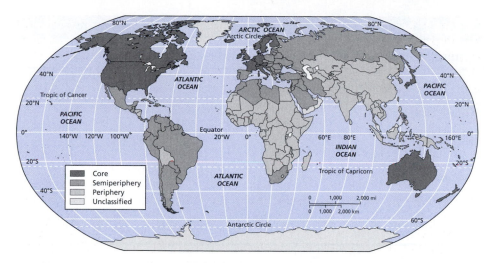

**FIGURE 16-3**   *The World System Today*

*SOURCE:* From Kottak, *Anthropology: The Exploration of Human Diversity,* 10th ed., Figure 23.5, p. 660. Reprinted by permission of The McGraw-Hill Companies.

resources to the use of fossil fuels. Fossil fuel energy, stored over millions of years, is being depleted rapidly to support a previously unknown and probably unsustainable level of consumption (Bodley 1985).

Table 16-2 compares energy consumption in various types of cultures. Americans are the world's foremost consumers of nonrenewable resources. In terms of energy consumption, the average American is about 35 times more expensive than the average forager or tribesperson. Since 1900, the United States has tripled its per capita energy use. It also has increased its total energy consumption thirtyfold.

Table 16-3 compares energy consumption, per capita and total, in the United States and selected other countries. The United States represents 22.5 percent of the world's annual energy consumption, compared with China's 13.4 percent, but the average American consumes 7 times the energy used by the average Chinese, and 24 times the energy used by the average inhabitant of India.

## TABLE 16-2

### Energy Consumption in Various Contexts

| Type of Society | Daily Kilocalories per Person |
| --- | --- |
| Bands and tribes | 4,000–12,000 |
| Preindustrial states | 26,000 (maximum) |
| Early industrial states | 70,000 |
| Americans in 1970 | 230,000 |
| Americans in 1990 | 275,000 |

*SOURCE:* From Bodley, *Anthropology and Contemporary Human Problems,* 1985. Reprinted by permission of The McGraw-Hill Companies.

## TABLE 16-3

### Energy Consumption in Selected Countries, 2004

|                | Total   | Per Capita |
|----------------|---------|------------|
| World          | 446.4*  | 70†        |
| United States  | 100.4   | 342        |
| China          | 59.6    | 46         |
| Russia         | 30.1    | 209        |
| India          | 15.4    | 14         |
| Germany        | 14.7    | 178        |
| Canada         | 13.6    | 418        |
| France         | 11.2    | 186        |
| United Kingdom | 10.0    | 166        |

*446.4 quadrillion (446,400,000,000,000,000) Btu.
†70 million Btu.
SOURCE: Based on data in *Statistical Abstract of the United States, 2007* (Table 1355), p. 860.

## Industrial Degradation

Industrialization and factory labor now characterize many societies in Latin America, Africa, the Pacific, and Asia. One effect of the spread of industrialization has been the destruction of indigenous economies, ecologies, and populations. Two centuries ago, as industrialization was developing, 50 million people still lived in politically independent bands, tribes, and chiefdoms. Occupying vast areas, those nonstate societies, although not totally isolated, were only marginally affected by nation-states and the world capitalist economy. In 1800 bands, tribes, and chiefdoms controlled half the globe and 20 percent of its population (Bodley, ed. 1988). Industrialization tipped the balance in favor of states.

As industrial states have conquered, annexed, and "developed" nonstates, there has been genocide on a grand scale. *Genocide* refers to a deliberate policy of exterminating a group through warfare or murder. Examples include the Holocaust, Rwanda in 1994, and Bosnia in the early 1990s. Bodley (1988) estimates that an average of 250,000 indigenous people perished annually between 1800 and 1950. Besides warfare, the causes included foreign diseases (to which natives lacked resistance), slavery, land grabbing, and other forms of dispossession and impoverishment.

Many native groups have been incorporated within nation-states, in which they have become ethnic minorities. Some such groups have been able to recoup their population. Many indigenous peoples survive and maintain their ethnic identity despite having lost their ancestral cultures to varying degrees (partial ethnocide). And many descendants of tribespeople live on as culturally distinct and self-conscious colonized peoples, many of whom aspire to autonomy. As the original inhabitants of their territories, they are called **indigenous peoples** (see Maybury-Lewis 2002).

Around the world many contemporary nations are repeating—at an accelerated rate—the process of resource depletion that started in Europe and the United States during the Industrial Revolution. Fortunately, however, today's world has some

As industrialization spreads, environmental resources, such as forests and their biodiversity, are threatened. Here women take part in a reforestation project in coastal Tanzania near Dar es Salaam.

environmental watchdogs that did not exist during the first centuries of the Industrial Revolution. Given national and international cooperation and sanctions, the modern world may benefit from the lessons of the past.

## ANTHROPOLOGY TODAY

### The World System Meets "The Noble Savage"

*The following news story brings into focus an anthropological debate about the origin and nature of warfare and the role of European contact in fostering violence among indigenous peoples. Violence among Native Americans increased after contact with Europeans. Note that as the article begins, it suggests, mistakenly, that Native Americans lived in prehistory and lacked "civilization." In fact, Native Americans developed states and "ancient civilizations" (e.g., Aztec,*

*Maya, Inca) comparable to those of the Old World (e.g., Mesopotamia and Egypt). Native Americans, most notably the Maya, also developed writing, which they used to record their history—rendering the label* prehistory *inaccurate.*

A romantic-sounding notion dating back more than 200 years has it that people in prehistory, such as Native Americans, lived in peace and harmony.

Then "civilization" showed up, sowing violence and discord. Some see this claim as naive. It even has a derisive nickname,

*Continued*

## ANTHROPOLOGY TODAY

the "noble savage myth." But new research seems to suggest the "myth" contains at least some truth. Researchers examined thousands of Native American skeletons and found that those from after Christopher Columbus landed in the New World showed a rate of traumatic injuries more than 50 percent higher than those from before the Europeans arrived.

"Traumatic injuries do increase really significantly," said Philip L. Walker, an anthropology professor at the University of California at Santa Barbara, who conducted the study with Richard H. Steckel of Ohio State University.

The findings suggest "Native Americans were involved in more violence after the Europeans arrived than before," Walker said. But he emphasized there was also widespread violence before the Europeans came. Nevertheless, he said, "probably we're just seeing the tip of the iceberg" as far as the difference between violence levels before and after. That's because as many as half of bullet wounds miss the skeleton. Thus, the study couldn't detect much firearm violence, though some tribes wiped each other out using European-supplied guns.

The findings shed light on a controversy that has stirred not only living room discussions, but also an intense, sometimes ugly debate among anthropologists.

It involves two opposing views of human nature: Are we hard-wired for violence, or pushed into it?

Anthropologists who believe the latter seized on the findings as evidence for their view. "What it all says to me is that humans aren't demonic. Human males don't have an ingrained propensity for war. . . . They can learn to be very peaceful, or terribly violent," said R. Brian Ferguson, a professor of anthropology at Rutgers University in Newark. Ferguson contends that before about 10,000 years ago, war was virtually nonexistent. But experts on the opposing side also said the findings fit their views.

"A 50 percent increase is the equivalent of moving from a suburb to the city, in terms of violence," said Charles Stanish, a professor of anthropology at the University of California at Los Angeles. "This shows the Native Americans were like us. Under stress, they fought more." Both sides called the study, which was presented Friday at the annual meeting of the American Association of Physical Anthropologists in Buffalo, a valuable contribution. . . .

Walker and colleagues examined the skeletons of 3,375 pre-Columbian and 1,165 post-Columbian Native Americans, from archaeological sites throughout North and Central America. . . .

Pre-Columbian skeletons showed an 11 percent incidence of traumatic injuries,

## SUMMARY

1. Local societies increasingly participate in wider systems—regional, national, and global. The capitalist world economy depends on production for sale, with the goal of maximizing profits. The key claim of world-system theory is that an identifiable social system, based on wealth and power differentials, extends beyond individual countries. That system is formed by a set of economic and political relations that has characterized much of the globe since the 16th century. World capitalism has political and economic specialization at the core, semiperiphery, and periphery.

he said, compared with almost 17 percent for the post-Columbians.

Walker said his findings surprised him. "I wasn't really expecting it," he said. Yet it undeniably suggests violence, he added. Most of the increase consisted of head injuries in young males, "which conforms pretty closely to the pattern you see today in homicides."

The researchers defined "traumatic injury" as anything leaving a mark on the skeleton, such as a skull fracture, a healed broken arm, or an embedded arrow point or bullet.

Walker said that although part of the increased injury rate doubtless stems from violence by whites themselves, it probably reflects mostly native-on-native violence. "In a lot of cases, such as in California, there weren't that many Europeans around—just a few priests, and thousands of Indians," he said.

Walker said the higher injury rate could have many explanations. Increased violence is normally associated with more densely populated, settled life, which Native Americans experienced in modernity, he said. Disease could also touch off war, he said.

"Here in California, there was a lot of inter-village warfare associated with the introduction of European diseases. People would attribute the disease to evil shamanic activity in another village," he said. Ferguson cited other factors. The Europeans often drew natives into their imperial wars. . . .

"You're also going to get competition over access to the Europeans, who are a form of wealth." . . . Native Americans fought over areas rich in fur, which the whites would buy.

Yet Native American warfare was widespread long before that, Stanish said. . . .

Keith F. Otterbein, an anthropology professor at the State University of New York at Buffalo, said the skeleton findings contribute to a balanced, middle-of-the-road view.

"The folks who are saying there was no early warfare—they're wrong, too. There is, in fact, a myth of the peaceful savage," he said. Otterbein said the controversy won't end here; both sides are too ideologically entrenched.

"Underlying the 'noble savage' myth," Stanish said, "is a political agenda by both the far right and far left. The right tries to turn the 'savages' into our little brown brothers, who need to be pulled up. . . . On the left, they have another agenda, that the Western world is bad."

*Source:* Jack Lucentini, "Bones Reveal Some Truth in 'Noble Savage Myth,'" *Washington Post*, April 14, 2002, p. A09. Reprinted by permission.

2. Columbus's voyages opened the way for a major exchange between the Old and New Worlds. Seventeenth-century plantation economies in the Caribbean and Brazil were based on sugar. In the 18th century, plantation economies based on cotton arose in the southeastern United States.

3. The Industrial Revolution began in England around 1760. Transoceanic commerce supplied capital for industrial investment. Industrialization hastened the separation of workers from the means of production. Marx saw a sharp division between the bourgeoisie and the proletariat. Class consciousness was a key feature of Marx's

view of this stratification. Weber believed that social solidarity based on ethnicity, religion, race, or nationality could take priority over class. Today's capitalist world economy maintains the contrast between those who own the means of production and those who don't, but the division is now worldwide. There is a substantial contrast between not only capitalists but workers in the core nations and workers on the periphery.

4. Imperialism is the policy of extending the rule of a nation or empire over other nations and of taking and holding foreign colonies. Colonialism is the domination of a territory and its people by a foreign power for an extended time. European colonialism had two main phases. The first started in 1492 and lasted through 1825. For Britain this phase ended with the American Revolution. For France it ended when Britain won the Seven Years' War, forcing the French to abandon Canada and India. For Spain, it ended with Latin American independence. The second phase of European colonialism extended approximately from 1850 to 1950. The British and French empires were at their height around 1914, when European empires controlled 85 percent of the world. Britain and France had colonies in Africa, Asia, Oceania, and the New World.

5. Many geopolitical labels and identities were created under colonialism that had little or nothing to do with existing social demarcations. The new ethnic or national divisions were colonial inventions, sometimes aggravating conflicts.

6. Like colonialism, economic development has an intervention philosophy that provides a justification for outsiders to guide native peoples toward particular goals. Development usually is justified by the idea that industrialization and modernization are desirable evolutionary advances. Neoliberalism revives and extends classic economic liberalism: the idea that governments should not regulate private enterprise and that free market forces should rule. This intervention philosophy currently dominates aid agreements with postsocialist and developing nations.

7. Spelled with a lowercase *c*, communism describes a social system in which property is owned by the community and in which people work for the common good. Spelled with an uppercase *C*, Communism indicates a political movement and doctrine seeking to overthrow capitalism and to establish a form of communism such as that which prevailed in the Soviet Union from 1917 to 1991. The heyday of Communism was between 1949 and 1989. The fall of Communism can be traced to 1989–1990 in eastern Europe and 1991 in the Soviet Union. Postsocialist states have followed the neoliberal agenda, through privatization, deregulation, and democratization.

8. By 1900 the United States had become a core nation. Mass production gave rise to a culture that valued acquisitiveness and conspicuous consumption. One effect of industrialization has been the destruction of indigenous economies, ecologies, and populations. Another has been the accelerated rate of resource depletion.

# KEY TERMS

bourgeoisie (p. 352)
capital (p. 347)
capitalist world economy (p. 347)
colonialism (p. 354)
communism (p. 360)
Communism (p. 360)
core (p. 348)
imperialism (p. 354)
indigenous peoples (p. 364)

Industrial Revolution (p. 350)
intervention philosophy (p. 359)
neoliberalism (p. 359)
periphery (p. 349)
postcolonial (p. 358)
semiperiphery (p. 348)
working class, or proletariat (p. 352)
world-system theory (p. 348)

# CHAPTER 17

# ETHNICITY AND RACE

❖ **Ethnic Groups and Ethnicity**
　Shifting Identities
❖ **Race**
❖ **The Social Construction of Race**
　Hypodescent: Race in the United States
　Not Us: Race in Japan
　Phenotype and Fluidity: Race in Brazil
❖ **Ethnic Groups, Nations, and
　Nationalities**
　Nationalities and Imagined Communities

❖ **Ethnic Tolerance and Accommodation**
　Assimilation
　The Plural Society
　Multiculturalism and Ethnic Identity
❖ **Roots of Ethnic Conflict**
　Prejudice and Discrimination
　Chips in the Mosaic
　Aftermaths of Oppression
　*Anthropology Today: The Basques*

Ethnicity is based on cultural similarities and differences in a society or nation. The similarities are with members of the same ethnic group; the differences are between that group and others. Ethnic groups must deal with other such groups in the nation or region they inhabit, so that interethnic relations are important in the study of that nation or region. (Table 17-1 lists American ethnic groups, based on 2005 figures.)

## ❖ ETHNIC GROUPS AND ETHNICITY

As with any culture, members of an **ethnic group** *share* certain beliefs, values, habits, customs, and norms because of their common background. They define themselves as different and special because of cultural features. This distinction may arise from language, religion, historical experience, geographic placement, kinship, or "race" (see Spickard, ed. 2004). Markers of an ethnic group may include a collective name, belief in common descent, a sense of solidarity, and an association with a specific territory, which the group may or may not hold (Ryan 1990, pp. xiii, xiv).

According to Fredrik Barth (1969), ethnicity can be said to exist when people claim a certain ethnic identity for themselves and are defined by others as having that identity. **Ethnicity** means identification with, and feeling part of, an ethnic group and exclusion from certain other groups because of this affiliation. Ethnic feelings and associated behavior vary in intensity within ethnic groups and countries and over time. A change in the degree of importance attached to an ethnic identity may reflect political changes (Soviet rule ends—ethnic feeling rises) or individual life-cycle changes (young people relinquish, or old people reclaim, an ethnic background).

## TABLE 17-1

### Racial/Ethnic Identification in the United States, 2005 (as Claimed in Census)

| Claimed Identity | Millions of People | Percentage |
|---|---|---|
| Hispanic | 42.7 | 14.4% |
| Asian | 12.7 | 4.3 |
| Two or more races | 4.6 | 1.6 |
| Pacific Islander | 0.5 | 0.2 |
| American Indian | 2.9 | 1.0 |
| Black | 37.9 | 12.8 |
| White (non-Hispanic) | 198.4 | 66.9 |
| Total population | 296.4 | |

SOURCE: *Statistical Abstract of the United States 2007*, p. 14.

Cultural differences may be associated with ethnicity, class, region, or religion. Individuals often have more than one group identity. People may be loyal (depending on circumstances) to their neighborhood, school, town, state or province, region, nation, continent, religion, ethnic group, or interest group (Ryan 1990, p. xxii). In a complex society such as the United States or Canada, people constantly negotiate their social identities. All of us "wear different hats," presenting ourselves sometimes as one thing, sometimes as another.

## Shifting Identities

Sometimes our identities (aka social statuses) are mutually exclusive. It's hard to be both black and white or male and female. Sometimes, assuming an identity or joining a group requires a conversion experience, acquiring a new and overwhelming primary identity, such as becoming a "born again" Christian.

Some statuses aren't mutually exclusive, but contextual. People can be both black and Hispanic or both a mother and a senator. One identity is used in certain settings, another in different ones. We call this the *situational negotiation of social identity* (Leman 2001). Hispanics, for example, may shift ethnic affiliations as they negotiate their identities. "Hispanic" is an ethnic category based mainly on language. It includes whites, blacks, and "racially" mixed Spanish speakers and their ethnically conscious descendants. (There also are Native American and even Asian Hispanics.) "Hispanic," representing the fastest-growing ethnic group in the United States, lumps together millions of people of diverse geographic origin—Puerto Rico, Mexico, Cuba, El Salvador, Guatemala, the Dominican Republic, and other Spanish-speaking countries of Central and South America and the Caribbean. "Latino" is a broader category, which also can include Brazilians (who speak Portuguese). The national origins of American Hispanics/Latinos in 2002 were as shown in Table 17-2.

Mexican Americans (Chicanos), Cuban Americans, and Puerto Ricans may mobilize to promote general Hispanic issues (e.g., opposition to "English-only" laws)

## TABLE 17-2

### American Hispanics, Latinos, 2002

| National Origin | Percentage |
| --- | --- |
| Mexican American | 66.9% |
| Puerto Rican | 8.6 |
| Cuban | 3.7 |
| Central & South American | 14.3 |
| Other Hispanic/Latino origin | 6.5 |
| Total | 100.0% |

SOURCE: Ramirez and de la Cruz, 2003.

but act as three separate interest groups in other contexts. Cuban Americans are richer on average than Chicanos and Puerto Ricans are, and their class interests and voting patterns differ. Cubans often vote Republican, but Puerto Ricans and Chicanos are

The ethnic label "Hispanic" lumps together millions of people of diverse racial types and countries of origin. People of diverse national backgrounds may mobilize to promote general Hispanic issues (such as opposition to "English-only" laws), but act as separate interest groups in other contexts. Shown here are Salvadorians in downtown Los Angeles watching a Central American Independence Day parade on September 19, 2004.

more likely to favor Democrats. Some Mexican Americans whose families have lived in the United States for generations have little in common with new Hispanic immigrants, such as those from Central America. Many Americans (especially those fluent in English) claim Hispanic ethnicity in some contexts but shift to a general "American" identity in others.

In many societies a racial, ethnic, or caste status is associated with a position in the social–political hierarchy. Certain groups, called **minority groups,** are subordinate. They have inferior power and less secure access to resources than do **majority groups** (which are superordinate, dominant, or controlling). Often ethnic groups are minorities. When an ethnic group is assumed to have a biological basis (distinctively shared "blood" or genes), it is called a **race.** Discrimination against such a group is called **racism** (Cohen 1998; Montagu 1997; Scupin 2003; Shanklin 1995; Wade 2002).

## ✦ RACE

Race, like ethnicity in general, is a cultural category rather than a biological reality. That is, ethnic groups, including "races," derive from contrasts perceived and perpetuated in particular societies, rather than from scientific classifications based on common genes (see Wade 2002).

It is not possible to define human races biologically. Only cultural constructions of race are possible—even though the average person conceptualizes "race" in biological terms. The belief that human races exist and are important is much more common among the public than it is among scientists. Most Americans, for example, believe that their population includes biologically based races to which various labels have been applied. These labels include "white," "black," "yellow," "red," "Caucasoid," "Negroid," "Mongoloid," "Amerindian," "Euro-American," "African American," "Asian American," and "Native American."

We hear the words *ethnicity* and *race* frequently, but American culture doesn't draw a very clear line between them. As illustration, consider two articles in *The New York Times* of May 29, 1992. One, discussing the changing ethnic composition of the United States, explains (correctly) that Hispanics "can be of any race" (Barringer 1992, p. A12). In other words, "Hispanic" is an ethnic category that cross-cuts racial contrasts such as that between "black" and "white." The other article reports that during the Los Angeles riots of spring 1992, "hundreds of Hispanic residents were interrogated about their immigration status on the basis of their *race* alone [emphasis added]" (Mydans 1992*a*, p. A8). Use of "race" here seems inappropriate because "Hispanic" usually is perceived as referring to a linguistically based (Spanish-speaking) ethnic group, rather than a biologically based race. Since these Los Angeles residents were being interrogated because they were Hispanic, the article is actually reporting on ethnic, not racial, discrimination. However, given the lack of a precise distinction between race and ethnicity, it is probably better to use the term "ethnic group" instead of "race" to describe *any* such social group, for example, African Americans, Asian Americans, Irish Americans, Anglo Americans, or Hispanics.

## ✦ THE SOCIAL CONSTRUCTION OF RACE

Races are ethnic groups assumed (by members of a particular culture) to have a biological basis, but actually race is socially constructed. The "races" we hear about every day are cultural, or social, rather than biological categories. In Charles Wagley's terms (Wagley 1959/1968), they are **social races** (groups assumed to have a biological basis but actually defined in a culturally arbitrary, rather than a scientific, manner). Many Americans mistakenly assume that whites and blacks, for example, are biologically distinct and that these terms stand for discrete races. But these labels, like racial terms used in other societies, really designate culturally perceived rather than biologically based groups.

## Hypodescent: Race in the United States

How is race culturally constructed in the United States? In American culture, one acquires his or her racial identity at birth, as an ascribed status, but race isn't based on biology or on simple ancestry. Take the case of the child of a "racially mixed" marriage involving one black and one white parent. We know that 50 percent of the child's genes come from one parent and 50 percent from the other. Still, American culture overlooks heredity and classifies this child as black. This rule is arbitrary. On the basis of genotype (genetic composition), it would be just as logical to classify the child as white.

American rules for assigning racial status can be even more arbitrary. In some states, anyone known to have any black ancestor, no matter how remote, is classified as a member of the black race. This is a rule of **descent** (it assigns social identity on the basis of ancestry), but of a sort that is rare outside the contemporary United States. It is called **hypodescent** (Harris and Kottak 1963) because it automatically places the children of a union between members of different groups in the minority group (*hypo* means "lower"). Hypodescent divides American society into groups that have been unequal in their access to wealth, power, and prestige.

The following case from Louisiana is an excellent illustration of the arbitrariness of the hypodescent rule and of the role that governments (federal or, in this case, state) play in legalizing, inventing, or eradicating race and ethnicity (B. Williams 1989). Susie Guillory Phipps, a light-skinned woman with Caucasian features and straight black hair, discovered as an adult that she was black. When Phipps ordered a copy of her birth certificate, she found her race listed as "colored." Since she had been "brought up white and married white twice," Phipps challenged a 1970 Louisiana law declaring anyone with at least one-thirty-second "Negro blood" to be legally black. Although the state's lawyer admitted that Phipps "looks like a white person," the state of Louisiana insisted that her racial classification was proper (Yetman, ed. 1991, pp. 3–4).

Cases like Phipps's are rare because racial identity usually is ascribed at birth and doesn't change. The rule of hypodescent affects blacks, Asians, Native Americans, and Hispanics differently (see Hunter 2005). It's easier to negotiate Indian or Hispanic identity than black identity. The ascription rule isn't as definite, and the assumption of a biological basis isn't as strong.

To be considered Native American, one ancestor out of eight (great-grandparents) or out of four (grandparents) may suffice. This depends on whether the assignment is by federal or state law or by an Indian tribal council. The child of a Hispanic may (or may not, depending on context) claim Hispanic identity. Many Americans with an Indian or Latino grandparent consider themselves white and lay no claim to minority group status.

The U.S. Census Bureau has gathered data by race since 1790. Initially this was done because the Constitution specified that a slave counted as three-fifths of a white person, and because Indians were not taxed. The racial categories included in the 1990 census were "White," "Black or Negro," "Indian (American)," "Eskimo," "Aleut or Pacific Islander," and "Other." A separate question was asked about Spanish–Hispanic heritage. Check out Figure 17-1 for the racial categories in the 2000 census.

Attempts by social scientists and interested citizens to add a "multiracial" census category have been opposed by the National Association for the Advancement of Colored People (NAACP) and the National Council of La Raza (a Hispanic advocacy group). Racial classification is a political issue (Goldberg 2002) involving access to resources, including jobs, voting districts, and federal funding of programs aimed at minorities. The hypodescent rule results in all the population growth being attributed to the minority category. Minorities fear their political clout will decline if their numbers go down.

But things are changing. Choice of "some other race" in the U.S. Census more than doubled from 1980 (6.8 million) to 2000 (over 15 million)— suggesting imprecision in and dissatisfaction with the existing categories (Mar 1997). In the 2000 census, 2.4 percent of Americans, or 6.8 million people, chose a first-ever option of identifying

→ **NOTE: Please answer BOTH Questions 5 and 6.**

5. **Is this person Spanish/Hispanic/Latino?** *Mark* ☒ *the "No" box if **not** Spanish/Hispanic/Latino.*
   ☐ **No,** not Spanish/Hispanic/Latino        ☐ Yes, Puerto Rican
   ☐ Yes, Mexican, Mexican Am., Chicano        ☐ Yes, Cuban
   ☐ Yes, other Spanish/Hispanic/Latino —Print group. ⬈

6. **What is this person's race?** *Mark* ☒ *one or more races to indicate what this person considers himself/herself to be.*
   ☐ White
   ☐ Black, African Am., or Negro
   ☐ American Indian or Alaska Native —*Print name of enrolled or principal tribe.* ⬈

   ☐ Asian Indian ☐ Japanese        ☐ Native Hawaiian
   ☐ Chinese      ☐ Korean          ☐ Guamanian or Chamorro
   ☐ Filipino     ☐ Vietnamese      ☐ Samoan
   ☐ Other Asian —*Print race.* ⬈   ☐ Other Pacific Islander —*Print race.* ⬈

   ☐ Some other race —*Print race.* ⬈

**FIGURE 17-1**    *Reproduction of Questions on Race and Hispanic Origin from Census 2000*

*SOURCE:* U.S. Census Bureau, Census 2000 questionnaire.

themselves as belonging to more than one race. The number of interracial marriages and children is increasing, with implications for the traditional system of American racial classification. "Interracial," "biracial," or "multiracial" children who grow up with both parents undoubtedly identify with particular qualities of either parent. It is troubling for many of them to have so important an identity as race dictated by the arbitrary rule of hypodescent. It may be especially discordant when racial identity doesn't parallel gender identity, for instance, a boy with a white father and a black mother, or a girl with a white mother and a black father.

## Not Us: Race in Japan

American culture ignores considerable diversity in biology, language, and geographic origin as it socially constructs race in the United States. North Americans also overlook diversity by seeing Japan as a nation that is homogeneous in race, ethnicity, language, and culture—an image the Japanese themselves cultivate. Thus in 1986 former Prime Minister Nakasone created an international furor by contrasting his country's supposed homogeneity (responsible, he suggested, for Japan's success at that time in international business) with the ethnically mixed United States.

Japan is hardly the uniform entity Nakasone described. Scholars estimate that 10 percent of Japan's national population are minorities of various sorts. These include aboriginal Ainu, annexed Okinawans, outcast *burakumin,* children of mixed marriages, and immigrant nationalities, especially Koreans, who number more than 700,000 (De Vos, Wetherall, and Stearman 1983; Lie 2001).

To describe racial attitudes in Japan, Jennifer Robertson (1992) uses Kwame Anthony Appiah's (1990) term "intrinsic racism"—the belief that a (perceived) racial difference is a sufficient reason to value one person less than another. In Japan the valued group is majority ("pure") Japanese, who are believed to share "the same blood." Thus, the caption to a printed photo of a Japanese American model reads: "She was born in Japan but raised in Hawaii. Her nationality is American but no foreign blood flows in her veins" (Robertson 1992, p. 5). Something like hypodescent also operates in Japan, but less precisely than in the United States, where mixed offspring automatically become members of the minority group. The children of mixed marriages between majority Japanese and others (including Euro-Americans) may not get the same "racial" label as their minority parent, but they are still stigmatized for their non-Japanese ancestry (De Vos and Wagatsuma 1966).

How is race culturally constructed in Japan? The (majority) Japanese define themselves by opposition to others, whether minority groups in their own nation or outsiders—anyone who is "not us." The "not us" should stay that way; assimilation generally is discouraged. Cultural mechanisms, especially residential segregation and taboos on "interracial" marriage, work to keep minorities "in their place."

In its construction of race, Japanese culture regards certain ethnic groups as having a biological basis, when there is no evidence that they do. The best example is the *burakumin,* a stigmatized group of at least 4 million outcasts, sometimes compared to India's untouchables. The burakumin are physically and genetically indistinguishable from other Japanese. Many of them "pass" as (and marry) majority Japanese, but a deceptive marriage can end in divorce if burakumin identity is discovered (Aoki and Dardess, eds. 1981).

Burakumin are perceived as standing apart from majority Japanese. Through ancestry, descent (and thus, it is assumed, "blood," or genetics) burakumin are "not us." Majority Japanese try to keep their lineage pure by discouraging mixing. The burakumin are residentially segregated in neighborhoods (rural or urban) called *buraku,* from which the racial label is derived. Compared with majority Japanese, the burakumin are less likely to attend high school and college. When burakumin attend the same schools as majority Japanese, they face discrimination. Majority children and teachers may refuse to eat with them because burakumin are considered unclean.

In applying for university admission or a job and in dealing with the government, Japanese must list their address, which becomes part of a household or family registry. This list makes residence in a buraku, and likely burakumin social status, evident. Schools and companies use this information to discriminate. (The best way to pass is to move so often that the buraku address eventually disappears from the registry.) Majority Japanese also limit "race" mixture by hiring marriage mediators to check out the family histories of prospective spouses. They are especially careful to check for burakumin ancestry (De Vos et al. 1983).

The origin of the burakumin lies in a historical tiered system of stratification (from the Tokugawa period—1603–1868). The top four ranked categories were warrior-administrators (*samurai*), farmers, artisans, and merchants. The ancestors of the

Japan's stigmatized burakumin are physically and genetically indistinguishable from other Japanese. In response to burakumin political mobilization, Japan has dismantled the legal structure of discrimination against burakumin. This Sports Day for burakumin children is one kind of mobilization.

burakumin were below this hierarchy, an outcast group who did unclean jobs such as animal slaughter and disposal of the dead. Burakumin still do similar jobs, including work with leather and other animal products. The burakumin are more likely than majority Japanese to do manual labor (including farm work) and to belong to the national lower class. Burakumin and other Japanese minorities are also more likely to have careers in crime, prostitution, entertainment, and sports (De Vos et al. 1983).

Like blacks in the United States, the burakumin are class-stratified. Because certain jobs are reserved for the burakumin, people who are successful in those occupations (e.g., shoe factory owners) can be wealthy. Burakumin also have found jobs as government bureaucrats. Financially successful burakumin can temporarily escape their stigmatized status by travel, including foreign travel.

Discrimination against the burakumin is strikingly like the discrimination that blacks have experienced in the United States. The burakumin often live in villages and neighborhoods with poor housing and sanitation. They have limited access to education, jobs, amenities, and health facilities. In response to burakumin political mobilization, Japan has dismantled the legal structure of discrimination against burakumin and has worked to improve conditions in the buraku. (The Web site http://blhrri.org/index_ e.htm is sponsored by the Buraku Liberation and Human Rights Research Institute and includes the most recent information about the Buraku liberation movement.) Still Japan has yet to institute American-style affirmative action programs for education and jobs. Discrimination against nonmajority Japanese is still the rule in companies. Some employers say that hiring burakumin would give their company an unclean image and thus create a disadvantage in competing with other businesses (De Vos et al. 1983).

## Phenotype and Fluidity: Race in Brazil

There are more flexible, less exclusionary ways of constructing social race than those used in the United States and Japan. Along with the rest of Latin America, Brazil has less exclusionary categories, which permit individuals to change their racial classification. Brazil shares a history of slavery with the United States, but it lacks the hypodescent rule. Nor does Brazil have racial aversion of the sort found in Japan.

Brazilians use many more racial labels—over 500 have been reported (Harris 1970)—than Americans or Japanese do. In northeastern Brazil, I found 40 different racial terms in use in Arembepe, a village of only 750 people (Kottak 2006). Through their classification system Brazilians recognize and attempt to describe the physical variation that exists in their population. The system used in the United States, by recognizing only three or four races, blinds Americans to an equivalent range of evident physical contrasts. The system Brazilians use to construct social race has other special features. In the United States one's race is an ascribed status; it is assigned automatically by hypodescent and usually doesn't change. In Brazil racial identity is more flexible, more of an achieved status. Brazilian racial classification pays attention to phenotype. **Phenotype** refers to an organism's evident traits, its "manifest biology"—physiology and anatomy, including skin color, hair form, facial features, and eye color. A Brazilian's phenotype and racial label may change because of environmental factors, such as the tanning rays of the sun or the effects of humidity on the hair.

These photos, taken in Brazil by the author in 2003 and 2004, give just a glimpse of the spectrum of phenotypical diversity encountered among contemporary Brazilians.

As physical characteristics change (sunlight alters skin color, humidity affects hair form), so do racial terms. Furthermore, racial differences may be so insignificant in structuring community life that people may forget the terms they have applied to others. Sometimes they even forget the ones they've used for themselves. In Arembepe, I made it a habit to ask the same person on different days to tell me the races of others in the village (and my own). In the United States I am always "white" or "Euro-American," but in Arembepe I got lots of terms besides *branco* ("white"). I could be *claro* ("light"), *louro* ("blond"), *sarará* ("light-skinned redhead"), *mulato claro* ("light mulatto"), or *mulato* ("mulatto"). The racial term used to describe me or anyone else varied from person to person, week to week, even day to day. My best informant, a man with very dark skin color, changed the term he used for himself all the time—from *escuro* ("dark") to *preto* ("black") to *moreno escuro* ("dark brunet").

The American and Japanese racial systems are creations of particular cultures, rather than scientific—or even accurate—descriptions of human biological differences. Brazilian racial classification also is a cultural construction, but Brazilians have developed a way of describing human biological diversity that is more detailed, fluid, and flexible than the systems used in most cultures. Brazil lacks Japan's racial aversion, and it also lacks a rule of descent like that which ascribes racial status in the United States (Degler 1970; Harris 1964).

For centuries the United States and Brazil have had mixed populations, with ancestors from Native America, Europe, Africa, and Asia. Although races have mixed in both countries, Brazilian and American cultures have constructed the results differently. The historical reasons for this contrast lie mainly in the different characteristics of the settlers of the two countries. The mainly English early settlers of the United States came as women, men, and families, but Brazil's Portuguese colonizers were mainly men—merchants and adventurers. Many of these Portuguese men married Native American women and recognized their racially mixed children as their heirs. Like their North American counterparts, Brazilian plantation owners had sexual relations with their slaves. But the Brazilian landlords more often freed the children that resulted—for demographic and economic reasons. (Sometimes these were their only children.) Freed offspring of master and slave became plantation overseers and foremen and filled many intermediate positions in the emerging Brazilian economy. They were not classed with the slaves, but were allowed to join a new intermediate category. No hypodescent rule developed in Brazil to ensure that whites and blacks remained separate (see Degler 1970; Harris 1964).

## ❖ ETHNIC GROUPS, NATIONS, AND NATIONALITIES

The term **nation** once was synonymous with *tribe* or *ethnic group*. All three of these terms referred to a single culture sharing a single language, religion, history, territory, ancestry, and kinship. Thus one could speak interchangeably of the Seneca (American Indian) nation, tribe, or ethnic group. Now *nation* has come to mean state—an independent, centrally organized political unit, or a government. *Nation* and *state* have become synonymous. Combined in **nation-state** they refer to an autonomous political entity, a country—like the United States, "one nation, indivisible" (see Farner, ed. 2004; Gellner 1997; Hastings 1997).

Because of migration, conquest, and colonialism, most nation-states are not ethnically homogeneous. Of 132 nation-states existing in 1971, Connor (1972) found just 12 (9 percent) to be ethnically homogeneous. In another 25 (19 percent) a single ethnic group accounted for more than 90 percent of the population. Forty percent of the countries contained more than five significant ethnic groups. In a later study, Nielsson (1985) found that in only 45 of 164 states did one ethnic group account for more than 95 percent of the population.

## Nationalities and Imagined Communities

Ethnic groups that once had, or wish to have or regain, autonomous political status (their own country) are called **nationalities.** In the words of Benedict Anderson (1991), they are "imagined communities." Even when they become nation-states, they remain imagined communities because most of their members, though feeling comradeship, will never meet (Anderson 1991, pp. 6–10). They can only imagine they all participate in the same unit.

Anderson traces Western European nationalism, which arose in imperial powers such as England, France, and Spain, back to the 18th century. He stresses that language and print played a crucial role in the growth of European national consciousness. The novel and the newspaper were "two forms of imagining" communities (consisting of all the people who read the same sources and thus witnessed the same events) that flowered in the 18th century (Anderson 1991, pp. 24–25).

Over time, political upheavals, wars, and migration have divided many imagined national communities that arose in the 18th and 19th centuries. The German and Korean homelands were artificially divided after wars, according to communist and capitalist ideologies. World War I split the Kurds, who remain an imagined community, forming a majority in no state. Kurds are a minority group in Turkey, Iran, Iraq, and Syria.

In creating multitribal and multiethnic states, colonialism often erected boundaries that corresponded poorly with preexisting cultural divisions. But colonial institutions also helped created new "imagined communities" beyond nations. A good example is the idea of *négritude* ("Black identity") developed by African intellectuals in Francophone (French-speaking) West Africa. Négritude can be traced to the association and common experience in colonial times of youths from Guinea, Mali, the Ivory Coast, and Senegal at the William Ponty school in Dakar, Senegal (Anderson 1991, pp. 123–124).

## ❖ ETHNIC TOLERANCE AND ACCOMMODATION

Ethnic diversity may be associated with positive group interaction and coexistence or with conflict (discussed shortly). There are nation-states in which multiple cultural groups live together in reasonable harmony, including some less developed countries.

## Assimilation

**Assimilation** describes the process of change that a minority ethnic group may experience when it moves to a country where another culture dominates. By assimilating, the minority adopts the patterns and norms of its host culture. It is incorporated into the dominant culture to the point that it no longer exists as a separate cultural unit. Some countries, such as Brazil, are more assimilationist than others. Germans, Italians, Japanese, Middle Easterners, and East Europeans started migrating to Brazil late in the 19th century. These immigrants have assimilated to a common Brazilian culture, which has Portuguese, African, and Native American roots. The descendants of these immigrants speak the national language (Portuguese) and participate in the national culture. (During World War II, Brazil, which was on the Allied side, forced assimilation by banning instruction in any language other than Portuguese—especially in German.)

## The Plural Society

Assimilation isn't inevitable, and there can be ethnic harmony without it. Ethnic distinctions can persist despite generations of interethnic contact. Through a study of three ethnic groups in Swat, Pakistan, Fredrik Barth (1958/1968) challenged an old idea that interaction always leads to assimilation. He showed that ethnic groups can be in contact for generations without assimilating and can live in peaceful coexistence.

Barth (1958/1968, p. 324) defines **plural society** (an idea he extended from Pakistan to the entire Middle East) as a society combining ethnic contrasts, ecological specialization (i.e., use of different environmental resources by each ethnic group), and the economic interdependence of those groups. Consider his description of the Middle East (in the 1950s): "The 'environment' of any one ethnic group is not only defined by natural conditions, but also by the presence and activities of the other ethnic groups on which it depends. Each group exploits only part of the total environment, and leaves large parts of it open for other groups to exploit." The ecological interdependence (or, at least, the lack of competition) between ethnic groups may be based on different activities in the same region or on long-term occupation of different regions in the same nation-state.

In Barth's view, ethnic boundaries are most stable and enduring when the groups occupy different ecological niches. That is, they make their living in different ways and don't compete. Ideally, they should depend on each other's activities and exchange with one another. When different ethnic groups exploit the *same* ecological niche, the militarily more powerful group will normally replace the weaker one. If they exploit more or less the same niche, but the weaker group is better able to use marginal environments, they also may coexist (Barth 1958/1968, p. 331). Given niche specialization, ethnic boundaries and interdependence can be maintained, although the specific cultural features of each group may change. By shifting the analytic focus from individual cultures or ethnic groups to *relationships* between cultures or ethnic groups, Barth (1958/1968, 1969) has made important contributions to ethnic studies.

## Multiculturalism and Ethnic Identity

The view of cultural diversity in a country as something good and desirable is called **multiculturalism** (see Kottak and Kozaitis 2008). The multicultural model is the opposite of the assimilationist model, in which minorities are expected to abandon their cultural traditions and values, replacing them with those of the majority population. The multicultural view encourages the practice of cultural–ethnic traditions. A multicultural society

socializes individuals not only into the dominant (national) culture but also into an ethnic culture. Thus in the United States millions of people speak both English and another
language, eat both "American" (apple pie, steak, hamburgers) and "ethnic" foods, and
celebrate both national (July 4, Thanksgiving) and ethnic–religious holidays.

In the United States and Canada multiculturalism is of growing importance. This
reflects an awareness that the number and size of ethnic groups have grown dramatically
in recent years. If this trend continues, the ethnic composition of the United States will
change dramatically. (See Figure 17-2.)

Even now, because of immigration and differential population growth, whites are outnumbered by minorities in many urban areas. For example, of the 8,085,742 people living in
New York City in 2003, 27 percent were black, 27 percent Hispanic, 10 percent Asian, and
36 percent other—including non-Hispanic whites. The comparable figures for Los Angeles
(which had 3,819,951 people) were 11 percent black, 46 percent Hispanic, 10 percent Asian,
and 33 percent other, including non-Hispanic whites (U.S. Census Bureau 2006).

In October 2006, the population of the United States reached 300 million people,
just 39 years after reaching 200 million and 91 years after reaching the 100 million
mark (in 1915). The country's ethnic composition has changed dramatically in the past
40 years. The 1970 census, the first to attempt an official count of Hispanics, found they

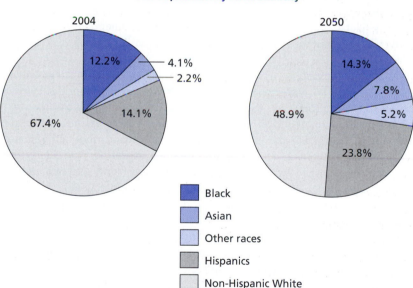

**FIGURE 17-2**   *Ethnic Composition of the United States*  The proportion of the
American population that is white and non-Hispanic is declining. The projection for
2050 shown here comes from a U.S. Census Bureau report issued in March 2004.
Note especially the dramatic rise in the Hispanic portion of the American population
between 2004 and 2050.

*SOURCE*: Based on data from U.S. Census Bureau, International Data Base, Table 094, http://www.census.
gov/ipc/www.idbprint.html; Files 2005.

represented no more than 4.7 percent of the American population, compared with 14.4 percent in 2006. The number of African Americans increased from 11.1 percent in 1967 to 13.4 percent in 2006, while (non-Hispanic) whites ("Anglos") declined from 83 to 67 percent. In 1967 fewer than 10 million people in the United States (5 percent of the population) had been born elsewhere, compared with more than 36 million immigrants (12 percent) today. (All figures are from Ohlemacher 2006).

In 1973, 78 percent of the students in American public schools were white, and 22 percent were minorities: blacks, Hispanics, Asians, Pacific Islanders, and "others." By 2004, only 57 percent of public school students were white, and 43 percent were minorities. If current trends continue, minority students will outnumber (non-Hispanic) white students by 2015. They already do in California, Hawaii, Mississippi, New Mexico, and Texas (Dillon 2006).

Immigration, mainly from southern and eastern Europe, had a similar effect on classroom diversity, at least in the largest American cities, a century ago. A study of American public schools in 1908–09 found that only 42 percent of those urban students were native-born, while 58 percent were immigrants. In a very different (multicultural now versus assimilationist then) context, today's American classrooms have regained the ethnic diversity they demonstrated in the early 1900s, when this author's German-speaking Austro-Hungarian-born father and grandparents immigrated to the United States.

One response to ethnic diversification and awareness has been for many whites to reclaim ethnic identities (Italian, Albanian, Serbian, Lithuanian, etc.) and to joint ethnic associations (clubs, gangs). Some such groups are new. Others have existed for decades, although they lost members during the assimilationist years of the 1920s through the 1950s.

Multiculturalism seeks ways for people to understand and interact that don't depend on sameness but rather on respect for differences. Multiculturalism stresses the interaction of ethnic groups and their contribution to the country. It assumes that each group has something to offer to and learn from the others. Several forces have propelled North America away from the assimilationist model toward multiculturalism. First, multiculturalism reflects the fact of recent large-scale migration, particularly from the "less developed countries" to the "developed" nations of North America and Western Europe. The global scale of modern migration introduces unparalleled ethnic variety to host nations. Multiculturalism is related to globalization: People use modern means of transportation to migrate to nations whose lifestyles they learn about through the media and from tourists who increasingly visit their own countries.

Migration also is fueled by rapid population growth, coupled with insufficient jobs (both for educated and uneducated people), in the less developed countries. As traditional rural economies decline or mechanize, displaced farmers move to cities, where they and their children often are unable to find jobs. As people in the less developed countries get better educations, they seek more skilled employment. They hope to partake of an international culture of consumption that includes such modern amenities as refrigerators, televisions, and automobiles (Ahmed 2004).

In a world with growing rural–urban and transnational migration, ethnic identities are used increasingly to form self-help organizations focused mainly on enhancing the group's economic competitiveness (Williams 1989). People claim and express ethnic identities for political and economic reasons. Michel Laguerre's (1984, 1998) studies of Haitian immigrants in the United States show that they mobilize to deal with the discriminatory structure (racist in this case, since Haitians tend to be black) of American society. Ethnicity (their common Haitian creole language and cultural background) is a basis for their mobilization. Haitian ethnicity helps distinguish them from African Americans and other ethnic groups.

In the face of globalization, much of the world, including the entire "democratic West," is experiencing an "ethnic revival." The new assertiveness of long-resident ethnic groups extends to the Basques and Catalans in Spain, the Bretons and Corsicans in France, and the Welsh and Scots in the United Kingdom. The United States and Canada are becoming increasingly multicultural, focusing on their internal diversity (see Laguerre 1999). "Melting pots" no longer, they are better described as ethnic "salads" (each ingredient remains distinct, although in the same bowl, with the same dressing).

## ✦ ROOTS OF ETHNIC CONFLICT

Ethnicity, based on perceived cultural similarities and differences in a society or nation, can be expressed in peaceful multiculturalism or in discrimination or violent interethnic confrontation. Culture can be both adaptive and maladaptive. The perception of cultural differences can have disastrous effects on social interaction.

The roots of ethnic differentiation—and therefore, potentially, of ethnic conflict— can be political, economic, religious, linguistic, cultural, or racial (see Kuper 2006). Why do ethnic differences often lead to conflict and violence? The causes include a sense of injustice because of resource distribution, economic or political competition, and reaction to discrimination, prejudice, and other expressions of devalued identity (see Friedman 2003; Ryan 1990, p. xxvii).

In Iraq, under the dictator Saddam Hussein, there was discrimination by one Muslim group (Sunnis) against others (Shiites and Kurds). Sunnis, although a numeric minority within Iraq's population, enjoyed privileged access to power, prestige, and position. After the elections of 2005, which many Sunnis chose to boycott, Shiites gained political control. A civil war developed out of "sectarian violence" (conflicts among sects of the same religion) as Sunnis (and their foreign supporters) fueled an insurgency against the new government and its foreign supporters, including the United States. The civil war was evident by 2006. Shiites retaliated against Sunni attacks and a history of Sunni privilege and perceived discrimination against Shiites, as Shiite militias engaged in ethnic (sectarian) cleansing of their own. The situation remains unresolved as of this writing.

### Prejudice and Discrimination

Ethnic conflict often arises in reaction to prejudice (attitudes and judgments) or discrimination (action). **Prejudice** means devaluing (looking down on) a group because of its assumed behavior, values, capabilities, or attributes. People are prejudiced when they hold stereotypes about groups and apply them to individuals. (**Stereotypes** are fixed ideas—often unfavorable—about what the members of a group are like.) Prejudiced people assume that members of the group will act as they are "supposed to act" (according to the stereotype) and interpret a wide range of individual behaviors as evidence of the stereotype. They use this behavior to confirm their stereotype (and low opinion) of the group.

**Discrimination** refers to policies and practices that harm a group and its members. Discrimination may be *de facto* (practiced, but not legally sanctioned) or *de jure* (part of the law). An example of de facto discrimination is the harsher treatment that American minorities (compared with other Americans) tend to get from the police and the judicial system. This unequal treatment isn't legal, but it happens anyway. Segregation in the southern United States and *apartheid* in South Africa provide two examples of de jure discrimination, which no longer are in existence. In both systems, by law, blacks and whites had different rights and privileges. Their social interaction ("mixing") was legally curtailed.

## Chips in the Mosaic

Although the multicultural model is increasingly prominent in North America, ethnic competition and conflict also are evident. There is conflict between newer arrivals, for instance, Central Americans and Koreans, and longer-established ethnic groups, such as African Americans. Ethnic antagonism flared in South-Central Los Angeles in spring 1992 in rioting that followed the acquittal of four white police officers who were tried for the videotaped beating of Rodney King (see Abelmann and Lie 1995).

Angry blacks attacked whites, Koreans, and Latinos. This violence expressed frustration by African Americans about their prospects in an increasingly multicultural society. A *New York Times* CBS News Poll conducted May 8, 1992, just after the Los Angeles riots, found that blacks had a bleaker outlook than whites about the effects of immigration on their lives. Only 23 percent of the blacks felt they had more opportunities than recent immigrants, compared with twice that many whites (Toner 1992).

Korean stores were hard hit during the 1992 riots, and more than a third of the businesses destroyed were Latino-owned. A third of those who died in the riots were Latinos. These mainly recent migrants lacked deep roots to the neighborhood and, as Spanish speakers, faced language barriers (Newman 1992). Many Koreans also had trouble with English.

Koreans interviewed on ABC's *Nightline* on May 6, 1992, recognized that blacks resented them and considered them unfriendly. One man explained, "It's not part of our culture to smile." African Americans interviewed on the same program did complain about Korean unfriendliness. "They come into our neighborhoods and treat us like dirt." These comments suggest a shortcoming of the multicultural perspective: Ethnic groups (blacks here) expect other ethnic groups in the same nation-state to assimilate to some extent to a shared (national) culture. The African Americans' comments invoked a general American value system that includes friendliness, openness, mutual respect, community participation, and "fair play." Los Angeles blacks wanted their Korean neighbors to act more like generalized Americans—and good neighbors.

## Aftermaths of Oppression

Fueling ethnic conflict are such forms of discrimination as genocide, forced assimilation, ethnocide, and cultural colonialism. The most extreme form of ethnic discrimination is **genocide,** the deliberate elimination of a group (such as Jews in Nazi Germany,

Two faces of ethnic difference in the former Soviet empire. A propaganda poster depicts a happy mix of nationalities that make up the population of Kyrgyzstan, Central Asia (top). On September 3, 2004, in Beslan, Russia, two men carry young hostages who managed to escape after Russian special forces entered a school that had been occupied for three days by terrorists, who demanded that Russian troops pull out of Chechnya, a Russian republic with a large Islamic population.

Muslims in Bosnia, or Tutsi in Rwanda) through mass murder. A dominant group may try to destroy the cultures of certain ethnic groups (**ethnocide**) or force them to adopt the dominant culture (*forced assimilation*). Many countries have penalized or banned the language and customs of an ethnic group (including its religious observances). One example of forced assimilation is the anti-Basque campaign that the dictator Francisco Franco (who ruled between 1939 and 1975) waged in Spain. Franco banned Basque books, journals, newspapers, signs, sermons, and tombstones and imposed fines for using the Basque language in schools. His policies led to the formation of a Basque terrorist group and spurred strong nationalist sentiment in the Basque region (Ryan 1990).

A policy of *ethnic expulsion* aims at removing groups who are culturally different from a country. There are many examples, including Bosnia-Herzegovina in the 1990s. Uganda expelled 74,000 Asians in 1972. The neofascist parties of contemporary Western Europe advocate repatriation (expulsion) of immigrant workers (West Indians in England, Algerians in France, and Turks in Germany) (see Friedman 2003; Ryan 1990, p. 9). A policy of expulsion may create **refugees**—people who have been forced (involuntary refugees) or who have chosen (voluntary refugees) to flee a country, to escape persecution or war.

In many countries, colonial nation-building left ethnic strife in its wake. Thus, over a million Hindus and Muslims were killed in the violence that accompanied the division of the Indian subcontinent into India and Pakistan. Problems between Arabs and Jews in Palestine began during the British mandate period.

## ANTHROPOLOGY TODAY

### The Basques

Having maintained a strong ethnic identity, perhaps for millennia, the Basques of France and Spain are linguistically unique; their language is unrelated to any other known language. Their homeland lies in the western Pyrenees Mountains, straddling the French–Spanish border (Figure 17-3). Of the seven Basque provinces, three are in France and four are in Spain. Although these provinces have not been unified politically for nearly a millennium, the Basques remain one of Europe's most distinctive ethnic groups.

The French Revolution of 1789 ended the political autonomy of the three Basque provinces in France. During the 19th century in Spain the Basques fought on the losing side in two internal wars, yielding

much of their political autonomy in defeat. When the Spanish Civil War broke out in 1936 the Basques remained loyal to the republic, opposing the Spanish dictator, Francisco Franco, who eventually defeated them. Under Franco's rule (1936–1975), Basques were executed, imprisoned, and exiled, and Basque culture was systematically repressed.

In the late 1950s disaffected Basque youths founded ETA (*Euskadi Ta Azkatasuna*, or "Basque Country and Freedom"). Its goal was complete independence from Spain (Zulaika 1988). The ETA's opposition to Franco escalated into violence, which continued thereafter, diminishing in recent years. Effective March 24, 2006, the leaders of ETA announced a cease-fire, which held through early 2007. They planned thereafter to seek full

Multiculturalism may be growing in the United States and Canada, but the opposite is happening in the former Soviet Union, where ethnic groups (nationalities) want their own nation-states. The flowering of ethnic feeling and conflict as the Soviet empire disintegrated illustrates that years of political repression and ideology provide insufficient common ground for lasting unity. **Cultural colonialism** refers to internal domination—by one group and its culture or ideology over others. One example is the domination over the former Soviet empire by Russian people, language, and culture, and by communist ideology. The dominant culture makes itself the official culture. This is reflected in schools, the media, and public interaction. Under Soviet rule ethnic minorities had very limited self-rule in republics and regions controlled by Moscow. All the republics and their peoples were to be united by the oneness of "socialist internationalism." One common technique in cultural colonialism is to flood ethnic areas with members of the dominant ethnic group. Thus, in the former Soviet Union, ethnic Russian colonists were sent to many areas, to diminish the cohesion and clout of the local people.

The Commonwealth of Independent States (CIS), founded in 1991 and headquartered in Minsk, Belarus, is what remains of the once-powerful Soviet Union (see Yurchak 2005). In Russia and other formerly Soviet nations, ethnic groups (nationalities) have sought, and continue to seek, to forge separate and viable nation-states based on cultural boundaries. This celebration of ethnic autonomy is part of an ethnic florescence that—as surely as globalization and transnationalism—is a trend of the late 20th and early 21st centuries.

independence from Spain through the political process.

Franco's death in 1975 had ushered in an era of democracy in Spain. Mainline Basque nationalists collaborated in framing a new constitution which gave considerable autonomy to the Basque regions (Trask 1996).

Since 1979 three Spanish Basque provinces have been united as the more or less self-governing Basque Autonomous Region. The Basque language is co-official with Spanish in this territory. Spain's fourth Basque province, Navarra, formed its own autonomous region, where the Basque language has a degree of official standing. In France, like other regional languages, Basque has been victimized for centuries by laws hostile to languages other than French (Trask 1996).

After generations of decline, the number of Basque speakers is increasing today. Much education, publishing, and broadcasting now proceeds in Basque in the Autonomous Region. Still, Basque faces the same pressures that all other minority languages do: Knowledge of the national language (Spanish or French) is essential, and most education, publishing, and broadcasting is in the national language (Trask 1996).

How long have the Basques been in their homeland? Archaeological evidence suggests that a single group of people lived in the Basque country continuously from late Paleolithic times through the Bronze Age (about 3,000 years ago). There is no evidence to suggest that any new population entered the area after that (La Fraugh n.d.).

*Continued*

# ANTHROPOLOGY TODAY

**FIGURE 17-3** *Location of the Basque homeland*

Historically the Basques have been farmers, herders, and fishers. (Today most of them work in business and industry.) The Basque *basseria* (family farm) once thrived as a mixed-farming unit emphasizing self-sufficiency. The farm family grew wheat, corn, vegetables, fruits, and nuts and raised poultry, rabbits, pigs, cows, and sheep. Subsistence pursuits increasingly have been commercialized, with the production of vegetables, dairy products, and fish aimed at urban markets (Greenwood 1976).

Basque immigrants originally entered North America as either Spanish or French nationals. Basque Americans, numbering some 50,000, now invoke Basqueness as their primary ethnic identity. They are concentrated in California, Idaho, and Nevada. First-generation immigrants usually are fluent in Basque. They are more likely to be bilingual in Basque and English than to have their parents' fluency in Spanish or French (Douglass 1992).

Building on a traditional occupation in Basque country, Basques in the United States are notable for their identification with sheepherding (see Ott 1981). Most of them settled and worked in the open-range livestock districts of the 13 states of the American West. Basques were among the Spanish soldiers, explorers, missionaries, and administrators in the American Southwest and Spanish California. More Basques came during the California gold rush, many from southern South America, where they were established sheepherders (Douglass 1992).

Restrictive immigration laws enacted in the 1920s, which had an anti-southern European bias, limited Basque immigration to the United States. During World War II, with the country in need of shepherds, the U.S. government exempted Basque herders from immigration quotas. Between 1950 and 1975, several thousand Basques entered the United States on three-year contracts. Later, the decline of the U.S. sheep industry would slow Basque immigration dramatically (Douglass 1992).

Catering to Basque sheepherders, western towns had one or more Basque boardinghouses. The typical one had a bar and a dining room, where meals were served family-style at long tables. A second floor of sleeping rooms was reserved for permanent boarders. Also lodged were herders in town for a brief visit, vacation, or employment layoff or in transit to an employer (Echeverria 1999).

Initially, few Basques came to the United States intending to stay. Most early immigrants were young, unmarried men. Their herding pattern, with solitary summers in the mountains, did not fit well with family life. Eventually, Basque men came with the intent to stay. They either sent back or went back to Europe for brides (few married non-Basques). Many brides, of the "mail order" sort, were sisters or cousins of an acquaintance made in the United States. Basque boardinghouses also became a source of spouses. The boardinghouse owners sent back to Europe for women willing to come to America as domestics. Few remained single for long (Douglass 1992). In these ways Basque Americans drew on their homeland society and culture in establishing the basis of their family and community life in North America.

Basques have not escaped discrimination in the United States. In the American West, sheepherding is an occupation that carries some stigma. Mobile sheepherders competed with settled livestock interests for access to the range. These were some of the sources of anti-Basque sentiment and even legislation. More recently, newspaper coverage of enduring conflict in the Basque country, particularly the activities of the ETA, has made Basque Americans sensitive to the possible charge of being terrorist sympathizers (Douglass 1992; see also Zulaika 1988).

## Summary

1. An ethnic group refers to members of a particular culture in a nation or region that contains others. Ethnicity is based on actual, perceived, or assumed cultural similarities (among members of the same ethnic group) and differences (between that group and others). Ethnic distinctions can be based on language, religion, history, geography, kinship, or race. A race is an ethnic group assumed to have a biological basis. Usually race and ethnicity are ascribed statuses; people are born members of a group and remain so all their lives.

2. Race is a cultural category, not a biological reality. Races derive from contrasts perceived in particular societies, rather than from scientific classifications based on common genes. In the United States racial labels such as "white" and "black" designate socially constructed races—categories defined by American culture. American racial classification, governed by the rule of hypodescent, is based neither on phenotype nor genes. Children of mixed unions, no matter what their appearance, are classified with the minority group parent.

3. Racial attitudes in Japan illustrate intrinsic racism—the belief that a perceived racial difference is a sufficient reason to value one person less than another. The valued group is majority (pure) Japanese, who are believed to share the same blood. Majority Japanese define themselves by opposition to others, such as Koreans and burakumin. These may be minority groups in Japan or outsiders—anyone who is "not us."

4. Such exclusionary racial systems are not inevitable. Although Brazil shares a history of slavery with the United States, it lacks the hypodescent rule. Brazilian racial identity is more of an achieved status. It can change during someone's lifetime, reflecting phenotypical changes. Given the correlation between poverty and dark skin, the class structure affects Brazilian racial classification. Someone with light skin who is poor will be classified as darker than a comparably colored person who is rich.

5. The term *nation* once was synonymous with *ethnic group*. Now nation has come to mean a state—a centrally organized political unit. Because of migration, conquest, and colonialism, most nation-states are not ethnically homogeneous. Ethnic groups that seek autonomous political status (their own country) are nationalities. Political upheavals, wars, and migrations have divided many imagined national communities.

6. Assimilation describes the process of change an ethnic group may experience when it moves to a country where another culture dominates. By assimilating, the minority adopts the patterns and norms of its host culture. Assimilation isn't inevitable, and there can be ethnic harmony without it. A plural society combines ethnic contrasts and economic interdependence between ethnic groups. The view of cultural diversity in a nation-state as good and desirable is multiculturalism. A multicultural society socializes individuals not only into the dominant (national) culture but also into an ethnic one.

7. Ethnicity can be expressed in peaceful multiculturalism, or in discrimination or violent confrontation. Ethnic conflict often arises in reaction to prejudice

(attitudes and judgments) or discrimination (action). The most extreme form of ethnic discrimination is genocide, the deliberate elimination of a group through mass murder. A dominant group may try to destroy certain ethnic practices (ethnocide), or to force ethnic group members to adopt the dominant culture (forced assimilation). A policy of ethnic expulsion may create refugees. Cultural colonialism refers to internal domination—by one group and its culture or ideology over others.

## KEY TERMS

assimilation (p. 381)
cultural colonialism (p. 389)
descent (p. 374)
discrimination (p. 386)
ethnic group (p. 370)
ethnicity (p. 370)
ethnocide (p. 388)
genocide (p. 386)
hypodescent (p. 374)
majority groups (p. 373)
minority groups (p. 373)
multiculturalism (p. 382)

nation (p. 380)
nation-state (p. 380)
nationalities (p. 381)
phenotype (p. 378)
plural society (p. 382)
prejudice (p. 385)
race (p. 373)
racism (p. 373)
refugees (p. 388)
social races (p. 374)
stereotypes (p. 385)

# CHAPTER 18

# APPLYING ANTHROPOLOGY

Applied anthropology is one of two dimensions of anthropology, the other being theoretical/academic anthropology. Applied, or *practical,* anthropology is the use of anthropological data, perspectives, theory, and methods to identify, assess, and solve contemporary problems involving human behavior and social and cultural forces, conditions, and contexts. For example, medical anthropologists have worked as cultural interpreters in public health programs, so as to facilitate their fit into local culture. Many applied anthropologists have worked for or with international development agencies, such as the World Bank and the U.S. Agency for International Development (USAID). In North America, garbologists help the Environmental Protection Agency, the paper industry, and packaging and trade associations. Archaeology is applied as well in cultural resource management and historic preservation. Biological anthropologists work in public health, nutrition, genetic counseling, substance abuse, epidemiology, aging, and mental illness. Forensic anthropologists work with the police, medical examiners, the courts, and international organizations to identify victims of crimes, accidents, wars, and terrorism. Linguistic anthropologists study physician–patient interactions and show how dialect differences influence classroom learning. The goal of most applied anthropologists is to find humane and effective ways of helping local people.

One of the most valuable tools in applying anthropology is the ethnographic method. Ethnographers study societies firsthand, living with and learning from ordinary people. Ethnographers are participant observers, taking part in the events they study in order to understand local thought and behavior. Applied anthropologists use ethnographic techniques in both foreign and domestic settings. Other "expert" participants in social-change programs may be content to converse with officials, read reports, and copy statistics. However, the applied anthropologist's likely early request is some variant of "take me to the local people." We know that people must play an active role in the changes that affect them and that "the people" have information "the experts" lack.

Anthropological theory, the body of findings and generalizations of the four subfields, also guides applied anthropology. Anthropology's holistic perspective—its interest in biology, society, culture, and language—permits the evaluation of many issues that affect people. Theory aids practice, and application fuels theory. As we compare social-change policy and programs, our understanding of cause and effect increases. We add new generalizations about culture change to those discovered in traditional and ancient cultures.

## ✦ THE ROLE OF THE APPLIED ANTHROPOLOGIST

### Early Applications

Application was a central concern of early anthropology in Great Britain (in the context of colonialism) and the United States (in the context of Native American policy). Before turning to the new, we should consider some dangers of the old. For the British empire, specifically its African colonies, Malinowski (1929) proposed that "practical anthropology" (his term for colonial applied anthropology) should focus on westernization, the diffusion of European culture into tribal societies. Malinowski questioned neither the legitimacy of colonialism nor the anthropologist's role in making it work. He saw nothing wrong with aiding colonial regimes by studying land tenure and land use, to recommend how much of their land local people should be allowed to keep and how much Europeans should get. Malinowski's views exemplify a historical association between early anthropology, particularly in Europe, and colonialism (Maquet 1964).

During World War II, American anthropologists studied Japanese and German "culture at a distance" in an attempt to predict the behavior of the enemies of the United States. After that war, applied anthropologists worked on Pacific islands to promote local-level cooperation with American policies in various trust territories.

### Academic and Applied Anthropology

Applied anthropology did not disappear during the 1950s and 1960s, but academic anthropology did most of the growing after World War II. The baby boom, which began in 1946 and peaked in 1957, fueled expansion of the American educational system and thus of academic jobs. New junior, community, and four-year colleges opened, and anthropology became a standard part of the college curriculum. During the 1950s and 1960s, most American anthropologists were college professors, although some still worked in agencies and museums.

This era of academic anthropology continued through the early 1970s. Especially during the Vietnam War, undergraduates flocked to anthropology classes to learn about other cultures. Students were especially interested in Southeast Asia, whose indigenous societies were being disrupted by war. Many anthropologists protested the superpowers' apparent disregard for non-Western lives, values, customs, and social systems.

During the 1970s, and increasingly thereafter, although most anthropologists still worked in academia, others found jobs with international organizations, government, business, hospitals, and schools. This shift toward application, though only partial, has benefited the profession. It has forced anthropologists to consider the wider social value and implications of their research.

## Applied Anthropology Today

Today, most applied anthropologists see their work as radically removed from the colonial perspective. Modern applied anthropology usually is seen as a helping profession, devoted to assisting local people, as anthropologists speak up for the disenfranchised in the international political arena. However, applied anthropologists also solve problems for clients who are neither poor nor powerless. Applied anthropologists working for businesses try to solve the problem of expanding profits for their employer or client. In market research, ethical issues may arise as anthropologists attempt to help companies operate more efficiently and profitably. Ethical ambiguities are present as well in cultural resource management (CRM), in deciding how to preserve significant remains and information when sites are threatened by development or public works. A CRM firm typically is hired by someone seeking to build a road or a factory. In such cases, the client may have a strong interest in an outcome in which no sites are found that need protecting. Contemporary applied anthropologists still face ethical questions: To whom does the researcher owe loyalty? What problems are involved in holding firm to the truth? What happens when applied anthropologists don't make the policies they have to implement? How does one criticize programs in which one has participated (see Escobar 1991, 1994)? Anthropology's professional organizations have addressed such questions by establishing codes of ethics and ethics committees. See http://www.aaanet. org for the Code of Ethics of the AAA. As Tice (1997) notes, attention to ethical issues is paramount in the teaching of applied anthropology today.

By instilling an appreciation for human diversity, the entire field of anthropology combats *ethnocentrism*—the tendency to view one's own culture as superior and to use one's own cultural values in judging the behavior and beliefs of people raised in other societies. This broadening, educational role affects the knowledge, values, and attitudes of people exposed to anthropology. This chapter focuses specifically on this question: What specific contributions can anthropology make in identifying and solving problems stirred up by contemporary currents of economic, social, and cultural change, including globalization?

Because anthropologists are experts on human problems and social change and because they study, understand, and respect cultural values, they are highly qualified to suggest, plan, and implement policy affecting people. Proper roles for applied anthropologists include (1) identifying needs for change that local people perceive, (2) working with those people to design culturally appropriate and socially sensitive change, and (3) protecting local people from harmful policies and projects that may threaten them.

Anthropology's systemic perspective recognizes that changes don't occur in a vacuum. A program or project always has multiple effects, some of which are unforeseen. In an American example of unintended consequences, a program aimed at enhancing teachers' appreciation of cultural differences led to ethnic stereotyping (Kleinfield 1975). Specifically, Native American students did not welcome teachers' frequent comments about their Indian heritage. The students felt set apart from their classmates and saw this attention to their ethnicity as patronizing and demeaning. Internationally, dozens of economic development projects intended to increase productivity through irrigation have worsened public health by creating waterways where diseases thrive.

# ✦ DEVELOPMENT ANTHROPOLOGY

**Development anthropology** is the branch of applied anthropology that focuses on social issues in, and the cultural dimension of, economic development. Development anthropologists do not just carry out development policies planned by others; they also plan and guide policy. (For more detailed discussions of issues in development anthropology, see Edelman and Haugerud 2004; Escobar 1995; Ferguson 1995; Nolan 2002; and Robertson 1995.)

However, ethical dilemmas often confront development anthropologists (Escobar 1991, 1995). Our respect for cultural diversity often is offended because efforts to extend industry and technology may entail profound cultural changes. Foreign aid usually doesn't go where need and suffering are greatest. It is spent on political, economic, and strategic priorities as international donors, political leaders and powerful interest groups perceive them. Planners' interests don't always coincide with the best interests of the local people. Although the aim of most development projects is to enhance the quality of life, living standards often decline in the target area (Bodley, ed. 1988).

## Equity

A commonly stated goal of recent development policy is to promote equity. **Increased equity** means reduced poverty and a more even distribution of wealth. However, if projects are to increase equity, they must have the support of reform-minded governments. Wealthy and powerful people typically resist projects that threaten their vested interests.

Some types of development projects, particularly irrigation schemes, are more likely than others to widen wealth disparities, that is, to have a negative equity impact. An initial uneven distribution of resources (particularly land) often becomes the basis for greater skewing after the project. The social impact of new technology tends to be more severe, contributing negatively to quality of life and to equity, when inputs are channeled to or through the rich.

Many fisheries projects also have had negative equity results (see Durrenberger and King, eds. 2000). In Bahia, Brazil (Kottak 2006), sailboat owners (but not nonowners) got loans to buy motors for their boats. To repay the loans, the owners increased the percentage of the catch they took from the men who fished in their boats. Over the years, they used their rising profits to buy larger and more expensive boats. The result was stratification—the creation of a group of wealthy people within a formerly egalitarian community. These events hampered individual initiative and interfered with further development of the fishing industry. With new boats so expensive, ambitious young men who once would have sought careers in fishing no longer had any way to obtain their own boats. They sought wage labor on land instead. To avoid such results, credit-granting agencies must seek out enterprising young fishers rather than giving loans only to owners and established businesspeople.

## ✦ STRATEGIES FOR INNOVATION

Development anthropologists, who are concerned with social issues in, and the cultural dimension of, economic development, must work closely with local people to assess and help them realize their own wishes and needs for change. Too many true local needs cry out for a solution to waste money funding development projects in area A that are inappropriate there but needed in area B, or that are unnecessary anywhere. Development anthropology can help sort out the needs of the As and Bs and fit projects accordingly. Projects that put people first by consulting with them and responding to their expressed needs must be identified (Cernea, ed. 1991). Thereafter, development anthropologists can work to ensure socially compatible ways of implementing a good project.

In a comparative study of 68 rural development projects from all around the world, I found the *culturally compatible* economic development projects to be twice as successful financially as the incompatible ones (Kottak 1990*b,* 1991). This finding shows that using anthropological expertise in planning to ensure cultural compatibility is cost effective. To maximize social and economic benefits, projects must (1) be culturally compatible, (2) respond to locally perceived needs, (3) involve men and women in planning and carrying out the changes that affect them, (4) harness traditional organizations, and (5) be flexible.

## Overinnovation

In my comparative study, the compatible and successful projects avoided the fallacy of **overinnovation** (too much change). We would expect people to resist development projects that require major changes in their daily lives. People usually want to change just enough to keep what they have. Motives for modifying behavior come from the traditional culture and the small concerns of ordinary life. Peasants' values are not such abstract ones as "learning a better way," "progressing," "increasing technical know-how," "improving efficiency," or "adopting modern techniques." (Those phrases exemplify intervention philosophy.)

Instead, their objectives are down-to-earth and specific ones. People want to improve yields in a rice field, amass resources for a ceremony, get a child through school, or have enough cash to pay the tax bill. The goals and values of subsistence producers differ from those of people who produce for cash, just as they differ from the intervention philosophy of development planners. Different value systems must be considered during planning.

In the comparative study, the projects that failed were usually both economically and culturally incompatible. For example, one South Asian project promoted the cultivation of onions and peppers, expecting this practice to fit into a preexisting labor-intensive

To maximize benefits, development projects should respond to locally perceived needs. Shown here (foreground) is the president of a Nicaraguan cooperative that makes and markets hammocks. This cooperative has been assisted by an NGO whose goals include increasing the benefits that women derive from economic development. What's an NGO?

system of rice-growing. Cultivation of these cash crops wasn't traditional in the area. It conflicted with existing crop priorities and other interests of farmers. Also, the labor peaks for pepper and onion production coincided with those for rice, to which the farmers gave priority.

Throughout the world, project problems have arisen from inadequate attention to, and consequent lack of fit with, local culture. Another naive and incompatible project was an overinnovative scheme in Ethiopia. Its major fallacy was to try to convert nomadic herders into sedentary cultivators. It ignored traditional land rights. Outsiders—commercial farmers—were to get much of the herders' territory. The pastoralists were expected to settle down and start farming. This project helped wealthy outsiders instead of the local people. The planners naively expected free-ranging herders to give up a generations-old way of life to work three times harder growing rice and picking cotton for bosses.

## Underdifferentiation

The fallacy of **underdifferentiation** is the tendency to view "the less-developed countries" as more alike than they are. Development agencies have often ignored cultural diversity (e.g., between Brazil and Burundi) and adopted a uniform approach to deal with very different sets of people. Neglecting cultural diversity, many projects also have tried to impose incompatible property notions and social units. Most often, the faulty social design assumes either (1) individualistic productive units that are privately owned by an individual or couple and worked by a nuclear family or (2) cooperatives that are at least partially based on models from the former Eastern bloc and Socialist countries.

One example of faulty Euro-American models (the individual and the nuclear family) was a West African project designed for an area where the extended family was the basic social unit. The project succeeded despite its faulty social design because the participants used their traditional extended family networks to attract additional settlers. Eventually, twice as many people as planned benefited as extended family members flocked to the project area. Here, settlers modified the project design that had been imposed on them by following the principles of their traditional society.

The second dubious foreign social model that is common in development strategy is the cooperative. In the comparative study of rural development projects, new cooperatives fared badly. Cooperatives succeeded only when they harnessed preexisting local-level communal institutions. This is a corollary of a more general rule: Participants' groups are most effective when they are based on traditional social organization or on a socioeconomic similarity among members.

Neither foreign social model—the nuclear family farm nor the cooperative—has an unblemished record in development. An alternative is needed: greater use of Third World social models for Third World development. These are traditional social units, such as the clans, lineages, and other extended kin groups of Africa, Oceania, and many other nations, with their communally held estates and resources. The most humane and productive strategy for change is to base the social design for innovation on traditional social forms in each target area.

## Third World Models

Many governments are not genuinely, or realistically, committed to improving the lives of their citizens. Interference by major powers has also kept governments from enacting needed reforms. In some nations, however, the government acts more as an agent of the people. Madagascar provides an example. The people of Madagascar, the Malagasy, had been organized into descent groups before the origin of the state. The Merina, creators of the major precolonial state of Madagascar, wove descent groups into its structure, making members of important groups advisers to the king and thus giving them authority in government. The Merina state made provisions for the people it ruled. It collected taxes and organized labor for public works projects. In return, it redistributed resources to peasants in need. It also granted them some protection against war and slave raids and allowed them to cultivate their rice fields in peace. The government maintained the water works for rice cultivation. It opened to ambitious peasant boys the chance of becoming, through hard work and study, state bureaucrats.

Throughout the history of the Merina state—and continuing in modern Madagascar—there have been strong relationships between the individual, the descent group, and the state. Local Malagasy communities, where residence is based on descent, are more cohesive and homogeneous than are communities in Latin America or North America. Madagascar gained political independence from France in 1960. Although it was still economically dependent on France when I first did research there in 1966–1967, the new government had an economic development policy aimed at increasing the ability of the Malagasy to feed themselves. Government policy emphasized increased production of rice, a subsistence crop, rather than cash crops. Furthermore, local communities, with their traditional cooperative patterns and solidarity based on kinship and descent, were treated as partners in, not obstacles to, the development process.

In a sense, the descent group is preadapted to equitable national development. In Madagascar, members of local descent groups have customarily pooled their resources to educate their ambitious members. Once educated, these men and women gain economically secure positions in the nation. They then share the advantages of their new positions with their kin. For example, they give room and board to rural cousins attending school and help them find jobs.

Malagasy administrations appear generally to have shared a commitment to democratic economic development. Perhaps this is because government officials are of the peasantry or have strong personal ties to it. By contrast, in Latin American countries, the elites and the lower class have different origins and no strong connections through kinship, descent, or marriage.

Furthermore, societies with descent-group organization contradict an assumption that many social scientists and economists seem to make. It is not inevitable that as nations become more tied to the world capitalist economy, native forms of social organization will break down into nuclear family organization, impersonality, and alienation. Descent groups, with their traditional communalism and corporate solidarity, have important roles to play in economic development.

Realistic development promotes change but not overinnovation. Many changes are possible if the aim is to preserve local systems while making them work better. Successful economic development projects respect, or at least don't attack, local cultural patterns. Effective development draws on indigenous cultural practices and social structures.

## ✦ ANTHROPOLOGY AND EDUCATION

Attention to culture also is fundamental to **anthropology and education,** involving research that extends from classrooms into homes, neighborhoods, and communities (see Spindler, ed. 2000, 2005). In classrooms, anthropologists have observed interactions among teachers, students, parents, and visitors. Jules Henry's classic account of the American elementary school classroom (1955) shows how students learn to conform to and compete with their peers. Anthropologists view children as total cultural creatures whose enculturation and attitudes toward education belong to a context that includes family and peers.

Sociolinguists and cultural anthropologists work side by side in education research. For example, in a study of Puerto Rican seventh-graders in the urban Midwest (Hill-Burnett 1978), anthropologists uncovered some misconceptions held by teachers. The teachers mistakenly had assumed that Puerto Rican parents valued education less than did non-Hispanics, but in-depth interviews revealed that the Puerto Rican parents valued it more.

In Peshawar, Pakistan, young boys receive instruction. What do you see here that differs from classrooms in your country?

The anthropologists also found that certain practices were preventing Hispanics from being adequately educated. For example, the teachers' union and the board of education had agreed to teach "English as a foreign language." However, they had provided no bilingual teachers to work with Spanish-speaking students. The school was assigning all students (including non-Hispanics) with low reading scores and behavior problems to the English-as-a-foreign-language classroom. This educational disaster brought together in the classroom a teacher who spoke no Spanish, children who barely spoke English, and a group of English-speaking students with reading and behavior problems. The Spanish speakers were falling behind not just in reading but in all subjects. They could at least have kept up in the other subjects if a Spanish speaker had been teaching them science, social studies, and math until they were ready for English-language instruction in those areas.

## ✦ URBAN ANTHROPOLOGY

Alan and Josephine Smart (2003) note that cities have long been influenced by global forces, including world capitalism and colonialism. However, the roles of cities in the world system have changed recently as a result of the time-space compression made possible by modern transportation and communication systems. That is, everything appears closer today because contact and movement are so much easier.

In the context of contemporary globalization, the mass media can become as important as local factors in guiding daily routines, dreams, and aspirations. People live in particular places, but their imaginations and attachments don't have to be locally confined (Appadurai 1996). Citizens of the semiperiphery and periphery migrate to cities of the core partly for economic reasons, but also to be where the action is. People seek experiences available only in cities, such as live theater or busy streets. Rural Brazilians routinely cite *movimento,* urban movement and excitement, as something to be valued. International migrants tend to settle in the largest cities, where the most is happening. For example, in Canada, which, after Australia, has the highest percentage of foreign-born population, 71.2 percent of immigrants settled in Toronto, Vancouver, or Montreal. Nearly half of Toronto's citizens were born outside Canada (Smart and Smart 2003).

The proportion of the world's population living in cities has been increasing ever since the Industrial Revolution. Only about 3 percent of people were city dwellers in 1800, compared with 13 percent in 1900, over 40 percent in 1980, and about 50 percent today (see Smart and Smart 2003). The More Developed Countries (MDCs) were 76 percent urbanized in 1999, compared with 39 percent for the Less Developed Countries (LDCs). However, the urbanization growth rate is much faster in the LDCs (Smart and Smart 2003). The world had only 16 cities with more than a million people in 1900, but there were 314 such cities in 2005. By 2025, 60 percent of the global population will be urban (Butler 2005; Stevens 1992).

About 1 billion people, one-sixth of Earth's population, live in urban slums, mostly without water, sanitation, public services, and legal security (Vidal 2003). If current trends continue, urban population increase and the concentration of people in slums will be accompanied by rising rates of crime, along with water, air, and noise pollution. These problems will be most severe in the LDCs.

As industrialization and urbanization spread globally, anthropologists increasingly study these processes and the social problems they create. **Urban anthropology,** which has theoretical (basic research) and applied dimensions, is the cross-cultural and ethnographic study of global urbanization and life in cities (see Aoyagi, Nas, and Traphagan, eds. 1998; Gmelch and Zenner, eds. 2002; Smart and Smart 2003; Stevenson 2003). The United States and Canada have become popular arenas for urban anthropological research on topics such as immigration, ethnicity, poverty, class, and urban violence (Mullings, ed. 1987; Vigil 2003).

## Urban versus Rural

Recognizing that a city is a social context that is very different from a tribal or peasant village, an early student of urbanization, the anthropologist Robert Redfield, focused on contrasts between rural and urban life. He contrasted rural communities, whose social relations are on a face-to-face basis, with cities, where impersonality characterizes many aspects of life. Redfield (1941) proposed that urbanization be studied along a rural–urban continuum. He described differences in values and social relations in four sites that spanned such a continuum. In Mexico's Yucatán peninsula, Redfield compared an isolated Maya-speaking Indian community, a rural peasant village, a small provincial city, and a large capital. Several studies in Africa (Little 1971) and Asia were influenced by Redfield's view that cities are centers through which cultural innovations spread to rural and tribal areas.

In any nation, urban and rural represent different social systems. However, cultural diffusion or borrowing occurs as people, products, images, and messages move from one to the other. Migrants bring rural practices and beliefs to cities and take urban patterns back home. The experiences and social forms of the rural area affect adaptation to city life. City folk also develop new institutions to meet specific urban needs (Mitchell 1966).

An applied anthropology approach to urban planning would start by identifying key social groups in the urban context. After identifying those groups, the anthropologist might elicit their wishes for change, convey those needs to funding agencies, and work with agencies and local people to realize those goals. In Africa relevant groups might include ethnic associations, occupational groups, social clubs, religious groups, and burial societies. Through membership in such groups, urban Africans maintain wide networks of personal contacts and support (Banton 1957; Little 1965). These groups also have links with, and provide cash support and urban lodging for, their rural relatives. Sometimes such groups think of themselves as a gigantic kin group, a clan that includes urban and rural members. Members may call one another "brother" and "sister." As in an extended family, rich members help their poor relatives. A member's improper behavior can lead to expulsion—an unhappy fate for a migrant in a large ethnically heterogeneous city.

One role for the urban applied anthropologist is to help relevant social groups deal with urban institutions, such as legal and social services, with which recent migrants may be unfamiliar. In certain North American cities, as in Africa, kin-based ethnic associations are relevant urban groups. One example comes from Los Angeles, which has the largest Samoan immigrant community (over 12,000 people) in the United States. Samoans in Los Angeles draw on their traditional system of *matai* (*matai* means "chief"; the matai system now refers to respect for elders) to deal with modern urban problems. One example: In 1992, a white police officer shot and killed two unarmed Samoan brothers. When a judge dismissed charges against the officer, local leaders used the matai system to calm angry youths (who have formed gangs, like other ethnic groups in the Los Angeles area). Clan leaders and elders organized a well-attended community meeting, in which they urged young members to be patient. The Samoans then used the American judicial system. They brought a civil case against the officer in question and pressed the U.S. Justice Department to initiate a civil rights case in the matter (Mydans 1992*b*). Not all conflicts involving gangs and law enforcement end so peacefully.

James Vigil (2003) examines gang violence in the context of large-scale immigrant adaptation to American cities. He notes that most gangs prior to the 1970s were located in white ethnic enclaves in Eastern and Midwestern cities. Back then, gang incidents typically were brawls involving fists, sticks, and knives. Today, gangs more often are composed of nonwhite ethnic groups, and handguns have replaced the less lethal weapons of the past. Gangs still consist mostly of male adolescents who have grown up together, usually in a low-income neighborhood, where it's estimated that about 10 percent of young men join gangs. Female gang members are much rarer—from 4 to 15 percent of gang members. With gangs organized hierarchically by age, older members push younger ones (usually 14- to 18-year-olds) to carry out violent acts against rivals (Vigil 2003).

In Ghana, a police officer talks to street children about their rights. In cities around the world, applied anthropologists work with formal and informal associations, including gangs, clubs, and youth groups.

The populations that include most of today's gang members settled originally in poorer urban areas. On the East Coast these usually were rundown neighborhoods where a criminal lifestyle already was present. Around Los Angeles, urban migrants created squatterlike settlements in previously empty spaces. Immigrants tend to reside in neighborhoods apart from middle-class people, thus limiting their opportunities for integration. Confined in this manner, and facing residential overcrowding, poor people often experience frustration, which can lead to aggressive acts (Vigil 2003). As well, industries and jobs have moved from inner cities to distant suburbs and foreign nations. Urban minority youth have limited access to entry-level jobs; often they receive harsh treatment from authorities, especially law enforcement. Frustration and competition over resources can spark aggressive incidents, fueling urban violence. For survival, many residents of abandoned neighborhoods have turned to informal and illegal economic arrangements, of which drug trafficking in particular has heightened gang violence (Vigil 2003). How might an applied anthropologist approach the problem of urban violence? Which groups would be need to be involved in the study?

## ✦ MEDICAL ANTHROPOLOGY

**Medical anthropology** is both academic/theoretical and applied/practical and includes anthropologists from all four subfields (see Anderson 1996; Briggs 2005; Brown 1998; Dressler et al. 2005; Joralemon 1999). Medical anthropologists examine such questions as which diseases and health conditions affect particular populations (and why) and how illness is socially constructed, diagnosed, managed, and treated in various societies.

**Disease** refers to a scientifically identified health threat caused genetically or by a bacterium, virus, fungus, parasite, or other pathogen. **Illness** is a condition of poor health perceived or felt by an individual (Inhorn and Brown 1990). Perceptions of good and bad health, along with health threats and problems, are culturally constructed. Various ethnic groups and cultures recognize different illnesses, symptoms, and causes and have developed different health care systems and treatment strategies.

The incidence and severity of *disease* vary as well (see Baer, Singer, and Susser 2003). Group differences are evident in the United States. Keppel, Pearch, and Wagener (2002) examined data between 1990 and 1998 using 10 health status indicators in relation to racial and ethnic categories used in the U.S. census: non-Hispanic white, non-Hispanic black, Hispanic, American Indian or Alaska Native, and Asian or Pacific Islander. Black Americans' rates for six measures (total mortality, heart disease, lung cancer, breast cancer, stroke, and homicide) exceeded those of other groups by a factor ranging from 2.5 to almost 10. Other ethnic groups had higher rates for suicide (white Americans) and motor vehicle accidents (American Indians and Alaskan Natives). Overall, Asians had the longest life spans (see Dressler et al. 2005).

Hurtado and colleagues (2005) note the prevalence of poor health and unusually high rates of early mortality among indigenous populations in South America. Life expectancy at birth is at least 20 years shorter among indigenous groups compared with other South Americans. In 2000, the life expectancy of indigenous peoples in Brazil and Venezuela was lower than that in Sierra Leone, which had the lowest reported national life expectancy in the world (Hurtado et al. 2005).

How can applied anthropologists help ameliorate the large health disparity between indigenous peoples and other populations? Hurtado and colleagues (2005) suggest three steps: (1) Identify the most pressing health problems that indigenous communities face; (2) gather information on solutions to those problems; and (3) implement solutions in partnership with the agencies and organizations that are in charge of public health programs for indigenous populations.

In many areas, the world system and colonialism worsened the health of indigenous peoples by spreading diseases, warfare, servitude, and other stressors. Traditionally and in ancient times, hunter-gatherers, because of their small numbers, mobility, and relative isolation from other groups, lacked most of the epidemic infectious diseases that affect agrarian and urban societies (Cohen and Armelagos, eds. 1984; Inhorn and Brown 1990). Epidemic diseases such as cholera, typhoid, and bubonic plague thrive in dense populations, and thus among farmers and city dwellers. The spread of malaria has been linked to population growth and deforestation associated with food production.

Certain diseases, and physical conditions such as obesity, have spread with economic development and globalization (Ulijaszek and Lofink 2006). *Schistosomiasis* or bilharzia (liver flukes) is probably the fastest-spreading and most dangerous parasitic infection now known. It is propagated by snails that live in ponds, lakes, and waterways, usually ones created by irrigation projects. A study done in a Nile Delta village in Egypt (Farooq 1966) illustrated the role of culture (religion) in the spread of schistosomiasis. The disease was more common among Muslims than among Christians because of an Islamic practice called *wudu,* ritual ablution (bathing) before prayer.

The applied anthropology approach to reducing such diseases is to see if local people perceive a connection between the vector (e.g., snails in the water) and the disease. If not, such information may be provided by enlisting active local groups, schools, and the media.

The highest global rates of HIV infection and AIDS-related deaths are in Africa, especially southern Africa. As it kills productive adults, AIDS leaves behind children and seniors who have difficulty replacing the lost labor force (Baro and Deubel 2006). In southern and eastern Africa, AIDS and other sexually transmitted diseases (STDs) have spread along highways, via encounters between male truckers and female prostitutes. STDs also are spread through prostitution, as young men from rural areas seek wage work in cities, labor camps, and mines. When the men return to their natal villages, they infect their wives (Larson 1989; Miller and Rockwell, eds. 1988). Cities also are prime sites of STD transmission in Europe, Asia, and North and South America (see Baer, Singer, and Susser 2003; French 2002). Cultural factors also affect the spread of HIV, which is less likely to be transmitted when men are circumcised than when they are not.

The kinds of and incidence of disease vary among societies, and cultures interpret and treat illness differently. Standards for sick and healthy bodies are cultural constructions that vary in time and space (Martin 1992). Still, all societies have what George Foster and Barbara Anderson call "disease-theory systems" to identify, classify, and explain illness. According to Foster and Anderson (1978), there are three basic theories about the causes of illness: personalistic, naturalistic, and emotionalistic. *Personalistic disease theories* blame illness on agents, such as sorcerers, witches, ghosts, or ancestral spirits. *Naturalistic disease theories* explain illness in impersonal terms. One example is Western medicine or *biomedicine,* which aims to link illness to scientifically demonstrated agents that bear no personal malice toward their victims. Thus Western medicine attributes illness to organisms (e.g., bacteria, viruses, fungi, or parasites), accidents, toxic materials, or genes.

Other naturalistic ethnomedical systems blame poor health on unbalanced body fluids. Many Latin societies classify food, drink, and environmental conditions as "hot" or "cold." People believe their health suffers when they eat or drink hot or cold substances together or under inappropriate conditions. For example, one shouldn't drink something cold after a hot bath or eat a pineapple (a "cold" fruit) when one is menstruating (a "hot" condition).

*Emotionalistic disease theories* assume that emotional experiences cause illness. For example, Latin Americans may develop *susto,* an illness caused by anxiety or fright (Bolton 1981; Finkler 1985). Its symptoms (lethargy, vagueness, distraction) are similar to those of "soul loss," a diagnosis of similar symptoms made by people in Madagascar. Modern psychoanalysis also focuses on the role of the emotions in physical and psychological well-being.

All societies have **health care systems** consisting of beliefs, customs, specialists, and techniques aimed at ensuring health and at preventing, diagnosing, and curing illness. A society's illness-causation theory is important for treatment. When illness has a personalistic cause, magicoreligious specialists may be good curers. They draw on varied techniques (occult and practical), which comprise their special expertise. A shaman

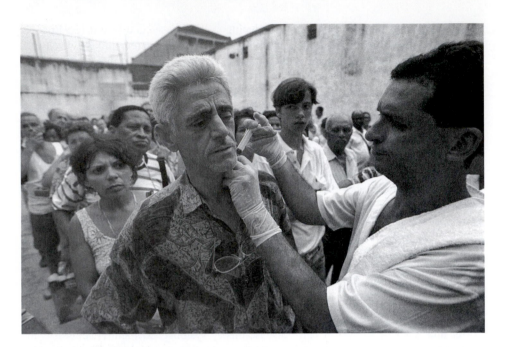

How do Western medicine and scientific medicine differ? Clinics provide antibiotics, minor surgery, and preventive medicine, such as this Brazilian campaign against cholera, through mass injection. What kind of medicine is being shown here? How can it coexist with the local healing system?

may cure soul loss by enticing the spirit back into the body. Shamans may ease difficult childbirths by asking spirits to travel up the birth canal to guide the baby out (Lévi-Strauss 1967). A shaman may cure a cough by counteracting a curse or removing a substance introduced by a sorcerer.

If there is a "world's oldest profession" besides hunter and gatherer, it is **curer,** often a shaman. The curer's role has some universal features (Foster and Anderson 1978). Thus curers emerge through a culturally defined process of selection (parental prodding, inheritance, visions, dream instructions) and training (apprentice shamanship, medical school). Eventually, the curer is certified by older practitioners and acquires a professional image. Patients believe in the skills of the curer, whom they consult and compensate.

We should not lose sight, ethnocentrically, of the difference between **scientific medicine** and Western medicine per se. Despite advances in technology, genomics, molecular biology, pathology, surgery, diagnostics, and applications, many Western medical procedures have little justification in logic or fact. Overprescription of drugs, unnecessary surgery, and the impersonality and inequality of the physician–patient relationship are questionable features of Western medical systems (see Briggs 2005 for linguistic aspects of this inequality). Also, overuse of antibiotics, not just for people but also in animal feed, seems to be triggering an explosion of resistant microrganisms, which may pose a long-term global public health hazard.

Still, biomedicine surpasses tribal treatment in many ways. Although medicines such as quinine, coca, opium, ephedrine, and rauwolfia were discovered in nonindustrial societies, thousands of effective drugs are available today to treat myriad diseases. Preventive health care improved during the twentieth century. Today's surgical procedures are much safer and more effective than those of traditional societies.

But industrialization and globalization have spawned their own health problems. Modern stressors include poor nutrition, dangerous machinery, impersonal work, isolation, poverty, homelessness, substance abuse, and noise, air, and water pollution (see McElroy and Townsend 2003). Health problems in industrial nations are caused as much by economic, social, political, and cultural factors as by pathogens. In modern North America, for example, poverty contributes to many illnesses, including arthritis, heart conditions, back problems, and hearing and vision impairment (see Bailey 2000). Poverty also is a factor in the differential spread of infectious diseases.

In the United States and other developed countries today, good health has become something of an ethical imperative (Foucault 1990). Individuals are expected to regulate their behavior and shape themselves in keeping with new medical knowledge. Those who do so acquire the status of sanitary citizens—people with modern understanding of the body, health, and illness, who practice hygiene, and depend on doctors and nurses when they are sick. People who act differently (e.g., smokers, overeaters, those who avoid doctors) are stigmatized as unsanitary and blamed for their own health problems (Briggs 2005; Foucault 1990).

Even getting an epidemic disease such as cholera or living in an infected neighborhood may be interpreted today as a moral failure. It's assumed that people who are properly informed and act rationally can avoid such "preventable" diseases. Individuals are expected to follow scientifically based imperatives (e.g., "boil water," "don't smoke"). People (e.g., gay men, Haitians, smokers, veterans) can become objects of avoidance and discrimination simply by belonging to a group seen as having a greater risk of getting a particular disease (Briggs 2005).

Medical anthropologists have served as cultural interpreters in public health programs, which must pay attention to local theories about the nature, causes, and treatment of illness. Health interventions cannot simply be forced on communities. They must fit into local cultures and be accepted by local people. When Western medicine is introduced, people usually retain many of their old methods while also accepting new ones (see Green 1987/1992). Native curers may go on treating certain conditions (spirit possession), whereas doctors may deal with others. If both modern and traditional specialists are consulted and the patient is cured, the native curer may get as much or more credit than the physician.

A more personal treatment of illness that emulates the non-Western curer-patient-community relationship could probably benefit Western systems. Western medicine tends to draw a rigid line between biological and psychological causation. Non-Western theories usually lack this sharp distinction, recognizing that poor health has intertwined physical, emotional, and social causes. The mind–body opposition is part of Western folk taxonomy, not of science (see also Brown 1998; Helman 2001; Joralemon 1999; Strathern and Stewart 1999).

Medical anthropologists increasingly are examining the impact of new scientific and medical techniques on ideas about life, death, and *personhood* (what is and is not a person). For decades, disagreements about personhood—about when life begins and ends—have been part of political and religious discussions of contraception, abortion, assisted suicide, and euthanasia (mercy killing). More recent additions to such discussions include stem cell research, frozen embryos, assisted reproduction, genetic screening, cloning, and life-prolonging medical treatments. Ideas about what it means to be human and to be alive or dead are being reformulated. In the United States, the controversy surrounding the death of Terri Schiavo in 2005 brought such questions into public debate. Kaufman and Morgan (2005) emphasize the contrast between what they call low-tech and high-tech births and deaths in today's world. A desperately poor young mother dies of AIDS in Africa while half a world away an American child of privilege is born as the result of a $50,000 in-vitro fertilization procedure. Medical anthropologists increasingly are concerned with new and contrasting conditions that allow humans to enter, live, and depart life, and with how the boundaries of life and death are being questioned and negotiated in the 21st century.

## ✦ ANTHROPOLOGY AND BUSINESS

At a major information technology company, Marietta Baba examines one of the world's fastest super-computers. She is studying that firm's adaptation to the rise of the service economy. Professor Baba, a prominent applied anthropologist and dean of the College of Social Science at Michigan State University, also has studied Michigan's automobile industry.

Carol Taylor (1987) discusses the value of an "anthropologist-in-residence" in a large, complex organization, such as a hospital or a business. A free-ranging ethnographer can be a perceptive oddball when information and decisions usually move through a rigid hierarchy. If allowed to observe and converse freely with all types and levels of personnel, the anthropologist may acquire a unique perspective on organizational conditions and problems. Also, high-tech companies, such as Xerox, IBM, and Apple, have employed anthropologists in various roles. Closely observing how people actually use computer products, anthropologists work with engineers to design products that are more user-friendly.

For many years anthropologists have used ethnography to study business settings (Arensberg 1987; Jordan 2003). For example, ethnographic research in an auto factory may view workers, managers, and executives as different social categories participating in a common social system. Each group has characteristic attitudes, values, and behavior patterns. These are transmitted through *microenculturation,* the process by which people learn particular roles in a limited social system. The free-ranging nature of ethnography takes the anthropologist back and forth from worker to executive. Each is an individual with a personal viewpoint and a cultural creature whose perspective is, to some extent, shared with other members of a group. Applied anthropologists have acted as "cultural brokers," translating managers' goals or workers' concerns to the other group (see Ferraro 2006).

For business, key features of anthropology include (1) ethnography and observation as ways of gathering data, (2) cross-cultural expertise, and (3) focus on cultural diversity. An important business application of anthropology has to do with knowledge of how consumers use products. Businesses hire anthropologists because of the importance of observation in natural settings and the focus on cultural diversity. Thus, Hallmark Cards has hired anthropologists to observe parties, holidays, and celebrations of ethnic groups to improve its ability to design cards for targeted audiences. Anthropologists go into people's homes to see how they actually use products.

---

## ✦ CAREERS AND ANTHROPOLOGY

Many college students find anthropology interesting and consider majoring in it. However, their parents or friends may discourage them by asking, "What kind of job are you going to get with an anthropology major?" The first step in answering this question is to consider the more general question, "What do you do with any college major?" The answer is "Not much, without a good bit of effort, thought, and planning." A survey of graduates of the literary college of the University of Michigan showed that few had jobs that were clearly linked to their majors. Medicine, law, and many other professions require advanced degrees. Although many colleges offer bachelor's degrees in engineering, business, accounting, and social work, master's degrees are often needed to get the best jobs in those fields. Anthropologists, too, need an advanced degree, almost always a Ph.D., to find gainful employment in academic, museum, or applied anthropology.

A broad college education, and even a major in anthropology, can be an excellent foundation for success in many fields. A recent survey of women executives showed that most had not majored in business but in the social sciences or humanities. Only after graduating did they study business, obtaining a master's degree in business administration. These executives felt that the breadth of their college educations had contributed to their business careers. Anthropology majors go on to medical, law, and business schools and find success in many professions that often have little explicit connection to anthropology.

Anthropology's breadth provides knowledge and an outlook on the world that are useful in many kinds of work. For example, an anthropology major combined with a master's degree in business is excellent preparation for work in international business. Breadth is anthropology's hallmark. Anthropologists study people biologically, culturally, socially, and linguistically, across time and space, in developed and underdeveloped nations, in simple and complex settings. Most colleges have anthropology courses that compare cultures and others that focus on particular world areas, such as Latin

America, Asia, and Native North America. The knowledge of foreign areas acquired in such courses can be useful in many jobs. Anthropology's comparative outlook, its longstanding Third World focus, and its appreciation of diverse lifestyles combine to provide an excellent foundation for overseas employment (see Omohundro 2001).

Even for work in North America, the focus on culture is valuable. Every day we hear about cultural differences and about social problems whose solutions require a multicultural viewpoint—an ability to recognize and reconcile ethnic differences. Government, schools, and private firms constantly deal with people from different social classes, ethnic groups, and tribal backgrounds. Physicians, attorneys, social workers, police officers, judges, teachers, and students can all do a better job if they understand social differences in a part of the world such as ours that is one of the most ethnically diverse in history.

Knowledge about the traditions and beliefs of the many social groups within a modern nation is important in planning and carrying out programs that affect those

## ANTHROPOLOGY TODAY

### *Culturally Appropriate Marketing*

Innovation succeeds best when it is culturally appropriate. This axiom of applied anthropology could guide the international spread not only of development projects but also of businesses, such as fast food. Each time McDonald's or Burger King expands to a new nation, it must devise a culturally appropriate strategy for fitting into the new setting.

McDonald's has been successful internationally, with more than a quarter of its sales outside the United States. One place where McDonald's is expanding successfully is Brazil, where more than 50 million middle-class people, most living in densely packed cities, provide a concentrated market for a fast-food chain. Still, it took McDonald's some time to find the right marketing strategy for Brazil.

In 1980 when I visited Brazil after a seven-year absence, I first noticed, as a manifestation of Brazil's growing participation in the world economy, the appearance of two McDonald's restaurants in Rio de Janeiro. There wasn't much difference between Brazilian and American McDonald's. The restaurants looked alike. The

menus were more or less the same, as was the taste of the quarter-pounders. I picked up an artifact, a white paper bag with yellow lettering, exactly like the take-out bags then used in American McDonald's. An advertising device, it carried several messages about how Brazilians could bring McDonald's into their lives. However, it seemed to me that McDonald's Brazilian ad campaign was missing some important points about how fast food should be marketed in a culture that values large, leisurely lunches.

The bag proclaimed, "You're going to enjoy the [McDonald's] difference," and listed several "favorite places where you can enjoy McDonald's products." This list confirmed that the marketing people were trying to adapt to Brazilian middle-class culture, but they were making some mistakes. "When you go out in the car with the kids" transferred the uniquely developed North American cultural combination of highways, affordable cars, and suburban living to the very different context of urban Brazil. A similar suggestion was "traveling to the country place." Even Brazilians who owned country places could not find McDonald's, still confined to the cities, on the road. The ad creator had apparently groups. Attention to social background and cultural categories helps ensure the welfare of affected ethnic groups, communities, and neighborhoods. Experience in planned social change—whether community organization in North America or economic development overseas—shows that a proper social study should be done before a project or policy is implemented. When local people want the change and it fits their lifestyle and traditions, it will be more successful, beneficial, and cost effective. There will be not only a more humane but also a more economical solution to a real social problem.

People with anthropology backgrounds are doing well in many fields. Even if one's job has little or nothing to do with anthropology in a formal or obvious sense, a background in anthropology provides a useful orientation when we work with our fellow human beings. For most of us, this means every day of our lives.

never attempted to drive up to a fast-food restaurant in a neighborhood with no parking spaces.

Several other suggestions pointed customers toward the beach, where *cariocas* (Rio natives) do spend much of their leisure time. One could eat McDonald's products "after a dip in the ocean," "at a picnic at the beach," or "watching the surfers." These suggestions ignored the Brazilian custom of consuming cold things, such as beer, soft drinks, ice cream, and ham and cheese sandwiches, at the beach. Brazilians don't consider a hot, greasy hamburger proper beach food. They view the sea as "cold" and hamburgers as "hot"; they avoid "hot" foods at the beach.

Also culturally dubious was the suggestion to eat McDonald's hamburgers "lunching at the office." Brazilians prefer their main meal at midday, often eating at a leisurely pace with business associates. Many firms serve ample lunches to their employees. Other workers take advantage of a two-hour lunch break to go home to eat with the spouse and children. Nor did it make sense to suggest that children should eat hamburgers for lunch, since most kids attend school for half-day sessions and have lunch at home. Two other suggestions—

"waiting for the bus" and "in the beauty parlor"—did describe common aspects of daily life in a Brazilian city. However, these settings have not proved especially inviting to hamburgers or fish filets.

The homes of Brazilians who can afford McDonald's products have cooks and maids to do many of the things that fast-food restaurants do in the United States. The suggestion that McDonald's products be eaten "while watching your favorite television program" is culturally appropriate, because Brazilians watch TV a lot. However, Brazil's consuming classes can ask the cook to make a snack when hunger strikes. Indeed, much televiewing occurs during the light dinner served when the husband gets home from the office.

Most appropriate to the Brazilian lifestyle was the suggestion to enjoy McDonald's "on the cook's day off." Throughout Brazil, Sunday is that day. The Sunday pattern for middle-class families is a trip to the beach, liters of beer, a full midday meal around 3 P.M., and a light evening snack. McDonald's found its niche in the Sunday evening meal, when families flock to the fast-food restaurant, and it is to this market that its advertising is now appropriately geared.

Continued

## ANTHROPOLOGY TODAY

McDonald's is expanding rapidly in Brazilian cities, and in Brazil as in North America, teenage appetites are fueling the fast-food explosion. As McDonald's outlets appeared in urban neighborhoods, Brazilian teenagers used them for after-school snacks, while families had evening meals there. As an anthropologist could have predicted, the fast-food industry has not revolutionized Brazilian food and meal customs. Rather, McDonald's is succeeding because it has adapted to preexisting Brazilian cultural patterns.

The main contrast with North America is that the Brazilian evening meal is lighter. McDonald's now caters to the evening meal rather than to lunch. Once McDonald's realized that more money could be made by fitting in with, rather than trying to Americanize, Brazilian meal habits, it started aiming its advertising at that goal.

## SUMMARY

1. Anthropology has two dimensions: academic and applied. Applied anthropology uses anthropological perspectives, theory, methods, and data to identify, assess, and solve problems. Applied anthropologists have a range of employers. Examples: government agencies; development organizations; NGOs; tribal, ethnic, and interest groups; businesses; social services and educational agencies. Applied anthropologists come from all four subfields. Ethnography is one of applied anthropology's most valuable research tools. A systemic perspective recognizes that changes have multiple consequences, some unintended.

2. Development anthropology focuses on social issues in, and the cultural dimension of, economic development. Development projects typically promote cash employment and new technology at the expense of subsistence economies. Not all governments seek to increase equality and end poverty. Resistance by elites to reform is typical and hard to combat. At the same time, local people rarely cooperate with projects requiring major and risky changes in their daily lives. Many projects seek to impose inappropriate property notions and incompatible social units on their intended beneficiaries. The best strategy for change is to base the social design for innovation on traditional social forms in each target area.

3. Anthropology and education researchers work in classrooms, homes, and other settings relevant to education. Such studies may lead to policy recommendations. Both academic and applied anthropologists study migration from rural areas to cities and across national boundaries. North America has become a popular arena for urban anthropological research on migration, ethnicity, poverty, and related topics. Although rural and urban are different social systems, there is cultural diffusion from one to the other.

4. Medical anthropology is the cross-cultural, biocultural study of health problems and conditions, disease, illness, disease theories, and health-care systems. Medical anthropology includes anthropologists from all four subfields and has theoretical

(academic) and applied dimensions. In a given setting, the characteristic diseases reflect diet, population density, economy, and social complexity. Native theories of illness may be personalistic, naturalistic, or emotionalistic. In applying anthropology to business, the key features are (1) ethnography and observation as ways of gathering data, (2) cross-cultural expertise, and (3) a focus on cultural diversity.

5. A broad college education, including anthropology and foreign-area courses, offers excellent background for many fields. Anthropology's comparative outlook and cultural relativism provide an excellent basis for overseas employment. Even for work in North America, a focus on culture and cultural diversity is valuable. Anthropology majors attend medical, law, and business schools and succeed in many fields, some of which have little explicit connection with anthropology.

## KEY TERMS

anthropology and education (p. 401)
applied anthropology (p. 394)
curer (p. 408)
development anthropology (p. 397)
disease (p. 406)
health care systems (p. 407)
illness (p. 406)

equity, increased (p. 397)
medical anthropology (p. 405)
overinnovation (p. 398)
scientific medicine (p. 408)
underdifferentiation (p. 399)
urban anthropology (p. 403)

# CHAPTER 19

# CULTURAL EXCHANGE
# AND SURVIVAL

❖ **Contact and Domination**

  Development and Environmentalism

  Religious Change

  Antimodernism

❖ **Resistance and Survival**

  Weapons of the Weak

  Cultural Imperialism

❖ **Making and Remaking Culture**

  Popular Culture

  Indigenizing Popular Culture

  A World System of Images

  A Transnational Culture of Consumption

❖ **People in Motion**

❖ **Indigenous Peoples**

  Identity in Indigenous Politics

❖ **The Continuance of Diversity**

  *Anthropology Today: Cultural
    Diversity Highest in Resource-
    Rich Areas*

---

This book has examined many aspects of increasing participation by local societies in wider systems—regional, national, colonial, and global. Since the 1920s anthropologists have been investigating the changes that arise from contact between industrial and nonindustrial societies. Studies of "social change" and "acculturation" are abundant. British and American ethnographers, respectively, have used those terms to describe the same process. *Acculturation* refers to changes that result when groups come into continuous firsthand contact—changes in the cultural patterns of either or both groups (Redfield, Linton, and Herskovits 1936, p. 149).

---

## ✛ CONTACT AND DOMINATION

Acculturation differs from diffusion, or cultural borrowing, which can occur without firsthand contact. For example, most North Americans who eat hot dogs ("frankfurters") have never been to Frankfurt, nor have most North American Toyota owners or sushi eaters ever visited Japan. Although acculturation can be applied to any case of cultural contact and change, the term most often has described **Westernization**—the influence of Western expansion on other societies. Thus people who wear store-bought clothes, learn Indo-European languages, and otherwise adopt Western customs are called acculturated. Acculturation may be voluntary or forced.

Different degrees of destruction, domination, resistance, survival, adaptation, and modification of local cultures may follow interethnic contact. In cases in which contact

**416**

between the indigenous societies and more powerful outsiders leads to destruction—a situation that is particularly characteristic of colonialist and expansionist eras—a "shock phase" often follows the initial encounter (Bodley, ed. 1988). Outsiders may attack or exploit the local people. Such exploitation may increase mortality, disrupt subsistence, fragment kin groups, damage social support systems, and inspire new religious movements, such as the cargo cults examined in the chapter on religion (Bodley, ed. 1988). During the shock phase, there may be civil repression backed by military force. Such factors may lead to the tribe's cultural collapse (*ethnocide*) or its physical extinction (*genocide*).

Outsiders often attempt to remake landscapes and cultures in their own image. Political and economic colonialists have tried to redesign conquered and dependent lands, peoples, and cultures, imposing their cultural standards on others. The aim of many agricultural development projects, for example, seems to have been to make the world as much like Iowa as possible, complete with mechanized farming and nuclear family ownership—despite the fact that these models may be inappropriate for settings outside the North American heartland.

## Development and Environmentalism

Today it often is multinational corporations, usually based in core nations, rather than the governments of those nations, that are changing the nature of Third World economies. Governments of many peripheral and semiperipheral nations, such as Brazil, have supported the predatory enterprises of some corporations that seek cheap labor and raw materials in their countries, where economic development often has contributed to ecological devastation.

Simultaneously, environmentalists from core nations increasingly state their case, promoting conservation, to the rest of the world. Akbar Ahmed (1992, 2004) finds the non-Western world to be cynical about Western ecological morality, seeing it as yet another imperialist message. "The Chinese have cause to snigger at the Western suggestion that they forgo the convenience of the fridge to save the ozone layer" (Ahmed 1992, p. 120). Brazilians complain that northerners talk about global needs and saving the Amazon after having destroyed their own forests for First World economic growth.

In the last chapter we saw that development projects usually fail if they try to replace local forms with culturally alien property concepts and productive units. A strategy that incorporates the local forms is more effective than the fallacies of overinnovation and underdifferentiation. The same caveats would seem to apply to an intervention philosophy that seeks to impose global ecological morality without due attention to cultural variation and autonomy. Countries and societies may resist interventionist philosophies aimed at either development or globally justified environmentalism.

A clash of cultures related to environmental change may occur when *development threatens indigenous peoples and their environments*. Hundreds of groups throughout the world, including the Kayapó Indians of Brazil and the Kaluli of Papua New Guinea, have been threatened by plans and forces, such as dam construction or commercially driven deforestation, that would *destroy* their homelands (see Johansen 2003).

A second clash of cultures related to environmental change occurs when *external regulation threatens indigenous peoples*. Local groups may actually be threatened by environmental plans that seek to *save* their homelands (see Harper 2002). By declaring certain resources off limits, outsiders may expect local people to give up customary economic and cultural activities without clear substitutes, alternatives, or incentives. The traditional approach to conservation has been to restrict access to certain (protected) areas, hire guards, and punish violators. Ironically, well-meaning conservation efforts can be as insensitive as development schemes that promote radical changes without involving local people in planning and carrying out the policies that affect them. When people are asked to give up the basis of their livelihood, they usually resist.

## Religious Change

Religious proselytizing can promote ethnocide, as local beliefs and practices are replaced by Western ones. Sometimes a religion and associated customs are replaced by ideology and behavior more compatible with Western culture. One example is the Handsome Lake religion (as described in the chapter on religion), which led the Iroquois to copy European farming techniques, stressing male rather than female labor. The Iroquois also gave up their communal longhouses and matrilineal descent groups for nuclear family households. The teachings of Handsome Lake led to a new church and religion. This revitalization movement helped the Iroquois survive in a drastically modified environment, but much ethnocide was involved.

Handsome Lake was an Iroquois man who created a new religion, drawing on Western models. More commonly, missionaries and proselytizers representing the major world religions, especially Christianity and Islam, are the proponents of religious change. Protestant and Catholic missionization continues even in remote corners of the world. Evangelical Protestantism, for example, is advancing in Peru, Brazil, and other parts of Latin America. It challenges an often jaded Catholicism that has too few priests and that is sometimes seen mainly as women's religion.

Sometimes the political ideology of a nation-state is pitted against traditional religion. Officials of the former Soviet empire discouraged Catholicism, Judaism, and Islam. In Central Asia, Soviet dominators destroyed Muslim mosques and discouraged religious practice. On the other hand, governments often use their power to advance a religion, such as Islam in Iran or Sudan.

## Antimodernism

**Antimodernism** describes the rejection of the modern in favor of what is perceived as an earlier, purer, and better way of life. This viewpoint reflects disillusionment with industrialization and globalization, including developments in science, technology, and consumption patterns. Antimodernists typically consider technology's use today to be misguided, or think technology should have a lower priority than religious and cultural values.

The modern and the antimodern are key ingredients in Benjamin R. Barber's (1992, 1995) contention that tribalism and globalism are the two key—and opposed—principles of our age. Tribalism, which Barber sums up with the term "Jihad" (borrowed loosely from Islam, where it means quest or struggle), is an antimodern force pitting culture against culture, tribe against tribe, and religion against religion. For Jihad's enemy, Barber coins the term "McWorld," which subsumes the modern forces that promote global integration and uniformity, including the diffusion of music, computers, and fast food—MTV, Macintosh, and McDonald's. Barber argues that Jihad and McWorld operate today with equal force in opposite directions. Jihad is driven by parochial hatreds; McWorld, by universalizing markets.

Jihad resists McWorld, which spans nations, cultures, and ideologies. Groups like al Qaeda exist in perpetual rebellion against McWorld and its perceived values and consumption patterns. To its warriors and adherents, Jihad offers an identity and a sense of community. But that social solidarity is grounded in exclusion, separation, opposition, and anger. Solidarity is achieved through war against outsiders. In places like Afghanistan under Taliban rule, solidarity might entail submission to an arbitrary hierarchy, fanaticism in beliefs, and the absorption or destruction of the individual self for the goals of the group.

## ✦ RESISTANCE AND SURVIVAL

Systems of domination—whether political, economic, cultural, or religious—have their more muted aspects along with their public dimensions. In studying systems of domination, we must pay attention to what lies beneath the surface of evident, public behavior. In public the oppressed may seem to accept their own domination, but they always question it offstage. James Scott (1990) uses the terms **public transcript** and **hidden transcript** to describe, respectively, the open, public interactions between dominators and oppressed—the outer shell of power relations—and the critique of power that goes on offstage: where the power holders can't see or hear it.

In public, the elites and the oppressed observe the etiquette of power relations. The dominants act like haughty masters while their subordinates show humility and defer. Antonio Gramsci (1971) developed the concept of **hegemony** for a stratified social order in which subordinates comply with domination by internalizing their rulers' values and accepting the "naturalness" of domination (this is the way things were meant to be). According to Pierre Bourdieu (1977, p. 164), every social order tries to make its own arbitrariness (including its oppression) seem natural. All hegemonic ideologies offer explanations about why the existing order is in everyone's interest. Often promises are made (things will get better if you're patient). Gramsci and others use the idea of hegemony to explain why people conform even without coercion.

Hegemony, the internalization of a dominant ideology, is one way to curb resistance. Another way is to let subordinates know they will eventually gain power—as young people usually foresee when they let their elders dominate them. Another way of curbing resistance is to separate or isolate subordinates and supervise them closely. According to Michel Foucault (1979), describing control over prisoners, solitude (as in solitary confinement) is one effective way to induce submission.

## Weapons of the Weak

Often, situations that seem to be hegemonic do have active resistance, but it is individual and disguised rather than collective and defiant. Scott (1985) uses Malay peasants, among whom he did fieldwork, to illustrate small-scale acts of resistance—which he calls "weapons of the weak." The Malay peasants used an indirect strategy to resist an Islamic tithe (religious tax). The goods (usually rice) that peasants had to give went to the provincial capital. In theory, the tithe would come back as charity to the peasants, but it never did. Peasants didn't resist the tithe by rioting, demonstrating, or protesting. Instead they used a "nibbling" strategy, based on small acts of resistance. For example, they failed to declare their land or lied about the amount they farmed. They underpaid or delivered rice contaminated with water, rocks, or mud, to add weight. Because of this resistance, only 15 percent of what was due was actually paid (Scott 1990, p. 89).

Subordinates also use various strategies to resist *publicly,* but again, usually in disguised form. Discontent may be expressed in public rituals and language, including metaphors, euphemisms, and folk tales. For example, trickster tales (such as the Brer Rabbit stories told by slaves in the southern United States) celebrate the wiles of the weak as they triumph over the strong.

Resistance is most likely to be expressed openly when the oppressed are allowed to assemble. The hidden transcript may be publicly revealed on such occasions. People see their dreams and anger shared by others with whom they haven't been in direct contact. The oppressed may draw courage from the crowd, from its visual and emotional impact and its anonymity. Sensing danger, the elites discourage such public gatherings. They try to limit and control holidays, funerals, dances, festivals, and other occasions that might unite the oppressed. Thus in the southern United States gatherings of five or more slaves were forbidden unless a white person was present.

Factors that interfere with community formation—such as geographic, linguistic, and ethnic separation—also work to curb resistance. Consequently, southern U.S. plantation owners sought slaves with diverse cultural and linguistic backgrounds. Despite the measures used to divide them, the slaves resisted, developing their own popular culture, linguistic codes, and religious vision. The masters taught portions of the Bible that stressed compliance, but the slaves seized on the story of Moses, the promised land, and deliverance. The cornerstone of slave religion became the idea of a reversal in the conditions of whites and blacks. Slaves also resisted directly, through sabotage and flight. In many New World areas slaves managed to establish free communities in the hills and other remote areas (Price, ed. 1973).

Hidden transcripts tend to be publicly expressed at certain times (festivals and *Carnivals*) and in certain places (for example, markets). Because of its costumed anonymity, Carnival is an excellent arena for expressing normally suppressed speech and aggression—antihegemonic discourse. (*Discourse* includes talk, speeches, gestures, and actions.) Carnivals celebrate freedom through immodesty, dancing, gluttony, and sexuality (DaMatta 1991). Carnival may begin as a playful outlet for frustrations built up during the year. Over time it may evolve into a powerful annual critique of domination and a threat to the established order (Gilmore 1987). (Recognizing that ceremonial license could turn into political defiance, the Spanish dictator Francisco Franco outlawed Carnival.)

## Cultural Imperialism

**Cultural imperialism** refers to the spread or advance of one culture at the expense of others, or its imposition on other societies, which it modifies, replaces, or destroys—usually because of differential economic or political influence (see Tomlinson 1991, 1999). Thus, children in the French colonial empire learned French history, language, and culture from standard textbooks also used in France. Tahitians, Malagasy, Vietnamese, and Senegalese learned the French language by reciting from books about "our ancestors the Gauls."

To what extent is modern technology, especially the mass media, an agent of cultural imperialism? Some commentators see modern technology as erasing cultural differences, as homogeneous products reach more people worldwide. But others see a role for modern technology in allowing social groups (local cultures) to express themselves (Marcus and Fischer 1999). Modern radio and TV, for example, constantly bring local happenings (for example, a "chicken festival" in Iowa) to the attention of a larger public. The North American media play a role in stimulating local activities of many sorts. Similarly in Brazil, local practices, celebrations, and performances are changing in the context of outside forces, including the mass media and tourism.

In the Brazilian town of Arembepe, TV coverage has stimulated participation in a traditional annual performance, the *Chegança*. This is a fishers' danceplay that reenacts the Portuguese discovery of Brazil. Arembepeiros have traveled to the state capital to perform the Chegança before television cameras, for a TV program featuring traditional performances from many rural communities.

One national Brazilian Sunday-night variety program (*Fantástico*) is especially popular in rural areas because it shows such local events. In several towns along the

Because of its costumed anonymity, Carnival is an excellent arena for expressing normally suppressed speech and behavior. Shown here is Carnival in Venice in 2001. Is there anything like Carnival in your society?

Amazon River, annual folk ceremonies are now staged more lavishly for TV cameras. In the Amazon town of Parantíns, for example, boatloads of tourists arriving any time of year are shown a videotape of the town's annual Bumba Meu Boi festival. This is a costumed performance mimicking bull-fighting, parts of which have been shown on *Fantástico*. This pattern, in which communities preserve, revive, and intensify the scale of traditional ceremonies to perform for TV and tourists, is expanding.

Brazilian television also has played a "top-down" role by spreading the popularity of holidays such as Carnival and Christmas (Kottak 1990*a*). TV has aided the national spread of Carnival beyond its traditional urban centers. Still, local reactions to the nationwide broadcasting of Carnival and its trappings (elaborate parades, costumes, and frenzied dancing) are not simple or uniform responses to external stimuli.

Rather than direct adoption of Carnival, local Brazilians respond in various ways. Often they don't take up Carnival itself but modify their local festivities to fit Carnival images. Others actively spurn Carnival. One example is Arembepe, where Carnival has never been important, probably because of its calendrical closeness to the main local festival, which is held in February to honor Saint Francis of Assisi. In the past, villagers couldn't afford to celebrate both occasions. Now, not only do the people of Arembepe reject Carnival, they are also increasingly hostile to their own main festival. Arembepeiros resent the fact that Saint Francis has become "an outsiders' event," because it draws thousands of tourists to Arembepe each February. The villagers think that commercial interests and outsiders have appropriated Saint Francis.

In opposition to these trends, many Arembepeiros now say they like and participate more in the traditional June festivals honoring Saint John, Saint Peter, and Saint Anthony. In the past these were observed on a much smaller scale than was the festival for Saint Francis. Arembepeiros celebrate them now with a new vigor and enthusiasm, as they react to outsiders and their celebrations, real and televised.

## ✦ MAKING AND REMAKING CULTURE

Any cultural product—a ceremony, an artifact, an ideology, an event, or a media-borne image such as Carnival—can be considered a **text.** This term applies to something that can be creatively "read," interpreted, and assigned meaning by *anyone* (a "reader") who receives it. The particular meanings that each of us finds in a given text can be very different from what the original creators of the text imagined. (The reading or meaning that the creators intended, or the one that the elites consider to be the right meaning, can be called the **hegemonic reading**).

The active role that individuals play in interpreting, using, making, and remaking culture is called **agency.** Illustrating agency, "readers" constantly produce their own meanings, some of which may resist or oppose the hegemonic meaning of the text. Sometimes readers focus on antihegemonic aspects of a text. Enslaved people in the American South did this with reference to the *Bible* when they preferred the biblical story of Moses and deliverance to the hegemonic lessons of patience and obedience their masters taught them (e.g., the book of *Job*).

## Popular Culture

In his book *Understanding Popular Culture* (1989), John Fiske argues that each individual's use of popular culture is a creative act (an original "reading" of a text). For example, *American Idol,* the World Cup, the Super Bowl, or *Harry Potter* means something different to each fan. As Fiske puts it, "The meanings I make from a text are pleasurable when I feel that they are *my* meanings and that they relate to *my* everyday life in a practical, direct way" (1989, p. 57). All of us creatively "read" magazines, books, music, television, films, celebrities, politicians, and other popular culture products.

Also illustrating agency, individuals manipulate ideas and images to express resistance. Popular culture allows people to oppose, symbolically at least, the unequal power relations they face each day—in the family, at work, and in the classroom. Variant forms, interpretations, and readings of culture, sometimes harnessed by political movements, can express discontent and resistance by individuals and groups who are or feel oppressed. Can you think of examples?

## Indigenizing Popular Culture

To understand culture change, it is important to recognize that meaning may be locally manufactured. People assign their own meanings and value to the texts, messages, and products they receive. Those meanings reflect their cultural backgrounds

December 26, 2003: Illustrating a process of indigenizing offerings of the modern world system, children dress as Colonel Sanders to promote egg tarts (a local dish now offered by an international restaurant chain) at a KFC store in Shanghai, China.

and experiences. When forces from world centers enter new societies, they are **indigenized**—modified to fit the local culture. This is true of cultural forces as various as fast food (see the box in the last chapter), music, housing styles, science, terrorism, celebrations, and political ideas and institutions (Appadurai 1990).

## A World System of Images

All societies express imagination—in dreams, fantasies, songs, myths, and stories. Today, however, more people in many more places imagine "a wider set of 'possible' lives than they ever did before. One important source of this change is the mass media, which present a rich, ever-changing store of possible lives" (Appadurai 1991, p. 197). The United States as a media center has been joined by Canada, Japan, Western Europe, Brazil, Mexico, Nigeria, Egypt, India, and Hong Kong (see Barker 1997).

As print has done for centuries (Anderson 1991), the electronic mass media can also spread, even help create, national and ethnic identities. Like print, television and radio can diffuse the cultures of countries within their own boundaries, thus enhancing national cultural identity. For example, millions of Brazilians who formerly were cut off (by geographic isolation or illiteracy) from urban and national events and information now participate in a national communication system, through TV networks (Kottak 1990a).

Cross-cultural studies of television contradict a belief Americans ethnocentrically hold about televiewing in other countries. This misconception is that American programs inevitably triumph over local products. This doesn't happen when there is appealing local competition. In Brazil, for example, the most popular network (TV Globo) relies heavily on Brazilian productions. TV Globo's most popular programs are *telenovelas,* locally made serials that are similar to American soap operas. Globo plays each night to the world's largest and most devoted audience (60 to 80 million viewers throughout the nation). The programs that attract this horde are made by Brazilians, for Brazilians. Thus it is not North American culture but a new pan-Brazilian national culture which Brazilian TV is propagating. Brazilian productions also compete internationally. They are exported to over 100 countries, spanning Latin America, Europe, Asia, and Africa.

We may generalize that programming that is culturally alien won't do very well anywhere, when a quality local choice is available. Confirmation comes from many countries. National productions are highly popular in Japan, Mexico, India, Egypt, and Nigeria. In a survey during the mid-1980s, 75 percent of Nigerian viewers preferred local productions. Only 10 percent favored imports, and the remaining 15 percent liked the two options equally. Local productions are successful in Nigeria because "they are filled with everyday moments that audiences can identify with. These shows are locally produced by Nigerians" (Gray 1986). Thirty million people watched one of the most popular series, *The Village Headmaster,* each week. That program brought rural values to the screens of urbanites who had lost touch with their rural roots (Gray 1986).

The mass media also can play a role in maintaining ethnic and national identities among people who lead transnational lives. As groups move, they stay linked to each other and to their homeland through the media. Diasporas have enlarged the markets for media and travel services targeted at specific ethnic, national, or religious audiences. For a fee, a PBS station in Fairfax, Virginia, offers more than thirty hours a week to immigrant groups in the D.C. area, to make programs in their own languages.

## A Transnational Culture of Consumption

Another key transnational force is finance. Multinational corporations and other business interests look beyond national boundaries for places to invest and draw profits. As Appadurai (1991, p. 194) puts it, "money, commodities, and persons unendingly chase each other around the world." Residents of many Latin American communities now depend on outside cash, remitted from international labor migration. Also, the economy of the United States increasingly is influenced by foreign investment, especially from Britain, Canada, Germany, the Netherlands, and Japan. The American economy also has increased its dependence on foreign labor—through both the immigration of laborers and the export of jobs.

Contemporary global culture is driven by flows of people, technology, finance, information, and ideology (Appadurai 1990; Appadurai, ed., 2001). Business, technology, and the media have increased the craving for commodities and images throughout the world (Appadurai, ed. 2001). This has forced most nation-states to open to a global culture of consumption. Almost everyone today participates in this culture. Few people

On November 14, 2003, crowds attend the opening of a shopping mall in the world's tallest building, the 101 Tower in Taipei, Taiwan. Throughout the world, business and the media have increased the craving for commercial products. How do you imagine people get to this shopping mall?

have never seen a T-shirt advertising a Western product. American and English rock stars' recordings blast through the streets of Rio de Janeiro, while taxi drivers from Toronto to Madagascar play Brazilian musical tapes. Peasants and tribal people participate in the modern world system not only because they have been hooked on cash but also because their products and images are appropriated by world capitalism (Giddens 2000; Gottdiener, ed. 2000; Marcus and Myers, eds. 1995; Root 1996). They are commercialized by others (like the San in the movie *The Gods Must Be Crazy*). Furthermore, indigenous peoples also market their own images and products, through outlets such as Cultural Survival.

## ✦ PEOPLE IN MOTION

The linkages in the modern world system have both enlarged and erased old boundaries and distinctions. Arjun Appadurai (1990, p. 1) characterizes today's world as a "translocal" "interactive system" that is "strikingly new." Whether as refugees, migrants, tourists, pilgrims, proselytizers, terrorists, laborers, business people, development workers, employees of nongovernmental organizations (NGOs), politicians, soldiers, sports figures, or media-borne images, people travel more than ever.

So important is transnational migration that many Mexican villagers find "their most important kin and friends are as likely to be living hundreds or thousands of miles away as immediately around them" (Rouse 1991). Most migrants maintain their ties with their homeland (phoning, e-mailing, visiting, sending money, watching "ethnic TV"). In a sense, they live multilocally—in different places at once. Dominicans in New York City, for example, have been characterized as living "between two islands"—Manhattan and the Dominican Republic (Grasmuck and Pessar 1991). Many Dominicans—like migrants from other countries—migrate to the United States temporarily, seeking cash to transform their lifestyles when they return to the Caribbean.

With so many people "in motion," the unit of anthropological study expands from the local community to the **diaspora**—the offspring of an area who have spread to many lands. Anthropologists increasingly follow descendants of the communities they have studied as they move from rural to urban areas and across national boundaries. For the 1991 annual meeting of the American Anthropological Association in Chicago, the anthropologist Robert Kemper organized a session of presentations about long-term ethnographic fieldwork. Kemper's own long-time research focus has been the Mexican village of Tzintzuntzan, which, with his mentor George Foster, Kemper has studied for decades. However, their database now includes not just Tzintzuntzan, but its descendants all over the world. Given the Tzintzuntzan diaspora, Kemper even was able to use some of his time in Chicago to visit people from Tzintzuntzan who had established a colony there. In today's world, as people move, they take their traditions and their anthropologists along with them.

**Postmodernity** describes our time and situation—today's world in flux, these people on the move who have learned to manage multiple identities depending on place and context. In its most general sense, **postmodern** refers to the blurring and breakdown of established canons (rules or standards), categories, distinctions, and boundaries. The word is taken from **postmodernism**—a style and movement in architecture that succeeded modernism, beginning in the 1970s. Postmodern architecture rejected the rules, geometric order, and austerity of modernism. Modernist buildings were expected to have a clear and functional design. Postmodern design is "messier" and more playful. It draws on a diversity of styles from different times and places—including popular, ethnic, and non-Western cultures. Postmodernism extends "value" well beyond classic, elite, and Western cultural forms. *Postmodern* now is used to describe comparable developments in music, literature, and visual art. From this origin, *postmodernity* describes a world in which traditional standards, contrasts, groups, boundaries, and identities are opening up, reaching out, and breaking down.

New kinds of political and ethnic units are emerging. In some cases, cultures and ethnic groups have banded together in larger associations. There is a growing pan-Indian identity (Nagel 1996) and an international Pantribal movement as well. Thus in June 1992 the World Conference of Indigenous Peoples met in Rio de Janeiro concurrently with the United Nations Conference on the Environment and Development (UNCED). Along with diplomats, journalists, and environmentalists came 300 representatives of the tribal diversity that survives in the modern world—from Lapland to Mali (Brooke 1992).

## ✦ INDIGENOUS PEOPLES

The term *indigenous people* entered international law with the creation in 1982 of the United Nations Working Group on Indigenous Populations (WGIP). This group, which meets annually, has members from six continents. The draft of the Declaration of Indigenous Rights, produced by the WGIP in 1989, was accepted by the UN for discussion in 1993. Convention 169, an ILO (International Labor Organization) document that supports cultural diversity and indigenous empowerment, was approved in 1989. Such documents, along with the work of the WGIP, have influenced governments, NGOs, and international agencies to adopt policies aimed at benefiting indigenous peoples. Social movements worldwide now use the term "indigenous people" as a self-identifying label in their quests for social, cultural, and political rights (de la Peña 2005).

In Spanish-speaking Latin America, social scientists and politicians now favor the term *indígena* (indigenous person) over *indio* (Indian). The latter is a colonial term that European conquerors used for Native Americans, whose situation did not necessarily improve after Latin American nations gained independence from Spain and Portugal, mostly by the 1820s. For the white and *mestizo* (mixed) elites of the new nations, *indios* and their lifestyle seemed alien to (European) civilization (de la Peña 2005).

Until the mid- to late 1980s, Latin American public policy emphasized assimilation. Indians were associated with a romanticized past, but marginalized in the present, except for museums, tourism, and folkloric events. Indigenous Bolivians and Peruvians were encouraged to self-identify as *campesinos* (peasants). The past 30 years have witnessed a dramatic shift. The emphasis has shifted from assimilation—*mestizaje*—to cultural difference. In Ecuador groups seen previously as Quichua-speaking peasants are classified now as indigenous communities with their own territories. Brazil has recognized 30 new indigenous communities in the northeast, a region previously seen as having lost its native population. Guatemala, Nicaragua, Brazil, Colombia, Mexico, Paraguay, Ecuador, Argentina, Bolivia, Peru, and Venezuela now are officially

La Paz, Bolivia, May 23, 2005: Bolivians claiming an Indian (indigenous) identity rally for indigenous rights and the nationalization of that country's natural gas resources. In December 2005, Bolivians elected as their president Evo Morales, the candidate of the Indigenous Movement toward Socialism party. The party made further gains in 2006 parliamentary elections.

multicultural (Jackson and Warren 2005). Several national constitutions recognize the rights of indigenous peoples to cultural distinctiveness and political representation. In Colombia, indigenous territories have the same benefits as any local government (de la Peña 2005).

The indigenous rights movement exists in the context of globalization, including transnational movements focusing on human rights, women's rights, and environmentalism. Transnational organizations have helped indigenous peoples to influence legislation. Since the 1980s there has been a general shift in Latin America from authoritarian to democratic rule. Still, inequality and discrimination persist, and there has been resistance to indigenous mobilization, including assassinations of leaders and their supporters. Guatemala, Peru, and Colombia have witnessed severe repression. There have been thousands of indigenous deaths, refugees, and internally displaced persons (Jackson and Warren 2005).

Ceuppens and Geschiere (2005) explore a recent upsurge, in multiple world areas, of the notion of *autochthony* (being native to, or formed in, the place where found), with an implicit call for excluding strangers. The terms *autochthony* and *indigenous* both go back to classical Greek history, with similar implications. Autochthony refers to self and soil. Indigenous literally means born inside, with the connotation in classical Greek of being born "inside the house." Both notions stress the need to safeguard ancestral lands (patrimony) from strangers, along with the rights of first-comers to special rights and protection versus later immigrants—legal or illegal (Ceuppens and Geschiere 2005).

During the 1990s, autochthony became an issue in many parts of Africa, inspiring violent efforts to exclude (European and Asian) "strangers." Simultaneously, autochthony became a key notion in debates about immigration and multiculturalism in Europe. European majority groups have claimed the label *autochthon*. This term highlights the prominence that the exclusion of strangers has assumed in day-to-day politics worldwide (Ceuppens and Geschiere 2005). One familiar example is the United States, as represented in the congressional debate in 2006–2007 over illegal immigration.

## Identity in Indigenous Politics

**Essentialism** describes the process of viewing an identity as established, real, and frozen, so as to hide the historical processes and politics within which that identity developed. Identities, emphatically, are not fixed. We saw in the chapter "Ethnicity and Race" that identities can be fluid and multiple. People seize on particular, sometimes competing, self-labels and identities. Some Peruvian groups, for instance, self-identify as *mestizos* but still see themselves as indigenous. Identity is a fluid, dynamic process, and there are multiple ways of being indigenous. Neither speaking an indigenous language nor wearing "native" clothing is required. Identities are asserted at particular times and places by particular individuals and groups and after various kinds of negotiations. Indigenous identity coexists with, and must be managed in the context of, other identity components, including religion, race, and gender. Identities always must be seen as (1) potentially plural, (2) emerging through a specific process, (3) ways of being someone or something in particular times and places (Jackson and Warren 2005).

## ❖ THE CONTINUANCE OF DIVERSITY

Anthropology has a crucial role to play in promoting a more humanistic vision of social change, one that respects the value of human biological and cultural diversity. The existence of anthropology is itself a tribute to the continuing need to understand similarities and differences among human beings throughout the world. Anthropology teaches us that the adaptive responses of humans can be more flexible than those of other species because our main adaptive means are sociocultural. However, the cultural forms, institutions, values, and customs of the past always influence subsequent adaptation, producing continued diversity and giving a certain uniqueness to the actions and reactions of different groups. With our knowledge and our awareness of our professional responsibilities, let us work to keep anthropology, the study of humankind, the most humanistic of all the sciences.

# ANTHROPOLOGY TODAY

## *Cultural Diversity Highest in Resource-Rich Areas*

*This chapter has focused on challenges to cultural diversity and cultural survival, and the resilience of people and cultures in the face of those challenges. Described in this box is a recent study of the origins and survival of cultural diversity. People tend to move, it is argued, for economic reasons. If resources are ample at home people tend to stay put and keep on doing what they always have done. This reinforces the point made in the last chapter that motives for modifying behavior come from the traditional culture and the small concerns of ordinary life.*

*An intriguing argument in this study is that patterns of cultural and biological diversity are similar, with diversity greatest in equatorial regions and least near the poles. Abundant resources in the tropics have allowed diverse societies to survive. When resources are less concentrated and abundant people have to range widely to meet their daily needs. This movement works to homogenize cultures, as people constantly come into contact with others. The study also draws attention to a tendency for cultures to maintain themselves, even in the face of migration to new areas, such as North American cities, so that ethnic and other cultural distinctions remain important in a globalizing world.*

We may rightfully beat our drums and toot our horns: No species come close to the wealth of culture that humans boast. We have different religions, marriage systems, languages, and dances.

"Humans are a very young species with very little genetic diversity, yet we've got enormous cultural diversity that other species really don't have," said Mark Pagel, a professor of evolutionary biology . . . at the University of Reading in England. But what explains our extreme cultural diversity?

In an article in this week's issue of the science journal *Nature,* Pagel and Ruth Mace, an anthropologist at the University College London, argue that our cultural evolution is driven in large part by a desire to control resources.

"Humans have a proclivity for drawing a ring around themselves and say[ing], 'This is my territory and I'm going to exclude others from occupying it,'" Pagel said. "That leads to different cultures arising through the usual processes of diversification and drifting apart when they're isolated from each other."

It may seem strange to talk about our great cultural diversity at a time when many of us fear that a cultural homogenization is sweeping the world. . . .

Pagel doesn't deny that a cultural erosion is taking place. But, he says, it's happened far less than it appears. In fact, unless they're tempted financially to move and assimilate into a new culture, most people prefer to stay where they are and continue doing what they have always done. "What's remarkable is how little movement we have seen in people, given the ability we have to move people," he said. "It's the natural tendency for cultures to be quite cohesive and exclusive that we want to draw attention to."

The study found that human cultures distribute themselves around the world in patterns similar to animal species. In animals, a trend known as Rapaport's rule holds that the density of species is highest in the equatorial regions and declines steadily toward the poles. Different languages—the standard by which the study differentiates cultures—are spoken every few square miles in some equatorial areas, while less climatologically hospitable regions have few languages.

Some 700 to 1,000 different languages, about 15 percent of the total on Earth, are spoken in Papua New Guinea. By comparison, only 90 languages are spoken in China.

"When resources are abundant, it is possible for a small group of humans to survive, while in areas where resources are not very abundant people have to range over large areas to meet their daily needs, and that seems to homogenize cultures, because they're constantly coming into contact with other people," Pagel said.

But how come humans don't form one large and homogeneous cultural group in ecologically rich areas like Papua New Guinea?

Pagel says that's because humans display forms of social behavior that favor living in small groups, such as rewarding cooperation, punishing those who deviate from the norms, and being wary of outsiders. "In trying to control resources and excluding others from using them, we have developed [sophisticated group behaviors such as] hunting and warfare," he said. "These things require enormous amounts of cooperation, coherence, and communication among individuals."

It may also be a matter of choice. While our genes are transmitted vertically and can't be chosen, cultural traits can be accepted or rejected. However, most people still get their traits from their ancestors rather than other cultures.

"People tend to speak the same language as their parents, and have the same political and religious beliefs," Pagel said.

Although our cultural diversity is still strong, it is perhaps only a fraction of what it was, say, 10,000 years ago, when agriculturists moved out of Mesopotamia and replaced hunter-gatherer cultures in Europe and elsewhere, wiping out languages in the process.

"There are only about 50 languages spoken in Europe today," Pagel said. "If it hadn't been for the advance of the agriculturists, we would probably have greater linguistic diversity in Europe, and probably greater cultural diversity too."

We may be in another state of transition now. While some experts suggest that mass migrations of people moving from poor regions to rich areas will dent our cultural diversity, Pagel is not so sure. "Whether things will change in the next hundred years and we'll have one big homogeneous world, we can't really say," he said. . . .

After all, Pagel says, you can walk down a street in Manhattan and find three generations of Italian speakers. Walk a few blocks more, and people are speaking Chinese. "The cultural differences in Manhattan still remain," he said.

*Source:* Stefan Lovgren, "Cultural Diversity Highest in Resource-Rich Areas, Study Says," *National Geographic News,* March 17, 2004, from http://news.nationalgeographic.com. Reprinted by permission.

## SUMMARY

1. Different degrees of destruction, domination, resistance, survival, and modification of local cultures may follow interethnic contact. This may lead to the tribe's cultural collapse (ethnocide) or its physical extinction (genocide). Multinational corporations have fueled economic development and ecological devastation. Either development or external regulation may pose a threat to indigenous peoples, their cultures, or their environments. The most effective conservation strategies pay attention to the needs, incentives, and customs of people living in the affected area.

2. "Public transcript" refers to the open, public interactions between the dominators and the oppressed. "Hidden transcript" describes the critique of power that goes on offstage, where the power holders can't see it. Discontent may also be expressed in public rituals and language. Hegemony describes a stratified social order in which subordinates comply with domination by internalizing its values and accepting its "naturalness." Often, situations that appear hegemonic have resistance that is individual and disguised rather than collective and defiant.

3. Cultural imperialism refers to the spread of one culture and its imposition on other societies, which it modifies, replaces, or destroys—usually because of differential economic or political influence. Some worry that modern technology, including the mass media, is destroying traditional cultures. But others see an important role for new technology in allowing local cultures to express themselves.

4. The term "text" is used here to describe anything that can be creatively "read," interpreted, and assigned meaning by someone who receives it. People may resist the hegemonic meaning of a text. Or they may seize on its antihegemonic aspects. When forces from world centers enter new societies, they are indigenized. Like print, the electronic mass media can help diffuse a national culture within its own boundaries. The media also play a role in preserving ethnic and national identities among people who lead transnational lives.

5. People travel more than ever. But migrants also maintain ties with home, so they live multilocally. With so many people "in motion," the unit of anthropological study expands from the local community to the diaspora. Postmodernity describes this world in flux, such people on the move who manage multiple social identities depending on place and context. New kinds of political and ethnic units are emerging as others break down or disappear.

6. The term *indigenous people* has gained legitimacy within international law. Governments, NGOs, and international agencies have adopted policies designed to recognize and benefit indigenous peoples. Social movements worldwide use this term as a self-identifying label signaling a search for social, cultural, and political rights. In Latin America, emphasis has shifted from assimilation to identities that value cultural difference. Several constitutions now recognize the rights of indigenous peoples. Recent use of the notion of *autochthony* (being native to, or formed, in the place where found) includes a call to exclude strangers, such as recent or illegal immigrants. Identity is a fluid, dynamic process, and there are multiple ways of being indigenous.

# KEY TERMS

agency (p. 422)
antimodernism (p. 418)
cultural imperialism (p. 420)
diaspora (p. 426)
essentialism (p. 429)
hegemonic reading (p. 422)
hegemony (p. 419)
hidden transcript (p. 419)

indigenized (p. 424)
postmodern (p. 426)
postmodernism (p. 426)
postmodernity (p. 426)
public transcript (p. 419)
text (p. 422)
Westernization (p. 416)

# CREDITS

## Photo

**Front Matter:** p. xxi © Barbara Salz

**Chapter 1:** p. 5: © National Anthropological Archives. Neg.#906-B; p. 7 (top left): © Paul Grebliunas/Getty Images; p. 7 (top right): © Darrell Gulin/Corbis; p. 7 (bottom left): © Sabine Vielmo/Argus Fotoarchiv/Peter Arnold; p. 7 (bottom right): © Penny Tweedie/ Woodfin Camp & Associates; p. 10 (left): © Jan Spieczny/Peter Arnold; p. 10 (right): © Hartmut Schwarzbach/Argus Fotoarchiv/Peter Arnold; p. 12: © Lauren Greenfield/VII; p. 14: © Randy Olson/Aurora Photos

**Chapter 2:** p. 27: © Dr. Jerome Rose, University of Arkansas; p. 29: © Kenneth Garrett/National Geographic Image Collection; p. 35: © Mary Evans Picture Library/Image Works; p. 37: © Michael Newman/PhotoEdit; p. 41: © Christopher M. O'Leary

**Chapter 3:** p. 48: © Noah's Ark by Edward Hicks, 1846, 261/2 × 301/2, oil on canvas, Philadelphia Museum of Art, Bequest of Lisa Norris Elkins [1950-92-7]; p. 51: © Michael Tweedie/Photo Researchers; p. 55: © Jean-Marc Giboux; p. 61: © AP Images/Tony Camerano; p. 62: © National Library of Medicine

**Chapter 4:** p. 76: © Kenneth Garrett/National Geographic Image Collection; p. 77: © Frans Lanting/Corbis; p. 78: © Karen Kasmauski/National Geographic Image Collection; p. 83: © Jane Goodall/National Geographic Image Collection; p. 94: © Russell L. Ciochon, University of Iowa

**Chapter 5:** p. 101: © Natural History Museum, London; p. 107: © John Reader/SPL/Photo Researchers; p. 110 (both): © Natural History Museum, London; p. 115 (both): © Peter Bostrom

**Chapter 6:** p. 121: © Kenneth Garrett; p. 124: © Kenneth Garrett/National Geographic Image Collection; p. 129 (left): © E.R. Degginger/Animals, Animals; p. 129 (right): © Tom McHugh/Photo Researchers

**Chapter 7:** p. 147: © Erich Lessing/Art Resource; p. 151: © Mike Yamashita/Woodfin Camp & Associates; p. 157: © 2005 Banco de Mexico Diego Rivera & Frida Kahlo Museums Trust. Av. Cinco de Mayo No. 2, Col. Centro, Del. Cuauhtemoc 06059, Mexico, D.F. Photo: Schalkwijk/Art Resource; p. 160: © Gerhard Hinterleitner/Gamma Press

**Chapter 8:** p. 170: © Ancient Art and Architecture Collection Ltd./Bridgeman Art Library; p. 175: © Barry Iverson/Woodfin Camp & Associates; p. 178: © Freer Gallery of Art, Smithsonian Institution, Washington, D.C. Purchase, F1936.6.; p. 181: © Jacques Jangoux/Peter Arnold; p. 183: © Kevin Schafer/Peter Arnold

**Chapter 9:** p. 189 (left): © Jason Homa/Getty Images; p. 189 (right): © Ted Spiegel/ Corbis Images; p. 193 (top): © William Gottlieb/Corbis; p. 193 (bottom): © Jamie Rose/ Aurora Photos; p. 196: © Kim Newton/Woodfin Camp & Associates

**Chapter 10:** p. 208: © Michael Nichols/Magnum Photos; p. 214: © Lonny Shavelson; p. 216: © Shaun Best/Reuters/ Corbis; p. 218: © Larry Downing/Reuters/Corbis; p. 221: © Jim Goldberg/Magnum Photos

**Chapter 11:** p. 233: © D. Halleux/Bios/Peter Arnold; p. 235: © Paul Chesley/Getty Images; p. 241: © Darcy Padilla/Redux Pictures; p. 247: Elbridge W. Merrill Collection Photograph Collection. /Alaska State Library and Archives [P57-028]

**Chapter 12:** p. 254: © Sarah Leen/National Geographic Image Collection; p. 261: © Burt Glinn/Magnum Photos; p. 263: © Douglas Kirkland; p. 267: © John A. Novak/ Animals Animals; p. 269: © Greg Ruffing/Getty Images

**Chapter 13:** p. 281: © Reuters; p. 285: © Najlah Feanny/ Stock Boston; p. 293: © National Pictures/Topham/Image Works; p. 299: © Earl & Nazima Kowall/Corbis Images

**Chapter 14:** p. 305: © Ziva Santop; p. 313: © George Holton/Photo Researchers; p. 317: © National Archives; p. 323: © Lindsay Hebberd/Corbis Images

**Chapter 15:** p. 330: © AP Images/Rick Silva; p. 332 (top): © Thierry Secretan/COSMOS/Woodfin Camp & Associates; p. 332 (bottom): © Joe McNally/IPNstock. com; p. 340: © R. Giling/Peter Arnold; p. 343: © Kal Muller/Woodfin Camp & Associates

**Chapter 16:** p. 348: © Denis Sinyakov/AFP/Getty Images; p. 351: © ARPL/Topham/Image Works; p. 356: © Hulton Archive/Getty Images; p. 365: © Ed Parker/Photographers Direct/Chris Fairclough Worldwide Ltd.

**Chapter 17:** p. 372: © A. Ramey/Woodfin Camp & Associates; p. 377: © PJ. Griffiths/Magnum Photos; p. 379 (all): Conrad P. Kottak; p. 387 (top): © Bradley Mayhew/Lonely Planet Images; p. 387 (bottom): © Yuri Kochetkov/EPA/Corbis

**Chapter 18:** p. 399: © Betty Press/Woodfin Camp & Associates; p. 402: © Hahn/laif/Aurora Photos; p. 405: © Ron Giling/Peter Arnold; p. 408: © John Maier, Jr./Image Works; p. 410: Courtesy Professor Marietta Baba, Michigan State University

**Chapter 19:** p. 421: © Pinnizzotto/Imapress/ Image Works; p. 423: © Hu Sheng/EPA/Corbis; p. 425: © Richard Chung/Reuters/Corbis; p. 428: © Jose Luis Quintana/ Reuters/Corbis.

# Text and Illustration

# Glossary

## A

**A. (Australopithecus) afarensis** Early form of *Australopithecus,* found in Ethiopia at Hadar ("Lucy") and in Tanzania at Laetoli; dating to the period between 3.8 and 3.0 m.y.a. 107

**A. africanus** First *Australopithecus* discovered, in South Africa; dating to 3.0–2.5 m.y.a. 104

**A. anamensis** Earliest form of *Australopithecus* yet discovered; found in Kenya and dating to 4.2 m.y.a. 104

**A. boisei** Late, hyperrobust form of *Australopithecus,* found in East Africa and dating to the period between 2.6 and 1.2 m.y.a. 104

**A. garhi** Found in Ethiopia in association with tools and dating to 2.5 m.y.a. 104

**A. robustus** Robust form of *Australopithecus,* found in South Africa and dating to the period between 2.6 and 2.0 m.y.a., aka Paranthropus. 104

**absolute dating** Dating techniques that establish dates in numbers or ranges of numbers; examples include the radiometric methods of $^{14}C$, K/A, $^{238}U$, TL, and ESR dating. 31

**acculturation** The exchange of cultural features that results when groups come into continuous firsthand contact; the original cultural patterns of either or both groups may be altered, but the groups remain distinct. 201

**Acheulian** Derived from the French village of St. Acheul, where these tools were first identified; Lower Paleolithic tool tradition associated with *H. erectus*. 125

**achieved status** Social status that comes through talents, actions, efforts, activities, and accomplishments, rather than ascription. 260

**adaptation** The process by which organisms cope with environmental stresses. 3

**adaptive** Favored by natural selection in a particular environment. 56

**agency** The active role that individuals play in interpreting, using, making, and remaking culture. 422

**age set** Group uniting all men or women (usually men) born during a certain time span; this group controls property and often has political and military functions. 263

**agriculture** Nonindustrial system of plant cultivation characterized by continuous and intensive use of land and labor. 234

**allele** A biochemical difference involving a particular gene. 53

**analogies** Similarities arising as a result of similar selective forces; traits produced by convergent evolution. 72

**anatomically modern humans (AMHs)** Including the Cro-Magnons of Europe (31,000 B.P.) and the older fossils from Skhūl (100,000) and Qafzeh (92,000); continue through the present; also known as *H. sapiens sapiens*. 133

**animism** Belief in souls or doubles. 327

**anthropoids** Members of Anthropoidea, one of the two suborders of primates; monkeys, apes, and humans are anthropoids. 73

**anthropology** The study of the human species and its immediate ancestors. 2

**anthropology and education** Anthropological research in classrooms, homes, and neighborhoods, viewing students as total cultural creatures whose enculturation and attitudes toward education belong to a larger context that includes family, peers, and society. 401

**anthropometry**    The measurement of human body parts and dimensions, including skeletal parts (*osteometry*). 26

**antimodernism**    The rejection of the modern in favor of what is perceived as an earlier, purer, and better way of life; based on disillusionment with industrialization, globalization, and developments in science, technology, and consumption patterns. 418

**applied anthropology**    The application of anthropological data, perspectives, theory, and methods to identify, assess, and solve contemporary social problems. 18, 394

**arboreal**    Tree-dwelling. 73

**archaeological anthropology**    The branch of anthropology that reconstructs, describes, and interprets human behavior and cultural patterns through material remains; best known for the study of prehistory. Also known as "archaeology." 13

**archaic *Homo sapiens***    Early *H. sapiens*, consisting of the Neandertals of Europe and the Middle East, the Neandertal-like hominids of Africa and Asia, and the immediate ancestors of all these hominids; lived from about 300,000 to 30,000 B.P. 129

***Ardipithecus kadabba***    Found in Ethiopia, earliest definite hominid; lived between 5.8 and 5.5 m.y.a. 104

***Ardipithecus ramidus***    Found in Ethiopia, dating to 4.4 m.y.a., successor to *Ardipithecus kadabba*. 105

**ascribed status**    Social status (e.g., race or gender) that people have little or no choice about occupying. 260

**assimilation**    The process of change that a minority group may experience when it moves to a country where another culture dominates; the minority is incorporated into the dominant culture to the point that it no longer exists as a separate cultural unit. 381

**australopithecines**    Varied group of Pliocene–Pleistocene hominids. The term is derived from their former classification as members of a distinct subfamily, the Australopithecinae; now they are distinguished from *Homo* only at the genus level. 105

**Aztec**    Last independent state in the Valley of Mexico; capital was Tenochtitlan. Thrived between A.D. 1325 and the Spanish conquest in 1520. 182

# B

**balanced polymorphism**    Two or more forms, such as alleles of the same gene, that maintain a constant frequency in a population from generation to generation. 57

**balanced reciprocity**    See *generalized reciprocity*. 245

**band**    Basic unit of social organization among foragers. A band includes fewer than one hundred people; it often splits up seasonally. 231, 255

**big man**    Figure often found among tribal horticulturalists and pastoralists. The big man occupies no office but creates his reputation through entrepreneurship and generosity to others. Neither his wealth nor his position passes to his heirs. 260

**biocultural**    Referring to the inclusion and combination (to solve a common problem) of both biological and cultural approaches—one of anthropology's hallmarks. 11

**biological anthropology**    The branch of anthropology that studies human biological diversity in time and space—for instance, hominid evolution, human genetics, human biological adaptation; also includes primatology (behavior and evolution of monkeys and apes). Also called *physical anthropology*. 15

**bipedalism**    Upright two-legged locomotion, the key feature differentiating early hominins from the apes. 100

**Black English Vernacular (BEV)**    A rule-governed dialect of American English with roots in southern English. BEV is spoken by African American youth and by many adults in their casual, intimate speech—sometimes called *ebonics*. 221

**blade tool**    The basic Upper Paleolithic tool type, hammered off a prepared core. 137

**bone biology**    The study of bone as a biological tissue, including its genetics; cell structure; growth, development, and decay; and patterns of movement (biomechanics). 26

**bourgeoisie**    One of Karl Marx's opposed classes; owners of the means of production (factories, mines, large farms, and other sources of subsistence). 352

**bridewealth**    A customary gift before, at, or after marriage from the husband and his kin to the wife and her kin; see also *progeny price*. 295

**broad-spectrum revolution**    Period beginning around 20,000 B.P. in the Middle East and 12,000 B.P. in Europe, during which a wider range, or broader spectrum, of plant and animal life was hunted, gathered, collected, caught, and fished; revolutionary because it led to food production. 144

**bronze**    An alloy of arsenic and copper or of tin and copper. 176

## C

**call systems**    Systems of communication among nonhuman primates, composed of a limited number of sounds that vary in intensity and duration. Tied to environmental stimuli. 206

**capital**    Wealth or resources invested in business, with the intent of producing a profit. 347

**capitalist world economy**    The single world system, which emerged in the 16th century, committed to production for sale, with the object of maximizing profits rather than supplying domestic needs. 347

**cargo cults**    Postcolonial, acculturative, religious movements common in Melanesia that attempt to explain European domination and wealth and to achieve similar success magically by mimicking European behavior. 341

**caste system**    Closed, hereditary system of stratification, often dictated by religion; hierarchical social status is ascribed at birth, so that people are locked into their parents' social position. 270

**catastrophism**    View that extinct species were destroyed by fires, floods, and other catastrophes. After each destructive event, God created again, leading to contemporary species. 48

**chiefdom**    Form of sociopolitical organization intermediate between the tribe and the state; kin-based with differential access to resources and a permanent political structure. A rank society in which relations among villages as well as among individuals are unequal, with smaller villages under the authority of leaders in larger villages; has a two-level settlement hierarchy. 172, 255

**chromosomes**    Basic genetic units, occurring in matching (homologous) pairs; lengths of DNA made up of multiple genes. 52

**clan**    Unilineal descent group based on stipulated descent. 287

**cline**    A gradual shift in gene frequencies between neighboring populations. 60

**Clovis tradition**    Stone technology based on a projectile point that was fastened to the end of a hunting spear; it flourished between 12,000 and 11,000 B.P. in North America. 139

**colonialism**    The political, social, economic, and cultural domination of a territory and its people by a foreign power for an extended time. 354

**communal religions**    In Wallace's typology, these religions have—in addition to shamanic cults—communal cults in which people organize community rituals such as harvest ceremonies and rites of passage. 338

**communism**    Spelled with a lowercase *c*, describes a social system in which property is owned by the community and in which people work for the common good. 360

**Communism**    Spelled with a capital *C*, a political movement and doctrine seeking to overthrow capitalism and to establish a form of communism such as that which prevailed in the Soviet Union (USSR) from 1917 to 1991. 360

**communitas**    Intense community spirit, a feeling of great social solidarity, equality, and togetherness; characteristic of people experiencing liminality together. 333

**complex societies**    Nations; large and populous, with social stratification and central governments. 42

**conflict resolution**    The means by which disputes are socially regulated and settled; found in all societies, but the resolution methods tend to be more formal and effective in states than in nonstates. 257

**convergent evolution**    Independent operation of similar selective forces; process by which analogies are produced. 72

**core**    Dominant structural position in the world system; consists of the strongest and most powerful states with advanced systems of production. 348

**core values**    Key, basic, or central values that integrate a culture and help distinguish it from others. 192

**correlation**    An association between two or more variables such that when one changes (varies), the other(s) also change(s) (covaries); for example, temperature and sweating. 231

**creationism**    Explanation for the origin of species given in Genesis:    God created the species during the original six days of Creation. 47

**cultural anthropology**    The study of human society and culture; describes, analyzes, interprets, and explains social and cultural similarities and differences. 12

**cultural colonialism**    Within a nation or empire, domination by one ethnic group or nationality and its culture/ideology over others—e.g., the dominance of Russian people, language, and culture in the former Soviet Union. 389

**cultural consultant**    Someone the ethnographer gets to know in the field, who teaches him or her about their society and culture, aka *informant*. 38

**cultural imperialism**    The rapid spread or advance of one culture at the expense of others, or its imposition on other cultures, which it modifies, replaces, or destroys—usually because of differential economic or political influence. 420

**cultural relativism**    The position that the values and standards of cultures differ and deserve respect. Anthropology is characterized by methodological rather than moral relativism:    In order to understand another culture fully, anthropologists try to understand its members' beliefs and motivations. Methodological relativism does

not preclude making moral judgments or taking action. 197

**cultural resource management (CRM)**    The branch of applied archaeology aimed at preserving sites threatened by dams, highways, and other projects. 18

**cultural rights**    Doctrine that certain rights are vested not in individuals but in identifiable groups, such as religious and ethnic minorities and indigenous societies. 198

**cultural transmission**    A basic feature of language; transmission through learning. 207

**culture**    Traditions and customs that govern behavior and beliefs; distinctly human; transmitted through learning. 2

**cuneiform**    Early Mesopotamian writing that used a stylus (writing implement) to write wedge-shaped impressions on raw clay; from the Latin word for "wedge." 174

**curer**    Specialized role acquired through a culturally appropriate process of selection, training, certification, and acquisition of a professional image; the curer is consulted by patients, who believe in his or her special powers, and receives some form of special consideration; a cultural universal. 408

## D

**daughter languages**    Languages developing out of the same parent language; for example, French and Spanish are daughter languages of Latin. 223

**descent**    Rule assigning social identity on the basis of some aspect of one's ancestry. 374

**descent group**    A permanent social unit whose members claim common ancestry; fundamental to tribal society. 286

**descriptive linguistics**    The scientific study of a spoken language, including its phonology, morphology, lexicon, and syntax. 211

**development anthropology**    The branch of applied anthropology that focuses on social issues in, and the cultural dimension of, economic development. 397

**diaspora**    The offspring of an area who have spread to many lands. 426

**differential access**    Unequal access to resources; basic attribute of chiefdoms and states. Superordinates have favored access to such resources, while the access of subordinates is limited by superordinates. 268

**diffusion**   Borrowing between cultures either directly or through intermediaries. 200

**diglossia**   The existence of "high" (formal) and "low" (familial) dialects of a single language, such as German. 217

**discrimination**   Policies and practices that harm a group and its members. 386

**disease**   A scientifically identified health threat caused by a bacterium, virus, fungus, parasite, or other pathogen. 406

**displacement**   A linguistic capacity that allows humans to speak of things and events that are not present. 209

**domestic–public dichotomy**   Contrast between women's role in the home and men's role in public life, with a corresponding social devaluation of women's work and worth. 310

**dominant**   Allele that masks another allele in a heterozygote. 52

**dowry**   A marital exchange in which the wife's group provides substantial gifts to the husband's family. 295

### E

**economy**   A population's system of production, distribution, and consumption of resources. 238

**egalitarian society**   A type of society, most typically found among foragers, that lacks status distinctions except for those based on age, gender, and individual qualities, talents, and achievements. 171

**emic**   The research strategy that focuses on native explanations and criteria of significance. 38

**enculturation**   The social process by which culture is learned and transmitted across the generations. 188

**endogamy**   Marriage between people of the same social group. 291

**equity, increased**   A reduction in absolute poverty and a fairer (more even) distribution of wealth. 397

**essentialism**   The process of viewing an identity as established, real, and frozen, so as to hide the historical processes and politics within which that identity developed. 429

**estrus**   Period of maximum sexual receptivity in female baboons, chimpanzees, and other primates, signaled by vaginal area swelling and coloration. 86

**ethnic group**   Group distinguished by cultural similarities (shared among members of that group) and differences (between that group and others); ethnic group members share beliefs, values, habits, customs, and norms, and a common language, religion, history, geography, kinship, and/or race. 370

**ethnicity**   Identification with, and feeling part of, an ethnic group, and exclusion from certain other groups because of this affiliation. 370

**ethnocentrism**   The tendency to view one's own culture as best and to judge the behavior and beliefs of culturally different people by one's own standards. 196

**ethnocide**   Destruction by a dominant group of the culture of an ethnic group. 388

**ethnography**   Field work in a particular culture. 12

**ethnology**   The theoretical, comparative study of society and culture; compares cultures in time and space. 13

**etic**   The research strategy that emphasizes the observer's rather than the natives' explanations, categories, and criteria of significance. 38

**evolution**   Descent with modification; change in form over generations. 49

**excavation**   Digging through the layers of deposits that make up an archaeo-logical site. 28

**exogamy**   Mating or marriage outside one's kin group; a cultural universal. 289

**extended family household**   Expanded household including three or more generations. 282

**extradomestic**   Outside the home; within or pertaining to the public domain. 314

### F

**family**   A group of people (e.g., parents, children, siblings, grandparents, grandchildren, uncles, aunts, nephews, nieces, cousins, spouses, siblings-in-law, parents-in-law, children-in-law) who are considered to be related in some way, for example by "blood" (common ancestry or descent) or marriage. 279

**family of orientation**    Nuclear family in which one is born and grows up. 279

**family of procreation**    Nuclear family established when one marries and has children. 279

**fiscal**    Pertaining to finances and taxation. 273

**focal vocabulary**    A set of words and distinctions that are particularly important to certain groups (those with particular foci of experience or activity), such as types of snow to Eskimos or skiers. 215

**food production**    Cultivation of plants and domestication (stockbreeding) of animals; first developed in the Middle East 10,000 to 12,000 years ago. 4, 144

**fossils**    Remains (e.g., bones), traces or impressions (e.g., footprints) of ancient life. 28

# G

**gender roles**    The tasks and activities that a culture assigns to each sex. 306

**gender stereotypes**    Oversimplified but strongly held ideas about the characteristics of males and females. 306

**gender stratification**    Unequal distribution of rewards (socially valued resources, power, prestige, and personal freedom) between men and women, reflecting their different positions in a social hierarchy. 306

**gene**    Area in a chromosome pair that determines, wholly or partially, a particular biological trait, such as whether one's blood type is A, B, AB, or O. 52

**gene flow**    Exchange of genetic material between populations of the same species through direct or indirect interbreeding. 59

**gene pool**    All the alleles and genotypes within a breeding population—the "pool" of genetic material available. 55

**genealogical method**    Procedures by which ethnographers discover and record connections of kinship, descent, and marriage, using diagrams and symbols. 37

**general anthropology**    The field of anthropology as a whole, consisting of cultural, archaeological, biological, and linguistic anthropology. 4

**generality**    Culture pattern or trait that exists in some but not all societies. 199

**generalized reciprocity**    Principle that characterizes exchanges between closely related individuals: As social distance increases, reciprocity becomes balanced and finally negative. 245

**genetic evolution**    Change in gene frequency within a breeding population. 55

**genocide**    Policies aimed at, and/or resulting in, the physical extinction (through mass murder) of a people perceived as a racial group, that is, as sharing defining physical, genetic, or other biological characteristics. 386

**genotype**    An organism's hereditary makeup. 53

**glacials**    The four or five major advances of continental ice sheets in northern Europe and North America. 131

**globalization**    The accelerating interdependence of nations in a world system linked economically and through mass media and modern transportation systems. 201

**gracile**    Opposite of *robust*. 111

# H

**H. (*Homo*) erectus**    Hominid type that lived from approximately 1.7 to 300,000 m.y.a.; widely distributed throughout the Old World; immediate predecessor of *Homo sapiens*. 122

**Halafian**    An early (7500–6500 B.P.) and widespread pottery style, first found in northern Syria; refers to a delicate ceramic style and to the period when the first chiefdoms emerged. 171

**head, village**    See *Village head*. 259

**health care systems**    Beliefs, customs, and specialists concerned with ensuring health and preventing and curing illness; a cultural universal. 407

**hegemonic reading**    The meaning of a text (including varied cultural products) as defined by its creators or other elites. 422

**hegemony**    As used by Antonio Gramsci, a stratified social order in which subordinates comply with domination by internalizing its values and accepting its "naturalness." 419

**heterozygous**    Having dissimilar alleles of a given gene. 53

**hidden transcript**    As used by James Scott, the critique of power by the oppressed that goes on offstage—in private—where the power holders can't see it. 419

**Hilly Flanks**    Woodland zone that flanks the Tigris and Euphrates rivers to the north; zone of wild wheat and barley and of sedentism (settled, nonmigratory life) preceding food production. 145

**historical linguistics**    Subdivision of linguistics that studies languages over time. 223

**holistic**    Interested in the whole of the human condition: past, present, and future; biology, society, language, and culture. 2

**hominid**    A member of the taxonomic family that includes humans and the African apes and their immediate ancestors. 73, 103

**hominin**    A member of the human lineage after its split from ancestral chimps; used to describe all the human species that ever have existed, including the extinct ones, but excluding chimps and gorillas. 73, 103

*Homo habilis*    Term coined by L. S. B. and Mary Leakey; immediate ancestor of *H. erectus;* lived from about 2 to 1.7 or 1.6 m.y.a. 114, 121

**homologies**    Traits that organisms have jointly inherited from their common ancestor. 70

**homozygous**    Possessing identical alleles of a particular gene. 53

**horticulture**    Nonindustrial system of plant cultivation in which plots lie fallow for varying lengths of time. 232

**human rights**    Doctrine that invokes a realm of justice and morality beyond and superior to particular countries, cultures, and religions. Human rights, usually seen as vested in individuals, would include the right to speak freely, to hold religious beliefs without persecution, and not to be enslaved. 197

**hypervitaminosis D**    Condition caused by an excess of vitamin D; calcium deposits build up on the body's soft tissues and the kidneys may fail; symptoms include gallstones and joint and circulation problems; may affect unprotected light-skinned individuals in the tropics. 11

**hypodescent**    A rule that automatically places the children of a union or mating between members of different socioeconomic groups in the less privileged group. 374

# I

**illness**    A condition of poor health perceived or felt by an individual. 406

**imperialism**    A policy of extending the rule of a nation or empire over foreign nations and of taking and holding foreign colonies. 354

**incest**    Sexual relations with a close relative. 289

**independent assortment (Mendel's law of)**    Chromosomes are inherited independently of one another. 54

**independent invention**    Development of the same culture trait or pattern in separate cultures as a result of comparable needs and circumstances. 201

**indigenized**    Modified to fit the local culture. 424

**indigenous peoples**    The original inhabitants of particular territories; often descendants of tribespeople who live on as culturally distinct colonized peoples, many of whom aspire to autonomy. 364

**Industrial Revolution**    The historical transformation (in Europe, after 1750) of "traditional" into "modern" societies through industrialization of the economy. 350

**informed consent**    Agreement to take part in research, after the people being studied have been told about that research's purpose, nature, procedures, and potential impact on them. 24

**intellectual property rights (IPR)**    Each society's cultural base—its core beliefs and principles. IPR is claimed as a group right—a cultural right, allowing indigenous groups to control who may know and use their collective knowledge and its applications. 198

**interglacials**   Extended warm periods between such major glacials as Riss and Würm. 131

**international culture**   Cultural traditions that extend beyond national boundaries. 195

**intervention philosophy**   Guiding principle of colonialism, conquest, missionization, or development; an ideological justification for outsiders to guide native peoples in specific directions. 359

**interview schedule**   Ethnographic tool for structuring a formal interview. A prepared form (usually printed or mimeographed) that guides interviews with households or individuals being compared systematically. Contrasts with a questionnaire because the researcher has personal contact and records people's answers. 36

### K

**key cultural consultant**   An expert on a particular aspect of local life who helps the ethnographer understand that aspect. Also called *key informant*. 38

**kinesics**   The study of communication through body movements, stances, gestures, and facial expressions. 210

### L

**law**   A legal code, including trial and enforcement; characteristic of state-organized societies. 257

**leveling mechanisms**   Customs and social actions that operate to reduce differences in wealth and thus to bring standouts in line with community norms. 336

**levirate**   Custom by which a widow marries the brother of her deceased husband. 296

**lexicon**   Vocabulary; a dictionary containing all the morphemes in a language and their meaning. 211

**life history**   Of a cultural consultant; provides a personal cultural portrait of existence or change in a culture. 38

**liminality**   The critically important marginal or in-between phase of a rite of passage. 331

**lineage**   Unilineal descent group based on demonstrated descent. 287

**linguistic anthropology**   The branch of anthropology that studies linguistic variation in time and space, including interrelations between language and culture; includes *historical linguistics* and *sociolinguistics*. 16

**longitudinal research**   Long-term study of a community, society, culture, or other unit, usually based on repeated visits. 40

### M

**magic**   Use of supernatural techniques to accomplish specific aims. 329

**maize**   Corn; domesticated in highland Mexico. 155

**majority groups**   Superordinate, dominant, or controlling groups in a social–political hierarchy. 373

**mana**   Sacred impersonal force in Melanesian and Polynesian religions. 338

**manioc**   Cassava; a tuber domesticated in the South American lowlands. 155

**market principle**   Profit-oriented principle of exchange that dominates in states, particularly industrial states. Goods and services are bought and sold, and values are determined by supply and demand. 244

**matrilineal descent**   Unilineal descent rule in which people join the mother's group automatically at birth and stay members throughout life. 286

**matrilocality**   Customary residence with the wife's relatives after marriage, so that children grow up in their mother's community. 288

**means (or factors) of production**   Land, labor, technology, and capital–major productive resources. 239

**medical anthropology**   Unites biological and cultural anthropologists in the study of disease, health problems, health care systems, and theories about illness in different cultures and ethnic groups. 405

**meiosis**   Special process by which sex cells are produced; four cells are produced from one, each with half the genetic material of the original cell. 54

**melanin**    Substance manufactured in specialized cells in the lower layers of the epidermis (outer skin layer); melanin cells in dark skin produce more melanin than do those in light skin. 9

**Mendelian genetics**    Studies ways in which chromosomes transmit genes across the generations. 52

**Mesoamerica**    Middle America, including Mexico, Guatemala, and Belize. 149

**Mesopotamia**    The area between the Tigris and Euphrates rivers in what is now southern Iraq and southwestern Iran; location of the first cities and states. 168

**metallurgy**    Knowledge of the properties of metals, including their extraction and processing and the manufacture of metal tools. 175

**minority groups**    Subordinate groups in a social–political hierarchy, with inferior power and less secure access to resources than majority groups have. 373

**mitosis**    Ordinary cell division; DNA molecules copy themselves, creating two identical cells out of one. 54

**mode of production**    Way of organizing production—a set of social relations through which labor is deployed to wrest energy from nature by means of tools, skills, and knowledge. 238

**molecular anthropology**    Genetic analysis, involving comparison of DNA sequences, to determine evolutionary links and distances among species and among ancient and modern populations. 27

**monotheism**    Worship of an eternal, omniscient, omnipotent, and omnipresent supreme being. 338

**morphology**    The study of form; used in linguistics (the study of morphemes and word construction) and for form in general—for example, biomorphology relates to physical form. 211

**Mousterian**    Middle Paleolithic tool-making tradition associated with Neandertals. 132

**multiculturalism**    The view of cultural diversity in a country as something good and desirable; a multicultural society socializes individuals not only into the dominant (national) culture, but also into an ethnic culture. 382

**multivariate**    Involving multiple factors, causes, or variables. 165

**mutation**    Change in the DNA molecules of which genes and chromosomes are built. 58

**m.y.a.**    Million years ago. 89

## N

**nation**    Once a synonym for "ethnic group," designating a single culture sharing a language, religion, history, territory, ancestry, and kinship; now usually a synonym for "state" or "nation-state." 380

**nation-state**    An autonomous political entity, a country like the United States or Canada. 380

**national culture**    Cultural experiences, beliefs, learned behavior patterns, and values shared by citizens of the same nation. 195

**nationalities**    Ethnic groups that once had, or wish to have or regain, autonomous political status (their own country). 381

**Natufians**    Widespread Middle Eastern culture, dated to between 12,500 and 10,500 B.P.; subsisted on intensive wild cereal collecting and gazelle hunting and had year-round villages. 148

**natural selection**    Originally formulated by Charles Darwin and Alfred Russell Wallace; the process by which nature selects the forms most fit to survive and reproduce in a given environment, such as the tropics. 9, 49

**Neandertals**    *H. sapiens neanderthalensis*, representing an archaic *H. sapiens* subspecies, lived in Europe and the Middle East between 130,000 and 30,000 B.P. 130

**negative reciprocity**    See *generalized reciprocity*. 245

**neoliberalism**    Revival of Adam Smith's classic economic liberalism, the idea that governments should not regulate private enterprise and that free market forces should rule; a currently dominant intervention philosophy. 359

**Neolithic**    "New Stone Age," coined to describe techniques of grinding and polishing stone tools; the first cultural period in a region in which the first signs of domestication are present. 145

**neolocality**   Postmarital residence pattern in which a couple establishes a new place of residence rather than living with or near either set of parents. 281

**nomadism, pastoral**   Movement throughout the year by the whole pastoral group (men, women, and children) with their animals. More generally, such constant movement in pursuit of strategic resources. 237

## O

**office**   Permanent political position. 266

**Oldowan pebble tools**   Earliest (2.0 to 2.5 m.y.a.) stone tools; first discovered in 1931 by L. S. B. and Mary Leakey at Olduvai Gorge. 114

**Olympian religions**   In Wallace's typology, develop with state organization; have full-time religious specialists—professional priesthoods. 338

**open-class system**   Stratification system that facilitates social mobility, with individual achievement and personal merit determining social rank. 270

**opposable thumb**   A thumb that can touch all the other fingers. 74

**overinnovation**   Characteristic of development projects that require major changes in people's daily lives, especially ones that interfere with customary subsistence pursuits. 398

## P

**paleoanthropology**   The study of hominid evolution and human life as revealed by the fossil record. 24

**Paleolithic**   Old Stone Age (from Greek roots meaning "old" and "stone"); divided into Lower (early), Middle, and Upper (late). 124

**paleontology**   Study of ancient life through the fossil record. 25

**paleopathology**   Study of disease and injury in skeletons from archaeological sites. 26

**pantribal sodality**   A non-kin-based group that exists throughout a tribe, spanning several villages. 262

**participant observation**   A characteristic ethnographic technique; taking part in the events one is observing, describing, and analyzing. 33

**particularity**   Distinctive or unique culture trait, pattern, or integration. 199

**pastoralists**   People who use a food-producing strategy of adaptation based on care of herds of domesticated animals. 237

**patriarchy**   Political system ruled by men in which women have inferior social and political status, including basic human rights. 315

**patrilineal descent**   Unilineal descent rule in which people join the father's group automatically at birth and stay members throughout life. 286

**patrilineal–patrilocal complex**   An interrelated constellation of patrilineality, patrilocality, warfare, and male supremacy. 312

**patrilocality**   Customary residence with the husband's relatives after marriage, so that children grow up in their father's community. 288

**peasant**   Small-scale agriculturist living in a state, with rent fund obligations. 243

**periphery**   Weakest structural position in the world system. 349

**phenotype**   An organism's evident traits; its "manifest biology"—anatomy and physiology. 6, 378

**phenotypical adaptation**   Adaptive biological changes that occur during the individual's lifetime, made possible by biological plasticity. 63

**phoneme**   Significant sound contrast in a language that serves to distinguish meaning, as in minimal pairs. 211

**phonemics**   The study of the sound contrasts (phonemes) of a particular language. 212

**phonetics**   The study of speech sounds in general; what people actually say in various languages. 212

**phonology**   The study of sounds used in speech. 211

**physical anthropology**   See *biological anthropology*.

**Pleistocene** Epoch of *Homo's* appearance and evolution; began 2 million years ago; divided into Lower, Middle, and Upper. 130

**plural marriage** Marriage of a man to two or more women (polygyny) or marriage of a woman to two or more men (polyandry)—at the same time; see also *polygamy.* 296

**plural society** A society that combines ethnic contrasts, ecological specialization (i.e., use of different environmental resources by each ethnic group), and the economic interdependence of those groups. 382

**polyandry** Variety of plural marriage in which a woman has more than one husband. 296

**polygamy** Marriage with three or more spouses, at the same time; see also *plural marriage.* 296

**polygyny** Variety of plural marriage in which a man has more than one wife. 296

**polytheism** Belief in several deities who control aspects of nature. 338

**population genetics** Field that studies causes of genetic variation, maintenance, and change in breeding populations. 52

**postcolonial** Referring to interactions between European nations and the societies they colonized (mainly after 1800); more generally, "postcolonial" may be used to signify a position against imperialism and Eurocentrism. 358

**postmodern** In its most general sense, describes the blurring and breakdown of established canons (rules, standards), categories, distinctions, and boundaries. 426

**postmodernism** A style and movement in architecture that succeeded modernism. Compared with modernism, postmodernism is less geometric, less functional, less austere, more playful, and more willing to include elements from diverse times and cultures; *post-modern* now describes comparable developments in music, literature, and visual art. 426

**postmodernity** Condition of a world in flux, with people on-the-move, in which established groups, boundaries, identities, contrasts, and standards are reaching out and breaking down. 426

**potlatch** Competitive feast among Indians on the North Pacific Coast of North America. 246

**power** The ability to exercise one's will over others—to do what one wants; the basis of political status. 270

**prejudice** Devaluing (looking down on) a group because of its assumed behavior, values, capabilities, or attributes. 385

**prestige** Esteem, respect, or approval for acts, deeds, or qualities considered exemplary. 270

**primary states** States that arise on their own (through competition among chiefdoms), and not through contact with other state societies. 172

**primates** Monkeys, apes, and prosimians; members of the zoological order that includes humans.

**primatology** The study of the biology, behavior, social life, and evolution of monkeys, apes, and other nonhuman primates. 69

**productivity** The ability to use the rules of one's language to create new expressions comprehensible to other speakers; a basic feature of language. 208

**progeny price** A gift from the husband and his kin to the wife and her kin before, at, or after marriage; legitimizes children born to the woman as members of the husband's descent group. 295

**prosimians** The primate suborder that includes lemurs, lorises, and tarsiers. 73

**protolanguage** Language ancestral to several daughter languages. 223

**public transcript** As used by James Scott, the open, public interactions between dominators and oppressed—the outer shell of power relations. 419

**punctuated equilibrium** Model of evolution; long periods of equilibrium, during which species change little, are interrupted by sudden changes—evolutionary jumps. 122

# R

**race** An ethnic group assumed to have a biological basis. 373

**racial classification** The attempt to assign humans to discrete categories (purportedly) based on common ancestry. 6

**racism** Discrimination against an ethnic group assumed to have a biological basis. 373

**random genetic drift** Change in gene frequency that results not from natural selection but from chance; most common in small populations. 58

**random sample** A sample in which all members of the population have an equal statistical chance of being included. 42

**ranked society** A type of society with hereditary inequality but not social stratification; individuals are ranked in terms of their genealogical closeness to the chief, but there is a continuum of status, with many individuals and kin groups ranked about equally. 172

**recessive** Genetic trait masked by a dominant trait. 52

**reciprocity** One of the three principles of exchange. Governs exchange between social equals; major exchange mode in band and tribal societies. 244

**recombination** Following independent assortment of chromosomes, new arrangements of hereditary units produced through bisexual reproduction. 54

**redistribution** Major exchange mode of chiefdoms, many archaic states, and some states with managed economies. 244

**refugees** People who have been forced (involuntary refugees) or who have chosen (voluntary refugees) to flee a country, to escape persecution or war. 388

**relative dating** Dating technique (e.g., stratigraphy) that establishes a time frame in relation to other strata or materials, rather than absolute dates in numbers. 31

**religion** Beliefs and rituals concerned with supernatural beings, powers, and forces. 326

**revitalization movements** Movements that occur in times of change, in which religious leaders emerge and undertake to alter or revitalize a society. 341

**rites of passage** Culturally defined activities associated with the transition from one place or stage of life to another. 331

**ritual** Behavior that is formal, stylized, repetitive, and stereotyped, performed earnestly as a social act; rituals are held at set times and places and have liturgical orders. 330

**robust** Large, strong, sturdy; said of skull, skeleton, muscle, and teeth; opposite of *gracile*. 111

# S

**sample** A smaller study group chosen to represent a larger population. 41

**Sapir-Whorf hypothesis** Theory that different languages produce different ways of thinking. 214

**science** A systematic field of study or body of knowledge that aims, through experiment, observation, and deduction, to produce reliable explanations of phenomena, with reference to the material and physical world. 17

**scientific medicine** As distinguished from Western medicine, a health care system based on scientific knowledge and procedures, encompassing such fields as pathology, microbiology, biochemistry, surgery, diagnostic technology, and applications. 408

**sedentism** Settled (sedentary) life; preceded food production in the Old World and followed it in the New World. 147

**semantics** A language's meaning system. 215

**semiperiphery** Structural position in the world system intermediate between core and periphery. 348

**settlement hierarchy** A ranked series of communities differing in size, function, and type of building; a three-level settlement hierarchy indicates state organization. 181

**sexual dimorphism** Marked differences in male and female biology, besides the contrasts in breasts and genitals, and temperament. 304

**sexual orientation** A person's habitual sexual attraction to, and activities with: persons of the opposite sex (*heterosexuality*), the same sex (*homosexuality*), or both sexes (*bisexuality*). 319

**sexual selection**   Based on differential success in mating, the process in which certain traits of one sex (e.g., color in male birds) are selected because of advantages they confer in winning mates. 56

**shaman**   A part-time religious practitioner who mediates between ordinary people and supernatural beings and forces. 337

**slavery**   The most extreme, coercive, abusive, and inhumane form of legalized inequality; people are treated as property. 271

**smelting**   The high-temperature process by which pure metal is produced from an ore. 175

**social race**   A group assumed to have a biological basis but actually perceived and defined in a social context—by a particular culture rather than by scientific criteria. 374

**society**   Organized life in groups; typical of humans and other animals. 171

**sociolinguistics**   Study of relationships between social and linguistic variation; study of language in its social context. 17, 217

**sociopolitical typology**   Classification scheme based on the scale and complexity of social organization and the effectiveness of political regulation; includes band, tribe, chiefdom, and state. 255

**sodality**   See *pantribal sodality*.

**sororate**   Custom by which a widower marries the sister of the deceased wife. 296

**speciation**   Formation of new species; occurs when subgroups of the same species are separated for a sufficient length of time. 60

**species**   Population whose members can interbreed to produce offspring that can live and reproduce. 60

**state (nation-state)**   Complex sociopolitical system that administers a territory and populace with substantial contrasts in occupation, wealth, prestige, and power. An independent, centrally organized political unit; a government. A form of social and political organization with a formal, central government and a division of society into classes. 164, 255

**status**   Any position that determines where someone fits in society; may be ascribed or achieved. 260

**stereotypes**   Fixed ideas—often unfavorable—about what members of a group are like. 385

**stratification**   Characteristic of a system with socioeconomic strata; see also *stratum*. 172, 270

**stratigraphy**   Science that examines the ways in which earth sediments are deposited in demarcated layers known as strata (singular, stratum). 31

**style shifts**   Variations in speech in different contexts. 217

**subcultures**   Different cultural symbol-based traditions associated with subgroups in the same complex society. 195

**subgroups**   Languages within a taxonomy of related languages that are most closely related. 224

**subordinate**   The lower, or underprivileged, group in a stratified system. 270

**superordinate**   The upper, or privileged, group in a stratified system. 270

**survey research**   Characteristic research procedure among social scientists other than anthropologists. Studies society through sampling, statistical analysis, and impersonal data collection. 41

**symbol**   Something, verbal or nonverbal, that arbitrarily and by convention stands for something else, with which it has no necessary or natural connection. 189

**syntax**   The arrangement and order of words in phrases and sentences. 211

**systematic survey**   Information gathered on patterns of settlement over a large area; provides a regional perspective on the archaeological record. 28

# *T*

**taboo**   Prohibition backed by supernatural sanctions. 328

**taphonomy**   The study of the processes—biological and geological—by which dead animals become fossils; from the Greek *taphos*, which means "tomb." 30

**taxonomy**    Classification scheme; assignment to categories (*taxa*; singular, *taxon*). 70

**teocentli**    Wild grass; apparent ancestor of maize. Also called teosinte. 156

**Teotihuacan**    First state in the Valley of Mexico and earliest major Mesoamerican empire, A.D. 100 to 700. 181

**terrestrial**    Ground-dwelling. 69

**text**    Something that is creatively "read," interpreted, and assigned meaning by each person who receives it; includes any media-borne image, such as Carnival. 422

**theory**    An explanatory framework, containing a series of statements, that helps us understand why (something exists); theories suggest patterns, connections, and relationships that may be confirmed by new research. 49

**transhumance**    One of two variants of pastoralism; part of the population moves seasonally with the herds while the other part remains in home villages. 237

**tribe**    Form of sociopolitical organization usually based on horticulture or pastoralism. Socioeconomic stratification and centralized rule are absent in tribes, and there is no means of enforcing political decisions. 255

**tropics**    Geographic belt extending about 23 degrees north and south of the equator, between the Tropic of Cancer (north) and the Tropic of Capricorn (south). 9

**typology, sociopolitical**    See *sociopolitical typology.*

## U

**urban anthropology**    The anthropological study of life in and around world cities, including urban social problems, differences between urban and other environments, and adaptation to city life. 403

**underdifferentiation**    Planning fallacy of viewing less developed countries as an undifferentiated group; ignoring cultural diversity and adopting a uniform approach (often ethnocentric) for very different types of project beneficiaries. 399

**uniformitarianism**    Belief that explanations for past events should be sought in ordinary forces that continue to work today. 49

**unilineal descent**    Matrilineal or patrilineal descent. 286

**universal**    Something that exists in every culture. 199

**Upper Paleolithic**    Blade-toolmaking traditions associated with early *H. sapiens sapiens;* named from their location in upper, or more recent, layers of sedimentary deposits. 137

## V

**variables**    Attributes (e.g., sex, age, height, weight) that differ from one person or case to the next. 42

**vertical mobility**    Upward or downward change in a person's social status. 270

**village head**    Leadership position in a village (as among the Yanomami, where the head is always a man); has limited authority; leads by example and persuasion. 259

## W

**wealth**    All a person's material assets, including income, land, and other types of property; the basis of economic status. 270

**Westernization**    The acculturative influence of Western expansion on other cultures. 416

**working class (or proletariat)**    Those who must sell their labor to survive; the antithesis of the bourgeoisie in Marx's class analysis. 352

**world-system theory**    Argument for the historic and contemporary social, political, and economic significance of an identifiable global system, based on wealth and power differentials, that extends beyond individual countries. 348

# BIBLIOGRAPHY

Abelmann, N., and J. Lie 1995. *Blue Dreams: Korean Americans and the Los Angeles Riots*. Cambridge, MA: Harvard University Press.

Adams, R. M. 1981. *Heartland of Cities*. Chicago: Aldine.

Adherents.com 2002. Major Religions of the World Ranked by Number of Adherents. http://www.adherents.com/Religions_By_Adherents.html.

Ahmed, A. S. 1992. *Postmodernism and Islam: Predicament and Promise*. New York: Routledge.

———. 2004. *Postmodernism and Islam: Predicament and Promise*, rev. ed. New York: Routledge.

Aiello, L., and M. Collard 2001. Our Newest Oldest Ancestor? *Nature* 410 (March 29):526–527.

Akazawa, T. 1980. *The Japanese Paleolithic: A Techno-Typological Study*. Tokyo: Rippo Shobo.

Akazawa, T., and C. M. Aikens, eds. 1986. *Prehistoric Hunter-Gatherers in Japan: New Research Methods*. Tokyo: University of Tokyo Press.

Amadiume, I. 1987. *Male Daughters, Female Husbands*. Atlantic Highlands, NJ: Zed.

American Anthropological Association *Anthropology Newsletter*. Published 9 times annually by the American Anthropological Association, Washington, DC.

Anderson, B. 1991. *Imagined Communities: Reflections on the Origin and Spread of Nationalism,* rev. ed. London: Verso.

Anderson, R. 1996. *Magic, Science, and Health: The Aims and Achievements of Medical Anthropology*. Fort Worth, TX: Harcourt Brace.

Angier, N. 1998. When Nature Discovers the Same Design Over and Over, Lookalike Creatures Spark Evolutionary Debate. *New York Times,* December 15, pp. D1, D6.

Annenberg/CPB Exhibits 2000. Collapse, Why Do Civilizations Fall? http://www.learner.org/exhibits/collapse/.

Aoki, M. Y., and M. B. Dardess, eds. 1981. *As the Japanese See It: Past and Present*. Honolulu: University Press of Hawaii.

Aoyagi, K., P. J. M. Nas, and J. Traphagan, eds. 1998. *Toward Sustainable Cities: Readings in the Anthropology of Urban Environments*. Leiden: Leiden Development Studies, Institute of Cultural and Social Studies, University of Leiden.

Appadurai, A. 1990. Disjuncture and Difference in the Global Cultural Economy. *Public Culture* 2(2):1–24.

———. 1991. Global Ethnoscapes: Notes and Queries for a Transnational Anthropology. In *Recapturing Anthropology: Working in the Present,* R. G. Fox, ed., pp. 191–210. Santa Fe, NM: School of American Research Advanced Seminar Series.

———. 1996. *Modernity at Large. Cultural Dimensions of Globalization*. Minneapolis: University of Minnesota Press.

Appadurai, A., ed. 2001. *Globalization*. Durham, NC: Duke University Press.

Appiah, K. A. 1990. Racisms. In *Anatomy of Racism,* David Theo Goldberg, ed., pp. 3–17. Minneapolis: University of Minnesota Press.

Applebome, P. 1996. English Unique to Blacks Is Officially Recognized. *The New York Times,* December 20, http://www.nytimes.com.

Arensberg, C. 1987. Theoretical Contributions of Industrial and Development Studies. In *Applied Anthropology in America,* 2nd ed., E. M. Eddy and W. L. Partridge, eds. New York: Columbia University Press.

Arieff, I. 2001. Developing Nations' Share of World Population Rising. Reuters, February 28. http://www.forests.org/archive/general/denashw1.htm.

Arrighi, G. 1994. *The Long Twentieth Century; Money, Power, and the Origins of Our Times*. New York: Verso.

Asfaw, B., T. White, and O. Lovejoy 1999. *Australopithecus garhi:* A New Species of Early Hominid from Ethiopia. *Science* 284 (April 23):629.

Ashcroft, B., G. Griffiths, and H. Tiffin 1989. *The Empire Writes Back: Theory and Practice in Post-colonial Literatures*. New York: Routledge.

Baer, H. A., M. Singer, and I. Susser 2003. *Medical Anthropology and the World System*. Westport, CT: Praeger.

Bailey, E. J. 2000. *Medical Anthropology and African American Health*. Westport, CT: Bergin and Garvey.

Bailey, R. C. 1990. *The Behavioral Ecology of Efe Pygmy Men in the Ituri Forest, Zaire*. Ann Arbor: Anthropological Papers, Museum of Anthropology, University of Michigan, no. 86.

Bailey, R. C., G. Head, M. Jenike, B. Owen, R. Rechtman, and E. Zechenter 1989. Hunting and Gathering in Tropical Rain Forests: Is It Possible? *American Anthropologist* 91:59–82.

Banton, M. 1957. *West African City. A Study in Tribal Life in Freetown*. London: Oxford University Press.

Barber, B. R. 1992. Jihad vs. McWorld. *Atlantic Monthly* 269(3):53–65, March 1992.

———. 1995. *Jihad vs. McWorld*. New York: Times Books.

Barker, C. 1997. *Global Television: An Introduction*. Malden, MA: Blackwell.

———. 2003. *Cultural Studies: Theory and Practice*. Thousand Oaks, CA: Sage.

Barnaby, F., ed. 1984. *Future War: Armed Conflict in the Next Decade*. London: M. Joseph.

Baro, M., and T. F. Deubel 2006. Persistent Hunger: Perspectives on Vulnerability, Famine, and Food Security in Sub-Saharan Africa. *Annual Review of Anthropology* 35:521–538.

Barringer, F. 1992. New Census Data Show More Children Living in Poverty. *The New York Times,* May 29, pp. A1, A12–A13.

Barth, F. 1968. (orig. 1958). Ecologic Relations of Ethnic Groups in Swat, North Pakistan. In *Man in Adaptation: The Cultural Present,* Yehudi Cohen, ed., pp. 324–331. Chicago: Aldine.

———. 1969. *Ethnic Groups and Boundaries: The Social Organization of Cultural Difference*. London: Allen & Unwin.

Beeman, W. 1986. *Language, Status, and Power in Iran*. Bloomington: Indiana University Press.

Bell, W. 1981. Neocolonialism. In *Encyclopedia of Sociology,* p. 193. Guilford, CT: DPG Publishing.

Bellah, R. N. 1978. Religious Evolution. In *Reader in Comparative Religion: An Anthropological Approach,* 4th ed., W. A. Lessa and E. Z. Vogt, eds., pp. 36–50. New York: Harper and Row.

Bellwood, P. S. 2004. *The First Farmers: Origins of Agricultural Societies*. Malden, MA: Blackwell.

Berkeleyan 1999. Berkeley Researchers Head Team That Discovers New Species of Human Ancestor: Earliest Evidence of Meat-Eating, Early Beings Has Been Unearthed in Ethiopia. April 28–May 4, 1999 (27,32); http://www.berkeley.edu/news/berkeleyan/1999/0428/species.html.

Berlin, B., and P. Kay 1992. (orig. 1969). *Basic Color Terms: Their Universality and Evolution,* 2nd ed. Berkeley: University of California Press.

Bernard, H. R. 2002. *Research Methods in Anthropology: Qualitative and Quantitative Methods,* 3rd ed. Walnut Creek, CA: AltaMira.
———. 2006. *Research Methods in Anthropology: Qualitative and Quantitative Approaches.* 4th ed. Lanham, MD: AltaMira.

Bernard, H. R., ed. 1998. *Handbook of Methods in Cultural Anthropology,* Walnut Creek, CA: AltaMira.

Bicker, A., P. Sillitoe, and J. Pottier, eds. 2004. *Investigating Local Knowledge: New Directions, New Approaches.* Burlington, VT: Ashgate.

Binford, L. R. 1968. Post-Pleistocene Adaptations. In *New Perspectives in Archeology,* S. R. Binford and L. R. Binford, eds., pp. 313–341. Chicago: Aldine.
———. 1981. *Bones: Ancient Men and Modern Myths.* New York: Academic Press.

Binford, L. R., and S. R. Binford 1979. Stone Tools and Human Behavior. In *Human Ancestors, Readings from Scientific American,* G. L. Isaac and R. E. F. Leakey, eds., pp. 92–101. San Francisco: W. H. Freeman.

Bird-David, N. 1992. Beyond "The Original Affluent Society": A Culturalist Reformulation. *Current Anthropology* 33(1):25–47.

Bjuremalm, H. 1997. Rattvisa kan skippas i Rwanda: Folkmordet 1994 gar attt forklara och analysera pa samma satt som forintelsen av judarna. *Dagens Nyheter* [06-03-19777, p. B3].

Blackwood, E., and S. Wieringa, eds. 1999. *Female Desires: Same-Sex Relations and Transgender Practices across Cultures.* New York: Columbia University Press.

Blanton, R. E. 1999. *Ancient Oaxaca: The Monte Alban State.* New York: Cambridge University Press.

Bloch, M., ed. 1975. *Political Language and Oratory in Traditional Societies.* London: Academic Press.

Blum, H. F. 1961. Does the Melanin Pigment of Human Skin Have Adaptive Value? *Quarterly Review of Biology* 36:50–63.

Boas, F. 1966. (orig. 1940). *Race, Language, and Culture.* New York: Free Press.

Boaz, N. T. 1997. *Eco Homo: How the Human Being Emerged from the Cataclysmic History of the Earth.* New York: Basic Books.

Boaz, N. T., and R. L. Ciochon 2004. Headstrong Hominids. *Natural History* 113(1):28–34.

Bodley, J. H. 1985. *Anthropology and Contemporary Human Problems,* 2nd ed. Palo Alto, CA: Mayfield.
———. 2003. *The Power of Scale: A Global History Approach.* Armonk, NY: M. E. Sharpe.

Bodley, J. H., ed. 1988. *Tribal Peoples and Development Issues: A Global Overview.* Mountain View, CA: Mayfield.

Bogaard, A. 2004. *Neolithic Farming in Central Europe: An Archaeobotanical Study of Crop Husbandry Practices.* New York: Routledge.

Bogin, B. 2001. *The Growth of Humanity.* New York: Wiley.

Bogoras, W. 1904. The Chukchee. In *The Jesup North Pacific Expedition,* F. Boas, ed. New York: Memoir of the American Museum of Natural History.

Bolinger, D., and D. Sears 1981. *Aspects of Language,* 3rd ed. New York: Harcourt Brace Jovanovich.

Bolton, R. 1981. Susto, Hostility, and Hypoglycemia. *Ethnology* 20(4): 227–258.

Bonnichsen, R., and A. L. Schneider 2000. *Battle of the Bones.* New York Academy of Sciences, *The Sciences,* July–August, http://www.friendsofpast.org/forum/battle.html.

Bonvillain, N. 2001. *Women and Men: Cultural Constructions of Gender,* 3rd ed. Upper Saddle River, NJ: Prentice Hall.
———. 2003. *Language, Culture, and Communication: The Meaning of Messages,* 4th ed. Upper Saddle River, NJ: Prentice Hall.

Boserup, E. 1970. *Women's Role in Economic Development.* London: Allen & Unwin.

Bourdieu, P. 1977. *Outline of a Theory of Practice.* R. Nice (trans.). Cambridge: Cambridge University Press.

———. 1982. *Ce Que Parler Veut Dire.* Paris: Fayard.

———. 1984. *Distinction: A Social Critique of the Judgment of Taste.* R. Nice (trans.). Cambridge, MA: Harvard University Press.

Bourque, S. C., and K. B. Warren 1987. Technology, Gender and Development. *Daedalus* 116(4): 173–197.

Bowie, F. 2006. *The Anthropology of Religion: An Introduction.* Malden, MA: Blackwell.

Brace, C. L. 1995. *The Stages of Human Evolution,* 5th ed. Upper Saddle River, NJ: Prentice Hall.

Bradley, B., D. M. Doran-Sheehy, D. Lukas, C. Boesch, and L. Vigilant 2004. Dispersed Male Networks in Western Gorillas. *Current Biology* 14 (March):510–513.

Braidwood, R. J. 1975. *Prehistoric Men,* 8th ed. Glenview, IL: Scott, Foresman.

Braudel, F. 1981. *Civilization and Capitalism, 15th–18th Century,* Volume I, *The Structure of Everyday Life: The Limits.* S. Reynolds (trans.). New York: Harper and Row.

———. 1982. *Civilization and Capitalism, 15th–18th Century,* Volume II, *The Wheels of Commerce.* New York: Harper and Row.

———. 1992. *Civilization and Capitalism, 15th–18th Century,* Volume III, *The Perspective of the World.* Berkeley: University of California Press.

Bremen, J., and A. Shimizu, eds. 1999. *Anthropology and Colonialism in Asia and Oceania.* London: Curzon.

Brenneis, D. 1988. Language and Disputing. *Annual Review of Anthropology* 17:221–237.

Brettell, C. B., and C. F. Sargent, eds. 2005. *Gender in Cross-Cultural Perspective.* Upper Saddle River, NJ: Pearson/ Prentice Hall.

Briggs, C. L. 2005. Communicability, Racial Discourse, and Disease. *Annual Review of Anthropology* 34:269–291.

Brooke, J. 1992. Rio's New Day in Sun Leaves Laplander Limp. *The New York Times,* June 1, p. A7.

Brown, A. 2001. Communism. *International Encyclopedia of the Social & Behavioral Sciences,* pp. 2323–2326. New York: Elsevier.

Brown, D. 1991. *Human Universals.* New York: McGraw-Hill.

Brown, P. J. 1998. *Understanding and Applying Medical Anthropology.* Mountain View, CA: Mayfield.

Brown, R. W. 1958. *Words and Things.* Glencoe, IL: Free Press.

Burns, J. F. 1997. A Year of Harsh Islamic Rule Weighs Heavily for Afghans. September 24, www.nytimes.com

Butler, R. 2005. World's Largest Cities: [Ranked by City Population]. http://www.mongabay.com/cities_ pop_01.htm.

Buvinic, M. 1995. The Feminization of Poverty? Research and Policy Needs. In *Reducing Poverty through Labour Market Policies.* Geneva: International Institute for Labour Studies.

Cann, R. L., M. Stoneking, and A. C. Wilson 1987. Mitochondrial DNA and Human Evolution. *Nature* 325:31–36.

Carneiro, R. L. 1956. Slash-and-Burn Agriculture: A Closer Look at Its Implications for Settlement Patterns. In *Men and Cultures,* Selected Papers of the Fifth International Congress of Anthropological and Ethnological Sciences, pp. 229–234. Philadelphia: University of Pennsylvania Press.

———. 1968. (orig. 1961). Slash-and-Burn Cultivation among the Kuikuru and Its Implications for Cultural Development in the Amazon Basin. In *Man in Adaptation: The Cultural Present,* Y. A. Cohen, ed., pp. 131–145. Chicago: Aldine.

———. 1970. A Theory of the Origin of the State. *Science* 69:733–738.

———. 1990. Chiefdom-Level Warfare as Exemplified in Fiji and the Cauca Valley. In *The Anthropology of War,* J. Haas, ed., pp. 190–211. Cambridge: Cambridge University Press.

———. 1991. The Nature of the Chiefdom as Revealed by Evidence from the Cauca Valley of Colombia. In *Profiles in Cultural Evolution,* A. T. Rambo and K. Gillogly, eds. Anthropological Papers 85, pp. 167–190. Ann Arbor: University of Michigan Museum of Anthropology.

Carsten, J. 2004. *After Kinship.* New York: Cambridge University Press.

Carter, J. 1988. Freed from Keepers and Cages, Chimps Come of Age on Baboon Island. *Smithsonian,* June, pp. 36–48.

Cartmill, M. 1974. Rethinking Primate Origins. *Science* (April 26):436–437.

———. 1992. New Views on Primate Origins. *Evolutionary Anthropology* 1: 105–111.

Cernea, M., ed. 1991. *Putting People First: Sociological Variables in Rural Development,* 2nd ed. New York: Oxford University Press (published for the World Bank).

Ceuppens, B., and P. Geschiere 2005. Autochthony: Local or Global? New Modes in the Struggle over Citizenship and Belonging in Africa and Europe. *Annual Review of Anthropology* 34:385–407.

Chagnon, N. A. 1967. *Yanomamo Warfare: Social Organization and Marriage Alliances.* Ann Arbor, MI: University Microfilms.

Chagnon, N. A. 1992 (orig. 1983). *Yanomamo: The Fierce People,* 4th ed. New York: Harcourt Brace.

———. 1997. *Yanomamo,* 5th ed. Fort Worth, TX: Harcourt Brace.

Chambers, E. 1987. Applied Anthropology in the Post-Vietnam Era: Anticipations and Ironies. *Annual Review of Anthropology* 16: 309–337.

Chang, K. C. 1977. *The Archaeology of Ancient China.* New Haven, CT: Yale University Press.

Chatterjee, P. 2004. *The Politics of the Governed: Reflections on Popular Politics in Most of the World.* New York: Columbia University Press.

Cheney, D. L., and R. M. Seyfarth 1990. In the Minds of Monkeys: What Do They Know and How Do They Know It? *Natural History,* September, pp. 38–46.

Childe, V. G. 1951. *Man Makes Himself.* New York: New American Library.

Chiseri-Strater, E., and B. S. Sunstein. 2001. *Fieldworking: Reading and Writing Research,* 2nd ed. Upper Saddle River, NJ: Prentice Hall.

Chomsky, N. 1957. *Syntactic Structures,* The Hague: Mouton.

Christensen, L. 2003. The Politics of Correction. *Rethinking Schools Online.* Fall. http://www.rethinkingschools. org/archive/18_01/corr181.shtml.

Ciochon, R. L. 1983. Hominoid Cladistics and the Ancestry of Modern Apes and Humans. In *New Interpretations of Ape and Human Ancestry,* R. L. Ciochon and R. S. Corruccini, eds., pp. 783–843. New York: Plenum.

Ciochon, R. L., J. Olsen, and J. James 1990. *Other Origins: The Search for the Giant Ape in Human Prehistory.* New York: Bantam Books.

Coates, J. 1986. *Women, Men, and Language.* London: Longman.

Cody, D. 1998. British Empire. http://www .stg. brown.edu/projects/hypertext/ landow/victorian/history/Empire.html, May 18.

Cohen, M. 1998. *Culture of Intolerance: Chauvinism, Class, and Racism.* New Haven, CT: Yale University Press.

Cohen, M. N., and G. J. Armelagos, eds. 1984. *Paleopathology at the Origins of Agriculture.* New York: Academic Press.

Cohen, R. 1967. *The Kanuri of Bornu.* New York: Holt, Rinehart & Winston.

Cohen, Y. 1974. Culture as Adaptation. In *Man in Adaptation: The Cultural Present,* 2nd ed., Y. A. Cohen, ed., pp. 45–68. Chicago: Aldine.

Colson, E., and T. Scudder 1975. New Economic Relationships between the Gwembe Valley and the Line of Rail. In *Town and Country in Central and Eastern Africa,* David Parkin, ed., pp. 190–210. London: Oxford University Press.

———. 1988. *For Prayer and Profit: The Ritual, Economic, and Social Importance of Beer in Gwembe District, Zambia, 1950–1982.* Stanford, CA: Stanford University Press.

Connor, W. 1972. Nation-Building or Nation-Destroying. *World Politics* 24(3).

Cooper, F., and A. L. Stoler, eds. 1997. *Tensions of Empire: Colonial Cultures in a Bourgeois World*. Berkeley: University of California Press.

Crapo, R. H. 2006. *Anthropology of Religion: The Unity and Diversity of Religions*. Boston: McGraw-Hill.

Cresswell, T. 2006. *On the Move: Mobility in the Modern West*. New York: Routledge.

Crosby, A. W., Jr. 2003. *The Columbian Exchange: Biological and Cultural Consequences of 1492*. Westport, CT: Praeger.

Cunningham, G. 1999. *Religion and Magic: Approaches and Theories*. New York: New York University Press.

*Cultural Survival Quarterly*. Quarterly journal. Cambridge, MA: Cultural Survival, Inc.

DaMatta, R. 1991. *Carnivals, Rogues, and Heroes: An Interpretation of the Brazilian Dilemma*. Translated from the Portuguese by John Drury. Notre Dame, IN: University of Notre Dame Press.

D'Andrade, R. 1984. Cultural Meaning Systems. In *Culture Theory: Essays on Mind, Self, and Emotion,* R. A. Shweder and R. A. Levine, eds., pp. 88–119. Cambridge: Cambridge University Press.

Darwin, C. 1958 (orig. 1859). *On the Origin of Species*. New York: Dutton.

Das, V., and D. Poole, eds. 2004. *Anthropology in the Margins of the State*. Santa Fe, NM: School of American Research Press.

Degler, C. 1970. *Neither Black nor White: Slavery and Race Relations in Brazil and the United States*. New York: Macmillan.

de la Peña, G. 2005. Social and Cultural Policies toward Indigenous Peoples: Perspectives from Latin America. *Annual Review of Anthropology* 34:717–739.

DeMarco, E. 1997. New Dig at 9,000-Year-Old City Is Changing Views on Ancient Life. November 11, http://www.nytimes.com.

Dentan, R. K. 1979. *The Semai: A Nonviolent People of Malaya,* Fieldwork edn. New York: Harcourt Brace.

De Vos, G. A., and H. Wagatsuma 1966. *Japan's Invisible Race: Caste in Culture and Personality*. Berkeley: University of California Press.

De Vos, G. A., W. O. Wetherall and K. Stearman 1983. *Japan's Minorities: Burakumin, Koreans, Ainu and Okinawans*. Report no. 3. London: Minority Rights Group.

De Waal, F. B. M. 1995. Bonobo Sex and Society: The Behavior of a Close Relative Challenges Assumptions about Male Supremacy in Human Evolution. *Scientific American,* March, pp. 82–88.

———. 1997. *Bonobo: The Forgotten Ape*. Berkeley: University of California Press.

———. 1998. *Chimpanzee Politics: Power and Sex among Apes,* rev. ed. Baltimore: Johns Hopkins University Press.

Di Leonardo, M., ed. 1991. *Toward a New Anthropology of Gender*. Berkeley: University of California Press.

Diamond, J. M. 1997. *Guns, Germs, and Steel: The Fates of Human Societies*. New York: Norton.

Dillon, S. 2006. In School Across U.S., the Melting Pot Overflows. *New York Times,* August 27, http://www.nytimes.com.

Divale, W. T., and M. Harris 1976. Population, Warfare, and the Male Supremacist Complex. *American Anthropologist* 78: 521–538.

Douglass, W. A. 1969. *Death in Murelaga: Funerary Ritual in a Spanish Basque Village*. Seattle: University of Washington Press.

———. 1975. *Echalar and Murelaga: Opportunity and Rural Exodus in Two Spanish Basque Villages*. London: C. Hurst.

———. 1992. Basques. *Encyclopedia of World Cultures,* V.4. Boston: G. K. Hall.

Draper, P. 1975. !Kung Women: Contrasts in Sexual Egalitarianism in Foraging and Sedentary Contexts. In *Toward an Anthropology of Women,* R. Reiter, ed., pp. 77–109. New York: Monthly Review Press.

Dreifus, C. 2000. Saving the Orangutan: Preserving Paradise. *The New York Times,* March 21. http://www.nytimes.com/library/national/science/032100sci-animal-orangutan.html.

Dressler, W. W., K. S. Oths, and C. C. Gravlee 2005. Race and Ethnicity in Public Health Research. *Annual Review of Anthropology* 34:231–252.

Durkheim, E. 1951 (orig. 1897). *Suicide: A Study in Sociology.* Glencoe, IL: Free Press.

————. 1961 (orig. 1912). *The Elementary Forms of the Religious Life.* New York: Collier Books.

————. 2001 (orig. 1912). *The Elementary Forms of the Religious Life.* Translated by Carol Cosman. Abridged with an introduction and notes by Mark S. Cladis. New York: Oxford University Press.

Durrenberger, E. P., and T. D. King, eds. 2000. *State and Community in Fisheries Management: Power, Policy, and Practice.* Westport, CT: Bergin and Garvey.

Earle, T. K. 1987. Chiefdoms in Archaeological and Ethnohistorical Perspective. *Annual Review of Anthropology* 16:279–308.

————. 1997. *How Chiefs Come to Power: The Political Economy in Prehistory.* Stanford, CA: Stanford University Press.

Eastman, C. M. 1975. *Aspects of Language and Culture.* San Francisco: Chandler and Sharp.

Echeverria, J. 1999. *Home Away from Home: A History of Basque Boardinghouses.* Reno: University of Nevada Press.

Eckert, P. 1989. *Jocks and Burnouts: Social Categories and Identity in the High School.* New York: Teachers College Press, Columbia University.

————. 2000. *Linguistic Variation as Social Practice: The Linguistic Construction of Identity in Belten High.* Malden, MA: Blackwell.

Eckert, P., and S. McConnell-Ginet 2003. *Language and Gender.* New York: Cambridge University Press.

Edelman, M., and A. Haugerud 2004. *The Anthropology of Development and Globalization: From Classical Political Economy to Contemporary Neoliberalism.* Malden, MA: Blackwell.

Edwards, D. N. 2004. *The Nubian Past: An Archaeology of Sudan.* New York: Routledge.

Ervin, A. M. 2005. *Applied Anthropology: Tools and Perspectives for Contemporary Practice,* 2nd ed. Boston: Pearson/Allyn & Bacon.

Escobar, A. 1991. Anthropology and the Development Encounter: The Making and Marketing of Development Anthropology. *American Ethnologist* 18:658–682.

————. 1995. *Encountering Development: The Making and Unmaking of the Third World.* Princeton, NJ: Princeton University Press.

Eskridge, W. N., JR. 1996. *The Case for Same-Sex Marriage: From Sexual Liberty to Civilized Commitment.* New York: Free Press.

Evans-Pritchard, E. E. 1970. Sexual Inversion among the Azande. *American Anthropologist* 72:1428–1433.

Fagan, B. M. 1996. *World Prehistory: A Brief Introduction,* 3rd ed. New York: HarperCollins.

————. 1998. *World Prehistory: A Brief Introduction,* 4th ed. New York: Longman.

————. 2002. *World Prehistory: A Brief Introduction,* 5th ed. Upper Saddle River, NJ: Prentice Hall.

————. 2003. *Archeology: A Brief Introduction,* 8th ed. Upper Saddle River, NJ: Prentice Hall.

————. 2004. *People of the Earth: A Brief Introduction to World Prehistory,* 12th ed. Upper Saddle River NJ: Prentice Hall.

Farner, R. F., ed. 2004. *Nationalism, Ethnicity, and Identity: Cross-National and Comparative Perspectives.* New Brunswick, NJ: Transaction Publishers.

Farooq, M. 1966. Importance of Determining Transmission Sites in Planning Bilharziasis Control: Field Observations from the Egypt-49 Project

Area. *American Journal of Epidemiology* 83:603–612.

Farr, D. M. L. 1980. British Empire. *Academic American Encyclopedia.* Princeton, NJ: Arete, volume 3, pp. 495–496.

Fasold, R. W. 1990. *The Sociolinguistics of Language.* Oxford: Blackwell.

Fedigan, L. M. 1992. *Primate Paradigms: Sex Roles and Social Bonds.* Chicago: University of Chicago Press.

Ferguson, R. B. 1995. *Yanomami Warfare: A Political History.* Santa Fe, NM: School of American Research.

———. 2002. *The State, Identity, and Violence: Political Disintegration in the Post-Cold War Era.* New York: Routledge.

Ferraro, G. P. 2002. *The Cultural Dimension of International Business,* 4th ed. Upper Saddle River, NJ: Prentice Hall.

Fields, J. M. 2004. America's Families and Living Arrangements: 2003. U.S. Census Bureau. *Current Population Reports,* P20–553, November. http://www.census.gov.

Fields, J. M., and L. M. Casper 2001. America's Families and Living Arrangements: Population Characteristics, 2000. U.S. Census Bureau. *Current Population Reports,* P20–537, June. http://www.census.gov/prod/2001pubs/p20–537.pdf.

Files, J. 2005. Report Describes Immigrants as Younger and More Diverse. *The New York Times,* National ed., June 10, p. A11.

Finkler, K. 1985. *Spiritualist Healers in Mexico: Successes and Failures of Alternative Therapeutics.* South Hadley, MA: Bergin and Garvey.

Finnstrom, S. 1997. Postcoloniality and the Postcolony: Theories of the Global and the Local. http://www.stg. brown. edu/projects/hypertext/landow/post/poldiscourse/finnstrom/finnstrom1.html.

Fisher, A. 1988. On the Emergence of Humanness. *MOSAIC* 19(1):34–45.

Fiske, J. 1989. *Understanding Popular Culture.* Boston: Unwin Hyman.

Fiske, J., and J. Hartley 2003. *Reading Television.* New York: Routledge.

Flannery, K. V. 1969. Origins and Ecological Effects of Early Domestication in Iran and the Near East. In *The Domestication and Exploitation of Plants and Animals,* P. J. Ucko and G. W. Dimbleby, eds., pp. 73–100. Chicago: Aldine.

———. 1973. The Origins of Agriculture. *Annual Review of Anthropology* 2: 271–310.

———. 1995. Prehistoric Social Evolution. In *Research Frontiers in Anthropology,* C. R. Ember and M. Ember, eds., pp. 1–26. Upper Saddle River, NJ: Prentice Hall.

———. 1999. Chiefdoms in the Early Near East: Why It's So Hard to Identify Them. In *The Iranian World: Essays on Iranian Art and Archaeology,* A. Alizadeh, Y. Majidzadeh, and S. M. Shahmirzadi, eds. Tehran: Iran University Press.

Flannery, K. V., ed. 1986. *Guila Naquitz: Archaic Foraging and Early Agriculture in Oaxaca, Mexico.* Orlando, FL: Academic Press.

Flannery, K. V., and J. Marcus 2000. Formative Mexican Chiefdoms and the Myth of the "Mother Culture." *Journal of Anthropological Archaeology* 19:1–37.

Flannery, K. V., J. Marcus, and R. G. Reynolds 1989. *The Flocks of the Wamani: A Study of Llama Herders on the Punas of Ayacucho, Peru.* San Diego: Academic Press.

Fleisher, M. L. 2000. *Kuria Cattle Raiders: Violence and Vigilantism on the Tanzania/Kenya Frontier.* Ann Arbor: University of Michigan Press.

Ford, C. S., and F. A. Beach 1951. *Patterns of Sexual Behavior.* New York: Harper Torchbooks.

Fortes, M. 1950. Kinship and Marriage among the Ashanti. In *African Systems of Kinship and Marriage,* A. R. Radcliffe-Brown and D. Forde, eds., pp. 252–284. London: Oxford University Press.

Fossey, D. 1983. *Gorillas in the Mist.* Boston: Houghton Mifflin.

Foster, G. M., and B. G. Anderson 1978. *Medical Anthropology*. New York: McGraw-Hill.

Foucault, M. 1979. *Discipline and Punish: The Birth of the Prison*. A. Sheridan (trans.). New York: Vintage Books.

———. 1990. *The History of Sexuality, Volume 2, The Use of Pleasure*. R. Hurley (trans.). New York: Vintage.

Fountain, H. 2002. Iceman's Last Meal. *New York Times*, September 17 http://www.nytimes.com/2002/09/17/science/17OBSE.html.

Fouts, R. S. 1997. *Next of Kin: What Chimpanzees Have Taught Me about Who We Are*. New York: William Morrow.

Fouts, R. S., D. H. Fouts, and T. E. Van Cantfort 1989. The Infant Loulis Learns Signs from Cross-Fostered Chimpanzees. In *Teaching Sign Language to Chimpanzees,* R. A. Gardner, B. T. Gardner, and T. E. Van Cantfort, eds., pp. 280–292. Albany: State University of New York Press.

Franke, R. 1977. Miracle Seeds and Shattered Dreams in Java. In *Readings in Anthropology,* pp. 197–201. Guilford, CT: Dushkin.

French, H. W. 2002. Whistling Past the Global Graveyard. *New York Times,* July 14, http://www.nytimes.com/2002/01/14.weekinreview/14FREN.html.

Fricke, T. 1994. *Himalayan Households: Tamang Demography and Domestic Processes,* 2nd ed. New York: Columbia University Press.

Fried, M. H. 1960. On the Evolution of Social Stratification and the State. In *Culture in History,* S. Diamond, ed., pp. 713–731. New York: Columbia University Press.

Friedl, E. 1975. *Women and Men: An Anthropologist's View*. New York: Holt, Rinehart & Winston.

Friedman, J., ed. 2003. *Globalization, the State, and Violence*. Walnut Creek, CA: AltaMira.

Frisancho, A. R. 1993. *Human Adaptation and Accommodation*. Ann Arbor: University of Michigan Press.

Futuyma, D. J. 1995. *Science on Trial,* updated ed. New York: Pantheon.

Gal, S. 1989. Language and Political Economy. *Annual Review of Anthropology* 18:345–367.

Gardner, R. A., B. T. Gardner, and T. E. Van Cantfort, eds. 1989. *Teaching Sign Language to Chimpanzees*. Albany: State University of New York Press.

Gates, C. 2003. *Ancient Cities: The Archaeology of Urban Life in the Ancient Near East, Egypt, Greece, and Rome*. New York: Routledge.

Geertz, C. 1973. *The Interpretation of Cultures*. New York: Basic Books.

Geis, M. L. 1987. *The Language of Politics*. New York: Springer-Verlag.

Gellner, E. 1997. *Nationalism*. New York: New York University Press.

Giddens, A. 1973. *The Class Structure of the Advanced Societies*. New York: Cambridge University Press.

———. 2000. *Runaway World: How Globalization Is Reshaping Our Lives*. New York: Routledge.

Gillespie, J. H. 2004. *Population Genetics: A Concise Guide,* 2nd ed. Baltimore: Johns Hopkins University Press.

Gilmore, D. D. 1987. *Aggression and Community: Paradoxes of Andalusian Culture*. New Haven, CT: Yale University Press.

———. 2001. *Misogyny: The Male Malady*. Philadelphia: University of Pennsylvania Press.

Gilmore-Lehne, W. J. 2000. Pre-Sumerian Cultures: Natufian through Ubaid Eras: 10,500–3500 B.C.E. http://www.stockton.edu/~gilbmorew/consorti/1bnear.htm.

Gledhill, J. 2000. *Power and Its Disguises: Anthropological Perspectives on Politics*. Sterling, VA: Pluto Press.

Gmelch, G. 1978. Baseball Magic. *Human Nature* 1(8):32–40.

———. 2001. *Inside Pitch: Life in Professional Baseball*. Washington, DC: Smithsonian Institution Press.

Gmelch, G., and W. Zenner, eds. 2002. *Urban Life: Readings in the*

*Anthropology of the City*. Prospect Heights, IL: Waveland.

Goldberg, D. T. 2002. *The Racial State*. Malden, MA: Blackwell.

Golden, T. 1997. Oakland Revamps Plan to Teach Black English. *The New York Times,* January 14, http://www.nytimes.com.

Goleman, D. 1992. Anthropology Goes Looking for Love in All the Old Places. *The New York Times,* November 24, 1992, p. B1.

Goodall, J. 1986. *The Chimpanzees of Gombe: Patterns of Behavior*. Cambridge, MA: Belknap Press of Harvard University Press.

————. 1996. *My Life with the Chimpanzees*. New York: Pocket Books.

Gottdiener, M., ed. 2000. *New Forms of Consumption: Consumers, Culture, and Commodification*. Lanham, MD: Rowman & Littlefield.

Gough, E. K. 1959. The Nayars and the Definition of Marriage. *Journal of the Royal Anthropological Institute* 89:23–34.

Gould, S. J. 1999. *Rock of Ages: Science and Religion in the Fullness of Life*. New York: Ballantine Books.

Gowlett, J. A. J. 1993. *Ascent to Civilization: The Archaeology of Early Humans*. New York: McGraw-Hill.

Gramsci, A. 1971. *Selections from the Prison Notebooks*. Q. Hoare and G. N. Smith, ed. and trans. London: Wishart.

Grasmuck, S., and P. Pessar 1991. *Between Two Islands: Dominican International Migration*. Berkeley: University of California Press.

Gray, J. 1986. With a Few Exceptions, Television in Africa Fails to Educate and Enlighten. *Ann Arbor News,* December 8.

Greaves, T. C. 1995. Problems Facing Anthropologists: Cultural Rights and Ethnography. *General Anthropology* 1(2):1, 3–6.

Green, E. C. 1992. (orig. 1987). The Integration of Modern and Traditional Health Sectors in Swaziland. In *Applying Anthropology,* A. Podolefsky and P. J. Brown, eds., pp. 246–251. Mountain View, CA: Mayfield.

Green, G. M., and R. W. Sussman 1990. Deforestation History of the Eastern Rain Forests of Madagascar from Satellite Images. *Science* 248 (April 13): 212–215.

Green, T. 2006. Archaeologist Makes the Case for Burying Dominant Theory of First Americans. Austin: University of Texas Research, http://www.utexas.edu/research/impact/collins/html.

Greenwood, D. J. 1976. *Unrewarding Wealth: The Commercialization and Collapse of Agriculture in a Spanish Basque Town*. Cambridge: Cambridge University Press.

Grekova, M. 2001. Postsocialist Societies. *International Encyclopedia of the Social & Behavioral Sciences,* pp. 11877–11881. New York: Elsevier.

Griffin, P. B., and A. Estioko-Griffin, eds. 1985. *The Agta of Northern Luzon: Recent Studies*. Cebu City, Philippines: University of San Carlos.

Gudeman, S., ed. 1999. *Economic Anthropology*. Northhampton, MA: E. Elgar.

Gugliotta, G. 2002. Earliest Human Ancestor? Skull Dates to When Apes, Humans Split. *The Washington Post,* July 11, p. A01.

————. 2005. Tools Found in Britain Show Much Earlier Human Existence. *Washington Post,* December 15, p. A24.

Gumperz, J. J., and S. C. Levinson, eds. 1996. *Rethinking Linguistic Relativity*. New York: Cambridge University Press.

Gupta, A., and J. Ferguson 1997a. Culture, Power, Place: Ethnography at the End of an Era. In *Culture, Power, Place: Explorations in Critical Anthropology,* A. Gupta and J. Ferguson, eds., pp. 1–29. Durham, NC: Duke University Press.

————. 1997b Beyond "Culture": Space, Identity, and the Politics of Difference. In *Culture, Power, Place: Explorations* in *Critical Anthropology,* A. Gupta and J. Ferguson, eds., pp. 33–51. Durham, NC: Duke University Press.

Gupta, A., and J. Ferguson, eds. 1997c *Anthropological Locations: Boundaries and Grounds of a Field Science.* Berkeley: University of California Press.

———. 1997d *Culture, Power, Place: Explorations in Critical Anthropology.* Durham, NC: Duke University Press.

Hallowell, A. I. 1955. *Culture and Experience.* Philadelphia: University of Pennsylvania Press.

Hansen, K. V. 2004. *Not-So-Nuclear Families: Class, Gender, and Networks of Care.* New Brunswick, NJ: Rutgers University Press.

Hansen, K. V., and A. I. Garey, eds. 1998. *Families in the U.S.: Kinship and Domestic Politics.* Philadelphia: Temple University Press.

Harcourt, A. H., D. Fossey, and J. Sabater-Pi 1981. Demography of Gorilla gorilla. *Journal of Zoology* 195:215–233.

Harding, S. 1975. Women and Words in a Spanish Village. In *Toward an Anthropology of Women,* R. Reiter, ed., pp. 283–308. New York: Monthly Review Press.

Harlan, J. R., and D. Zohary 1966. Distribution of Wild Wheats and Barley. *Science* 153:1074–1080.

Harlow, H. F. 1971. *Learning to Love.* San Francisco: Albion.

Harper, J. 2002. *Endangered Species: Health, Illness, and Death among Madagascar's People of the Forest.* Durham, NC: Carolina Academic Press.

Harris, M. 1964. *Patterns of Race in the Americas.* New York: Walker.

———. 1970. Referential Ambiguity in the Calculus of Brazilian Racial Identity. *Southwestern Journal of Anthropology* 26(1):1–14.

———. 1974. *Cows, Pigs, Wars, and Witches: The Riddles of Culture.* New York: Random House.

———. 1978. *Cannibals and Kings.* New York: Vintage Books.

———. 2001 (orig. 1968). *The Rise of Anthropological Theory:* Walnut Greek, CA: AltaMira.

Harris, M., and C. P. Kottak 1963. The Structural Significance of Brazilian Racial Categories. *Sociologia* 25:203–209.

Hart, C. W. M., A. R. Pilling, and J. C. Goodale 1988. *The Tiwi of North Australia* 3rd ed. Fort Worth, TX: Harcourt Brace.

Hartl, D. L. 2000. *A Primer of Population Genetics,* 3rd ed. Sunderland, MA: Sinauer Associates.

Hartl, D. L., and E. W. Jones 2002. *Essential Genetics,* 3rd ed. Sudbury, MA: Jones and Bartlett.

Harvey, D. J. 1980. French Empire. *Academic American Encyclopedia.* Princeton, NJ: Arete, volume 8, pp. 309–310.

Hassig, R. 1985. *Trade, Tribute, and Transportation: The Sixteenth-Century Political Economy of the Valley of Mexico.* Norman: University of Oklahoma Press.

Hastings, A. 1997. *The Construction of Nationhood: Ethnicity, Religion, and Nationalism.* New York: Cambridge University Press.

Hawkes, K., J. O'Connell, and K. Hill 1982. Why Hunters Gather: Optimal Foraging and the Ach of Eastern Paraguay. *American Ethnologist* 9:379–398.

Hayden, B. 1981. Subsistence and Ecological Adaptations of Modern Hunter/ Gatherers. In *Omnivorous Primates: Gathering and Hunting in Human Evolution,* R. S. Harding and G. Teleki, eds., pp. 344–421. New York: Columbia University Press.

Hedges, C. 1992. Sudan Presses Its Campaign to Impose Islamic Law on Non-Muslims. *The New York Times,* June 1, p. A7.

Helman, C. 2001. *Culture, Health, and Illness: An Introduction for Health Professionals,* 4th ed. Boston: Butterworth-Heinemann.

Henry, D. O. 1989. *From Foraging to Agriculture: The Levant at the End of the Ice Age*. Philadelphia: University of Pennsylvania Press.

———. 1995. *Prehistoric Cultural Ecology and Evolution: Insights from Southern Jordan*. New York: Plenum Press.

Henry, J. 1955. Docility, or Giving Teacher What She Wants. *Journal of Social Issues* 2:33–41.

Herdt, G. H. 1981. *Guardians of the Flutes*. New York: McGraw-Hill.

Herdt, G. H., ed. 1984. *Ritualized Homosexuality in Melanesia*. Berkeley: University of California Press.

Heyerdahl, T. 1971. *The Ra Expeditions*. Translated by P. Crampton. Garden City, NY: Doubleday.

Hill, J. H. 1978. Apes and Language. *Annual Review of Anthropology* 7:89–112.

Hill, K., H. Kaplan, K. Hawkes, and A. Hurtado 1987. Foraging Decisions among Ache Hunter-gatherers: New Data and Implications for Optimal Foraging Models. *Ethology and Sociobiology* 8:1–36.

Hill-Burnett, J. 1978. Developing Anthropological Knowledge through Application. In *Applied Anthropology in America,* E. M. Eddy and W. L. Partridge, eds., pp. 112–128. New York: Columbia University Press.

Hinde, R. A. 1983. *Primate Social Relationships: An Integrated Approach*. Sunderland, MA: Sinauer.

Hobhouse, L. T. 1915. *Morals in Evolution,* rev. ed. New York: Holt.

Hoebel, E. A. 1954. *The Law of Primitive Man*. Cambridge, MA: Harvard University Press.

———. 1968 (orig. 1954). The Eskimo: Rudimentary Law in a Primitive Anarchy. In *Studies in Social and Cultural Anthropology,* J. Middleton, ed., pp. 93–127. New York: Crowell.

Hoge, W. 2001. Kautokeino Journal; Reindeer Herders, at Home on a (Very Cold) Range. *The New York Times,* March 26, late ed.—final, sec. A, p. 4.

Holden, A. 2005. *Tourism Studies and the Social Sciences*. New York: Routledge.

Hole, F., K. V. Flannery, and J. A. Neely 1969. *The Prehistory and Human Ecology of the Deh Luran Plain*. Memoir no. 1. Ann Arbor: University of Michigan Museum of Anthropology.

Hopkins, T., and I. Wallerstein 1982. Patterns of Development of the Modern World System. In *World System Analysis: Theory and Methodology,* by T. Hopkins, I. Wallerstein, R. Bach, C. Chase-Dunn, and R. Mukherjee, eds., pp. 121–141. Thousand Oaks, CA: Sage.

Hunter, M. L. 2005. *Race, Gender, and the Politics of Skin Tone*. New York: Routledge.

Hurtado, A. M., C. A. Lambourne, P. James, K. Hill, K. Cheman, and K. Baca 2005. Human Rights, Biomedical Science, and Infectious Diseases among South American Indigenous Groups. *Annual Review of Anthropology* 34:639–665.

Ingraham, C. 1999. *White Weddings: Romancing Heterosexuality in Popular Culture*. New York: Routledge.

Inhorn, M. C., and P. J. Brown 1990. The Anthropology of Infectious Disease. *Annual Review of Anthropology* 19:89–117.

Jackson, J., and K. B. Warren 2005. Indigenous Movements in Latin America, 1992–2004: Controversies, Ironies, New Directions. *Annual Review of Anthropology* 34:549–573.

Jenks, C. 2003. *Culture*, 2nd ed. New York: Routledge.

Johansen, B. E. 2003. *Indigenous Peoples and Environmental Issues: An Encyclopedia*. Westport, CT: Greenwood.

Johanson, D. C., and T. D. White 1979. A Systematic Assessment of Early African Hominids. *Science* 203:321–330.

Johnson, A. W. 1978. *Quantification in Cultural Anthropology: An Introduction to Research Design*. Stanford, CA: Stanford University Press.

Johnson, A. W., and T. K. Earle 2000. *The Evolution of Human Societies: From*

*Foraging Group to Agrarian State,* 2nd ed. Stanford, CA: Stanford University Press.

Jolly, C. J., and R. White 1995. *Physical Anthropology and Archaeology,* 5th ed. New York: McGraw-Hill.

Jones, D. 1999. Hot Asset in Corporate: Anthropology Degrees. *USA Today,* February 18, p. B1.

Joralemon, D. 1999. *Exploring Medical Anthropology.* Boston: Allyn & Bacon.

Jordan, A. 2003. *Business Anthropology.* Prospect Heights, IL: Waveland.

Kan, S. 1986. The 19th-Century Tlingit Potlatch: A New Perspective. *American Ethnologist* 13:191–212.

———. 1989. *Symbolic Immortality: The Tlingit Potlatch of the Nineteenth Century.* Washington, DC: Smithsonian Institution Press.

Katzenberg, M. A., and S. R. Saunders, eds. 2000. *Biological Anthropology of the Human Skeleton.* New York: Wiley.

Kaufman, S. R., and L. M. Morgan 2005. The Anthropology of the Beginnings and Ends of Life. *Annual Review of Anthropology* 34:317–341.

Kearney, M. 1996. *Reconceptualizing the Peasantry: Anthropology in Global Perspective.* Boulder, CO: Westview Press.

———. 2004. *Changing Fields of Anthropology: From Local to Global.* Lanham, MD: Rowman & Littlefield.

Kelly, R. C. 1976. Witchcraft and Sexual Relations: An Exploration in the Social and Semantic Implications of the Structure of Belief. In *Man and Woman in the New Guinea Highlands,* P. Brown and G. Buchbinder, eds., pp. 36–53. Special Publication no. 8. Washington, DC: American Anthropological Association.

Kelly, R. L. 1995. *The Foraging Spectrum: Diversity in Hunter-Gatherer Lifeways.* Washington, DC: Smithsonian Institution Press.

Kent, S. 1992. The Current Forager Controversy: Real versus Ideal Views of Hunter-gatherers. *Man* 27:45–70.

———. 1996. *Cultural Diversity among Twentieth-Century Foragers: An African Perspective.* New York: Cambridge University Press.

Keppel, K. G., J. N. Pearch, and D. K. Wagener 2002. Trends in Racial and Ethnic-Specific Rates for the Health Status Indicators: United States, 1990–98. *Healthy People Statistical Notes No. 23.* Hyattsville, MD: National Center for Health Statistics.

Keynes, J. M. 1927. *The End of Laissez-Faire.* London: L and Virginia Woolf.

———. 1936. *General Theory of Employment, Interest, and Money.* New York: Harcourt Brace.

Kimmel, M., J. Hearn, and R. W. Connell 2004. *Handbook of Studies on Men and Masculinities.* Thousand Oaks, CA: Sage.

Kimmel, M., and R. Plante 2004. *Sexualities: Identities, Behaviors, and Society.* New York: Oxford University Press.

Kimmel, M. S., and M. A. Messner, eds. 2004. *Men's Lives,* 6th ed. Boston: Pearson.

Kinsey, A. C., W. B. Pomeroy, and C. E. Martin 1948. *Sexual Behavior in the Human Male.* Philadelphia: W. B. Saunders.

Klass, M. 2003. *Mind over Mind: The Anthropology and Psychology of Spirit Possession.* Lanham, MA: Rowman & Littlefield.

Kleinfeld, J. 1975. Positive Stereotyping: The Cultural Relativist in the Classroom. *Human Organization* 34:269–274.

Kluckhohn, C. 1944. *Mirror for Man: A Survey of Human Behavior and Social Attitudes.* Greenwich, CT: Fawcett.

Kopytoff, V. G. 1995. Meat Viewed as Staple of Chimp Diet and Mores. *The New York Times,* June 27, pp. B5–B6.

Kottak, C. P. 1980. *The Past in the Present: History, Ecology, and Social Organization in Highland Madagascar.* Ann Arbor: University of Michigan Press.

———. 1990a. Culture and "Economic Development." *American Anthropologist* 93(3):723–731.

————. 1990b. *Prime-Time Society: An Anthropological Analysis of Television and Culture*. Belmont, CA: Wadsworth.

————. 1991. When People Don't Come First: Some Lessons from Completed Projects. In *Putting People First: Sociological Variables in Rural Development,* 2nd ed., M. Cernea, ed., pp. 429–464. New York: Oxford University Press.

————. 1999. The New Ecological Anthropology. *American Anthropologist* 101(1):23–35.

————. 2004. An Anthropological Take on Sustainable Development: A Comparative Study of Change. *Human Organization* (63, 4): 501–510.

————. 2006. *Assault on Paradise: The Globalization of a Little Community in Brazil,* 4th ed. New York: McGraw-Hill.

Kottak, C. P., and K. A. Kozaitis 2008. *On Being Different: Diversity and Multiculturalism in the North American Mainstream,* 3rd. ed. Boston: McGraw-Hill.

Kottak, C. P., L. L. Gezon, and G. Green 1994. Deforestation and Biodiversity Preservation in Madagascar: The View from Above and Below. *CIESIN Human Dimensions Kiosk*—an electronic publication. http://www.ciesin.com.

Kreider, R. M., and J. M. Fields 2002. Number, Timing and Duration of Marriages and Divorces: 1996. U.S. Census Bureau. *Current Population Reports,* P70–80, February. http://www.census.gov/prod/2002pubs/p70–80.pdf.

Kretchmer, N. 1975 (orig. 1972). Lactose and Lactase. In *Biological Anthropology, Readings from Scientific American,* S. H. Katz, ed., pp. 310–318. San Francisco: W. H. Freeman.

Kulick, D. 1998. *Travesti: Sex, Gender, and Culture among Brazilian Transgendered Prostitutes.* Chicago: University of Chicago Press.

Kuper, L. 2006. *Race, Class, and Power: Ideology and Revolutionary Change in Plural Societies.* New Brunswick, NJ: Transaction Publishers.

Kurtz, D. V. 2001. *Political Anthropology: Power and Paradigms.* Boulder, CO: Westview Press.

Kutsche, P. 1998. *Field Ethnography: A Manual for Doing Cultural Anthropology.* Upper Saddle River, NJ: Prentice Hall.

Labov, W. 1972a. *Language in the Inner City: Studies in the Black English Vernacular.* Philadelphia: University of Pennsylvania Press.

————. 1972b. *Sociolinguistic Patterns.* Philadelphia: University of Pennsylvania Press.

La Fraugh, R. J. n.d. Euskara: The History, a True Mystery. The La Fraugh Name History. http://planetrjl. tripod. com/LaFraughName/id5.html.

Laguerre, M. 1984. *American Odyssey: Haitians in New York.* Ithaca, NY: Cornell University Press.

————. 1998. *Diasporic Citizenship: Haitian Americans in Transnational America.* New York: St. Martin's Press.

————. 1999. *The Global Ethnopolis: Chinatown, Japantown, and Manilatown in American Society.* New York: St. Martin's Press.

————. 2001. *Urban Multiculturalism and Globalization in New York City.* New York: Palgrave Macmillan.

Laird, S. A. 2002. *Biodiversity and Traditional Knowledge: Equitable Partnerships in Practice.* Sterling, VA: Earthscan.

Lakoff, R. 2004. *Language and Women's Place: Text and Commentaries,* rev. ed. New York: Oxford University Press.

Lakoff, R. T. 2000. *The Language War.* Berkeley: University of California Press.

————. 2004. *Language and Woman's Place,* rev. ed. New York: Oxford University Press.

Lancaster, R. N., and M. Di Leonardo, eds. 1997. *The Gender/Sexuality Reader: Culture, History, Political Economy.* New York: Routledge.

Larsen, C. S. 2000. *Skeletons in Our Closet: Revealing Our Past through Bioarchaeology.* Princeton, NJ: Princeton University Press.

Larson, A. 1989. Social Context of Human Immunodeficiency Virus Transmission in Africa: Historical and Cultural Bases of East and Central African Sexual Relations. *Review of Infectious Diseases* 11:716–731.

Lassiter, L. E. 1998. *The Power of Kiowa Song: A Collaborative Ethnography*. Tucson: University of Arizona Press.

Laughlin, J. C. H. 2003. *Fifty Major Cities of the Bible*. New York: Routledge.

Leach, E. R. 1955. Polyandry, Inheritance and the Definition of Marriage. *Man* 55:182–186.

———. 1961. *Rethinking Anthropology*. London: Athlone Press.

Lee, R. B. 1979. *The !Kung San: Men, Women, and Work in a Foraging Society*. New York: Cambridge University Press.

———. 1984. *The Dobe !Kung*. New York: Harcourt Brace.

———. 1993. *The Dobe Ju/'hoansi,* 2nd ed. Fort Worth, TX: Harcourt Brace.

———. 2003. *The Dobe Ju/'hoansi,* 3rd ed. Belmont, CA: Wadsworth.

Lee, R. B., and R. H. Daly 1999. *The Cambridge Encyclopedia of Hunters and Gatherers*. New York: Cambridge University Press.

Lehmann, A. C., J. E. Meyers, and P. A. Moro eds. 2005. *Magic, Witchcraft, and Religion: An Anthropological Study of the Supernatural,* 6th ed. Boston: McGraw-Hill.

Leman, J. 2001. *The Dynamics of Emerging Ethnicities: Immigrant and Indigenous Ethnogenesis in Confrontation*. New York: Peter Lang.

Lemonick, M. D., and A. Dorfman 1999. Up from the Apes: Remarkable New Evidence Is Filling in the Story of How We Became Human. *Time* 154(8):5–58.

Lenski, G. 1966. *Power and Privilege: A Theory of Social Stratification*. New York: McGraw-Hill.

Lévi-Strauss, C. 1963. *Totemism*. R. Needham (trans.). Boston: Beacon Press.

———. 1967. *Structural Anthropology*. New York: Doubleday.

Levy, J. E., with B. Pepper 1992. *Orayvi Revisited: Social Stratification in an "Egalitarian" Society*. Santa Fe, NM: School of American Research Press, and Seattle: University of Washington Press.

Lewellen, T. C. 2003. *Political Anthropology: An Introduction,* 3rd ed. Westport, CT: Praeger.

Lie, J. 2001. *Multiethnic Japan*. Cambridge, MA: Harvard University Press.

Lieban, R. W. 1977. The Field of Medical Anthropology. In *Culture, Disease, and Healing: Studies in Medical Anthropology,* D. Landy, ed., pp. 13–31. New York: Macmillan.

Lindenbaum, S. 1972. Sorcerers, Ghosts, and Polluting Women: An Analysis of Religious Belief and Population Control. *Ethnology* 11:241–253.

Linton, R. 1943. Nativistic Movements. *American Anthropologist* 45:230–240.

Little, K. 1965. *West African Urbanization: A Study of Voluntary Associations in Social Change*. Cambridge: Cambridge University Press.

———. 1971. Some Aspects of African Urbanization South of the Sahara. Reading, MA: Addison-Wesley, McCaleb Modules in Anthropology.

Livingstone, F. B. 1969. Gene Frequency Clines of the b Hemoglobin Locus in Various Human Populations and Their Similarities by Models Involving Differential Selection. *Human Biology* 41:223–236.

Lockwood, W. G. 1975. *European Moslems: Economy and Ethnicity in Western Bosnia*. New York: Academic Press.

Lohr, S. 2005. Cutting Here, but Hiring Over There. *The New York Times,* June 24. http://www.nytimes.com/2005/06/24/technology/24blue.html?pagewanted=print.

Loomis, W. F. 1967. Skin-Pigmented Regulation of Vitamin-D Biosynthesis in Man. *Science* 157:501–506.

Lowie, R. H. 1961 (orig. 1920). *Primitive Society*. New York: Harper & Brothers.

Lucentini, J. 2002. Bones Reveal Some Truth in "Noble Savage Myth." *Washington Post,* April 15, p. A09.

Lugaila, T. 1999. Married Adults Still in the Majority, Census Bureau Reports. http://www.census.gov/Press-Release/www/1999/cb9903.html.

Lyell, C. 1969 (orig. 1830–1837). *Principles of Geology*. New York: Johnson.

MacKinnon, J. 1974. *In Search of the Red Ape*. New York: Ballantine Books.

Madra, Y. M. 2004. Karl Polanyi: Freedom in a Complex Society. *Econ-Atrocity Bulletin: In the History of Thought*. http://www.fguide.org/Bulletin/polanyi.htm.

Malinowski, B. 1929. Practical Anthropology. *Africa* 2:23–38.

———. 1961 (orig. 1922). *Argonauts of the Western Pacific*. New York: Dutton.

———. 1978 (orig. 1931). The Role of Magic and Religion. In *Reader in Comparative Religion: An Anthropological Approach,* 4th ed., W. A. Lessa and E. Z. Vogt, eds., pp. 37–46. New York: Harper and Row.

Malkin, C. 2004. Earliest Primate Discovered in China. *Science Now,* January 5, American Association for the Advancement of Science. http://cmbi.bjmu.edu.cn/news/0401/13.htm.

Malkki, Liisa H. 1995. *Purity and Exile: Violence, Memory, and National Cosmology among Hutu Refugees in Tanzania*. Chicago: University of Chicago Press.

Maquet, J. 1964. Objectivity in Anthropology. *Current Anthropology* 5:47–55.

Mar, M. E. 1997. Secondary Colors: The Multiracial Option. *Harvard Magazine,* May–June, pp. 19–20.

Marcus, G. E., and M. M. J. Fischer. 1986. *Anthropology as Cultural Critique: An Experimental Moment in the Human Sciences*. Chicago: University of Chicago Press.

———. 1999. *Anthropology as Cultural Critique: An Experimental Moment in the Human Sciences,* 2nd ed. Chicago: University of Chicago Press.

Marcus, G. E., and F. R. Myers, eds. 1995. *The Traffic in Culture: Refiguring Art and Anthropology*. Berkeley: University of California Press.

Marcus, J., and K. V. Flannery 1996. *Zapotec Civilization: How Urban Society Evolved in Mexico's Oaxaca Valley*. New York: Thames and Hudson.

Margolis, M. L. 1984. *Mothers and Such: American Views of Women and How They Changed*. Berkeley: University of California Press.

———. 2000. *True to Her Nature: Changing Advice to American Women*. Prospect Heights, IL: Waveland.

Margolis, M. L. 2003. The Relative Status of Men and Women. In *Encyclopedia of Sex and Gender: Men and Women in the World's Cultures,* C. Ember and M. Ember, eds., pp. 137–145. New York: Kluwer Academic/Plenum.

Martin, E. 1992. The End of the Body? *American Ethnologist* 19:121–140.

Martin, K., and B. Voorhies 1975. *Female of the Species*. New York: Columbia University Press.

Martinez, E., and A. Garcia 2000. What Is "Neo-Liberalism"? A Brief Definition. http://www.globalexchange.org/campaigns/econ101/neoliberalDefined.html.pdf.

Marx, K., and F. Engels 1976 (orig. 1948). *Communist Manifesto*. New York: Pantheon.

Mascia-Lees, F., and N. J. Black 2000. *Gender and Anthropology*. Prospect Heights, IL: Waveland.

Maybury-Lewis, D. 2002. *Indigenous Peoples, Ethnic Groups, and the State,* 2nd ed. Boston: Allyn & Bacon.

Mayell, H. 2003. Orangutans Show Signs of Culture, Study Says. *National Geographic News,* January 3.

———. 2004a Wild Orangs, Extinct by 2023? *National Geographic News,*

March 9. http://news.national-geographic. com/news/2003/09/0930_030930_ orangutanthreat.html.

———. 2004b. Is Bead Find Proof Modern Thought Began in Africa? *National Geographic News,* March 31. http://news.national-geographic. com/news/2004/03/0331_040331_ ostrichman.html.

Mayr, E. 2001. *What Evolution Is.* New York: Basic Books.

McElroy, A., and P. K. Townsend 2003. *Medical Anthropology in Ecological Perspective,* 4th ed. Boulder, CO: Westview Press.

McKinnon, S. 2005. On Kinship and Marriage: A Critique of the Genetic and Gender Calculus of Evolutionary Psychology. In *Complexities: Beyond Nature and Nurture,* S. McKinnon and S. Silverman, eds., pp. 106–131. Chicago: The University of Chicago Press.

Meadow, R., ed. 1991. *Harappa Excavations 1986–1990: A Multidisciplinary Approach to Third Millennium Urbanism.* Monographs in World Archeology, no. 3. Madison, WI: Prehistory Press.

Meadow, R. H., and J. M. Kenoyer 2000. The Indus Valley Mystery: One of the World's First Great Civilizations Is Still a Puzzle. *Discovering Archaeology,* March/April 2000. http://www/ discoveringarchaeology.com/0800toc/ 8feature1-indus.shtml.

Mercader, J., M. Panger, and C. Boesch 2002. Excavation of a Chimpanzee Stone Tool Site in the African Rainforest. *Science* 296 (May 24):1452–1455.

Merry, S. E. 2006. Anthropology and International Law. *Annual Review of Anthropology* 35:99–116.

Miles, H. L. 1983. Apes and Language: The Search for Communicative Competence. In *Language in Primates,* J. de Luce and H. T. Wilder, eds., pp. 43–62. New York: Springer Verlag.

Miller, B. D. 1997. *The Endangered Sex: Neglect of Female Children in Rural North India.* New York: Oxford University Press.

Miller, N., and R. C. Rockwell, eds. 1988. *AIDS in Africa: The Social and Policy Impact.* Lewiston, NY: Edwin Mellen.

Mintz, S. 1985. *Sweetness and Power: The Place of Sugar in Modern History.* New York: Viking Penguin.

Mitani, J. C., and D. P. Watts 1999. Demographic Influences on the Hunting Behavior of Chimpanzees. *American Journal of Physical Anthropology* 109: 439–454.

Mitchell, J. C. 1966. Theoretical Orientations in African Urban Studies. In *The Social Anthropology of Complex Societies,* M. Banton, ed., pp. 37–68. London: Tavistock.

Moerman, M. 1965. Ethnic Identification in a Complex Civilization: Who Are the Lue? *American Anthropologist* 67(5 Part I):1215–1230.

Moncure, S. 1998. Anthropologist Assists in Police Investigations. *University of Delaware Update.* 17(39, August 20). http://www.udel.edu/PR/UpDate/98/39/ anthrop.html.

Montagu, A., ed. 1997. *Man's Most Dangerous Myth: The Fallacy of Race.* Walnut Creek, CA: AltaMira.

Morgen, S., ed. 1989. *Gender and Anthropology: Critical Reviews for Research and Teaching.* Washington, DC: American Anthropological Association.

Motseta, S. 2006. Botswana Gives Bushmen Tough Conditions. *Tulsa World,* December 14.

Moyà-Solà, S., M. Köhler, D. M. Alba, I. Casanovas-Vilar, and J. Galindo 2004. *Pierolapithecus catalaunicus,* a New Middle Miocene Great Ape from Spain. *Science* 306 (November 19):1339–1344.

Mukhopadhyay, C., and P. Higgins 1988. Anthropological Studies of Women's Status Revisited: 1977–1987. *Annual Review of Anthropology* 17:461–495.

Mullings, L., ed. 1987. *Cities of the United States: Studies in Urban Anthropology.* New York: Columbia University Press.

Murdock, G. P. 1934. *Our Primitive Contemporaries*. New York: Macmillan.

———. 1957. World Ethnographic Sample. *American Anthropologist* 59: 664–687.

Murdock, G. P., and C. Provost 1973. Factors in the Division of Labor by Sex: A Cross-Cultural Analysis. *Ethnology* XII(2):203–225.

Murray, S. O., and W. Roscoe, eds. 1998. *Boy-wives and Female Husbands: Studies in African Homosexualities*. New York: St. Martin's Press.

Mydans, S. 1992a. Criticism Grows over Aliens Seized during Riots. *The New York Times,* May 29, p. A8.

———. 1992b. Judge Dismisses Case in Shooting by Officer. *The New York Times,* June 4, p. A8.

Nafte, M. 2000. *Flesh and Bone: An Introduction to Forensic Anthropology*. Durham, NC: Carolina Academic Press.

Nagel, J. 1996. *American Indian Ethnic Renewal: Red Power and the Resurgence of Identity and Culture*. New York: Oxford University Press.

Nanda, S. 2000. *Gender Diversity Crosscultural Variations*. Prospect Heights, IL: Waveland.

Naylor, L. L. 1996. *Culture and Change: An Introduction*. Westport, CT: Bergin and Garvey.

Nazarea, V. D. 2006. Local Knowledge and Memory in Biodiversity Conservation. *Annual Review of Anthropology* 35:317–335.

Newman, M. 1992. Riots Bring Attention to Growing Hispanic Presence in South-Central Area. *The New York Times,* May 11, p. A10.

*The New York Times* 1992. Alexandria Journal: TV Program for Somalis Is a Rare Unifying Force. December 18.

Ni, X., W. Wang, Y. Hu, and C. Li 2004. A Euprimate Skull from the Early Eocene of China. *Nature* 427 (January 1): 65–68.

Nielsson, G. P. 1985. States and Nation-Groups: A Global Taxonomy. In *New Nationalisms of the Developed World,*

E. A. Tiryakian and R. Rogowski, eds., pp. 27–56. Boston: Allen & Unwin.

Nolan, R. W. 2002. *Development Anthropology: Encounters in the Real World*. Boulder, CO: Westview Press.

———. 2003. *Anthropology in Practice*. Boulder, CO: Lynne Rienner.

Nordstrom, C. 2004. *Shadows of War: Violence, Power, and International Profiteering in the Twenty-First Century*. Berkeley: University of California Press.

Nugent, D., and J. Vincent, eds. 2004. *A Companion to the Anthropology of Politics*. Malden, MA: Blackwell.

O'Leary, C. 2002. *Class Formation, Diet and Economic Transformation in Two Brazilian Fishing Communities*. Unpublished Ph.D. dissertation, University of Michigan, Ann Arbor.

Ohlemacher, S. 2006. 2006: The Year of the 300M Mark: Face of America Changes as Country Grows. *Charleston Post and Courier,* June 26, pp. 1A, 11A.

Omohundro, J. T. 2001. *Careers in Anthropology,* 2nd ed. Boston: McGraw-Hill.

Ong, A. 1987. *Spirits of Resistance and Capitalist Discipline: Factory Women in Malaysia*. Albany: State University of New York Press.

———. 1989. Center, Periphery, and Hierarchy: Gender in Southeast Asia. In *Gender and Anthropology: Critical Reviews for Research and Teaching*, S. Morgen, ed., pp. 294–312. Washington, DC: American Anthropological Association.

Ong, A., and S. J. Collier, eds. 2005. *Global Assemblages: Technology, Politics, and Ethics as Anthropological Problems*. Malden, MA: Blackwell.

Ontario Consultants on Religious Tolerance 1996. Religious Access Dispute Resolved. Internet Mailing List, April 12, http://www.religious tolerance.org/news_694.htm.

———. 2001. Religions of the World: Number of Adherents; Rates of Growth. http://www.religioustolerance.org/worldrel.htm.

Ortner, S. B. 1984. Theory in Anthropology Since the Sixties. *Comparative Studies in Society and History* 126(1):126–166.

Ott, S. 1981. *The Circle of Mountains: A Basque Shepherding Community*. Oxford: Clarendon Press.

Parkin, R., and L. Stone, eds. 2004. *Kinship and Family: An Anthropological Reader*. Malden, MA: Blackwell.

Parsons, J. R. 1974. The Development of a Prehistoric Complex Society: A Regional Perspective from the Valley of Mexico. *Journal of Field Archaeology* 1:81–108.

———. 1976. The Role of Chinampa Agriculture in the Food Supply of Aztec Tenochtitlan. In *Cultural Change and Continuity: Essays in Honor of James Bennett Griffin,* C. E. Cleland, ed., pp. 233–262. New York: Academic Press.

Patterson, F. 1978. Conversations with a Gorilla. *National Geographic,* October, pp. 438–465.

Peletz, M. 1988. *A Share of the Harvest: Kinship, Property, and Social History among the Malays of Rembau*. Berkeley: University of California Press.

Pelto, P. 1973. *The Snowmobile Revolution: Technology and Social Change in the Arctic*. Menlo Park, CA: Cummings.

Peplau, L. A., ed. 1999. *Gender, Culture, and Ethnicity: Current Research about Women and Men*. Mountain View, CA: Mayfield.

Perlman, D. 2004. Fossil Find May Be the Father of Us All: It's Hailed as Last Common Kin of the Great Apes and Humans. *San Francisco Chronicle,* November 22, p. A-4. http://www.sfgate.com/cgibin/article.cgi?file=/chronicle/archive/2004/11/22/MNGIV9VF 3G1. DTL.

Peters-Golden, H. 2002. *Culture Sketches: Case Studies in Anthropology,* 3rd ed. New York: McGraw-Hill.

Petraglia-Bahri, D. 1996. Introduction to Postcolonial Studies. http://www.emory.edu/ENGLISH/Bahri/.

Piddocke, S. 1969. The Potlatch System of the Southern Kwakiutl: A New Perspective. In *Environment and Cultural Behavior,* A. P. Vayda, ed., pp. 130–156. Garden City, NY: Natural History Press.

Plattner, S., ed. 1989. *Economic Anthropology*. Stanford, CA: Stanford University Press.

Polanyi, K. 1968. *Primitive, Archaic and Modern Economies: Essays of Karl Polanyi,* G. Dalton, ed., Garden City, NY: Anchor Books.

Pollock, S. 1999. *Ancient Mesopotamia: The Eden That Never Was*. Cambridge: Cambridge University Press.

Pospisil, L. 1963. *The Kapauku Papuans of West New Guinea*. New York: Holt, Rinehart & Winston.

Potash, B., ed. 1986. *Widows in African Societies: Choices and Constraints*. Stanford, CA: Stanford University Press.

Prag, J., and R. Neave 1997. *Making Faces: Using Forensic and Archaeological Evidence*. College Station: Texas A&M University Press.

Price, R., ed. 1973. *Maroon Societies*. New York: Anchor Press/Doubleday.

Price, T. D., ed. 2000. *Europe's First Farmers*. New York: Cambridge University Press.

Radcliffe-Brown, A. R. 1965. (orig. 1962). *Structure and Function in Primitive Society*. New York: Free Press.

Rak, Y. 1986. The Neandertal: A New Look at an Old Face. *Journal of Human Evolution* 15(3):151–164.

Ramirez, R. R., and G. P. de la Cruz 2003. The Hispanic Population in the United States, U.S. Census Bureau. *Current Population Reports,* P20–545, March. http://www.census.gov/prod/2003 pubs/p20-545.pdf.

Ranger, T. O. 1996. Postscript. In *Postcolonial Identities,* R. Werbner and T. O. Ranger, eds. London: Zed.

Rappaport, R. A. 1974. Obvious Aspects of Ritual. *Cambridge Anthropology* 2:2–60.

————. 1999. *Holiness and Humanity: Ritual in the Making of Religious Life.* New York: Cambridge University Press.

Rathus, S. A., J. S. Nevid, and J. Fichner-Rathus 2005. *Human Sexuality in a World of Diversity,* 6th ed. Boston: Pearson.

Redfield, R. 1941. *The Folk Culture of Yucatan.* Chicago: University of Chicago Press.

Redfield, R., R. Linton, and M. Herskovits 1936. Memorandum on the Study of Acculturation. *American Anthropologist* 38:149–152.

Reese, W. L. 1999. *Dictionary of Philosophy and Religion: Eastern and Western Thought.* Amherst, NY: Humanities Books.

Reiter, R. 1975. Men and Women in the South of France: Public and Private Domains. In *Toward an Anthropology of Women,* R. Reiter, ed., pp. 252–282. New York: Monthly Review Press.

Rice, P. 2002. Paleoanthropology 2001—Part II. *General Anthropology* 8(2): 11–14.

Rickford, J. R. 1997. Suite for Ebony and Phonics, *Discover*, December. http://www.stanford.edu/~rickford/papers/SuiteForEbony AndPhonics.html.

————. 1999. *African American Vernacular English: Features, Evolution, Educational Implications.* Malden, MA: Blackwell.

Rickford, J. R., and R. J. Rickford 2000. *Spoken Soul: The Story of Black English.* New York: Wiley.

Robertson, A. F. 1995. *The Big Catch: A Practical Introduction to Development.* Boulder, CO: Westview Press.

Robertson, J. 1992. Koreans in Japan. Paper presented at the University of Michigan Department of Anthropology, Martin Luther King Jr. Day Panel, January. Ann Arbor: University of Michigan Department of Anthropology (unpublished).

Rodseth, L., R. W. Wrangham, A. M. Harrigan, and B. Smuts 1991. The Human Community as a Primate Society. *Current Anthropology* 32:221–254.

Romaine, S. 1999. *Communicating Gender.* Mahwah, NJ: Erlbaum.

————. 2000. *Language in Society: An Introduction to Sociolinguistics,* 2nd ed. New York: Oxford University Press.

Root, D. 1996. *Cannibal Culture: Art, Appropriation, and the Commodification of Difference.* Boulder, CO: Westview Press.

Rosaldo, M. Z. 1980a. *Knowledge and Passion: Notions of Self and Social Life.* Stanford, CA: Stanford University Press.

————. 1980b. The Use and Abuse of Anthropology: Reflections on Feminism and Cross-Cultural Understanding. *Signs* 5(3): 389–417.

Rose, M. 1997. Neandertal DNA. Newsbriefs. *Archaeology* 50 (September/October): 5. http://www.archaeology.org/9709/newsbriefs/dna.html.

Roth, N. L., and L. K. Fuller 1998. *Women and AIDS: Negotiating Safer Practices, Care, and Representation.* Binghampton, NY: Harrington Park Press.

Rouse, R. 1991. Mexican Migration and the Social Space of Postmodernism. *Diaspora* 1(1):8–23.

Royal Anthropological Institute 1951. *Notes and Queries on Anthropology,* 6th ed. London: Routledge and Kegan Paul.

Ryan, S. 1990. *Ethnic Conflict and International Relations.* Brookfield, MA: Dartmouth.

Sahlins, M. D. 1968. *Tribesmen.* Englewood Cliffs, NJ: Prentice Hall.

————. 2004. *Stone Age Economics.* New York: Routledge.

Salzman, P. C. 1974. Political Organization among Nomadic Peoples. In *Man in Adaptation: The Cultural Present*, 2nd ed., Y. A. Cohen, ed., pp. 267–284. Chicago: Aldine.

————. 2004. *Pastoralists: Equality, Hierarchy, and the State.* Boulder, CO: Westview.

Salzmann, Z. 1993. *Language, Culture, and Society: An Introduction to Linguistic Anthropology.* Boulder, CO: Westview.

Sanday, P. R. 1974. Female Status in the Public Domain. In *Woman, Culture, and Society,* M. Z. Rosaldo and L. Lamphere, eds., pp. 189–206. Stanford, CA: Stanford University Press. Albuquerque: University of New Mexico Press.

Santley, R. S. 1985. The Political Economy of the Aztec Empire. *Journal of Anthropological Research* 41(3): 327–337.

Sapir, E. 1931. Conceptual Categories in Primitive Languages. *Science* 74:578–584.

Schaller, G. 1963. *The Mountain Gorilla: Ecology and Behavior.* Chicago: University of Chicago Press.

Scheidel, W. 1997. Brother-Sister Marriage in Roman Egypt. *Journal of Biosocial Science* 29(3):361–371.

Scheinman, M. 1980. Imperialism. *Academic American Encyclopedia.* Princeton, NJ: Arete, volume 11, pp. 61–62.

Schneider, D. M. 1967. Kinship and Culture: Descent and Filiation as Cultural Constructs. *Southwestern Journal of Anthropology* 23:65–73.

Scholte, J. A. 2000. *Globalization: A Critical Introduction.* New York: St. Martin's, Press.

Scott, J. C. 1985. *Weapons of the Weak.* New Haven, CT: Yale University Press.
———. 1990. *Domination and the Arts of Resistance.* New Haven, CT: Yale University Press.

Scudder, T., and E. Colson 1980. *Secondary Education and the Formation of an Elite: The Impact of Education on Gwembe District, Zambia.* London: Academic Press.

Scupin, R. 2003. *Race and Ethnicity: An Anthropological Focus on the United States and the World.* Upper Saddle River, NJ: Prentice Hall.

Sebeok, T. A., and J. Umiker-Sebeok, eds. 1980. *Speaking of Apes: A Critical Anthropology of Two-Way Communication with Man.* New York: Plenum.

Senut, B., M. Pickford, D. Gommery, P. Mein, K. Cheboi, and Y. Coppens 2001. First Hominid from the Miocene (Lukeino Formation, Kenya). Comptes Rendus de l'Academie des Sciences, Series IIA - Earth and Planetary Science 332. 2 (January 30): 137–144.

Service, E. R. 1962. *Primitive Social Organization: An Evolutionary Perspective.* New York: McGraw-Hill.
———. 1966. *The Hunters.* Englewood Cliffs, NJ: Prentice Hall.

Shanklin, E. 1995. *Anthropology and Race.* Belmont, CA: Wadsworth.

Shannon, T. R. 1996. *An Introduction to the World-System Perspective,* 2nd ed. Boulder, CO: Westview Press.

Sharma, A., and A. Gupta, eds. 2006. *The Anthropology of the State: A Reader.* Malden, MA: Blackwell.

Shermer, M. 2002. *In Darwin's Shadow: The Life and Science of Alfred Russel Wallace.* New York: Oxford University Press.

Shivaram, C. 1996. Where Women Wore the Crown: Kerala's Dissolving Matriarchies Leave a Rich Legacy of Compassionate Family Culture. *Hinduism Today,* http://www.spiritweb.org/HinduismToday/96_02_Women _Wore_Crown.html.

Shreeve, J. 1992. The Dating Game: How Old Is the Human Race? *Discover* 13(9):76–83.

Silberbauer, G. 1981. *Hunter and Habitat in the Central Kalahari Desert.* New York: Cambridge University Press.

Simons, E. L., and P. C. Ettel 1970. Gigantopithecus. *Scientific American,* January, pp. 77–85.

Sinnott, M. J. 2004. *Toms and Dees: Transgender Identity and Female Same-Sex Relationships in Thailand.* Honolulu: University of Hawaii Press.

Slade, M. 1984. Displaying Affection in Public. *The New York Times,* December 17.

Smart, A., and J. Smart 2003. Urbanization and the Global Perspective. *Annual Review of Anthropology* 32:263–285.

Smith, A. T. 2003. *The Political Landscape: Constellations of Authority in Early Complex Polities*. Westport, CT: Praeger.

Smith, B. D. 1995. *The Emergence of Agriculture*. New York: Scientific American Library, W. H. Freeman.

Smitherman, G. 1986 (orig. 1977). *Talkin and Testifyin: The Language of Black America*. Detroit: Wayne State University Press.

Solway, J., and R. Lee 1990. Foragers, Genuine and Spurious: Situating the Kalahari San in History (with CA treatment). *Current Anthropology* 31(2): 109–146.

Spickard, P., ed. 2004. *Race and Nation: Ethnic Systems in the Modern World*. New York: Routledge.

Spindler, G. D., ed. 2000. *Fifty Years of Anthropology and Education, 1950–2000: A Spindler Anthology*. Mahwah, NJ: Erlbaum.

Srivastava, J., N. J. H. Smith, and D. A. Forno 1998. *Integrating Biodiversity in Agricultural Intensification. Toward Sound Practices*. Washington, DC: World Bank.

Stack, C. B. 1975. *All Our Kin: Strategies for Survival in a Black Community*. New York: Harper Torchbooks.

Stanford, C. B. 1999. *The Hunting Apes: Meat Eating and the Origins of Human Behavior*. Princeton, NJ: Princeton University Press.

Stanford, C. B., and H. T. Bunn, eds. 2001. *Meat-eating and Human Evolution*. New York: Oxford University Press.

*Statistical Abstract of the United States* 1991. 111th ed. Washington, DC: U.S. Bureau of the Census, U.S. Government Printing Office.

———. 1996. 116th ed. Washington, DC: U.S. Bureau of the Census, U.S. Government Printing Office.

———. 1999. 119th ed. Washington, DC: U.S. Bureau of the Census, U.S. Government Printing Office.

———. 2001. http://www.census.gov/prod/www/statistical-abstract-us.html.

———. 2002. http://www.census.gov/prod/www/statistical-abstract-us.html.

———. 2003. http://www.census.gov/prod/www/statistical-abstract-04.html.

———. 2004–2005. http://www.census.gov/prod/www/statistical-abstract-04.html.

———. 2007. http://www.census.gov/prod/www/statistical-abstract.html.

*Statistics Canada* 2003. Religions in Canada. 2001 Census—Release 8, May 13, 2003. http://www12.statcan.ca/english/census01/release/index.cfm.

Stein, R. L., and P. L. Stein 2005. *The Anthropology of Religion, Magic, and Witchcraft*. Boston: Pearson/Allyn & Bacon.

Stern, A. 2000. Experts Say 138 World Primate Species Endangered. *Reuters*. http://www.forests.org/archive/general/exsay138.htm.

Stevens, W. K. 1992. Humanity Confronts Its Handiwork: An Altered Planet. *The New York Times*, May 5, pp. B5–B7.

Stevenson, D. 2003. *Cities and Urban Cultures*. Philadelphia, PA: Open University Press.

Stevenson, R. F. 1968. *Population and Political Systems in Tropical Africa*. New York: Columbia University Press.

Stoler, A. 1977. Class Structure and Female Autonomy in Rural Java. *Signs* 3:74–89.

Strathern, A., and P. J. Stewart 1999. *Curing and Healing: Medical Anthropology in Global Perspective*. Durham, NC: Carolina Academic Press.

Susman, R. L. 1987. Pygmy Chimpanzees and Common Chimpanzees: Models for the Behavioral Ecology of the Earliest Hominids. In *The Evolution of Human Behavior: Primate Models*, W. G. Kinzey, ed., pp. 72–86. Albany: State University of New York Press.

Suttles, W. 1960. Affinal Ties, Subsistence, and Prestige among the Coast Salish. *American Anthropologist* 62:296–305.

Swift, M. 1963. Men and Women in Malay Society. In *Women in the New Asia*, B. Ward, ed., pp. 268–286. Paris: UNESCO.

Tague, R. G., and C. O. Lovejoy 1986. The Obstetric Pelvis of A. L. 288-1 (Lucy). *Journal of Human Evolution* 15:237–255.

Tanaka, J. 1980. *The San Hunter-Gatherers of the Kalahari.* Tokyo: University of Tokyo Press.

Tannen, D. 1990. *You Just Don't Understand: Women and Men in Conversation.* New York: Ballantine Books.

Tannen, D., ed. 1993. *Gender and Conversational Interaction.* New York: Oxford University Press.

Taylor, C. 1987. Anthropologist-in-Residence. In *Applied Anthropology in America,* 2nd ed., E. M. Eddy and W. L. Partridge, eds. New York: Columbia University Press.

Terrace, H. S. 1979. *Nim.* New York: Knopf.

Thomas, L. 1999. *Language, Society and Power.* New York: Routledge.

Thomas, L., and S. Wareing, eds. 2004. *Language, Society, and Power: An Introduction.* New York: Routledge.

Thompson, W. 1983. Introduction: World System with and without the Hyphen. In *Contending Approaches to World System Analysis,* W. Thompson, ed., pp. 7–26. Thousand Oaks, CA: Sage.

Tice, K. 1997. Reflections on Teaching Anthropology for Use in the Public and Private Sector. In *The Teaching of Anthropology: Problems, Issues, and Decisions,* C. P. Kottak, J. J. White, R. H. Furlow, and P. C. Rice, eds., pp. 273–284. Mountain View, CA: Mayfield.

Tishkov, V. A. 2004. *Chechnya: Life in a War-Torn Society.* Berkeley: University of California Press.

Titiev, M. 1992. *Old Oraibi: A Study of the Hopi Indians of Third Mesa.* Albuquerque: University of New Mexico Press.

Tomlinson, J. 1991. *Cultural Imperialism: A Critical Introduction.* Baltimore: Johns Hopkins University Press.

———. 1999. *Globalization and Culture.* Chicago: University of Chicago Press.

Toner, R. 1992. Los Angeles Riots Are a Warning, Americans Fear. *The New York Times,* May 11, pp. A1, A11.

Trask, L. 1996. FAQs about Basque and the Basques. http://www.cogs.susx. ac.uk/users/larryt/basque.faqs.html.

Trigger, B. G. 2003. *Understanding Early Civilizations: A Comparative Study.* Cambridge: Cambridge University Press.

Trudgill, P. 2000. *Sociolinguistics: An Introduction to Language and Society,* 4th ed. New York: Penguin Books.

Turner, V. W. 1974 (orig. 1967). *The Ritual Process.* Harmondsworth, England: Penguin Press.

———. 1995 (orig. 1969). *The Ritual Process.* Hawthorne, NY: Aldine de Gruyter.

Turnbull, C. 1965. *Wayward Servants: The Two Worlds of the African Pygmies.* Garden City, NY: Natural History Press.

Tylor, E. B. 1958 (orig. 1871). *Primitive Culture.* New York: Harper Torchbooks.

U.S. Census Bureau 2006. http://quickfacts. census.gov/qfd/index.html.

Ulijaszek, S. J., and H. Lofink 2006. Obesity in Biocultural Perspective. *Annual Review of Anthropology* 35:337–360.

Van Cantfort, T. E., and J. B. Rimpau 1982. Sign Language Studies with Children and Chimpanzees. *Sign Language Studies* 34:15–72.

Van der Elst, D., and P. Bohannan 2003. *Culture as Given, Culture as Choice,* 2nd ed. Prospect Heights, IL: Waveland.

Vayda, A. P. 1968 (orig. 1961). Economic Systems in Ecological Perspective: The Case of the Northwest Coast. In *Readings in Anthropology,* 2nd ed., volume 2, M. H. Fried, ed., pp. 172–178. New York: Crowell.

Veblen, T. 1934. *The Theory of the Leisure Class: An Economic Study of Institutions.* New York: The Modern Library.

Verdery, K. 2001. Socialist Societies: Anthropological Aspects. *International Encyclopedia of the Social & Behavioral Sciences,* pp. 14496–14500. New York: Elsevier.

Vekua, A., D. Lordkipanidze, and G. P. Rightmire. 2002. A Skull of Early Homo from Dmanisi, Georgia, *Science,* July 5, pp. 85–89.

Vidal, J. 2003. Every Third Person Will Be a Slum Dweller within 30 Years, UN Agency Warns: Biggest Study of World's Cities Finds 940 Million Already Living in Squalor. *The Guardian,* October 4, 2003. http://www.guardian.co.uk/international/story/0,3604,1055785,00.html.

Viegas, J. 2000. Planet of the Dying Apes: Conference Reveals Steep Decline in Primate Populations. http://abcnews.go.com/sections/science/DailyNews/apeconference000512.html.

Vigil, J. D. 2003. Urban Violence and Street Gangs. *Annual Review of Anthropology* 32:225–242.

Viola, H. J., and C. Margolis 1991. *Seeds of Change: Five Hundred Years since Columbus, a Quincentennial Commemoration.* Washington, DC: Smithsonian Institution Press.

Von Daniken, E. 1971. *Chariots of the Gods: Unsolved Mysteries of the Past.* New York: Bantam.

Wade, N. 2005. For Gay Men, Different Scent of Attraction. *The New York Times,* Late ed.—Final, May 10, p. A1.

Wade, P. 2002. *Race, Nature, and Culture: An Anthropological Perspective.* Sterling, VA: Pluto Press.

Wagley, C. W. 1968 (orig. 1959). The Concept of Social Race in the Americas. In *The Latin American Tradition,* by C. Wagley, pp. 155–174. New York: Columbia University Press.

Wallace, A. F. C. 1956. Revitalization Movements. *American Anthropologist* 58: 264–281.

———. 1966. *Religion: An Anthropological View.* New York: McGraw-Hill.

———. 1969. *The Death and Rebirth of the Seneca.* New York: Knopf.

Wallerstein, I. M. 1982. The Rise and Future Demise of the World Capitalist System: Concepts for Comparative Analysis. In *Introduction to the Sociology of "Developing Societies,"* H. Alavi and T. Shanin, eds., pp. 29–53. New York: Monthly Review Press.

———. 2004a. *The Decline of American Power: The U.S. in a Chaotic World.* New York: New Press.

———. 2004b. *World-Systems Analysis: An Introduction.* Durham, NC: Duke University Press.

Ward, M. C. 2003. *A World Full of Women,* 3rd ed. Needham Heights, MA: Allyn & Bacon.

Watson, P. J. 1983. The Halafian Culture: A Review and Synthesis. In *The Hilly Flanks and Beyond: Essays on the Prehistory of Southwestern Asia,* T. C. Young, Jr., P. E. L. Smith, and P. Mortensen, eds. Studies in Ancient Oriental Civilization 36: 231–250. Oriental Institute, University of Chicago.

Watzman, H. 2006. The Echoes of Ancient Humans. *Chronicle of Higher Education,* January 27, http://chronicle.com/weekly/v52/i21/21a01601.htm.

Weber, M. 1958 (orig. 1904). *The Protestant Ethic and the Spirit of Capitalism.* New York: Scribner.

———. 1968 (orig. 1922). *Economy and Society.* E. Fischoff et al. (trans.). New York: Bedminster Press.

*Webster's New World Encyclopedia* 1993. College Edition. Englewood Cliffs, NJ: Prentice Hall.

Wedel, J. 2002. Blurring the Boundaries of the State-Private Divide: Implications for Corruption. Paper presented at the European Association of Social Anthropologists (EASA) Conference in Copenhagen, August 14–17, 2002. http://www.anthrobase.com/Txt/W/Wedel_J_01.htm.

Weiner, J. 1994. *The Beak of the Finch: A Story of Evolution in Our Time.* New York: Alfred A. Knopf.

Weise, E. 1999. Anthropologists Adapt Technology to World's Cultures. *USA Today,* May 26. http://www.usatoday.com/life/cyber/tech/ctf256.htm.

Weiss, H. 2005. *Collapse.* New York: Routledge.

Weiss, R. 2005. More Evidence of Skull's Link to Humans: Remains Believed to Be from Earliest Known Ancestor. *Washington Post,* April 7, p. A03.

Wendorf, F., and R. Schild 2000. Late Neolithic Megalithic Structures at Nabta Playa (Sahara), Southwestern Egypt. http://www.comp-archaeology.org/ WendorfSAA98.html.

Wenke, R. J. 1996. *Patterns in Prehistory: Mankind's First Three Million Years,* 4th ed. New York: Oxford University Press.

Weston, K. 1991. *Families We Choose: Lesbians, Gays, Kinship.* New York: Columbia University Press.

White, L. A. 1959. *The Evolution of Culture: The Development of Civilization to the Fall of Rome.* New York: McGraw-Hill.

Whorf, B. L. 1956. A Linguistic Consideration of Thinking in Primitive Communities. In *Language, Thought, and Reality: Selected Writings of Benjamin Lee Whorf,* J. B. Carroll, ed., pp. 65–86. Cambridge, MA: MIT Press.

Whyte, M. F. 1978. Cross-Cultural Codes Dealing with the Relative Status of Women. *Ethnology* XII(2): 203–225.

Wilford, J. N. 2000. Ruins Alter Ideas of How Civilization Spread. May 23, http://www.nytimes.com.

———. 2003. Big Teeth in Ancient Jaw Offer Clues About Our Ancestors. *New York Times* September 30, 2003, Late Edition—Final, Section F, Page 4, Column 2.

Wilk, R. R. 1996. *Economies and Cultures: An Introduction to Economic Anthropology.* Boulder, CO: Westview Press.

Williams, B. 1989. A Class Act: Anthropology and the Race to Nation across Ethnic Terrain. *Annual Review of Anthropology* 18:401– 444.

Williams, L. M., and D. Finkelhor 1995. Paternal Caregiving and Incest: Test of a Biosocial Model. *American Journal of Orthopsychiatry* 65(1):101–113.

Willie, C. V. 2003. *A New Look at Black Families.* Walnut Creek, CA: AltaMira.

Wilmsen, E. N. 1989. *Land Filled with Flies: A Political Economy of the Kalahari.* Chicago: University of Chicago Press.

Wilson, D. S. 2002. *Darwin's Cathedral: Evolution, Religion, and the Nature of Society.* Chicago: University of Chicago Press.

Wilson, M. L., and R. W. Wrangham 2003. Intergroup Relations in Chimpanzees. *Annual Review of Anthropology* 32:363–392.

Wilson, R., ed. 1996. *Human Rights: Culture and Context: Anthropological Perspectives.* Chicago: Pluto Press.

Winter. R. 2001. Religions of the World: Number of Adherents; Names of Houses of Worship; Names of Leaders; Rates of Growth. http://www.religioustolerance. org/worldrel.htm.

Wittfogel, K. A. 1957. *Oriental Despotism: A Comparative Study of Total Power.* New Haven, CT: Yale University Press.

Wolpoff, M., B. Senut, M. Pickford, and J. Hawks 2002. Sahelanthropus or "Sahelpithecus"? *Nature* 419: 581–582.

Wolf, E. R. 1966. *Peasants.* Englewood Cliffs, NJ: Prentice Hall.

———. 1982. *Europe and the People without History.* Berkeley: University of California Press.

Wolf, E. R., with S. Silverman 2001. *Pathways of Power: Building an Anthropology of the Modern World.* Berkeley: University of California Press.

Wolpoff, M. H. 1980a *Paleoanthropology.* New York: McGraw-Hill.

———. 1980b. Cranial Remains of Middle Pleistocene Hominids. *Journal of Human Evolution* 9:339–358.

———. 1999. *Paleoanthropology,* 2nd ed. New York: McGraw-Hill.

Worsley, P. 1985 (orig. 1959). Cargo Cults. In *Readings in Anthropology* 85/86. Guilford, CT: Dushkin.

Wrangham, R., W. McGrew, F. de Waal, and P. Heltne, eds. 1994. *Chimpanzee Cultures.* Cambridge, MA: Harvard University Press.

Wright, H. T. 1994. Prestate Political Formations. In *Chiefdoms and Early States in the Near East: The Organizational Dynamics of Complexity,* ed. G. Stein and M. S. Rothman, *Monographs in World Archaeology* 18:67–84. Madison, WI: Prehistory Press.

Wright, H. T., and G. A. Johnson 1975. Population, Exchange, and Early State Formation in Southwestern Iran. *American Anthropologist* 77:267–289.

Yellen, J. E., A. S. Brooks, and E. Cornelissen 1995. A Middle Stone Age Worked Bone Industry from Katanda, Upper Semliki Valley, Zaire. *Science* 268:553–556.

Yetman, N., ed. 1991. *Majority and Minority: The Dynamics of Race and Ethnicity in American Life,* 5th ed. Boston: Allyn and Bacon.

Yurchak, A. 2002. Entrepreneurial Governmentality in Postsocialist Russia. In *The New Entrepreneurs of Europe and Asia,* V. Bonnell and T. Gold, eds., p. 301. Armonk, NY: M. E. Sharpe.

———. 2005. *Everything Was Forever until It Was No More: The Last Soviet Generation.* Princeton, NJ: Princeton University Press.

Zimmer-Tamakoshi, L. 1997. The Last Big Man: Development and Men's Discontents in the Papua New Guinea Highlands. *Oceania* 68(2):107–122

Zou, Y., and E. T. Trueba 2002. *Ethnography and Schools: Qualitative Approaches to the Study of Education.* Lanham, MD: Rowman & Littlefield.

Zulaika, J. 1988. *Basque Violence: Metaphor and Sacrament.* Reno: University of Nevada Press.

# INDEX

*Note:* Boldface numbers indicate pages on which glossary definitions appear; page numbers followed by *f* indicate figures; page numbers followed by *t* indicate tables; page numbers in italic indicate photos.